The Berlin Aging Study

The present and future of our society are shaped by an ever increasing proportion of old and very old people. The Berlin Aging Study is one of the largest interdisciplinary efforts to explore old age and aging. Unique aspects of the Berlin Aging Study are the spectrum of scientific disciplines involved, the range of discipline-specific and interdisciplinary research topics, the focus on very old age (70 to over 100 years), and the empirical reference to a representative heterogeneous urban population. The study's first cross-sectional findings on intellectual abilities, self and personality, social relationships, physical health, functional capacity, medical treatment, mental disorders such as depression and dementia, socioeconomic conditions, activities, everyday competence, subjective well-being, and gender differences are reported in depth in this book. The study was carried out in the context of the Berlin-Brandenburg Academy of Sciences study group on "Aging and Social Development." The authors primarily conduct their research at the Berlin Max Planck Institute for Human Development, the Free University of Berlin, and the Humboldt University, Berlin.

Paul B. Baltes is the Director of the Center for Lifespan Psychology at the Max Planck Institute for Human Development and Professor of Psychology at the Free University of Berlin. Baltes has spent extensive time in the United States (e.g., at the Center for Advanced Study in the Behavioral Sciences at Stanford University and at Pennsylvania State University). For his work, he has received the International Psychology Award of the American Psychological Association, the Aristotle Award of the European Federation of Psychological Associations, and the Kleemeier Award of the Gerontological Society of America. A member of several academies, including the European Academy of Sciences and the Royal Swedish Academy of Sciences, Baltes has directed his research toward a life-span view of human development. Currently, he is also coeditor-in-chief of the *International Encyclopedia of the Social and Behavioral Sciences*.

Karl Ulrich Mayer is the Director of the Center for Sociology and the Study of the Life Course at the Max Planck Institute for Human Development in Berlin. He currently holds a chair at the German Science Council, and he has been a visiting scientist and lecturer at Nuffield College, Oxford, Harvard University, the University of Zurich, and the Center for Advanced Study in the Behavioral Sciences at Stanford University. He is a member of several academies, among them the Academia Europaea. He is also a Foreign Corresponding Member of the American Academy of Arts and Sciences. In addition to research on social stratification and mobility, education, training, and labor market processes, Mayer's primary academic interests have been the sociology of aging and the impact of welfare state policies on the life course.

The Berlin Aging Study
Aging from 70 to 100

Edited by

PAUL B. BALTES

KARL ULRICH MAYER

A Research Project of the Berlin-Brandenburg Academy of Sciences

Coordinating Editor: Julia Delius

CAMBRIDGE
UNIVERSITY PRESS

PUBLISHED BY THE PRESS SYNDICATE OF THE UNIVERSITY OF CAMBRIDGE
The Pitt Building, Trumpington Street, Cambridge, United Kingdom

CAMBRIDGE UNIVERSITY PRESS
The Edinburgh Building, Cambridge CB2 2RU, UK
40 West 20th Street, New York, NY 10011–4211, USA
10 Stamford Road, Oakleigh, VIC 3166, Australia
Ruiz de Alarcón 13, 28014 Madrid, Spain
Dock House, The Waterfront, Cape Town 8001, South Africa

http://www.cambridge.org

First published 1999
First paperback printing 2001

Printed in the United States of America

Typeface Times 10/12 pt.   *System* Quark XPress™   [CS]

A catalogue record for this book is available from the British Library

Library of Congress Cataloguing-in-Publication Data is available

ISBN 0 521 62134 8 hardback
ISBN 0 521 00003 3 paperback

We dedicate this book to the 516 women and men who participated in the Berlin Aging Study (BASE), as well as to those more than 1,000 individuals who took part in pilot work and the first phases of data collection. These people gave us much of their precious time and energy.

Contents

vii

Acknowledgments

On behalf of the study group "Aging and Societal Development" of the Berlin-Brandenburg Academy of Sciences, the editors would like to express their gratitude to numerous people and several institutions. Our initial thanks go to the Berlin residents who participated in the study. They gave us their trust, their commitment, and their time, and received our research staff with great openness. In a time when science and research are sometimes viewed with skepticism, they generously provided the information that is the foundation of the Berlin Aging Study (BASE).

We are equally grateful to the two academies sponsoring the research group: the former Academy of Sciences and Technology in Berlin and the Berlin-Brandenburg Academy of Sciences. Without the Academy of Sciences and Technology and the active support of its president, Horst Albach, its general secretary, Wolfgang Holl, and the staff at its central office, the Berlin Aging Study would never have been started. After the closure of the West Berlin academy following German unification, the Berlin-Brandenburg Academy of Sciences, founded in 1993 as the successor to the former Prussian Academy of Sciences, included the Berlin Aging Study in its first portfolio of activities. We are grateful to its first president, Hubert Markl, and his successor, Dieter Simon, for this decision, as well as to the general secretary, Diepold Salvini-Plawen, and the academy's excellent administrative staff.

We are certain that without the context of these two academies, neither the participating institutions nor the many scientists from such a broad range of disciplines would have been able to cooperate adequately in the preparation and realization of the Berlin Aging Study. Without the academies, it would not have been possible to incorporate such a wide spectrum of scientific perspectives in the planning of the Berlin Aging Study, or to attract such a stellar group of scientists to serve on the study group. Among the members of the initial study group, Ursula Lehr (University of Heidelberg) and Wolfgang Gerok (University of Freiburg) were particularly helpful in the formulation of the aims of the Berlin Aging Study and the shaping of the necessary financial, administrative, and interdisciplinary conditions.

A project of the size of the Berlin Aging Study requires a benevolent supporter with many resources. Besides institutions belonging to the Free University of Berlin (and now also to the Humboldt University Berlin) and the Max Planck Institute for Human Development, two federal ministries took this role. After initial funding by the Federal Ministry for Research and Technology (1989–91), the Federal Ministry for Family Affairs, Senior Citizens, Women, and Youth (Federal Ministry for Family Affairs and Senior Citizens until 1994) generously financed this project. In particular, we are very grateful to senior members of the ministry staff such as Annette Niederfranke, who was responsible for the project at the Federal Ministry for Family Affairs and Senior Citizens and accompanied the study with expertise and individual initiative. It was through her efforts that the project funding followed the course of the study, rather than being subject to revision due to difficult developments within federal and departmental budgets.

We express particular gratitude, however, to our home institution, the Max-Planck-Institut für Bildungsforschung (Max Planck Institute for Human Development). Not only have our directorial colleagues (Wolfgang Edelstein, Peter M. Roeder, Jürgen Baumert, and, more recently, Gerd Gigerenzer) treated the financial and infrastructural concerns of the Berlin Aging Study with consideration and encouragement, but the institute's administrative staff was generously committed to helping us to solve the many problems posed by the Berlin Aging Study's financial, administrative, and spatial needs.

The organizational coordination of the study required a high degree of social competence and administrative efficiency in the maintenance of good relations with the sponsors, the supporting institutions, and the research departments and hospitals involved, in providing the basis for interaction between participating scientists, in supporting the work of the research assistants, and in attending to the study participants' concerns and individual life circumstances. These tasks were fulfilled by several persons, in concert or in succession: Hans-Werner Wahl (1988–89), Reinhard Nuthmann (1989–96), assisted by Cornelia Borchers (1991–93), and Karl Mathias Neher (since 1997). They fulfilled the role of administrative project coordinator with great personal dedication, tolerance, loyalty, and a high degree of social intelligence. In particular, Reinhard Nuthmann ensured the stability and continuity of the Berlin Aging Study in the face of extremely difficult external conditions for the project and an equally complex and dynamic internal situation. Above and beyond praise, he earned respect and appreciation.

The BASE Project Coordination Center, headed in succession by Hans-Werner Wahl, Reinhard Nuthmann, and Karl Mathias Neher, was supported by the staff of the BASE secretarial office (who are named below). Data processing and organization for the Coordination Center were carried out with great dedication and efficiency by Alexa Breloer, Gregor Caregnato, Wolfgang Otto, and later by Andrea Barth and Christine Drkosch.

A fundamental part of the Berlin Aging Study was the fieldwork involving more than 30 persons. We are grateful to the project physicians and dentists involved in the first wave of the study: Markus Borchelt, Sabine Englert, Johannes Fischer-Pauly, Dieter Felsenberg, Franz Fobbe, Bernhard Geiselmann, Heiko Hennersdorf, Jürgen Lüthje, Alexandre Mochine, Ina Nitschke, Hans-Peter Stahl, Mathias Taupitz, Thomas Wernicke, and Jens Zanther.

The largest share of the fieldwork was carried out by the research and medical assistants. Their commitment, loyalty, and skills were widely judged to be outstanding. We thank those who took part in field research activities to various degrees of intensity and duration: Rosemarie Adair, Doris Barth, Alexandra zu Bentheim, Heike Borkenhagen, Christine Dautert, Simone Elsing, Gabriele Faust, Ursula Feierabend, Noëlle Gielen, Lutz Groh, Anita Günther, Kerstin Haenel, Klaus Häring, Sabine Kahle, Christiane Kahnt, Günter Kleinknecht, Jürgen Menzel, Bärbel Mucke, Iris Nentwig, Annette Rentz, Alexandra Schlüter, Rudi Scholz, Dorothea Schrader, Gisela Schubert, Ralf Straßburger, Katharina Tamborini, Felicitas Thiel, and Jacqueline Umlauf. The field staff was supported by Renate Gebhardt and Hasso Klimitz who provided psychological supervision and offered guidance in situations requiring careful ethical review. Hans Peter Rosemeier, Professor of Psychological Medicine at the Free University of Berlin, was the main consultant in planning this external supervision.

Several scientists played important roles at the beginning stages of the Berlin Aging Study, in formulating basic concepts, developing new measures, and training the research assistants. Because their careers took them on to other institutions, they were then less involved in the analyses presented in this book. In particular, we thank Gisela Clausen, Reinhold Kliegl, and Ulrich Mayr for their many contributions in the initial phases of the Berlin Aging Study.

This book represents the revised and modified version of a German monograph on the Berlin Aging Study published in 1996. The authors of the chapters are the creators of this book and, together with a few others, were the makers of its precursor. We are grateful to them on many counts, but especially for their willingness to subject their texts to repeated internal and external criticism. In accordance with the goals of the Berlin-Brandenburg Academy and its study groups, the chapters were not written by individual scientists in seclusion. Instead, they are the result of project meetings, an evaluation conference at Schloß Ringberg in 1994, internal commentaries, and external written reviews.

Reviewers and their helpful criticism have indeed played a vital role in the production of this book. Therefore, we thank the scientists who engaged their competence as reviewers and commentators: Jutta Allmendinger, Anton Amann, Bernhard Badura, Axel Börsch-Supan, Erika Brückner, Angelika Callaway, Charles Chappuis, Christoph Conrad, Brian Cooper, Helmut Coper, John F. Corso, D. Yves von Cramon, Margret Dieck, Martin Diewald, Hanneli Döhner, Georg Elwert, Alexander von Eye, Sigrun-Heide Filipp, Insa Fooken, James L. Fozard, Dieter Frey, Angela Friederici, Vjenka Garms-Homolová, Matthias Geiser, Wolfgang Glatzer, Werner Greve, Heinz Häfner, Richard Hauser, William J. Hoyer, Hartmut Kaelble, Hans-Joachim von Kondratowitz, Andreas Kruse, Adelheid Kuhlmey, Hans Lauter, Elisabeth Minnemann, Jürgen Mittelstraß, Walter Müller, Joep Munnichs, Gerd Naegele, John Nesselroade, Dieter Neumeier, Annette Niederfranke, Erhard Olbrich, Wolf D. Oswald, Klaus Poeck, Jürgen Reulecke, Dorothea Roether, Leopold Rosenmayr, Georg Rudinger, Timothy Salthouse, Günther Schlierf, Dietrich Seidel, Annemette Sørensen, Georg Strohmeyer, Andreas Stuck, Hans Thomae, Klaus-Peter Wefers, Siegfried Weyerer, Brita Willershausen-Zönnchen, Hans-Ulrich Wittchen, and Jürgen Wolf. We express our gratitude and respect for their constructive comments. However, we must emphasize that the authors and not the reviewers are responsible for any remaining shortcomings.

The Berlin Aging Study's day-to-day organizational work mainly took place in the BASE project office, housed at the Max Planck Institute for Human Development. We are grateful to Jane Johnston, Natalia Geb, Noëlle Gielen, Christoph Emmrich, and particularly Susannah Goss for their dedicated work as research secretaries. This involved the manifold organizational and coordination tasks associated with the project as well as work on manuscripts and graphics. We are grateful also to Jörg Metze at Chamäleon Design in Berlin for preparing the figures. Christine Drkosch and Florian Grüter as well as Holger Sweers deserve our thanks for their excellent work on the indexes.

The German-language predecessor to this book was published by the Akademie Verlag in Berlin, which is headed by Gerd Giesler. His competence and flexibility in making time adjustments during the preparation of the German-language edition were impressive, as was his cooperative spirit in paving the administrative way for the present English version.

Our collaboration with the publisher of this English version, Cambridge University Press, and its staff was equally splendid. Julia Hough, as our responsible editor, provided the kind of organizational help that authors and editors hope for. The production process was supported by the excellent work of Brian R. MacDonald. We thank them.

Many of the chapters in the present volume are based on translations of the original German chapters, though all chapters underwent major revisions and editorial refinements. In addition to the coordinating editor (Julia Delius, see below), several persons were involved in this task. Susannah Goss provided first translations of Chapters 3 and 10 and many suggestions for editorial improvements in other chapters. Irmgard Pahl assisted with the translation of Chapters 7 and 17 and helped with the proofreading. Anne Tschida offered feedback on English style in nearly all chapters with a particular focus on reducing overly technical language. The final versions of the chapters were reviewed by Michael Marsiske, a former BASE scientist and now an assistant professor at Wayne State University, Detroit. Together with his graduate students Jason Allaire, Jennifer Margrett, and Benjamin Mast, he painstakingly reviewed all chapters and provided detailed editorial but also substantive commentaries. We thank him and his student colleagues for their outstanding work.

There is one person who deserves more than anyone else the deep gratitude of the editors and authors of this book: Julia Delius. As shown on the title page, Julia Delius served as coordinating editor. Just as Reinhard Nuthmann was the singular person in charge of the administrative coordination of the data collection of the Berlin Aging Study, Julia Delius was the mastermind of the editorial coordination of the many steps resulting in the present publication. Apart from functioning as first translator of ten chapters, Julia Delius was responsible for organizing the review process, keeping time schedules, attending to the idiosyncrasies of individual authors, alerting the editors to specific problems and inconsistencies, organizing the preparation of indexes and graphic materials, maintaining excellent relations with the two publishing houses involved, and, not least, compensating for the deficits of the two editors. In each of these tasks and their orchestration, Julia Delius was outstanding. Not surprisingly, Julia Delius has provided the editorial foundation on which the present book could be built, and a building process it was. We thank her with deep gratitude and unqualified respect.

Our expression of gratitude to our colleagues and especially Julia Delius, however, are not meant to detract from our own responsibilities as editors. Let us hasten to add, therefore, that those whom we acknowledge deserve much of the credit but none of the blame for whatever shortcomings remain.

Paul B. Baltes
Karl Ulrich Mayer
Berlin and Palo Alto, November 1997

Introduction

The present and future of our society are characterized by a rising proportion of old and very old people. Hopes for a longer life are not only justified but real. They are often associated, however, with negative views about old age – expectations of declining intellectual abilities and physical health, of social isolation and inactivity, economic insecurity, and social dependency. Increased quantity of life in old age, in other words, is combined with a concern about its quality. The increase in number and proportion of old and very old people in the population – often described as a slow demographic revolution – is also coupled with worries that society may have to struggle to deal with difficult issues such as the financial burden of providing for old age, increasing demands on social and medical care, growing needs for assistance and care in cases of disability, and the potential loss of a sense of purpose as individuals reach advanced old age.

On closer examination, of course, it becomes clear that many of our images of old age and aging, and the associated stresses and opportunities, are based on rather uncertain knowledge. What is old age? How is chronological age related to functional age? What is the range of aging patterns for different individuals? Are old age and aging different for men and women or for members of various social, educational, and ethnic groups and classes? In which sense is aging unavoidable, and which intervention chances are realistic? Is there a difference between young old age and old old age, between what one of us has recently called the third and fourth ages of life (P. B. Baltes, 1997)? The answers to such questions will have far-reaching consequences on future changes resulting from the aging of societies.

These and other questions led the former West Berlin Academy of Sciences and Technology to initiate a study group "Aging and Societal Development" (P. B. Baltes & Mittelstraß, 1992). A project group emanating from this panel designed and carried out the Berlin Aging Study (BASE), whose first results are presented in this volume. The Berlin Aging Study is unique in several regards: the wide spectrum of scientific disciplines involved, the focus on very old age (70- to over 100-year-olds), and the empirical study of a heterogeneous (representative) urban population. Among other topics, this book includes findings on intellectual functioning, personality, and social relationships in old age; on physical health, medical treatment, and dental health; on psychiatric disorders such as dementia and depression; on socioeconomic conditions, social and cultural activities; and on everyday competence, subjective well-being, and differences between men and women.

The present English-language publication is the successor to a German publication (Mayer & Baltes, 1996). To retain some of the contextual flavor of the German publication and illustrate the role of the Berlin Aging Study in the context of German society and the German gerontological research community, we have made an effort to keep this Introduction close to its original form and content.

1

1   Aging in Science and Society

The research of aging (gerontology) presents a challenge not only because it is a relatively new field, but also because it is one of the few domains of research that are accessible from nearly all sides of sciences and the humanities and are directly related to numerous facets of our lives.

The challenge to the scientific analysis of aging is its multidimensionality in structure and function. In order to comprehend old age and aging in its multifarious physical, psychological, socioeconomic, and public policy aspects, special multi- and interdisciplinary efforts are required. The approaches chosen by the individual disciplines – for example, biology, internal medicine, psychiatry, psychology, economics, sociology, or anthropology – provide an essential research basis. However, what is at least equally important, and likely to be associated with greater intellectual and organizational problems, is to bring these lines of research together, concentrating scientific analysis on the uncovering of systemic links and interactions in order to understand old age and aging in its entirety.

The challenge to society, mainly to social policy, consists in the search for structures and rules that allow people at *all* stages of life to have fair chances of further development and a good (fulfilled) life. The underlying fact that the population is aging is often negatively characterized as the increasing "senescence" of society. However, we need to be aware that this does not give cause for resignation and pessimism. Only in this century has human civilization made it possible for most people in Western societies to reach the age of 70 and over. Therefore, the shaping of what is possible in old age does not have a long tradition. As a society, we are only at the beginning of a learning process about old age. In this sense, old age is still young, its potential is not fully realized, and institutions, norms, and resources advantageous for old age still need to be developed.

2   "Aging and Societal Development": A Berlin-Brandenburg Academy of Sciences Study Group

As old age and aging have come to be a focus of interest in modern societies, it is not surprising that the Academy of Sciences and Technology in Berlin, which was founded in 1987 and emphasized the close links between basic science and societal practice, turned to this topic. Supported by the academy's president Horst Albach, the multidisciplinary study group "Aging and Societal Development" was constituted during one of the academy's first assemblies. In 1993, the Berlin-Brandenburg Academy of Sciences was founded and took over from the West Berlin academy. Under its president Hubert Markl, the study group "Aging and Societal Development" was integrated into the new academy's work program.

Of the 30 founding members of the academy, 6 formed the initial study group: the psychologist Paul B. Baltes (chair), Max Planck Institute for Human Development in Berlin; the internist Wolfgang Gerok, University of Freiburg; the economist Hans-Jürgen Krupp, (formerly) German Institute for Economic Research in Berlin; the gerontologist Ursula Lehr (until 1990), University of Heidelberg; the philosopher Jürgen Mittelstraß, University of Konstanz; and the biologist Heinz-Günter Wittmann, Max Planck Institute for Molecular Genetics in Berlin. Three external experts soon joined the group: the psychiatrist Hanfried Helmchen, Free University of Berlin; the sociologist Karl Ulrich

Mayer (deputy chair of the study group), Max Planck Institute for Human Development in Berlin; and the internist Elisabeth Steinhagen-Thiessen, (formerly) Free University of Berlin. Ursula M. Staudinger, research scientist at the Max Planck Institute for Human Development, joined as the coordinator of the study group.

Following intensive discussions, the study group set itself two closely related goals in 1988 (see the academy's yearbook, Akademie der Wissenschaften zu Berlin, 1989, pp. 412–431). The first goal was a volume on general research and social perspectives on human aging. This book, *Zukunft des Alterns und gesellschaftliche Entwicklung* [The future of aging and societal development], was published in 1992 as the fifth research report of the Academy of Sciences and Technology (P. B. Baltes & Mittelstraß, 1992), and reissued as a textbook in 1994 (P. B. Baltes, Mittelstraß, & Staudinger, 1994).

Second, together with a project group of scientists from various Berlin research institutions, the study group decided to carry out an empirical and representative study of old and very old people in Berlin: the Berlin Aging Study (BASE). The findings from the first wave of this study were initially presented in German in an extensive monograph published in 1996 (Mayer & Baltes, 1996). The present book represents a revised and modified translation of the German book and provides the first detailed account of this study in English (but see also the special issue of the journal *Ageing and Society* on the Berlin Aging Study: P. B. Baltes, Mayer, Helmchen, & Steinhagen-Thiessen, 1993; and a featured section in the journal *Psychology and Aging*: P. B. Baltes & Smith, 1997).

3   The Berlin Aging Study (BASE)

Within the second project, the Berlin Aging Study (BASE), the academy study group "Aging and Societal Development" cooperates with institutions of the Free University (FU) of Berlin and with the Max Planck Institute (MPI) for Human Development. (Changes of institutional affiliations led to the addition of the Humboldt University [HU] Berlin in 1994.) The following scientists are primarily responsible for the Berlin Aging Study, which is organized into four research units (Internal Medicine/Geriatrics, Psychiatry, Psychology, and Sociology/Social Policy): Paul B. Baltes (chair of the study group and codirector of the Psychology Research Unit, MPI for Human Development), Karl Ulrich Mayer (deputy chair of the study group and codirector of the Sociology and Social Policy Unit, MPI for Human Development), Hanfried Helmchen (director of the Psychiatry Unit, Department of Psychiatry, FU Berlin), and Elisabeth Steinhagen-Thiessen (director of the Internal Medicine and Geriatrics Unit, Virchow Clinic, HU Berlin, and Evangelisches Geriatriezentrum Berlin). This core group was joined by Markus Borchelt (Internal Medicine/Geriatrics), Michael Linden (Psychiatry), Jacqui Smith (Psychology), and Michael Wagner (Sociology/Social Policy) to form the steering committee of the study. The sociologist Reinhard Nuthmann was responsible for the administrative organization and coordination of the Berlin Aging Study until the end of 1996, when psychologist Karl Mathias Neher took over this task.

The Berlin Aging Study project group consists of more than 40 scientists (see Table I.1 at the end of the Introduction) and represents a broad spectrum of research disciplines (biochemistry, internal medicine and geriatrics, dentistry, radiology, psychiatry, neuropsychology, psychology, sociology, economics, and social policy). The members of the project group are assigned to the study's four research units and have cooperated at every stage of the study: at the theoretical and methodological planning stage, during the assessment phases, for the work on data analysis, and for publication of the BASE findings. Regular project meetings, which have taken place at the MPI for Human Development once or twice a month from 1989 onward and are regularly attended by 20 to 25 scientists, are a particularly important component of this collaboration.

The conception of the Berlin Aging Study (see P. B. Baltes et al., Chapter 1 in this volume) takes up central gerontological issues and aims to contribute toward the development of a gerontological knowledge base with four foci: (1) a broadly based multi- and interdisciplinarity of assessment and analysis, (2) a concentration on very old age (70–100+ years), (3) a locally representative and heterogeneous sample, and (4) the collection of a reference data set for the elderly population of a large city. When embarking on this project, the BASE research units – Internal Medicine and Geriatrics, Psychiatry, Psychology, and Sociology and Social Policy (demonstrating the multidisciplinarity of the study) – agreed on the following theoretical orientations as a connecting framework for research questions, hypotheses, and measures: (1) differential aging, (2) continuity and discontinuity over the life course and in old age, (3) reserve capacity and action potential of older adults, and (4) aging as a systemic phenomenon. Initially, these theoretical orientations implied different connotations depending on the research units' discipline-specific approaches and interests. Nevertheless, the orientations have proved able to provide structure to the discourse of the research team and to subsequent analyses.

4   Contents of This Volume

This book is divided into four parts. In the first part, basic information is presented about the Berlin Aging Study. The first chapter by P. B. Baltes, Mayer, Helmchen, and Steinhagen-Thiessen introduces the conceptual and methodological framework of the study and presents the different BASE samples. The question of data weighting, which results from the stratification of the sample by age and gender, is discussed as well as the important but frequently neglected problem of sample selectivity. By comparing available information about participants and nonparticipants, we examined the degree to which persons with certain features (e.g., very poor health) were underrepresented in the main BASE sample. The topic of sample selectivity is dealt with in more detail in Chapter 2 (Lindenberger et al.).

The findings presented in this book are based on cross-sectional data. It is therefore important to note that the age differences reported in many chapters may be due to cohort differences, at least in part. In order to make this point obvious, Maas, Borchelt, and Mayer (Chapter 3) present a quantitative analysis of birth cohort differences that result from having experienced the historical events and changes of this century at different stages of the life course. This quantitative approach to cohort differences is supplemented by qualitative analysis. To this end, Schütze, Tesch-Römer, and Borchers (Chapter 4) focus on six selected biographies of BASE participants and remind the reader that the statistical values presented in most other chapters are based on data about *individuals*. On the one hand, the individual life histories reflect the historical events and societal developments of the 20th century. On the other hand, they are shaped by the origins of the older persons, as well as their very different personal decisions and experiences.

In the second part, the four research units of the Berlin Aging Study (Internal Medicine/Geriatrics, Psychiatry, Psychology, and Sociology/Social Policy) report their results from discipline-specific perspectives. In these four chapters, many of the instruments, measures, and terms used in BASE and referred to in later chapters are introduced.

In Chapter 5, Steinhagen-Thiessen and Borchelt present the main topics examined by the Internal Medicine and Geriatrics Unit. First, findings about the prevalence of somatic illnesses are discussed. It is then examined whether the cardiovascular risk-factor model developed for younger adults remains valid for older adults. Further sections deal with biochemical reference values, older adults' dental health, geriatric drug therapy, and functional capacity. In Chapter 6, Helmchen et al. present findings on the types and frequencies of psychiatric disorders in old age and their predictors and consequences. The most frequent psychiatric disorders in old age, dementia and depression, are particularly closely examined. Special emphasis is also placed on so-called subdiagnostic psychiatric morbidity, which has everyday relevance for the people affected. In Chapter 7, Smith and P. B. Baltes consider aging from a psychological perspective, focusing on three areas of psychological research, namely, intelligence, self and personality, and social relationships. After providing descriptive results from the three domains, a systemic perspective is taken in order to illustrate links between these domains of functioning. Finally, in Chapter 8, Mayer, Maas, and Wagner present findings from the Sociology and Social Policy Unit. The relationships between older adults' socioeconomic conditions, their life circumstances, and social activities are at the center of attention. For example, the consequences of socioeconomic characteristics (such as social class and social prestige) for social participation and for aspects of physical and mental health are examined.

The third, longest part of the monograph includes chapters by authors from different research fields who deal with topics covering more than one discipline. The discussions of their findings are often guided by the theoretical orientations introduced in Chapter 1.

In Chapter 9, M. M. Baltes, Freund, and Horgas analyze the differences between old men and women, a topic that is particularly interesting because of the demographic "feminization of old age." Surprisingly, relatively few gender differences were observed on separate dimensions (one exception is a higher degree of disability in old women). However, gender differences become more obvious if the analysis takes the entire pattern of functioning into account, rather than being restricted to individual variables (cf. Smith & Baltes, Chapter 7; Mayer et al., Chapter 18). Such a wholistic viewpoint reveals that older women are particularly often represented in what can be considered as risk groups.

In Chapter 10, Wagner, Schütze, and Lang consider older adults' social relationships, their embeddedness in networks of family and friends, as well as aspects such as perceived support and loneliness. In Chapter 11, Staudinger, Freund, Linden, and Maas examine psychological resilience. They find that self-regulatory processes play an important role in dealing with restrictions in old age and, to a certain degree, contribute toward the maintenance of adaptation in later life. In Chapter 12, Lindenberger and Reischies focus on aspects of intellectual functioning in old age. Although intellectual abilities generally decline with old age, a considerable amount of interindividual variability and potential to learn new things remains. However, individual learning capacity is reduced more conspicuously for persons diagnosed with dementia. Among persons aged 90 and above, almost 50% are affected by some form of dementia. Lindenberger and Reischies also discuss the close association found between sensory functioning and intelligence in old age. This intimate connection between sensory and intellectual functioning in old age is probably due to the biological aging of the brain influencing both systems in a similar way. Specific attention to questions about vision, hearing, and balance/gait is given in Chapter 13 by Marsiske et al. They describe the relationships between sensory impairments, which become very frequent in old age, and domains such as everyday competence and well-being.

Two components of everyday competence are identified using a multidisciplinary approach in Chapter 14 by M. M. Baltes, Maas, Wilms, Borchelt, and Little. The basic competence to care for oneself is mainly determined by more physical indicators of health and mobility, whereas expanded competence, which includes the capacity to participate in more complex social activities, is found to be more dependent on psychosocial factors. In Chapter 15, Borchelt, Gilberg, Horgas, and Geiselmann concentrate on the interactions between physical and mental health and between health-related and psychosocial factors. With age there is an increasing discrepancy between objective and subjective health. In Chapter 16 by Linden, Horgas, Gilberg, and Steinhagen-Thiessen, conditions for the utilization of medical and nursing care are examined. A complex web of social-structural, medical, and psychological factors play a role in determining the use of formal and informal assistance.

In Chapter 17, Smith, Fleeson, Geiselmann, Settersten, and Kunzmann examine subjective well-being. Again, a marked discrepancy between older people's objective life circumstances and their subjective evaluations is found. In general, older adults report remarkably high life satisfaction considering their objective situation. However, if one takes into account additional aspects of their psychological status (including emotional loneliness; cf. Smith & Baltes, Chapter 7), there is a stronger negative age trend. Still, it seems that where subjective life satisfaction is concerned, individual perceptions of different life domains (e.g., health, social relationships) play a more important role than the respective objective situation.

Finally, in the fourth part of the book, Mayer et al. summarize and discuss the central findings from the Berlin Aging Study in Chapter 18. Furthermore, using cluster analysis, interrelationships between domains of functioning, which are of interest to all of the disciplines involved in BASE, are illustrated and subgroups with characteristic profiles of functioning are identified.

5   Limitations of This Book

The aim of this book is to document the goals, theoretical orientations, methodological framework, and initial findings of the Berlin Aging Study's first cross-sectional wave. The analyses we present here are selected to provide an overview of important topics examined so far in BASE. In the meantime (see P. B. Baltes et al., Chapter 1), the Berlin Aging Study has been extended as a longitudinal project. First results of longitudinal studies are expected to be available in late 1998. Further, although 14 of the 18 chapters were written in interdisciplinary collaboration, work on several topics that cross the boundaries of scientific fields, such as the question of socioeconomically based differences in morbidity, is still in progress.

A sense of scientific responsibility makes it necessary for us to point out very explicitly to the reader the restrictions and limitations that we see in the evidence offered, including its generalizability (cf. P. B. Baltes et al., Chapter 1, Sections 6 and 7). The major systematic limitation affecting the validity of the statements made in this book results from the fact that the data base is restricted to the first cross-sectional phase of the Berlin

Aging Study. We compare age groups and do not follow individual courses of aging. We have tried to make this limitation as clear as possible in the presentation of our findings, but possible misunderstandings of phrasings can not always be excluded. Moreover, a complete abstinence from using cross-sectional age differences to estimate age changes is not warranted.

Second, the reader should be aware of the fact that the BASE Intensive Protocol sample consists of only 516 people. For some questions, this may be considered a large sample; for others, the available sample is small. In comparison with most other studies, we have exceptionally many participants in the oldest age groups and among old men. Still, with a sample size such as this, it cannot be excluded that we are not able to substantiate weak but systematic relationships. Likewise it is possible that rare but important phenomena are only insufficiently captured.

Third, the fact that very old and frail persons are difficult to reach or cannot be examined is an insurmountable hurdle for studies of very old age. In planning and carrying out the study, we made a special effort to clarify the potential consequences of selective participation (cf. P. B. Baltes et al., Chapter 1; Lindenberger et al., Chapter 2) and to correct for it (e.g., Helmchen et al., Chapter 6). In many chapters, biases caused by selectivity are reflected in the interpretation of findings. On the whole, the selectivity analyses indicate that the image of old age outlined by our findings tends to be too positive. At the same time, we must emphasize that, in our opinion, the size of these bias effects is small rather than large. For instance, our selectivity analyses have shown that differences caused by selectivity remain within narrow boundaries. Particularly important is the finding that statements about relationships between variables and the diversity (heterogeneity) of aging appear justified despite the selectivity obtained on average levels of analysis. In some cases, however, correcting for selectivity possibly leads to alterations in our conclusions that are theoretically significant (e.g., regarding the prevalence of dementia).

The generalizability of the BASE findings is also compromised by the restriction of the study to the districts of former West Berlin. After the collapse of the Berlin Wall in 1989, we held detailed discussions about whether the organizational and financial conditions would allow the extension of this complex study to the eastern districts of Berlin. Unfortunately, the infrastructure was not available to make this possible. Some of the particularities of West Berlin as a large city and as a historical exception are discussed in Chapter 1 with regard to the issue of generalizability. Summarily, it seems reasonable to conclude that the unique aspects of West Berlin appear to be smaller than often assumed.

Finally, we want to make the reader aware of the pair of terms that we have used to characterize the frequently distinguished two large age groups in our study. To reflect what is often called young old age and old old age, we refer to *old* (aged 70 to 84 years) and *very old* people (aged 85 and over). Furthermore, it should be clear that, based on our sample, we mean persons aged 70 and over when we speak about the population of old people.

Judging by the time and effort spent, the number of scientists involved, and, not least, by the amount of financial resources invested, the scope and intensity of multidisciplinary assessments in the Berlin Aging Study make this an important research project. We hope the first yield documented in this book justifies this undertaking. However, in view of the current state of interdisciplinary gerontological research (cf. P. B. Baltes & Baltes, 1992), we are very aware of the fact that we are closer to the beginning of this work than to its completion. For a first impression and overview of the BASE findings, we recommend reading the first and last chapters.

References

Akademie der Wissenschaften zu Berlin. (1989). *Jahrbuch 1988*. Berlin: de Gruyter.

Baltes, P. B. (1997). On the incomplete architecture of human ontogeny: Selection, optimization, and compensation as foundation of developmental theory. *American Psychologist, 52*, 366–380.

Baltes, P. B., & Baltes, M. M. (1992). Gerontologie: Begriff, Herausforderung und Brennpunkte. In P. B. Baltes & J. Mittelstraß (Eds.), *Zukunft des Alterns und gesellschaftliche Entwicklung* (pp. 1–34). Berlin: de Gruyter.

Baltes, P. B., Mayer, K. U., Helmchen, H., & Steinhagen-Thiessen, E. (1993). The Berlin Aging Study (BASE): Overview and design. *Ageing and Society, 13*, 483–515.

Baltes, P. B., & Mittelstraß, J. (Eds.). (1992). *Zukunft des Alterns und gesellschaftliche Entwicklung*. Berlin: de Gruyter.

Baltes, P. B., Mittelstraß, J., & Staudinger, U. M. (Eds.). (1994). *Alter und Altern: Ein interdisziplinärer Studientext zur Gerontologie*. Berlin: de Gruyter.

Baltes, P. B., & Smith, J. (1997). A systemic-wholistic view of psychological functioning in very old age: Introduction to a collection of articles from the Berlin Aging Study. *Psychology and Aging, 12*, 395–409.

Mayer, K. U., & Baltes, P. B. (Eds.). (1996). *Die Berliner Altersstudie*. Berlin: Akademie Verlag.

Table I.1. *Persons involved in the study group "Aging and Societal Development" and in the Berlin Aging Study (BASE) as of November 1997*

Berlin-Brandenburg Academy of Sciences Study Group "Aging and Societal Development"

Prof. Dr. P. B. Baltes (chair)	Max Planck Institute (MPI) for Human Development, Berlin
Prof. Dr. G. Elwert	Free University (FU) of Berlin
Prof. Dr. A. Friederici	MPI for Cognitive Neuroscience, Leipzig
Prof. Dr. W. Gerok	Freiburg University
Prof. Dr. H. Helmchen	FU Berlin – Department of Psychiatry[a]
Prof. Dr. K. U. Mayer (deputy chair)	MPI for Human Development, Berlin
Prof. Dr. J. Mittelstraß	Konstanz University
Prof. Dr. E. Steinhagen-Thiessen	Humboldt University (HU) Berlin – Virchow Clinic[a] and Evangelisches Geriatriezentrum Berlin (EGZB)
Dr. R. Nuthmann (BASE coordinator until 1996)	MPI for Human Development
Dr. K. M. Neher (BASE coordinator since 1997)	MPI for Human Development
Priv. Doz. Dr. U. M. Staudinger (coordinator of the study group)	MPI for Human Development

Project Coordination Center of the Berlin Aging Study (BASE)

Dr. R. Nuthmann, Dipl.-Soz. (until 1996)	MPI for Human Development
Dr. K. M. Neher, Dipl.-Psych. (since 1997)	MPI for Human Development
Dr. J. Delius, physician – coordinating editor	MPI for Human Development

Scientists involved in the Berlin Aging Study

Internal Medicine and Geriatrics Unit

Prof. Dr. E. Steinhagen-Thiessen, physician (director)	HU Berlin – Virchow Clinic[a] and EGZB
Dr. M. Borchelt, physician (deputy director)	EGZB
Dr. T. Hillen, physician	Berlin-Brandenburg Academy of Sciences
Prof. Dr. D. Huhn, physician	HU Berlin – Virchow Clinic[a]
Dr. A. Kage, physician	HU Berlin – Virchow Clinic[a]
Prof. Dr. E. Köttgen, physician	HU Berlin – Virchow Clinic[a]
Dr. H. Münzberg, physician	EGZB
Dr. R. Nieczaj, Dipl.-Biol.	EGZB
Associate	
Dr. I. Nitschke, dentist	HU Berlin – Center for Dentistry[b]

Psychiatry Unit

Prof. Dr. H. Helmchen, physician (director)	FU Berlin – Department of Psychiatry[a]
Prof. Dr. M. Linden, physician, Dipl.-Psych. (deputy director)	FU Berlin – Department of Psychiatry[a]
Prof. Dr. M. M. Baltes, Dipl.-Psych.	FU Berlin – Department of Psychiatry[a]
Dr. B. Geiselmann, physician	Max Bürger Center, Berlin
Prof. Dr. S. Kanowski, physician	FU Berlin – Department of Psychiatry[a]
H. Krüger, Dipl.-Math.	FU Berlin – Department of Psychiatry[a]
Dr. F. R. Lang, Dipl.-Psych.	FU Berlin – Department of Psychiatry[a]

Table I.1. (*cont.*)

Priv. Doz. Dr. F. M. Reischies, physician	FU Berlin – Department of Psychiatry[a]
Dr. R. T. Schaub, physician	Berlin-Brandenburg Academy of Sciences
Dr. T. Wernicke, physician	FU Berlin – Department of Psychiatry[a]
Associate	
Dr. A. L. Horgas, R.N.	Wayne State University, Detroit, MI

Psychology Unit

Prof. Dr. P. B. Baltes, Dipl.-Psych. (codirector)	MPI for Human Development
Dr. J. Smith, B.A., Hons.: Psychology (codirector)	MPI for Human Development
Dr. A. M. Freund, Dipl.-Psych.	MPI for Human Development
Priv. Doz. Dr. U. Lindenberger, Dipl.-Psych.	MPI for Human Development
Dr. T. D. Little, M.A. (psychology)	MPI for Human Development
Dr. H. Maier, Dipl.-Psych.	MPI for Human Development
Priv. Doz. Dr. U. M. Staudinger, Dipl.-Psych.	MPI for Human Development
Associates	
Dr. W. Fleeson, M.A. (psychology)	Wake Forest University, Winston-Salem, NC
Dr. U. Kunzmann, Dipl.-Psych.	MPI for Human Development
Dr. S.-C. Li, M.A. (psychology)	MPI for Human Development
Dr. M. Marsiske, M.S. (psychology)	Wayne State University, Detroit, MI
Prof. Dr. H. Scherer, physician	FU Berlin – University Clinic Benjamin Franklin[c]
Prof. Dr. Y. Schütze, Dipl.-Soz.	HU Berlin
T. Singer, Dipl.-Psych.	MPI for Human Development
Priv. Doz. Dr. C. Tesch-Römer, Dipl.-Psych.	German Center of Gerontology, Berlin

Sociology and Social Policy Unit

Prof. Dr. K. U. Mayer, M.A. (codirector)	MPI for Human Development
Prof. Dr. M. Wagner, Dipl.-Soz. (codirector)	MPI for Human Development and University of Cologne
Prof. Dr. G. Wagner, Dipl.-Volksw.	German Institute for Economic Research, Berlin and European University Viadrina, Frankfurt (Oder)
Dr. I. Maas, Dipl.-Soz.	MPI for Human Development
Associates	
A. Bukov, Dipl.-Soz.	MPI for Human Development
Dr. R. Gilberg, Dipl.-Soz.	Infas, Bonn
T. Lampert, Dipl.-Soz.	MPI for Human Development

Research assistants and medical staff[d]

R. Adair (until 1993)	FU Berlin – University Clinic Rudolf Virchow
D. Barth (until 1992)	Academy of Sciences and Technology, Berlin
A. zu Bentheim (until 1992)	Academy of Sciences and Technology, Berlin
H. Borkenhagen (until 1992)	Academy of Sciences and Technology, Berlin
C. Dautert (until 1993)	Academy of Sciences and Technology, Berlin
S. Elsing	Berlin-Brandenburg Academy of Sciences
G. Faust (until 1992)	Academy of Sciences and Technology, Berlin
U. Feierabend (until 1991)	Academy of Sciences and Technology, Berlin

Table I.1. (*cont.*)

N. Gielen (until 1993)	Academy of Sciences and Technology, Berlin
L. Groh (until 1993)	Academy of Sciences and Technology, Berlin
A. Günther (until 1991)	MPI for Human Development
K. Haenel (until 1992)	MPI for Human Development
K. Häring (until 1991)	Academy of Sciences and Technology, Berlin
S. Kahle (until 1991)	Academy of Sciences and Technology, Berlin
C. Kahnt (until 1992)	Academy of Sciences and Technology, Berlin
G. Kleinknecht (until 1991)	Academy of Sciences and Technology, Berlin
J. Menzel (until 1992)	MPI for Human Development
B. Mucke (until 1993)	FU Berlin – Northern Dental Clinic
I. Nentwig (until 1990)	Academy of Sciences and Technology, Berlin
A. Rentz (until 1991)	MPI for Human Development
A. Schlüter (until 1993)	Academy of Sciences and Technology, Berlin
R. Scholz (until 1992)	Academy of Sciences and Technology, Berlin
D. Schrader	MPI for Human Development
G. Schubert	MPI for Human Development
R. Straßburger (until 1995)	Academy of Sciences and Technology, Berlin
K. Tamborini (until 1992)	Academy of Sciences and Technology, Berlin
F. Thiel (until 1991)	MPI for Human Development
J. Umlauf (until 1993)	Academy of Sciences and Technology, Berlin

Scientists formerly involved in the Berlin Aging Study[d]

C. Borchers, M.A. (until 1993)	Academy of Sciences and Technology, Berlin
Dr. G. Clausen, Dipl.-Soz. (until 1992)	MPI for Human Development
Prof. Dr. R. Eckstein (until 1993)	FU Berlin – University Clinic Rudolf Virchow
Dr. S. Englert, physician (until 1995)	FU Berlin – Department of Psychiatry[a]
Dr. S. Fimmel, Dipl.-Biochem. (until 1994)	HU Berlin – Virchow Clinic[a]
J. Fischer-Pauly, physician (until 1993)	Academy of Sciences and Technology, Berlin
Dr. W. Hopfenmüller, physician (until 1996)	FU Berlin – University Clinic Benjamin Franklin
Prof. Dr. R. Kliegl, Dipl.-Psych. (until 1994)	MPI for Human Development
Dr. B. Klingenspor, Dipl.-Psych. (until 1995)	MPI for Human Development
J. Lüthje, physician (until 1992)	Max Bürger Hospital, Berlin
Dr. U. Mayr, Dipl.-Psych. (until 1993)	MPI for Human Development
Dr. A. Mochine, physician (until 1992)	Academy of Sciences and Technology, Berlin
Dr. R. Nuthmann, Dipl.-Soz. (until 1996)	MPI for Human Development
Dr. R. A. Settersten Jr., M.A. (until 1993)	MPI for Human Development
Prof. Dr. H.-W. Wahl, Dipl.-Psych. (until 1989)	Academy of Sciences and Technology, Berlin
Dr. H.-U. Wilms, Dipl.-Psych. (until 1997)	FU Berlin – Department of Psychiatry[a]
Dr. G. Wittmann (until 1994)	HU Berlin – Virchow Clinic[a]

[a]FU Berlin, University Clinic Rudolf Virchow until April 1995.
[b]FU Berlin, Northern Dental Clinic until April 1994.
[c]FU Berlin, Klinikum Steglitz until April 1995.
[d]Institutional affiliations at the time of their involvement in BASE.

PART A

Theoretical Orientations and Methods

CHAPTER 1

The Berlin Aging Study (BASE): Sample, Design, and Overview of Measures

Paul B. Baltes, Karl Ulrich Mayer, Hanfried Helmchen, and Elisabeth Steinhagen-Thiessen

This introductory chapter describes the general basis, goals, and methods of the Berlin Aging Study (BASE). Three features represent the special characteristics of BASE: (1) sample heterogeneity through local representativeness (for West Berlin), (2) a focus on very old people (70–105 years), and (3) broadly based interdisciplinarity (internal medicine, geriatrics, psychiatry, psychology, sociology, and social policy). Apart from discipline-specific topics, four common and intersecting theoretical orientations guide the study: (1) differential aging, (2) continuity versus discontinuity of aging, (3) range and limits of plasticity and reserve capacity, and (4) old age and aging as interdisciplinary and systemic phenomena.

1 Outline

After presenting a theoretical overview and discussing some methodological limitations of cross-sectional studies, this chapter presents three empirical aspects of BASE that are relevant to all chapters in this volume: (1) an overview of the measures used in the 14 sessions of data collection, (2) a summary of the findings of sample selectivity analyses, and (3) issues of generalizability, with a special emphasis on problems such as selective mortality and statistical weighting.

In general, the selectivity analyses indicate that the BASE data are characterized by a considerable degree of heterogeneity and generalizability. Furthermore, there is little evidence of interactions between selectivity effects and the primary design variables – that is, chronological age and gender. Furthermore, there are also few indications that sample selection processes imply major effects on information about interindividual variability and covariation among variables. This conclusion is based on selectivity analyses involving 25 indicators. Thus, the results of the Berlin Aging Study can be considered as a good approximation of the entire population of older people in West Berlin. Where this is not the case, and for the selection variables considered, the extent and direction of the bias can be estimated by using the selectivity analyses to obtain adequate correction formulae (cf. Fig. 1.3; see Lindenberger et al., Chapter 2 in this volume). We view the explicitness of the selectivity analyses as a particular strength of the Berlin Aging Study and intend to continue this line of research as the study is extended to a longitudinal design.

Finally in this chapter, we turn to another methodological topic, that of objective and subjective measurement. It is particularly important to us to point out that the human psyche does not strive to achieve perfect representation of objective (internal and external) reality. On the contrary, the adaptation and coping strategies of the human self include the transformation of objective life conditions and events for the creation of a self-relevant reality. It is important to keep in mind the dual nature of "self-reports" – reality and its psychological transformation.

2   The Berlin Aging Study (BASE)

The Berlin Aging Study (BASE) is an interdisciplinary gerontological study focusing on a representative sample of 516 persons aged 70 to over 100 years, stratified by age and gender (cf. P. B. Baltes, Mayer, Helmchen, & Steinhagen-Thiessen, 1993, 1994). The assessments reported in this volume took place from May 1990 to June 1993 as a cross-sectional study. The protocol included internal/geriatric, psychiatric, psychological, sociological, and economic information collected in 14 sessions. Since then, the study has been continued as a longitudinal study (1993–98). Longitudinal information, however, is not part of this first overall report.

The Berlin Aging Study deals with old age and aging. When the term *old age* is employed, we focus on old people and the result of aging, old age as a phase of life, and old people as a part of society. When we speak of *aging*, we refer to processes and mechanisms associated with, or causally related to, growing old. As we present cross-sectional data from the first wave of the study, strictly speaking, we cannot make statements about individual courses of the aging process. This will be possible with the longitudinal data currently being collected.

2.1   *Main Foci of BASE*

Because BASE was initiated before the unification of Germany, the data collection is restricted to the area of former West Berlin. Of course, the limitation to the West Berlin population of older people has disadvantages, particularly with regard to the use of the present findings for the planning of social-political measures for the whole of Berlin. However, it seems that some of the differences between former East and West Berlin are overestimated. For example, a recent World Health Organization study (Linden & Helmchen, 1995) has shown remarkable similarities in the psychological and psychiatric profiles of East and West Berliners. The differences were far less pronounced than expected (cf. P. B. Baltes et al., 1994).

From a scientific perspective, the question of sample size and contextual (geographic) background of the sample is always relative (cf. Rendtel & Pötter, 1992). Its answer depends on the adequacy of the sample with respect to a study's scientific goals. In our view, the limitation of our sample to former West Berlin is of minor importance for most of the research issues examined in BASE. For most gerontological questions, it is of much greater significance that, because of random sampling, the BASE sample approaches the variability (heterogeneity) existing in the general population and that, because of sample stratification by age and gender, it also allows reliable statements on old men and the very old.

The special characteristics of the Berlin Aging Study are:

(1)   local representativeness and *heterogeneity* of the participants through random sampling from the obligatory city register;

(2)   a focus on the *full range of old age,* including *very old* people through the assessment of six equal age groups from 70 to over 100;

(3) *interdisciplinarity* through wide-ranging and intensive data sets collected in 14 sessions; and

(4) the collection of a *reference data set* for the population of older people in a German city.

With these foci, the Berlin Aging Study aligns itself with efforts in gerontology to achieve subject heterogeneity (Maddox, 1987) and to include the very old (Poon, 1992) in investigations. For instance, our goals are similar to those of the Health and Retirement Study initiated by the U.S. National Institute on Aging, and especially the aging research funded by the MacArthur Foundation Network on Aging (Berkman et al., 1993; Rowe & Kahn, 1987).

2.2   *Local Representativeness and Sample Heterogeneity*

With its first focus on local representativeness and sample heterogeneity, the Berlin Aging Study responds to the often stated need for gerontological research to be based on samples drawn from the population at large rather than on convenience samples of volunteers, or clinical or health insurance populations (Maddox, 1987; Nelson & Dannefer, 1992; Rowe & Kahn, 1987). Estimating local representativeness and sample heterogeneity is feasible in BASE because there is an obligatory state register, the aim of which is to include all those residing in Berlin. Although this register is not flawless, it offers the best entry to the population as a whole.

2.3   *A Focus on Advanced Old Age*

With its second focus on the full range of old age and especially on *very old people,* BASE responds to the criticism that the majority of current gerontological research is based on "young old" samples of individuals aged 65 to 85 years (P. B. Baltes & Baltes, 1990b; Bromley, 1988; Neugarten, 1974; Svanborg, 1985). There is good reason to assume that data about advanced old age (85+ years) may offer new insights into mechanisms and regularities of human aging because of increasing proximity to death. In fact, it has long been argued that proximity to death may be a more important variable for the determination of adult age variance than distance from birth (cf. Kleemeier, 1962; Riegel & Riegel, 1972; Siegler, 1975).

To obtain a good overview of the full age spectrum of old age, we decided to stratify the BASE sample by age and gender, examining equal numbers of men and women in each age group. This procedure, which we describe in more depth below, enables us to make sufficiently precise statements about subgroups (such as the very old), who would only have been sampled in relatively small numbers in a nonstratified random sample from the population. In particular, men are hardly represented in samples of the very old because of the fact that their life-spans are on average shorter than women's. This effect is even stronger in Germany because of the loss of comparatively more men than women in the two world wars.

2.4   *Interdisciplinarity*

Third, BASE attempts to achieve a broad range of *interdisciplinarity.* Although multi-, inter-, and transdisciplinarity are frequently stated objectives of gerontological research (P. B. Baltes & Mittelstraß, 1992; Birren, 1959; Birren & Bengtson, 1988; Cowdry, 1939; Lehr & Thomae, 1987; Maddox, 1987; Olbrich, Sames, & Schramm, 1994; Oswald, Herrmann, Kanowski, Lehr, & Thomae, 1984), the desired disciplinary spectrum is only rarely achieved in data collection and analysis.

Over the years of existence of the Berlin Aging Study, more than 50 scientists from the fields of biochemistry, internal medicine, dentistry, psychiatry, neuropsychology, psychology, sociology, and economics (cf. Table I.1) have attempted inter- and multidisciplinary collaboration in addition to more discipline-specific work. The scientists constitute four closely cooperating research units (Internal Medicine/Geriatrics, Psychiatry, Psychology, and Sociology/Social Policy) with equal participation in planning and decision making. One means to achieve equality was to assign comparable amounts of time for the examination of study participants to the four research units. In contrast to many previous studies on aging and old age, then, no single discipline claimed a special leadership status.

2.5   Reference Data Set

The fourth focus, the collection of a set of reference or baseline data from a well-defined and heterogeneous urban population of older adults, is primarily motivated by questions of practical application and social policy (Alber, 1992; P. B. Baltes & Mittelstraß, 1992; Bundesministerium für Familie und Senioren [BMFuS; Federal Ministry for Family Affairs and Senior Citizens], 1993; Dieck, Igl, & Schwichtenberg-Hilmert, 1993; Klose, 1993a; Mayer et al., 1992). German practitioners in health care, medical and social services, and the field of social policies are very interested in information on functional indicators of old age and aging that could be relevant for their work.

For example, physicians require authoritative information about laboratory parameters in advanced old age; human-service professionals in charge of local agencies or clinical services need accurate data on old people's everyday needs, their living conditions, and the prevalence of physical or mental illnesses; and policy makers want to know about macrodevelopments such as societal aging or about changes in morbidity patterns (e.g., regarding the age-related prevalence of Alzheimer's disease).

With the BASE data, we are trying to contribute toward answering these and similar questions. Thus, BASE also has an epidemiological emphasis. However, this is not an epidemiological study in the "classical" sense (Häfner, 1992). Because of our primary interest in achieving interdisciplinary depth and intensity of assessment, we had to limit the size of our sample. Such a focus on in-depth study of individuals has disadvantages. For instance, it is possible that low-prevalence phenomena are not adequately represented or did not become manifest in BASE. However, these reservations do not apply to the central epidemiological issues in BASE. Regarding topics such as the need for health and nursing care, depression, and dementia, the BASE sample is large enough to offer good evidence.

2.6   Longitudinal Perspectives

Although the data reported in this volume come from the first cross-sectional phase of BASE (i.e., old age and aging are assessed by observing people of different ages on one occasion), BASE also has longitudinal characteristics. First, the assessment protocol includes the retrospective collection of life history data. Thus, the assessment schedules of the Internal Medicine/Geriatrics and Sociology/Social Policy Units encompass the study participants' previous characteristics and life events as well as their past social, economic, educational, and health environments. Second, the duration of the assessment phase (four to five months for each participant) enables a short-term prospective follow-up that could be important in cases of accelerated age-specific changes in subgroups of the very old or in cases of severe illness.

Third, BASE was designed such that it could be transformed into a longitudinal study (P. B. Baltes, Reese, & Nesselroade, 1988; Magnusson & Bergman, 1990; Nesselroade & Baltes, 1979; Rutter, 1988; Schaie, 1965, 1996). To date, three steps have been taken in the direction of longitudinal extension. A first, single-session repeat of the Intake Assessment (session 1; see below) was completed in 1994. A second, more extensive longitudinal observation of the survivors of the $N = 516$ sample, involving a total of five 90-minute sessions, was completed in 1996. A second repetition of this shortened Intensive Protocol was begun in 1997 and is expected to be completed in 1998. In addition, the BASE sample has been continuously monitored regarding its long-term survival and mortality characteristics.

3   The Study's Design and Strategic Concept

Figure 1.1 summarizes the cross-sectional study's basic design, the three prototypical questions, and the stratified sample.

3.1   On the BASE Sample

The parent sample was randomly drawn from the West Berlin city register and stratified by age and gender. For the complete assessment schedule (Intensive Protocol, see below), six age categories (70–74, 75–79, 80–84, 85–89, 90–94, and 95+ years) were selected, with equal numbers ($n = 43$) of men and women in each of the twelve cells. The BASE sample thus comprised 516 participants. More persons from the parent sample took part in less intensive measurements (cf. Nuthmann & Wahl, 1996, 1997).

Why did we decide to stratify our sample by age and gender? Many studies, which, like BASE, aim to achieve representativeness, examine a sample whose composition (e.g., regarding age, gender, and education) mirrors the demography of the parent population. This strategy always makes sense when the study's statements are to be generalized directly to the entire population, for example, regarding questions about how many over-70-year-olds have Alzheimer's disease or vote for a certain political party. Note, however, that because of the disproportionate distribution of age and gender in the older population, a strict random sampling approach aiming for representation of the population includes far more younger than older persons and far more women than men (e.g., about five times more persons in their 70s than those in their 90s and five times more women than men aged 90 and over; cf. Table 1.11).

However, gerontological research is not only interested in parameters involving the total population of older adults and its distributional characteristics. On the contrary, many gerontologists focus on chronological age as a causal factor (P. B. Baltes et al., 1988; Birren, 1959; Maddox, 1987). Therefore, gerontologists strive for comparable statistical power for the analysis of age effects. In general, two age samples of equal size are most useful for such age comparisons. For this reason, we chose to stratify the BASE

Figure 1.1. The design of the Berlin Aging Study and its prototypical questions. In each of the age-by-gender cells, 43 participants were examined (N=516).

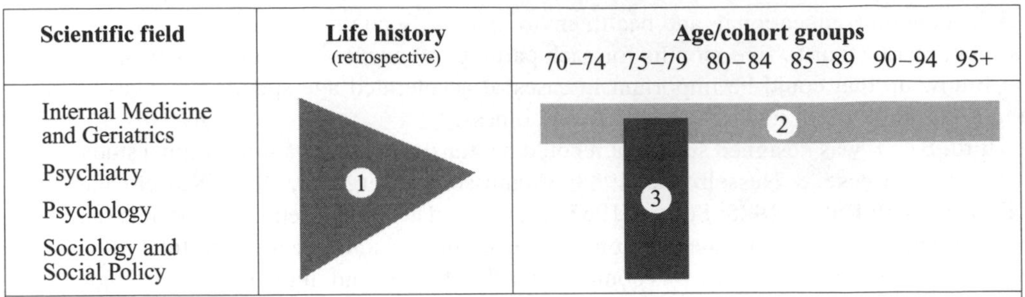

Scientific field	Life history (retrospective)	Age/cohort groups 70–74 75–79 80–84 85–89 90–94 95+					
Internal Medicine and Geriatrics Psychiatry Psychology Sociology and Social Policy							

1. Are individual age differences predictable on the basis of life history data?

2. How large are age differences within domains, and which direction do they take?

3. What is the nature of transdisciplinary relationships across different domains?

sample by age, thus statistically overrepresenting the very old. And because of the general importance of gender differences, we applied the same logic to the gender variable. Oversampling old men makes it possible for us to examine gender differences up into advanced old age with comparable statistical precision (see M. M. Baltes et al., Chapter 9).

Of course, our stratification approach does not preclude estimates of population distribution. When distributions of certain indicators, such as well-being, in the population need to be estimated (i.e., distributions of indicators existing in the elderly population at the time of measurement), they are produced by a posteriori weighting. We discuss the special opportunities, but also the problems, of this weighting procedure in Section 7.4.

3.2   Potentials and Limits of Cross-Sectional Studies

Although we know that age comparisons based on cross-sectional data can only provide first (and sometimes false) estimates of age changes and do not include information on individual patterns of change, we try to give a first summary of aging among old people in West Berlin in this book. What is feasible, what are the pitfalls, and what is impossible in this venture that initially has to rely on cross-sectional data?

In cross-sectional studies, it is possible to estimate *average age differences*. The validity of these average age effects is mainly dependent on two basic conditions (cf. P. B. Baltes et al., 1988). First, the findings on different age groups should not be the result of selective mortality; that is, age groups should distinguish themselves not only on the variable of interest because they represent different compositions of the initial birth cohorts due to selective mortality. For example, an inappropriate interpretation of cross-sectional age differences would occur if a high correlation between income and length of life corresponded to the age effect observed in a cross-sectional analysis.

So-called cohort differences are a second source of error in the evaluation of cross-sectionally obtained age differences. Cross-sectionally observed age groups differ not only in their chronological age, but also in the life contexts associated with different historical periods. Such cohort differences can begin with differences in genetic makeup due to historical changes in fertility patterns. Certainly they include historical changes in life contexts, be they physical, social, or technological. For instance, the centenarians examined in BASE experienced their first 20 years of life from 1890 to 1910, whereas the octogenarians' first two life decades lay in the time from 1910 to 1930 (cf. Maas et al., Chapter 3). Since first scientific discussions of methodology in gerontological life-span research (P. B. Baltes, 1968; Riley, 1973; Ryder, 1965; Schaie, 1965), it is known that cross-sectionally obtained age differences represent bad estimates of average age changes when historically anchored conditions dominate the shaping of the life course of the variables under consideration.

Despite such shortcomings, cross-sectional information carries valuable information. For instance, it is also possible to analyze *correlational associations across domains of functioning* using cross-sectional data. The relationship between intelligence and health is one example. There is little evidence from previous research that such correlational "systemic" covariance patterns are much altered when they are calculated separately for younger and older persons using longitudinal data. Furthermore, it is feasible to utilize cross-sectional data as a first estimate of causal temporal connections, especially if these are hypothesized on the basis of theory. The question whether earlier objective life circumstances influence the relationship between ill health and intellectual functioning in old age is one example; another refers to the association between educational attainment and dementia in old age. In both cases, however, the temporal and causal structure of the relationship pattern can only be "simulated" and not tested directly.

How cross-sectional data can be utilized in the examination of certain issues is also very much dependent on the state of knowledge in the individual scientific fields. For example, there are good opportunities to compare cross-sectional and longitudinal data sets in gerontological intelligence research (Lindenberger & Baltes, 1997; Salthouse, 1991), and it has become clear that the differences between cohorts are often smaller than expected. In the field of cognitive aging, therefore, cross-sectional findings appear to provide quite good estimates of average changes with age.

The authors of chapters in this book were asked to take into account what is known in their fields about long-term stability of interindividual differences and cohort and selective mortality effects and to keep these issues in mind when interpreting their findings. They were requested to avoid conclusions about individual aging processes and causal effects and to emphasize that the reported results represent first estimates of aging processes. At the same time, we recognize that continuous reminders of the restrictions of cross-sectional data interpretation can lead to a kind of intellectual sterility that is likely to hinder scientific progress. Thus, we hope that, on the whole, we have managed to achieve a sensible balance with regard to this important methodological issue (see also Kruse, Lindenberger, & Baltes, 1993).

3.3   *Prototypical Questions*

Of course, any multidisciplinary project has many streams of intellectual motivation that occasionally flow in different or even opposing directions. It is therefore important for such a large project to stake out common territory in order to generate an in-

Table 1.1. *Common theoretical orientations of the Berlin Aging Study*

Theoretical orientation	
Differential aging	a) By domains of functioning
	b) By subgroups of individuals
Continuity versus discontinuity of aging	a) Quantitative versus qualitative changes
	b) Prediction of old age based on characteristics and events of the life course
Range and limits of plasticity and reserve capacity in old age	a) Developmental reserve capacity in old age
	b) Internal versus external action resources
Old age and aging as systemic and interdisciplinary phenomena	a) Relationships between physical, mental, social, and psychological aging
	b) Normal versus optimal versus pathological aging

tellectual basis for long-term integration and collaboration. As shown in Figure 1.1, early in the planning of BASE we formulated three (purposely atheoretical) prototypical questions. These derive mainly from the study's design.

(1)   Are individual age differences predictable on the basis of life history data?
(2)   How large are age differences within domains, and which direction do they take?
(3)   What is the nature of transdisciplinary relationships across different domains?

Of course, these questions represent a subset selected from the variety of possible ones. They are closely linked to the role of chronological age in the study of aging. But as a first approach, these prototypical questions provided research guidelines and explicated the continuing need for interdisciplinary discourse. In addition, they facilitated analysis of the differences between the "young old" and "old old."

4   Common Theoretical Orientations

In addition to these three prototypical questions, the BASE research group adopted four common theoretical orientations (see Table 1.1). Whenever we were lost in the complexity of the study and the diverging preferences and biases of our various disciplines, we returned to them for commonality and direction. These four orientations are:

(1)   differential aging;
(2)   continuity versus discontinuity of aging;
(3)   the search for range and limits of plasticity and reserve capacity; and
(4)   the conceptualization of old age and aging as a systemic and interdisciplinary phenomenon.

These theoretical orientations have a long-standing tradition in gerontology, and they should not be considered as independent of each other. For example, there is a close link between the first two. More extensive information on each of these theoretical orientations is contained in the companion book project initiated by the Berlin Academy of Sciences and Technology study group "Aging and Societal Development" (P. B. Baltes & Mittelstraß, 1992).

At the time of the study initiation, the first theoretical orientation, *differential aging*, reflected two of the main topics of gerontological research (P. B. Baltes & Baltes, 1992; Birren & Bengtson, 1988; Bromley, 1988; Gerok & Brandtstädter, 1992; Kohli, 1992; Lehr, 1991; Lehr & Thomae, 1987; Maddox, 1987; Nelson & Dannefer, 1992; Oswald et al., 1984; Rowe & Kahn, 1987; Schaie, 1996; Steen & Djurfeldt, 1993; Steinhagen-Thiessen, Gerok, & Borchelt, 1992; Thomae, 1976, 1992; Weinert, 1992). While our focus on chronological age as a primary design variable underlines our assumption that aging can, to a significant degree, be captured by a measure of lifetime, emphasizing variability of aging clarifies that chronological age neither depicts the variance of aging in a unified way nor represents the source of all "aging phenomena." In fact, there are many factors influencing old age and aging processes that are hardly correlated with chronological age.

One illustration of the considerable individual variation in age changes is the differentiation between "normal," "pathological," and "optimal" aging. Are changes occurring in old age the expression of normal development or indications of illness? What can aging look like if life conditions are optimized? Another example from social sciences is "social differentiation" associated with social class, ethnicity, gender, education, and work (Kohli, 1992; Kohli & Meyer, 1986; Mayer, 1992; Nelson & Dannefer, 1992; Riley, 1987; Riley, Kahn, & Foner, 1994; Tews, 1990). A further illustration of differential aging involves interdomain differences in age gradients. Even in a given domain, such as intelligence, age gradients for subcomponents can differ dramatically (e.g., P. B. Baltes, 1993; Horn, 1970).

Like many others in the field, we are interested in exploiting the existence of individual and domain variability for questions of theory and social policy. This has additional significance in view of the societal stereotype of old age that typically considers the group of older adults as homogeneous (P. B. Baltes & Staudinger, 1993; Tews, 1991). In contrast, scientists often claim that the extent of interindividual variability (heterogeneity) increases with old age (Nelson & Dannefer, 1992).

The second theoretical orientation, *continuity versus discontinuity* of aging, brings at least two historical issues of gerontological work into focus (P. B. Baltes, 1973; Birren, 1959; Brim & Kagan, 1980; Neugarten, 1969). First is the question of whether and to what degree the phenomena of old age are characterized by qualitatively new aspects or whether they involve essentially quantitative shifts within a set of parameters that also determined earlier phases of life. The "development" of wisdom as an innovative form of knowledge in old age represents a case of positively evaluated qualitative discontinuity, whereas the development of manifest dementia or the need for nursing care is an example of negatively assessed qualitative discontinuity.

The second question associated with the continuity-discontinuity distinction refers to the relative predictability of aging phenomena from earlier life history. If, on the one hand, states in old age could, to a large extent, be predicted from earlier life characteristics, this would represent an example of continuity. If, on the other hand, aging and interindividual variations of functioning in old age were expressions of determinants that had little to do with previous conditions, but rather had developed in old age on the basis of new constellations of determining factors, this would be an example for predictive discontinuity. It should be noted that continuity-discontinuity aspects are also dependent on societal and contextual factors (e.g., the structure of the life course). This is a key issue in comparative international gerontology (e.g., Guillemard, 1992) and cultural anthropology (Elwert, 1992).

The third common theoretical orientation, the identification of the *range and limits of plasticity and reserve capacity* in old age, is more recent (P. B. Baltes & Graf, 1996; Coper, Jänicke, & Schulze, 1985). It was developed in reaction to the long-standing position, prominent especially among biologists, that losses in adaptivity or plasticity are *the* essential feature of aging (Finch, 1990; Shock, 1977). A new perspective on the investigation of plasticity has been developed in the last decade, not least stimulated by psychological and sociological research. Increasingly, "two faces" of plasticity in old age (P. B. Baltes, 1987, 1993, 1997) are recognized. Because of the many intellectual and cultural facets of aging and the opportunities for the development of a positive culture of old age, more attention is paid to the identification of potential gains and latent reserves of aging (P. B. Baltes & Baltes, 1992; P. B. Baltes & Staudinger, 1993; Bortz, 1991; Fries, 1990; Gerok & Brandtstädter, 1992; Kliegl & Baltes, 1991; Kruse, 1992a, 1992b; Lehr, 1991; Mayer, 1992; Perlmutter, 1990; Riley & Riley, 1992; Rowe & Kahn, 1987; Steinhagen-Thiessen et al., 1992; Svanborg, 1985). In this way, a new "dual" research perspective has developed, which we express in the juxtaposition of "range and limits" of plasticity.

According to this theoretical orientation, aging is typically associated with increasing limits to, and restrictions in, physical, neurobiological, mental, and social capacities. However, gerontological research of the past decade has also presented impressive evidence of plasticity and thereby pointed to sizable untapped reserves of elderly people in a variety of domains, ranging from biochemical status to physical performance and cognitive as well as social functioning.

The search for latent reserves and plasticity of aging is of paramount importance because the current ecology or "culture" of old age is likely to underestimate the potential of the last segments of the life-span. There is a kind of paradox about old age (P. B. Baltes & Baltes, 1990a, 1992). In a certain cultural-historical sense, old age is "young" because its cultural history is the shortest of all life phases. As a result, there is not yet a highly developed, positive culture for or among old people. This applies to advanced old age, in particular. In Germany, public policy proposals and party-political manifestos are strongly influenced by this situation and focus on the search for a better life for future senior citizens (BMFuS, 1993; Dieck, 1992; Klose, 1993b; Kohli, 1993; Mayer et al., 1992; Tews, 1990; Thomae & Maddox, 1982).

In BASE, therefore, we are interested in learning more about what, in principle, is possible in old age at present and what could be if individual and cultural conditions were different. This applies to both the "internal" or endogenous personal characteristics of aging individuals and the "external" or exogenous conditions of the material, institutional, and cultural world in which aging takes place. Because of the large individual differences in old age and aging, the challenge of avoiding a unified definition of societal and personal aims for old age is equally significant in this context. For instance, one issue refers to whether the vitality-striving image of the young old (Karl & Tokarski, 1989) should also be propagated for advanced old age.

The fourth theoretical orientation, a commitment to *interdisciplinarity,* continues the long-standing belief of gerontologists that the study of aging is an enterprise that calls for rich multi-, inter-, and transdisciplinary discourse and collaboration (P. B. Baltes &

Baltes, 1992; Birren & Bengtson, 1988; Cowdry, 1939; Lehr & Thomae, 1987; Maddox, 1987; Mittelstraß et al., 1992; Olbrich et al., 1994; Oswald et al., 1984). Old age and aging are simultaneously characterized by biological, psychological, social, and societal features. From this perspective, no discipline holds supremacy in understanding the nature of aging. Every discipline has but a partial and limited view.

Old age and aging are inherently determined by a system of interacting physical, psychological, social, and institutional phenomena, each of which is at the center of a different scientific discipline (biology, medicine, psychology, sociology, etc.). Moreover, aging and old age are also characteristic of both individuals and groups. One speaks of the aging of individuals, of society, and of the population (Kohli, 1992; Mayer et al., 1992; Myles, 1984). In highlighting the systemic aspect of aging, not only do we wish to combine the analytical and empirical perspectives of different disciplines, we also wish to elaborate the recognition that aging is embedded in a multilevel system ranging from molecular biology to political economy and technological application. As the biology of aging sets very basic constraints and opportunities for health and mobility, the sociocultural environment determines constraints and opportunities for education, leisure, income, and technology use (Dieck, 1992; Krämer, 1992; Mayer et al., 1992).

The likelihood of successful interdisciplinarity is enhanced in BASE by the organizational structure of the sponsoring institutions and our commitment to equality among research units (as in the MacArthur Study on Aging: Berkman et al., 1993; Rowe & Kahn, 1987). In the end, however, only the quality of our work and publications will show to what degree we have been successful in our efforts at interdisciplinarity.

At the same time, interdisciplinarity should not be the primary assessment criterion. As one of the reviewers of our first larger publication on BASE (P. B. Baltes et al., 1993) pointed out, interdisciplinarity is not the only goal of a study that involves collaboration among scientists from rather diverse disciplines. This collaboration can also reflect the added value of studying "in an integrated design the sociological, psychological, and medical facets of aging," thereby focusing on "wholism and integration" without expecting interdisciplinarity in the theoretical sense (cf. Mittelstraß et al., 1992). Furthermore, it is important to recognize that the state of discipline-specific knowledge should also be enhanced by interdisciplinary projects. Indeed, from a science-theoretical perspective, it is hardly imaginable that gerontological research and progress can be primarily based on interdisciplinarity. On the contrary, good discipline-specific work is a prerequisite for fruitful interdisciplinarity.

5   Methods: Intake Assessment and Intensive Protocol

This section provides an overview of measures and strategies of assessment used in the Berlin Aging Study. The full data protocol applied in BASE is summarized in Table 1.2. Each of the four research units was primarily responsible for three to four sessions. The content of the sessions was, however, not entirely divided according to discipline; practical and organizational considerations also played a role.

All sessions were organized by the Project Coordination Center and lasted about 90 minutes each (for details, see Nuthmann & Wahl, 1996, 1997). Most sessions took place at the participants' place of residence, be it a private household or an institution. The major exceptions were three sessions involving internal medicine, geriatrics, and dentistry, where study participants were taken to various medical units of the Free University of Berlin.

Table 1.2. *Typical sequence of data collection in the Berlin Aging Study (BASE) at the first occasion of measurement*

Session	Content
Multidisciplinary Intake Assessment (session 1)	
1	Short Initial Assessment/Baseline protocol/Observational protocol
Intensive Protocol (sessions 2–14)	
2	Sociology I (Family of origin and employment history)
3	Sociology II (Family history and family relationships)
4	Sociology III (Economic situation and activities)
5	Psychology I (Intelligence and intellectual functioning)
6	Psychology II (Social relationships)
7	Psychiatry I (Neuropsychological tests)
8	Psychology III (Self and personality)
9	Psychiatry II (Yesterday Interview and psychiatric scales)
10	Internal Medicine and Geriatrics I (Medical anamnesis)
11	Internal Medicine and Geriatrics II (Physical examination)
12	Psychiatry III (Psychiatric examination)
13	Internal Medicine and Geriatrics III (Dental examination)
14	Internal Medicine and Geriatrics IV (qCT, ultrasound imaging)

Note. Sessions lasted an average of 1.5 hours. Except for sessions 11, 13, and 14, all sessions were conducted at the participants' residence.

The data collection staff consisted of a highly trained team of full-time research assistants, and medical personnel including internists and psychiatrists. Throughout the four- to five-month period needed to collect all data for a given individual, each participant was assigned to one of the research assistants who served as a continuing liaison person.

Special emphasis was put on the issue of research ethics (cf. Geiselmann & Helmchen, 1994; Helmchen & Lauter, 1995; Nuthmann & Wahl, 1996, 1997). Apart from a review of medical procedures by the Committee on Research Ethics of the Berlin Medical Council, the research assistants were regularly supervised by an outside expert, for instance, in dealing with situations of conflict between the needs of subjects and interests of research. In addition, there were explicit procedures for the appraisal of each potential participant's cognitive ability to give consent to take part in the study and for assessment of the feasibility of examinations in cases of severe health impairment.

In 61 cases, the decision was made that, for physical or mental health reasons, it was not ethically justifiable to assume the potential participant's ability to give consent or capacity to undergo examination. In these cases, the data used in the study were restricted to the person's demographic characteristics or any data available from previous assessment stages. To what degree these decisions may have affected the sample composition is discussed later in this chapter, in Chapter 2, and in subsequent chapters where relevant.

5.1   *Multidisciplinary Intake Assessment (Session 1)*

The assessment schedule began with a multidisciplinary Intake Assessment session, which, in time and effort, corresponded to a typical multidisciplinary survey study of older adults. It contained objective and subjective measures from all four research units (cf. Table 1.3).

Two rationales guided the construction of the Intake Assessment (session 1). The first goal was to monitor sample attrition and selective dropout. Because we expected dropout in the course of the 14 sessions, we wanted to have a data base available early in the data collection process that could provide us with a wide range of information permitting the examination of sample heterogeneity and selectivity. A second consideration concerned the possibility of a later longitudinal follow-up with a less intensive assessment battery.

As shown in Table 1.3, the Intake Assessment contained objective and subjective measures of physical status, mental health, psychological functioning, socioeconomic status, and social participation. In addition, the interviewers were trained to record their observations of the participants' general appearance, disabilities, behavior, and residential situation. For most BASE participants, this Intake Assessment was completed in one session, but there were large variations. The need for more than one session was correlated with age and the level of pathology. In order to obtain full baseline information from as many people as possible, we decided to spend as many sessions as necessary for the completion of the Intake Assessment. The maximal number needed was seven for one participant (see Nuthmann & Wahl, 1996, 1997).

5.2   *Intensive Protocol (Sessions 2–14)*

Tables 1.4–7 summarize the data protocol of the remaining 13 sessions of the BASE assessment battery. In our in-house language we label these additional sessions as the Intensive Protocol, although at later points in this book we also use the term Intensive Protocol to refer to all 14 sessions.

The specific measurement procedures, observation strategies, and interview methods are described in detail in the following chapters of this book. However, in order to give an impression of the scope of the study in this introductory chapter, we present a table for each research unit, showing the key domains, the general formats of assessment, and the major theoretical constructs that motivate the study. In addition to characterizing the scope of assessment, each table provides more specific examples to illustrate its depth. The italics identify the constructs selected to indicate the depth of assessment.

In the following section, we describe the sessions with a focus on the research units primarily responsible for their planning and implementation. We need to underscore, however, that the selection of measures was often based on interdisciplinary considerations. Thus, commonality in interest and development efforts is greater than might seem, based on the organizational format of presentation.

The three sessions following the Intake Assessment covered topics and constructs developed primarily by the Sociology and Social Policy Unit (cf. Mayer et al., Chapter 8). As shown in Table 1.4, the main topics and constructs were (1) retrospective accounts of the life course and generational differences, (2) later phases of the family life cycle, (3) financial and social security conditions, and (4) social resources and social participation. The construction of these components of the data protocol benefited from earlier research carried out by Mayer and his colleagues, which dealt with life history analysis of German adults differing in age and cohort membership (e.g., Brückner & Mayer, 1998; Mayer, 1990; Mayer & Brückner, 1989).

Table 1.5 summarizes the assessments developed and carried out primarily by the Psychology Unit (sessions 5, 6, and 8; cf. Smith & Baltes, Chapter 7; see also P. B.

Table 1.3. *The multidisciplinary BASE Intake Assessment (session 1)*

Research units and their key domains			
Internal Medicine and Geriatrics	**Psychiatry**	**Psychology**	**Sociology and Social Policy**
Objective health	**Assessment of psychiatric age-related morbidity**	**Intelligence**	**Socioeconomic status**
Body Mass Index	SMMS[b]	Digit Letter test	Educational level
Drug consumption	Self-reported depressivity	Backward digit span	Social prestige
Last doctor's appointment	Fears and worries		Income and savings
		Social relationships	Family members
Subjective health	**Dealing with psychiatric age-related morbidity**	Number of close companions	Housing conditions
	Drug consumption	Loss of close companions	
Functional capacity	Yesterday Interview (short form)		**Social participation**
ADL[a]	Previous contact with psychiatrist	**Self and personality**	Voting behavior
Grip strength		PGCMS[c] (life satisfaction, satisfaction with aging, emotional balance)	
Wrist measurement		Control beliefs	
Subjective walking distance			
Vision and hearing			

Concurrent observation of study participant by field staff

Health risk factors
Disability/frailty
Behavior and speech characteristics
Housing conditions
Residential environment

[a]ADL: Activities of Daily Living.
[b]SMMS: Short form of the Mini Mental State Examination.
[c]PGCMS: Philadelphia Geriatric Center Morale Scale.

Table 1.4. *Topics examined by the Sociology and Social Policy Unit and a selection of the instruments used to measure them in the Intensive Protocol*

Main topics/constructs	Detailed example	Instruments
Life history and generational dynamics		
Social background	*Career mobility*	Magnitude Prestige Scale
Migration history	*Labor force participation*	Life history instrument
Educational history	*Career continuity*	
Employment history	*Unemployment*	
Partnership history	*Transitions (employment/*	
Family life history	*retirement)*	
Later phases of the family life cycle		
Current social structure	*Size of the family*	Family history inventory
of the family	*Living distance and contacts*	Social relations and sup-
Social structure of	*Household structure*	port questionnaire
the generations	*Familial support*	
Changes of familial		
social structure		
Economic situation and social security		
Assets	*Savings*	German Socioeconomic
Sources of income	*Property*	Panel questionnaire
Transfers		(SOEP)
Income expenditure		
Consumer sovereignty		
Social resources and social participation		
Social status	*Formal and informal care*	Inventory of care needs
Housing standards/	*Household help*	
environment	*Institutionalization*	
Social care	*Institutionalization career*	
Social and cultural		
participation		

Note. To illustrate the depth of assessment, more details are given for selected topics or constructs (in italics). Cf. Mayer et al., Chapter 8, for references and further details.

Baltes & Smith, 1997). They cover three areas of psychological functioning: (1) intelligence and intellectual functioning, (2) self and personality, and (3) social relationships. The choice of constructs examined was guided by life-span developmental theory (P. B. Baltes, 1987) and by models of successful aging (M. M. Baltes, 1987; P. B. Baltes & Baltes, 1990a). We also included some of the topics central to the Bonn Gerontological Longitudinal Study (Lehr & Thomae, 1987; Thomae, 1976). Instruments were selected and developed to accommodate a wide range of psychological functioning and to allow comparison with younger age groups. Methods ranged from a computerized battery of standard intelligence tests (Lindenberger & Baltes, 1994, 1997; Lindenberger, Mayr, & Kliegl, 1993), standard measures of personality and self-related beliefs, open-ended self-

Table 1.5. *Topics examined by the Psychology Unit and a selection of the instruments used to measure them in the Intensive Protocol*

Main topics/constructs	Detailed example	Instruments
Intelligence and intellectual functioning		
Mechanics of intelligence	*Reasoning*	Letter Series
Pragmatics of intelligence	*Memory*	Figural Analogies
	Perceptual speed	Activity Recall
		Paired Associates
		Digit Letter test
Self and personality		
Self-concept	*Personal life investment*	"Who am I?"
Personality dimensions	*Changes in life investment*	Possible selves
Emotional state/affect	*Control beliefs*	NEO[a]
Self-regulatory processes	*Coping patterns*	PANAS[b]
Social relationships		
Network structure	*Closeness/distance*	Social network and sup-
Social support	*Size*	port questionnaire
Changes of the network	*Age structure*	
Negative aspects	*Losses*	
Satisfaction with relationships	*Homogeneity*	
Relationships in retrospect		

Note. To illustrate the depth of assessment, more details are given for selected topics or constructs (in italics). Cf. Smith & Baltes, Chapter 7, for references and further details.
[a]NEO: Neuroticism, Extraversion, Openness.
[b]PANAS: Positive and Negative Affect Schedule.

descriptions, and a questionnaire about coping styles, to a structured interview about social life and support networks (Kahn & Antonucci, 1980).

Table 1.6 identifies the key domains and methods developed and implemented primarily by the Psychiatry Unit (Helmchen et al., Chapter 6). This part of the assessment usually took place in sessions 7, 9, and 12. Session 12 was carried out by psychiatrists, sessions 7 and 9 by research assistants. The central foci of psychiatric assessment were: (1) evaluation of the spectrum of psychiatric morbidity, including depression and dementia, but also so-called subdiagnostic morbidity (psychiatric disturbances that bear real-life significance despite not fulfilling the established criteria of psychiatric diagnosis); (2) assessment of life history antecedents and current correlates of psychiatric morbidity and comorbidity; and (3) appraisal of persons' coping with their psychiatric morbidity. The third focus included assessment of the utilization of medication as well as examination of everyday competence and daily activity profiles. The selection of topics and methods was based on previous research on psychiatric diagnosis (Helmchen, 1991; Reischies, von Spiess, & Hedde, 1990), on utilization of medical and nursing care (Geiselmann, Linden, & Sachs-Ericsson, 1989; Heinrich, Linden, & Müller-Oerling-hausen, 1989; Helmchen & Linden, 1992), and on behavioral competence using the Yes-

Table 1.6. *Topics examined by the Psychiatry Unit and a selection of the instruments used to measure them in the Intensive Protocol*

Main topics/constructs	Detailed example	Instruments
Spectrum of age-related psychiatric morbidity		
Mental illness	*Clinical diagnosis*	GMS-A/HAS[a]
Depression syndrome	*Degree of depression*	DSM-III-R[b]
Dementia syndrome	*Differential diagnosis with respect*	ICD-10[c]
Psychopathology	*to somatic health or dementia*	HAMD[d]
(subdiagnostic)		CES-D[e]
Predictors of psychiatric morbidity		
Previous illnesses	*Psychopathological morbidity*	Psychiatric history/diagnosis
Multi-/comorbidity	*Somatic morbidity*	Medical history/diagnosis
	Subdiagnostic morbidity	Consensus conference
Consequences of psychiatric morbidity		
Health/illness behavior	*Utilization of medical care*	Health behavior question-
Everyday competence	*Drug consumption*	naire
Self-efficacy	*Health perception*	Interview with family
	Illness concepts	physician

Note. To illustrate the depth of assessment, more details are given for selected topics or constructs (in italics). Cf. Helmchen et al., Chapter 6, for references and further details.
[a]GMS-A/HAS: Geriatric Mental State, Version A/History and Aetiology Schedule.
[b]DSM-III-R: *Diagnostic and Statistical Manual of Mental Disorders,* third revision.
[c]ICD-10: *International Classification of Mental and Behavioural Disorders,* 10th version.
[d]HAMD: Hamilton Depression Scale.
[e]CES-D: Center for Epidemiologic Studies-Depression Scale.

terday Interview (M. M. Baltes & Lang, 1997; M. M. Baltes, Mayr, Borchelt, Maas, & Wilms, 1993; Marsiske, Klumb, & Baltes, 1997; cf. M. M. Baltes et al., Chapter 14).

The primary methods applied in the psychiatric field included the "Geriatric Mental State, Version A" interview (GMS-A; Copeland, Dewey, & Griffiths-Jones, 1986), various scales such as the Center for Epidemiologic Studies-Depression Scale (CES-D; Radloff, 1977), and questionnaires dealing with, for example, medication use, the use of medical care, and subjective illness beliefs. To validate the diagnostic categories and to evaluate the medication, *consensus conferences* were conducted jointly with the Internal Medicine/Geriatrics Unit. Information about each study participant was presented and discussed in these consensus conferences and, where necessary, diagnostic evaluations were specified or modified. The information collected at each stage of the diagnostic effort was stored separately to prevent contamination of the data and artifacts resulting from cumulative and tautological reasoning.

Table 1.7 summarizes the assessment in sessions 10, 11, 13, and 14, which were developed and arranged primarily by the Internal Medicine and Geriatrics Unit (Steinhagen-Thiessen & Borchelt, 1993; cf. Steinhagen-Thiessen & Borchelt, Chapter 5). In addition to a standardized medical anamnesis, a full-body, noninvasive medical and den-

Table 1.7. *Topics examined by the Internal Medicine and Geriatrics Unit and a selection of the instruments used to measure them in the Intensive Protocol*

Main topics/constructs	Detailed example	Instruments
Objective health	*Symptoms*	Standardized medical history
Cardiovascular system	*Objective status*	Medical and neurological
Musculoskeletal system	*Cardiovascular risk factors*	examination
Immune system	*Comorbidity*	Resting ECG, blood
Dental status		pressure
Multimorbidity		Color-coded ultrasound
Subjective health		
Subjective physical health	*Retrospective interindividual comparison*	Standardized subjective health interview
Subjective vision and hearing	*Comparison with age peers*	
Functional capacity		
Activities of Daily Living	*Objective coordination and balance*	Subjective walking distance
Physical performance		Grip strength
	Objective strength	Use of aids
	Subjective ratings	Bending, turning
	Compensation strategies	Standing and walking with closed eyes
Risk profile		
Cardiovascular risks	*Smoking*	Medical anamnesis and
	Diet	examination
	Lipid metabolism	Diet questionnaire
	Hypertension	Blood chemistry
Treatment needs		
Medication	*Drug treatment needs*	Analysis of medication
Dental treatment	*Dental treatment needs*	Dental examination
Integration of treatment needs	*Needs for medical and nursing care*	Interview with family physician
		Consensus conferences
Reference values		
Physical performance	*Pulmonary function*	Spirometry
Organ functioning	*Renal function*	Blood chemistry
Metabolism	*Hepatic function*	Immunological analysis
	Immune function	

Note. To illustrate the depth of assessment, more details are given for selected topics or constructs (in italics). Cf. Steinhagen-Thiessen & Borchelt, Chapter 5, for references and further details.

tal examination was conducted. Furthermore, methods ranging from biochemical analysis to computer scanning were applied. Portions of the blood and saliva samples were saved for subsequent analyses when new methods become available in the field of molecular biology, permitting more refined forms of chemical and genetic analysis. Furthermore, tests of sensory acuity and sensorimotor functioning (balance/gait) were performed. Finally, for about half of the participants, radiological examinations were carried out to study bone structure and brain morphology (computer tomography), and blood flow patterns and morphology of the extracranial arteries (color-coded ultrasound).

6 The BASE Sample: Methods and Problems

Questions of subject and context generalizability are central to any research effort in the human sciences. However, judgments about the importance of certain dimensions of generalizability (e.g., observation methods, time points, assessment contexts, sampling of participants, etc.) vary, depending on discipline-specific preferences and the type of issue under consideration (P. B. Baltes et al., 1988; Magnusson & Bergman, 1990). Not surprisingly, the scientists involved in BASE also set different priorities. For example, the sociologists were most anxious about the size and composition of the sample, the psychologists were most concerned about the issue of measurement validity and replication, the psychiatrists worried most about the selective loss of persons suffering from dementia, and the internists felt most troubled about the refusal rates for medical examinations.

In this spirit, we now concentrate on general methodological aspects of BASE that are important for each of the following chapters. These include questions of measurement validity, the method of sampling, and potential sample selectivity. Capturing the heterogeneity of old age and aging is one of the aims and intended strengths of BASE. We have tried to achieve this by examining a representative local sample, and our effectiveness in accomplishing this is one of our major concerns. In addition to the summary presented below, Chapter 2 by Lindenberger et al. deals with this topic in more depth. First, however, we present some of the procedures used in BASE to enlist as many people as possible to participate in the study (cf. Nuthmann & Wahl, 1996, 1997).

6.1 Procedures Applied in BASE to Maximize Participation

Persons who, on the basis of the sampling procedure, were to be asked to participate in the study were first sent a letter suggesting a date for a first appointment. This initial letter was intended to prepare the potential participants for a first contact – on the one hand, to preclude older persons' fears about answering the door to someone unknown and, on the other hand, to give bedridden or very frail persons interested in participation the chance to arrange help for the first meeting. The pilot studies had also shown that visits to inhabitants of homes were much more likely to be successful if they had been announced in writing previously. Enclosed photographs of BASE staff made it possible for the addressees to identify the interviewers not only by their written documentation (project identification card and a copy of the letter), but also personally.

The letter included statements on old age and aging chosen to present some of the topics and aims of the study in an appealing manner. The request for participation in BASE was the key target, but its voluntary nature was emphasized. At the end of the letter, which also mentioned the institutions and head scientists involved in BASE, a date was proposed on which a named BASE interviewer would visit the recipient and talk to him or her about the study and potential participation. An encouraging letter from two high-level Berlin government officials and a color brochure on the study with photographs of the interviewers and project physicians were also enclosed in this first mail contact.

This initial letter was usually sent off about five to seven days before the date suggested for the first appointment. Contacts with the recipients were then carried out according to a standardized routine. If the recipient did not answer the letter, the interviewer tried to make a personal visit at the announced time. This was repeated a half hour later if no one answered the door. If this attempt was also unsuccessful, the interviewers left a letter announcing further contact attempts, but also asking the recipients to call the field coordinator or the interviewer on the telephone. If further contact attempts were equally unsuccessful, the interviewer tried to find the potential participant's telephone number in the directory and to call him or her up at varying times. If this did not lead to contact either, a new letter was sent with another date for an appointment about four or five weeks after the first. And if no contact could be made at that time (and a half hour later), the address was given back to the field coordinator. In all, no less than six contact attempts (usually more) were made before the address was declared inactive.

If the letter led to an initial contact face-to-face or on the telephone, the interviewers introduced themselves and asked for a chance to present the study in more detail, thereby trying to motivate the potential participants. During face-to-face contacts, the addressees were given an additional information sheet listing typical questions on the study and worries about participation, which could be discussed in detail. They were also told that study participants would have a specific liaison person during all of the study's sessions and would receive 500 DM payment (equivalent to about $300 at the time) for completion of the entire protocol.

The interviewers usually had to involve persons already in the old people's surroundings during the process of enticing them to participate. In the case of institutionalized persons, the homes' directors were informed about the study before making contact with potential participants. The addressees themselves sometimes asked spouses, children, or friends to join the first meeting with interviewers. Often, the older persons' physicians played an important part as confidants. Therefore, a special information sheet was designed giving general information on BASE and more detailed descriptions of the planned medical examinations. A copy of an article which had previously appeared in the Berlin Medical Council's journal was also provided.

The encounters made via telephone contacts were usually not the most effective. First, it was often difficult to find the correct number in the directory. Second, it was obviously much easier for people to decline participation in the study on the phone than in a face-to-face conversation. It also became clear that people with hearing impairments did not like to speak with unknown callers on the phone. It was helpful for interviewers to be able to refer to the previously sent letter. Sometimes, a specially designed version of the Intake Assessment (or at least the Short Initial Assessment) was conducted on the telephone. In these cases, of course, tests such as the measurements of grip strength and visual acuity or the Digit Letter test could not be carried out. Despite all of our attempts to minimize sample loss, many people did not agree to take part in the study. This again emphasizes the necessity of selectivity analyses. The methods used are introduced in the following sections.

6.2   Drawing the BASE Sample

As already mentioned, the parent sample was randomly drawn from the West Berlin city register and stratified by age and gender (see Table 1.8). For age-related com-

Table 1.8. *The most important BASE samples*

	Age/cohort group					
	70–74	75–79	80–84	85–89	90–94	95+
Intake Assessment sample (*N* = 928)						
Men	58	69	82	83	85	
Women	60	74	76	85	79	97
Total	118	143	158	168	159	182
Intensive Protocol sample (*N* = 516 of 928)						
Men	43	43	43	43	43	43
Women	43	43	43	43	43	43
Total	86	86	86	86	86	86

Note. These samples stem from a verified parent sample of *N* = 1,908 persons randomly drawn from the West Berlin city register (stratified by age and gender). A Short Initial Assessment was carried out with 1,264 persons (66%; see Fig. 1.2). Most data reported in this book are based on the *N* = 516 Intensive Protocol sample.

parisons, the sample is divided into six age/cohort groups (each *n* = 86): 70–74 years (born 1915–22), 75–79 years (born 1910–17), 80–84 years (born 1905–13), 85–89 years (born 1900–1908), 90–94 years (born 1896–1902), and 95–103 years (born 1883–97). Because of the three-year time interval required for testing, there is some overlap in birth cohort membership across adjacent age groups.

Within the framework of our budget and the anticipated duration of the examination schedule, it was our aim to complete the entire 14-session Intensive Protocol with at least 500 participants. In the end, we were able to achieve a sample of *N* = 516: 258 men and 258 women who all completed the entire data protocol. There are 43 persons in each of the study design's 12 age-by-gender cells.

Of course, we had to begin with a much larger parent sample in order to reach this number of 516 participants. The problem of selective recruitment means that not all individuals approached actually take part in studies. Moreover, not all persons can be expected to continue participation when the assessment schedule – as in BASE – comprises at least 14 sessions over four to five months. This results in the problem of selective "experimental" dropout.

Figure 1.2 summarizes the drawing of the sample. We began with a verified parent sample of 1,908 persons. In fact, our initial sample from the city register included 2,297 persons, but only 1,908 (83%) were verifiable: 194 had died before the study began; in 180 cases, the addresses were wrong or the persons had moved elsewhere without leaving a forwarding address; and 15 had moved out of Berlin (see Table 1.9; cf. Nuthmann & Wahl, 1996, 1997).

Of the 1,908 (100%) verified individuals, 66% (i.e., 1,264 persons) could be approached for a Short Initial Assessment, which preceded the actual assessment schedule. Of these 1,264 persons, 928 (49% of the verified parent sample) were prepared to take part in the multidisciplinary Intake Assessment (session 1). Of these 928, 516 persons

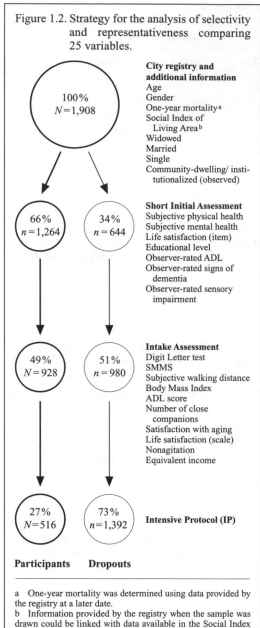

Figure 1.2. Strategy for the analysis of selectivity and representativeness comparing 25 variables.

100%
$N = 1,908$

City registry and additional information
Age
Gender
One-year mortality[a]
Social Index of
    Living Area[b]
Widowed
Married
Single
Community-dwelling/ insti-
    tutionalized (observed)

66%
$n = 1,264$

34%
$n = 644$

Short Initial Assessment
Subjective physical health
Subjective mental health
Life satisfaction (item)
Educational level
Observer-rated ADL
Observer-rated signs of
    dementia
Observer-rated sensory
    impairment

49%
$N = 928$

51%
$n = 980$

Intake Assessment
Digit Letter test
SMMS
Subjective walking distance
Body Mass Index
ADL score
Number of close
    companions
Satisfaction with aging
Life satisfaction (scale)
Nonagitation
Equivalent income

27%
$N = 516$

73%
$n = 1,392$

Intensive Protocol (IP)

Participants   Dropouts

a   One-year mortality was determined using data provided by the registry at a later date.
b   Information provided by the registry when the sample was drawn could be linked with data available in the Social Index (Meinlschmidt, Imme, & Kramer, 1990).

(27% of the verified parent sample, respectively 56% of the 928 Intake Assessment participants) completed the entire Intensive Protocol.

Although we had expected sizable sample losses both because this was a study of old and very old people, and also demanded considerable time and effort on the part of each

Table 1.9. *Summary of the numbers of men and women in six age/cohort groups at various stages of enlisting the BASE Intensive Protocol sample (N = 516)*

Group	Persons registered in West Berlin	Addresses drawn from the register	Addresses used in the field	Incorrect addresses/ no contact made	Verified parent sample[a]	Participants in Intake Assessment	Participants in Intensive Protocol	% of verified parent sample
Men								
70–74	22,694	245	119	10	109	58	43	39.4
75–79	20,895	245	137	18	119	69	43	36.1
80–84	18,020	245	175	23	152	82	43	28.3
85–89	8,765	265	182	25	157	82	43	27.4
90–94	2,306	268	197	56	141	80	43	30.5
95+	422	239	239	70	169	85	43	25.4
Subtotal	73,102	1,504	1,049	202	842	456	258	30.4
Women								
70–74	50,851	245	136	5	131	60	43	32.8
75–79	55,398	245	178	18	160	74	43	26.9
80–84	55,582	245	197	19	178	76	43	24.2
85–89	31,282	265	227	23	204	86	43	21.1
90–94	11,398	265	194	41	153	79	43	28.1
95+	2,646	391	316	81	235	97	43	18.3
Subtotal	207,157	1,656	1,248	187	1,061	472	258	24.3
Total	280,259	3,160	2,297	389	1,908	928	516	27.0

[a]Persons who could be contacted directly or indirectly (i.e., via a third party) to determine their participation status.

participant, we were disappointed about the high proportion of nonparticipants (51%, if the Intake Assessment is taken as the criterion). The relatively low participation rate becomes less surprising considering (1) the advanced age of the approached individuals and the intensity of assessment (as far as we know, no one has previously tried to recruit a random, stratified sample of 70- to over 100-year-olds for participation in 14 sessions of interdisciplinary data collection); (2) that this is a sample from a large city; and (3) that German surveys (usually involving brief interviews) based on random samples normally report participation rates of 50–70%.

6.3   Selectivity Analyses

Our general approach to the issue of sampling bias and selectivity is not to hide the problem, but to bring it into focus in order to understand it as fully as possible. In our opinion, this is necessary for two reasons. First, aging is a selection process by its very nature – not all individuals reach the same age. Moreover, we have the impression that the majority of gerontological studies (even if they concentrate on the young old and are less intensive) have similar problems, but do not refer to them in depth. Several aspects of the BASE design and schedule enable the examination of sample characteristics and selectivity: (1) the presence of an obligatory city register, (2) the design of the Short Initial Assessment and Intake Assessment, and (3) follow-up information (e.g., about mortality) from the register. These pools of information are outlined in Figure 1.2.

Having a population register available as the sample frame, as we do in Germany, has special advantages for studying a locally representative and heterogeneous sample. The register includes information on age, gender, marital status, and place of residence for all citizens of Berlin. Potential subjects were drawn at random and stratified to achieve equal representation in the 12 age-by-gender groups. The data from the register enable BASE, unlike many previous studies, to analyze the extent of selection effects.

Figure 1.2 presents our general approach (cf. Lindenberger et al., Chapter 2). Proceeding from the verified parent sample ($N = 1,908$), we can trace the history of contacts with participants and check representativeness and selectivity with increasing levels of precision. For instance, the initial comparison between the verified parent sample ($N = 1,908$) and the subjects contacted and recruited for a first level of information ($n = 1,264$) was based on registry variables (age, gender, three categories of marital status), categorization of the place of residence (community-dwelling vs. institutionalized), an index of the social structure of residential areas (Social Index of Living Area; Meinlschmidt, Imme, & Kramer, 1990), and follow-up information on mortality within a year after first contact. Later comparisons between persons who completed the entire Intensive Protocol ($N = 516$) and those who participated only in the Intake Assessment ($N = 928$) can be based on all variables from the Intake Assessment. In this way, up to 25 variables were considered.

6.4   The BASE Samples

How heterogeneous and representative are the resulting BASE samples, and the core BASE sample in particular? Table 1.10 summarizes sociodemographic characteristics of the BASE sample and compares them with data from the German 1991 Microcensus (Statistisches Bundesamt [Federal Statistical Office], 1993).

Table 1.10. *Characteristics of the BASE sample* (N = *516) compared with information from the 1991 Microcensus for West Berlin*

Demographic characteristics	Men (*n = 258*)	Women (*n = 258*)	Total (*N = 516*)	BASE (weighted)	1991 Microcensus
Gender (in %)	50.0	50.0	—	—	—
Age in years					
M	84.7	85.1	84.9	—	—
SD	8.4	8.9	8.7	—	—
Education (in %)					
Primary	61.8	67.6	64.7	63.6	73.5
Lower secondary	26.4	28.9	27.6	29.6	19.5
Higher secondary	11.8	3.5	7.7	6.8	7.0
Occupational training (in %)	74.8	42.0	58.4	56.6	55.1
Income[a] (in %)					
Under 1,000 DM	4.7	5.0	4.8	17.6	16.3
1,000 to 1,399 DM	18.2	19.8	19.0	13.3	20.3
1,400 to 1,799 DM	18.2	20.5	19.4	16.0	22.2
1,800 to 2,199 DM	15.1	26.4	20.7	24.3	19.2
2,200 DM and over	43.8	28.3	36.0	33.9	22.0
M (in DM)	2,208	1,877	2,042	—	—
SD (in DM)	1,294	664	980	—	—
Marital status (in %)					
Married	52.3	7.4	29.8	23.5	28.7
Widowed	39.9	69.8	54.8	56.2	54.3
Divorced	4.3	10.5	7.4	11.3	7.5
Single	3.5	12.4	7.9	9.0	9.5
Type of residence (in %)					
Community- dwelling	90.3	82.5	86.5	91.1	94.2
Living alone	37.6	65.4	51.6	62.7	57.2
Living with others	52.7	17.1	34.9	28.8	37.0
Institutionalized	9.7	17.5	13.6	8.4	5.8
Mortality (in %)					
Died within one year	7.7	3.5	5.6	—	—

[a]Equivalent income: monthly per capita income weighted according to size of household (cf. Mayer et al., Chapter 8).

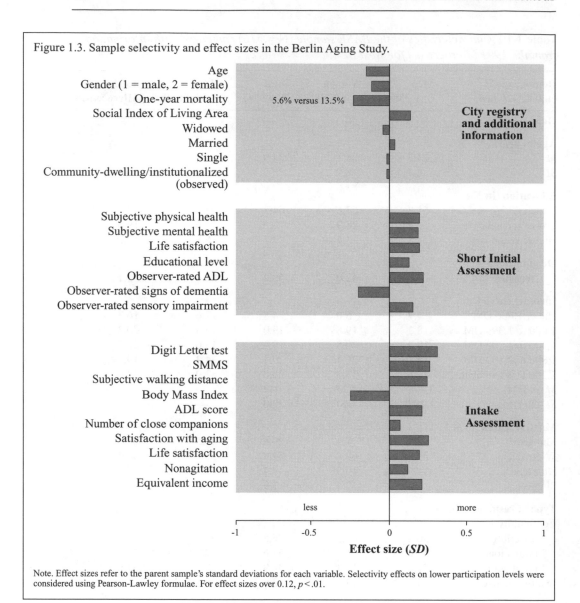

Figure 1.3. Sample selectivity and effect sizes in the Berlin Aging Study.

Note. Effect sizes refer to the parent sample's standard deviations for each variable. Selectivity effects on lower participation levels were considered using Pearson-Lawley formulae. For effect sizes over 0.12, $p < .01$.

At the beginning of data collection, the average age of the sample was 85 years. At the time of the study, 30% of the sample were married, 55% widowed, 7% divorced, and 8% had never married. A proportion of 86% lived in their own homes and 14% in institutions (i.e., senior citizens' homes, nursing homes, hospitals for the chronically ill). Representative for these cohorts in Germany, 65% had primary-level, 28% lower-secondary-level, and 8% higher-secondary-level education (cf. Max Planck Institute for Human Development and Education, 1983, for information about the German education system). The percentage of non-German participants in the BASE sample was low (4.5%), matching the population distribution for this age range. During the 12-month period after study participation, 5.6% of the sample had died, a mortality rate similar to age-mortality statistics for these age groups.

Table 1.10 also includes a comparison of BASE data (weighted by age and gender, see below) with 1991 Microcensus data for the population aged 70 and over living in West Berlin. In Germany, the Microcensus is a national survey conducted with a smaller representative sample in between the major national surveys. The major national survey purports to be exhaustive of the total population.

6.5   *Results of Selectivity Analyses*

Figure 1.3 summarizes the extensive selectivity analyses that are reported in more detail in Chapter 2 (Lindenberger et al.). Their results are based on successive comparisons of the Intensive Protocol sample ($N = 516$, 27%) with the samples out of which it was recruited, that is, with the verified parent sample ($N = 1,908$), the Short Initial Assessment sample ($n = 1.264$, 66%), and the Intake Assessment sample ($N = 928$, 49%).

Strictly speaking, the validity of statements based on data from the Intensive Protocol are restricted to those persons who actually completed the entire assessment schedule. This leads to the question whether one would reach other conclusions if all, or at least more, members of the verified parent sample had taken part. This would be the case if characteristics predicting dropout were nonrandomly related to the features of interest (nonrandom missing data; cf. Little & Rubin, 1987).

So far, three different methods have been applied to study sample selectivity: (1) logistic regression to test differences of frequencies and means, (2) structural equation models to test differences of variances and covariances, and (3) the use of Pearson-Lawley selectivity formulae for the projection of selectivity effects onto constructs of the Intensive Protocol (Lawley, 1943; Pearson, 1903; cf. Little & Rubin, 1987). As explained by Lindenberger et al. in Chapter 2, the simultaneous application of all three procedures provides a good picture of the extent and quality of sample selectivity.

The most important findings of these analyses are as follows:

(1)   The members of the Intensive Protocol sample were characterized by *reduced mortality.* Whereas 5.6% of the BASE Intensive Protocol sample died within a year following initial contact, the rate in the verified parent sample was 13.5%. However, it should be noted that some of this selectivity is a necessary consequence of the study design because the assessment took, on average, four to five months.

(2)   The logistic regressions and the cumulative selectivity analysis using Pearson-Lawley formulae show that, regarding *mean levels* of functioning, the BASE sample was positively selected in all considered domains. However, the extent of these selectivity effects on means were relatively small and all remained well below 0.5 of a standard deviation.

(3)   The selectivity analyses did not give strong indications that the *correlation patterns* and *variability* of features of the final BASE sample differed much from those of samples on lower participation levels. With the exception of a slight decrease of the variance in the Social Index of Living Area, there was no evidence of variance reduction. This indicates that the differential forms of aging and life con-

ditions were retained in the BASE sample. This is of great importance for the correlational analyses of BASE data. As there were no signs of salient selectivity effects on interindividual variance, it is likely that the generalizability of *correlational patterns* is high, despite selectivity effects on the level of means or averages.

Figure 1.3 also illustrates the size and pattern of the observed selectivity effects. It presents estimated mean differences (using the Pearson-Lawley formulae) between the verified parent sample ($N = 1,908$) and the Intensive Protocol sample ($N = 516$) from variables on each level of participation. The effect size is represented in standard deviation units (E_{SD}). A value of +0.2, for example, indicates that the mean of the Intensive Protocol sample lies 0.2 standard deviations above that of the parent sample.

As can be seen in the figure, none of the selectivity effects was larger than a third of the standard deviation estimated for the parent sample. Among variables of the first participation level ($N = 1,908$), one-year mortality has to be emphasized; the risk of death within 12 months after first contact was clearly reduced in the BASE sample (5.6% vs. 13.5% in the verified parent sample). Among the remaining variables, the Digit Letter test, measuring general intellectual functioning, had the largest effect ($E_{SD} = 0.31$).

When all variables listed in Figure 1.3 were entered simultaneously in a linear regression model, they significantly predicted participation in the Intensive Protocol, accounting for 12.2% of the variance (multiple $R = .35$, $p < .01$). Inspection of the regression coefficients revealed that eight of the 25 variables significantly contributed to the prediction in this analysis (age: $\beta = .09$, one-year mortality: $\beta = -.07$, institutionalization: $\beta = .12$, Social Index of Living Area: $\beta = .06$, equivalent income: $\beta = .09$, Body Mass Index: $\beta = -.10$, satisfaction with aging: $\beta = .08$, SMMS [short form of the Mini Mental State Examination]: $\beta = .08$).

Although the effects are relatively small, it must be said that the 516 participants in the full BASE protocol represented a "positively" selected sample. However, these selectivity effects appeared neither to reduce sample heterogeneity nor to change the structural (correlational) relationships between variables. Of course, strictly speaking, these conclusions refer only to the 25 variables examined so far. It may well be that other indicators reveal greater selectivity effects and that selection includes aspects of interindividual variability and covariation as well. It is clearly possible that longitudinal information (beyond mortality) will provide new insights. We intend to pursue these questions in further work.

7 Further Problems of Generalizability

In the following, we turn to three further aspects of generalizability. Recognizing them and appreciating their possible impact on the interpretation of findings reported in the following chapters of this book is important as a general framework for evaluating the generalizability of results from the Berlin Aging Study.

7.1 *Is West Berlin Unique?*

Despite our efforts to work with a heterogeneous and representative sample, the question of generalizability may be regarded as a particular problem of a *Berlin* Aging

Study. Of course ours is not only a German but also a metropolitan sample. Therefore, we need to highlight that the results are city-specific and do not provide generalizable information for variables affected by distinctions between urban and rural settings. Moreover, the results are restricted to a sample from the now former city of West Berlin. For example, the proportion of house owners is especially low in West Berlin, whereas the proportion of old people without children is especially high. We can also assume that poverty is less widespread among old people in West Berlin than in rural areas. Furthermore, we can not exclude that levels of intellectual functioning are higher and the prevalence of dementia is lower among elderly West Berliners than in regions with lower average educational levels in the older population.

However, questions concerning sample and ecological generalizability are possibly more fundamental (cf. P. B. Baltes et al., 1994). For many, Berlin is a "special" city with historically unique conditions. Aside from arguing that the quest for generalizability is a "never-ending story," we cannot refute this objection.

In our assessment, the criticism of lacking generalizability has most weight for social scientists whose research focuses on different societal conditions and the characterization of populations. In contrast, biologists, medical scientists, and psychologists, who are more interested in universal principles and mechanisms, will feel more secure in accepting findings gained from the West Berlin population of older adults as important for general progress in gerontological knowledge. For example, the intersystemic analysis linking sensory functioning (hearing, vision, and balance/gait) to intellectual functioning in old age that was possible with the multidisciplinary BASE data set yielded new evidence that demonstrated a remarkably high correlation between these two systems of functioning (P. B. Baltes & Lindenberger, 1997; Lindenberger & Baltes, 1994; see also Lindenberger & Reischies, Chapter 12). It is not likely that this intersystemic correlation is very different in West Berlin than in other areas of Germany.

Moreover, social-scientific research may well be less limited by the restriction to West Berlin than is often imagined. Demographically speaking, West Berlin is less different from (former) West Germany than assumed. The following information is from the 1989 Microcensus for West Germany (Statistisches Bundesamt, 1990) and the West Berlin city register of 1991. Whereas 12.1% of West Berlin residents were aged 70 and above, 10.5% of the West German population was in this age range. The difference was mainly due to the higher proportion of women in the oldest age groups. In West Berlin, 17.1% of the female population was 70 and older, in comparison to 14.0% in West Germany. Old people in West Berlin score higher on measures of educational and economic attainment than their West German counterparts. In this respect, West Berlin resembles other large West German cities such as Hamburg.

In our opinion, then, the question of generalizability is less problematic for many of the BASE findings than one might have expected. One could even argue that the observed differences between the West Berlin and West German populations of older adults (e.g., the higher proportion of old people in West Berlin and their educational and economic advantages) have a certain attraction because these differences resemble the demographic changes foreseen for the future (P. B. Baltes & Mittelstraß, 1992). Nevertheless, in our interpretations, we will consider the possibility that life and aging in West Berlin had different aspects than in other cities (Schröder, 1995; Senatsverwaltung für Soziales, Berlin [Berlin Senate Department for Social Affairs], 1995).

7.2   *Aging and Selective Mortality*

A further problem of generalizability that particularly concerns a study dealing with old age is the question of selective survival (mortality). A given birth cohort decreases in size as it ages. Apart from cohort differences, life-expectancy-based selectivity effects represent the second important issue impairing internal and external validity of cross-sectional studies.

A study dealing with aging has to take special account of issues of survival and mortality (P. B. Baltes et al., 1988; Hertzog, 1996; Manton & Vaupel, 1995; Mayer & Huinink, 1990). As the present study's design determined the age of 70 as the lower age limit, strictly speaking, its results only refer to persons who actually reached 70 and more years of age. Thus, the BASE findings do not pertain to the aging of all members of a certain birth cohort (e.g., those born in 1900). For example, more than half of the birth cohort of persons aged 85 in BASE had already died before the study began. This cohort's "potential" aging could no longer be examined. By and large, those persons live longer who are biologically and socioeconomically "better off" (Riegel & Riegel, 1972; Siegler, 1975). Thus, it is reasonable to assume that on average, the older age groups, that is, the "longer" survivors, displayed and display better functioning in some domains than members of their cohorts who have died or are close to death.

Statistically speaking, these selective mortality effects can lead to both positive and negative biases involving the shape and level of age gradients (P. B. Baltes et al., 1988; Firebaugh, 1989). The direction of bias is dependent on the direction of the correlation between the variables considered in age functions and length of life. Where this longevity correlation is positive (e.g., health), the survival bias favors those with higher levels of functioning. In other words, older age groups include people who were healthier, on average, than the total population. Where this correlation between a given variable (e.g., blood pressure) and length of life is negative, the survival bias favors those with lower scores. Of course, there are instances of curvilinear and discontinuous relationships, which present more complicated dynamics. Furthermore, mortality itself is also cohort-dependent so that selective longevity is subject to historical change (Manton & Vaupel, 1995; Vaupel & Lundström, 1994). In fact, some propose that today's old cohorts are socioeconomically better off, but are biologically and genetically more vulnerable (or less selected) than cohorts of earlier times (e.g., Krämer, 1992). When interpreting our data with regard to prognoses for the aging of the "entire" population, in particular, we always need to consider the possibility of bias through selective survival.

Are there strategies we can use to deal with the issue of selective mortality adequately? In our opinion, there are three main ways to control or estimate such effects:

(1)   the comparison of data on BASE cohorts with earlier census findings on the same birth cohorts, that is, with census information about the same birth cohort collected at a younger age (cf. Maas et al., Chapter 3);

(2)   the utilization of data from other studies that dealt explicitly with questions of age- and cohort-specific selective survival and were able to do so based on longitudinal and cohort-sequential data; and

(3)   carrying out differentiated selectivity analyses on the present data set and continuing this work on the longitudinal BASE data that are currently being collected (see above; cf. Lindenberger et al., Chapter 2).

Table 1.11. *Sampling rates of the core BASE sample (Intensive Protocol, N = 516) from the population of West Berliners aged 70 and above (January 1, 1991) by age group and gender, and the resulting weighting factors*

Age group	*n*	Men *n = 258*	Women *n = 258*	Total *N = 516*	Men	Women	Total
		Percentage			**Weighting factor**		
70–74	86	0.18	0.08	0.12	532	1,296	860
75–79	86	0.20	0.08	0.11	488	1,296	892
80–84	86	0.24	0.08	0.12	422	1,188	859
85–89	86	0.49	0.14	0.21	205	733	469
90–94	86	1.83	0.38	0.62	55	266	160
95+	86	12.25	1.62	2.86	8	62	35
Total	516	0.35	0.12	0.18	353	1,001	546

Note. On the left-hand side, this table shows the percentages of the West Berlin elderly population that the core BASE sample represents. Stratification by age and gender leads to higher representation of men and of very old people, (e.g., the oldest male age group represents 12% of all men aged 95 and above). On the right-hand side, the factors are shown by which, ceteris paribus, the frequencies observed in BASE are multiplied in order to estimate the frequency of a phenomenon in the West Berlin population of old people (e.g., to obtain the number of older adults with a diagnosis of dementia). Each of the 12 cells of the design contains $n = 43$.

7.3   *Statistical Reliability and Validity of Subsamples*

Generalizing from samples to a population is, among other things, dependent on how well and reliably the sample represents the population. This problem is often discussed under the heading of sample reliability and validity. In total, approximately 282,000 people aged 70 and above lived in West Berlin at the time of the data collection (about 208,000 women and 74,000 men).

Because of the stratification of our sample by age and gender, there is a special problematic in BASE. As shown in Table 1.11, the relative sampling rates in the six age and two gender categories varied because of the decision to achieve 12 cells of identical size ($n = 43$). For example, the sampling rate for the entire sample was 0.18%, but 0.12% for 70- to 74-year-olds, and 2.86% for those aged 95 and above (i.e., about 23 times higher). Similar differences apply to the two gender groups ($n = 258$), with the sampling rates for men (see last row of Table 1.11) approximately three times those for women (0.35% vs. 0.12%).

By and large, the statistical reliability (power) of generalization from our sample to the population is characterized by two trends: (1) Reliability becomes larger with older age groups; and (2) reliability is larger for men than for women. Thus, despite their equal size ($n = 43$), the subsamples have different generalizability.

Of course, these general statements about different reliability among the subsamples have to be seen in the validity context of the selectivity analyses described above and in Chapter 2. It is important to note that these analyses only indicate small interactions between the selectivity effects observed for 23 variables and age and gender. On the contrary, the selectivity effects (cf. Fig.1.3) generally apply across all age groups and for men and women. In Chapter 2, Lindenberger et al. report further analyses and possible correction strategies.

7.4   Generalization from the BASE Sample to the Population of Old People: The Issue of Weighting

A further problem arises from the stratification of the sample and the resulting unequal sampling rate for age and gender groups. The relevant information is presented on the left-hand side of Table 1.11.

At the beginning of this chapter, we pointed out that, for certain questions, it is important to be able to estimate the distribution of a phenomenon in the entire West Berlin population of old people. In this case it is necessary to *weight* the individuals measured in the BASE sample ($N = 516$) so that frequencies are obtained for the entire West Berlin population of old people (approximately 74,000 men and 208,000 women aged 70 and above living in West Berlin). The weighting factors are a direct function of the relative sampling rates.

The weighting factors for the BASE Intensive Protocol sample are listed on the right-hand side of Table 1.11. The relative reliability of generalization to the population of senior citizens living in West Berlin is again reflected in these numbers. They range from a weighting factor of 8 (for men aged 95+) to a factor of 1,296 (for 70- to 74-year-old and 75- to 79-year-old women).

In Figure 1.4 we show three examples to illustrate the problem and strategy of weighting: dementia, marital status, and institutionalization. However, we refrain from further specification of these variables because, at this point, our goal is a demonstration of the weighting issue. Because the problem of weighting is familiar to many social scientists, one may wonder why we explicate this problem at such length. We do so because these issues are less familiar to behavioral and medical scientists.

The shaded columns in Figure 1.4 show how often (in percentage) a certain phenomenon occurred based on the data from the BASE sample ($N = 516$), for men and women respectively. It is helpful to remember that the BASE sample is, on average, older than the West Berlin population of old people. The white columns show how the findings are altered by weighting to estimate occurrences in the respective reference population. Clear differences become obvious between age-weighted and unweighted rates of dementia, the proportion of married persons (particularly among men), and the proportion of persons living in institutional settings. Relatively speaking, the proportions of BASE participants who were diagnosed with dementia, who were married (taking men and women together), and who were institutionalized, are higher than in the West Berlin population of old people. For example, the lower rate of married people estimated in the population is due to the fact that weighting by age and gender brings forward the women, who are much more frequent than men in the older population, but are rarely still married. In short, if one is interested in making generalizations from the BASE sample regarding the frequency of a phenomenon's occurrence in the entire West Berlin population of old people, weighting steps that vary by age and gender need to be carried out based on the factors given in Table 1.11.

It is important to note that, for many of the issues examined in BASE, weighting neither makes sense nor is necessary. It is only important when the frequency of a certain phenomenon in the population of old people or in a specified subgroup (e.g., among old

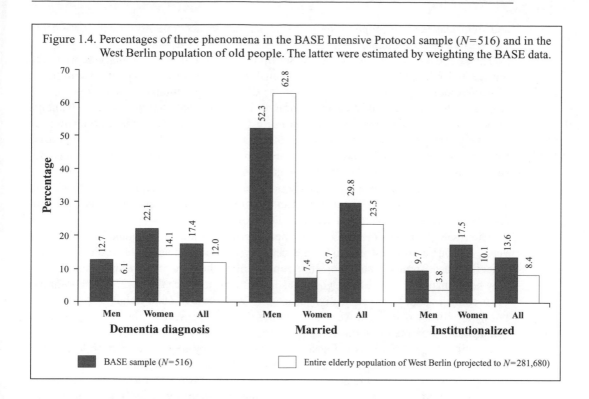

Figure 1.4. Percentages of three phenomena in the BASE Intensive Protocol sample (N=516) and in the West Berlin population of old people. The latter were estimated by weighting the BASE data.

women) is of interest. In contrast, when a question refers to whether 70-, 80-, and 90-year-olds differ (e.g., in visual acuity or blood pressure), it is typically appropriate to compare the age groups examined in BASE directly or other age groups that are corrected for unwanted age-correlated confounds. Indeed, it is advantageous for such age comparisons if the statistical reliability (power) of the subsamples is equivalent. In this book, the authors have tried to clarify when and why they report weighted or unweighted data. Occasionally, both kinds of information are provided.

We do not want to conceal the fact that the issue of adequate weighting is methodologically more complex than stated here. Apart from the problem of age and gender differences in the sampling rate (Table 1.11), there are sample selectivity effects that could have confounding consequences. For example, the success of recruitment within age and gender groups was unequal – that is, different numbers of contacts with potential participants were needed (ranging from n = 119 addresses for 70- to 74-year-old men to n = 316 for women aged 95 and above) in order to realize the final cell size of n = 43 (Table 1.9; cf. Nuthmann & Wahl, 1996, 1997). Again, we expect to pursue these issues in more depth as longitudinal data become available.

7.5   *On Measurement Subjectivity and Objectivity*

A detailed discussion of validity and reliability of the BASE assessments is beyond the scope of this chapter. The individual chapters provide detailed information and evaluation. However, we want to point out a basic problem associated with the validity and significance of self-reports (participants' subjective accounts) and their relationship to objective life conditions.

The BASE assessment protocol was set up to enable a multidisciplinary approach to old age and aging. Methods vary along dimensions such as disciplinary/interdisciplinary, subjective/objective, subject-driven/response-driven, or qualitative/quantitative. In research work, multimethod assessments of a topic are desirable because of the advantage of being able to evaluate a phenomenon more fully, while at the same time testing the relative convergence of different methodological approaches. Disadvantages can arise from two sources. First, different disciplines sometimes imply different phenomena despite using identical terms. The distinct meanings attached to the concepts of anxiety and depression in psychology and psychiatry provide a good example. Second, subjectively and objectively measured phenomena can become inappropriately exchanged or confounded. The latter problem is discussed in the following.

The issue at stake is the "objective" meaning of "subjective" statements and the reverse, of course, as constructivist and especially postmodern scholars would argue. Do objective measurements and subjective reports of a phenomenon always coincide; can they be exchanged? Or are there good reasons for this not to be the case? As the joint use of so-called objective and subjective measures plays a role in most chapters of this book, but is not always discussed, we want to make the reader aware of the issue by offering some general comments on this topic.

Imagine that older adults are asked how much money they give their children each month or how much they receive, or how satisfied they are with their life. In these instances, it is important to realize that the validity of answers to these questions is not only influenced by subjects' potentially inadequate memory or a lack of accessible knowledge (i.e., they cannot remember how much money they gave or received, or they just do not know how satisfied they are and therefore fluctuate in assessment). Apart from these nonintentional errors, there are other reasons for incongruence of objective and subjective measures.

These lie in the fact that achieving perfect correspondence between objectivity and subjectivity is *not* always the goal of human behavior (in contrast to what scientists sometimes like to believe – e.g., when taking subjects' answers about the number of cigarettes they smoke for the literal truth). On the contrary, the possibility of construction and transformation of reality is an inherent quality of the human psyche, and this fact is relevant for adaptive processes of development and aging (e.g., P. B. Baltes, 1991; Brandtstädter & Greve, 1994; Markus & Wurf, 1987; Thomae, 1992). For instance, responses to questions about life satisfaction, physical health, or monetary transfers between the generations are also the result of self-referential processes (e.g., self-protective processes of life management; cf. Staudinger et al., Chapter 11; Borchelt et al., Chapter 15; Smith et al., Chapter 17). Thus, the fact that older adults present themselves as, on average, equally satisfied with life as younger people can also indicate that maintenance of life satisfaction in old age is considered an important life goal. In the same way, old individuals' statements that they give more money than they receive can be the expression of psychological discourse between the generations. Each of these possibilities of self-initiated transformation of reality stands in the way of scientists' expectation of congruence between objectivity and subjectivity.

Therefore, the relationship between objective and subjective measurement is not just an issue of methodological inadequacy. It is also a problem of individual construction of reality and its embeddedness in the subjectivity of life. For example, it can be part of "good" life management to disregard or reinterpret objective reality for the self to feel in control, or to transform life conditions and events retro- and proactively for a sense of meaningfulness. For these reasons, it is always important to consider cognitive and motivational frames when interpreting self-reports.

Often the researchers' aims to find consistency between objectivity and subjectivity are at cross-purposes with subjects' intentions or with basic psychological processes of adaptation and mastery. And this is precisely the reason why it would be wrong to conclude that respondents must have been "lying" if discrepancies between (differently measured) objectivity and subjectivity emerge. Such incongruencies not only exist because human memory and the access to knowledge are imperfect. Objective and subjective measures collected in BASE do not always form identical representations of a phenomenon because the study participants are likely to process the object (reality) psychologically and thereby transform it according to adaptation goals (e.g., the maintenance of an intact sense of self). Indeed, this mechanism also has an individual-differences component. Individuals can differ in the level and direction of such transformational processes.

The chapters of this book have different expectations and aims concerning the problem of objective and subjective measures and their congruence. In some (cf. Staudinger et al., Chapter 11; Borchelt et al., Chapter 15; Smith et al., Chapter 17), the dynamics between objectivity and subjectivity are the explicit focus of interest – for example, when trying to understand why persons rate their life satisfaction similarly, although they appear to live in objectively completely different conditions. In other chapters, subjective statements are used as valid indicators of objective events and psychological phenomena. This is feasible when the measures have been carefully developed and are well tested in terms of validity and reliability. In an interdisciplinary study, it is a particular challenge not to play off the complex relationships of objective and subjective measures against each other, but to keep both lines of interpretation in mind and, where theoretically meaningful, to exploit their commonalities and differences.

References

Alber, J. (1992). *Social and economic policies for the elderly in Germany*. Konstanz: University of Konstanz, Department of Administrative Studies.

Baltes, M. M. (1987). Erfolgreiches Altern als Ausdruck von Verhaltenskompetenz und Umweltqualität. In C. Niemitz (Ed.), *Der Mensch im Zusammenspiel von Anlage und Umwelt* (pp. 353–377). Frankfurt/M.: Suhrkamp.

Baltes, M. M., & Lang, F. R. (1997). Everyday functioning and successful aging: The impact of resources. *Psychology and Aging, 12*, 433–443.

Baltes, M. M., Mayr, U., Borchelt, M., Maas, I., & Wilms, H.-U. (1993). Everyday competence in old and very old age: An inter-disciplinary perspective. *Ageing and Society, 13*, 657–680.

Baltes, P. B. (1968). Longitudinal and cross-sectional sequences in the study of age and generation effects. *Human Development, 11*, 145–171.

Baltes, P. B. (1973). Prototypical paradigms and questions in life-span research on development and aging. *The Gerontologist, 13*, 458–467.

Baltes, P. B. (1987). Theoretical propositions of life-span developmental psychology: On the dynamics between growth and decline. *Developmental Psychology, 23*, 611–626.

Baltes, P. B. (1991). The many faces of human ageing: Toward a psychological culture of old age. *Psychological Medicine, 21*, 837–854.

Baltes, P. B. (1993). The aging mind: Potential and limits. *The Gerontologist, 33*, 580–594.

Baltes, P. B. (1997). On the incomplete architecture of human ontogeny: Selection, optimization, and compensation as foundation of developmental theory. *American Psychologist, 52*, 366–380.

Baltes, P. B., & Baltes, M. M. (1990a). Psychological perspectives on successful aging: The model of selective optimization with compensation. In P. B. Baltes & M. M. Baltes (Eds.), *Successful aging: Perspectives from the behavioral sciences* (pp. 1–34). Cambridge: Cambridge University Press.

Baltes, P. B., & Baltes, M. M. (Eds.). (1990b). *Successful aging: Perspectives from the behavioral sciences*. Cambridge: Cambridge University Press.

Baltes, P. B., & Baltes, M. M. (1992). Gerontologie: Begriff, Herausforderung und Brennpunkte. In P. B. Baltes & J. Mittelstraß (Eds.), *Zukunft des Alterns und gesellschaftliche Entwicklung* (pp. 1–34). Berlin: de Gruyter.

Baltes, P. B., & Graf, P. (1996). Psychological aspects of aging: Facts and frontiers. In D. Magnusson (Ed.), *The life-span development of individuals: Behavioral, neurobiological and psychosocial perspectives* (pp. 427–460). Cambridge: Cambridge University Press.

Baltes, P. B., & Lindenberger, U. (1997). Emergence of a powerful connection between sensory and cognitive functions across the adult life span: A new window to the study of cognitive aging? *Psychology and Aging, 12*, 12–21.

Baltes, P. B., Mayer, K. U., Helmchen, H., & Steinhagen-Thiessen, E. (1993). The Berlin Aging Study (BASE): Overview and design. *Ageing and Society, 13*, 483–515.

Baltes, P. B., Mayer, K. U., Helmchen, H., & Steinhagen-Thiessen, E. (1994). The Berlin Aging Study: Reply to and reflections on commentaries. *Ageing and Society, 14*, 604–617.

Baltes, P. B., & Mittelstraß, J. (Eds.). (1992). *Zukunft des Alterns und gesellschaftliche Entwicklung*. Berlin: de Gruyter.

Baltes, P. B., Reese, H. W., & Nesselroade, J. R. (1988). *Life-span developmental psychology: Introduction to research methods*. Hillsdale, NJ: Erlbaum.

Baltes, P. B., & Smith, J. (1997). A systemic-wholistic view of psychological functioning in very old age: Introduction to a collection of articles from the Berlin Aging Study. *Psychology and Aging, 12*, 395–409.

Baltes, P. B., & Staudinger, U. M. (1993). Über die Gegenwart und Zukunft des Alterns: Ergebnisse und Implikationen psychologischer Forschung. *Berichte und Mitteilungen der Max-Planck-Gesellschaft, 4*, 154–185.

Berkman, L. F., Seeman, T. E., Albert, M., Blazer, D., Kahn, R., Mohs, R., Finch, C., Schneider, E., Cotman, C., McClearn, G., et al. (1993). Successful, usual and impaired functioning in community-dwelling elderly: Findings from the MacArthur Foundation Research Network on Successful Aging. *Journal of Clinical Epidemiology, 46*, 1129–1140.

Birren, J. E. (Ed.). (1959). *Handbook of aging and the individual: Psychological and biological aspects*. Chicago: University of Chicago Press.

Birren, J. E., & Bengtson, V. L. (1988). *Emergent theories of aging*. New York: Springer.

Bortz, W. M. (1991). *Living short and dying long*. New York: Bantam.

Brandtstädter, J., & Greve, W. (1994). The aging self: Stabilizing and protective processes. *Developmental Review, 14*, 52–80.

Brim, O. G., Jr., & Kagan, J. (1980). Constancy and change: A view of the issues. In O. G. Brim, Jr. & J. Kagan (Eds.), *Constancy and change in human development* (pp. 1–25). Cambridge, MA: Harvard University Press.

Bromley, D. B. (1988). Approaching the limits. *Social Behavior, 3*, 71–84.

Brückner, E., & Mayer, K. U. (1998). Collecting life history data: Experiences from the German Life History Study. In J. L. Giele & G. H. Elder Jr. (Eds.), *Methods of life course research: Qualitative and quantitative approaches* (pp. 152–181). Thousand Oaks, CA: Sage.

Bundesministerium für Familie und Senioren (Ed.). (1993). *Erster Altenbericht: Die Lebenssituation älterer Menschen in Deutschland*. Bonn.

Copeland, J. R., Dewey, M. E., & Griffiths-Jones, H. M. (1986). A computerized psychiatric diagnostic system and case nomenclature for elderly subjects: GMS and AGECAT. *Psychological Medicine, 16*, 89–99.

Coper, H., Jänicke, B., & Schulze, G. (1985). Adaptivität. In D. Bente, H. Coper, & S. Kanowski (Eds.), *Hirnorganische Psychosyndrome im Alter: Vol. II. Methoden zur Objektivierung pharmakotherapeutischer Wirkungen* (pp. 159–170). Berlin: Springer-Verlag.

Cowdry, E. V. (1939). *Problems of ageing*. Baltimore: Williams & Wilkins.

Dieck, M. (1992). Besondere Perspektiven des Alterns und des Alters im vereinten Deutschland. In P. B. Baltes & J. Mittelstraß (Eds.), *Zukunft des Alterns und gesellschaftliche Entwicklung* (pp. 640–667). Berlin: de Gruyter.

Dieck, M., Igl, G., & Schwichtenberg-Hilmert, B. (Eds.). (1993). *Dokumente der internationalen Altenpolitik*. Berlin: Deutsches Zentrum für Altersfragen.

Elwert, G. (1992). Alter im interkulturellen Vergleich. In P. B. Baltes & J. Mittelstraß (Eds.), *Zukunft des Alterns und gesellschaftliche Entwicklung* (pp. 260–282). Berlin: de Gruyter.

Finch, C. E. (1990). *Longevity, senescence, and the genome*. Chicago: University of Chicago Press.

Firebaugh, G. (1989). Methods for estimating cohort replacement effects. *Sociological Methodology, 19*, 243–262.

Fries, J. F. (1990). Medical perspectives upon successful aging. In P. B. Baltes & M. M. Baltes (Eds.), *Successful aging: Perspectives from the behavioral sciences* (pp. 35–49). Cambridge: Cambridge University Press.

Geiselmann, B., & Helmchen, H. (1994). Demented subjects' competence to consent to participate in field studies: The Berlin Aging Study. *Medicine and Law, 13*, 177–184.

Geiselmann, B., Linden, M., & Sachs-Ericsson, N. (1989). Benzodiazepine prescription and therapist non-compliance. *European Archives of Psychiatry and Neurological Sciences, 239*, 180–187.

Gerok, W., & Brandtstädter, J. (1992). Normales, krankhaftes und optimales Altern: Variations- und Modifikationsspielräume. In P. B. Baltes & J. Mittelstraß (Eds.), *Zukunft des Alterns und gesellschaftliche Entwicklung* (pp. 356–385). Berlin: de Gruyter.

Guillemard, A.-M. (1992). Europäische Perspektiven der Alternspolitik. In P. B. Baltes & J. Mittelstraß (Eds.), *Zukunft des Alterns und gesellschaftliche Entwicklung* (pp. 614–639). Berlin: de Gruyter.

Häfner, H. (1992). Psychiatrie des höheren Lebensalters. In P. B. Baltes & J. Mittelstraß (Eds.), *Zukunft des Alterns und gesellschaftliche Entwicklung* (pp. 151–179). Berlin: de Gruyter.

Heinrich, K., Linden, M., & Müller-Oerlinghausen, B. (1989). *Werden zu viele Psychopharmaka verbraucht? Methoden und Ergebnisse der Pharmakoepidemiologie und Phase-IV-Forschung*. Stuttgart: Thieme.

Helmchen, H. (1991). The impact of diagnostic systems on treatment planning. *Integrative Psychiatry, 7*, 16–20.

Helmchen, H., & Lauter, H. (Eds.). (1995). *Dürfen Ärzte mit Demenzkranken forschen? Analyse des Problemfeldes: Forschungsbedarf und Einwilligungsproblematik*. Stuttgart: Thieme.

Helmchen, H., & Linden, M. (Eds.). (1992). *Die jahrelange Behandlung mit Psychopharmaka.* Berlin: de Gruyter.

Hertzog, C. (1996). Research design in studies of aging and cognition. In J. E. Birren & K. W. Schaie (Eds.), *Handbook of the psychology of aging* (4th ed., pp. 24–37). New York: Academic Press.

Horn, J. L. (1970). Organization of data on life-span development of human abilities. In L. R. Goulet & P. B. Baltes (Eds.), *Life-span developmental psychology: Research and theory* (pp. 423–466). New York: Academic Press.

Kahn, R. L., & Antonucci, T. C. (1980). Convoys over the life course: Attachment, roles, and social support. In P. B. Baltes & O. G. Brim Jr. (Eds.), *Life-span development and behavior* (Vol. 3, pp. 253–283). New York: Academic Press.

Karl, F., & Tokarski, W. (1989). *Die neuen Alten.* Kassel: Gesamthochschulbibliothek.

Kleemeier, R. W. (1962). Intellectual change in the senium. *Proceedings of the Social Statistics Section of the American Statistical Association, 1,* 290–295.

Kliegl, R., & Baltes, P. B. (1991). Testing the limits: Kognitive Entwicklungskapazität in einer Gedächtnisleistung. *Zeitschrift für Psychologie, 11* (Suppl.), 84–92.

Klose, H.-U. (Ed.). (1993a). *Altern der Gesellschaft: Antworten auf den demographischen Wandel.* Cologne: Bund.

Klose, H.-U. (Ed.). (1993b). *Altern hat Zukunft: Bevölkerungsentwicklung und Wirtschaftsdynamik.* Opladen: Westdeutscher Verlag.

Kohli, M. (1992). Altern in soziologischer Perspektive. In P. B. Baltes & J. Mittelstraß (Eds.), *Zukunft des Alterns und gesellschaftliche Entwicklung* (pp. 231–259). Berlin: de Gruyter.

Kohli, M. (1993). *Engagement im Ruhestand: Rentner zwischen Erwerb, Ehrenamt und Hobby.* Opladen: Leske + Budrich.

Kohli, M., & Meyer, J. W. (1986). Social structure and social construction of life stages. *Human Development, 29,* 145–180.

Krämer, W. (1992). Altern und Gesundheitswesen: Probleme und Lösungen aus der Sicht der Gesundheitsökonomie. In P. B. Baltes & J. Mittelstraß (Eds.), *Zukunft des Alterns und gesellschaftliche Entwicklung* (pp. 563–580). Berlin: de Gruyter.

Kruse, A. (1992a). Alter im Lebenslauf. In P. B. Baltes & J. Mittelstraß (Eds.), *Zukunft des Alterns und gesellschaftliche Entwicklung* (pp. 331–355). Berlin: de Gruyter.

Kruse, A. (1992b). *Kompetenz im Alter in ihren Bezügen zur objektiven und subjektiven Lebenssituation.* Darmstadt: Steinkopff.

Kruse, A., Lindenberger, U., & Baltes, P. B. (1993). Longitudinal research on human aging: The power of combining real-time, microgenetic, and simulation approaches. In D. Magnusson & P. Casaer (Eds.), *Longitudinal research on individual development: Present status and future perspectives* (pp. 153–193). Cambridge: Cambridge University Press.

Lawley, D. N. (1943). A note on Karl Pearson's selection formulae. *Proceedings of the Royal Society of Edinburgh, 62,* 28–30.

Lehr, U. (1991). *Psychologie des Alterns* (7th ed.). Heidelberg: Quelle & Meyer.

Lehr, U., & Thomae, H. (Eds.). (1987). *Formen seelischen Alterns: Ergebnisse der Bonner Gerontologischen Längsschnittstudie (BOLSA).* Stuttgart: Enke.

Linden, M., & Helmchen, H. (1995). WHO International Collaborative Study on psychological problems in general health care: Results from the Berlin centre. In T. B. Üstün & N. Sartorius (Eds.), *Mental illness in general health care: An international study* (pp. 99–119). Chichester: Wiley.

Lindenberger, U., & Baltes, P. B. (1994). Sensory functioning and intelligence in old age: A strong connection. *Psychology and Aging, 9,* 339–355.

Lindenberger, U., & Baltes, P. B. (1997). Intellectual functioning in old and very old age: Cross-sectional results from the Berlin Aging Study. *Psychology and Aging, 12,* 410–432.

Lindenberger, U., Mayr, U., & Kliegl, R. (1993). Speed and intelligence in old age. *Psychology and Aging, 8,* 207–220.

Little, R. J. A., & Rubin, D. B. (1987). *Statistical analysis with missing data.* New York: Wiley.

Maddox, G. L. (1987). Aging differently. *The Gerontologist, 27,* 557–564.

Magnusson, D., & Bergman, L. (Eds.). (1990). *Data quality in longitudinal research.* Cambridge: Cambridge University Press.

Manton, K. G., & Vaupel, J. W. (1995). Survival after the age of 80 in the United States, Sweden, France, England, and Japan. *New England Journal of Medicine, 333,* 1232–1235.

Markus, H., & Wurf, E. (1987). The dynamic self-concept: A social psychological perspective. In M. R. Rosenzweig & L. W. Porter (Eds.), *Annual review of psychology* (Vol. 38, pp. 299–337). Palo Alto, CA: Annual Reviews.

Marsiske, M., Klumb, P., & Baltes, M. M. (1997). Everyday activity patterns and sensory functioning in old age. *Psychology and Aging, 12,* 444–457.

Max Planck Institute for Human Development and Education. (1983). *Between elite and mass education: Education in the Federal Republic of Germany.* Albany: State University of New York Press.

Mayer, K. U. (Ed.). (1990). Lebensverläufe und sozialer Wandel. *Kölner Zeitschrift für Soziologie und Sozialpsychologie, 31* (Special issue).

Mayer, K. U. (1992). Bildung und Arbeit in einer alternden Bevölkerung. In P. B. Baltes & J. Mittelstraß (Eds.), *Zukunft des Alterns und gesellschaftliche Entwicklung* (pp. 518–543). Berlin: de Gruyter.

Mayer, K. U., Baltes, P. B., Gerok, W., Häfner, H., Helmchen, H., Kruse, A., Mittelstraß, J., Staudinger, U. M., Steinhagen-Thiessen, E., & Wagner, G. (1992). Gesellschaft, Politik und Altern. In P. B. Baltes & J. Mittelstraß (Eds.), *Zukunft des Alterns und gesellschaftliche Entwicklung* (pp. 721–757). Berlin: de Gruyter.

Mayer, K. U., & Brückner, E. (1989). *Lebensverläufe und Wohlfahrtsentwicklung: Konzeption, Design und Methodik der Erhebung von Lebensverläufen der Geburtsjahrgänge 1929–1931, 1939–1941, 1949–1951* (Materialien aus der Bildungsforschung, Vol. 35, Parts I–III). Berlin: Max Planck Institute for Human Development.

Mayer, K. U., & Huinink, J. (1990). Age, period and cohort in the study of the life course: A comparison of classical A-P-C-analysis with event history analysis, or farewell to Lexis? In D. Magnusson & L. R. Bergman (Eds.), *Data quality in longitudinal research* (pp. 211–232). Cambridge: Cambridge University Press.

Meinlschmidt, G., Imme, U., & Kramer, R. (1990). *Sozialstrukturatlas Berlin (West): Eine statistisch-methodische Analyse mit Hilfe der Faktorenanalyse.* Berlin: Senats-verwaltung für Gesundheit und Soziales.

Mittelstraß, J., Baltes, P. B., Gerok, W., Häfner, H., Helmchen, H., Kruse, A., Mayer, K. U., Staudinger, U. M., Steinhagen-Thiessen, E., & Wagner, G. (1992). Wissenschaft und Altern. In P. B. Baltes & J. Mittelstraß (Eds.), *Zukunft des Alterns und gesellschaftliche Entwicklung* (pp. 695–720). Berlin: de Gruyter.

Myles, J. (1984). *Old age in the welfare state: The political economy of public pensions.* Boston, MA: Little, Brown.

Nelson, A. E., & Dannefer, D. (1992). Aged heterogeneity: Fact or fiction? The fate of diversity in gerontological research. *The Gerontologist, 32,* 17–23.

Nesselroade, J. R., & Baltes, P. B. (Eds.). (1979). *Longitudinal research in the study of behavior and development.* New York: Academic Press.

Neugarten, B. L. (1969). Continuities and discontinuities of psychological issues into adult life. *Human Development, 12,* 121–130.

Neugarten, B. L. (1974). Age groups in American society and the rise of the young-old. *Annals of the American Academy of Political and Social Sciences, 9,* 187–198.

Nuthmann, R., & Wahl, H.-W. (1996). Methodische Aspekte der Erhebungen der Berliner Altersstudie. In K. U. Mayer & P. B. Baltes (Eds.), *Die Berliner Altersstudie* (pp. 55–83). Berlin: Akademie Verlag.

Nuthmann, R., & Wahl, H.-W. (1997). *Methodological aspects of the Berlin Aging Study* (Technical report). Berlin: Max Planck Institute for Human Development.

Olbrich, E., Sames, K., & Schramm, A. (1994). *Kompendium der Gerontologie: Interdisziplinäres Handbuch für Forschung, Klinik und Praxis.* Landsberg/Lech: Ecomed.

Oswald, W. D., Herrmann, W. M., Kanowski, S., Lehr, U. M., & Thomae, H. (1984). *Gerontologie.* Stuttgart: Kohlhammer.

Pearson, K. (1903). Mathematical contributions to the theory of evolution: XI. On the influence of natural selection on the variability and correlation of organs. *Philosophical Transactions of the Royal Society of London (Series A), 200,* 1–66.

Perlmutter, M. (Ed.). (1990). *Late-life potential.* Washington, DC: Gerontological Society of America.

Poon, L. W. (Ed.). (1992). *The Georgia Centenarian Study.* Amityville, NY: Baywood.

Radloff, L. S. (1977). The CES-D Scale: A self-report depression scale for research in the general population. *Applied Psychological Measurement, 1,* 385–401.

Reischies, F. M., Spiess, P. von, & Hedde, J. P. (1990). Cognitive deterioration and dementia outcome in depression: The search for prognostic factors. In K. Maurer, P. Riederer, & H. Beckmann (Eds.), *Alzheimer's disease, epidemiology, neuropathology, neurochemistry and clinics* (pp. 687–691). Wien: Springer.

Rendtel, U., & Pötter, U. (1992). *Über Sinn und Unsinn von Repräsentativitätsstudien* (Discussion paper No. 61). Berlin: Deutsches Institut für Wirtschaftsforschung.

Riegel, K. F., & Riegel, R. M. (1972). Development, drop, and death. *Developmental Psychology, 6,* 306–319.

Riley, M. W. (1973). Aging and cohort succession: Interpretations and misinterpretations. *Public Opinion Quarterly, 37,* 35–49.

Riley, M. W. (1987). On the significance of age in sociology. *American Sociological Review, 52,* 1–14.

Riley, M. W., Kahn, R. L., & Foner, A. (Eds.). (1994). *Age and structural lag.* New York: Wiley.

Riley, M. W., & Riley, J. W., Jr. (1992). Individuelles und gesellschaftliches Potential des Alterns. In P. B. Baltes & J. Mittelstraß (Eds.), *Zukunft des Alterns und gesellschaftliche Entwicklung* (pp. 437–460). Berlin: de Gruyter.

Rowe, J. W., & Kahn, R. L. (1987). Human aging: Usual and successful. *Science, 237,* 143–149.

Rutter, M. (1988). *Studies of psychosocial risk: The power of longitudinal data.* Cambridge: Cambridge University Press.

Ryder, N. B. (1965). The cohort as a concept in the study of social change. *American Sociological Review, 30,* 843–861.

Salthouse, T. A. (1991). *Theoretical perspectives on cognitive aging.* Hillsdale, NJ: Erlbaum.

Schaie, K. W. (1965). A general model for the study of developmental problems. *Psychological Bulletin, 64,* 92–107.

Schaie, K. W. (1996). *Intellectual development in adulthood: The Seattle Longitudinal Study.* Cambridge: Cambridge University Press.

Schröder, H. (1995). Materiell gesichert, aber häufig isoliert: Zur Lebenssituation älterer Menschen in Deutschland. *Informationsdienst Soziale Indikatoren, 13,* 11–15.

Senatsverwaltung für Soziales, Berlin. (1995). *Bericht zur sozialen Lage im Land Berlin.* Berlin.

Shock, N. W. (1977). System integration. In C. E. Finch & L. Hayflick (Eds.), *Handbook of the biology of aging* (pp. 639–665). New York: Van Nostrand Reinhold.

Siegler, I. C. (1975). The terminal drop hypothesis: Fact or artifact? *Experimental Aging Research, 1,* 169–185.

Statistisches Bundesamt (Ed.). (1990). *Bevölkerung und Erwerbstätigkeit.* Stuttgart: Metzler-Poeschel.

Statistisches Bundesamt (Ed.). (1993). *Bevölkerung und Erwerbstätigkeit.* Stuttgart: Metzler-Poeschel.

Steen, B., & Djurfeldt, H. (1993). Die gerontologischen und geriatrischen Populationsstudien in Göteborg. *Zeitschrift für Gerontologie, 26,* 163–169.

Steinhagen-Thiessen, E., & Borchelt, M. (1993). Health differences in advanced old age. *Ageing and Society, 13,* 619–655.

Steinhagen-Thiessen, E., Gerok, W., & Borchelt, M. (1992). Innere Medizin und Geriatrie. In P. B. Baltes & J. Mittelstraß (Eds.), *Zukunft des Alterns und gesellschaftliche Entwicklung* (pp. 124–150). Berlin: de Gruyter.

Svanborg, A. (1985). The Gothenburg longitudinal study of 70-year-olds: Clinical reference values in the elderly. In M. Bergener, M. Ermini, & H. B. Stähelin (Eds.), *Thresholds in aging* (pp. 231–239). London: Academic Press.

Tews, H. P. (1990). Leistung im Strukturwandel des Alters. In R. Schmitz-Scherzer, A. Kruse, & E. Olbrich (Eds.), *Altern: Ein lebenslanger Prozeß der sozialen Interaktion* (pp. 357–363). Darmstadt: Steinkopff.

Tews, H. P. (1991). *Altersbilder: Über Wandel und Beeinflussung von Vorstellungen vom und Einstellungen zum Alter* (KDA Forum, Vol. 16). Cologne: Kuratorium Deutsche Altershilfe.

Thomae, H. (1976). *Patterns of aging: Findings from the Bonn Longitudinal Study of Aging. Contributions to human development.* Basel: Karger.

Thomae, H. (1992). Emotion and personality. In J. E. Birren, R. B. Sloane, & G. D. Cohen (Eds.), *Handbook of mental health and aging* (2nd ed., pp. 355–375). San Diego, CA: Academic Press.

Thomae, H., & Maddox, G. L. (Eds.). (1982). *New perspectives on old age: A message to decision makers.* New York: Springer.

Vaupel, J. W., & Lundström, H. (1994). The future of mortality at older ages in developed countries. In W. Lutz (Ed.), *The future population of the world* (pp. 295–315). London: Earthscan.

Weinert, F. E. (1992). Altern in psychologischer Perspektive. In P. B. Baltes & J. Mittelstraß (Eds.), *Zukunft des Alterns und gesellschaftliche Entwicklung* (pp. 180–203). Berlin: de Gruyter.

CHAPTER 2

Sample Selectivity and Generalizability of the Results of the Berlin Aging Study

Ulman Lindenberger, Reiner Gilberg, Todd D. Little, Reinhard Nuthmann, Ulrich Pötter, and Paul B. Baltes

In epidemiological investigations, one common but rarely analyzed threat to generalizability is sample selectivity or nonrandom sample attrition. In this chapter, we describe our approach to the study of selectivity and provide in-depth analyses of the magnitude of sample selectivity in the Berlin Aging Study. Of all individuals eligible for participation (the verified parent sample, $N = 1,908$), 27% reached the highest level of participation (the Intensive Protocol, $N = 516$). With respect to levels of performance, projection of selectivity observed on lower levels of participation onto Intensive Protocol constructs indicates that the Intensive Protocol sample was, indeed, positively selected on medical, social, and psychological dimensions. However, the magnitude of observed selectivity effects did not exceed 0.5 standard deviations for any construct. In addition, variances and covariance relations observed in the Intensive Protocol sample were not markedly different from those found at lower levels of participation. We conclude that the degree of selectivity in BASE fell within the usual range and did not result in a decrease of sample heterogeneity. Given the magnitude of sample attrition and the high mean age of the sample, this is a satisfactory result.

1   Introduction

A major goal in science is to ensure that the validity of empirical patterns does not remain restricted to the observed events, but can be generalized to a larger space of potential measurements. In this sense, *measurement representativeness* characterizes the degree to which observations can stand for other nonmeasured events (cf. McArdle, 1994).

In this chapter, our main intention is to document and analyze one important factor endangering representativeness and generalizability: the sample selectivity that can occur with sample loss or sample attrition. *Sample attrition* describes the fact that not all persons asked to take part in the Berlin Aging Study (BASE) passed through the entire assessment protocol. This sample loss can lead to *selectivity* (or bias) of the sample if participants differ from dropouts in characteristics relevant to the study (Kessler, Little, & Groves, 1995; Little, 1995; Little & Rubin, 1987). This selectivity associated with sample attrition should not be confused with selectivity related to the *sampling* procedure itself ("selective sampling" vs. "selective dropout"; cf. P. B. Baltes, Reese, & Nesselroade, 1988). The random sampling procedure used in BASE, by which every element has an equal chance of being selected, is generally accepted as being the best way of minimizing systematic sampling-related biases (Kruskal & Mosteller, 1979a, 1979b, 1979c).[1]

Independent of the degree of generalizability associated with *sampling* – which is large in BASE – is the risk of *sample attrition*, which makes it possible that the statements made on the basis of reduced samples can no longer be applied to the parent sample. In that case, sample attrition would lead to sample selectivity, and the generalizability of BASE results would need to be qualified. The main task of the analyses reported in this chapter is to determine the type and extent of sample selectivity and, in turn, contribute to the adequate interpretation of statements based on the BASE data set.

In the following, we first define our concept of selectivity. We then present an overview of the participation levels in BASE and introduce the statistical methods and variables used in the analyses. After reporting the results of the selectivity analyses, we finally discuss how the findings from the BASE Intensive Protocol data are influenced by sample selectivity.

2   Focuses of Interest

2.1   On the Examination of Sample Selectivity

In a study such as BASE, values on variables are assigned to persons and groups of persons. Depending on the topic of examination and the type of variable, these assignments can usually be summarized by statistical reference values such as means, frequency distributions (prevalence rates), variances, and correlations. The following examples illustrate this: (a) How large are the social networks of men and women? (mean); (b) What proportion of individuals aged 95 and above have dementia? (prevalence); (c) How large are individual differences in intellectual abilities among 70- to 80-year-olds? (variance); (d) How closely are sensory and intellectual functioning linked? (correlation).

The validity of these statements is initially restricted to those participants who were actually measured on the relevant variables. However, not all of the people selected for BASE went through the whole assessment sequence; therefore, the question arises as to whether the examination of the entire parent sample would have yielded different results. This would be the case if variables predicting dropout versus further participation in the study were systematically related to the variables under scrutiny (Little & Rubin, 1987). For example, persons with dementia could be less likely to reach the part of the assessment during which they would receive a clinical diagnosis of dementia (i.e., the Intensive Protocol). In this case, statements on dementia rates based on the Intensive

---

[1] Specifically, the verified sample of BASE is based on random sampling of addresses from the obligatory Berlin city register according to certain criteria. This form of random sampling is advantageous because systematic biases connected to the investigators' research interests are much less likely to occur than with nonrandom samples. However, even if 100% of the parent sample took part in the study (i.e., if there were no sample losses), there would be no guarantee that the persons selected by chance would represent a perfect "miniature" of the Berlin population aged 70 and above (cf. Kruskal & Mosteller, 1979a, 1979b, 1979c; Rendtel & Pötter, 1992; Rudinger & Wood, 1990). Therefore, questions about generalizability of the statements based on analyses of BASE data cannot be answered with a sweeping reply. Instead, generalizability will vary by domain, the type of statement made, and our current state of knowledge, and will sometimes refer to rather small (e.g., the elderly population of West Berlin) or larger (e.g., old people in Western industrial societies) groups (cf. P. B. Baltes et al., Chapter 1 in this volume).

Protocol would underestimate the prevalence rate in the parent sample (cf. Helmchen et al., Chapter 6 in this volume).

Thus, the analysis of sample selectivity represents a methodological precaution to reduce the likelihood of false conclusions and misleading generalizations. Do we overestimate educational levels because fewer people with a low education level take part in the study than those with a higher level? Do we underestimate the variability of intelligence because both good performers and persons with dementia participate less often than individuals with average abilities?

In trying to answer these questions, the *analysis* of sample selectivity is confronted with a fundamental paradox: In order to quantify optimally the degree and nature of selectivity, we would need precisely the information that is missing. We would have to know the characteristics of the nonparticipants – but if they provided this information, they would no longer be nonparticipants. In the methodological literature, this paradoxical situation has led to the demand that at least some basic pieces of information should be gathered on *all* persons, including potential nonparticipants (Dalenius, 1988; Esser, Grohman, Müller, & Schäffer, 1989; von Eye, 1989; Herzog & Rodgers, 1988; Oh & Scheuren, 1983; Panel on Incomplete Data, 1983; Tennstedt, Dettling, & McKinlay, 1992; Weaver, Holmes, & Glenn, 1975). An empirical examination of selectivity – without reference to external sources such as census information – is only possible when this condition is fulfilled.

For a study stretching over a longer period of time such as BASE, it makes sense to replace the dichotomy of participation versus nonparticipation by the graded concept of "participation levels" or *participation depth*. From the outset, the design of BASE was structured to allow the distinction of an ordered sequence of participation levels with increasing amounts of information (cf. P. B. Baltes et al., Chapter 1). For selectivity analyses, this has the important advantage that, at every step from one participation level to the next, the persons continuing participation can be compared with the dropouts on previously measured variables. In this way, we can identify variables on which the two groups differ. This eventually allows the calculation of estimates for constructs assessed later in the protocol which take account of observed sample selectivity at all previous levels.

2.2   Definition of Participation Levels

The parent sample of BASE is based on addresses drawn randomly from the West Berlin city registry. (In Germany, every citizen must register with the police.) The Intensive Protocol sample constitutes the highest participation level and offers the data for most analyses reported in this volume ($N = 516$). It is stratified by age and gender, meaning that the manifestations of these variables are distributed equally. Therefore, on the level of the Intensive Protocol, there are 43 men and 43 women in each of six age groups (70–74, 75–79, 80–84, 85–89, 90–94, and 95+ years).

As opposed to a random distribution, sample stratification has the advantage that age differences can be registered across the entire age range and in both sexes with equal reliability. A comparison with the expected numbers in a nonstratified random sample may illustrate this: If 516 persons aged 70 and above had been drawn in a nonstratified manner from the West Berlin population, there would have been approximately 94 70- to 74-

Figure 2.1. Sample attrition by age and gender. The columns in the 12 cells represent the five participation levels: (1) city registry ($N = 1,908$); (2) Short Initial Assessment ($n = 1,264$); (3) complete Intake Assessment ($n = 928$); (4) consent to take part in the Intensive Protocol ($n = 638$); (5) complete Intensive Protocol ($N = 516$). There are exactly 43 people in each of the 12 cells on the level of the Intensive Protocol.

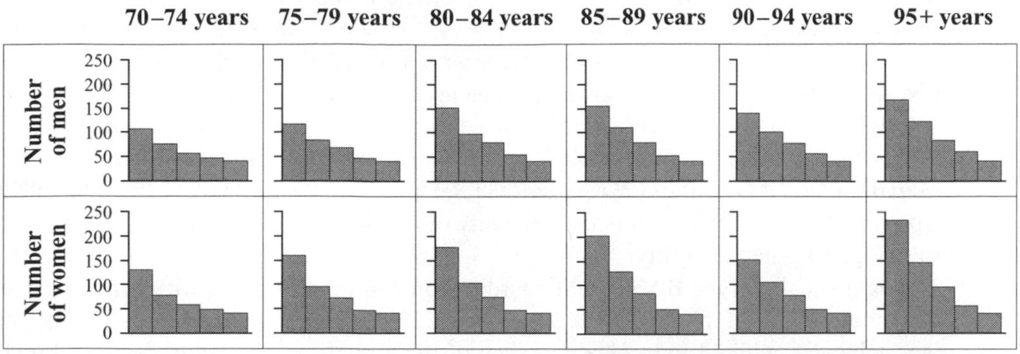

year-old women and 42 70- to 74-year-old men, but only 5 women and 1 man aged 95 and above in the sample.

The equal distribution by age and gender on the level of the Intensive Protocol was achieved by drawing a different number of addresses for each of the 12 design cells, thereby compensating for differences in sample attrition between the cells (see Figure 2.1). As outlined above, we distinguish five participation levels (see also Fig. 1.2 in P. B. Baltes et al., Chapter 1). From May 1990 until May 1993, a total of 2,297 persons received letters asking them to participate in BASE. *Participation level 1* comprises the subset of 1,908 individuals who could be contacted personally or indirectly (via information from relatives or third parties such as friends, neighbors, or nursing personnel). The fact that 389 persons could not be reached indicates that even an obligatory register does not necessarily constitute a perfect record of the population. Specifically, 50% of those 389 had already died. Others had moved to an unknown address (28%) or away from Berlin (4%). The remaining 18% could not be contacted at the given address despite many attempts. Therefore, we feel justified in designating those 1,908 individuals who were still alive and, in principle, recruitable, as constituents of the *verified parent sample*. By definition, participation at this level was 100%.

Participation level 2 ($n = 1,264$, or 66% of the verified sample of $N = 1,908$) contained all persons who completed all or most of the Short Initial Assessment. This consists of the first 16 questions of the multidisciplinary Intake Assessment, which were either posed by the interviewers during an initial contact or sent to participants as a questionnaire. In addition, interviewers carried out a standardized concurrent observation of the participants and their living conditions. For the selectivity analyses, we considered the 1,219 participants who answered all of the 16 questions as well as an additional group consisting of 45 individuals for whom information on most of those questions was available (sometimes from interviews with relatives, but always including direct observational information from the interviewers). The criterion for reaching *participation level 3* ($n = 928$, or 49% of $N = 1,908$) was the completion of the Intake Assessment (an instrument developed in BASE assessing core constructs of all involved disciplines in 100 questions; cf. P. B. Baltes et al., Chapter 1).

The fourth and fifth participation levels are distinguished by the amount of information available from the Intensive Protocol. All participants who agreed to take part in the Intensive Protocol reached *participation level 4* ($n = 638$, or 33% of $N = 1,908$). Only those who actually *completed the entire protocol* consisting of the Intake Assessment and an additional 13 sessions were assigned to *participation level 5* ($N = 516$, 27% of $N = 1,908$). The multidisciplinary data set available for these persons is extensive (see P. B. Baltes et al., Chapter 1, Tables 1.4–7, for an overview of the measured constructs). *Participation level 5 constitutes the core of the Berlin Aging Study.* The extent of sample attrition at this level underscores the necessity of conducting selectivity analyses in order to safeguard generalizability.

The main aim of the BASE field coordination was to ensure stratification by age and gender at level 5 (cf. Nuthmann & Wahl, 1996, 1997). As can be seen in Figure 2.1, this was achieved, with 43 individuals in each of the 12 cells of the study design's highest participation level. Variations from equal distributions at lower levels show that different numbers of addresses had to be entered in each cell to reach stratification at the highest level.[2] For example, 235 women aged 95 and above had to be selected, whereas only 109 70- to 74-year-old men had to be selected on participation level 1 to achieve equal distribution on the level of completed Intensive Protocols.

The variation of sample attrition by age and gender raises the question whether the degree of sample *selectivity* is also associated with age and gender. For example, sample selectivity could be larger for the very old (aged 85 and above) than for the old (aged 70 to 84), or larger for women than men. This makes it methodologically necessary to consider the design variables age and gender systematically in the selectivity analyses.

2.3   Summary

The validity of statements made on the basis of the Intensive Protocol is initially restricted to those individuals who actually went through the entire measurement process. Therefore, the question arises as to whether the observations made about these persons are also true for the parent sample. Validity would be limited according to the extent that observed (but also nonobserved) characteristics that predict study participation or dropout are correlated with variables of interest, such as constructs from the Intensive Protocol. In itself, the fact that a complete data set from the Intensive Protocol is not available for 73% of the verified parent sample does not prove the existence of *selec-*

---

[2] From a theoretical perspective, redrawing addresses at a later time according to participation rates is problematic because observations can no longer be seen as being stochastically independent of each other. In the context of selectivity analyses, a dependency of observations would have to be examined more closely if persons recruited later in time differed in measured characteristics from those selected earlier. To test this, the variables presented in Table 2.1 were correlated with the date of the letter asking people to participate. No strong associations between that date and the observed characteristics were found within or across the 12 design cells. This indicates that the redrawing of addresses according to participation rates did not have any significant influence on the composition of the sample.

tivity, it only documents sample attrition. One can only speak of selectivity if sample loss was not random. The statistical methods presented below concentrate on this question.

3 Methods

First, we present the variables used in the selectivity analyses (Section 3.1). Second, we summarize expectations regarding the direction and pattern of selectivity effects on the basis of previous gerontological research (Section 3.2). Finally, we give an overview of statistical methods applied for the analysis of selectivity (Section 3.3).

3.1 Choice of Variables

The variables used in the following analyses are listed in Table 2.1. Our choice of variables was aimed at capturing selectivity as early (i.e., on low participation levels) and as comprehensively as possible.

All information available on level 1 was included. As can be seen in Table 2.1, the data from the city register were supplemented by an assessment of the living area based on an index developed for West Berlin by Meinlschmidt, Imme, and Kramer (1990), as well as an interviewers' description of the living quarters, which allowed the distinction between community dwellers (private households or sheltered housing for old people) and the institutionalized (senior citizens' homes, nursing homes, or hospitals for the chronically ill).

The one-year mortality variable is particularly important. It conveys information on mortality given to us by the city registry later on, and shows whether a person was still alive one year after he or she was sent the initial letter asking him or her to participate in BASE.

At the higher levels of participation, the selection of additional variables was guided by the consideration that information pertinent to important constructs be available as early as possible (e.g., health, functional capacity, intelligence, everyday competence, social networks, education, and well-being).

3.2 Predictions

The analyses reported in this chapter are mainly exploratory and descriptive. Nonetheless, some predictions on the direction of selectivity effects can be made on the basis of selectivity analyses carried out in previous gerontological research. In these (mainly longitudinal) studies, it has been shown that participation likelihood and duration are usually positively correlated with the many dimensions that can be subsumed under the terms of "fitness" or "competence." Thus, on average, persons taking part in studies for a longer time are *younger* (DeMaio, 1980; Hawkins, 1975; Lowe & McCormick, 1955; Mercer & Butler, 1967/68; Weaver et al., 1975) and *healthier* (Goudy, 1976; Hertzog, Schaie, & Gribbin, 1978; McArdle, Hamagami, Elias, & Robbins, 1991; Norris, 1985; Powers & Bultena, 1972; Schaie, Labouvie, & Barrett, 1973; Siegler & Botwinick, 1979) and come from a *higher social class* (Goudy, 1976; Powers & Bultena, 1972; Streib, 1966) than persons who do not agree to participate or who drop out during the course of the protocol. Moreover, participants often have *higher intelligence* (P. B. Baltes, Schaie, & Nardi, 1971; Cooney, Schaie, & Willis, 1988; Goudy, 1976; Norris,

Table 2.1. *List of variables used in selectivity analyses*

	Participation level				
	1 **N = 1,908**	**2** **n = 1,264**	**3** **n = 928**	**4** **n = 638**	**5** **N = 516**
City registry and additional information					
Age at time of contact (in years)	86.1 (8.6)	86.3 (8.7)	86.0 (8.6)	85.5 (8.8)	84.9 (8.7)
Gender (proportion of women in %)	55.6	52.6	50.9	48.4	50.0
One-year mortality (in %)	13.5	12.0	10.7	9.9	5.6
Married (in %)	28.6	28.6	28.0	29.5	30.4
Widowed (in %)	55.9	56.8	55.3	54.4	53.9
Single (in %)	8.2	7.8	9.1	7.8	7.9
Divorced (in %)	7.2	6.8	7.7	8.3	7.7
Institutionalized (in %)	14.9	15.1	15.4	16.3	14.5
Social Index of Living Area	24.2 (117.8)	24.7 (114.7)	31.4 (110.1)	36.1 (109.6)	40.7 (107.2)
Short Initial Assessment					
Observer-rated ADL[a]	—	3.9 (1.3)	4.0 (1.3)	4.1 (1.2)	4.2 (1.2)
Observer-rated signs of dementia	—	4.3 (5.8)	3.7 (5.6)	3.7 (5.5)	3.1 (4.9)
Observer-rated sensory impairment	—	3.2 (0.8)	3.2 (0.8)	3.2 (0.8)	3.3 (0.8)
Rough index of education	—	1.9 (0.7)	1.9 (0.7)	1.9 (0.7)	1.9 (0.7)
Life satisfaction (item)	—	3.5 (1.1)	3.6 (1.0)	3.6 (1.0)	3.7 (1.0)
Subjective physical health (item)	—	2.7 (1.1)	2.8 (1.1)	2.9 (1.1)	2.9 (1.1)
Subjective mental health (item)	—	3.3 (1.1)	3.5 (1.0)	3.5 (1.0)	3.5 (1.0)

Intake Assessment

ADL score	4.4 (1.3)	4.4 (1.3)	4.5 (1.2)
Subjective walking distance (in km)	4.2 (1.4)	4.3 (1.4)	4.4 (1.3)
Body Mass Index	1.2 (0.2)	1.2 (0.2)	1.2 (0.2)
SMMS[b]	0.45 (1.3)	0.51 (1.3)	0.59 (1.2)
Digit Letter test	68.1 (28.3)	70.3 (29.1)	73.3 (28.2)
Equivalent income (in DM)	1,979 (981)	2,020 (1,078)	2,042 (1,037)
Number of close companions	2.1 (3.0)	2.2 (3.3)	2.2 (3.3)
Depressivity (short scale)	10.4 (5.8)	10.1 (5.6)	10.0 (5.5)
Nonagitation	4.0 (0.9)	4.0 (0.9)	4.1 (0.8)
Satisfaction with aging	4.0 (0.8)	4.1 (0.8)	4.1 (0.8)
Life satisfaction (scale)	4.0 (0.8)	4.1 (0.8)	4.1 (0.8)

Intensive Protocol

Number of moderate to severe illnesses	—	—	8.1 (4.0)
ADL/IADL[a] (T-score)	—	—	50.0 (10.0)
Visual acuity (in Snellen decimals)	—	—	0.32 (0.18)
Hearing (threshold in decibels)	—	—	54.4 (16.0)
Dementia (clinical diagnosis; proportion in %)	—	—	21.1
Intellectual functioning (T-score)	—	—	50.0 (10.0)
Education (in years)	—	—	10.8 (2.4)
Activities (number in previous year)	—	—	2.9 (2.4)
Social network size (number of persons)	—	—	10.9 (7.2)
Neuroticism (T-score)	—	—	50.0 (10.0)
Openness (T-score)	—	—	50.0 (10.0)
Depressivity (HAMD)[c]	—	—	5.7 (6.1)
Depression (clinical diagnosis; proportion in %)	—	—	25.6

Note. Data are given in means, with standard deviations in parentheses. All variables are introduced in more detail in the discipline-specific chapters of this book (cf. Steinhagen-Thiessen & Borchelt, Chapter 5; Helmchen et al., Chapter 6; Smith & Baltes, Chapter 7; Mayer et al., Chapter 8).

[a] ADL/IADL: Activities of Daily Living/Instrumental Activities of Daily Living.
[b] SMMS: Short Mini Mental State Examination; dementia screening.
[c] HAMD: Hamilton Depression Scale.

1985; Powers & Bultena, 1972; Schaie et al., 1973; Siegler & Botwinick, 1979), and a *lower mortality risk* (Cooney et al., 1988; Manton & Woodbury, 1983; Powell et al., 1990; Siegler & Botwinick, 1979). Finally, there are indications that the duration of participation is positively correlated with desirable personality characteristics, such as flexibility (Cooney et al., 1988).[3]

Selectivity in BASE most likely resembles this pattern. However, BASE has two special features which make it likely that the *observed* selectivity effects should be *larger* than in most other studies: (a) the stratification by age – leading to an unusually high proportion of very old people in the sample – and (b) the initial random sampling of addresses by the city registry. First, in the examined age range, age is negatively correlated with health and intelligence, and positively associated with the likelihood of death (Siegler & Botwinick, 1979). Therefore, health- and mortality-related selectivity should be stronger in an elderly sample stratified by age than in a random sample of older adults. Second, it can be argued that the random sampling by the city registry has probably resulted in a parent sample of little bias. There is no reason to suppose that the persons selected randomly were particularly intelligent, healthy, or educated. This may stand in contrast to studies whose parent samples were selected using other criteria, such as membership in a private health insurance (Schaie, 1983) or profession (Shock et al., 1984). Thus, random sampling of the parent sample reduces the likelihood of selectivity having taken place before it could even be observed. Compared with other studies, then, both the age stratification and the random drawing of addresses should increase, rather than decrease, the extent of *observable* selectivity effects in BASE.

3.3　Methodological Considerations

3.3.1　Overview of Statistical Methods Used

Sample selectivity is examined using three interrelated methods:[4] (a) logistic regressions to determine differences in means and frequency distributions (Aldrich & Nelson, 1984; Kühnel, Jagodzinski, & Terwey, 1989); (b) the comparison of variance-covariance matrices to measure differences in variability and correlations (Bentler, 1989); (c) Pearson-Lawley formulae to estimate statistical reference values for the parent sample on Intensive Protocol variables (Lawley, 1943; Neale, 1991). Looking at results obtained with all three methods should comprehensively document selectivity effects in BASE.

To clarify the relations between the three methods, it is helpful to formalize the data structure. With x_i, we refer to vectors of variables related to the four different participation levels (e.g., x_1 = city registry variables, x_2 = variables from the Short Initial Assessment, x_3 = variables from the Intake Assessment, x_5 = variables from the Intensive Protocol; x_4 is excluded because the willingness to participate in the Intensive Protocol is not associated with a unique vector of variables). For example, for persons at the highest level of participation ($N = 516$ of $N = 1,908$), we have observations (i.e., value assign-

---

[3] So far, not many empirical findings covering selectivity effects on correlation patterns have been reported in the gerontological literature (but see McArdle et al., 1991). Furthermore, there have been hardly any attempts to quantify selectivity effects on variables measured later using estimation techniques (but see McArdle & Hamagami, 1991; McArdle et al., 1991).

[4] The methods are recapitulated in Section 4. Readers not interested in procedural details may skip this section.

ments on variables) for vectors x_1, x_2, x_3, and x_5. For persons who did not even reach level 2, only observations on the vector x_1 are available.

Furthermore, let y_i be an indicator of observation loss (i.e., dropout) immediately after the ith participation level. Thus, $y_i = 1$ if a person reaches level i, but not level $i + 1$. If a person reaches level $i + 1$, $y_i = 0$. If a person is without observation on level i, y_i is not defined.

The three statistical methods are based on the assumption that x_i and y_i can be described as samples from a "superpopulation" characterized by a probability distribution (Cassel, Särndal, & Wretman, 1977). Assuming a superpopulation makes it possible to express aspects of the population as parameters and to use classical statistical procedures for their estimation. In particular, after making further assumptions, three different questions can be posed to clarify sample selectivity:

(1) *Sample attrition depending on means and frequency distributions of previously observed variables.* Can the likelihood of observation loss be described as a function of values on previously observed variables?

$$\text{E}\,(y_i \mid x_i) = \text{Pr}\,(y_i = 1 \mid x_i) \tag{1}$$

(2) *Differences in variances and covariances between samples of different participation levels.* Do continuing participants differ from dropouts in terms of variances and covariances on the previously observed variables?

$$\text{cov}\,(x_i \mid y_i = 0) \neq \text{cov}\,(x_i \mid y_i = 1) \tag{2}$$

(3) *Cumulative effects of sample attrition on Intensive Protocol constructs.* Are there differences in the expected values E (i.e., in means and frequency distributions) on Intensive Protocol variables between persons who reached this level and persons whose participation ended on a lower level?

$$\text{E}\,(x_5 \mid x_i, y_i = 0) \neq \text{E}\,(x_5 \mid x_i) \tag{3}$$

Thus, the questions refer to: (1) the relationship between the dropout indicator and previously measured variables; (2) the differences between persons continuing participation and dropouts on second moments (i.e., variances and covariances) of previously observed features; and (3) the relationship between features assessed on the highest participation level and features of previous levels, including the dropout indicator.

If differences between the groups of continuing participants and dropouts on the analyzed variables become apparent using the adequate statistical procedures, this would indicate that sample loss was associated with selectivity whose extent can be represented by statistical reference values. However, the reverse does not necessarily hold: If no differences are found, this *cannot* be taken as evidence that there is no sample selectivity. For instance, we cannot exclude the possibility that some features relevant to BASE that predict sample attrition were not assessed in the first place, and therefore could not be analyzed. This problem is particularly important for the analysis of sample loss at the step from participation level 1 to level 2 for which only the variables measured on the first level are available. In addition, the applied procedures do not capture all forms of sample selectivity possible in principle, but are limited to means, frequency distributions, variances, and covariances. However, as the analyses of BASE concentrate on these aspects of the data anyway, this restriction to first and second moments seems to be acceptable.

3.3.2   Selectivity Depending on Age Group and Gender

The variables age and gender are of special significance in BASE. On the one hand, they define the design of BASE as stratification variables. On the other hand, the description and explanation of differences by age and gender across all domains are among the study's central goals.

The validity of statements on age gradients and gender differences would be impaired if the magnitude of selectivity effects was a function of age or gender. In other words, if the selectivity of women differed from that of men, or if selectivity decreased or increased with age, the age and gender differences observed on the level of the Intensive Protocol would at least partially reflect this differential selectivity.

Estimates of prevalence rates represent a good example for this problem. It is possible that selectivity effects lead to a general underestimation of the prevalence of a disease. An examination of selectivity for each age group could show that the degree of underestimation is quite low at younger ages but becomes considerable at higher ages. In this case, the results of selectivity analysis would not only influence the interpretation of the observed prevalence rate, but also the interpretation of the age trend.

Therefore, possible consequences of sample attrition need to be examined for each age group, and for men and women separately. Ideally, one would analyze selectivity for each of the 12 cells of the study design (i.e., for men and women in each of the six age groups) in order to capture *interactions* between age and gender on selectivity, too. However, such analyses are associated with a marked reduction of statistical power due to relatively low numbers in each of the 12 cells. Mainly for this reason, we restrict our analyses to a comparison of selectivity between men and women across all age groups, and between the six age groups (70–74, 75–79, 80–84, 85–89, 90–94, 95+) across both sexes.

Statements concerning means, distributions, and other statistical reference values can either refer directly to the observed sample or, by weighting, can take into account that there are more women than men, and more younger than older persons among West Berliners aged 70 and above as compared with a sample stratified by age and gender. If not stated otherwise, all results presented here refer to *unweighted* data.

4   Results

In the following, we report the results of the selectivity analyses under three aspects: (1) means and distributions; (2) variability and covariance patterns; (3) cumulative selectivity effects on Intensive Protocol constructs. Because of its particular importance we begin with a separate consideration of mortality.

4.1   One-Year Mortality and Participation Depth

In a study of old age, the associations between participation likelihood and mortality are especially relevant. Figure 2.2 shows one-year mortality as a function of participation depth. Whereas one-year mortality is over 13% in the verified parent sample (participation level 1), it is under 6% in the Intensive Protocol sample (level 5).

Direct interpretation of these numbers is difficult because the mortality rate of persons who reached higher participation levels has to be lower than for those on lower levels anyway, due to the longer period of time necessary for the collection of more detailed data. Thus, it would be possible to find differences in one-year mortality even if persons on various participation levels did not differ in their mortality risk. Therefore, it is necessary to compare empirically observed values with estimates that consider different examination durations under the assumption that the mortality risk is independent of participation level.

As illustrated by the comparison of observed and estimated values (see Fig. 2.2), *one-year mortality remains lower for persons reaching participation level 5 even if longer participation durations are taken into account.* The difference between the one-year mortality observed in the Intensive Protocol sample and the mortality expected due to the longer participation period is 3%. Accordingly, the mortality rates on lower participation levels are slightly higher than expected from participation durations.[5]

In summary, the Intensive Protocol sample's one-year mortality is clearly reduced in comparison to the parent sample. Considering the high mortality rate among older adults, this result is to be expected due to the duration of the Intensive Protocol (median = 133 days). Statistical analysis shows that most of the observed reduction of one-year mortality in the Intensive Protocol sample ($N = 516$) versus the parent sample ($N = 1,908$) is indeed due to the time taken for data collection. However, participants in the Intensive Protocol still had a lower mortality risk than persons in the parent sample. This finding is consistent with other studies' results (Cooney et al., 1988; Manton & Woodbury, 1983; Powell et al., 1990; Siegler & Botwinick, 1979). A more detailed analysis and discussion of this finding would require the identification of variables related to both participation depth and mortality (cf. P. B. Baltes et al., 1971; Kruse, Lindenberger, & Baltes, 1993; Maier & Smith, in press; Manton & Woodbury, 1983) and are beyond the rationale of the present investigation.

4.2 *Means and Frequency Distributions*

Logistic regressions were used to analyze the relationship between sample attrition and previously measured characteristics. The regression coefficient exponentials can be interpreted as "odds ratios." In the following, we briefly introduce this term to facilitate the understanding of our results.

For two-point (dichotomous) independent variables, an odds ratio can be interpreted directly as the probability quotient for manifestations of these variables. Thus, an odds ratio of 2.0 on the gender variable with 0 for men and 1 for women indicates that the dropout likelihood is twice as large for women as for men. For continuous, independent

---

[5] The estimates of one-year mortality taking into account differential participation duration shown in Figure 2.2 were calculated as follows. For every person who at least reached participation level 2, the duration of participation in days (s) was subtracted from 365 to determine the period of time during which death could have occurred. Given the one-year mortality rate (m) for the parent sample ($m = .1347$) and under the simplifying assumption of a constant mortality risk, the survival probability for the remaining days of the year (Pr) can be expressed in the following equation:

$$Pr = (1 - m)^{(365 - s)/365}$$

By subtracting this survival probability from one, one obtains the required mortality likelihood corrected for duration of participation. The expected values shown in Figure 2.2 are based on the mean of these probabilities.

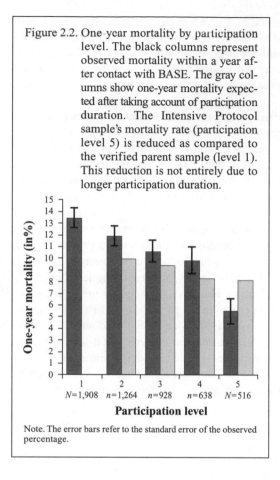

Figure 2.2. One-year mortality by participation level. The black columns represent observed mortality within a year after contact with BASE. The gray columns show one-year mortality expected after taking account of participation duration. The Intensive Protocol sample's mortality rate (participation level 5) is reduced as compared to the verified parent sample (level 1). This reduction is not entirely due to longer participation duration.

Note. The error bars refer to the standard error of the observed percentage.

variables, the probability quotients expressed by odds ratios are scaled in the units of the independent variables. For example, if age is measured in years and the odds ratio is 1.1, the likelihood of dropout before the next participation level is 1.1 times higher for 71-year-olds than for 70-year-olds, and $1.1^{10} = 2.59$ times higher for 80-year-olds than for 70-year-olds.[6]

4.2.1   Contrast 1: Participation Level 1 Only (n = 644) versus Higher Participation Levels (n = 1,264)

The variables available on level 1 (age, gender, marital status, Social Index of Living Area, place of residence, and one-year mortality) were entered into the model as covariates. The variables age and Social Index of Living Area are continuous, whereas gender, place of residence, and one-year mortality are dichotomous variables with the manifestations 0 and 1. Marital status was divided into four dummy variables, with the group of

---

[6] Note that results of logistic regression coincide with those of discriminant analysis if the independent variables are more or less normally distributed (cf. Haggstrom, 1983).

the married as the reference category. We calculated the coefficients, their standard deviations *(SD)*, *p*-scores, odds ratios, and pseudo-R^2.

With respect to this first contrast, the explanatory power of the total model was remarkably low, with a pseudo-R^2 of .014. Selectivity effects on the variables available on this participation level thus only explain a very small part of the attrition process. Significant differences between persons continuing to participate and dropouts were only found on the variables gender and one-year mortality. The likelihood of dropping out of the study was 1.68 times larger for persons who died within a year than for those who survived. For women, the dropout probability was 1.65 times larger than for men. The latter means that, initially, a larger number of addresses needed to be drawn for women to end up with equal numbers of men and women in the Intensive Protocol sample. There was no systematic association between participation likelihood and marital status, or place of residence on this participation level. Surprisingly, the same was true for age.

4.2.2 Contrast 2: Up to Participation Level 2 Only (n = 336) versus Higher Participation Levels (n = 928)

In addition to the variables listed in Section 4.2.1, the following variables could be considered on level 2: observer-rated ADL (Activities of Daily Living), dementia, and sensory impairment; education; and the subjective variables life satisfaction, physical health, and mental health (cf. Table 2.1).

As is to be expected, the inclusion of further variables resulted in greater explanatory power of the model than that on the first level (pseudo-R^2 = .19). This was mainly due to the Social Index of Living Area, the observational dementia rating, and subjective mental health. The higher the Social Index of Living Area (i.e., the "better" the residential area), the lower the dropout likelihood was (odds ratio = .73, $p < .01$). The probability of dropout also decreased with better subjective mental health (odds ratio = .70, $p < .01$). As for the dementia rating, where higher scores indicate a greater likelihood of dementia, dropout became more likely with higher scores (odds ratio = 1.09, $p < .01$). Persons with dementia symptoms were therefore more likely not to continue participation in the study. In addition, a larger probability of dropout for women was again found on this level (but with a greater standard deviation; odds ratio = 1.85, $p < .05$). A higher education level reduced the probability of dropout (odds ratio = .64, $p < .05$). For the remaining variables, no additional significant selectivity effects were found.

4.2.3 Contrast 3: Up to Participation Level 3 Only (n = 290) versus Higher Participation Levels (n = 638)

Core variables from the Intake Assessment were added in this model (see Table 2.1). In comparison to the model on contrast 2, this model's explanatory power is considerably lower (pseudo-R^2 = .05). Accordingly, the likelihood of ending participation after the Intake Assessment was not strongly related to the examined variables. On this level, place of residence and life satisfaction had an influence. Community-dwelling persons were nearly twice as likely to end participation on this level than the institutionalized (odds ratio = 0.49, $p < .05$). As to be expected, the dropout likelihood decreased with higher scores on the life satisfaction scale (odds ratio = 0.70, $p < .05$). None of the other variables examined in this model made significant additional contributions to the probability of further participation.

4.2.4   *Contrast 4: Dropout During the Intensive Protocol* (n = 122) *versus Highest Participation Level* (N = 516).

In this model, no additional variables were examined. The pseudo-R^2 of .16 indicates that this model describes dropout much better than the previous one. Here, one-year mortality had the largest effect (odds ratio = 7.07, $p < .01$). As explained above, to a large extent, this is due to the duration of the Intensive Protocol. In addition, the Social Index of Living Area was found to be relevant (odds ratio = 0.80, $p < .05$). Persons from "better" residential areas were less likely to drop out on this final level. Effects of the Body Mass Index and the Digit Letter test were also significant. Those with higher intellectual abilities (as measured by the Digit Letter test) were less likely to drop out during the Intensive Protocol (odds ratio = 0.99, $p < .05$). The same holds for the Body Mass Index,[7] an indicator of physical health: Dropout probability decreased with higher scores (odds ratio = 0.17, $p < .05$). No systematic associations between dropout likelihood during the Intensive Protocol and the other examined variables were found.

4.2.5   *Summary of the Analyses of Means and Frequency Distributions*

Relations between participation likelihood and observed variables were rather weak. The most prominent selectivity effect concerned one-year mortality. Dropout in the course of the Intensive Protocol is determined by this feature to a considerable degree and can be linked in part, but not completely, to the duration of data collection. Significant effects of the Social Index of Living Area on participation likelihood were observed on the second and fourth participation level. Accordingly, persons from "better" areas are slightly overrepresented in the final Intensive Protocol sample. Together with the positive association between education and participation likelihood, this indicates a slight overrepresentation of the higher social classes. However, this education effect is only significant on the second participation level and has a high standard deviation.

On the third level, neither education nor income had an effect on participation likelihood, thus contradicting the hypothesis of clear selectivity by social class. The effects of the dementia rating score and of subjective mental health on the second level, of life satisfaction on the third, and of the Digit Letter test on the fourth participation level indicate an overrepresentation of healthier and more satisfied people, and of those with higher intellectual performance.

However, it must be added that many of the analyzed variables were not significantly related to participation probability. In particular, of the health measures, only the Body Mass Index had an influence on participation likelihood, so that one cannot assume a general overrepresentation of healthy individuals. Instead, a higher participation likelihood for persons living in institutional settings was found on level 3, thus counteracting the positive selectivity for good health. Surprisingly, there was no age effect on selectiv-

---

[7] The relationship between Body Mass Index and indicators of risk is known to be curvilinear in the general population (Andres, 1985); that is, both very high and very low values on the Body Mass Index are associated with higher mortality risks. In the present sample of old and very old people, however, individuals with very high Body Mass Index scores (e.g., very obese persons) were virtually absent (Andres, 1985; Borchelt & Steinhagen-Thiessen, 1992). Therefore, the selection effect on the Body Mass Index in the positive direction helps to explain the observed reduction of mortality risk among continuing participants.

ity independent of the variables included in the models (but see Section 5 for an explanation of this finding). The gender effects on the first and second participation level correspond to the higher dropout likelihood of women described in the literature. However, because of the stratification of the Intensive Protocol sample by gender, this does not influence the sample's composition.

4.3 *Variability and Correlational Patterns*

A comparison of variances and covariances can give further information on sample selectivity. It is possible that logistic regressions indicate that persons with especially low or high scores on certain variables are less likely to continue to participate in the study. However, this selectivity effect based on means does not necessarily imply that the two groups differ in their variability.

Another possibility is that consequences of sample attrition are more pronounced in variances and covariances than in means. If, for example, particularly healthy and particularly ill persons were, for different reasons, less likely to reach the next participation level than persons of average health, dropouts would not necessarily differ, on average, from the original sample on health variables. A selectivity effect like this can hardly be proved using logistic regression (i.e., the logit-model would be misspecified). However, the inconsistency of the attrition process should lead to a decrease of variance on the health variables, with the consequence that the variances of dropouts and those continuing participation would need to be estimated by two different parameters, rather than one common parameter. Hence, the comparison of variance-covariance matrices allows the examination of sample selectivity in terms of variances and covariances.[8]

Comparing variances and covariances, we again tested whether the group of dropouts differs from the group of those continuing participation. Three contrasts were defined for this purpose. In the *first contrast*, we examined whether persons on whom we only have information from level 1 ($n = 644$) differ from persons on whom more information is available, at least from level 2 ($n = 1,264$). The *second contrast* captures differences between persons on whom we have information from level 2, but not from level 3 ($n = 336$), and those for whom at least a complete Intake Assessment is available (level 3 and above; $n = 928$). Finally, the *third contrast* compares persons with a complete Intake Assessment, but no more ($n = 412$), with persons who completed the entire protocol ($N = 516$). Because of the low number of cases ($n = 122$), no separate contrast was defined for the participants who began the Intensive Protocol but did not complete it.

For the sake of clarity, we dispensed with a complete list of statistical reference values. Instead, group differences on single variables were only reported when their significance reached an α-level of $p = .01$. Dichotomous variables such as marital status dummies were not considered, because, in these cases, variance differences are statistically dependent on previously tested differences in means. Also, some variables were rescaled to yield well-conditioned variance-covariance matrices. For instance, the Social Index of

---

[8] The comparison of variance-covariance matrices was carried out using the statistics program EQS which was developed for structural equation models (Bentler, 1989). The main advantage of this program in comparison to standard procedures (e.g., the Box-M-test in SPSSX) is the option of carrying out tests of significance for single matrix elements or groups of elements selected by the user. A printout of the applied programs can be requested from the first author.

Living Area was divided by 100. The Comparative Fit Index (CFI; cf. Bentler, 1989) was used as an overall measure of fit of the models in which the variances and covariances of the compared groups are constrained to be equal. Generally, a CFI above 0.95 is taken as indicating good model fit.

4.3.1   Contrast 1: Participation Level 1 Only (n = 644) versus Higher Participation Levels (n = 1,264).

Here, only differences of variances and covariances in age and the Social Index of Living Area could be tested (the only nondichotomous variables on this level). For this purpose, a model was specified in which variances and covariances for both groups were each estimated with the *same* parameter. Then we examined whether the estimation with two *different* parameters significantly improved the model's fit. This was not the case ($\chi^2(3) = 5.25$, $p = .15$). The fit of the model with across-group equality constraints was good (CFI = 1.000).

4.3.2   Contrast 2: Participation Level 2 Only (n = 336) versus Higher Participation Levels (n = 928)

Variance and covariance differences were tested for age, gender, education (the rough index in the Short Initial Assessment), life satisfaction (item), and subjective physical and mental health. No significant differences between the two groups were found. Again, the fit of the constrained model was good (CFI = 0.979).

4.3.3   Contrast 3: Participation Level 3 Only (n = 412) versus Highest Participation Level (N = 516)

In addition to the variables mentioned earlier, subjective walking distance, equivalent income, the number of close companions, ADL score, Body Mass Index, nonagitation, satisfaction with aging, life satisfaction (scale), Short Mini Mental State Examination (SMMS), Digit Letter test, and the depressivity score were considered (see Table 2.1). The overall test across all 17 variances was statistically significant ($\chi^2(17) = 62.13$, $p < .01$). Inspection of individual variances showed that this was due to two parameters. First, the variance in the Social Index of Living Area was lower in the Intensive Protocol sample than in the group of persons who only reached participation level 3 ($SD = 1.07$ vs. $SD = 1.15$, $\chi^2(1) = 26.24$, $p < .001$). Second, the variance in income was *higher* in the Intensive Protocol sample than in the comparison group ($SD = 1,037$ vs. $SD = 898$, $\chi^2(1) = 10.23$, $p < .001$).

The overall test for covariances was also significant ($\chi^2(136) = 204.45$, $p < .01$). Of the 136 individual comparisons 3 proved to be significant: the relationships between subjective physical health and nonagitation ($\chi^2(1) = 11.38$, $p < .01$), between subjective mental health and life satisfaction (scale; $\chi^2(1) = 7.36$, $p < .01$), and between subjective walking distance and depressivity score ($\chi^2(1) = 9.73$, $p < .01$). In all three cases, the covariance relationship was stronger in the Intensive Protocol sample than in the group of persons who only reached level 3.

Thus, in this contrast, there were indications of a significant overall difference in variance-covariance relations between dropouts and continuers. At the level of individual comparisons, however, only 5 of 153 resulted in significant differences between the two groups. Therefore, the impression of a relatively high degree of similarity in variances and covariances of both groups prevails. This is again underlined by the good fit of the model with across-group equality constraints (CFI = 0.983).

4.4   Cumulative Selectivity Effects on Intensive Protocol Constructs

The formulae on selectivity developed by Pearson (1903) and Lawley (1943) allow the estimation, using linear regressions, of statistical reference values (means, variances, and covariances) that take account of observed selectivity (Meredith, 1964, 1993; Muthén, Kaplan, & Hollis, 1987; Smith, Holt, & Smith, 1989). Independent (or selection) variables are distinguished from dependent variables (i.e., variables on which only persons continuing participation have scores). Means, variances, and covariances of the parent sample on the dependent variables are estimated on the basis of the linear relationships between selection variables and dependent variables and of the differences in selection variable means between the parent and the selected sample.

The Pearson-Lawley method uses the results presented above on the relationships between expected values (means, distributions), variances, and covariances, with the understanding that the regressions of the dependent variables on selection variables are linear and that the conditional variances are constant (homoscedasticity). Under these assumptions, the method allows a direct estimation of selectivity effects on the Intensive Protocol constructs central to BASE. Within the framework of the linear model, this projection makes optimal use of all of the available information (cf. Meredith, 1964).

Aitkin (1934) and Lawley (1943) showed that these formulae can be applied *repeatedly*. For our selectivity analyses this means that the variables available on participation level 1 can be used to estimate the parent sample's manifestations on level 2 variables. Then, the variables of level 1 *and* 2 (i.e., the *observed* values on level 1, and the *estimated* values on level 2) serve as selection variables, and the variables available on level 3 become the dependent variables. Finally, the variables on the first three levels are the selection variables by which the manifestations of the parent sample on the Intensive Protocol constructs can be estimated.[9]

When the results obtained with this method are interpreted, the following rule, related to the basic paradox of selectivity analysis mentioned in Section 2.1, needs to be kept in mind: The more closely features on lower participation levels (i.e., the selection variables) are associated with variables on the following level (i.e., the independent variables), the more meaningful the calculated estimates become. Dependent variables for which there are no "precursors" on previous participation levels cannot be corrected and inevitably maintain the means that were observed in the selected subsample.

Therefore, we first examined how well the selection variables to be considered explained the variance in the chosen Intensive Protocol constructs. This analysis was based on the Intensive Protocol sample ($N = 516$) and, accordingly, does not involve any kind of estimation procedure.

As shown in Figure 2.3, the proportion of explained variance in the Intensive Protocol constructs was generally quite high. The lowest value (28% explained variance) was found for the number of moderate to severe illnesses, and the highest was observed for

---

[9] The statistical program Mx (Neale, 1991) was used for the calculation of the estimates using the Pearson-Lawley formulae. The printout of the program can be requested from the first author.

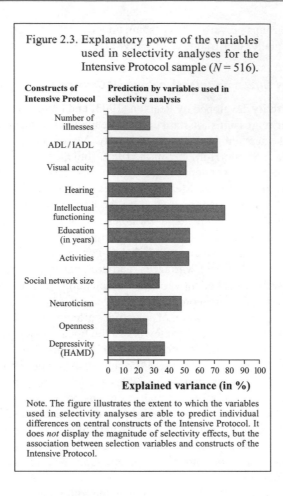

Figure 2.3. Explanatory power of the variables used in selectivity analyses for the Intensive Protocol sample ($N = 516$).

Note. The figure illustrates the extent to which the variables used in selectivity analyses are able to predict individual differences on central constructs of the Intensive Protocol. It does *not* display the magnitude of selectivity effects, but the association between selection variables and constructs of the Intensive Protocol.

general intelligence (78%). An inspection of correlations and semipartial regression co-efficients (which are not presented here in detail) showed that the variables deemed to function as "precursors" were indeed the ones that mainly contributed toward explaining variance in the constructs assigned to them. For instance, the observational ratings of de-mentia, sensory functioning, and ADL on participation level 2 played an important role in explaining variance in the corresponding Intensive Protocol constructs. Thus, insofar as there is selectivity, the predictive power of the selection variables is definitely large enough to detect it.

4.4.1   *Effects of Selectivity on the Entire Sample*

Figure 2.4 shows the discrepancies between the means estimated for the parent sample and the means observed in the Intensive Protocol. The normed standard deviation E_{SD} is the measure used for this comparison (estimated mean of the parent sample minus ob-served mean of the selected sample, divided by the parent sample's estimated standard deviation; cf. Hedges & Olkin, 1985). It indicates the distance between the mean of the

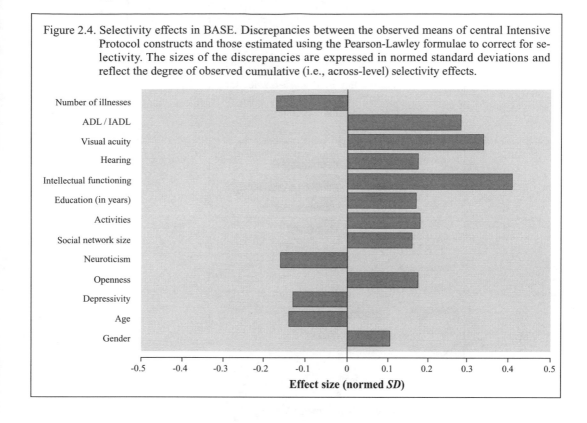

Figure 2.4. Selectivity effects in BASE. Discrepancies between the observed means of central Intensive Protocol constructs and those estimated using the Pearson-Lawley formulae to correct for selectivity. The sizes of the discrepancies are expressed in normed standard deviations and reflect the degree of observed cumulative (i.e., across-level) selectivity effects.

selected sample and the mean of the parent sample. Thus, E_{SD} = 0.5 would signify that the selected sample's mean is half a standard deviation above the parent sample's mean. The variables age and gender (0 = men, 1 = women) are also listed because some of the effects could be linked to the design variables. For these two variables, effect sizes could be directly calculated because these features are known for every participation level.

The pattern of effects confirms the picture reported in the literature: Persons with better intellectual functioning, better vision and hearing, more self-reliance in everyday activities (ADL/IADL), less illnesses, and a higher education level were more likely to proceed through the entire Intensive Protocol. The findings on less frequently examined domains such as social network size, number of activities, neuroticism, openness, and depressivity also fit into this general pattern.

If one assumes a normal distribution, an effect size of .14 (the smallest effect size for depressivity) indicates that 56% of the observations in the Intensive Protocol – instead of chance 50% – lie above the mean of the parent sample. The effect size of .42 (the largest effect size for intellectual functioning) signifies a proportion of 66%. The effect sizes therefore represent relatively small deviations from the values estimated for the parent sample.

The estimated prevalence rates for the clinical diagnoses of dementia and depression are not shown in Figure 2.4. A prevalence estimate of 30% was made for dementia –

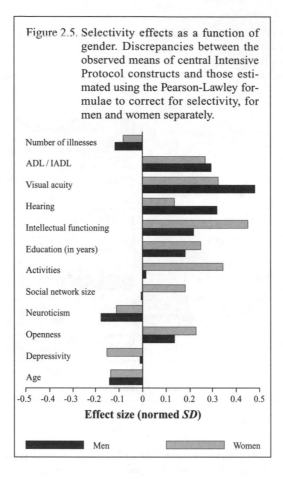

Figure 2.5. Selectivity effects as a function of gender. Discrepancies between the observed means of central Intensive Protocol constructs and those estimated using the Pearson-Lawley formulae to correct for selectivity, for men and women separately.

considerably higher than the observed 21%. For depression, there was little difference between the estimated prevalence and the observed prevalence (27% estimated for the parent sample vs. 26% observed).

4.4.2   Effects of Selectivity on Gender Differences

Figure 2.5 refers to possible gender differences in selectivity. The clearest differences were found on the constructs social activities (men: .02, women: .35), intellectual functioning (men: .22, women: .45), and social network size (men: -.01, women: .19). With respect to these three variables, women in the Intensive Protocol were more positively selected than men.

4.4.3   Effects of Selectivity on Age Differences

An inspection of the effect sizes calculated separately for the six age groups showed little selectivity differences as a function of age. The clinical diagnosis of dementia was a notable exception (cf. Helmchen et al., Chapter 6). Figure 2.6 shows the observed and estimated dementia prevalence rates. The *observed* values suggest that prevalence does

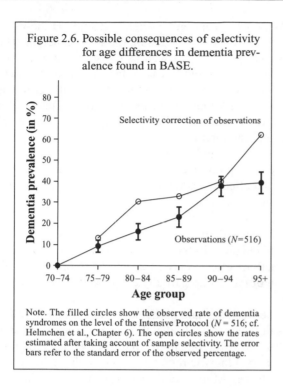

Figure 2.6. Possible consequences of selectivity for age differences in dementia prevalence found in BASE.

Note. The filled circles show the observed rate of dementia syndromes on the level of the Intensive Protocol (N = 516; cf. Helmchen et al., Chapter 6). The open circles show the rates estimated after taking account of sample selectivity. The error bars refer to the standard error of the observed percentage.

not increase any further in the two highest age groups. In contrast, the *estimated* values support the hypothesis that dementia prevalence continues to rise, even beyond the age of 90. In this case, taking account of selectivity leads to a quite different conclusion. The examination of the regression coefficients revealed that the observer rating of dementia on participation level 2, as well as the SMMS and the Digit Letter test on level 3, made the largest contributions to the prediction of these estimates.

5   Discussion

Before we summarize and comment on our results, we expressly want to point out the limits of selectivity analyses. Selectivity analyses show the extent of observed selectivity, but not the extent of selectivity that is possible in principle. They try to relate *available* data to each other and to make optimal use of available information, but obviously cannot deal with issues for which additional information is necessary. This necessary deficit is especially relevant for the step from the first (N = 1,908) to the second participation level (n = 1,264) which is documented by only a few variables. The question of whether the availability of more variables on level 1 would have resulted in the observation of more selectivity at this step (and thus overall) cannot be answered conclusively. With this limitation in mind, the results of the selectivity analyses can be summarized as follows:

First, the selectivity analyses indicate that neither variances nor covariance relations in the Intensive Protocol sample (N = 516) are very different from those of the samples on lower participation levels. With one exception – a slight reduction of the variance in the Social Index of Living Area – there were no signs of variance reduction. Thus, the manifold forms of aging and social situations, as well as the structure of associations among variables, appear to be maintained in the Intensive Protocol sample. Concerning selectivity, it seems permissible to generalize statements about associations among variables observed in the Intensive Protocol sample to the parent sample. This result is particularly important for systemic (e.g., multidisciplinary) analyses examining relationships between different domains of functioning.

Second, in comparison with variances and covariances, selectivity effects in means and frequency distributions were more pronounced. Judging by the number of variables analyzed, the number of significant effects was rather low. Across all participation levels, there were indications of positive selection by social class, subjective mental health, and life satisfaction, as well as intelligence and dementia. There were no signs of selectivity with respect to health measures, with the exception of Body Mass Index on the last level. The higher participation likelihood observed for individuals in institutional settings suggests that different selectivity effects may have worked in opposite directions. Possibly, the higher participation of this group partially evens out the positive selection effect for health and intelligence.

Surprisingly, no strong links between age and participation likelihood were found on any participation level. This result seems to contradict the varying pattern of sample loss by age group shown in Figure 2.1. However, one needs to remember that only linear age effects can be captured by the reported logistic regressions (i.e., either a linear decrease or increase of sample attrition with age). More detailed analyses of the data in Figure 2.1 indicate *nonlinear* relationships (Gilberg & Pötter, 1994). For example, sample loss in the age group of the 85- to 89-year-olds was larger than in the two adjacent groups.

More clear-cut selection effects were observed by gender. However, because of the study's stratified design, women's lower participation likelihood had no influence on the proportion of men and women in the Intensive Protocol sample.

Third, the participants in the BASE Intensive Protocol sample have a lower mortality rate in comparison to the parent sample (see Fig. 2.2). This result is largely, but not completely, due to the duration of the Intensive Protocol. Further interpretation of this mortality-associated sample selectivity requires the identification of measures that predict both participation depth and death rates. In the examined age range, of course, the population composition already alters so much by age that the assumption of a uniform parent sample is not really tenable. In Germany, 81% of women and 66% of men reach age 70, but only about 18% of women and 7% of men reach age 90 (Statistisches Bundesamt [Federal Statistical Office], 1993). It is well known that individual differences in longevity are correlated with features such as health, intelligence, and well-being (Siegler & Botwinick, 1979; for first analyses of the BASE data set regarding this issue, cf. Maier & Smith, in press). Thus, mortality is a selective process. Inevitably, age-related analyses of the BASE data set confound the aging process of the survivors with the selectivity of mortality (cf. Keiding, 1991; Mulder, 1993).

Fourth, the cumulative analysis of selectivity and its projection onto Intensive Protocol constructs using the Pearson-Lawley formulae shows that the Intensive Protocol sample is positively selected in all considered domains. However, the extent of these selectivity effects never exceeded half a standard deviation, and varied only slightly by age. For the interpretation of results presented in other chapters, this means that the values found empirically on the level of the Intensive Protocol tend to show old age and aging in a slightly too positive light.

An important exception from the general rule of rather low and age-stable selectivity effects is dementia prevalence. In this case, there was quite a substantial discrepancy between the rate observed in the Intensive Protocol sample (21%) and the rate estimated using the Pearson-Lawley formulae (30%). Clearly, sample attrition led to an underestimation of dementia prevalence in the parent sample, especially for the group aged 95 and above (40% vs. 62%).

Unfortunately, it is nearly impossible to compare the extent of selectivity in BASE directly with results from other studies. First, a comparison is impeded by many differences in methodology and content. Second, mentions of selectivity are often so fragmentary that one can only speculate on effect sizes. In general, the impression prevails that the extent of selectivity effects in BASE is more or less within the usual range. In view of the considerable degree of sample attrition (see Fig. 2.1) and of BASE participants' particularly old age, this is certainly a satisfactory result.

References

Aitkin, A. C. (1934). Note on selection from a multivariate normal population. *Proceedings of the Edinburgh Mathematical Society, 4*, 106–110.

Aldrich, J. H., & Nelson, F. D. (1984). *Linear probability, logit and probit models*. Beverly Hills, CA: Sage.

Andres, R. (1985). Mortality and obesity: The rationale for age specific height-weight tables. In R. Andres, E. L. Bierman, & W. R. Hazzard (Eds.), *Principles of geriatric medicine* (pp. 311–318). New York: McGraw-Hill.

Baltes, P. B., Reese, H. W., & Nesselroade, J. R. (1988). *Life-span developmental psychology: Introduction to research methods*. Hillsdale, NJ: Erlbaum.

Baltes, P. B., Schaie, K. W., & Nardi, A. H. (1971). Age and experimental mortality in a seven-year longitudinal study of cognitive behavior. *Developmental Psychology, 5*, 18–26.

Bentler, P. M. (1989). *EQS: Structural equations manual (Version 3.0)*. Los Angeles: BMDP Statistical Software.

Borchelt, M., & Steinhagen-Thiessen, E. (1992). Physical performance and sensory functions as determinants of independence in activities of daily living in the old and the very old. *Annals of the New York Academy of Sciences, 673*, 350–361.

Cassel, C. M., Särndal, C. E., & Wretman, J. H. (1977). *Foundations of inference in survey sampling*. New York: Wiley.

Cooney, T. M., Schaie, K. W., & Willis, S. K. (1988). The relationships between prior functioning on cognitive and personality dimensions and subject attrition in longitudinal research. *Journal of Gerontology: Psychological Sciences, 43*, P12–P17.

Dalenius, T. (1988). A first course in survey sampling. In P. Krishnaiah & C. R. Rao (Eds.), *Handbook of statistics: Vol. 6. Sampling* (pp. 15–46). Oxford: North-Holland.

DeMaio, T. J. (1980). Refusals: Who, where and why. *Public Opinion Quarterly, 44*, 223–233.

Esser, H., Grohmann, H., Müller, W., & Schäffer, K.-A. (1989). *Mikrozensus im Wandel: Untersuchungen und Empfehlungen zur inhaltlichen und methodischen Gestaltung* (Schriftenreihe Forum der Bundesstatistik, Vol. 11). Stuttgart: Metzler-Poeschel.

Eye, A. von. (1989). Zero-missing non-existing data: Missing data problems in longitudinal research and categorical data solutions. In M. Brambring, F. Lösel, & H. Skowronek

(Eds.), *Children at risk: Assessment, longitudinal research, and intervention* (pp. 336–355). Berlin: de Gruyter.

Gilberg, R., & Pötter, U. (1994). *Poststratifizierungsgewichte für die BASE-Studie.* Unpublished manuscript, Max Planck Institute for Human Development, Berlin.

Goudy, W. J. (1976). Nonresponse effects on relationships between variables. *Public Opinion Quarterly, 40*, 360–369.

Haggstrom, G. W. (1983). Logistic regression and discriminant analysis by ordinary least squares. *Journal of Business and Economic Statistics, 1*, 229–238.

Hawkins, D. F. (1975). Estimation of nonresponse bias. *Sociological Methods and Research, 3*, 461–488.

Hedges, L. V., & Olkin, I. (1985). *Statistical methods for meta-analysis.* Orlando, FL: Academic Press.

Hertzog, C., Schaie, K. W., & Gribbin, K. (1978). Cardiovascular disease and changes in intellectual functioning from middle to old age. *Journal of Gerontology, 33*, 872–883.

Herzog, A. R., & Rodgers, W. L. (1988). Age and response rates to interview sample surveys. *Journal of Gerontology: Social Sciences, 43*, S200–S205.

Keiding, N. (1991). Age-specific incidence and prevalence: A statistical perspective. *Journal of the Royal Statistical Society, Series A, 154*, 371–412.

Kessler, R. C., Little, R. J., & Groves, R. M. (1995). Advances in strategies for minimizing and adjusting for survey nonresponse. *Epidemiologic Reviews, 17*, 192–204.

Kruse, A., Lindenberger, U., & Baltes, P. B. (1993). Longitudinal research on human aging: The power of combining real-time, microgenetic, and simulation approaches. In D. Magnusson & P. Casaer (Eds.), *Longitudinal research on individual development: Present status and future perspectives* (pp. 153–193). Cambridge: Cambridge University Press.

Kruskal, W., & Mosteller, F. (1979a). Representative sampling: I. Non-scientific literature. *International Statistical Review, 47*, 13–24.

Kruskal, W., & Mosteller, F. (1979b). Representative sampling: II. Scientific literature, excluding statistics. *International Statistical Review, 47*, 111–127.

Kruskal, W., & Mosteller, F. (1979c). Representative sampling: III. The current statistical literature. *International Statistical Review, 47*, 245–265.

Kühnel, S. M., Jagodzinski, W., & Terwey, M. (1989). Teilnehmen oder boykottieren: Ein Anwendungsbeispiel der binären logistischen Regression mit SPSSX. *ZA-Information, 25*, 44–75.

Lawley, D. N. (1943). A note on Karl Pearson's selection formulae. *Proceedings of the Royal Society of Edinburgh, 62*, 28–30.

Little, R. J. A. (1995). Modeling the drop-out mechanism in repeated-measures studies. *Journal of the American Statistical Association, 90*, 1112–1121.

Little, R. J. A., & Rubin, D. B. (1987). *Statistical analysis with missing data.* New York: Wiley.

Lowe, F. E., & McCormick, T. C. (1955). Some survey sampling biases. *Public Opinion Quarterly, 19*, 303–315.

Maier, H., & Smith, J. (in press). Psychological predictors of mortality in old age. *Journal of Gerontology: Psychological Sciences.*

Manton, K. G., & Woodbury, M. A. (1983). A mathematical model of the physiological dynamics of aging and correlated mortality selection: II. Application to Duke Longitudinal Study. *Journal of Gerontology, 38*, 406–413.

McArdle, J. J. (1994). Structural factor analysis experiments with incomplete data. *Multivariate Behavioral Research, 29*, 409–454.

McArdle, J. J., & Hamagami, F. (1991). Modeling incomplete longitudinal and cross-sectional data using latent growth structural models. In L. M. Collins & J. L. Horn (Eds.), *Best methods for the analysis of change: Recent advances, unanswered questions, future directions* (pp. 276–298). Washington, DC: American Psychological Association.

McArdle, J. J., Hamagami, F., Elias, M. F., & Robbins, M. A. (1991). Structural modeling of mixed longitudinal and cross-sectional data. *Experimental Aging Research, 17*, 29–51.

Meinlschmidt, G., Imme, U., & Kramer, R. (1990). *Sozialstrukturatlas Berlin (West): Eine statistisch-methodische Analyse mit Hilfe der Faktorenanalyse*. Berlin: Senatsverwaltung für Gesundheit und Soziales.

Mercer, J. R., & Butler, E. W. (1967/68). Disengagement of the aged population and response differentials in survey research. *Social Forces, 46*, 89–96.

Meredith, W. (1964). Notes on factorial invariance. *Psychometrika, 29*, 177–185.

Meredith, W. (1993). Measurement invariance, factor analysis, and factorial invariance. *Psychometrika, 58*, 525–543.

Mulder, P. G. H. (1993). The simultaneous processes of ageing and mortality. *Statistica Nederlandica, 47*, 253–267.

Muthén, B. O., Kaplan, D., & Hollis, M. (1987). On structural equation modeling with data that are not completely missing at random. *Psychometrika, 52*, 431–462.

Neale, M. C. (1991). *Mx: Statistical modelling*. Department of Human Genetics, Box 3MCV, Richmond, VA 23298.

Norris, F. H. (1985). Characteristics of nonrespondents over five waves of a panel study. *Journal of Gerontology, 40*, 627–636.

Nuthmann, R., & Wahl, H.-W. (1996). Methodische Aspekte der Erhebungen der Berliner Altersstudie. In K. U. Mayer & P. B. Baltes (Eds.), *Die Berliner Altersstudie* (pp. 55–83). Berlin: Akademie Verlag.

Nuthmann, R., & Wahl, H.-W. (1997). *Methodological aspects of the Berlin Aging Study* (Technical report). Berlin: Max Planck Institute for Human Development.

Oh, H. L., & Scheuren, F. J. (1983). Weighting adjustment for unit non-response. In W. G. Madow, I. Olkin, & D. B. Rubin (Eds.), *Incomplete data in sample surveys: Vol. 2. Theory and bibliographies* (pp. 143–184). New York: Academic Press.

Panel on Incomplete Data. (1983). Part I: Report. In W. G. Madow, I. Olkin, & D. B. Rubin (Eds.), *Incomplete data in sample surveys: Vol. 1. Report and case studies* (pp. 3–106). New York: Academic Press.

Pearson, K. (1903). Mathematical contributions to the theory of evolution: XI. On the influence of natural selection on the variability and correlation of organs. *Philosophical Transactions of the Royal Society of London (Series A), 200*, 1–66.

Powell, D. A., Furchtgott, E., Henderson, M., Prescott, L., Mitchell, A., Hartis, P., Valentine, J. D., & Milligan, W. L. (1990). Some determinants of attrition in prospective studies on aging. *Experimental Aging Research, 16*, 17–24.

Powers, E. A., & Bultena, G. L. (1972). Characteristics of deceased dropouts in longitudinal research. *Journal of Gerontology, 27*, 350–353.

Rendtel, U., & Pötter, U. (1992). *Über Sinn und Unsinn von Repräsentativitätsstudien* (Discussion paper No. 61). Berlin: Deutsches Institut für Wirtschaftsforschung.

Rudinger, G., & Wood, P. K. (1990). N's, times and number of variables in longitudinal research. In D. Magnusson & L. R. Bergman (Eds.), *Data quality in longitudinal research* (pp. 157–180). Cambridge: Cambridge University Press.

Schaie, K. W. (1983). The Seattle Longitudinal Study: A twenty-one year exploration of psychometric intelligence in adulthood. In K. W. Schaie (Ed.), *Longitudinal studies of adult psychological development* (pp. 64–135). New York: Guilford.

Schaie, K. W., Labouvie, G. V., & Barrett, T. J. (1973). Selective attrition effects in a fourteen-year study of adult intelligence. *Journal of Gerontology, 28*, 328–334.

Shock, N. W., Greulich, R. C., Costa, P. T., Jr., Andres, R., Lakatta, E. G., Arenberg, D., & Tobin, J. D. (1984). *Normal human aging: The Baltimore Longitudinal Study on Aging* (NIH Publication No. 84-2450). Washington, DC: Government Printing Office.

Siegler, I. C., & Botwinick, J. (1979). A long-term longitudinal study of intellectual ability of older adults: The matter of selective subject attrition. *Journal of Gerontology, 34*, 242–245.

Smith, C. J., Holt, D., & Smith, T. M. F. (1989). *Analysis of complex surveys*. New York: Wiley.

Statistisches Bundesamt. (1993). *Statistisches Jahrbuch 1993*. Stuttgart: Metzler-Poeschel.

Streib, G. F. (1966). Participants and dropouts in a longitudinal study. *Journal of Gerontology, 21*, 200–209.

Tennstedt, S. L., Dettling, U., & McKinlay, J. B. (1992). Refusal rates in a longitudinal study of older people: Implications for field methods. *Journal of Gerontology: Social Sciences, 47*, S313–S318.

Weaver, C. N., Holmes, S. L., & Glenn, N. D. (1975). Some characteristics of inaccessible respondents in a telephone survey. *Journal of Applied Psychology, 60*, 260–262.

CHAPTER 3

Generational Experiences of Old People in Berlin

Ineke Maas, Markus Borchelt, and Karl Ulrich Mayer

In this chapter we discuss those characteristics of the participants in the Berlin Aging Study which can be attributed to their belonging to different birth cohorts. We ask whether general trends in societal development can be discerned by examining the educational achievement, employment and occupational careers, family formation, and health impairments of three cohort groups (born 1887–1900, 1901–10, and 1911–22). We further investigate the differential effects of historical events and periods, in particular the two world wars and the Great Depression, and examine how these effects are still perceptible in old age. We would like to highlight two of the many descriptive findings. First, the younger cohorts did not have more successful career paths than the older ones. Although the younger men and women had a better education, they were hit harder by historical events, and ended their careers on the same level as the older cohorts. Second, we invalidate the myth of the "golden age" where large families cared for the oldest cohorts. In fact, older cohorts more often remained single, had less children, and were at a higher risk of losing their children at an early age.

1   Introduction

The Berlin Aging Study (BASE) focuses both on the present situation of elderly people and on the correlates and determinants of aging processes. However, the older adults observed in the study are characterized not only by their age, but also by being members of certain birth cohorts, and sharing the collective life history of their generation.[1] When observing differences between age groups – as is done frequently in this book – we can rarely be certain if these differences stem from age or constitute differences between birth cohorts (P. B. Baltes, 1968; Mayer & Huinink, 1990; Riley, 1987; Schaie, 1965). In this chapter, we therefore describe the collective generational life histories of the BASE sample. Our main purpose is to provide background information for the other chapters in this book. We aim to draw attention to the potentially unique historical features of our elderly population and guard against making unfounded generalizations about aging effects when it could be that our observations are only due to the par-

---

[1] In the following we will use the concepts of birth cohort (Ryder, 1965) and generation interchangeably to denote a group of persons born at about the same historical time. It should be noted, however, that the concept of generation has a number of further meanings in the social sciences, such as relationships between parents and children (Bengtson, Cutler, Mangen, & Marshall, 1985), or very self-aware and active groups identified by certain historical periods, for example, the 1968 generation (Mannheim, 1928).

ticular experiences of Germans or, more specifically, Berliners who were born in certain periods and lived through extraordinary times.

Because of methodological problems with mortality and selectivity that will be discussed in Section 2, it is difficult to tell whether observed generational differences in life histories are historical or simply artifacts of our method. External data must be assessed to solve this problem. We concentrate on data from the 1% Microcensus Supplementary Survey 1971 (1%-Mikrozensus-Zusatzerhebung, MZ71; Tegtmeyer, 1976) which, unlike most other studies, includes an adequate number of Berlin residents from the relevant birth cohorts.

Generational differences can come about in different ways. First, the 20th century is characterized by trends toward what is often called a more "modern" society; living conditions, educational opportunities, and economic and social security improved, while family size declined. Second, differences between cohorts develop because their members experience different historical events, or the same historical event at different times in their lives (Elder, 1974, 1975). Third, the influences of historical circumstances on members of different birth cohorts are not necessarily lifelong. It is possible that those affected most negatively by a historical event will adapt and later catch up with the others (Elder, 1974).

This chapter does not aim to show direct or indirect links between aging outcomes and previous generation-specific experiences. This would require us either to compare a broader range of birth cohorts on the aggregate level – an analysis for which we do not have the necessary data – or to trace the impact of collective conditions on aging outcomes via individual life courses (cf. Maas & Staudinger, 1996).

The BASE participants were between 70 and 103 years old at the time of the interviews (1990–93), which means that they were born between 1887 and 1922. The fewer years included in a birth cohort, the more precisely the effects of historical events can be traced. However, with a total number of 516 subjects, and allowing for separate analyses for men and women, we are only able to distinguish between three cohort groups. Because we wish to describe life course characteristics as varied as educational and occupational attainment, marriage, birth of children, and surgical interventions, it is impossible to define the cohorts in a theoretical way that would do justice to the effects of historical circumstances on all of these characteristics.

We therefore chose to use three cohorts of approximately the same size. The members of these cohorts were born in 1887–1900, 1901–10, and 1911–22. In the following, we will examine whether trends exist in educational achievement, employment and occupational careers, family formation, and health impairment. We will further investigate the differential effects of historical events and periods, and will examine whether these are still perceptible in old age. The domains of educational and occupational success, family relations, and health were chosen because of the large and direct impact that they have on material, social, and physical well-being in old age (see Smith et al., Chapter 17 in this volume). Although numerous other historical events may have shaped the lives of these cohorts – the building of the Berlin Wall, for example – we will focus on World War I, the Great Depression, and World War II.

The three BASE cohorts were in different phases of their lives when these historical events occurred. At the onset of World War I, many of the 1911–22 cohort (hereafter the youngest cohort) were not yet born, the members of the 1901–10 cohort (middle cohort) were at school, and those born between 1887 and 1900 (oldest cohort) were – if not called into military service – in the labor market and starting families of their own (see

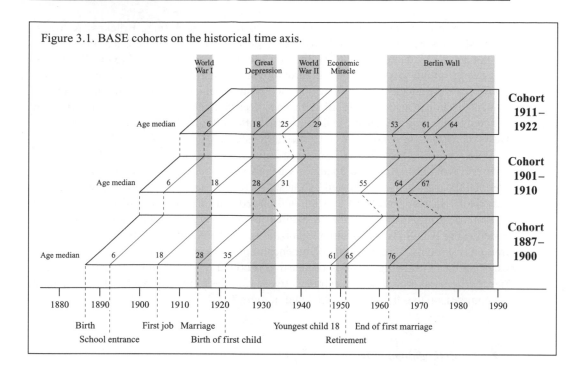

Figure 3.1. BASE cohorts on the historical time axis.

Fig. 3.1).[2] In the middle of the Great Depression, the age range of the BASE participants was 8 to 43 years. The youngest cohort members were at school or in occupational training, middle cohort members had just started their first jobs, and those in the oldest cohort were in the middle of their occupational careers and having children. World War II hit the youngest cohort members as they were leaving school or in their first jobs. Many hurried to marry and have a first child before the men left for the war. Middle cohort members had young children at this time, while the children of the oldest cohort were approaching adulthood and themselves at risk of being called into military service. After the economic slump of the postwar years, the beginning of the 1950s brought decided economic growth ("the economic miracle"; Abelshauser, 1983). Members of the youngest cohort started their careers anew, while the oldest cohort reached retirement age. When the Berlin Wall was built in 1961, only very few of the oldest cohort were still working. The period of German division seemed almost lifelong to the youngest cohort, whereas the oldest cohort had already reached old age when it began.

2   Methods

2.1   *Life Course Data in the Berlin Aging Study*

Data on educational, occupational, and family histories were gathered in the sociological section of the BASE Intensive Protocol. The questionnaire was developed on the

---

[2] Although there are some differences, the main patterns of occupational and family events are similar for men and women. With the exception of school entrance, all events occur somewhat earlier in a woman's life course.

basis of experience gained from previous life history research (e.g., Brückner & Mayer, 1998; Mayer & Brückner, 1989). A basic principle of the questionnaire is that interviewees are not asked about single events within their life history, but are asked to recall activities and events within given domains in chronological order. After the interviews, the questionnaires were checked for missing and inconsistent data. If necessary, participants were contacted again in an attempt to fill in the gaps. Research has shown that life histories constructed in this way are reliable and consistent with findings of cross-sectional research, at least where younger cohorts are concerned (Blossfeld, 1987; Brückner, 1994).

Data on health over the life-span were collected in the medical section of the Intensive Protocol. The structured anamnesis began with standardized questions on present complaints and diseases, followed by questions on fractures and surgical operations, tuberculosis, strokes, and heart attacks, and ended with an open question on "other illnesses." The month and year of all medical events were recorded, and illnesses were coded using ICD-9 (World Health Organization, 1978). Answers to the final, open question are used only to identify the commencement of illnesses present at the time of the examination. Following this comprehensive reconstruction of individual health histories, participants were asked to retrospectively rate their physical health at the age of 40 (in comparison to other 40-year-olds) and in their 20s.

2.2   Methodological Issues

Four methodological problems should be discussed at this point: data quality, selective mortality, selective migration, and weighting. A fifth problem – selective participation – is discussed in Chapter 2 (Lindenberger et al.). Data quality is dependent on whether the participants were able to recall systematic information about their life course. Not only is the period of time to be recalled quite long, but in some cases the ability to give an orderly overview of one's life is negatively influenced by psychiatric impairments such as dementia. Indeed, Helmchen et al. (1996) showed that the data gathered from persons with severe dementia are marked by a high number of missing values. We tested the quality of the occupational history data in a similar way. It was possible to construct complete occupational histories for almost all persons without a diagnosis of dementia. On average, these consist of nine episodes (of work or interruptions). The starting and finishing points of an episode are recorded in all but 2% of cases.

With increasing dementia, however, the number of episodes mentioned decreases. One way of handling recall difficulties, thus, seems to be representing one's own life history in a less complex manner.[3] In particular, persons with severe dementia have gaps in their occupational history, periods for which they remember neither their occupational activity nor its duration. For persons with severe dementia, data on the timing of a certain episode are missing in 44% of cases. We therefore decided to exclude persons with severe dementia from all analyses in this chapter. This leaves us with 477 of the 516 BASE participants; 244 men (72, 79, and 93 in the three cohorts) and 233 women (64, 75, and 94). We do not believe this exclusion to be as significant for the generalization of

---

[3] An alternative explanation is that an occupational career with only few episodes and a high risk of dementia could have a common cause (e.g., low level of education).

the findings as it might first appear, as dementia seems to be a primarily genetically controlled process.

Selective mortality, selective migration, and weighting all relate to the representativeness of the sample. We describe only the collective histories of survivors now living in Berlin. What effect does this have on our cohort analyses? Selective mortality can cause cohort differences in other variables either to appear or to disappear. If, for example, persons with a lower level of education are less likely to reach the age of 100 than those with a higher educational level, differences in educational attainment at the beginning of this century will no longer be discernible by the time the cohorts reach old age. Conversely, the development of treatment for certain diseases could mean that we encounter survivors of these diseases in the youngest cohort, but not in the oldest. It would be wrong to conclude that the disease did not play a role in the lives of the oldest cohort. We cannot solve the problem of selective mortality, but we have two ways of dealing with it. First, we employ knowledge about selective mortality in the interpretation of the results. Second, it is sometimes possible to estimate the effect of selective mortality using earlier data on the same cohorts; here we can use data from the MZ71.

Selective migration also makes the interpretation of the results more difficult. Although all participants lived in Berlin at the time of the study, they did not necessarily spend their whole lives in the city. Only 36% of the BASE participants were born in Berlin, 46% lived in Berlin at age 20, 82% at 50, and 97% at 70. A considerable number of BASE participants lived outside Berlin at some point in their lives, in smaller towns or even rural areas. Biographies include migration from rural to urban areas, periods as refugees, and phases spent in former East Germany.

We decided against weighting the data (see P. B. Baltes et al., Chapter 1), as almost all analyses will be carried out separately for men and women. Moreover, each of our three cohorts largely overlaps with two of the study's age groups. Weighting would therefore only generate minor changes in the results. An alternative would be to weight the data so as to be representative for the original cohorts, but practical reasons make this alternative impossible. It would require nonexistent information on the characteristics of the many men who died during the war and on selective mortality in old age.

3   Cohort Differences in Education

The trend toward higher educational attainment is one of the best documented changes of the 20th century (e.g., Handl, 1984; Mayer, 1980). Today's older people experienced the beginning of this trend at the turn of the century (Table 3.1). In the oldest cohort (born before 1901), 31% of men and 57% of women attended only elementary school. The younger cohorts attained a distinctly higher level of education then the oldest cohort. The main difference between the oldest and the middle cohort is an increase in the number of persons who took occupational training after their elementary schooling. Comparing the middle and youngest cohort, we see an increase in the number of men with a high school certificate ("Abitur"), and in the number of women who took occupational training following their intermediate school certificate ("Mittlere Reife").

There is a marked difference in the educational levels of men and women. Women received less occupational training and very few of them obtained a high school certificate.

Table 3.1. *Education and occupational training of men and women*

	Birth cohorts		
	1887–1900 (in %)	1901–1910 (in %)	1911–1922 (in %)
Men			
Elementary school[a]	31	18	24
Elementary school and occupational training	43	55	38
Intermediate school certificate	6	3	3
Intermediate school certificate and occupational training	14	19	20
High school certificate	1	0	4
High school certificate and occupational training	4	5	11
Women			
Elementary school[a]	57	47	32
Elementary school and occupational training	16	27	28
Intermediate school certificate	13	14	14
Intermediate school certificate and occupational training	12	10	23
High school certificate	0	1	1
High school certificate and occupational training	2	1	2

Note. Includes only education completed before entering the labor market.
[a]Includes "elementary school without certificate." At the beginning of the century pupils did not necessarily have to formally complete their elementary education, and it is not possible to distinguish precisely between those with and without a formal certificate.

Apart from some minor differences,[4] the general pattern of the BASE data is consistent with both general knowledge on the development of educational opportunities, and trends in educational attainment observed in the Berlin participants in MZ71.

Handl (1984) and Mayer (1988) describe how the educational attainment of some birth cohorts was negatively affected by historical circumstances. World War I resulted in inferior educational opportunities for men and women born around 1906. The Great Depression had a similar, if smaller, impact on those born around 1920. Political restrictions after 1933 hindered women born between 1919 and 1922 from taking occupational training and entering the labor market (Handl, 1984; Mayer, 1980). Since these historical

---

[4] As is known from many other studies, men and women with a higher level of education are more likely to participate in surveys. This also holds true for BASE. In comparison with the Berlin participants in MZ71, we overestimate the percentage of women with an intermediate school certificate (in the oldest and youngest cohort) and the percentage of men with occupational training (in the middle cohort). This means that the historical trend toward higher educational attainment is less visible in our data. Findings pertaining to women with occupational training are particularly interesting. We overestimate the percentages in all cohorts, but particularly in the older ones. This suggests that women without occupational training have a higher risk of dying at a relatively young age (Maas, 1994).

events cut through our cohort groups, we cannot establish precisely how these circumstances affected them.

We conclude that the BASE cohorts show differences in educational achievement, mainly as a result of the trend toward higher educational levels that developed in the first decades of the century. Cohort differences in educational attainment are slight compared with gender differences.

4   Employment History

4.1   The Career Histories of Men

Though less well documented than the changes in education, occupational structure also underwent tremendous changes in the past century. There was a continuous flow out of self-employment (particularly farmers and those helping out with family businesses) and into white-collar work and the civil service. The size of the working class did not change much until the 1970s (Kleber, 1983; Statistisches Bundesamt [Federal Statistical Office], 1972).

The first jobs taken by the BASE men do not reflect these changes (Table 3.2). The differences between cohorts are only slight (considering the number of men in each cohort), but contrary to the general trend, the men from the youngest cohort – who entered the labor market just before World War II – were more likely than those from the oldest cohort to begin their careers as blue-collar workers and less likely to start as white-collar workers.

In the course of their careers, men of all three cohorts progressed from worker and lower-level white-collar status to civil service and higher-level white-collar work (e.g., as bookkeepers, department heads, or draftsmen). According to an overall (χ^2) test, the cohorts do not differ with respect to their final occupational position. However, self-employment was still an important career path for the oldest cohort but not for the younger cohorts (cf. Kleber, 1983).[5]

Using the schema of five social classes developed by Mayer and Wagner (1996; see Mayer et al., Chapter 8), we can comment on upward and downward mobility. More upward than downward mobility can be observed over the life course. Over 80% of men moved into a higher class at least once in their life. Downward mobility is somewhat less common. Nevertheless 62% of men made at least one downward move, most often for a temporary period during the Depression and/or after World War II. Again, the cohorts do not differ greatly.

Considering the differential effects of World War I, the Great Depression, World War II, and the economic slump that followed, the similarity of the three cohorts with respect to their first and last jobs, and their upward or downward mobility is surprising – even when we take selective mortality into account as a force counteracting occupational change. World War I interrupted the occupational careers of many of the oldest men; 53% of the BASE men from this cohort served as soldiers. On average, they were away from home for three years, either in active service or as prisoners of war. World War II disrupted the careers of members of all three cohorts, in particular the youngest cohort,

---

[5] An important factor in the lack of change in occupational structure could be selective mortality. Compared with the Berlin participants in MZ71, the older cohorts in BASE comprise consistently fewer skilled and unskilled workers, and more white-collar workers and civil servants (Maas, 1994). Similar occupation-specific mortality has been demonstrated with other data (e.g., Klein, 1993b).

Table 3.2. *Features of men's career histories by birth cohort*

	Birth cohorts		
	1887–1900	1901–1910	1911–1922
First position (%)			
Self-employed	3	4	7
Helpers in family business	7	6	2
Civil servants	6	5	5
Qualified employees	24	28	19
White-collar workers	18	8	12
Skilled blue-collar workers	23	35	31
Unskilled blue-collar workers	20	14	24
Final position (%)			
Self-employed	20	13	8
Helpers in family business	0	0	0
Civil servants	24	14	15
Qualified employees	34	38	36
White-collar workers	6	6	8
Skilled blue-collar workers	10	23	20
Unskilled blue-collar workers	7	6	14
Upwardly mobile (%)	78	85	82
Number of moves[a]	2	2	2
Downwardly mobile (%)	53	66	65
Number of moves[a]	2	2	2
Downwardly mobile 1945–50 (%)	33	38	33
Soldier in World War I (%)	53	0	0*
Duration (in months)[a]	36	—	—
Soldier in World War II (%)	46	66	86*
Duration (in months)[a]	54	55	73*
Unemployment			
Unemployed 1928–32 (%)	11	28	8*
Unemployed 1945–50 (%)	18	17	24
Unemployed at another time (%)	24	29	31
Total unemployed (%)	38	57	47
Duration (in months)[a]	41	43	37

* Differences between cohorts significant, $p < .05$.
[a] Only where applicable.

of which 86% served (or were held prisoner) for an average of six years. Only 34% of the middle cohort did not actively participate in the war; 46% of the oldest cohort served. Of course, these percentages apply only to men who reached 70 years of age. Many men from these cohorts did not survive the war at all, or died in the following years.

The wars not only produced gaps in career paths, but also caused unemployment and downward mobility, as did the economic depressions (Fig. 3.2). Men's occupational

Figure 3.2. a) Upward mobility, b) downward mobility, and c) unemployment of men by year (percentage of the men on the labor market).

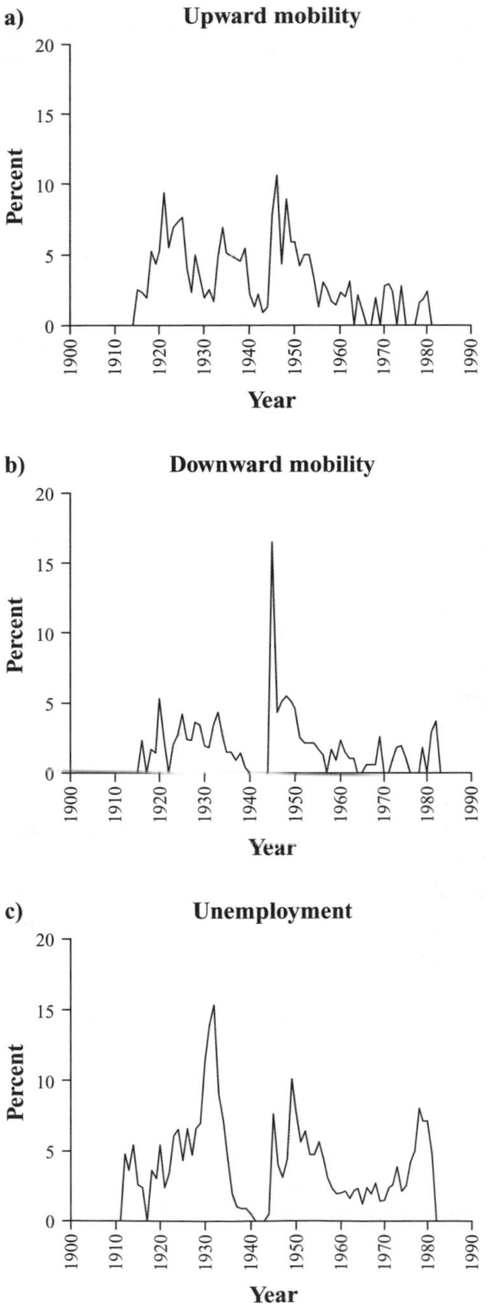

careers were characterized by high unemployment around 1930. Of all BASE men already in the labor market,[6] 15% experienced at least one period of unemployment in
1932 when unemployment rates peaked. However, cohorts were affected differently
(Table 3.2). During the Depression, 28% of the middle cohort men experienced unemployment, compared with only 11% of the oldest cohort. This confirms the hypothesis
that the occupational careers of those who entered the labor market during the Great Depression were affected most profoundly (Elder, 1974; Mayer, 1988). The low percentage
of unemployment in the youngest cohort (8%) stems from the fact that most of its members were still in school during the Depression. There was barely any occupational mobility in any of the cohorts during the Great Depression.

From 1933 onward, occupational opportunities improved, as can be seen from the decrease in unemployment and downward mobility, and the increase in upward mobility. In
the year 1935 alone, 7% of all BASE men in the labor market moved into a higher class.
The level of upward mobility was high until the beginning of World War II. During the
war, mobility and unemployment figures approached zero, as the majority of men were
in the army. When they began to come home in 1945, many were not able to return to
their old jobs, but were forced to reenter the labor market at a lower position. The timing
of the war within individual life-spans does not seem to have made a difference; respectively, 33%, 38%, and 33% of the three cohorts were downwardly mobile between 1945
and 1950 (Table 3.2). In 1949, 10% of all BASE men were unemployed for a time. But in
contrast to the Great Depression, the postwar economic slump hit all cohorts equally
hard. Between 1945 and 1950, 18% of the oldest cohort, 17% of the middle cohort, and
24% of the youngest cohort were unemployed. This bears out the earlier finding that the
negative effects of World War II on men's occupational careers are not dependent on the
number of years spent in military service (Mayer, 1988).

However, the postwar years were not only characterized by downward mobility and
unemployment; many men were upwardly mobile. During the years 1945–50, the rate of
upward mobility was as high as at the beginning of their careers. The reshuffling of occupational positions brought about by the war was soon followed by the restoration of
the old occupational structure.

After 1955 upward and downward mobility figures remained at a constant, relatively
low level. Unemployment, on the other hand, increased for the last time for our cohorts
at the end of the 1970s. Although the figures should be interpreted with caution,[7] they indicate that the end of the occupational careers of the youngest cohort was affected by
economically less favorable circumstances.

A further question is whether the war really reshuffled occupational opportunities.
Were the men who lost high positions after the war replaced by others, or were they able
to recover their positions within a short time? In fact, the latter is the case. Of those who
were downwardly mobile in 1945, more than 50% managed to improve their occupational status between 1946 and 1950. Of those who did not experience downward mobility in 1945, only 27% were upwardly mobile in the following five years.

Thus, the main changes in occupational structure over the working lives of BASE
men were primarily caused by high occupational mobility within all cohorts and not by

---

[6] Men were considered to be in the labor market from the start of their first job until retirement.
[7] Since most members of the older cohorts and some of the youngest cohort had already retired, the
number of men in the labor market is rather small (1978: 50, 1979: 42, 1980: 28, 1981: 21).

the replacement of older, traditional cohorts by younger, more modern ones. Most note-worthy is the great similarity across cohorts with respect to the class distribution of first and final jobs, and the amount of upward and downward mobility – in spite of the fact that they experienced turbulent historical events at different points in their lives.

4.2   The Career Histories of Women

Contrary to popular belief, the total participation of women in the labor market has remained extremely constant since the beginning of the century (Willms, 1983). Be-tween 1907 and 1980, around 50% of women between the ages of 15 and 60 were en-gaged in paid labor. However, there were marked changes in the type of work these women performed. There was a shift from part-time toward full-time work, and away from more dependent positions (such as helping out in family businesses).

The proportion of women who never had full-time work (20 hours or more per week for at least three months) decreased over the BASE cohorts (Table 3.3) – 14% of the old-est, 4% of the middle, and 3% of the youngest cohort. Those who worked were in the la-bor market for an average of 25 years. This figure is somewhat higher than that calcu-lated by Allmendinger, Brückner, and Brückner (1993) for the 1919–21 West German cohort (22 years on average). Figure 3.3 illustrates the rates of female employment by year and birth cohort. The curves of all three cohorts have a similar shape: high employ-ment in young adulthood, lower rates during the phase of family formation (but not less than 40%!), and an increase thereafter. The younger cohorts had a higher probability of returning to the labor market after having children.[8]

Eventually, 78% of women received pensions as a result of their own occupational ac-tivities (compared with 100% of men). This reflects the fact that many women, having worked for considerable periods, still did not fulfill the criteria for a pension. Compared with the results of a study on Germans born in 1920 (Allmendinger et al., 1993), how-ever, a relatively large proportion of the BASE women were able to secure a pension from their own earnings. This could be due to the relatively high proportion of white-collar and blue-collar workers among Berlin women or, to a lesser degree, the revised pension laws of 1992 (Bundesminister für Arbeit und Sozialordnung [Federal Minister of Labor and Social Affairs], 1992). The number of women who did manage to earn their own pension is markedly larger in the younger cohort than in the older ones.

The class distribution of the first job was fairly constant over the cohorts. More than 40% of women began their occupational career as lower-level white-collar workers, and a quarter as higher-level white-collar workers. The service sector was obviously already the best place for Berlin women to find a job in the first half of the century. More women than men started their careers in the most traditional kind of jobs (helping out with fam-ily businesses), but even here, the number is small (10%). The general trend in the first half of the century of German women leaving positions as helpers in family businesses and taking up blue-collar and white-collar positions (Statistisches Bundesamt, 1972) had obviously already ended in Berlin.

---

[8] The percentages of Berlin women in the labor market in 1939, 1950, and 1960 are very similar in the BASE data and the MZ71 data. There are no signs of selective mortality or selective participa-tion of either women with paid jobs or housewives (Maas, 1994).

Table 3.3. *Features of women's career histories by birth cohort*

	Birth cohorts		
	1887–1900	**1901–1910**	**1911–1922**
On the labor market (%)	86	96	97*
Duration (in years)[a]	26	24	24
First position (%)			
Self-employed	3	3	0
Helpers in family business	9	15	8
Civil servants	3	0	0
Qualified employees	22	23	26
White-collar workers	45	43	46
Skilled blue-collar workers	5	6	8
Unskilled blue-collar workers	12	11	13
Final position (%)			
Self-employed	5	7	5
Helpers in family business	10	8	3
Civil servants	9	1	1
Qualified employees	26	30	38
White-collar workers	35	25	27
Skilled blue-collar workers	3	7	4
Unskilled blue-collar workers	12	22	22
Upwardly mobile (%)	33	48	53*
Number of moves[a]	2	1	2
Downwardly mobile (%)	30	43	47
Number of moves[a]	2	1	1
Pension from own earnings (%)	67	79	85*
Unemployment			
Unemployed 1928–32 (%)	6	11	1*
Unemployed 1945–50 (%)	5	23	18*
Unemployed at another time (%)	14	25	19
Total unemployed (%)	17	40	34*
Duration (in months)[a]	48	65	64

* Differences between cohorts significant, $p < .05$.
[a] Only where applicable.

If we compare first with last jobs, two important shifts seem to have taken place. First, 29% of lower-level white-collar workers moved on to higher-level positions as qualified employees. Second, many women ended their occupational career as unskilled blue-collar workers (22% of the youngest cohort). Upward mobility increased over the cohorts. Among BASE women, 33% (oldest cohort), 48%, and 53% (youngest cohort) were upwardly mobile at least once in their life, most frequently from lower-level to higher-level white-collar worker. Downward mobility was less common than up-

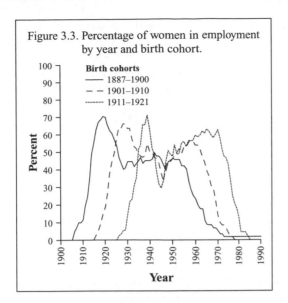

Figure 3.3. Percentage of women in employment by year and birth cohort.

ward mobility. The number of downward moves does not differ significantly among cohorts.

During the Great Depression and the years thereafter, it was difficult for women to stay in paid jobs. A political campaign with the slogan "double income earners" was conducted against their employment and occupational training (Allmendinger et al., 1993; Handl, 1984; Lehr, 1987). As was also the case for men, the highest rates of unemployment at this time can be seen in the middle cohort of BASE women (11% vs. 6% of the oldest and 1% of the youngest cohort; see Table 3.3). The extent of the Depression's impact on women's occupational careers was obviously dependent on its timing within their career history (Müller, 1985; Müller, Handl, & Willms, 1983).

In general, World War II afforded women new occupational opportunities, as their labor was required while most of the men were away at war. However, it is difficult to discern any stimulating effects World War II may have had on the paid labor of BASE women (Fig. 3.3). There is only a marginal increase in the percentage of the middle and oldest cohort members in the labor market. The number of Berlin women in work was probably already so high that it could not rise any further. However, the difficulties for women in the labor market directly after the war are clearly visible. The postwar economic crisis, combined with the return of many of the men, forced women out of the labor market (Meyer & Schulze, 1984, 1985). In 1945, more than 10% of BASE women were unemployed. The unemployment figures were much higher in the two younger cohorts than in the older one (5%, 23%, and 18%; see Table 3.3); it seems to have been easier for older women to keep their jobs.

Men not only experienced high unemployment and downward mobility in the postwar years, but also substantial upward mobility. This was not the case for women. With the exception of slightly more downward mobility between 1945 and 1950, female upward and downward mobility rates remained very stable.

It can be concluded that the occupational careers of BASE women show remarkably modern characteristics. Participation in the labor force was high, as was the number of women working in the service sector. The younger cohorts were more modern in the sense that it was even more common for them to participate in the labor force, they were more likely to return to the labor market after having children, and more of them earned their own pension. The Great Depression, and especially the economic slump after World War II, forced women out of the labor market. In both cases older women were more likely to retain their jobs than younger women.

5   Family History

Characteristics of the family are among the most important determinants of many aspects of life in old age. For example, men and women with a partner run a lower risk of institutionalization; children are important caregivers for older parents; and losing a partner leads to a higher mortality risk, at least temporarily (Gärtner, 1990; Klein, 1993a; Mellström, Nilsson, Odén, Rundgren, & Svanborg, 1982).

In this section we describe aspects of the family histories of the three BASE birth cohorts (1887–1900, 1901–10, and 1911–22) within their historical context. Since they play the most important role in old age, we concentrate on partners and children, and do not discuss parents, siblings, or grandchildren. Relationships between BASE participants and the members of their extended families are discussed in Chapter 10 (Wagner et al.).

5.1   *Marriage*

Current marital status reveals only a fraction of family history. The life histories of the men and women in BASE show 15 different patterns of marriage, widowhood, and divorce. Two differences in the marriage patterns of men and women are evident. Very few women married more than twice, and men were more likely to have a pattern ending with an existing marriage (for details, see Maas, 1995).

Almost all BASE participants were married at least once. This applies particularly to the men (99%, 98%, and 95%) and to the younger cohorts of women (83%, 91%, and 89%; see Table 3.4). Men married somewhat later than women. Men and women from the youngest cohort married earlier than the older cohorts. Looking at the historical time axis (cf. Fig. 3.1), it is possible that these marriages were accelerated by National Socialist family policies and the war.

At the time of the interviews, 32% of the men were still in their first marriage, compared with only 5% of the women. When comparing cohorts, however, it is more interesting to look at marital status at the age of 70 (the last age for which we have data on all respondents). More than half of the men were still in their first marriage when they reached the age of 70. The women's situation is less positive, with only 25% still in their first marriage at 70. This is undoubtedly due mainly to the generally higher mortality of men (combined with the fact that they married later). There are, however, also historical influences, as we observe from the differences between the cohorts. At age 70, 70% of the oldest male cohort were still in their first marriage, compared with only 49% of the middle cohort, and 55% of the youngest. For women, the percentages are 28, 35, and 20, respectively.

The distinct difference between the oldest and the middle cohort in the number of men still married to their first partner at 70 (70% vs. 49%), can be explained mainly by the

Table 3.4. *Characteristics of family history (marriages) by gender and birth cohort*

	Birth cohorts		
	1887–1900	1901–1910	1911–1922
Men			
First marriage (%)	99	98	95
Age at first marriage	29	29	27*
Still in first marriage at age 70 (%)	70	49	55
Divorce from first partner before age 70 (%)	13	28	27
Death of first partner before age 70 (%)	16	22	13
Second marriage before age 70 (%)	21	33	28
Second marriage among divorced men and (%) widowers	70	65	62
Still in second marriage at age 70 (%)	19	28	22
Women			
First marriage (%)	83	91	89
Age at first marriage	27	27	24*
Still in first marriage at age 70 (%)	28	35	20
Divorce from first partner before age 70 (%)	5	16	27
Death of first partner before age 70 (%)	50	40	42
Second marriage before age 70 (%)	9	16	29
Second marriage among divorcées and widows (%)	13	25	36
Still in second marriage at age 70 (%)	2	5	10

* Differences between cohorts significant, $p < .05$.

large number of men in the second cohort who divorced during or directly after the war. The intermediate position of the youngest cohort (55%) is the result of high divorce rates, particularly after the war (comparable with rates of the middle cohort), but lower death rates.[9]

The marital histories of the women show some parallels, but also some major differences. As mentioned above, the number of women who remained single is larger than the number of unmarried men. In the oldest BASE cohort, the cumulative percentage of married women is only 83. Barely any of these marriages still existed at the time of the interviews.

The increase in divorce rates over the cohorts was even larger for women than men. This should not be interpreted as a "modernization trend," however, but as a consequence of World War II, which broke up many young marriages. On the other hand, the

[9] The cohort differences observed are also partly due to selective mortality. It is well known that married men live longer than unmarried men, who in turn live longer than divorced men and widowers (Gärtner, 1990; Klein, 1993b). A comparison of the male BASE cohorts with the male Berlin participants in MZ71 shows similar differences. Compared with the Microcensus data, more of the men in the oldest BASE cohort were married in 1971 and fewer were widowers. In the younger cohorts there are no such differences (Maas, 1994).

number of women in the oldest cohort widowed before the age of 70 is surprisingly high. Although many of the younger women's partners died during the war, there are fewer widows in the younger cohorts than in the oldest one.[10] This finding may reflect the trend to longevity.

Nearly 28% of men married for a second time before reaching the age of 70. This means that around 65% of men who lost their first wife found a new one (Table 3.4). In all three cohorts, almost all men who lost their partner at a relatively young age remarried within a few years. Most of the second marriages were still intact when the interviewees reached age 70. Of the few men who lost their second partner, some married for a third or even fourth time.

In contrast, we observe clear cohort differences where women's second marriages are concerned. Most widows/divorcées from the 1887–1900 cohort remained alone for the rest of their lives; only 13% remarried. Moreover, almost all of these second marriages ended before the women reached the age of 70 years. The likelihood of remarriage was somewhat higher in the 1901–10 cohort (25%) and higher again in the 1911–22 cohort (36%). The absolute number of men and women from this cohort who entered second marriages does not differ (28% vs. 29%). Since many more women had lost their first partner, however, their chances of remarrying were much smaller (36% vs. 62%). An explanation for these gender differences in remarriage is of course the extreme shortage of men after World War II. Another striking difference is that almost all of the women who remarried lost their second partner before the age of 70, whereas most of the men who remarried were still with their partner at this age.

We conclude that – as expected – the effects of World War II on family life were disastrous. Almost all German men left their families for military service. Many never returned. Death of the partner was not the only reason marriages ended in the war years, however. The changes in divorce rates we see among the BASE cohorts are similar to those described by the Statistisches Bundesamt (1972). The divorce rate increased only slightly between World Wars I and II, but rose temporarily to a much higher level after World War II. This is most relevant for women in old age, as many more women than men lost their partner, and their chances of remarriage were much slimmer. We observe two contrasting cohort differences for women. Women from the youngest cohort (1911–22) were at a very high risk of losing their partner during or shortly after World War II. On the other hand, they had considerably better chances of remarrying than the women in the older cohorts (1887–1900, 1901–10). The differences in marriage patterns among men of the BASE cohorts were caused partly by the higher mortality risk of widowed men.

5.2   Children

Aside from the partner, children are probably the most important people in the lives of older people. For this reason, concern is often expressed that declining family size will have a negative influence on the quality of life of the older generations. Family size and especially childlessness are therefore important topics of gerontological research.

---

[10] A comparison of MZ71 data on women's marital status in 1971 and BASE findings for the same year reveals no differences. Selective mortality by marital status is generally found to be less significant for women than for men (Gärtner, 1990), and is not discernible in the BASE data.

Table 3.5. *Children of the BASE cohorts*

	Birth cohorts		
	1887–1900	1901–1910	1911–1922
Average number of children alive at time of interview	0.9	1.2	1.5*
Average number of children born	1.2	1.5	1.6*
Proportion of persons who never had children	40%	29%	26%*
Average number of children (excluding the childless)	2.0	2.0	2.2

*Differences between cohorts significant, $p < .05$.

There are clear differences between the BASE cohorts in the number of children alive at the time of the interviews (Table 3.5). On average, the members of the youngest cohort have 1.5 living children, the middle cohort 1.2, and the oldest cohort 0.9. Many factors need to be considered in order to understand these differences.

We start with differences in birthrates. First, we know that fewer children were born in Germany during wartime and, to a lesser extent, during periods of economic depression (Statistisches Bundesamt, 1972). In contrast to other countries, the wars were not followed by a period of increased fertility. We also know that fertility decreased in the first decades of this century, but that a reversal of this trend began around 1930 (Knodel, 1974). The fertility of the BASE cohorts will have been affected by both types of historical change.

From the perspective of family size, it is interesting to distinguish between childless families and the number of children in families. Table 3.5 shows that only the percentage of people who never had children differs between cohorts (cf. Wagner et al., Chapter 10). Compared with 29% and 26% respectively of the younger cohorts, 40% of the oldest cohort (1887–1900) remained childless. In all cohorts, those who did have children had an average of two.[11] Are these results concurrent with the reversal of the trend to lower fertility, and the influence of historical events?

The BASE cohorts started their family formation process at about 28 years of age. The oldest cohort reached this age between 1915 and 1928. Our findings that so many of its members remained childless (and that so many women never married) are in accordance with the general trend in Germany. The 1901–10 cohort was hit more severely by the Great Depression (as shown by the unemployment figures), but was probably also influenced by the National Socialist policy of promoting childbirth. This policy seems to have worked, as fertility increased. The 1911–22 cohort reached age 28 during and directly after World War II, a comparatively bad time to have children. Furthermore, as we have seen, the marriages of these younger cohorts were rather unstable. Nevertheless, more of them had children than the older cohorts – an unexpected finding.

[11] The MZ71 data also shows a high number of childless people in the oldest cohort and a constant family size throughout cohorts.

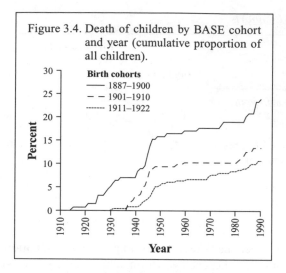

Figure 3.4. Death of children by BASE cohort and year (cumulative proportion of all children).

Birth cohorts
—— 1887–1900
– – 1901–1910
······ 1911–1922

Another reason for cohort differences in family size in old age is that some parents outlive their children. Apart from accidents and other random causes of death, there are three main causes of children's death: (1) infant mortality, (2) World War II, and (3) age-related illnesses. Figure 3.4 shows the cumulative percentages of children who did not survive. There are clear cohort differences. More than 20% of the children of the 1887–1900 cohort died before the time of the interviews, compared with only 13% and 10% of the children of the 1901–10 and 1911–22 cohorts respectively. All three of the aforementioned causes of death played a role. Infant mortality (not caused by World War II) was much more common in the oldest cohort than in the younger ones (cf. Knodel, 1974). All three cohorts lost children in the war. The children of the 1911–22 cohort were still very young in the war years, whereas some of the children of the 1887–1900 cohort were already soldiers. The first children of the 1887–1900 cohort were born in 1911. By 1990 they were 79 years old and, as to be expected, some of these children died from age-related diseases between 1980 and 1990. This effect is not yet visible in the two younger cohorts.

We can conclude that the data on the children of the BASE cohorts show some of the assumptions mentioned earlier to be quite inaccurate. Contrary to popular belief, the members of the oldest cohort were much more likely to grow old without children than the younger cohorts. They were more likely to be childless, they did not have larger families than younger cohorts, and they lost more children at an early age. The fact that they lost more children in the past few years is a clear age effect.

6   Health History

In this context, we consider both chronic and acute diseases that occurred over the participants' life course under the following aspects: First, although the BASE participants are "long-term survivors" of the two world wars (Mayer, 1988), their health histories were heavily influenced by wartime events. Second, some conditions are more common in certain phases of life (Brody & Schneider, 1986). For example, appendicitis

Table 3.6. *Characteristics of the health histories of the BASE cohorts by gender*

	Birth cohorts		
	1887–1900	1901–1910	1911–1922
Men			
Number of operations	1.0	1.5	2.3**
Number of fractures	0.3	0.5	0.8**
Tuberculosis (%)	5.6	6.3	7.5
Myocardial infarction/stroke (%)	5.6	7.6	15.1
Subjective health[a]			
At age 40	2.5	2.5	2.6
Between ages 20 and 30	1.9	1.8	1.6*
Number of chronic illnesses at age 70	0.9	1.1	1.7**
Women			
Number of operations	0.9	1.3	2.5**
Number of fractures	0.2	0.4	0.6*
Tuberculosis (%)	7.8	5.3	6.4
Myocardial infarction/stroke (%)	3.6	4.0	9.6
Subjective health[a]			
At age 40	2.5	2.6	2.8
Between ages 20 and 30	1.8	1.9	2.0
Number of chronic illnesses at age 70	0.7	1.5	1.9**

Note. Only information given on the calendar years 1887–1989 and up to the age of 70 is used.
* $p < .05$, ** $p < .01$.
[a]Measured retrospectively on a five-point scale: 1 = "very good," 5 = "poor."

typically occurs in late childhood as opposed to cholelithiasis (gallstones) and cataracts, which occur more often in middle adulthood and old age, respectively. All three are routinely treated by surgical intervention.[12] Third, the general improvement (modernization) of medical treatment in the 20th century has made operations safer, for example. Because these developments occurred at different phases of life for the three BASE cohorts, and because the risks of many modern treatments still increase with age, we can assume that each BASE cohort profited from this progress to a differing extent. A combination of these three aspects provides us with the fourth, selective mortality, which is largely dependent upon historical events, acute and chronic diseases, and possibilities of intervention (Dinkel, 1992).

In this section we will therefore analyze several characteristics of the health history (operations, fractures, myocardial infarctions, strokes, tuberculosis, chronic illnesses, and subjective health; see Table 3.6). For the period from 1887 to 1989, we calculate a total of 1,150 operations and 334 fractures for the 477 BASE participants in question.

---

[12] Because the three birth cohorts are so close to each other in time, we do not expect to find any great differences in the ages at which the illnesses are most prevalent. When a historical event associated with an increased level of illness (e.g., World War II) falls in an otherwise "healthy" or uneventful phase for one cohort, but in a more eventful period for another cohort, then – when viewed cumulatively – the latter seems to have been harder hit by the historical event.

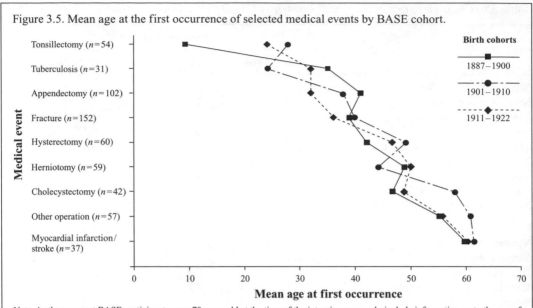

Figure 3.5. Mean age at the first occurrence of selected medical events by BASE cohort.

Note. As the youngest BASE participants were 70 years old at the time of the interviews, we only include information up to the age of 70. There are no significant differences in the means ($p > .05$).

Before the age of 70, 31 had tuberculosis and 37 had a myocardial infarction or stroke. The most common operations up to the age of 70 were tonsillectomy, appendectomy, hysterectomy, herniotomy, and cholecystectomy. Figure 3.5 shows the mean ages at which these surgical interventions were carried out. There are no significant age differences between the cohorts. This finding can also be interpreted as important evidence of the consistency of the data, even where the oldest cohort is concerned.

A systematic comparison of the health histories of the cohorts up to the age of 70 reveals no differences for some characteristics, but very distinct differences for others. There is no significant difference between cohorts where tuberculosis, myocardial infarctions, and strokes are concerned. The same can be said for the participants' retrospective assessments of their own health at the age of 40. The men of the youngest (1911–22) cohort, however, evaluated their physical health between the ages of 20 and 30 significantly better than the other cohorts. This may be a result of their subjective experience of selective survival, as this cohort was 20 to 30 years old directly before, during, and after World War II; many of their contemporaries did not survive. Memories of want and deprivation at the front line and in captivity may have convinced the men of the youngest cohort that they were only able to survive because of their excellent physical health.

Clearer cohort differences can be seen in the number of operations and fractures. The men and women of the youngest cohort had an average of 2.4 operations – more than the middle (about 1.5), and more than twice as many as the oldest cohort (about 1 operation). The number of fractures is also higher in the youngest cohort than in either of the others. These findings must be interpreted in the correct historical and biological context. The

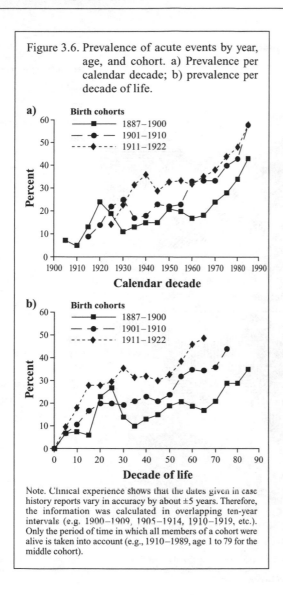

Figure 3.6. Prevalence of acute events by year, age, and cohort. a) Prevalence per calendar decade; b) prevalence per decade of life.

Note. Clinical experience shows that the dates given in case history reports vary in accuracy by about ±5 years. Therefore, the information was calculated in overlapping ten-year intervals (e.g. 1900–1909, 1905–1914, 1910–1919, etc.). Only the period of time in which all members of a cohort were alive is taken into account (e.g., 1910–1989, age 1 to 79 for the middle cohort).

prevalence of medical events – the majority of which are operations – is known to vary according to the calendar decade and the chronological age of the patient (cf. Fig. 3.6). The number of medical events peaks initially for the oldest cohort in the decade 1915–24, the time of World War I; for the middle cohort in the decade 1925–34, during the Great Depression; and for the youngest cohort in the decade 1935–44, the World War II period (Fig. 3.6a). These phases are not shown so clearly against the chronological age of the patient, at least not where the middle and youngest cohorts are concerned. This can be interpreted as evidence that historical events are very significant (Fig. 3.6b).

The extreme increase in prevalence of events when the members of the oldest cohort were about 20 years old, however, reflects the peak at about 1920, and is probably due to

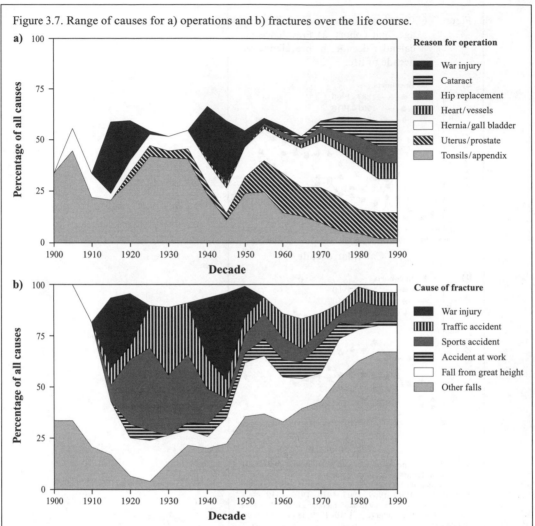

Figure 3.7. Range of causes for a) operations and b) fractures over the life course.

Note. The absolute number of operations and fractures was much lower in the first decades than in the later ones. Percentages refer to all acute medical events mentioned for each decade which were calculated in overlapping five-year intervals (e.g., 1900–1909, 1905–1914, 1910–1919, etc.). Where the total is under 100%: other causes.

the fact that about 30% of the men in this cohort were born in the year 1896 and were therefore old enough to serve in the military when World War I broke out. The distribution of causes of operations and fractures shows that this peak is definitely influenced by war wounds here (Fig. 3.7).

However, we must add that the relative decline in the number of tonsillectomies and appendectomies during wartime, and the increase following the wars had a corresponding effect on the absolute number of operations carried out. The end of World War II, on the other hand, marks a shift in the causes of fractures; the "youthful" profile seen between the wars (with sport and traffic accidents representing the main causes) is replaced by an aged profile (with falls causing even more fractures). Hence, the historical influence of wartime on the BASE cohorts makes itself known in many ways – the increase in injuries, the change in causes of injury, the reduction in the number of "normal" operations during wartime, and the postwar increase of "normal" operations, leading to peak levels. When looking at the number of events according to age, and at the first seven decades of the survivors of the oldest cohort in particular (Fig. 3.6b), we gain the impression that World War I alone led to a sharp increase in the prevalence of acute medical events, compared with an otherwise steady upwards trend with a 2–3% increase per decade among the two younger cohorts. The fact that Figure 3.6a shows a continually steeper increase in the number of events after 1960 – an increase that cannot be discerned from the age-dependent data – could be due to a combination of modernization (more possibilities for surgical intervention, particularly in the younger cohorts) and age effects (more fractures, cardiovascular disease, and cataracts, especially in the oldest cohort).

Finally, we would like to highlight the fact that the estimated number of chronic illnesses in the seventh decade of life is much higher among the youngest cohort than the two older ones (see Table 3.6). This estimate is based on information on the duration of diseases present at the time of the examination, corrected to allow for the illnesses for which no starting point can be ascertained, the proportion of which varies by cohort.[13] Despite the very conservative estimate that results, the cohort differences are significant. That is to say that those born in 1887–1900 and 1901–10 were healthier between the ages of 60 and 69 than the youngest (1911–22) cohort. These findings appear very plausible when we consider selective mortality. We can assume that a relatively small proportion of the youngest BASE cohort will reach the age of 90 or 100, specifically, those who had few or no chronic illnesses at the time of the interviews (i.e., a group of persons with a much lower mean number of chronic illnesses in the seventh decade of life). This hypothesis is supported by the finding that the calculated number of diagnoses for members of the oldest cohort in their seventh decade of life is significantly lower than the mean number for the entire youngest cohort (see Fig. 3.8).

The potential effect of selective mortality is very significant for the interpretation of other findings on morbidity presented in this book. The more dependent selective mortality is on morbidity in old age, the less suitable morbidity trends shown by cross-sectional figures are for estimating the actual development of morbidity in very old age. This important aspect is clearly illustrated by our retrospective data (see Fig. 3.8). For all cohorts, the retrospectively estimated rise in morbidity is much steeper than indicated by the trend in morbidity shown in the cross-sectional figures. The retrospective data are, however, certainly consistent with recent theories on the development of morbidity and mortality in old age (Brody & Miles, 1990; Fries, 1980; Palmore, 1986; Perls, 1995).

---

[13] The relative proportion of illnesses for which the starting point could not be ascertained was 49% in the oldest cohort, 18% in the middle cohort, and 1% in the youngest. The large proportion in the oldest cohort is not directly due to memory loss, but largely to the fact that the oldest BASE participants were only actually aware of approximately half of their illnesses. This has much to do with the fact that more and more illnesses go undiagnosed with increasing age (cf. Steinhagen-Thiessen & Borchelt, Chapter 5). To correct for this, the retrospectively estimated number of illnesses was multiplied by 1.96 for the oldest cohort, 1.22 for the middle cohort, and 1.10 for the youngest cohort.

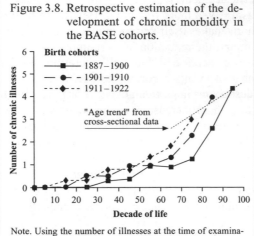

Figure 3.8. Retrospective estimation of the development of chronic morbidity in the BASE cohorts.

Note. Using the number of illnesses at the time of examination (1990–1992) and knowledge of the duration of the illnesses, the mean number of chronic illnesses in past decades was calculated, and corrected to allow for illnesses for which no starting point could be ascertained (the proportion of which varied according to cohort; factor 1.96 for the 1887–1900 cohort; 1.22 for the 1901–1910 cohort; 1.01 for the 1911–1922 cohort). The mean difference in the seventh decade of life is statistically significant ($p < .001$).

We are aware that the aspects of cohort-specific health histories presented in this section can only be regarded as illustrations. Whether and how memory loss of the BASE participants affects the results, for example, is just as difficult to assess as the influence of the manner in which the data were collected. However, this is largely because of the lack of studies with comparable methodological approaches. The fact that the data are generally consistent and plausible is an important indicator of their validity. The same can be said for the fact that there is no sign of a continuous bias in one direction, and that significant cohort differences cannot be statistically explained by cognitive deficits. Moreover, all participants were given a thorough physical examination during which operation scars and other points of the case history could be verified, even if this was not done systematically. In conclusion we must stress that we can only assume that the data represent the BASE participants' detailed recollections of medical events over the past century. But even if this is not the case, we still have a unique record of the particular historical period in which BASE cohorts lived.

7   Cohort Differences and Aging

The aim of this chapter is to outline cohort-specific characteristics of the participants in the Berlin Aging Study. This should not only help us to avoid interpreting cohort differences as age differences, but also to direct our attention to possible explanatory factors for individual differences. Three sources of differences between cohorts have been investigated: trends toward a more modern society, permanent consequences of historical events, and temporary effects of events.

Several modernization trends have been observed. The younger cohorts were better educated, and the women among them had more modern occupational careers. They were more likely to be in the labor market, usually returned to work after caring for their young children, and earned their own pension rights. In younger cohorts more women remarried, had more operations, and fewer of their children died in infancy.

However, stability and trends in unexpected directions are just as interesting as modernization trends. The growth in educational attainment was not accompanied by a shift in occupational structure toward more highly qualified jobs. To a large extent, men and women from the younger cohorts began and ended their occupational careers in the same occupational classes as the older cohorts. The older cohorts did not have larger families than the younger ones – on the contrary, they were more likely to remain childless.

World War I interrupted the occupational careers of the oldest cohort (1887–1900), and caused an increase in the number of operations. The Great Depression led to a high rate of unemployment, especially for men and women of the middle cohort (1901–10). World War II had the greatest and most universal impact on the lives of older people in Berlin. Many of the men from all three cohorts, but especially the youngest, served as soldiers and were taken prisoner; many of the women from the middle and younger cohorts were widowed, and many of the remaining marriages broke down. So many injured persons had to be operated on that "normal" operations were reduced to a minimum. Members of all cohorts lost children during the war. Effects of the war extended into the postwar years, with high unemployment and much upward and downward mobility among men of all cohorts, and high unemployment among women of the 1901–10 and 1911–22 cohorts.

Some cohort differences are no longer discernible in old age. Men who were downwardly mobile directly after the war often did not end their occupational career in a lower occupational class, but managed to regain a higher position. Widowers from all cohorts found new partners. This was nearly impossible for women in the oldest cohort, but more feasible for increasing numbers of younger women.

Before discussing how these cohort differences can be of significance to the aging process, we will consider the problems of selective mortality. In general, selective mortality makes it more difficult to discern modernization trends in old age. Modernization means that younger cohorts do better with respect to education, material well-being, health, and so on. As these characteristics also correlate with mortality, however, those from the oldest cohort with a high level of education, better material conditions, and better health are more likely to survive. We saw the effect of selective mortality very clearly in our consideration of health. If a trend is still discernible, for example, in the educational levels of the oldest cohort, we have reasonable evidence that modernization really did take place. Nevertheless, we should not disregard the fact that there are exceptions to the rule that modernization increases longevity. For example, the higher divorce rates in the younger cohorts could have negative effects on their survival chances. The same is true for smoking, a habit that is more widespread among the younger cohorts than the older ones (Brenner, 1993). Hence, trends of this kind are easily overestimated if we take only frequencies in old age into consideration.

Although we cannot recapitulate all findings described in this chapter, we wish to make two summarizing statements. First, it is not generally the case that younger cohorts had more successful career paths than older ones. Although men and women from the younger cohorts were better educated, they were hit harder by historical circumstances. Considering they had better starting positions than their elders but still ended their careers at the same level, we can even deem the younger cohorts to be comparatively less successful. Since material well-being in old age largely depends on occupational success, differences in old age are very likely not due to cohort differences in occupational careers, but to other factors such as changes in social security laws.

Second, it is not generally accurate to assume that older cohorts have more children to care for them. The myth of a "golden age" where older people were cared for by large families does not apply to the oldest BASE cohort. As shown in numerous studies (Bengtson & Schütze, 1992), many families are still willing to care for their older relatives, but the members of the oldest BASE cohort more often remained unmarried, had fewer children than older or younger cohorts, and were at a higher risk of losing their children at an early age. Thus, it is definitely feasible that age group differences in loneliness, social network size, and institutionalization, for example, have their roots in family formation processes in the first half of this century.

References

Abelshauser, W. (1983). *Wirtschaftsgeschichte der Bundesrepublik Deutschland 1945–1980.* Frankfurt/M.: Suhrkamp.

Allmendinger, J., Brückner, H., & Brückner, E. (1993). The production of gender disparities over the life course and their effects in old age: Results from the West German Life History Study. In A. B. Atkinson & M. Rein (Eds.), *Age, work, and social security* (pp. 188–223). New York: St. Martin's Press.

Baltes, P. B. (1968). Longitudinal and cross-sectional sequences in the study of age and generation effects. *Human Development, 11*, 145–171.

Bengtson, V. L., Cutler, N. E., Mangen, D. J., & Marshall, V. W. (1985). Generations, cohorts, and relations between age groups. In R. H. Binstock & E. Shanas (Eds.), *Handbook of aging and the social sciences* (2nd ed., pp. 304–338). New York: Van Nostrand Reinhold.

Bengtson, V. L., & Schütze, Y. (1992). Altern und Generationenbeziehungen: Aussichten für das kommende Jahrhundert. In P. B. Baltes & J. Mittelstraß (Eds.), *Zukunft des Alterns und gesellschaftliche Entwicklung* (pp. 492–517). Berlin: de Gruyter.

Blossfeld, H.-P. (1987). Zur Repräsentativität der Sfb-3-Lebensverlaufsstudie: Ein Vergleich mit Daten aus der amtlichen Statistik. *Allgemeines Statistisches Archiv, 71*, 126–144.

Brenner, H. (1993). A birth cohort analysis of the smoking epidemic in West Germany. *Journal of Epidemiology and Community Health, 47*, 54–58.

Brody, J. A., & Miles, T. P. (1990). Mortality postponed and the unmasking of age-dependent non-fatal conditions. *Aging, 2*, 283–289.

Brody, J. A., & Schneider, E. L. (1986). Diseases and disorders of aging: A hypothesis. *Journal of Chronic Diseases, 39*, 871–876.

Brückner, E. (1994). Erhebung ereignisorientierter Lebensverläufe als retrospektive Längsschnittrekonstruktion. In R. Hauser, N. Ott, & G. Wagner (Eds.), *Mikroanalytische Grundlagen der Gesellschaftspolitik: Vol. 2. Erhebungsverfahren, Analysemethoden und Mikrosimulation* (pp. 38–69). Berlin: Akademie Verlag.

Brückner, E., & Mayer, K. U. (1998). Collecting life history data: Experiences from the German Life History Study. In J. L. Giele & G. H. Elder Jr. (Eds.), *Methods of life course research: Qualitative and quantitative approaches* (pp. 152–181). Thousand Oaks, CA: Sage.

Bundesminister für Arbeit und Sozialordnung (Ed.). (1992). *Die Rente '92*. Bonn.

Dinkel, R. H. (1992). Demographische Alterung: Ein Überblick unter besonderer Berücksichtigung der Mortalitätsentwicklungen. In P. B. Baltes & J. Mittelstraß (Eds.), *Zukunft des Alterns und gesellschaftliche Entwicklung* (pp. 62–93). Berlin: de Gruyter.

Elder, G. H., Jr. (1974). *Children of the Great Depression: Social change in life experience.* Chicago: University of Chicago Press.

Elder, G. H., Jr. (1975). Age differentiation and the life course. In A. Inkeles, J. Coleman, & N. Smelser (Eds.), *Annual review of sociology* (Vol. 1, pp. 165–190). Palo Alto, CA: Annual Reviews.

Fries, J. F. (1980). Aging, natural death and the compression of morbidity. *New England Journal of Medicine, 303*, 130–135.

Gärtner, K. (1990). Sterblichkeit nach dem Familienstand. *Zeitschrift für Bevölkerungswissenschaft, 16*, 53–66.

Handl, J. (1984). Educational chances and occupational opportunities of women: A sociohistorical analysis. *Journal of Social History, 17*, 463–487.

Helmchen, H., Baltes, M. M., Geiselmann, B., Kanowski, S., Linden, M., Reischies, F. M., Wagner, M., & Wilms, H.-U. (1996). Psychische Erkrankungen im Alter. In K. U. Mayer & P. B. Baltes (Eds.), *Die Berliner Altersstudie* (pp. 185–219). Berlin: Akademie Verlag.

Kleber, W. (1983). Die sektorale und sozialrechtliche Umschichtung der Erwerbsstruktur in Deutschland, 1882–1970. In M. Haller & W. Müller (Eds.), *Beschäftigungssystem im gesellschaftlichen Wandel* (pp. 24–75). Frankfurt/M.: Campus.

Klein, T. (1993a). Familienstand und Lebenserwartung: Eine Kohortenanalyse der Bundesrepublik Deutschland. *Zeitschrift für Familienforschung, 5*, 99–114.

Klein, T. (1993b). Soziale Position und Lebenserwartung: Eine kohortenbezogene Analyse mit den Daten des Sozio-ökonomischen Panels. *Zeitschrift für Gerontologie, 26*, 313–320.

Knodel, J. E. (1974). *The decline of fertility in Germany, 1871–1939*. Princeton, NJ: Princeton University Press.

Lehr, U. (1987). *Zur Situation der älterwerdenden Frau: Bestandsaufnahme und Perspektiven bis zum Jahre 2000*. Munich: Beck.

Maas, I. (1994). *Selektive Mortalität: Ein Vergleich der Berliner Altersstudie und der Mikrozensus-Zusatzerhebung 1971*. Unpublished manuscript, Max Planck Institute for Human Development, Berlin.

Maas, I. (1995). Demography and aging: Long term effects of divorce, early widowhood, and migration on resources and integration in old age. *Korea Journal of Population and Development, 24*, 275–299.

Maas, I., & Staudinger, U. M. (1996). Lebensverlauf und Altern: Kontinuität und Diskontinuität der gesellschaftlichen Beteiligung, des Lebensinvestments und ökonomischer Ressourcen. In K. U. Mayer & P. B. Baltes (Eds.), *Die Berliner Altersstudie* (pp. 543–572). Berlin: Akademie Verlag.

Mannheim, K. (1928). Das soziologische Problem der Generationen. *Kölner Vierteljahreshefte für Soziologie, 7*, 168–185/309–321.

Mayer, K. U. (1980). Sozialhistorische Materialien zum Verhältnis von Bildungs- und Beschäftigungssystemen bei Frauen. In U. Beck, K. H. Hörning, & W. Thomssen (Eds.), *Bildungsexpansion und betriebliche Beschäftigungspolitik: Aktuelle Entwicklungstendenzen im Vermittlungszusammenhang von Bildung und Beschäftigung* (pp. 60–79). Frankfurt/M.: Campus.

Mayer, K. U. (1988). German survivors of World War II: The impact on the life course of the collective experience of birth cohorts. In M. W. Riley (Ed.), *Social structures and human lives: Vol. 1. Social change and the life course* (pp. 229–246). Newbury Park, CA: Sage.

Mayer, K. U., & Brückner, E. (1989). *Lebensverläufe und Wohlfahrtsentwicklung: Konzeption, Design und Methodik der Erhebung von Lebensverläufen der Geburtsjahrgänge 1929–1931, 1939–1941, 1949–1951* (Materialien aus der Bildungsforschung, Vol. 35, Parts I–III). Berlin: Max Planck Institute for Human Development.

Mayer, K. U., & Huinink, J. (1990). Age, period and cohort in the study of the life course: A comparison of classical A-P-C-analysis with event history analysis, or farewell to Lexis? In D. Magnusson & L. R. Bergman (Eds.), *Data quality in longitudinal research* (pp. 211–232). Cambridge: Cambridge University Press.

Mayer, K. U., & Wagner, M. (1996). Lebenslagen und soziale Ungleichheit im hohen Alter. In K. U. Mayer & P. B. Baltes (Eds.), *Die Berliner Altersstudie* (pp. 251–275). Berlin: Akademie Verlag.

Mellström, D., Nilsson, Å., Odén, A., Rundgren, Å., & Svanborg, A. (1982). Mortality among the widowed in Sweden. *Scandinavian Journal of Social Medicine, 10*, 33–41.

Meyer, S., & Schulze, E. (1984). *Wie wir das alles geschafft haben: Alleinstehende Frauen berichten über ihr Leben nach 1945*. Munich: Beck.

Meyer, S., & Schulze, E. (1985). *Von Liebe sprach damals keiner: Familienalltag in der Nachkriegszeit*. Munich: Beck.

Müller, W. (1985). Women's labor force participation over the life course: A model case of social change? In P. B. Baltes, D. L. Featherman, & R. M. Lerner (Eds.), *Life-span development and behavior* (Vol. 7, pp. 43–67). Hillsdale, NJ: Erlbaum.

Müller, W., Handl, J., & Willms, A. (1983). Frauenarbeit im Wandel: Forschungsfragen und Datenbasis. In W. Müller, A. Willms, & J. Handl (Eds.), *Strukturwandel der Frauenarbeit 1880–1980* (pp. 7–24). Frankfurt/M.: Campus.

Palmore, E. B. (1986). Trends in the health of the aged. *The Gerontologist, 26*, 289–302.

Perls, T. T. (1995). The oldest old. *Scientific American, 272*, 50–55.

Riley, M. W. (1987). On the significance of age in sociology. *American Sociological Review, 52*, 1–14.

Ryder, N. B. (1965). The cohort as a concept in the study of social change. *American Sociological Review, 30*, 843–861.

Schaie, K. W. (1965). A general model for the study of developmental problems. *Psychological Bulletin, 64*, 92–107.

Statistisches Bundesamt. (1972). *Bevölkerung und Wirtschaft 1872–1972*. Stuttgart: Kohlhammer.

Tegtmeyer, H. (1976). Berufliche und soziale Umschichtung der Bevölkerung: Methodische Anmerkung zur Planung, Durchführung und Aufbereitung der Befragung. *Zeitschrift für Bevölkerungswissenschaft, 76*, 4–33.

Willms, A. (1983). Grundzüge der Entwicklung der Frauenarbeit von 1880 bis 1980. In W. Müller, A. Willms, & J. Handl (Eds.), *Strukturwandel der Frauenarbeit 1880–1980* (pp. 25–54). Frankfurt/M.: Campus.

World Health Organization (WHO). (1978). *Manual of the international statistical classification of diseases, injuries, and causes of death. Based on the recommendations of the Ninth Revision Conference, 1975, and adopted by the 29th World Health Assembly*. Geneva.

CHAPTER 4

Six Individual Biographies from the Berlin Aging Study

Yvonne Schütze, Clemens Tesch-Römer, and Cornelia Borchers

Each of the 516 participants in the Berlin Aging Study (BASE) has a unique biography and his or her own way of dealing with the positive and negative aspects of old age. At the same time, subgroups in BASE have also had some "objectively" common experiences. Cohorts have lived through the same historical events and changes in German society and, in old age, subgroups of individuals often have an apparently similar status with regard to some life domains (e.g., marital or financial status). This chapter aims to provide an initial sense of the diverse life trajectories in the biographies of BASE participants that arise from the interplay between common and unique life experiences. Three men and three women were selected for deeper consideration in this chapter because of their above- or below-average status on objective life conditions or because they represented statistically normative cases.

1 Introduction

Other chapters of this book describe group-level differences across a broad range of life conditions and domains of functioning. The unique characteristics of the lives and subjective experiences of individuals have only been hinted at (e.g., in scatterplots). In this chapter the biographies of six participants in BASE take center stage. The technique of using biographical approaches to supplement quantitative nomothetic methods has received renewed attention in recent years, and there has been much discussion about appropriate methods (for an overview see the *Ageing and Society* Special Issue on Ageing, Biography and Practice, 1996; Birren, Kenyon, Ruth, Schroots, & Svensson, 1996; Reker & Wong, 1988). The data collection strategy adopted in the BASE Intensive Protocol was not specifically derived from a biographical approach. Participants, for example, were not asked directly, in an open-ended interview, to narrate their life story or to describe their personal experiences of illness or family life in old age. Instead, this information was obtained using tasks and questionnaire items designed to capture subjective experiences in a standardized way (e.g., the life history inventory described in Mayer et al., Chapter 8; the network questionnaire described in Wagner et al., Chapter 10; the "Who am I?" task described in Smith & Baltes, Chapter 7; and various measures of self and personality described in Staudinger et al., Chapter 11 in this volume).

Our primary motive for piecing together six life reports was to consider the extent to which each biography reflected continuity or discontinuity (one of the central theoretical perspectives in BASE; see P. B. Baltes et al., Chapter 1). Could the current life situation be seen as a consequence of earlier conditions and events in these individuals' lives? Did new influences appear in old age that magnified or leveled out interindividual differences? While it is easy to imagine, for instance, that individual differences in early life history (e.g., educational opportunity and attainment, professional and marital career) predict the objective socioeconomic status of an old adult, it is more difficult to foretell individuals' subjective experience of their financial security or life satisfaction. Individuals with apparently similar socioeconomic status may have different subjective needs. Furthermore, personal plans to make use of accumulated resources to enjoy life in old age may be constrained or moderated by unforeseen challenges (e.g., change in health status or functional capacity).

To discover whether old persons' lives reflect aspects of developmental continuity or discontinuity, we looked for three types of information in the available biographical material. First, we reconstructed a chronological lifeline of "social clock" events for each individual (e.g., Elder, 1995; Hagestad & Neugarten, 1985; Kohli, 1986; Mayer, 1981). This encompassed information about family of origin, education, occupational career, family life cycle, and participation in activities. Second, we gathered information to describe the individual's current life situation: for instance, present socioeconomic situation, level of physical and mental functioning, and reported social network. Third, we examined the participants' responses to various questions asking for their subjective evaluations of different aspects of their lives. We also listened to the tape-recordings of the interviews with the selected participants in order to gain a more complete impression of each individual. What do they consider to be the high and low points of their lives at present and in the past? How do they describe themselves? What are their hopes and fears? How do they deal with everyday life?

These three types of information were then pieced together to form a "story." We established two criteria for the completion of each story. First, the story should provide both a picture of the individual's unique characteristics and the societal context and underpinnings of his or her life trajectory. Second, in order to make the theme of continuity versus discontinuity salient, the story should highlight any links or apparent disparities between the individual's past and present life. As a result of our efforts to fulfill these criteria, we concluded that life trajectory conditions contributing to continuity and age-related conditions contributing to discontinuity may not necessarily be mutually exclusive, because they can affect different life domains.

2   Selection of Individual Cases

In order to avoid arbitrary selection, we decided to choose individuals based on their present objective life situation and reported life satisfaction. Six variables were considered: present marital status, place of residence (i.e., community-dwelling vs. institutionalized), education, income, functional capacity (the ability to perform Activities of Daily Living, ADL), and reported life satisfaction (see Table 4.1). Furthermore, we decided to present the biographies of men and women who had statistically "above-average," "average," and "below-average" profiles for their gender across all six of these variables (i.e., relative to the BASE sample). As can be seen in Table 4.1, averages were defined differently for categorical (mode) and continuous variables (a score between the 25th and 75th percentile).

To further explicate this selection procedure, we consider the variables marital status and income as exemplars. More than half (52%) of the men in BASE were married. The modal marital status for men was thus "married." For women, the modal status was

Table 4.1. *Average status on the six selected variables by gender*

	Averages	Men	Women
Marital status	Mode	52.1% married	70.0% widowed
Place of residence	Mode	86.1% in private household	73.0% in private household
Education	Mode	62.0% elementary school	67.4% elementary school
Income	Values between 25th and 75th percentiles	50% lie between 1,800 and 3,275 DM	50% lie between 1,200 and 2,069 DM
Functional capacity (ADL)[a]	Values between 25th and 75th percentiles	50% reach a score of 5	50% lie between 4 and 5
Life satisfaction[b]	Values between 25th and 75th percentiles	50% lie between 3 and 4	50% lie between 3 and 4

[a] A score of 5 signifies the ability to perform five Activities of Daily Living without assistance (cf. Steinhagen-Thiessen & Borchelt, Chapter 5; M. M. Baltes et al., Chapter 14).
[b] Subjective satisfaction with life rated on a five-point scale (max. = 5; cf. Smith et al., Chapter 17).

"widowed" (70% of women in BASE were widowed). Thus, married men and widowed women are statistically typical or average in terms of their marital status. Average income was also determined separately for men and women. Men receiving 1,800 DM per month belonged to the 25th percentile for income, those receiving 3,275 DM to the 75th. Statistically average men therefore have an income between these amounts, whereas statistically average women have between 1,200 and 2,069 DM.

Based on this descriptive categorization, the following normative profiles emerged. The average man is married, lives in a private household, has completed an elementary school education, receives a monthly income between 1,800 and 3,275 DM, has good functional capacity, and expresses positive life satisfaction (response of good [= 4] or satisfactory [= 3] on a five-point scale; cf. Smith et al., Chapter 17). Using these criteria, we narrowed the potential sample of 258 men down to an "average" subgroup of $n = 21$. The average woman is a widow, lives in a private household, has elementary-level schooling, receives an income between 1,200 and 2,069 DM, has good functional capacity, and positive life satisfaction (good or satisfactory). Of the 258 women in BASE, 26 fulfilled these criteria. One man (Mr. Steiner) and one woman (Mrs. Ebener) aged between 80 and 85 were selected from these identified subgroups.

Men and women representing extreme profiles (above-average or below-average) were also identified, although it is interesting to note that no cases were found that satisfied the criteria of being above- or below-average on all six criteria. The first person to be presented below (Ms. Simon) reports high life satisfaction, has an above-average income, and is in excellent physical and mental health. The second (Mrs. Gärtner) is in bad physical and mental health and rates her life satisfaction as "so-so." The third (Mr. Bruckner) is in relatively good health, has an above-average income, and is very dissatisfied with his life. The fourth (Mr. Kleiber) is in need of care, is nearly blind, is very badly off economically, and is not very satisfied with life.

It is important to note that all personal information has been changed so that participants can not be reidentified.

3   Biographies of "Extreme" Cases

3.1   *Ms. Simon – "Auntie Bluestocking"*

Age at the time of the interview: 78
Income: above average
Physical health: above average
Mental abilities: above average
Life satisfaction: above average

Ms. Simon was born in Berlin in 1912. Her father was a white-collar worker with a lower secondary education. Her mother had the same level of formal education, but no occupational training. Ms. Simon herself received a higher secondary education which she completed in 1932 with the "Abitur" (high school certificate) like her two younger siblings. Her brother, who has since died, worked in the same job as her father, and her sister was a teacher.

After the "Abitur" Ms. Simon took a one-year course at a business college. She worked as a secretary until 1945. In 1942, she also began studying at a university, and she completed postsecondary training in 1944 with credentials as an academically trained translator. After the war she was forced to live off her savings until beginning part-time work as a translator at the end of 1945. She completed her doctoral thesis in Romance languages and literature in 1955, and then worked as a freelance translator. From 1965 until her retirement in 1979, she was employed at a university library as an academic assistant.

Out of love for her former job she still performs several hours of unpaid library work a week. She is fully satisfied with her financial situation – she receives a pension of 3,800 DM per month, but has no additional income from other sources.

Apart from her voluntary work at the library, which she can schedule at her convenience, she takes continuing education courses. She is particularly interested in linguistics and archaeology. She enjoys going for long walks and is enthusiastic about the new excursions outside Berlin that were made possible following the collapse of the Berlin Wall and the opening of the East.

Ms. Simon represents an interesting mixture of two seemingly incompatible social types from the early 20th century. As an unmarried woman with many intellectual interests and a high degree of commitment to her work, she can be put in the category of women once labeled "bluestockings." However, she is also the family-oriented aunt who plays a kinkeeper role as an important confidante for numerous relatives – her sister, nieces, first and second cousins. She is well aware of, and accepts, this aspect of her personality: "My sister calls me 'Auntie' – well, that's it really, that does characterize it; I'm basically very close to my family." Her social relationships are not restricted to the family. She also has many friends, particularly women. She mentions 15 female friends and 1 male friend. These friendships are not just incidental acquaintances; they each have endured for at least 30 years.

Ms. Simon was never married, but she does discuss a relationship with a "dominant," complicated man. This was "the most difficult thing" in her life. The sources of her difficulties are easily understood. Ms. Simon was nearly 43 when she finished her doctorate, indicating a strong will, ambition, and persistence – traits that a dominant man presumably could not accept. Describing herself, Ms. Simon says, "I am a person led by emotions, I am strongly attached to people; that is, to some people." And further: "Personal relationships are always important to me, never mind where, even at work and so on." This seems to be the key to the difficult relationship with her partner; on the one hand, she is led by emotions and oriented toward relationships as the feminine stereotype demands; on the other hand, talking about her emotional life immediately reminds her of her work where she can unite her interest in people with her interest in academic topics. Thus, her work has an equal status with her personal relationships – and to this day this does not correspond with the feminine stereotype.

Unquestionably, Ms. Simon's life course has strong features of continuity. The foundation for this continuity was laid in her parental home, where it was made possible for her to complete the "Abitur" and to receive sound occupational training. Although a university degree was not part of her parents' plan, she was able to finance her education independently, and even completed it with a doctorate at a relatively advanced age. Her social relationships with relatives and friends are characterized by the same continuity. Nevertheless, she feels that the continuity of her life, so filled with work and educational and social activities at the time of the interview, could be threatened. When asked, "What is the most difficult thing in your life at present?" she answers that she needs to decide whether to give up the apartment in which she has lived since 1969 in order to move into sheltered housing for senior citizens. Her biggest fear is that she might lose her mental capacities and end up in a crowded hospital ward. Ironically, it is this sense of realistic self-evaluation, her ability to consider all of the possibilities of her situation, that casts a shadow over her life. Objectively, this sober assessment of future developments may facilitate important future planning, for instance, by leading her to select accommodation that includes nursing care should the need arise. Still, it may be the case that for someone like Ms. Simon, who could always rely on herself and her intellectual abilities, the fear of losing these capacities looms larger than for someone who sees life as being determined by fate, God, or by other people.

3.2   Mrs. Gärtner – "One day is just like the next here"

> Age at the time of the interview: 95
> Income: below average
> Physical health: below average
> Mental abilities: below average
> Life satisfaction: "so-so"

In clinical terms, Mrs. Gärtner is diagnosed as having a moderate level of dementia. This means that she cannot remember most of the events that are seen as constituting a biography. Nonetheless, we will try to sketch her life course with the help of the fragments of information we have. In this case, another issue seems more important to us. The label "demented" often evokes the image of mental deterioration, incoherent speech, and complete loss of the capacity to make oneself understood. Mrs. Gärtner is one of many examples we encountered who show that this assumption is not necessarily true, and that an impairment of mental abilities does not mean that one is unable to describe one's situation or to talk about everyday matters.

Mrs. Gärtner was born in Berlin in 1895. She cannot remember her father's occupation, but knows her mother was a domestic servant. Both parents had an elementary school education. Mrs. Gärtner had four brothers, two of whom are certainly dead. She cannot recall whether the other two are still alive.

After finishing elementary education, Mrs. Gärtner completed an apprenticeship at a grocery store and worked there until her marriage in 1916. Her husband was a printer. Her daughter was born in 1917, and her husband died two or three years later. Apparently she can hardly remember her husband or their first meeting. It is not even clear that he really did die so early: At a later point in the interview, she states that she lived with her husband before moving into the nursing home where she is at present. She refers to a two- or three-year period of work as a switchboard operator for the post office, but does not remember the date or whether she had other jobs during her working life. Thus, the period between 1920 and 1961, when she claims to have retired, as well as the date of her move to the nursing home, remain unknown. She was transferred to the facility by a doctor; it was not her own decision.

Her self-definition, "Who am I?" consists of only one succinct and unambiguous sentence: "I am old and frail." All of the following statements refer to the situation in the home and not to herself. First, she remembers special occasions: there used to be singing and music, and a summer party, which appears to have provided a break in the daily monotony, recently took place. "Here, one day is just like the next," she says. For the party, however, they were taken outside "for several hours," and were served "coffee and goulash." She clearly also remembers events that affect her directly. For instance, a male nurse comes into her room during the interview, greets each of the five roommates loudly and says a few words to them. He asks Mrs. Gärtner, "Who am I, what's my name?" She laughs a little and says, "Christian." "That's right," says Christian, in the manner of a schoolteacher, and then asks her something he should know, "When are you going home, then?" She answers, "Not at all, I haven't got an apartment anymore." "Well, then you can stay with me," he says, and she laughs in agreement. One has the feeling that this is a little ritual, perhaps the nurse is testing her. When asked whether there are people she feels very close to, she immediately mentions the home's director. She lists two other nurses as less close friends, but can not remember their names. When asked whether she has spoken to someone about personal matters during the three previous months, she names her son-in-law, Rolf, who visits her every four weeks. Allegedly, Rolf is 90 years old. After further questioning by the interviewer, Mrs. Gärtner also assigns him the status of a person who is very close to her.

Mrs. Gärtner has a blind roommate whom she tries to cheer up. She herself does not receive comfort, but says that she does not need any. When asked about visitors in the four weeks before the interview, she immediately remembers her son-in-law and then her daughter. Asked for her daughter's name, there is a little pause, an embarrassed smile, and then she remembers: "Ingrid." Ingrid's year of birth is no problem, however: 1917. The fact that she mentions Rolf when talking about personal conversations, but not her daughter, and that she immediately recalls his name but not hers, suggests that she feels closer to her son-in-law than to her daughter. It seems clear that her relationship with her daughter is not particularly close. Answering the question "How would you describe your relationship with your children?" she replies, half laughing, half sighing, "What can I say?" and is silent. On other occasions, remarks such as "That's hard to say," or "so-so," serve as generic responses when answering questions she has not understood. Thus she replies to the question about "the most difficult thing" in her life with "so-so." This strategy allows her to maintain a façade of communication and to cover up her memory gaps and her difficulties in understanding with dignity. She is also able to cope with everyday life and to enjoy the little variety of life that there is in a nursing home.

3.3   Mr. Bruckner – "Patching things up with my family, that's my main problem"

Age at the time of the interview: 84
Income: above average
Physical health: below average
Mental abilities: above average
Life satisfaction: below average

Mr. Bruckner was born in Berlin in 1908. Both parents had an elementary school education. His mother was a tailor, his father began as an apprentice weaver and worked his way up to become the technical manager at a weaving mill. Twin siblings were born a year before Mr. Bruckner's birth, but died after a few days. Mr. Bruckner also mentions two younger "stepbrothers" – orphaned cousins who were adopted by his parents. Both cousins have died.

Mr. Bruckner finished school with a lower secondary education ("Mittlere Reife," an intermediate school certificate) and took up a business apprenticeship. He also took courses at a textile and clothing college. After his training he was a white-collar worker at a textile factory; two years later he became its manager. There he met his future wife, who worked as a secretary and bookkeeper until their marriage in 1935. He moved to a different firm that year and became a sales representative. A daughter was born in 1938, but died within a month. In 1940 he was called up for military service. His first son was born the same year. His second son was born in 1942, but died two years later.

Mr. Bruckner served on almost all fronts during World War II; in France, Italy, Russia, and Rumania. After three years as a prisoner of war in Siberia he returned to what had since become East Berlin. After a three-month recovery period, he worked as a gardener for six months. He then became a sales representative in the textile industry in 1949, and in 1961, he moved on to a state-owned firm where he was responsible for buying, selling, and bookkeeping. In 1971 he was promoted to deputy director. Seven years after retiring in 1973, he moved from East to West Berlin. His wife became very ill in 1985, and he nursed her until her death in 1990. Looking back, he sees this phase as "the most difficult thing" he experienced in his life.

His financial situation at the time of the interview is good, with a monthly pension of more than 2,800 DM. In addition, he has money invested in stocks and shares. Mr. Bruckner has already given his son a large sum of money in advance of his inheritance. His physical health is satisfactory given that he can carry out all ADL without help. However, he suffered a heart attack three weeks after his wife's death and then two attacks of sudden weakness requiring an emergency doctor. His biggest fear is that he could one day be in permanent need of nursing. "I don't want to become a burden to anyone." Nevertheless, neither his health nor his fear of needing permanent care worry him most. Instead, he sees his attacks of weakness as being indicators of his psychological situation. On the one hand, his feelings of stress result from the loss of his wife, which has left him feeling lonely. On the other hand, he mentions a troubled relationship with his son, daughter-in-law, and granddaughter as being the main reason for his lack of life satisfaction, his depressive mood, and his physical symptoms.

His loneliness and dissatisfaction are not compensated for by his many relationships with friends and relatives. He met most of these friends at an activities club to which he has belonged for over 10 years. His social network comprises 39 persons and he has contacts of varying frequency with all of them. However, he believes that his relationships have diminished "a great deal" during the past five years.

We do not know what had happened between him and his children, but it must have caused a deep rift between them. When asked, "What is the most difficult thing in your life at present?" he replies, "Well, the relationship with my children." Answering the question about hopes and fears, he responds, "Patching things up with my family – well, yes, that's my main problem, yes." All his thoughts and energies seem centered on this problem, and regardless of the topic of conversation, he always returns to it. However, it is not clear whether he is actually attempting to achieve reconciliation himself, or whether he is waiting for his family to take the first step. At the end of his life – and this is the way he sees it himself – he is not comforted by his many friends and relatives; he only really feels close to his son and his family, who appear not to want to keep up the contact anymore.

This suggests that his lack of life satisfaction is not directly associated with his age. Presumably he would have been able to cope with his wife's death better were it not for the argument with his son. Since the conflict arose after his wife's death, there may be some connection between the two events.

3.4   Mr. Kleiber – Methodical Life Planning

Age at the time of the interview: 96
Income: below average
Physical health: below average
Mental abilities: above average
Life satisfaction: below average

Mr. Kleiber was born in 1896 in East Prussia. His father was a shoemaker and, as was usual at the time, his mother had no occupational training. His father died in 1928, his mother in 1943. Mr. Kleiber had seven siblings, five of whom were half brothers and half sisters. All have died. After finishing elementary school, Mr. Kleiber was apprenticed as a retail salesman in the food trade. At 17 he moved to Düsseldorf where one of his half brothers lived. In his own words, he wanted to "settle down" there, but realized within a week that things were not ideal for him and immediately moved on to the city of S. (now in Poland). There he took up work as a shop assistant at a grocery. Because he had a hernia, he avoided conscription for military service during World War I. In 1923 he met his future wife, also an assistant at a grocery, at a dance. In 1924, the year of his marriage, he was able to open a shop himself. Most likely this was only possible because his wife then worked in the shop with him. However, this woman does not seem to have left any traces in his life. When asked about people to whom he still feels very close despite their deaths, he mentions four friends, but not his wife. She neither belongs to the persons who played an important role in his life nor to those he likes to think of.

Their first daughter was born a year after their wedding, followed by a second daughter two years later. Eight years after that, a son was born; his existence may well be due to the political situation at the time. During the Nazi period, there was a massive propaganda campaign to raise birthrates through financial and other incentives. In the Kleiber family this may have led to the planning of a third child a relatively long time after the first two.

The city of S. became Polish in 1945, and Mr. Kleiber's shop was taken over, in his words, by the "Poles." He sees this event as "the most difficult thing" in his life. He left S. with his family and moved to Berlin. First he ran a horse-and-cart business. In 1948 he leased a grocery shop, which he gave up in 1952 to lease another in a different part of the city. His first wife died at this time. In 1961 he retired and passed on the shop to his son; however, he continued to work eight and a half hours a day until 1973, earning 1,200 DM a month. Upon his retirement he moved to a different part of town, into a house of which he owned half. In 1965 he put a "lonely hearts ad" in the personal column of a newspaper, and met a woman 12 years younger than himself. Although she had been a shop assistant in a jewelry store, she soon found herself working in the son's grocery shop. Mr. Kleiber's entire interest is focused on the food trade. He has no hobbies and belonged to no organizations except for a shopkeepers' trade association. About himself he says, "My job was my hobby." And answering the question about "the best thing" in his life, he mentions his successful business.

Mr. Kleiber's strong identification with his job must have had a great influence on his children. All three completed a lower secondary education; in those days this was not common for children of someone with a elementary education, particularly not for daughters born in the 1920s. Mr. Kleiber's son took over the shop, and the daughters also remained in the food trade. The elder, a widow, had her own grocery store, and the second, who is married, still has a butcher shop. Even the grandchildren continued the family tradition of educational aspirations within the context of changing societal trends. Mr. Kleiber's grandson, born in 1950, also has a lower secondary education, and his granddaughter, born in 1956, has a higher secondary education, the "Abitur." Considering the change of the times (i.e., a limited future for the small-scale food trade), the grandson's choice of work is not really very different from his grandfather's; he is an estate agent. The granddaughter broke with family tradition and became a social worker. Although Mr. Kleiber sees both grandchildren several times a month, they do not appear to play an important role in his life as he does not mention them as persons to whom he feels close or with whom he is in regular contact.

Until around 1986 Mr. Kleiber was reasonably fit and could still work in his garden, but he has increasingly needed nursing care. He separated from his partner in 1988, but the relationship does not seem to have been completely severed, as he still mentions her as a friend and speaks of monthly phone calls with her.

Mr. Kleiber always knew how to connect his business and private goals. With the help of his first wife he was able to start his own business, his second partner was selected purposefully and also put to work in the family shop, and it was presumably no coincidence that all three children chose careers in the food trade. Despite being bedridden, nearly blind, and almost without income (he receives a monthly pension of 740 DM), his planning competence remains. He has managed to arrange an unparalleled schedule of nursing care for himself. A sister-in-law and two other women, all aged over 60, and all living in former East Germany, take turns in staying with him and nursing him for one to three months.

As a consequence, despite his frailty and need for care, his life is as well organized and planned as in his more active days. In the morning, one of his caregivers readies him for the day and moves him into another room for lunch. In the afternoon he watches television and drinks coffee. He is put to bed early. Even his contacts with his children are well organized: "Every Sunday my children come for coffee and we chat until the evening." Just as they followed his career footsteps as a matter of course, they appear to find it completely natural to visit their father every Sunday, and only then. Relations between father and children are thus confined to a regular pattern of contacts on a certain day, at a predetermined time, with no spontaneous visits in between. However, there are some indications that relations with his daughters are slightly closer. His son visits a little less frequently, and Mr. Kleiber would ask his daughters and not his son for advice if a decision had to be made.

Conversely, Mr. Kleiber assumes that all three children would ask him for counsel if necessary. This indicates that he himself feels that he is still in control. His children do not help him financially or with his nursing care. It is not clear whether he does not want assistance or whether they prefer to restrict their involvement to their Sunday visits. Their participation could presumably muddle up the tight caregiving schedule, for example, through arguments between his children and helpers about practical questions.

How does this man, whose entire life was determined by nonstop work, cope with his enforced passivity? He has not been able to leave his apartment for three and a half years due to bad health. Despite having arranged his own care, he has become an object of his nursing schedule and feels governed by his helpers. He also misses activities like gardening that were possible only a few years ago.

His feeling of dependency on others, and on fate, become clear in his answer to the question about hopes for the future: "I hope I'll be sent for soon. A lump of flesh like me shouldn't be left like this." He does not say, "I wish I could die," but "I hope I'll be sent for soon." Just as he needs someone to put him to bed or to help him with meals, he feels dependent on death fetching him, but death has kept him waiting. Describing himself as "a lump of flesh," he distances himself from his body, seeing it as inanimate material. In other words, as his body no longer functions according to his will, it has become an object that needs to be administered by others, a lump that he no longer wants anything to do with.

Recognizing his dependency on others, his second hope is that his caregivers will not leave him. Although he cannot rely on his body anymore, his spirit is unbroken. Accordingly his greatest fear is that he could become "mentally disturbed" in the future.

In its structured activity pattern and planned sobriety, Mr. Kleiber's biography represents what Weber (1964) calls methodical life planning or what Riesman (1950) describes as typical for the internally guided individual. From an outside perspective, this life is characterized by continuity into very old age. From an inside perspective, enforced passivity in old age due to bad physical health obviously signifies a discontinuity that is linked to an ambivalence toward the self. Since the interview, death has fulfilled Mr. Kleiber's expectations and "sent for" him.

4   Biographies of Statistically "Average" Cases

4.1   Hildegard Ebener – "After all, one has to cope with one's situation"

Age at the time of the interview: 83
Income: average
Physical health: average
Mental abilities: average
Life satisfaction: average

Mrs. Ebener was born in 1909 as the first of three children in a small town in Saxony. Her father was a self-employed instrument-maker and her mother had completed an apprenticeship as a milliner. The family moved to Berlin in the year of Mrs. Ebener's birth. Her two brothers Heinz and Horst were born there in 1911 and 1920. Her relationship with her parents was the only one to remain intact until their deaths. Mrs. Ebener has not been in contact with the older of her two brothers for years. She remarks that he was very much changed by his wartime experiences and his injuries. Although her younger brother and his family live in Berlin, she has not seen him for over one and a half years.

The family moved from a working-class area to a middle-class district in the south of Berlin in 1911. When her father was called up for military service in 1915, the children were sent to stay with their grandparents in Saxony for three years. Hildegard Ebener finished elementary school in 1923. Although she wanted to work in the "fashion trade" like her mother, she eventually decided to do something "more respectable" and trained to become a bookkeeper. Because she worked hard and was committed to her job, her employers kept her on after her apprenticeship and gave her more and more responsibility in the ensuing years.

In 1932 Hildegard married Johannes Ebener, a textile trader who had been a school friend of hers. She applied for the pension money she had already accumulated and they used it to set up a home. In 1935 the Jewish-owned firm she worked for went bankrupt following the increased persecution of Jewish citizens and the so-called Aryanization of Jewish shops. This brought her job and her career to an end. The time then seemed ripe to start a family. Thus, Hildegard Ebener's life developed in a way that is only now becoming a matter of course for women – even if her decision was determined mainly by economic and political developments. She first sought recognition in her work and then decided to become a mother.

The family became her new focus in life. In 1936 her first child died after only two months. A year later her daughter Beate was born. When her son Bernhard was born in 1942, her husband was in military service. Hildegard experienced the fate of all mothers whose husbands were away at war; she had to cope on her own. She describes the city's bombardment, which she witnessed directly, as "the most difficult thing" in her life. "Just getting out of there in one piece. . . . It was terrible. How can they just exterminate people like that?" Her husband returned from a prisoner-of-war camp in the autumn of 1945.

Johannes Ebener's career forced the family to move frequently. Between 1951 and 1974 Hildegard had to pack up the family belongings approximately every three years. When the family moved to West Germany in 1953, their 17-year-old daughter Beate stayed in Berlin with her future husband. After Mr. Ebener retired in 1974, the Ebeners returned to Berlin. Mr. Ebener carried on doing odd jobs until 1981, the last of which was as a "man Friday" at a supermarket. Having brought up the children, a new phase of life began for Mrs. Ebener; she had much more time for her husband, friends, and acquaintances. The Ebeners traveled abroad, went hiking with friends, and often visited the theater. At home they frequently played cards with an aunt. A coffee afternoon with female friends became a regular fixture.

Johannes Ebener died in 1984 after a short stay in the hospital. His widow moved to the smaller and cheaper apartment which is still her home. Although her living standard is somewhat lower than before, she is satisfied. "One just has to make ends meet." Her grandson Peter, whom the Ebeners adopted when he was 11 after their son's divorce in 1974, moved in with his grandmother (and adoptive mother) after his grandfather died. Having lost her husband, Mrs. Ebener created a new role for herself, one that required a great deal of commitment. Peter has a drug problem that his grandmother describes euphemistically: "The boy can't cope with life." She adds, "When I stand by someone, I really do." Peter's difficulties forced Mrs. Ebener to confront problems that were completely unknown to her before. She feels she has been left in the lurch by her son Bernhard, who lives in western Germany. But she cannot, and does not want to, avoid this family responsibility. "At the end of the day, you have to take things as they are," she says, hoping that "everything will change for the better."

As she is in good health she manages everyday activities well. Her unstable blood pressure worries her less than the visual impairment caused by cataracts, because she does not want to be "dependent on help from others." Hildegard Ebener knows that she would have to move to a nursing home if she needed continuous nursing care. Supporting Peter has used up her financial reserves. The two of them live on her widow's pension and his social security payments; a total of 2,200 DM a month. Mrs. Ebener finds this sufficient.

Good social relationships are of vital importance to her. One of her closest confidantes is her daughter Beate who lives in the United States. They write and telephone regularly. Mrs. Ebener visits her daughter in the States once a year. In contrast, her relationship with her son (who is also the father of her adoptive son), owner of a clothes shop in western Germany, is strained, partly due to his new wife. Nevertheless, mother and son are in regular but "much too infrequent" contact. The great distance from her daughter and the unsatisfactory relationship with Bernhard sometimes make her fear that she could "suddenly be all alone." However, she says, "I am a person who can suppress a lot of worries in any situation, and for some time; you can't always be worried." Mrs. Ebener compensates for the failures in her familial relations by maintaining close friendships with several women.

In the five years before the interview, Hildegard Ebener has also made some new friends. For instance, she mentions a female friend to whom she has only recently "really grown close." However, she believes that she has less contacts than other women of her age. While her relationships within the family have remained the same, she finds that friends and acquaintances who have enough time for her have gained importance. She feels very content with her friendships, but only partly satisfied with her familial relationships. Nevertheless, looking back, Mrs. Ebener describes "the long years living with my husband and my children" as "the best thing," and her own family, her parents, and parents-in-law as "the most important thing" in her life. These memories help her to "shake off worries" and to cope with the present.

Mrs. Ebener goes hiking with her female friends several times a month; she takes day trips and attends lectures. The coffee afternoons which began in the 1970s still take place. She has also kept up the hobby of her childhood years, collecting stamps. Despite being interested in current affairs, there is no sign that Mrs. Ebener was ever committed to a cause beyond her circle of family and friends. She was never a member of a club, association, or political party. In accordance with the stereotypical female role, her activities were always restricted to her private world and her immediate surroundings.

Mrs. Ebener does not want to "have any more bad experiences." She notes an increasing loss of energy and lack of drive. However, she accepts these changes without giving way to them. Characteristically, she says, "After all, one has to cope." As regards the future, she remarks optimistically and concisely, "I've got a lot to live for and don't want to die for a long time yet."

4.2   Karl Steiner – A Settled Worker with Daydreams

Age at the time of the interview: 82
Income: average
Physical health: average
Mental abilities: average
Life satisfaction: average

Karl Steiner was born in 1910 in a part of Berlin to which he has remained loyal throughout his life. The only three homes he ever inhabited were within a 500-yard radius. He moved into the first place of his own in 1938, and lived there for 32 years, and has lived in the "new" apartment for 22 years since. The two places where he worked until his retirement, a factory making furniture and a Berlin theater, are also close by.

Karl Steiner's parents married in 1909 and their two sons were born in 1910 and 1917. His mother, who died at the age of 89 in 1977, was a nurse, and his father, who died at 68, two years after the end of World War II, was a tram driver. Education was highly regarded in the Steiner family and Karl's parents made it possible for him to learn to play the violin. His parents often read newspapers and sometimes books. Among the activities of his youth were sports (he was a member of a workers' sports club), but also visits to concerts, museums, exhibitions, the theater, and the cinema. Mr. Steiner was influenced by the family's interests and wanted to become a musician.

However, he could not fulfill his dream and, upon leaving elementary school in 1924, took up an apprenticeship at a Berlin furniture factory. While training to be a joiner, he went to an evening school where he also learned drawing and furniture design. At 18 he passed his examination to become a journeyman and continued work at the factory until losing his job in December 1929 due to the economic crisis. Mr. Steiner suffered the fate of many workers at the time, remaining unemployed for three and a half years. In 1933, at the very beginning of the Nazi regime, he again found work at the firm which had dismissed him three years earlier. He joined the Storm Troopers ("Sturmabteilung," SA) the same year, but left again in 1939. We do not have any information about Karl Steiner's reasons for joining the SA, and leaving again at the peak of National Socialism, but it is possible that joining the SA was a reaction to the economic rise under Hitler, which brought him work and a steady income once again. After four years Steiner left his old firm and moved closer to fulfilling his musical dreams; he became a stagehand at a theater. He worked there for nearly 40 years until his retirement in 1974, only interrupted by four years of military service.

As a soldier Karl Steiner also experienced the fate typical for his generation. He was called up in December 1939 at the age of 29. He was sent to Holland, Belgium, and France, and then in 1940–41 to the eastern front in Poland and Russia. He fell ill in 1942 and was so badly injured in 1943 that he had to be sent home. This probably saved his life. His brother was killed in 1943. From Mr. Steiner's point of view, the war was "the most difficult thing" in his life.

Mr. Steiner met his first wife Else several years before the war at a dance near his home. Else was pregnant when they married in August 1937 and set up their own home. Their only daughter Anna was born in January 1938. Else was a tailor and later also worked in a theater as a costume maker. Mr. Steiner does not say much about his first marriage, but when asked what "the best thing" in his life was, he replies, "love." Else died in 1965 after one and a half years in the hospital.

Mr. Steiner met his second wife Eva two years after Else's death during a stay at a health resort. Eva was a factory worker, but became an administrative employee in local government offices during the course of their marriage. Mr. Steiner was 57 and his wife 29, the same age as his daughter, when they married. However, Mr. Steiner's relationship with his daughter does not seem to have suffered from the presence of a young "stepmother." Mr. Steiner sees Anna at least once a week. The relationship with Eva's daughter from a previous marriage, born in 1956, is completely different. For unknown reasons Mr. Steiner has no contact at all with his stepdaughter or her three children, his only grandchildren.

His second wife Eva and his daughter Anna are the two most important people in Mr. Steiner's social network, which consists of 14 people altogether. His close connections to these two women are reflected in the pattern of the day he describes in the Yesterday Interview (cf. M. M. Baltes et al., Chapter 14). In the morning he gets up with his wife, prepares breakfast, and makes the beds after she has left for work. Being a lot younger than her husband, Eva does the rest of the housework; for example, she makes lunch and supper after coming home from her job. On the day described by Mr. Steiner, his daughter Anna picked him up and took him to a doctor's appointment. Afterward the two of them had coffee together in a café. This day seems typical. Karl Steiner phones Anna daily, sees her once a week, and asks for her advice on important decisions. What is more, Anna has retired early due to illness and lives very near to her father. The relationships with his wife and daughter are "the best thing" in Mr. Steiner's life at the time of the interview. However, Anna's bad health casts a dark shadow. Answering the question about "the best thing" in his life he says, "The present situation, really, as long as my daughter stays healthy and my wife and I have the energy to go on another holiday together, in the south."

Mr. Steiner's financial situation would certainly allow a trip to the south. His health is also satisfactory. Although he needs crutches to walk following a hip operation, his mobility is not much impaired. This becomes obvious in his choice of a hobby, which shows signs of continuity from his working life. Mr. Steiner is restoring an old boat in association with a friend who was a boatbuilder. Working in his garden plot and collecting coins are some of his other hobbies. Further education and music also remain important to him. Asked to describe himself, the lifelong interest in education and music that he could never fully express come to the fore: "I'm someone who, having reached old age, thinks a lot about the past. I realize that one probably should have done things differently in the younger years, as this could have been to one's advantage now. For instance, one could have done more schoolwork." And, "What interests me are today's events in world politics; and things that are related to my old job, for example, new theater productions."

5 Differences and Common Features

At first glance it is the diversity of these life histories and situations in old age that is most noticeable. This variety manifests itself most clearly in the different physical and mental functioning of these six BASE participants. Looking at the extreme cases first, we found Ms. Simon representing the ideal of successful aging. She is healthy and as mentally fit as younger people – as can be seen from the fact that she is still active in her old job. In contrast, Mrs. Gärtner embodies a very negative image of old age. She is virtually immobile and very impaired in her mental functioning. Mr. Kleiber's physical (but not mental) health is possibly even worse than Mrs. Gärtner's. He is not only bedridden but also nearly blind. Although Ms. Simon also differs from Mrs. Gärtner and Mr. Kleiber in her socioeconomic status, the main difference between them is surely their health. Of course, Ms. Simon is 16–17 years younger than the other two.

However, despite the major health impairments affecting both Mrs. Gärtner and Mr. Kleiber, large differences in their situations are obvious. Our hypothesis is that these differences are based on differential coping strategies (cf. Bandura, 1982). Mr. Kleiber does not wait for things to happen to him. When his health became worse, he made sure that there were people to nurse him. In contrast, Mrs. Gärtner seems not to have registered her loss of competence and was sent to a nursing home. It is unclear whether she was as badly impaired when first admitted to the home, but it can be assumed that her abilities decreased further due to her limited communication opportunities. In other words, there seems to be a reciprocal distance between self and environment in Mrs. Gärtner's case. Mr. Kleiber distances himself from his body, but not from his surroundings. With his caregiving arrangement he created a situation in which his three caregivers reappear at regular intervals. This meant that he always has "new" communication partners who, in turn, are not worn out by the dreary routine of daily nursing.

Mrs. Ebener and Mr. Bruckner also exemplify different ways of dealing with structurally similar situations. Both are about the same age, in reasonably good health, and do not have any mental impairments. However, their relationships with other family members are difficult. Whereas Mrs. Ebener manages to deal with the strained relationship with her son and with the difficulties due to her adoptive son's drug problems by maintaining emotionally satisfying relationships with her female friends, Mr. Bruckner concentrates almost exclusively on the broken relations with his son, thus losing sight of old friendships.

After emphasizing interindividual differences in dealing with structurally similar life situations, we now consider the roles of social background, historical events, gender, and generation in the course of these lives (cf. Maas et al., Chapter 3). We then ask which factors, over and above personality traits, appear to be important for life satisfaction (cf. Smith et al., Chapter 17).

Looking at these life courses through the filter of educational and occupational careers, it is clear that each individual's social background set the stage for his or her later position in the social hierarchy (Mayer, 1981). Only Ms. Simon came from a middle-class background, only she took the "Abitur" and could thus begin a university education. All of the others came from a craftsman's, working-class or petit bourgeois background. The tendency toward a certain upward mobility in comparison to the family of origin – as exemplified by the careers in small businesses – is perhaps not atypical for this generation. Of course, all six participants shared the experience of the Great Depression, unemployment, and war. However, the continuity of their occupational careers seems only to have been disturbed, not completely disrupted, by these events (Maas et al., Chapter 3). This applies to the men and to the unmarried Ms. Simon, who was even able to continue her career at a higher level after the war. Starting a family ended the careers of the other two women, as was the case for the majority of this generation of women. Mrs. Ebener had her children after losing her job and Mrs. Gärtner stopped work when she married (it is not clear whether she resumed work later on). Even though the war did not completely shatter the lives of any of these individuals, it is often remembered as "the most difficult thing" in their lives. Something else the members of this generation seem to have in common is their work ethic. None of them took early retirement, and Ms. Simon and Mr. Kleiber even continued working after their retirement. In some ways Mrs. Ebener did so too, by taking care of her addicted grandson.

The educational and occupational careers are also the main determinants of the economic situation in old age. Ms. Simon receives the highest pension, but does not own any property. Typically for his trade, the self-employed shopkeeper Mr. Kleiber receives very little pension, but owns half of a house. Mrs. Gärtner and Mrs. Ebener are in the lower income bracket, as is typical for widows from the lower social classes (Allmendinger, Brückner, & Brückner, 1991; cf. Mayer et al., Chapter 8). This is not true for Mr. Bruckner and Mr. Steiner who, due to their lifelong employment, both have a pension guaranteeing them a reasonably comfortable position in old age (Brückner & Mayer, 1987). However, the members of this generation seem to be rather undemanding and content with a more modest standard of living; none of them are dissatisfied with their financial situation.

The economic situation does not play the decisive role in determining the life satisfaction of these six individuals (see Smith et al., Chapter 17). Health seems to be a much more important factor, with respect to the current situation (for Mrs. Gärtner and Mr. Kleiber), the deterioration that can be expected, and the fear of becoming dependent on others (for Ms. Simon, Mrs. Ebener, and Mr. Bruckner).

Coming back to our first question on the extent to which age and aging conditions can level out differences in life histories and subjective interpretation, we see that the otherwise considerable differences between five of these six cases are smoothed out in their common rejection of an existing or anticipated dependency on others. Being afraid of dependency on others means not being able to hope for (much less being able to expect) assistance and nursing care from members of one's own informal social network. Dependency on others thus stands for dependency on institutions. This means that an anticipated loss of functioning is itself less threatening than its association with dependency on anonymous caregivers. The case of Mr. Steiner, who already uses crutches and therefore has every reason to fear a decline in health, exemplifies that differences between individuals can also increase in old age. In contrast to all five others, Mr. Steiner lives with the certainty that he can rely on the people close to him for nursing care when the need arises. (Answering the question "Who would look after you, should you become bedridden?" he names his relatively young wife and his daughter.) The possibility of needing permanent nursing care does not appear to be "the most difficult thing" in his life, and he thus differs from the others presented here. In other words, the dependency on unknown others, who have had no role in one's biography, versus the knowledge that one can rely on close friends and relations not only produces differences between persons in otherwise similar circumstances, but also disrupts the continuity of everyday life and of one's self-image.

However, enjoyment of life is not only diminished by a real or imagined loss of self-determination; emotional ties to others also have an important influence. Although Mr. Kleiber suffers because of his immobility and his dependency on his nurses, his distress is reduced somewhat by the good relations he maintains with his children and caregivers. Vice versa, problems with people one actually feels close to can have a negative influence on life satisfaction. This particularly applies to Mr. Bruckner, whose financial situation is good, but whose health and happiness is primarily marred by the dispute within his family. In a way, this is also true for Mrs. Ebener, although she compensates for her disturbed family relations with friendships.

These six biographies do not allow us to draw conclusions about the general life situation of all older people. However, they direct our attention to the conditions that seem to be necessary for today's elderly people to form a positive attitude toward life. The first is a state of health that allows a certain measure of independence and mobility. Emotionally satisfying ties to others are, however, possibly even more important. Such relationships not only provide a feeling of security and reliability, but also help to make sense of one's own life history.

References

Ageing and Society Special Issue on Ageing, Biography and Practice. (1996). *Ageing and Society, 16* (6).

Allmendinger, J., Brückner, H., & Brückner, E. (1991). Arbeitsleben und Lebensarbeitsentlohnung: Zur Entstehung von finanzieller Ungleichheit im Alter. In K. U. Mayer, J. Allmendinger, & J. Huinink (Eds.), *Vom Regen in die Traufe: Frauen zwischen Beruf und Familie* (pp. 423–459). Frankfurt/M.: Campus.

Bandura, A. (1982). Self-efficacy mechanism in human agency. *American Psychologist, 37,* 122–147.

Birren, J. E., Kenyon, G. M., Ruth, J.-E., Schroots, J. J. F., & Svensson, T. (Eds.). (1996). *Aging and biography: Explorations in adult development.* New York: Springer.

Brückner, E., & Mayer, K. U. (1987). Lebensgeschichte und Austritt aus der Erwerbstätigkeit im Alter: Am Beispiel der Geburtsjahrgänge 1919–21. *Zeitschrift für Sozialisationsforschung und Erziehungssoziologie, 2,* 101–116.

Elder, G. H., Jr. (1995). The life course paradigm: Social change and individual development. In P. Moen, G. H. Elder Jr., & K. Lüscher (Eds.), *Examining lives in context: Perspectives on the ecology of human development* (pp. 101–139). Washington, DC: American Psychological Association.

Hagestad, G. O., & Neugarten, B. L. (1985). Age and the life course. In R. H. Binstock & E. Shanas (Eds.), *Handbook of aging and the social sciences* (2nd ed., pp. 35–61). New York: Van Nostrand Reinhold.

Kohli, M. (1986). Social organization and subjective construction of the life course. In A. B.
        Sorensen, F. E. Weinert, & L. R. Sherrod (Eds.), *Human development and the life
        course* (pp. 271–292). Hillsdale, NJ: Erlbaum.
Mayer, K. U. (1981). Gesellschaftlicher Wandel und soziale Struktur des Lebenslaufs. In J.
        Matthes (Ed.), *Lebenswelt und soziale Probleme* (pp. 492–501). Frankfurt/M.: Campus.
Reker, G. T., & Wong, P. T. P. (1988). Aging as an individual process: Toward a theory of personal
        meaning. In J. E. Birren & V. L. Bengtson (Eds.), *Emergent theories of aging* (pp.
        214–246). New York: Springer.
Riesman, D. (1950). *The lonely crowd: A study of the changing American character.* New Haven,
        CT: Yale University Press.
Weber, M. (1964). *Wirtschaft und Gesellschaft* (Vol. 1). Cologne: Kiepenheuer & Witsch.

Major Results from the Four Research Units

CHAPTER 5

Morbidity, Medication, and Functional Limitations in Very Old Age

Elisabeth Steinhagen-Thiessen and Markus Borchelt

This chapter provides a brief overview of the main research topics, applied methods, and basic results of the Internal Medicine and Geriatrics Unit of the Berlin Aging Study (BASE). It focuses on (a) physical illnesses, (b) medication and related risks, and (c) functional incapabilites with regard to performance-oriented functional limitations and need for help with Activities of Daily Living (ADL). Profiles of functioning in each domain are presented from various perspectives. Particular emphasis lies on the recognition of potential determinants of morbidity in old age, exemplified by the atherosclerosis risk profile, and on the analysis of qualitative aspects of medication (over-, under-, and inappropriate medication). Finally, based on a recently proposed model of the disablement process in old age, these domains are considered from an integrated (systemic) perspective of health in old age with functional capacity at its center.

The results show a high degree of morbidity, but also indicate many modifiable risk factors for illness and disability, opening new vistas of prevention and therapy in old and very old age.

1   Introduction

Past decades of geriatric research have revealed much evidence indicating that morbidity is not only increased by age-related factors alone, but by modifiable organic risk factors such as fat metabolism disorders (Sorkin, Andres, Muller, Baldwin, & Fleg, 1992; Zimetbaum et al., 1992), functional risk factors such as falls (Tinetti, 1986), or iatrogenic risk factors such as inappropriate drug therapy (Beers et al., 1991; Williamson & Chopin, 1980). The age-related increase of morbidity is accompanied by an increase in the utilization of drugs (Chrischilles et al., 1992; Gilchrist, Lee, Tam, MacDonald, & Williams, 1987). Multimedication associated with multimorbidity poses a particular problem in geriatric medicine because of the many potential adverse drug reactions and drug-drug interactions (Vestal, 1985). Therefore, the development of criteria allowing assessment of medication quality in old age has become an important topic in geriatric research in recent years (Beers et al., 1991; Stuck et al., 1994).

Perhaps the single most essential component in gerontological research and geriatric practice is the emphasis on functional aspects of physical health (Lachs et al., 1990; Rubenstein & Rubenstein, 1992; Stuck, Siu, Wieland, Adams, & Rubenstein, 1993). Significant correlations between physical illness and functional limitations have been described for several chronic diseases such as stroke or coronary heart disease (Pinsky et al., 1985; Pinsky, Jette, Branch, Kannel, & Feinleib, 1990), and osteoarthritis (Jette, Branch, & Berlin, 1990). Apart from these examples, however, representative information is scarce on

131

causal pathways and interactions among multiple illnesses, multiple medications, and multiple functional limitations at ages between 70 and above 100 years (Heikkinen et al., 1984; Manton & Soldo, 1985; Nagi, 1976; Palmore, Nowlin, & Wang, 1985; Verbrugge, 1988).

Recently, a theoretical model of the disablement process in old age has been proposed by Verbrugge and Jette (1994). It emphasizes an integrated perspective of morbidity as a risk factor for functional limitations, which in turn increase the risk for disability and loss of independence in everyday activities. This theoretical framework can be viewed as an important prerequisite in facing the challenge stemming from the increase in life expectancy and the associated increase of very old people in the population (Rosenwaike, 1985). This will further necessitate a better understanding of the differentiation between morbidity-associated development of disability and morbidity-independent development of physical "frailty" (Mor et al., 1989). Each phenomenon will presumably demand different strategies of prevention and intervention and needs further investigation (Rubenstein, Josephson et al., 1984).

2   Central Topics of the Internal Medicine and Geriatrics Unit

With regard to highest ages, no representative studies are available that have collected information on a broad range of clinical and functional indicators allowing detailed analyses on all aspects of somatic health, including intervention and interventional risks. Thus, the Internal Medicine and Geriatrics Unit has reached beyond previous studies (Cornoni-Huntley, Brock, Ostfeld, Taylor, & Wallace, 1986; Shock et al., 1984; Svanborg, 1985) in obtaining a comprehensive overview of somatic multimorbidity, multimedication, and functional limitations on the basis of standardized objective medical and functional assessments for a representative sample of old and very old adults.

The assessment of somatic health focused on six key domains (see Table 5.1): (1) objective health, (2) functional capacity, (3) subjective health, (4) risk profiles, (5) need for medical treatment, and (6) reference values.

Selection of these domains was closely related to the four theoretical orientations of BASE (see P. B. Baltes et al., Chapter 1 in this volume). For example, the medical data protocol was designed (a) to examine *differential aging* in terms of differences between individuals and between domains of health and functioning (Steinhagen-Thiessen & Borchelt, 1993), (b) to analyze *continuity and discontinuity* of health in old age as compared with reported health in younger years (Maas et al., Chapter 3), (c) to estimate specific functional *reserve capacities* in old age (Kage, Nitschke, Fimmel, & Köttgen, 1996), and (d) to analyze *aging as a systemic phenomenon* in a multidisciplinary context (M. M. Baltes et al., Chapter 14; Borchelt et al., Chapter 15).

In order to complete the wide-ranging medical examination schedule with all participants, including those house-bound and bedridden, it was necessary to develop a mobile assessment program. By making extensive use of portable equipment, all participants were visited at their place of residence by geriatricians and dentists who completed basic medical and dental testing, including physical examination, blood sampling, functional assessment, and technical procedures (e.g., electrocardiography [ECG], spirometry, and audiometry) on almost all participants. In contrast, radiological examinations (ultrasound imaging of carotid arteries, quantitative computer tomography [qCT] of the lumbar spine) had to be carried out at the university hospital and could therefore be completed only with mobile and healthy participants ($n = 283$).

The focus was on the examination of the extent and direction of health differences in old age, mainly in terms of multimorbidity (key domain: objective health), multimedica-

Table 5.1. *Key domains, topics, and measurement methods of the Geriatrics Unit in BASE*

Domain	Topic	Methods
Objective health	Cardiovascular system	Interview, examination, resting ECG, Doppler ultrasound, blood pressure
	Musculoskeletal system	Interview, examination, qCT
	Immune system	Flow cytometry, lymphocyte stimulation, MHC-types
	Dental status	Interview, examination, X-ray
Functional capacity	Independence	ADL/IADL scores, aids, and devices
	Physical vigor	Walking distance, grip strength
	Sensorimotor functioning	Balance and gait
	Sensory functioning	Visual acuity, audiometry
Subjective health	General	Standardized interviews
	Comparative	
	Health behavior	
Risk profiles	Genetic determinants	MHC-types, blood group serology, apo-E-types
	Anthropometry	Body Mass Index (BMI), arm span, hip/waist ratio
	Diet	Questionnaire (qualitative)
	Utilization of drugs	Interview
Treatment needs	General	Consensus conferences
	Pharmaceutical	Medication analysis
	Dental treatment needs	Assessment by dentist
Reference values	Functional diagnosis	ECG, spirometry, audiometry
	Clinical chemistry	Serum, plasma, urinalyses
	Radiology	qCT, Doppler ultrasound
	Dentistry	Dental status, X-ray

tion (treatment needs), and disability (functional capacity). In addition to these descriptive aspects, a central question addressed modifiable risk factors for illness and disability in old and very old age.

3   Physical Illnesses in Very Old Age

Laboratory testing is of major importance for the diagnosis of physical illness in old age. Due to the lack of age-adjusted reference values, all clinical interpretations made during the data collection phase were based on unadjusted reference values. However, first results from BASE concerning reference values are now available and are briefly summarized in the following section.

3.1   *Reference Values for Laboratory Screening Parameters*

Virtually all participants consented to venipuncture for laboratory testing ($n =$ 504). The entire procedure (blood withdrawal, storage, transportation, analysis) was conducted in strict adherence to recommendations of the International Federation of Clinical Chemistry (IFCC). A description of laboratory methods used, as well as a detailed report on initial analyses of all parameters investigated are provided elsewhere (Kage et al., 1996).

In brief, the initial analyses indicated that reference values for laboratory tests in old age do not deviate much from those in younger ages. With regard to considered covariates, fasting serum glucose levels were significantly influenced by specific medications and by morbidity. Morbidity also altered many other parameters, for example, electrolytes and protein. Indicators of kidney function (serum creatinine, serum urea) were found to be significantly age-correlated, which is consistent with findings from previous studies and points to a continuous decline in renal function up to highest ages independent of morbidity and medication. Additionally, a negative age correlation was found for blood formation indicators (hemoglobin, erythrocyte count, hematocrit) and for serum calcium. These findings can be interpreted as manifestations of the negative consequences of increasing renal failure with age. In this case, renal dysfunction could be viewed as one reason for other age-related changes in body function, and as an indicator for aging as a systemic phenomenon.

With regard to geriatrics, a definition of "health" as the absence of disease is no longer meaningful because of the high prevalence of diagnosable disorders in old age. For the calculation of reference values, another definition is necessary to identify a reference sample of "rather healthy" subjects. Despite sound research on this topic, a consensus definition of health in old age is still lacking (Rowe & Kahn, 1987). Therefore, based on theoretical considerations and empirical findings, explicit criteria were chosen that stem from analyses on the meaning of health and disability in old age (cf. Borchelt et al., Chapter 15). "Rather healthy" older adults were thus defined as those having less than five somatic diagnoses, less than five prescription drugs, no diagnosis of dementia or depression, no severe loss of vision or hearing, who were mobile, continent, and not restricted in ADL. This subgroup comprises 119 individuals (67 men and 52 women) aged 70 to 96 years, with a mean age of 78.9 years ($SD = 6.9$). The four-year mortality rate in this group was 18% compared with 50% in the rest of the sample ($\chi^2(1) = 38.4, p < .001$). Based on this subgroup, Table 5.2 provides an overview of reference ranges for most frequently used laboratory screening parameters. According to IFCC recommendations, interfractal 95% intervals are provided in addition to means and standard deviations. Gender-specific ranges are noted for parameters with distributions that significantly differ between both sexes (F-test, $p < .01$).

3.2   *The Assessment and Evaluation of Somatic Disease Profiles in BASE*

In preparation for consensus conferences on final diagnoses and treatment needs conducted with the Psychiatry Unit for every participant, all pathological findings were printed out in a list provided to the physicians for identification of diagnoses that were based on a standardized summary of clinical findings from all diagnostic procedures.[1] For every diagnosed illness, consensus ratings were made for certainty of diagnosis (five-point scale, "certain" to "very uncertain"), medical severity (three-point scale,

---

[1] An examination of interrater reliability of diagnoses indicated high agreement between different physicians (85% for three-digit ICD codes and 90% for the ICD ranges shown in Table 5.3).

Table 5.2. *Reference values for laboratory screening parameters in subjects aged 70 years and older*

Parameter	Mean	SD	Percentiles 2.5	Percentiles 50	Percentiles 97.5	n^a
Electrolytes						
Sodium (mmol/L)	141.1	2.3	135	141	146	118
Potassium (mmol/L)	4.18	0.57	3.4	4.1	5.2	118
Calcium (mmol/L)	2.310	0.097	2.15	2.31	2.54	116
Iron (µmol/L)	16.38	5.41	6.3	16.1	28.2	117
Metabolism						
Glucose (mg/dl)	100.6	23.4	72	97	165	118
Uric acid (mg/dl)						
Men	5.54	1.13	3.8	5.3	9.0	65
Women	4.27	1.14	1.6	4.2	6.3	51
Total protein (g/dl)	7.11	0.46	6.3	7.0	8.0	118
Albumin (g/dl)	4.47	0.44	3.3	4.6	5.1	116
Cholesterol (mg/dl)						
Men	223.6	39.0	140	221	302	65
Women	252.0	45.2	162	250	362	51
Triglycerides (mg/dl)	136.5	62.8	51	125	262	116
Renal function						
Urea (mg/dl)	38.6	10.6	20	39	62	117
Creatinine (mg/dl)						
Men	1.06	0.23	0.6	1.0	1.6	67
Women	0.80	0.17	0.4	0.8	1.3	51
Hepatobiliary system						
SGPT (ALT) (U/L)	10.8	6.5	4	9	29	118
GGT (U/L)	20.9	46.5	2	13	73	117
AP (U/L)	119.3	68.6	56	109	228	118
Blood formation						
Hemoglobin (g/dl)						
Men	14.80	1.10	12.6	14.7	17.0	65
Women	13.80	1.02	11.3	13.8	15.5	50
Hematocrit (L/L)						
Men	0.442	0.033	0.38	0.44	0.51	65
Women	0.415	0.029	0.33	0.41	0.46	50
RBC (/pl)						
Men	4.824	0.412	3.93	4.83	5.65	65
Women	4.494	0.410	3.23	4.50	5.28	50
WBC (/nl)	6.63	2.29	3.7	6.0	12.7	115
Platelets (10^3/mm^3)	220.2	59.2	103	213	350	115

Note. Values are based on a subsample of $n = 119$ "rather healthy" persons.
SGPT (ALT): alanine aminotransferase; GGT: gamma-glutamyl transpeptidase; AP: alkaline phosphatase; RBC: red blood cell count (erythrocytes); WBC: white blood cell count (leukocytes).
[a]Deviations from $n = 119$ are due to missing values.

"mild" to "severe"), subjective complaints (four-point scale, "none" to "severe"), and type of related medication including indication and potential undermedication.

Diagnoses were coded according to the four-digit code of the ICD-9 (World Health Organization [WHO], 1978). As a correction of the heterogeneous specificity conveyed in the ICD-9, prevalence rates were calculated on the basis of different aggregation levels (e.g., specifications of subtypes of "malignancy" span the ICD range 140.0–209.9, which will be collapsed here, whereas all subtypes of "osteoporosis" are subsumed under ICD-code 733.0, which is used unchanged).

3.3   *Prevalence Rates of Physical Illnesses in Very Old Age*

Table 5.3 shows the population prevalence rates of diagnosed diseases.[2] With respect to diagnostic certainty, the most frequent illnesses beyond the age of 70 were hyperlipidemia, varicosis, cerebral atherosclerosis, heart failure, osteoarthritis, dorsopathies, and hypertension with prevalences between 45% and 76%. With regard to severity, a comparison between objectively versus subjectively moderate to severe illnesses (second pair of columns in Table 5.3) reveals obvious differences in frequency profiles. From a subjective perspective, osteoarthritis, heart failure, dorsopathies, and osteoporosis head the list, followed by coronary heart disease and peripheral vascular disease. The subjective perspective thus emphasizes musculoskeletal disorders.

The third pair of columns considers pharmaceutical treatment independent of diagnostic certainty or illness severity. The most frequently drug-treated illnesses were heart failure, hypertension, coronary heart disease, osteoarthritis, peripheral vascular disease, and varicose veins. Here cardiovascular illnesses come to the fore.

Regardless of the type of "objective" perspective chosen to view morbidity in very old age, at least one diagnosis can be found in 87% to 96% of old persons, and at least one illness with subjectively experienced moderate to severe complaints is noted in 71%. Multimorbidity (arbitrarily defined as co-occurrence of at least five physical illnesses) is also very frequent: Again, using the criterion of diagnostic certainty first, the population prevalence estimate is 88%. With regard to severity, about 30% were diagnosed as having at least five coexisting, moderate to severe illnesses, and 21% had at least five simultaneously drug-treated illnesses.

3.4   *Undermedication of Physical Illness in Very Old Age*

The last column in Table 5.3 shows diagnosis-related prevalence rates of drug treatment needs. This was only assumed for moderate to severe illnesses, that are generally regarded as treatable and that were rated by consensus as being undermedicated and in clear need of additional causal or symptomatic drug treatment, after taking into account all other illnesses and medication. This conservative definition was chosen to avoid the impression often conveyed in the literature that drug treatment is too quickly prescribed in old age (Beers & Ouslander, 1989; Campion, Avorn, Reder, & Olins, 1987; Lisi, 1991).

---

[2] The "population prevalence" was obtained by weighting the BASE data in order to make up for the oversampling of the very old and of men (cf. P. B. Baltes et al., Chapter 1).

With the exception of hypertension (6%), no diagnosis-related undermedication prevalence above 5% was observed, so that the individual estimates are not of sufficient reliability for the population. Taking all diagnoses together, the population prevalence estimate of undermedication reaches 24%, despite the generally high medication rate. However, the picture only becomes complete when psychiatric (Helmchen et al., Chapter 6) and dental treatment needs are also considered.

3.5   Dental Treatment Needs

In Germany, geriatric dentistry has only recently developed within the field of general dentistry. Hence, descriptive data on the oral health of old people is of great importance. A comprehensive dental examination session was included in BASE, consisting of (a) a structured interview focused on case history, use of dental services, oral health habits, and control beliefs, (b) a full dental examination performed by experienced dentists, and (c) radiological and microbiological investigations. A detailed description of materials, methods, and initial results is provided elsewhere (Nitschke & Hopfenmüller, 1996).

In brief, the initial results indicated that approximately 43% of the population aged 70 years and older is edentulous. This prevalence increased from 34% among 70- to 74-year-olds to 65% among 95- to 103-year-olds. However, the highest prevalence rate was observed among 90- to 94-year-olds (76%). With regard to these numbers, it is evident that the single most important treatment needed in the aged population is the supply and maintenance of dentures. Taking full dentures and other fixed and removable tooth replacements together, only 78% of all participants needed no further restoration. That is, 22% of participants would require further prosthetic dental treatment. With regard to maintenance of dentures, BASE dentists judged 73% of all upper-jaw dentures and 85% of all lower-jaw dentures to be in need of repair or renewal according to specific criteria.

In contrast, analyses of participants' satisfaction with dentures revealed maximally discrepant results. Almost 80% of the participants with upper-jaw dentures and 65% of those with lower-jaw dentures were satisfied or very satisfied with their prostheses. These positive subjective evaluations may well influence oral health behavior in terms of lowered utilization of dental care services, which in turn would explain at least some of the qualitative denture deficiencies.

The period of time since the participants' last visit to a dentist varied widely, ranging between 14 days and 52 years with a median of 18 months. Nevertheless, this indicator of dental care utilization was strongly related to functional capacity. Physically or cognitively impaired older adults had significantly longer intervals between dentist visits than the nonimpaired ($p < .01$).

In total, an adjusted prosthetic treatment need (i.e., an objective need after taking account of individual functional limitations) was identified for 72% of all participants. Adjusted needs were also identified for surgical (23%), functional (8%), and periodontal (75%) treatment. Taking all categories together, adjusted treatment needs were identified for 88% of all participants.

In conclusion, the considerable dental treatment needs in the German population aged 70 years and above are not yet adequately dealt with. The development and further improvement of age-adjusted dental care, taking functional limitations into account, is of crucial importance with respect to future demographic changes.

Table 5.3. *Diagnosis prevalences (in %) by diagnostic certainty, objective and subjective severity, medication, and treatment needs (weighted data)*

Diagnosis	Certainty		Severity[a]		Medication	
	All categories	At least probable	Objective	Subjective	In use	Additional needs
Malignancies	11.2	10.8	2.5[b]	3.0	3.1	—
Thyroid disorders	11.4	7.6	0.7[b]	2.0	5.2	0.1
Diabetes mellitus	21.8	18.5	11.3	2.9	10.9	3.3
Hyperlipidemia	78.9	76.3	36.9	—	11.1	4.0
Gout/hyperuricemia	16.4	15.2	4.6	1.2	3.2	1.3
Anemia	13.9	13.1	2.9	0.9	2.4	1.7
CNS disorders	10.2	6.7	3.1[b]	3.5	3.2	—
PNS disorders	22.7	20.0	9.2	6.0	5.5	0.1
Hypertension	58.9	45.6	18.4	0.8	34.0	6.1
Past myocardial infarction	28.5	19.3	11.4	0.4	5.6	0.1
Coronary heart disease	45.4	23.3	17.6	10.4	30.2	3.1
Conduction block	36.5	35.7	16.7	0.6	—	—
Arrhythmia	34.6	33.0	13.4	2.2	5.7	0.4
Congestive heart failure	64.7	56.5	24.1	25.1	44.6	3.3
Cerebral atherosclerosis[c]	65.0	65.0	15.2	6.1	11.7	0.5

Peripheral vascular disease	40.4	35.6	18.4	10.4	18.1	1.3
Varicose veins	72.8	72.1	36.2	9.7	14.3	0.9
Postural hypotension	17.4	14.6	6.3	1.0	3.5	0.0
Chronic bronchitis	29.4	25.3	12.6	7.8	6.1	1.9
Chronic constipation	14.2	13.4	5.8	6.5	8.3	0.0
Hepatopathies	10.2	8.0	3.8	0.2	0.4	—
Nephropathies	11.2	9.0	5.5	0.6	1.0	0.4
Urinary incontinence	38.0	37.2	7.6[b]	6.8	3.1	—
Fecal incontinence	12.4	11.3	3.0[b]	4.1	3.5	—
Osteoarthritis	60.6	54.8	31.6	32.1	27.7	0.1
Dorsopathies[e]	49.5	46.0	20.6[b]	20.4	10.2	0.1
Osteoporosis	33.8	24.1	10.3[b]	12.3	8.1	1.6
Other[d]	32.6	28.9	7.6	7.1	12.6	—
Total						
At least one diagnosis	99.6	97.9	96.0	71.3	87.4	23.9
Five and more diagnoses	94.0	87.7	30.2	6.0	20.7	—

Note. CNS/PNS: central/peripheral nervous system.

[a]Moderate to severe.

[b]In most of these cases, objective severity could only be judged globally on the basis of clinical examination and the case history.

[c]Unweighted data; only persons with Doppler ultrasound ($n = 283$); including apoplexia.

[d]All remaining diagnoses of similar specificity with a prevalence of 10% or less.

[e]Degenerative diseases of the spine.

4   The Atherosclerosis Risk Factor Model in Very Old Age

Many studies have shown that the onset and progress of atherosclerosis, which clinically manifests itself mainly as coronary heart disease, peripheral vascular disease, or cerebral atherosclerosis, is influenced by various "risk" factors (Bühler, Vesanen, Watters, & Bolli, 1988; Castelli, 1988; Dahlöf et al., 1991; Kannel, D'Agostino, Wilson, Belanger, & Gagnon, 1990; Kannel & Higgins, 1990; Reid et al., 1976; Wilson et al., 1980). Most of these studies included participants of middle or at the beginning of old age, whereas an emphasis on the "old old" is scarce (Barrett-Connor, Suarez, Khaw, Criqui, & Wingard, 1984; Sorkin et al., 1992; Zimetbaum et al., 1992). The validity of the atherosclerosis risk factor model for aged subjects is still unclear and deserves further investigation (Hazzard, 1987).

**4.1   *Diagnostic Criteria for Atherosclerotic Illnesses
           and Associated Risk Factors***

Criteria for the diagnosis of coronary heart disease (CHD) were definite ECG signs of ischemia or of a previous myocardial infarction together with typical symptoms of angina pectoris. Peripheral vascular disease (PVD) was diagnosed from clinical signs of a peripheral arterial circulatory disorder based on physical examination. The diagnosis of cerebral atherosclerosis (CAS) was based on evidence of plaques and/or stenoses in ultrasound imaging of carotid arteries and on information about previous strokes. Since ultrasound imaging was carried out in the hospital, only 283 mobile subjects were examined in this way (54%). However, 33% of the subjects aged 85 and above ($n = 86$) were among them.

Assessment of atherosclerosis risk factors included a detailed serum lipid profile, health behavior, diabetes, hypertension, obesity, and family history of myocardial infarction or stroke. All participants currently smoking tobacco were considered as "smokers." Participants who did not take regular physical exercise (e.g., swimming, cycling, hiking, or gardening at least twice a week) were recorded as lacking exercise.

The recommendations of the European Atherosclerosis Society (EAS) were used as criteria for assuming an increased atherosclerosis risk (EAS Group, 1988; Recommendations of the EAS, 1992). Thresholds and the resulting population prevalences are shown in Table 5.4. Most frequently observed risk factors with a prevalence above 40% were increased LDL-cholesterol, hypertension, lack of physical exercise, and a positive family history. The apolipoprotein-E (Apo-E) genotypes 2/2 and 4/4 are known to be associated with a massive atherosclerosis risk. Their rare occurrence in this older population already indicates selective mortality effects as their prevalence in younger populations usually lies between 3% and 6%.

4.2   *Risk Profiles in Participants with Atherosclerotic Disease*

Although the initial BASE data (cross-sectional at baseline) are not suited for analyses of atherosclerosis incidence in relation to risk profiles, some important information can be gained by analysis of coincidences between diseases and risk factors. Therefore, risk profiles of participants with CHD, PVD, or CAS were compared with profiles of subjects free of any signs of these diseases ($n = 153$ for the whole sample and $n = 57$ for the ultrasound subgroup). As both presence of illness and risk factors were

Table 5.4. *Atherosclerosis risk factors by age and gender, and their population prevalences (in %)*

	Age group				Total (weighted)
	70–84		85+		
	Men	Women	Men	Women	
Total cholesterol > 250 mg/dl	25.6	41.9	11.6	33.3	36.9
LDL-cholesterol > 155 mg/dl	40.3	48.1	16.3	37.2	44.7
HDL-cholesterol < 35 mg/dl (men)					
or < 42 mg/dl (women)	10.1	12.4	10.1	23.3	13.8
Cholesterol/HDL > 5	42.6	31.0	22.5	28.7	33.4
Lipoprotein (a) > 15 mg/dl	27.4	21.3	17.9	19.3	22.0
Apo-E 2/2 or 4/4	2.4	4.1	0.8	—	2.9
Triglycerides > 200 mg/dl	24.8	26.4	16.3	26.4	26.5
Body Mass Index > 28 kg/m^2	31.8	26.4	15.5	16.3	25.6
Diabetes mellitus	14.7	20.2	20.2	15.5	18.5
Hypertension	39.5	43.4	38.8	57.4	45.6
Smoking	23.3	12.4	17.8	4.7	14.1
Lack of exercise	50.4	50.4	68.2	77.5	55.1
Positive family history	47.3	49.6	21.7	33.3	45.9
Four or more risk factors	54.3	51.9	32.6	45.7	51.6

Note. Apo-E 2/2 or 4/4: apolipoprotein-E genotype 2/2 or 4/4; LDL/HDL: low/high density lipoprotein.

coded dichotomously (yes/no), two-by-two tables were calculated to determine standardized residuals for the combination "risk factor and illness." The standardized residuals have positive signs when the observed rate of co-occurrence is higher than the expected rate estimated by chance alone, and have negative signs when the observed rate is lower. All distributions were tested for independence using χ^2-analyses. The results for the three groups are presented in Figure 5.1.

Two findings stand out. First, positive relationships predominate in all illness groups, that is, most of the risk factors occurred more frequently (on a descriptive level) in these groups than in the control group. Second, the groups' profiles are quite different from each other. For instance, in the CHD group (Fig. 5.1a) an unfavorably elevated ratio of total- to HDL-cholesterol, elevated triglycerides, and lack of exercise were significantly more common. In those with PVD, an elevated cholesterol ratio and elevated triglycerides were also found more frequently (Fig. 5.1b). However, hypertension exhibited an additional significant association, whereas lack of exercise and all other factors were not statistically significant. The associations are much less clear-cut for persons with CAS (Fig. 5.1c), which, to some degree, could be due to small sample sizes (184 cases with CAS versus 57 controls). Still, coincidence with hypertension, seen as the main risk factor for stroke (Besdine, 1993; Furmaga, Murphy, & Carter, 1993), is significant. Furthermore, diabetes and the presence of multiple risk factors were significantly more common.

Two further general findings should be emphasized. As expected, some effect of the cumulation of risk factors can be observed in all three groups. This finding corresponds

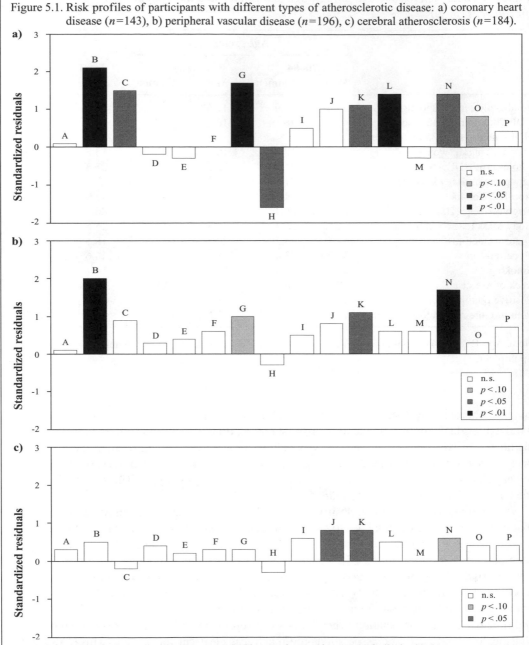

Figure 5.1. Risk profiles of participants with different types of atherosclerotic disease: a) coronary heart disease (*n*=143), b) peripheral vascular disease (*n*=196), c) cerebral atherosclerosis (*n*=184).

Note. Relative frequencies in the affected groups versus a healthy control group (shown as standardized residuals).
Risk factors: A) cholesterol >250 mg/dl, B) cholesterol/HDL-cholesterol >5, C) HDL-cholesterol <35 mg/dl (men) / <42 mg/dl (women), D) LDL-cholesterol >155 mg/dl, E) apolipoprotein-E genotype 2/2 or 4/4, F) Lp(a) >15 mg/dl, G) triglycerides >200 mg/dl, H) Body Mass Index >28 kg/m^2, I) positive family history, J) diabetes mellitus, K) hypertension, L) inactivity, M) smoking, N) four or more risk factors, O) aged 85 and above, P) male.

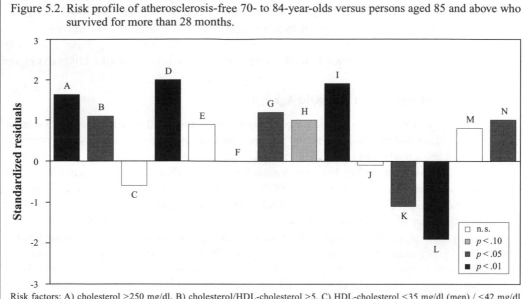

Figure 5.2. Risk profile of atherosclerosis-free 70- to 84-year-olds versus persons aged 85 and above who survived for more than 28 months.

Risk factors: A) cholesterol >250 mg/dl, B) cholesterol/HDL-cholesterol >5, C) HDL-cholesterol <35 mg/dl (men) / <42 mg/dl (women), D) LDL-cholesterol >155 mg/dl, E) apolipoprotein-E genotype 2/2 or 4/4, F) Lp(a) >15 mg/dl, G) triglycerides >200 mg/dl, H) Body Mass Index >28 kg/m², I) positive family history, J) diabetes mellitus, K) hypertension, L) inactivity, M) smoking, N) four or more risk factors.

to the hypothesized multifactorial genesis of atherosclerosis, especially of PVD (Robbins & Austin, 1993; Valentine, Grayburn, Vega, & Grundy, 1993). Typical gender differences, to men's disadvantage, that are found in younger age groups, seem to diminish in old age. This is consistent with other studies' reports of an increase in women's risk for atherosclerosis after menopause due to the decline in estrogen synthesis (Stampfer et al., 1985).

4.3   *Risk Profiles of Participants without Atherosclerosis by Age*

Under the assumption that a group of healthy very old persons represents a selection mainly determined by atherosclerotic mortality (Kannel, McGee, & Gordon, 1976), a risk profile comparison between healthy 70- to 84-year-olds and healthy persons aged 85 and above can serve as an estimate for the relevance of the atherosclerotic risk factor model in old age. For this purpose, "healthy" participants were defined as those free of CHD and PVD at the time of examination and surviving over the following 28 months. Cerebral atherosclerosis could not be included in these analyses due to small sample sizes.

The risk profiles of atherosclerosis-free ("healthy") 70- to 84-year-old survivors are compared with those of the corresponding older group in Figure 5.2. It turns out that the younger "healthy" group retains a statistically significant higher risk for atherosclerosis than the older group. In particular, this holds for elevated lipids (total cholesterol, cholesterol ratio, LDL-cholesterol, and triglycerides) and a positive family history. The significantly less frequent occurrence of hypertension in the younger group allows the assumption that a "benign" form of hypertension tends to develop in very old age. In conclusion, if one assumes selective survival due to atherosclerosis, these results are consistent with the hypothesis that the atherosclerosis risk factor model holds in old age.

5   Medication in Very Old Age

In some ways, the increase in morbidity is mirrored by multimedication in old age. Although there has been sound research on this topic, multimorbidity was rarely assessed objectively and in detail (Chrischilles et al., 1992; Gilchrist et al., 1987; Kruse et al., 1991). This may have been the reason for some studies to conclude that older adults generally receive too many drugs (Kruse et al., 1991; Lisi, 1991; Renner, Engle, & Graney, 1992). However, only few studies have dealt explicitly with the equally important question of undermedication in old age (Lipton, Bero, Bird, & McPhee, 1992).

In general, the improvement of geriatric prescription practice is of crucial importance since pharmacological research indicates important age-related changes in pharmacokinetics and -dynamics of many drugs (Greenblatt, Sellers, & Shader, 1982; Vestal, 1985). Nevertheless, these changes are not yet routinely acknowledged in clinical practice. Many handbooks on drug therapy as well as the most frequently used German *Physician's Desk Reference* (PDR) "Rote Liste" (1990) give no specific advice on the treatment of older adults. In contrast, recent perceptions of this issue in the United States have led to the development of specifically geriatric recommendations for several frequently used medications on the basis of experts' consensus (Beers et al., 1991; Stuck et al., 1994).

5.1   *Assessment of Drug History and Medication Analysis in BASE*

A differentiated protocol was applied to assess each participant's actual medication utilization. All interviews took place at the participants' homes, which was of utmost importance for verification of subjective reports by inspecting original drug containers. Participants cared for by others were asked for permission to question caregivers or to consult medical records. For every mentioned drug, the prescription status (doctor/self/others), form of administration, dosage, duration, and frequency of use was noted as well as information on its pharmaceutical composition (chemical/herbal/homeopathic/organic) and on all contraindications and potential adverse drug reactions (ADR).

For coding, the five-digit drug number of the German PDR was used where the first two digits denote the indication class. From an epidemiological perspective, drug classification by indication classes is neither better nor worse than other systems. So far, no classification system allows an unambiguous and meaningful distinction by pharmacology and indication.[3] In order to solve this dilemma at least partially, the German PDR system was slightly modified by merging some areas of indications for rarely used or related drugs (e.g., laxatives/bile acids, vitamins/minerals), and dividing others, frequently used and heterogeneous drugs (e.g., analgesics, cardiac drugs, psychotropics), into subgroups.

[3] For example, aspirin belongs to salicylates and is used as an analgesic, antipyretic, antirheumatic, and a platelet inhibitor. Other salicylates are only applied externally in rheumatoid arthritis.

5.2   Prevalence of Drug Utilization by Indication Classes

Table 5.5 gives an overview of the population prevalences of drug utilization by indication classes. The first column shows prevalence rates including all available information. Without exclusion of participants' imprecise statements such as "eye drops," ophthalmic drugs head the list (34%), followed by internally administered analgesics/ nonsteroidal anti-inflammatory drugs (NSAID), digitalis glycosides, diuretics, and vitamins/minerals.

A clear shift in this order occurs when prevalences are calculated only for chemically defined prescription drugs (fourth column). Cardiac drugs, mainly digitalis glycosides, were most frequently prescribed (31%), followed by diuretics, ophthalmics, vasodilators, and calcium antagonists. Internally administered analgesics/NSAID follow these groups with 22%. The comparison with the rate of 32% in the third column indicates that 10% use these drugs in self-medication only.

The fifth column presents prevalence rates of chemically defined drugs prescribed for daily use. The further decrease of internally administered analgesics/NSAID shows that about 50% of patients treated with these drugs received an "as needed" prescription scheme. In the case of diuretics (30% prescribed in total vs. 24% prescribed for daily use), however, this is due to more variable prescription schemes (usage on alternating days or weekly). Although reduction of dosage in elderly patients is nearly always appropriate, this type of complex prescription should be viewed critically with regard to compliance (Vestal, 1985). Finally, despite high hyperlipidemia prevalence, only a small proportion of older adults (7%) received specific treatment with lipid-lowering drugs.

Regarded cumulatively, the expected high general prevalence of medication becomes obvious – 96% of persons aged 70 and above took at least one drug and 87% took at least one chemically defined prescription drug daily (bottom of Table 5.5). Multimedication (utilization of five or more drugs at the same time) was also frequent with prevalences of 56% when all drugs were taken into account, or 23% for prescribed daily drugs.

5.3   Inappropriate and Individually Unnecessary Drugs

The final column of Table 5.5 shows prevalence estimates for drug-specific overmedication. Overmedication was only assumed for chemically defined prescription drugs that could either not be identified as causal, symptomatic, or substituting treatment for any of the diagnosed illnesses, or had to be classified as contraindicated because of one of these. No indication-specific overmedication reached a prevalence of more than 3%, so that no reliable population estimates can be derived. In the sample, psychotropic drugs, gastrointestinal drugs, diuretics, and vasodilators were most frequently identified as not indicated or contraindicated. Taken together, one in seven older adults (about 14%) had at least one such prescription drug. However, it should be pointed out that these assessments do not take into account any qualitative aspect of medication rated as being indicated. Other studies often emphasize this aspect and might therefore find overmedication prevalence rates between 25% and 50% (Campion et al., 1987; Kruse et al., 1991).

Recently, attempts have been made to define explicit criteria for medication that is inappropriate in old age, on principle, based on clinical and pharmacological research. An

Table 5.5. *Medication class prevalences by pharmaceutical definition and type of prescription (weighted data, in %)*

Indication class	Total	Pharmaceutical definition known		Prescription by physician (chemically defined)		
		Total	Chemically defined	Total	Daily	Over-medicated
Ophthalmic drugs	33.8	32.5	31.2	29.6	27.8	0.2
Analgesics/NSAID (internally administered)	32.8	32.8	31.7	22.1	12.5	0.1
Cardiac drugs	39.7	39.7	32.3	32.2	31.1	1.1
Digitalis glycosides	31.0	31.0	31.0	30.9	30.3	1.1
Diuretics	30.4	30.0	30.0	30.0	23.5	1.8
Vitamins/minerals	28.6	26.5	25.7	15.1	12.0	1.0
Drugs improving circulation/platelet aggregation inhibitors	28.3	28.3	22.7	22.7	21.3	1.5
Analgesics/NSAID (externally applied)	25.4	24.9	19.5	14.9	8.3	—
Calcium antagonists	22.8	22.8	22.8	22.7	22.3	1.1
Geriatrics/roborants	22.8	22.5	5.0	5.0	0.3	—
Antianginals	21.7	21.6	21.6	21.2	16.3	—
Laxatives/bile acids[a]	18.8	15.4	4.0	7.1	3.5	0.0
Medication for venous disorders	16.8	16.3	11.3	8.5	7.1	0.1
Gastrointestinal medication	25.1	25.1	24.8	18.0	9.6	2.2
Antacids/ulcer medication	16.3	16.3	16.3	10.2	4.5	0.7
Psychotropic drugs	25.1	24.6	23.4	21.7	15.7	3.0
Neuroleptics	4.4	4.4	4.4	4.4	4.3	0.1
Neurotropics	4.3	4.3	4.3	4.1	4.1	0.7
Antidepressants	3.3	3.3	3.3	3.3	2.8	0.3
Hypnotics/sedatives	12.4	11.9	7.7	4.5	2.3	0.9
Antidiabetics	11.4	11.4	11.4	11.4	11.4	0.6
Antihypertensives[b]	11.3	11.3	10.9	10.9	9.8	0.6
Urologic/gynecologic medication	10.9	9.4	3.4	3.2	2.2	0.5
Lipid-lowering drugs	7.5	7.5	7.5	7.3	7.3	—
Skin therapeutics	6.4	6.3	5.9	4.9	2.2	0.6
Hormone therapeutics	6.0	6.0	6.0	6.0	3.6	—
Cough medicines	5.6	5.6	4.2	3.8	3.5	0.1
Beta-blockers	5.5	5.5	5.5	5.5	5.5	0.6

Table 5.5. *(cont.)*

Indication class	Total	Pharmaceutical definition known		Prescription by physician (chemically defined)		
		Total	Chemically defined	Total	Daily	Over-medicated
Antiasthmatics	5.5	5.5	5.5	5.5	4.3	—
Thyroid therapeutics	5.4	5.4	5.4	5.4	4.9	—
ACE inhibitors	5.3	5.3	5.3	5.3	5.3	—
Other[c]	17.9	17.5	17.5	17.3	15.0	2.0
Total						
At least one drug	96.4	95.9	93.8	91.7	86.7	13.7
Five or more drugs	56.0	53.7	32.1	24.3	23.1	—

Note. ACE: Angiotensin Converting Enzyme; NSAID: nonsteroidal anti-inflammatory drugs.
[a]"Prescribed by physician" includes herbal preparations.
[b]Excluding diuretics, ACE inhibitors, beta-blockers, calcium antagonists.
[c]All remaining categories with a prevalence of 5% or less.

initial consensus could be reached for treatment of institutionalized (Beers et al., 1991) as well as ambulatory elderly patients (Stuck et al., 1994). Applying these explicit criteria to the BASE sample reveals an estimated prevalence rate of 19% taking age-inappropriate drugs. In detail, nearly one in five older adults is treated with at least one drug that, according to experts' consensus, either should not be used at all in old age (mainly reserpine, diazepam, amitriptyline, indomethacin) or should be administered at lower dosage (hydrochlorothiazide) or for a shorter period (oxazepam, ranitidine). Taking inappropriate medication and individually defined overmedication together results in a total prevalence of 28% of older adults receiving inadequate medications.

5.4   Risk for Adverse Drug Reactions (ADR) and Prevalence of ADR-Like Symptoms

Adverse drug reactions (ADR) represent an important aspect of geriatric pharmacotherapy. Although a direct association between age and ADR rate is a controversial issue (Hutchinson, Flegel, Kramer, Leduc, & Hopingkong, 1986; Klein et al., 1976; Weber & Griffin, 1986; Williamson & Chopin, 1980), it is well known that old people are more sensitive to certain adverse effects (Beers & Ouslander, 1989; Castleden & Pickles, 1988; Greenblatt et al., 1982; Meyer & Reidenberg, 1992).

Any identification of ADR is difficult to achieve, and many procedures have proved not to be particularly valid and/or reliable (Hutchinson et al., 1983). Therefore, standardized algorithms for measurement and assessment were introduced (Kramer, Leventhal, Hutchinson, & Feinstein, 1979; Pere, Begaud, Haramburu, & Albin, 1986). In contrast to

Table 5.6. *Rates (in %) of ADR-like symptoms or suspected ADR by indication class*

Indication class with ADR risk (population prevalence)	ADR-like symptoms	Suspected ADR
Aldosterone antagonists (1.9)	94.7	73.7
Diuretics (25.9)	100.0	69.7
Antihypertensives (13.7)	88.3	61.7
Lipid-lowering drugs (5.8)	75.0	50.0
Beta-blockers and calcium antagonists (25.5)	87.7	47.1
Psychotropic drugs (24.6)	68.9	34.9
Gout medications (3.9)	75.0	33.3
Vasodilators (22.0)	53.6	29.7
Antianginals (20.8)	46.9	29.2
Hypnotics/sedatives (9.3)	54.9	28.0
Analgesics/NSAID (36.5)	51.1	27.1
Sexual hormones and hormone inhibitors (5.4)	54.5	22.7
Antiasthmatics (4.9)	58.8	20.6
Ophthalmic drugs (17.5)	54.0	18.4
Cardiac drugs (33.5)	44.8	18.4
Other		
Total (87.2)	86.6	58.4

Example. 25.9% of older adults were treated with diuretics with ADR risk. In 100% of this group at least one ADR-like symptom typical for diuretics could be identified. In 69.7%, suspected ADR were presumed to be present – after taking all other medications and illnesses into account.

these algorithms, the medication analysis of the Geriatrics Unit started out from the present medication and not from symptoms or clinical findings (Borchelt & Horgas, 1994). Based on the computerized ADR classification provided by the German PDR, a list of all potential ADR for all drugs taken by a participant was automatically printed out. The project physicians compared this list with the one that listed all symptoms and clinical findings as described earlier (cf. Section 3.2). In this way, all "ADR-like" symptoms were first identified and then coded in terms of their assumed cause either as a "symptom of a preexisting disease" or as a "suspected ADR."

Summarized by drug indication classes, prevalences of ADR-like symptoms and suspected ADR are shown in Table 5.6. For instance, nearly 26% of persons aged 70 and above took a diuretic with an ADR risk. For everyone in this group (100%), at least one ADR-like symptom was indeed observed. In 70%, at least one such symptom was rated as a suspected ADR. Use of diuretics coincided most frequently with ADR-like symptoms (mainly hyperuricemia, azotemia, elevated creatinine, blurred vision). Detailed analyses have shown that this coincidence is clearly not explained by age effects alone (Borchelt & Horgas, 1994).

In total, symptoms and clinical findings are very often interpretable as potential ADR. Within the risk population (about 87% of older adults are at risk for ADR), at least one ADR-like symptom can be found in 87%, and a causal relationship (suspected ADR) can be assumed in 58%. However, verification of a true ADR is nearly impossible to achieve in context of concurrent multimorbidity and multimedication and without the discontinuation of individual drugs.

At first glance, the total prevalence of suspected ADR (58%) observed in the risk population seemed to be extremely high. However, this high rate becomes quite plausible on the basis of probability theory. If one assumes an ADR rate of only 5% per drug course (Hutchinson et al., 1986; Klein et al., 1976), an estimated total ADR rate of 22% would result for the BASE sample for which the average number of different drugs was about five per person ($Pr(\text{ADR}) = 1 - 0.95^5$). If instead the ADR rate per drug course is assumed to be 15% (Williamson & Chopin, 1980), the estimated total prevalence would reach 56% – quite close to the observed 58% suspected ADR cases. However, these probability models still infer that the likelihood of ADR occurrence per drug is not influenced by combinations of drugs, although such drug interactions are, of course, well known.

6   Functional Capacity in Very Old Age

The focus on "functional" aspects of health is a characteristic of geriatric medicine, setting it somewhat apart from other clinical specialties. The main issues are assessments of sensory and sensorimotor capabilities and evaluations of the need for help with so-called basic and instrumental Activities of Daily Living (ADL/IADL; Branch, Katz, Kniepmann, & Papsidero, 1984; Katz, Ford, Moskowitz, Jackson, & Jaffe, 1963; Lawton & Brody, 1969; Mahoney & Barthel, 1965; Reuben, Laliberte, Hiris, & Mor, 1990; Rubenstein & Rubenstein, 1992).

Although the original instruments were modified and extended during the past decades for theoretical and methodological reasons (Feinstein, Josephy, & Wells, 1986), the Barthel and the Katz Index have become standard ADL measures in clinical geriatrics (Katz, Downs, Cash, & Grotz, 1970) and in epidemiological research (Branch et al., 1984; Cornoni-Huntley et al., 1986). However, the geriatric interdisciplinary approach has chiefly led to a continuous extension of the instruments by adding dimensions such as social activities and psychological state (Applegate, Blass, & Williams, 1990; Nagi, 1976; Pearlman, 1987; Reuben & Siu, 1990). More recently, another aspect has been developed which is based on objective measures of physical mobility (Guralnik, Branch, Cummings, & Curb, 1989; Imms & Edholm, 1981; Tinetti, 1986). The most important argument for this shift in emphasis is the frequently questioned validity of (mostly subjective) ADL evaluations (Rubenstein, Schairer, Wieland, & Kane, 1984). However, there are several reports indicating good or even excellent congruence of subjective and objective measures of functioning (Harris, Jette, Campion, & Cleary, 1986; Myers & Huddy, 1986; Sager et al., 1992).

6.1   Functional Assessment in BASE

In the Geriatrics Unit, a multidimensional approach to the assessment of physical functional impairments and the need for help was chosen. The central indicators drew on different subjectively evaluated ADL measures, a questionnaire on the use of technical aids, and objective tests of visual acuity, hearing, gait, and mobility. ADLs were measured as self-reports with the Barthel Index (Mahoney & Barthel, 1965). The items "shopping" and "transportation" were selected from Lawton and Brody's (1969) IADL

Scale of more complex "instrumental" activities, because they neither differ by gender nor depend on living standards.

Four routine clinical tests following Tinetti's (1986) objective mobility tests were applied to assess balance, coordination, and gait: Romberg's trial (standing upright with eyes closed, feet together, and arms stretched out ahead) was qualitatively evaluated in terms of stance on a six-point scale ranging from "no sway" up to "can not stand without support." "Walking on the spot" (30 steps with eyes closed) was rated by the deviation from the original position, whereas "bending over" was assessed by the distance between the fingertips and the floor while bending over with one's feet together and legs stretched. The 360° turn was measured by the steps necessary to turn around one's body axis. Participants' subjective maximal walking distance that they claimed to be able to walk without pain and without interruption was also noted (Scheidegger, 1987). Grip strength was measured by standardized dynamometry (Borchelt & Steinhagen-Thiessen, 1992; Steinhagen-Thiessen & Borchelt, 1993). Audiometry for speech-range (0.5–2.0 kHz) and high-frequency (3.0–8.0 kHz) hearing was also performed. Distance vision was measured binocularly with a Snellen chart at least 2.5 m away. Close vision was assessed for each eye separately using a Snellen reading chart (individual reading distance, typically about 25 cm). These functional assessments were complemented by measures from the other research units (cf. Borchelt et al., Chapter 15), such as psychometric tests of intellectual functioning (Smith & Baltes, Chapter 7), DSM-III-R diagnoses of dementia and depression (Helmchen et al., Chapter 6), and sociological indicators of psychosocial resources and risks (Mayer et al., Chapter 8).

6.2   Prevalence of ADL Disabilities and Functional Impairments

The need for help in the eight ADLs and the two IADLs by age and gender are presented in the upper part of Table 5.7. The two frequently reported central findings for "younger" old populations are replicated for very old age: (1) a clearly negative age effect ($\chi^2 = 167.9$, $p < .001$) and (2) a strong gender effect disadvantageous to women ($\chi^2 = 13.1$, $p < .001$). However, beyond age 70, the negative age effect did not differ between both sexes (χ^2 [Age × Gender] = 2.8, $p > .09$). Since the numbers in all age and gender groups and, hence, the statistical power are equal in BASE, these results underpin the sharp increase in need for help in very old age for men and women alike. However, 66% of the entire population aged 70 and above claimed to be completely independent.

Differences in the use of technical aids are shown in the middle part of Table 5.7. The very high rate of persons having glasses is presumably mainly due to physiological aging of the visual system (cf. Marsiske et al., Chapter 13). Problems with reading and/or watching television were reported by 34% of the male and 46% of the female participants, and 7% underwent surgery for cataracts in the year preceding the study. The statistical comparison shows no gender-specific age differences in sensory functioning.

The results of objective mobility tests following Tinetti (1986) are compiled in Table 5.8. In nearly all tests, complete disability is measured almost twice as often in women than in men across both age groups. Taken together, these findings support the well-known paradox in gerontology that women have a higher disability and morbidity rate, but men have the higher mortality rate and shorter life expectancy (Verbrugge, 1988).

Table 5.7. *Population prevalence estimates for the need for help with ADL, use of technical aids, and sensory impairments by age and gender (in %)*

	Age group				Total (weighted)
	70–84		85+		
	Men	**Women**	**Men**	**Women**	
IADL					
Shopping	18.6	27.1	59.7	80.6	33.7
Transportation[a]	17.8	22.5	62.0	83.7	31.2
ADL					
Bathing	9.3	8.5	31.8	60.5	16.0
Climbing stairs	3.1	8.5	22.5	42.6	11.4
Going for walks	5.4	6.2	27.1	42.6	10.6
Getting dressed	5.4	3.1	11.6	24.0	5.9
Toileting	0.8	2.3	6.2	15.5	3.2
Transfer[b]	1.6	1.6	4.7	15.5	2.7
Grooming[c]	—	0.8	3.1	6.2	1.3
Eating	—	0.8	0.8	2.3	0.9
Technical aids					
Glasses[d]	99.2	96.9	86.6	85.5	95.6
Magnifying glass	14.3	15.0	39.7	28.0	16.9
Hearing aid	18.3	14.1	24.4	14.3	15.5
Walking stick	14.3	14.8	56.7	44.4	20.9
Crutches	4.8	3.1	10.2	7.9	4.6
Delta-wheel	—	2.3	3.9	14.3	2.4
Wheelchair	1.6	2.3	5.5	15.9	3.1
Sensory functioning					
Visual impairment[e]	18.6	20.9	56.6	65.9	26.6
Hearing impairment[f]	14.0	15.5	45.3	43.4	18.6

Note. Need for help includes "assistance needed" and "completely dependent on help."
[a]Traveling longer distances in town (beyond reach on foot).
[b]Getting into and out of bed.
[c]Including combing hair, shaving, etc.
[d]Glasses for close and/or distance vision.
[e]Close and/or distance vision below 0.2 Snellen decimals.
[f]Pure tone thresholds $\geq$ 55 dB (0.25–2 kHz) and/or $\geq$ 75 dB (3–8 kHz).

7   Morbidity, Medication, and Functional Limitations as Determinants of Need for Help in Very Old Age

Looking at the results, it seems as though nearly all people aged 70 and above are ill in some way, are treated pharmaceutically, and additionally suffer from adverse drug reactions. However, the previous section already indicates that these age groups also exhibit great variability in functional health. One of the reasons for this lies in the fact that most of the illnesses typically occurring in old age are not directly life-

Table 5.8. *Population prevalence estimates for objective mobility impairments by age and gender (in %)*

	Age group				Total (weighted)
	70–84		85+		
	Men	Women	Men	Women	
Walking on the spot[a]					
Unimpaired	44.2	41.1	32.8	25.2	39.7
Impaired	48.1	48.1	35.9	16.5	44.2
Unable	7.8	10.9	31.3	58.3	16.1
Romberg trial[b]					
Unimpaired	62.0	46.5	14.0	7.8	43.7
Impaired	34.1	47.3	63.6	47.7	46.2
Unable	3.9	6.2	22.5	44.5	10.0
360° turn[c]					
Quick	82.2	72.9	37.5	20.3	66.4
Slow	16.3	21.7	47.7	49.2	26.4
Unable	1.6	5.4	14.8	30.5	7.2
Bending over[d]					
Completely	18.6	47.6	11.7	18.1	35.2
Nearly	48.8	33.3	25.8	20.5	35.2
Hardly	28.7	13.5	38.3	12.6	17.4
Unable	3.9	5.6	24.2	48.8	10.8

[a]Taking at least 30 steps on the spot with closed eyes; "impaired" if deviation from original position exceeds 45°.
[b]Standing freely with eyes closed, feet together, and arms stretched out ahead for at least 30 seconds; "impaired" if strong sway with balancing movements occurs.
[c]Number of steps needed for a complete turn on the spot; "quick": under 11 steps, "slow": more than 10 steps.
[d]Distance between fingertips and the ground in centimeters: "completely" = 0 cm, "nearly" < 16 cm, "hardly" > 16 cm.

threatening (e.g., arthritis, varicose veins, constipation). This means that many older adults have to live permanently with chronic illnesses associated with varying complaints and disabilities.

7.1   A Theoretical Model of the Disablement Process

Somatic illnesses such as arthritis or circulation disorders are often regarded as risk factors for functional limitations (e.g., restricted mobility, hearing loss, or blurred vision) that in themselves can contribute to the development of disability and lead to the need for care (Nagi, 1976; WHO, 1980). In further work on this theoretical model by Verbrugge and Jette (1994), risk and intervention factors that accelerate or slow down

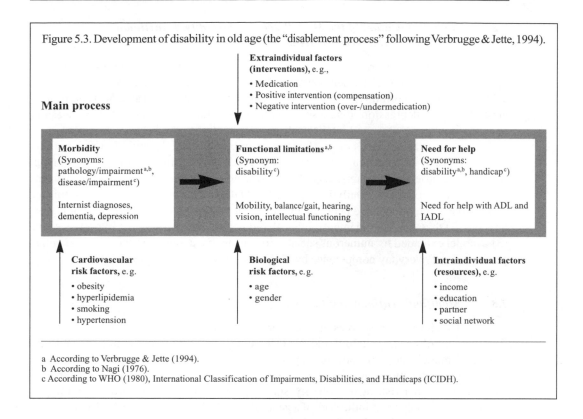

Figure 5.3. Development of disability in old age (the "disablement process" following Verbrugge & Jette, 1994).

Main process

Extraindividual factors (interventions), e.g.,
• Medication
• Positive intervention (compensation)
• Negative intervention (over-/undermedication)

Morbidity
(Synonyms: pathology/impairment[a,b], disease/impairment[c])

Internist diagnoses, dementia, depression

Functional limitations[a,b]
(Synonym: disability[c])

Mobility, balance/gait, hearing, vision, intellectual functioning

Need for help
(Synonyms: disability[a,b], handicap[c])

Need for help with ADL and IADL

Cardiovascular risk factors, e.g.
• obesity
• hyperlipidemia
• smoking
• hypertension

Biological risk factors, e.g.
• age
• gender

Intraindividual factors (resources), e.g.
• income
• education
• partner
• social network

a According to Verbrugge & Jette (1994).
b According to Nagi (1976).
c According to WHO (1980), International Classification of Impairments, Disabilities, and Handicaps (ICIDH).

the disablement process have gained importance (Fig. 5.3). The significance of this change in emphasis is clear: If risk factors accelerating the need for care and the efficacy of intervention strategies were known, effective preventive measures against dependency could be devised for an increasing proportion of the population.

Furthermore, Verbrugge and Jette's (1994) model takes a new direction by integrating and developing the theory-based model by Nagi (1976) and the International Classification of Impairments, Disabilities, and Handicaps (ICIDH; WHO, 1980), and also works toward unified terminology.

This model enables a systemic approach to the aspects of somatic health presented above and the analysis of potential consequences of morbidity, medication, and functional limitations in old age. It allows for the hypotheses that (a) morbidity is the main risk factor for functional limitations which, in turn, lead to need for help and (b) intraindividual psychosocial and biological risk factors and extraindividual interventions can influence this process at different points. Furthermore, it raises the question of whether or not the quality of drug therapy can limit the negative consequences of illnesses for functional capacity and independence in old age. This approach could be particularly fruitful because pharmaceutical treatment has mainly been examined from the negative perspective of overmedication, often without actually proving negative functional consequences (Lord, Clark, & Webster, 1991; Ray, Griffin, Schaffner, Baugh, & Melton, 1987; Studenski et al., 1994).

7.2   Global Indicators of the Main Process: Morbidity, Functional Limitations, and Need for Help

Following Verbrugge and Jette (1994), no distinction is made between pathology and organ dysfunction when operationalizing the model. These two constructs were subsumed under "morbidity," which is represented by somatic (cf. Table 5.3) and psychiatric (dementia, depression) diagnoses. Functional limitations are indicated by measures of sensorimotor, sensory, and intellectual capacity central to the BASE assessment.

In contrast to the model's original intention and the ICIDH definition, which both regard "disability" or "handicap" as subjectively experienced limitations in activities ranging across a variety of domains, disability is indicated by the need for help with basic and instrumental Activities of Daily Living (ADL/IADL) only. The main reasons for this are that (1) these measures have been used very frequently and are therefore thoroughly examined, (2) they are of fundamental clinical and health epidemiological importance, and (3) a model extended by numerous social activities is discussed from the complementary perspective of everyday competence by M. M. Baltes et al. in Chapter 14.

7.3   Modifiable Influencing Factors

Psychosocial resources and risks are important factors known to influence the development of need for help in old age (Mor et al., 1989; Palmore et al., 1985). In the statistical model, they are indicated by the presence of a partner, the number of close companions, education, and financial resources (income, assets, and home ownership). The cardiovascular risk factors obesity, smoking, fat metabolism disorders, and hypertension are considered as indicators of a general health risk (cf. Section 4). To prevent an overload of statistical analysis by including too many variables, only the number of risk factors present was entered.

Undermedication and the number of ADR-like symptoms (cf. Sections 3 and 5) are used as indicators of therapeutic intervention. This decision is based on a model analysis which confirmed that qualitative aspects of medication (not indicated, contraindicated, or age-inappropriate) moderate the relationship between morbidity and functional limitations via ADR, whereas undermedication (i.e., untreated moderate to severe illness) has a directly negative effect.

7.4   Testing the Model

Hierarchical regression analyses of the three global constructs (main effects) – need for help with ADL, functional limitations, and morbidity – were carried out to test the model. The first two constructs were represented by the unweighted negative mean of their z-transformed indicators (Barthel and IADL Index, balance/gait, subjective walking distance, close vision, speech-range hearing, Digit Letter test), whereas somatic morbidity was determined by the number of moderate to severe somatic illnesses.

In the hierarchical analyses, the indicator seen as more proximal in the theoretical "main pathway" of the model was entered before the more distal one. A theoretically motivated hierarchy was not assumed for the influence factors. Instead, their independent efficacy was tested groupwise by entering them into models already containing the main effects first or, alternatively, last. Significance was only accepted if the indicators contributed significantly to the explanation of variance in both steps. The results are presented in Tables 5.9 and 5.10.

Regarding the hypothesized main effects, indicators of functional limitations proved to explain more than 70% ($R^2 = .706$, $p < .001$) of the variability in the need for help with ADL, whereas somatic illnesses had no additional independent effect (Table 5.9). This needs to be seen in context with the direct multiple correlation of .41 ($p < .001$) between medical diagnoses and need for help. Thus, the effect of morbidity on the development of need for help can be explained completely by functional limitations in the sensorimotor, sensory, and intellectual domain. Accordingly, the regression analysis of functional limitations reveals a highly significant effect of somatic illnesses ($R^2 = .187$, $p < .001$), which was mainly due to coronary heart disease, heart failure, arthritis, and dorsopathy (Table 5.10). These findings confirm the model assumption of a main pathway as shown in Figure 5.3.

However, the standardized regression coefficients of the individual indicators shown in Table 5.10 indicate that this model is not equally valid for all illnesses. Direct effects on need for help that are not moderated by functional limitations were found for dementia ($\beta = .13$, $p < .001$), depression ($\beta = .08$, $p < .001$), and coronary heart disease ($\beta = .05$, $p < .05$). A more detailed analysis on coronary heart disease showed that the correlation with ADL/IADL is due to specific items (climbing stairs, going for walks, shopping, and transportation). Although this effect is plausible, as these activities are possible inducers of acute angina, the low effect size does not warrant fundamental modification of the model. However, in order to take into account the more robust direct effects of psychiatric morbidity on need for help, the model was changed to regard dementia and depression as modifying factors rather than part of the main process. In Figure 5.4, the modified model is presented and all effect sizes are provided (as estimated proportions of explained variance).

Significant effects on functional limitations were observed for most of the modifiable risk factors: medication (mainly ADR-like symptoms), psychiatric morbidity (dementia and depression), and psychosocial factors (financial resources and education). In addition to the main effect of morbidity, all of these factors explain 25% of variance in functional limitations if age and gender are taken into account (at least 20% of variance). Altogether, the indicators maximally explain about 65%.

Significant associations with all determinants of the main process (somatic morbidity, functional limitations, and need for help) could be shown for the biological markers. However, the direct effect on the development of need for help is rather small. Despite the large zero-order correlation between age and ADL status ($r = -.60$, $p < .001$), age itself is not a major risk factor for the development of need for help. The gender differences in ADL status disadvantaging women (zero-order correlation between ADL and female gender: $r = .17$, $p < .001$) can also be explained by other factors.

7.5   Summary of the Model

Three results need to be emphasized: (1) there is a significant relationship between medication quality and functional limitations in old age; (2) independent of other factors, psychiatric morbidity is associated with somatic morbidity, functional limitations, and the need for help; (3) in the disablement process, biological factors' (age, gender) largest effect is on the development of functional limitations.

Table 5.9. *Hierarchical regression analyses of need for help, functional limitations, and morbidity on other moderating factors influencing the disablement process in old age: Changes in* R²

	Need for help		Functional limitations		Morbidity	
	Maximal[a]	Minimal[a]	Maximal	Minimal	Maximal	Minimal
Main effects						
Functional limitations	.706***	—	—	—	—	—
Morbidity	.009	—	.187***	—	—	—
Moderating factors						
Intervention	.002	.000	.026***	.007**	.264***	.167***
Number of risk factors	.003*	.001	.037***	.000	.044***	.051***
Psychiatric morbidity	.017***	.017***	.150***	.035***	.037***	.010*
Psychosocial factors	.003	.004	.107***	.023***	.033**	.011†
Biological factors	.006**	.006	.392***	.208***	.067***	.020***
R	.862		.805		.590	
R^2	.744		.648		.349	
Adj. R^2	.729		.633		.334	
df	23, 488		22, 493		11, 504	
F	52.409***		41.393***		24.522***	

† $p < .10$, * $p < .05$, ** $p < .01$, *** $p < .001$.

[a] The moderating factors were each entered into the model first and then last to determine their maximal and minimal (specific) contribution toward explaining variance; the main effects were entered strictly hierarchically.

Table 5.10. *Hierarchical regression analyses of need for help, functional limitations, and morbidity as well as other modifying factors influencing the disablement process in old age: Standardized regression coefficients (β)*

	Need for help	Functional limitations	Morbidity
Functional limitations			
Balance/gait	.34***	—	—
Subjective walking distance	.31***	—	—
Vision	.09**	—	—
Hearing	.01	—	—
Cognitive functioning	.07*	—	—
Morbidity			
Diabetes	.02	.07*	—
Thyroid disorders	.01	-.01	—
Coronary heart disease	.05*	.06*	—
Peripheral vascular disease	.00	.02	—
Cerebral atherosclerosis	-.02	.03	—
Congestive heart failure	.00	.06*	—
Osteoarthritis	.01	.10***	—
Osteoporosis	.01	-.01	—
Dorsopathies	-.03	.07*	—
Chronic obstructive lung disease	-.01	.05†	—
Other	.02	.04	—
Intervention			
Undermedication	.00	.02	.29***
ADR-like symptoms	.02	.09**	.33***
Risk factors			
Number	-.04	.01	.24***
Psychiatric morbidity			
Dementia	.13***	.19***	.03
Depression	.08***	.09**	.10**
Psychosocial factors			
Financial resources	-.04	-.06*	.07†
Education	-.02	-.13***	-.05
Partner present	-.05†	-.05	.01
Close companions	.02	.00	-.05
Biological factors			
Age	.11**	.55***	.17***
Gender	.05	.04	.02

† $p < .1$, * $p < .05$, ** $p < .01$, *** $p < .001$.

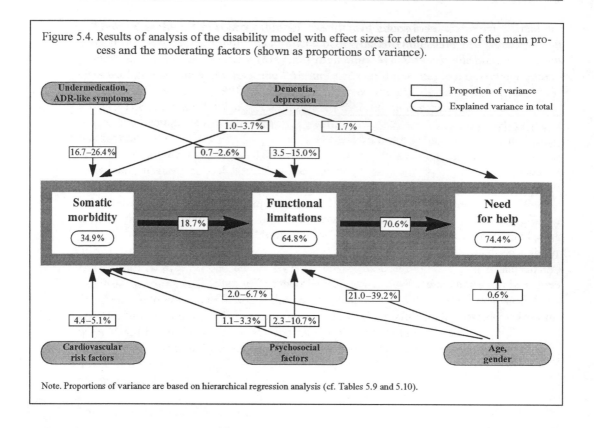

Figure 5.4. Results of analysis of the disability model with effect sizes for determinants of the main process and the moderating factors (shown as proportions of variance).

Note. Proportions of variance are based on hierarchical regression analysis (cf. Tables 5.9 and 5.10).

At first glance, medication quality explaining 0.7% to 2.6% of the variance does not seem to be an important risk factor for functional limitations. However, it should be considered that hierarchical analysis yields a very conservative estimate of the medication effect because of the intercorrelation between morbidity and medication ($r = .32$). One could also take the opposite position by hypothesizing that effects of somatic morbidity become obvious depending on the quality of pharmaceutical intervention. If medication quality is accordingly entered into the model first, it explains 10% of the variance in functional limitations while somatic morbidity explains 11%. Thus, medication quality could play an equally important role in the disablement process as did somatic morbidity.

Considering the significance of psychiatric morbidity in the present context, it should be stressed that dementia, independent of intellectual decline as measured by the Digit Letter test, contributes to the need for help with ADL. This may be due to the typical impairment of everyday functioning in dementia (cf. Lindenberger & Reischies, Chapter 12). The relationship between depression and the need for help could be explained by the decline in activities caused by depression (e.g., due to loss of interest, motivation, and drive). Vice versa, it could also indicate depressive reactions to the need for help (cf. Borchelt et al., Chapter 15).

In the disablement process, the biological factors of age and gender mainly have an effect on the development of functional limitations. Although a considerable proportion of the strong correlation between age and functional limitations ($r = .71, p < .001$) is also due to other factors, age remains the most effective single factor, contributing at least 21% to the explanation of variance in functional limitations.

8   General Discussion

In the context of the BASE theoretical orientations, the Geriatrics Unit's central findings can be interpreted as demonstrating *differential aging* both in the varying age correlations with considered health domains (morbidity, medication, functionality) and in their differing correlation with individual characteristics (risk factors, resources) and interventions (medication). Although health "in old age" appears to be characterized by multimorbidity, multimedication, and multiple functional limitations, its main feature is variability, which can be attributed to many different, sometimes age-independent factors. This complexity can only be grasped by a theoretical stance that interprets health in old age as a *systemic phenomenon*. Medically, the important roles shown for modifiable risk factors in the development of morbidity, functional limitations, and the need for help – which do not just represent gradual degrees of aging, but are *qualitatively discontinuous* – open important perspectives for primary and secondary prevention in old and very old age. This potential indicates the existence of a *reserve capacity* in somatic health which not only depends on intra- but also on extraindividual factors.

8.1   *Somatic Morbidity and the Significance of Risk Factors*
for Atherosclerosis

We could show that (1) the extent of morbidity and multimorbidity varies with the perspective selected (objective, subjective, or interventional), (2) somatic morbidity continues to increase by age after 70, and (3) modifiable risk factors are involved in illnesses in old age.

We were also able to show that in old and very old age (a) atherosclerotic disorders still coincide with "classical" risk factors and (b) atherosclerosis-free 70- to 84-year-olds with a low short-term mortality risk still carry a higher atherosclerosis risk than those aged 85 and over. This does not prove the validity of the atherosclerosis risk factor model for old age, but makes it very likely. Diagnostic procedures and therapy, particularly concerning fat metabolism disorders in old age, should be affected by this finding. In our opinion, our results (which are consistent with other studies; Benfante & Reed, 1990; Kafonek & Kwiterovich, 1990; Luepker, 1990; Scandinavian Simvastatin Survival Study Group, 1994) should provide sufficient reason to prescribe lipid-lowering medication to an elderly patient with a fat metabolism disorder not yet manifested in atherosclerosis. Of course, in cases of manifest atherosclerosis, further aspects need to be taken into account (life quality, life expectancy, medication risks).

Taken together, these findings indicate that maintenance of health is achievable for a large proportion of the aging population (Fries, 1990) through better intervention and prevention in the future. However, the present state of the examined cohorts can be characterized by illness, disability, and treatment needs (McKinlay, McKinlay, & Beaglehole, 1989).

8.2   *Medication Quality in Old Age: General and Individual Aspects*

Despite being somewhat more neutral than the terms polypharmacy or polypragmacy, multimedication has a clearly negative connotation in the gerontological literature. The BASE findings support the necessity of specifying qualitative aspects of geriatrically oriented pharmacotherapy. Multimedication can signify unnecessary or inappropriate medication, but also undermedication or optimal medication that can prevent negative functional consequences of somatic (multi)morbidity.

Even if there is no other study with a comparable range of detailed, explicitly defined, and standardized indicators of medication quality and objective morbidity, it is possible to put individual aspects of BASE findings into the context of previous research on medication. Our data on the prevalence of prescribed medication are consistent with the drug utilization figures published by the German health insurances for 1992 (Klauber & Selke, 1993). For community-dwelling participants, we observed inappropriate medication in 17% as compared with 14% reported by Stuck et al. (1994). The prevalence of ADR-like symptoms was discussed above and seems quite plausible. In fact, no methodologically comparable study exists. In view of the considerable coincidence of specific drugs with ADR-like symptoms in this sample, research work on this topic should have a high priority, particularly as the majority of prescriptions are for older adults – who, at the same time, are systematically excluded from clinical medication trials. Therefore, our methodological approach, which only takes account of previously recorded ADR for each drug, could even be considered too conservative.

8.3   *Functional Capacity and the Development of Disability*

The BASE findings show that functional health is the main "building block" for an integrating perspective on somatic health in old age. The need for help with basic and instrumental Activities of Daily Living is directly dependent on sensory (vision, hearing), sensorimotor (balance, coordination), and intellectual functioning, and only dependent on morbidity insofar as these functions are impaired. Although somatic morbidity in old age is a risk factor for functional limitations, it is not a sufficient causal factor for the development of the need for help. Psychiatric morbidity differs in this respect.

In this context, it is of great importance that the quality of pharmacotherapy influences functional health. Presumably, the cross-sectional analysis of this aspect under- rather than overestimates the effect. The distinction between primarily morbidity-induced and primarily drug-induced effects is not possible in this design so that false attributions will have occurred in both directions. Hierarchical analysis will therefore always underestimate the arbitrarily subordinated aspect.

Finally, one further finding on functional capacity needs to be mentioned, that is, the development of functional limitations associated with age. The strong independent effect of age on functional capacity indicates that the morbidity-unrelated development of "frailty" plays an important role in the final phase of life (Bortz, 1990; Mor et al., 1989). With regard to the comprehensive data analysis, it seems unlikely that additional explaining factors could be identified. Thus, age-related factors remain significant for the development of functional limitations and consecutive loss of independence.

References

Applegate, W. B., Blass, J. P., & Williams, T. F. (1990). Instruments for the functional assessment of older patients. *New England Journal of Medicine, 322*, 1207–1214.

Barrett-Connor, E., Suarez, L., Khaw, K. T., Criqui, M. H., & Wingard, D. L. (1984). Ischemic heart disease risk factors after age 50. *Journal of Chronic Diseases, 37*, 903–908.

Beers, M. H., & Ouslander, J. G. (1989). Risk factors in geriatric drug prescribing. *Drugs, 37*, 105–112.

Beers, M. H., Ouslander, J. G., Rollingher, I., Reuben, D. B., Brooks, J., & Beck, J. C. (1991). Explicit criteria for determining inappropriate medication use in nursing home residents. *Archives of Internal Medicine, 151*, 1825–1832.

Benfante, R., & Reed, D. (1990). Is elevated serum cholesterol level a risk factor for coronary heart disease in the elderly? *Journal of the American Medical Association, 263*, 393–396.

Besdine, R. W. (1993). Stroke prevention in the elderly. *Connecticut Medicine, 57*, 287–292.

Borchelt, M., & Horgas, A. L. (1994). Screening an elderly population for verifiable adverse drug reactions: Methodological approach and initial data analysis of the Berlin Aging Study (BASE). *Annals of the New York Academy of Sciences, 717*, 270–281.

Borchelt, M., & Steinhagen-Thiessen, E. (1992). Physical performance and sensory functions as determinants of independence in activities of daily living in the old and the very old. *Annals of the New York Academy of Sciences, 673*, 350–361.

Bortz, W. M. (1990). The trajectory of dying: Functional status in the last year of life. *Journal of the American Geriatrics Society, 38*, 146–150.

Branch, L. G., Katz, S., Kniepmann, K., & Papsidero, J. A. (1984). A prospective study of functional status among community elders. *American Journal of Public Health, 74*, 266–268.

Bühler, F. R., Vesanen, K., Watters, J. T., & Bolli, P. (1988). Impact of smoking and heart attack, strokes, blood pressure control, drug dose and quality of life aspects in the International Prospective Primary Prevention Study in Hypertension. *American Heart Journal, 115*, 282–287.

Campion, E. W., Avorn, J., Reder, V. A., & Olins, N. J. (1987). Overmedication of low-weight elderly. *Archives of Internal Medicine, 147*, 945–947.

Castelli, W. P. (1988). Cholesterol and lipids in the risk of coronary heart artery disease: The Framingham Heart Study. *Canadian Journal of Cardiology, 4*, 5A–10A.

Castleden, C. M., & Pickles, H. (1988). Suspected adverse drug reactions in elderly patients reported to the Committee on Safety of Medications. *British Journal of Clinical Pharmacology, 26*, 347–353.

Chrischilles, E. A., Foley, D. J., Wallace, R. B., Lemke, J. H., Semla, T. P., Hanlon, J. T., Glynn, R. J., Ostfeld, A. M., & Guralnik, J. M. (1992). Use of medications by persons 65 and over: Data from the Established Populations for Epidemiologic Studies of the Elderly. *Journal of Gerontology: Medical Sciences, 47*, M137–M144.

Cornoni-Huntley, J., Brock, D. B., Ostfeld, A. M., Taylor, J. O., & Wallace, R. B. (1986). *Established Populations for Epidemiologic Studies of the Elderly (EPESE): Resource data book* (NIH Publication No. 86–2443). Rockville, MD: U.S. Department of Health and Human Services.

Dahlöf, B., Lindholm, L. H., Hansson, L., Schersten, B., Ekbom, T., & Wester, P. O. (1991). Morbidity and mortality in the Swedish Trial in Old Patients with Hypertension (STOP-Hypertension). *The Lancet, 338*, 1281–1285.

European Atherosclerosis Society Group. (1988). The recognition and management of hyperlipidemia in adults: A policy statement of the European Atherosclerosis Society. *European Heart Journal, 9*, 571–600.

Feinstein, A. R., Josephy, B. R., & Wells, C. K. (1986). Scientific and clinical problems in indexes of functional disability. *Annals of Internal Medicine, 105*, 413–420.

Fries, J. F. (1990). Medical perspectives upon successful aging. In P. B. Baltes & M. M. Baltes (Eds.), *Successful aging: Perspectives from the behavioral sciences* (pp. 35–49). Cambridge: Cambridge University Press.

Furmaga, E. M., Murphy, C. M., & Carter, B. L. (1993). Isolated hypertension in older patients. *Clinical Pharmacy, 12*, 347–358.

Gilchrist, W. J., Lee, Y. C., Tam, H. C., MacDonald, J. B., & Williams, B. O. (1987). Prospective study of drug reporting by general practitioners for an elderly population referred to a geriatric service. *British Medical Journal, 294*, 289–290.

Greenblatt, D. J., Sellers, E. M., & Shader, R. I. (1982). Drug disposition in old age. *New England Journal of Medicine, 306*, 1081–1088.

Guralnik, J., Branch, L. G., Cummings, S. R., & Curb, J. D. (1989). Physical performance measures in aging research. *Journal of Gerontology: Medical Sciences, 44*, M141–M146.

Harris, B. A., Jette, A. M., Campion, E. W., & Cleary, P. D. (1986). Validity of self-report measures of functional disability. *Topics in Geriatric Rehabilitation, 1*, 31–41.

Hazzard, W. R. (1987). Aging, lipoprotein metabolism and atherosclerosis: A clinical conundrum. In S. R. Bates & E. C. Gangloff (Eds.), *Atherogenesis and aging* (pp. 75–103). New York: Springer.

Heikkinen, E., Arajarvi, R. L., Era, P., Jylha, M., Kinnunen, V., Leskinen, A., Leskinen, E., Masseli, E., Pohjolainen, P., Rahkila, P., et al. (1984). Functional capacity of men born in 1906–10, 1926–30 and 1946–50: A basic report. *Scandinavian Journal of Social Medicine, 33* (Suppl.), 1–97.

Hutchinson, T. A., Flegel, K. M., Hopingkong, H., Bloom, W. S., Kramer, M. S., & Trummer, E. G. (1983). Reasons for disagreement in the standardized assessment of suspected adverse drug reactions. *Clinical Pharmacology and Therapeutics, 34*, 421–426.

Hutchinson, T. A., Flegel, K. M., Kramer, M. S., Leduc, D. G., & Hopingkong, M. S. (1986). Frequency, severity and risk factors for adverse reactions in adult outpatients: A prospective study. *Journal of Chronic Diseases, 39*, 533–542.

Imms, F. J., & Edholm, O. G. (1981). Studies of gait and mobility in the elderly. *Age and Ageing, 10*, 147–156.

Jette, A. M., Branch, L. G., & Berlin, J. (1990). Musculoskeletal impairments and physical disablement among the aged. *Journal of Gerontology: Medical Sciences, 45*, M203–M208.

Kafonek, S. D., & Kwiterovich, P. O. (1990). Treatment of hypercholesterolemia in the elderly. *Annals of Internal Medicine, 112*, 723–725.

Kage, A., Nitschke, I., Fimmel, S., & Köttgen, E. (1996). Referenzwerte im Alter: Beeinflussung durch Alter, Medikation und Morbidität. In K. U. Mayer & P. B. Baltes (Eds.), *Die Berliner Altersstudie* (pp. 405–427). Berlin: Akademie Verlag.

Kannel, W. B., D'Agostino, R. B., Wilson, P. W., Belanger, A. J., & Gagnon, D. R. (1990). Diabetes, fibrinogen, and risk of cadiovascular disease: The Framingham Study. *American Heart Journal, 120*, 672–676.

Kannel, W. B., & Higgins, M. (1990). Smoking and hypertension as predictors of cardiovascular risk in population studies. *Journal of Hypertension, 8* (Suppl. 5), S3–S8.

Kannel, W. B., McGee, D., & Gordon, T. (1976). A general cardiovascular risk profile: The Framingham Study. *American Journal of Cardiology, 38*, 46–51.

Katz, S., Downs, T. D., Cash, H. R., & Grotz, R. C. (1970). Progress in development of the index of ADL. *The Gerontologist, 1*, 20–30.

Katz, S., Ford, A. B., Moskowitz, R. W., Jackson, B. A., & Jaffe, M. W. (1963). Studies of illness in the aged. The index of ADL: A standardized measure of biological and psychosocial function. *Journal of the American Medical Association, 185*, 914–919.

Klauber, J., & Selke, G. W. (1993). Arzneimittelverordnungen nach Altersgruppen. In U. Schwabe & D. Paffrath (Eds.), *Arzneiverordnungs-Report '93* (pp. 498–507). Stuttgart: Gustav Fischer.

Klein, U., Klein, M., Sturm, H., Rothenbühler, M., Huber, R., Stucki, P., Gikalov, I., Keller, M., & Hoigné, R. (1976). The frequency of adverse drug reactions is dependent upon age, sex, and duration of hospitalization. *International Journal of Clinical Pharmacology, 13*, 187–195.

Kramer, M. S., Leventhal, J. M., Hutchinson, T. A., & Feinstein, A. R. (1979). An algorithm for the operational assessment of adverse drug reactions: I. Background, description, and instructions for use. *Journal of the American Medical Association, 242*, 623–632.

Kruse, W., Rampmaier, J., Frauenrath-Volkers, C., Volkert, D., Wankmüller, I., Oster, P., & Schlierf, G. (1991). Drug-prescribing patterns in old age. *European Journal of Clinical Pharmacology, 41*, 441–448.

Lachs, M. S., Feinstein, A. R., Cooney, L. M., Drickamer, M. A., Marottoli, R. A., Pannill, F. C., & Tinetti, M. E. (1990). A simple procedure for general screening for functional disability in elderly patients. *Annals of Internal Medicine, 112*, 699–706.

Lawton, M. P., & Brody, E. M. (1969). Assessment of older people: Self-maintaining and instrumental activities of daily living. *The Gerontologist, 9*, 179–186.

Lipton, H. L., Bero, L. A., Bird, J. A., & McPhee, S. J. (1992). Undermedication among geriatric outpatients: Results of a randomized controlled trial. In J. W. Rowe & J. C. Ahronheim (Eds.), *Annual review of gerontology and geriatrics: Focus on medications and the elderly* (Vol. 12, pp. 95–108). New York: Springer.

Lisi, D. M. (1991). Reducing polypharmacy. *Journal of the American Geriatrics Society, 39*, 103–105.

Lord, S. R., Clark, R. D., & Webster, L. W. (1991). Physiological factors associated with falls in an elderly population. *Journal of the American Geriatrics Society, 39*, 1194–1200.

Luepker, R. V. (1990). Dyslipoproteinemia in the elderly: Special considerations. *Endocrinology and Metabolism Clinics of North America, 19*, 451–462.

Mahoney, F. I., & Barthel, D. W. (1965). Functional evaluation: The Barthel Index. *Maryland Medical Journal, 14*, 61 65.

Manton, K. G., & Soldo, B. J. (1985). Dynamics of health changes in the oldest old: New perspectives and evidence. *Milbank Quarterly: Health and Society, 63*, 206 285.

McKinlay, J. B., McKinlay, S. M., & Beaglehole, R. (1989). A review of the evidence concerning the impact of medical measures on recent mortality in the United States. *International Journal of Health Services, 19*, 181–208.

Meyer, B. R., & Reidenberg, M. M. (1992). Clinical pharmacology and ageing. In J. G. Evans & T. F. Williams (Eds.), *Oxford textbook of geriatric medicine* (pp. 107–116). Oxford: Oxford University Press.

Mor, V., Murphy, J., Masterson-Allen, S., Willey, C., Razmpour, A., Jackson, M. E., Greer, D., & Katz, S. (1989). Risk of functional decline among well elders. *Journal of Clinical Epidemiology, 42*, 895–904.

Myers, A. M., & Huddy, L. (1986). Evaluating physical capabilities in the elderly: The relationship between ADL self-assessments and basic abilities. *Canadian Journal on Aging, 4*, 189–200.

Nagi, S. Z. (1976). An epidemiology of disability among adults in the United States. *Milbank Quarterly, 54*, 439–467.

Nitschke, I., & Hopfenmüller, W. (1996). Die zahnmedizinische Versorgung älterer Menschen. In K. U. Mayer & P. B. Baltes (Eds.), *Die Berliner Altersstudie* (pp. 429–448). Berlin: Akademie Verlag.

Palmore, E. B., Nowlin, J. B., & Wang, H. S. (1985). Predictors of function among the old-old: A ten-year follow-up. *Journal of Gerontology, 40*, 242–250.

Pearlman, R. A. (1987). Development of a functional assessment questionnaire for geriatric patients: The Comprehensive Older Persons' Evaluation (COPE). *Journal of Chronic Diseases, 40*, 85S–94S.

Pere, J. C., Begaud, B., Haramburu, F., & Albin, H. (1986). Computerized comparison of six adverse drug reaction assessment procedures. *Clinical Pharmacology and Therapeutics, 40*, 451–461.

Pinsky, J. L., Branch, L. G., Jette, A. M., Haynes, S. G., Feinleib, M., Cornoni-Huntley, J. C., & Bailey, K. R. (1985). Framingham Disability Study: Relationship of disability to cardiovascular risk factors among persons free of diagnosed cardiovascular disease. *American Journal of Epidemiology, 122*, 644–656.

Pinsky, J. L., Jette, A. M., Branch, L. G., Kannel, W. B., & Feinleib, M. (1990). The Framingham Disability Study: Relationships of various coronary heart disease manifestations to disability in older persons living in the community. *American Journal of Public Health, 80*, 1363–1367.

Ray, W. A., Griffin, M. R., Schaffner, W., Baugh, D. K., & Melton, L. J. (1987). Psychotropic drug use and the risk of hip fracture. *New England Journal of Medicine, 316*, 363–369.

Recommendations of the European Atherosclerosis Society. (1992). Prevention of coronary heart disease: Scientific background and new clinical guidelines (Prepared by the International Task Force for Prevention of Coronary Heart Disease). *Nutrition, Metabolism and Cardiovascular Disease, 2*, 113–156.

Reid, D. D., McCartney, P., Hamilton, P. J. S., Rose, G., Jarrett, R. J., & Keen, H. (1976). Smoking and other risk factors for coronary heart disease in British civil servants. *The Lancet, 6*, 979–984.

Renner, E. A., Engle, V. F., & Graney, M. J. (1992). Prevalence and predictors of regularly scheduled presciption medications of newly admitted nursing home residents. *Journal of the American Geriatrics Society, 40*, 232–236.

Reuben, D. B., Laliberte, L., Hiris, J., & Mor, V. (1990). A hierarchical exercise scale to measure function at the Advanced Activities of Daily Living (AADL) level. *Journal of the American Geriatrics Society, 38*, 855–861.

Reuben, D. B., & Siu, A. L. (1990). An objective measure of physical function of elderly outpatients: The physical performance test. *Journal of the American Geriatrics Society, 38*, 1105–1112.

Robbins, J. M., & Austin, C. L. (1993). Common peripheral vascular disease. *Clinics in Podiatric Medicine & Surgery, 10*, 205–219.

Rosenwaike, I. (1985). A demographic portrait of the oldest old. *Milbank Quarterly: Health and Society, 63*, 187–205.

Rote Liste. (1990). Aulendorf: Editio Cantor.

Rowe, J. W., & Kahn, R. L. (1987). Human aging: Usual and successful. *Science, 237*, 143–149.

Rubenstein, L. Z., Josephson, K. R., Wieland, G. D., English, P. A., Sayre, J. A., & Kane, R. L. (1984). Effectiveness of a geriatric evaluation unit. *New England Journal of Medicine, 311*, 1664–1670.

Rubenstein, L. Z., & Rubenstein, L. V. (1992). Multidimensional geriatric assessment. In J. C. Brocklehurst, R. C. Tallis, & H. M. Fillit (Eds.), *Textbook of geriatric medicine and gerontology* (pp. 150–159). Edinburgh: Churchill Livingstone.

Rubenstein, L. Z., Schairer, C., Wieland, G. D., & Kane, R. (1984). Systematic biases in functional status assessment of elderly adults: Effects of different data sources. *Journal of Gerontology, 39*, 686–691.

Sager, M. A., Dunham, N. C., Schwantes, A., Mecum, L., Halverson, K., & Harlowe, D. (1992). Measurement of activities of daily living in hospitalized elderly: A comparison of self-report and performance-based measurements. *Journal of the American Geriatrics Society, 40*, 457–462.

Scandinavian Simvastatin Survival Study Group. (1994). Randomised trial of cholesterol lowering in 4444 patients with coronary heart disease: The Scandinavian Simvastatin Survival Study (4S). *The Lancet, 344*, 1383–1390.

Scheidegger, M. J. (1987). *Die St. Galler Seniorenbefragung von 1985/89* (Europäische Hochschulschriften Vol. 152). Bern: Peter Lang.

Shock, N. W., Greulich, R. C., Costa, P. T., Jr., Andres, R., Lakatta, E. G., Arenberg, D., & Tobin, J. D. (1984). *Normal human aging: The Baltimore Longitudinal Study on Aging* (NIH Publication No. 84–2450). Washington, DC: Government Printing Office.

Sorkin, J. D., Andres, R., Muller, D. C., Baldwin, H. L., & Fleg, J. L. (1992). Cholesterol as a risk factor for coronary heart disease in elderly men: The Baltimore Longitudinal Study of Aging. *Annals of Epidemiology, 2*, 59–67.

Stampfer, M. J., Willett, W. C., Colditz, G. A., Rosner, B., Speizer, F. E., & Hennekens, C. H. (1985). A prospective study of postmenopausal estrogen therapy and coronary heart disease. *New England Journal of Medicine, 313*, 1044–1049.

Steinhagen-Thiessen, E., & Borchelt, M. (1993). Health differences in advanced old age. *Ageing and Society, 13*, 619–655.

Stuck, A. E., Beers, M. H., Steiner, A., Aronow, H. U., Rubenstein, L. Z., & Beck, J. C. (1994). Inappropriate medication use in community-residing older persons. *Archives of Internal Medicine, 154*, 2195–2200.

Stuck, A. E., Siu, A. L., Wieland, G. D., Adams, J., & Rubenstein, L. Z. (1993). Comprehensive geriatric assessment: A meta-analysis of controlled trials. *The Lancet, 342*, 1032–1036.

Studenski, S., Duncan, P. W., Chandler, J., Samsa, G., Prescott, B., Hogue, C., & Bearon, L. B. (1994). Predicting falls: The role of mobility and nonphysical factors. *Journal of the American Geriatrics Society, 42*, 297–302.

Svanborg, A. (1985). The Gothenburg longitudinal study of 70-year-olds: Clinical reference values in the elderly. In M. Bergener, M. Ermini, & H. B. Stähelin (Eds.), *Thresholds in aging* (pp. 231–239). London: Academic Press.

Tinetti, M. E. (1986). A performance-oriented assessment of mobility problems in elderly patients. *Journal of the American Geriatrics Society, 34*, 119–126.

Valentine, R. J., Grayburn, P. A., Vega, G. L., & Grundy, S. M. (1993). Lp(a) lipoprotein is an independent, discriminating risk factor for premature peripheral atherosclerosis among white men. *Archives of Internal Medicine, 154*, 801–806.

Verbrugge, L. M. (1988). Unveiling higher morbidity for men: The story. In M. W. Riley (Ed.), *Social structures and human lives: Vol. 1. Social change and the life course* (pp. 138–160). Newbury Park, CA: Sage.

Verbrugge, L. M., & Jette, A. M. (1994). The disablement process. *Social Science and Medicine, 38*, 1–14.

Vestal, R. E. (1985). Clinical pharmacology. In R. Andres, E. L. Bierman, & W. R. Hazzard (Eds.), *Principles of geriatric medicine* (pp. 424–443). New York: McGraw-Hill.

Weber, J. C. P., & Griffin, J. P. (1986). Adverse reactions and the elderly. *The Lancet, 2*, 291–292.

Williamson, J., & Chopin, J. M. (1980). Adverse reactions to prescribed drugs in the elderly: A multicentre investigation. *Age and Ageing, 9*, 73–80.

Wilson, P. W., Garrison, R. J., Castelli, W. P., Feinleib, M., McNamara, P. M., & Kannel, W. B. (1980). Prevalence of coronary heart disease in the Framingham Offspring Study: Role of lipoprotein cholesterols. *American Journal of Cardiology, 46*, 649–654.

World Health Organization (WHO). (1978). *Manual of the international statistical classification of diseases, injuries, and causes of death. Based on the recommendations of the Ninth Revision Conference, 1975, and adopted by the 29th World Health Assembly.* Geneva.

World Health Organization (WHO). (1980). *International classification of impairments, disabilities, and handicaps.* Geneva.

Zimetbaum, P., Frishman, W. A., Ooi, W. L., Derman, M. P., Aronson, M., Gidez, L. I., & Eder, H. A. (1992). Plasma lipids and lipoproteins and the incidence of cardiovascular disease in the very elderly: The Bronx Aging Study. *Arteriosclerosis and Thrombosis, 12*, 416–423.

CHAPTER 6

Psychiatric Illnesses in Old Age

Hanfried Helmchen, Margret M. Baltes, Bernhard Geiselmann, Siegfried Kanowski, Michael Linden, Friedel M. Reischies, Michael Wagner, Thomas Wernicke, and Hans-Ulrich Wilms

In this chapter, we report empirical findings from the Berlin Aging Study (BASE) on the types and frequencies of psychiatric illnesses in old age, their somatic and social predictors, and their consequences.

Nearly half (44%) of the West Berliners aged 70 and above had no psychiatric disorders, whereas less than a quarter (24%) were clearly psychiatrically ill (specified DSM-III-R[1] diagnoses). The remaining third consisted of carriers of psychopathological symptoms without illness value (16%) and of psychiatric syndromes with illness value (17%). Because this last group (mainly affective disorders) differs from the psychiatrically healthy in indicators of health impairment (in prognosis and use of psychotropic drugs), despite not fulfilling the criteria of operationalized DSM-III-R diagnoses, we speak of "subdiagnostic psychiatric morbidity." In further analyses we tried to determine the thresholds defining gradations from mental health to subdiagnostic psychiatric morbidity. Thus, with the help of a consensus conference between internists and psychiatrists, which was specifically developed for the purpose of BASE, we have demonstrated that in the case of depression, scores on the Hamilton Depression Scale (HAMD) are half as great when cases that are probably of somatic origin are excluded.

The most frequent psychiatric illness in old age is dementia, affecting 14% of those aged 70 years and above. Recalculated for the population of over-65-year-olds, this corresponds to a prevalence of 6% (excluding mild forms). The number of dementia cases increases strongly with age. Whereas no cases were found in BASE at the age of 70, more than 40% of 90-year-olds were affected. Depressive illnesses are the second most frequent psychiatric diagnosis, affecting 9% of the elderly population. There is no clear relationship with age. On the level of diagnoses, there is no association between dementia and depression. On the syndromal level, however, one finds a positive correlation between mild cognitive disorders (Mini Mental State Examination [MMSE] score over 16) and depressivity (HAMD and Center for Epidemiologic Studies-Depression Scale [CES-D]). For severe cognitive disorders, this correlation is negative.

Persons with depressive illnesses or dementia have a higher rate of physical illnesses than the mentally healthy. It remains to be seen whether physical illnesses are the causes or consequences of mental illnesses. In terms of possible social risk factors, an important finding is that a lower level of education increases the likelihood of a dementia diagnosis. This is in agreement with other studies.

Mental illnesses differ with regard to their consequences for everyday functioning. With dementia, one observes a decrease in instrumental or practical ac-

---

[1] *Diagnostic and Statistical Manual of Mental Disorders*, 3rd revision (American Psychiatric Association, 1987).

tivities, a doubling of sleep and rest phases, and a reduction of time spent outdoors. In contrast, depressive disorders rarely have similar effects. Therapeutic consequences of mental disorders also differ. About two-thirds of older people take psychotropic drugs (defined broadly, including analgesics) and a quarter take strictly defined psychotropic drugs. More than two-thirds of the psychotropic drug prescriptions can be regarded as appropriate. Overdosages were not observed. A comparatively low rate of overall prescriptions (i.e., including medication for somatic disorders) was found for persons with dementia while the rate of neuroleptics was actually increased. In the case of depressive illnesses, the general medication rate was relatively high. However, only few depressive elderly patients were treated specifically with antidepressive medication, which is suggestive of undermedication.

According to these BASE findings, it must be emphasized that older adults need careful differential diagnosis and treatment of mental disorders, because the form, course, and treatment are just as varied – if not more, due to multimorbidity – in old age as in younger years.

1   Introduction

The Psychiatry Research Unit in BASE focuses (a) on the types and frequencies[2] of psychiatric illnesses, (b) on their predictors and determinants, and (c) on their consequences, particularly for everyday functioning and the utilization of medical treatment.

1.1   Psychiatric Morbidity in Old Age

Information regarding *types and frequencies of mental illnesses* is important for early recognition and differential diagnosis, as well as for the planning of social policies and service structures. Knowledge concerning predictors should improve the etiopathogenetic understanding of risk factors, and thereby improve prediction or perhaps prevention of mental disorders. Moreover, results regarding consequences should contribute toward an optimization of compensatory strategies, help, and treatment.

Mental disorders and illnesses are often regarded as a corollary of aging. According to representative field studies, overall *psychiatric morbidity*[3] affects 20–30% of over-65-year-olds (Cooper, 1986, 1992; Copeland et al., 1987; Meller, Fichter, Schröppel, & Beck-Eichinger, 1993; Weissman et al., 1985; Welz, Lindner, Klose, & Pohlmeier, 1989; Wernicke & Reischies, 1994). Despite the age-related increase of dementia, this rate is not substantially higher than at younger ages (Dilling, Mombour, & Schmidt, 1991; Dilling, Weyerer, & Castell, 1984; Weyerer & Dilling, 1984).

A particular problem of these prevalence studies concerns the diagnostic thresholds and criteria used, especially when it comes to the diagnosis of early phases or mild forms of psychiatric disorders. Some of the difficult issues include (1) the roles that educational level, birth cohort, or gender could play in making a diagnosis, (2) the insufficient

---

[2] We report the *frequency* of a disorder with respect to the total sample or certain age groups. *Prevalence* estimates are given when frequencies are weighted to represent the West Berlin population.

[3] Morbidity including all psychiatric illnesses at a certain time (point prevalence) or within a limited space of time (6–12 months: period prevalence).

distinction between age-related benign cognitive decline and beginning dementia, or (3) the lack of diagnostic specificity of somatoform depression symptoms in multimorbidity.

There is only limited information regarding the frequency and structure of "subdiagnostic syndromes." Despite the fact that they do not reach the criteria of operationalized diagnostic systems such as DSM-III-R or ICD-10[4] (Blazer, 1989, 1995; Blazer & Williams, 1980; Goldberg & Sartorius, 1990; Henderson et al., 1993), they are suspected as having a nontrivial negative effect on life quality or utilization of medical care. This applies particularly to depressive disorders, because depressivity is a continuously distributed phenomenon, so that prevalence rates depend directly on the definition of thresholds (Häfner, 1992; Helmchen, 1992). Therefore, it is necessary to analyze the influence of different case definitions as well as that of different measurement approaches (Newmann, Klein, Jensen, & Essex, 1996) on prevalence rates of depression, especially in relation to age. To date, some argue that depression is unrelated to age (Morgan et al., 1987), others that it becomes either less frequent in old age (Gurland, Copeland, & Kuriansky, 1983; Kramer, German, Anthony, von Korff, & Skinner, 1985; Weissman et al., 1988), or even more frequent (Gertz & Kanowski, 1989; Lindesay, Briggs, & Murphy, 1989; Welz et al., 1989).

In contrast, the association between age and dementia is clearly positive. The question of whether the exponential increase of dementia (Hofman et al., 1991; Jorm, Korten, & Henderson, 1987) continues into very old age (85 years and above) remains unresolved, however. The rates published in the literature are often very unreliable, due to the low numbers of very old participants in most studies (Fratiglioni et al., 1991; Lauter, 1992; Ritchie, Kildea, & Robine, 1992). The same indeterminacy applies to the question of whether dementias are more frequent in women and whether a gender difference in dementia prevalence persists up into very old age (Bachman et al., 1992; Fratiglioni et al., 1991).

Another unresolved question is whether depression and dementia in elderly persons coincide by chance or not. Many reports indicate that depression occurs more frequently in association with mild dementia or subdiagnostic cognitive disorders (Copeland et al., 1992; Henderson, 1990; Kay et al., 1985; Lindesay et al., 1989; Welz et al., 1989). However, the pathogenetic direction of this association is still unclear (Emery & Oxman, 1992; Helmchen, 1992; Henderson, 1990; Reischies & von Spiess, 1990).

1.2   Predictors and Determinants of Psychiatric Morbidity in Old Age

Very little is also known about *causes and pathogenetic determinants* of mental illnesses in old age; however, several hypotheses postulate associations with both physical impairments and social factors. Two examples illustrate this.

First, multimorbidity and multimedication increase in old age. Many physical illnesses such as hypothyroidism, pernicious anemia, uremia, diabetes, hypertension, stroke, or heart failure (Kukull et al., 1986; Murphy, Smith, Lindesay, & Slattery, 1988; Rodin & Voshart, 1986) are considered to be risk factors for dementia or depression, as are drugs such as beta-blockers, steroids, dopa, or sedatives (Naber & Hippius, 1989; Patten & Love, 1993). However, these assumptions are usually based on clinical rather than community-dwelling populations.

[4] *International Classification of Mental and Behavioural Disorders*, 10th revision (World Health Organization [WHO], 1992).

Second, a low level of education is seen as a risk factor for dementia (Fratiglioni et al., 1991; Kay, Beamish, & Roth, 1964; O'Connor, Pollitt, & Treasure, 1991; Parsons, 1965) although this is not undisputed (Moritz & Petitti, 1993). It is not clear whether educational level changes the threshold of manifestation and diagnostic identification of dementia (e.g., by compensating for cognitive deficits over a longer period of time) or whether it also influences the process of the illness, such that a higher level of education could be associated with a higher level of neuronal stimulation or a healthier way of life and thus be linked to a lower risk of dementia-associated chronic illnesses (Berkman et al., 1986; Mortimer, 1990).

1.3   Consequences of Psychiatric Morbidity in Old Age

So far, there is not sufficient information on the many *consequences of mental illnesses* in old age – for instance, on their significance for everyday functioning or treatment utilization. Although it seems obvious that cognitive deficits impair older adults' ability to master their everyday lives, surprisingly little is known about specific relationships between cognitive disorders and everyday functioning when understood as entailing more than basic Activities of Daily Living (ADL; cf. M. M. Baltes, Mayr, Borchelt, Maas, & Wilms, 1993; Wahl, 1990). This is even more true for depressive disorders.

Prescriptions of medication are known to increase beyond the age of 40 (Klauber & Selke, 1993). Only 21% of the German population is aged over 60, but 55% of the medication expenditures occur on behalf of this group in the German health care system. Privately paid medications are not included in this calculation. Such epidemiological data show that, in old age, medication in general (and psychotropic drugs in particular) constitutes a medically – and economically – relevant problem. However, it remains unclear whether these reported prescription rates signify over- or undermedication (von Herrath, 1992).

2   Methods

The interdisciplinary structure of BASE allows references to medical, psychological, and sociological findings when answering the questions raised above. The measures shown in Table 6.1 were used for the psychiatric examinations. The standardized examination according to GMS-A/HAS allows *case definitions* on three different diagnostic levels (cf. Table 6.2): (1) psychiatrically healthy, (2) subdiagnostic syndromes, and (3) specified DSM-III-R diagnosis.

All cases were clinically graded by degree of severity and an estimate of the need for medical intervention with the Global Assessment of Functioning Scale (GAF Scale) as mild (GAF score: 61–70), moderate (GAF score: 41–60), or severe (GAF score: < 41). To achieve high interrater reliability and consistency, each case was discussed by all three examining psychiatrists. A second psychiatrist observed 52 psychiatric examinations and rated them independently, resulting in 90% concordant ratings.

For cognitive disorders, no distinction was made between clinical (see 2b in Table 6.2) cases and specified (see 3 in Table 6.2) cases, and they were grouped together as DSM-III-R dementia diagnoses because the available information was insufficient for a nosological differentiation of degenerative and vascular dementia.

Psychiatrists and internists held a *consensus conference* to bring together all available information and to rate each illness's diagnostic certainty, and objective and subjective severity. In addition, all pharmacological treatments were assessed in terms of medica-

Table 6.1. *Psychiatric measures used in the BASE Intensive Protocol*

Function	Measure	Authors
Recognition of cases and diagnoses	Geriatric Mental State, Version A/History and Aetiology Schedule (GMS-A/HAS)	Copeland, Dewey, & Griffiths-Jones, 1986; McWilliam, Copeland, Dewey, & Wood, 1988
	Criteria of diagnosis according to DSM-III-R	American Psychiatric Association, 1987; Wittchen, Saß, Zaudig, & Koehler, 1989
	Criteria of diagnosis according to ICD-10	Dilling, Mombour, & Schmidt, 1991; WHO, 1992
	Additional medical information from the Geriatrics Unit and from family physicians	Cf. Steinhagen-Thiessen & Borchelt, Chapter 5
Observer-rating		
Psychopathology	Brief Psychiatric Rating Scale (BPRS)	Overall & Gorham, 1962; Collegium Internationale Psychiatriae Scalarum (CIPS), 1986
Depression	Hamilton Depression Scale (HAMD)	Hamilton, 1967; CIPS, 1986
Self-rating		
Depressivity	Center for Epidemiologic Studies-Depression Scale (CES-D)	Radloff, 1977; Hautzinger, 1988
Somatic complaints	Complaint List	von Zerssen, 1976; CIPS, 1986
Hypochondria	Whiteley Index	Pilowsky & Spence, 1983
Illness beliefs	Illness Concepts Scale	Linden, Nather, & Wilms, 1988
Complaints, medication, and utilization of medical care	Semistructured interview	Developed by Psychiatry Unit in BASE
Neuropsychology	Mini Mental State Examination (MMSE)	Folstein, Folstein, & McHugh, 1975
	Complex Figure	Osterrieth, 1944; Read, 1987
	Reitan Trail Making Test	Reitan, 1958
	Enhanced Cued Recall	Grober, Buschke, Crystal, Bank, & Dresner, 1988
Everyday competence	Yesterday Interview	After Moss & Lawton, 1982

tion type, dosage, duration, adverse drug reactions, and indication. This allowed clinical judgments to be made regarding whether there is adequate, inappropriate, under-, or overmedication. Internists also decided whether certain complaints recorded on psychopathological symptom scales could be symptoms of a somatic illness.

Table 6.2. *Case definitions of psychiatric morbidity*

Case definition	Criteria
1. Psychiatrically healthy	No psychopathological symptoms or only isolated symptoms under the threshold given in definition 2a
2. Subdiagnostic syndromes	
a. Symptom carriers	At least one leading psychopathological symptom
	For cognitive disorders: in addition, GMS-A dementia score with at least one further symptom
	For depressive disorders: in addition, GMS-A depression score with at least two further symptoms
	Persistent or recurring symptoms during the past four weeks
b. Psychiatric illness, diagnosis "not otherwise specified"	Criteria of definition 2a fulfilled
	Clinical diagnosis of illness (anamnesis, subjective perception of illness, objective impairment of functioning) and need for therapeutic intervention
	But no specified DSM-III-R diagnosis possible
3. Specified DSM-III-R diagnosis	First criteria of definition 2b fulfilled
	But specified DSM-III-R diagnosis possible

Indicators of everyday functioning and competence were recorded with the Yesterday Interview (Moss & Lawton, 1982). The type, frequency, and duration of activities were reconstructed from participants' reports of the day before the interview, leading to descriptions of the complexity and rhythm of daily life (cf. M. M. Baltes et al., Chapter 14 in this volume).

3   Results

In this section, we give a short overview of the major psychiatric findings. For more detailed reports, we refer to the cited articles from the Psychiatry Unit. The results are based on the Intensive Protocol sample (cf. P. B. Baltes et al., Chapter 1) consisting of 516 participants, with 43 men and 43 women in each age group (70–74, 75–79, 80–84, 85–89, 90–94, 95+). Seventy-four participants lived in senior citizens' or nursing homes, or hospitals for the chronically ill (see Linden et al., Chapter 16).

3.1   *Types and Frequencies of Mental Illnesses in Old Age*

The estimated *prevalence* of psychiatric morbidity in BASE (specified DSM-III-R diagnoses; see Table 6.3) amounts to 24% (Helmchen, Linden, & Wernicke, 1996). This is within the range of rates reported in the literature, particularly if one takes into account that these rates have mostly referred to populations aged 60 or 65 and above, with a much higher proportion of younger persons, and thus lower dementia prevalence. The inclusion of milder illnesses, that is illnesses "not otherwise specified" according to DSM-III-R, leads to a prevalence rate of 40%, which is also similar to the rates of total psychiatric morbidity given in the literature as varying between 20% and 40% (Cooper, 1992; Häfner, 1992).

The most frequent mental illnesses in old age are dementia and depression. In BASE, *dementia* prevalence was 14%, more than double the rates of 3–7% reported in other studies; but in contrast to BASE, those earlier rates refer only to moderate or severe cases of dementia in younger populations aged 60 and above. If dementia prevalence is calculated from the age of 60 onward using the BASE data, assuming a proportion of 0.5% persons with moderate or severe dementia in the 60- to 69-year-old population, one obtains estimated rates of 5% of the over-60-year-olds, 6% of the over-65-year-olds, and 8% of the over-70-year-olds, equivalent to other studies' findings.

Prevalence rates for dementia increase in our study from 0% in the 70- to 74-year-olds to about 40% in 90- to 94-year-olds. This age correlation remains if the analysis is restricted to moderate and severe cases (70–74: 0%, 80–84: 11%, 90–94: 32%). The increase is not exponential, and there is no further increase among men aged 95 and above (cf. Fig. 6.1). For the group of those aged 95 and above, the difference between the rate found in BASE and that assumed by Jorm et al. (1987) is statistically significant for both men and women.

This finding is important in view of the particularly high proportion of very old participants examined in BASE (86 persons aged 95 and above). It could indicate that the exponential increase of dementia with age that has been extrapolated rather than established in the literature is true neither for women nor for men aged 95 and above. This hypothesis is supported by the fact that the observed stabilization of the dementia rate is found despite a counteractive cohort effect in education (i.e., lower education levels in persons born before 1900). Although dementia-related selectivity effects were observed (i.e., BASE may underrepresent dementia cases in the parent population; see Lindenberger et al., Chapter 2), it remains unclear whether such selectivity can completely explain the flattening prevalence in very old age.

The prevalence of *major depression* in BASE is 5%, which is rather high in comparison with rates in other studies (Henderson et al., 1993; Meller et al., 1993). If depressive disorders of potentially somatic origin are disregarded, the prevalence of major depression is reduced to 1% ($n = 8$).

Subdiagnostic syndromes are more frequent (33%) than specified morbidity (24%). This is especially pertinent to depressive disorders, with a prevalence of 23% subdiagnostic syndromes as compared with 9% DSM-III-R specified morbidity. These subdiagnostic cases are distinguishable from psychiatrically healthy persons in terms of various indicators of morbidity, for instance, disruption of everyday activities or differences in medication (cf. Table 6.4).

There is no clear age-related trend in the prevalence of depression in old age. This applies to major depression and dysthymia as well as to the "not otherwise specified" depressive syndromes, which require therapeutic intervention according to clinical judgment, but do not fulfill the criteria of DSM-III-R (see Table 6.5).

An age trend was also not found for the average manifestation of depressive syndromes as measured by the observer-rating scale HAMD (see Table 6.5). However,

Table 6.3. *Frequencies of psychiatric disorders among West Berliners aged 70 and above, using data from BASE weighted by age and gender (data collection 1990–93)*

| | Diagnostic morbidity DSM-III-R specified diagnoses | | Subdiagnostic syndromes | |
| | | | Not otherwise specified illnesses | "Pure" symptom level[a] |
DSM-III-R No.	Name	*Prevalence in % (n total)* [n mild/moderate/severe]	*Prevalence in % (n total)* [n mild/moderate/severe]	*Prevalence in % (n)*
Depressive syndrome				
	Total	*9.1* (48) [13/31/4]	*17.8* (85) [47/38/–]	*5.2* (24)
296.22–296.24	Major depression[b]	*4.8* (23) [–/20/3]		
296.25, 296.35	Major depression, partially remitted	*0.6* (3) [not defined]		
300.40	Dysthymic disorder	*2.0* (11) [3/8/–]		
309.00	Depressive adjustment disorder	*0.7* (5) [4/1/–]		
290.21	Dementia with depression[c]	*1.0* (6) [2/3/1]		
Anxiety syndrome				
	Total	*1.9* (8) [3/5/–]	*2.5* (9) [9/–/–]	*6.0* (17)
300.02	Generalized anxiety disorder	*0.9* (2) [–/2/–]		
300.01	Panic disorder without agoraphobia	*0.0* (1) [–/1/–]		
300.22	Agoraphobia without panic disorder	*0.8* (3) [2/1/–]		
309.24	Anxious adaptation disorder	*0.0* (1) [–/1/–]		
300.30	Obsessive compulsive disorder	*0.2* (1) [1/–/–]		
Organically caused syndrome, cognitive				
290.00, 290.20, 290.21	Dementia	*13.9* (109) [37/33/39]	Not defined	*2.8* (20)

Organically caused syndrome, noncognitive

Code	Diagnosis	At least one DSM-III-R specified diagnosis	At least one not otherwise specified illness, but no DSM-III-R specified diagnosis	Symptoms, but neither specified nor not otherwise specified illness
	Total	0.6 (7) [2/5/–]	1.6 (8) [5/3/–]	2.0 (12)
293.81, 293.82	Organically caused delusional disorder or hallucinosis			
310.10	Organically caused personality disorder	0.6 (6) [1/5/–]		

Psychiatric syndrome due to psychotropic substances

Code	Diagnosis	At least one DSM-III-R specified diagnosis	At least one not otherwise specified illness, but no DSM-III-R specified diagnosis	Symptoms, but neither specified nor not otherwise specified illness
	Total	1.1 (9) [3/6/–]	0.0 (0) [–/–/–]	2.0 (9)
303.90, 305.00	Alcohol abuse			
304.10, 305.40	Abuse or dependence on sedatives, hypnotics, anxiolytics	0.7 (3) [–/3/–]		

Schizophrenic or paranoid syndrome

Code	Diagnosis	At least one DSM-III-R specified diagnosis	At least one not otherwise specified illness, but no DSM-III-R specified diagnosis	Symptoms, but neither specified nor not otherwise specified illness
	Total	0.0 (0)	0.0 (0) [–/–/–]	0.0 (0)
295.62	Chronic residual schizophrenia	0.2 (1) [not defined]		
297.10	Delusional (paranoid) disorder	0.5 (2) [–/2/–]		

Total

		At least one DSM-III-R specified diagnosis	At least one not otherwise specified illness, but no DSM-III-R specified diagnosis	Symptoms, but neither specified nor not otherwise specified illness
	All	23.5 (166)	16.9 (72)	16.0 (74)

Note. In cases of comorbidity, multiple diagnoses are possible; see, e.g., note b. Sleep disorders and somatoform disorders are not included.

a "Pure" symptom carriers: participants who neither have a diagnosis in the same row of the table nor a DSM-III-R specified or not otherwise specified diagnosis from another category.

b Including four cases with an additional diagnosis of a mild dementia, but whose depressive symptoms are so clear that a separate diagnosis of depression appears adequate.

c Cases that formally fulfill the criteria of major depression, but cannot be classified as such because of equally strong symptoms of dementia. Therefore, these cases are also included in the DSM-III-R dementia category.

Table 6.4. *Differences between different levels of depression regarding several morbidity indicators often associated with depression*

	Not depressive (*n* = 270)		Symptom level (*n* = 34)		Not otherwise specified depressive illness (*n* = 66)		DSM-III-R specified depressive illness (*n* = 37)	
ADL score[a]	95.5*	(8.8)	89.1	(16.7)	89.8	(13.6)	85.7	(16.3)
IADL score[a]	16.6	(5.4)	14.0	(7.3)	13.3*	(7.0)	9.7	(7.1)
Number of common somatic illnesses	2.9	(1.8)	3.5	(2.1)	3.9	(1.9)	3.6	(2.0)
Number of somatic drugs[b]	3.6	(2.5)	4.4	(3.0)	5.1	(2.8)	4.9	(3.0)
Number of psycho-tropic drugs (incl. sedatives/hypnotics)	0.25	(0.50)	0.38	(0.70)	0.48*	(0.64)	0.89	(1.00)

Note. Cases of dementia (*n* = 109) were excluded to eliminate an effect of dementia on the variables. All five variables change significantly with the level of depression diagnosis (ANOVA, *p* < .01). Values are given as means, with standard deviations in parentheses.
* Significant difference in comparison to following level (Scheffé Test, *p* < .05).
[a]ADL: Activities of Daily Living (Barthel Index); IADL: Instrumental Activities of Daily Living.
[b]Participants' reports in psychiatric interview about utilization of medication during the past fortnight (excluding externally applied drugs, psychotropic medication, and sedatives/hypnotics).

statistically significant age differences were found when analyzing the self-rating CES-D depressivity scores of men and women both together and separately. Further analysis using the Scheffé Test shows that the main distinction occurred between those aged 70 to 84 and the remaining older groups. This corresponds to findings from Wallace and O'Hara (1992), who also described a rise of CES-D scores with age, and partially to those from Fuhrer et al. (1992), who only observed a rise of scores in men.

In the interpretation of these findings one must consider all three measurement levels for depression in relation to each other; that is, self- and observer-rating of the depressive syndrome as well as the prevalence of depressive illnesses. Syndrome rating scales, and self-rating scales in particular, can be regarded as screening measures for depression (Radloff & Teri, 1986). This means that they have higher sensitivity than specificity; that is, they also record nondepressive, nonspecific complaints and feelings of strain (Wallace & O'Hara, 1992). This notion is supported by the significant negative correlation (*r* = -.64) found between CES-D scores and subjective well-being (see Smith et al., Chapter 17). It is also corroborated by a French study which recommends a six-point higher depressivity threshold for women than for men (23 vs. 17), because women appear to report more CES-D complaints that do not correspond to their observer-rated depressivity scores (Fuhrer & Rouillon, 1989).

Depressivity scales can also measure complaints caused by age-typical multimorbidity. The association of high CES-D scores with physical impairment (Berkman et al., 1986; Gatz & Hurwics, 1990) could be interpreted as an indication that CES-D also cap-

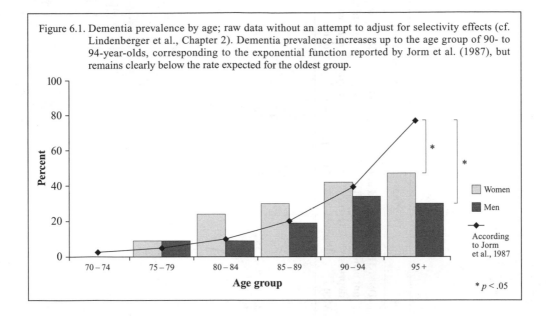

Figure 6.1. Dementia prevalence by age; raw data without an attempt to adjust for selectivity effects (cf. Lindenberger et al., Chapter 2). Dementia prevalence increases up to the age group of 90- to 94-year-olds, corresponding to the exponential function reported by Jorm et al. (1987), but remains clearly below the rate expected for the oldest group.

tures nondepressive complaints. A similar case could be made for the finding that CES-D scores are lower in men, but are more strongly correlated with physical impairments than in women (Fuhrer et al., 1992). In our sample, the number of somatic illnesses is more closely linked to the sum of somatic-type CES-D items than to the sum of psychiatric-type CES-D items (.23 vs. .16). An analogous observation was made for HAMD (.29 vs. .17). The assumption that these depression scales not only measure psychopathological but also somatic complaints is supported mainly by the fact that the average total score in HAMD is nearly halved from 5.7 to 2.9, and the percentage of nondepressed persons (with a score of 0–6) rises from 60% to 80% if one does not count the symptoms that could equally be caused by somatic morbidity (Linden, Borchelt, Barnow, & Geiselmann, 1995). It is likely that this applies even more to the self-rating CES-D scale. Of course, observer-rating scales measure different aspects than self-rating scales (Boyle, 1985; Steer, Beck, Riskind, & Brown, 1987), because the clinical judgment of the observer always plays a part in assessment, while complaints are reflected without a filter in self-rating scales. Thus, complaints can be biased by depressive cognitions or anosognosia. Accordingly, the correlation between CES-D and HAMD is not very strong ($r = .65$).

In summary we conclude that, judging from the cross-sectional BASE sample and despite the CES-D findings, there is no age association for depressive illnesses in old age. Furthermore, women tend to have more depressive symptoms and specified depressive illnesses than men, even though the gender difference in major depression prevalence is not significant in our study because of the small number of cases. Thus, the gender difference in depressive disorders observed in younger age groups (Gebhardt & Kliemitz, 1986) is also carried through into old age.

An important diagnostic question in old age is the *relationship between depression and dementia*. On the diagnostic-categorical level, that is, the level of specified DSM-III-R diagnoses, they are not linked to each other more than by chance (Helmchen & Linden, 1993). However, on the dimensional level of symptom manifestation, that is, the

Table 6.5. *Depression by age and gender*

| | Scores on syndrome rating scales | | | | | | Psychiatric diagnoses of depression | | | | | |
| | CES-D Self-rating | | | HAMD Observer-rating | | | DSM-III-R specified and not otherwise specified depressive illnesses | | | DSM-III-R major depression (acute and partially remitted) | | |
	Men	Women	All	Men	Women	All	Men	Women	All	Men	Women	All
70–74	10.1	11.7	10.9	3.7	5.0	4.4	16	26	23	2.3	4.7	3.9
75–79	11.3	15.6	13.4	3.8	7.9	5.9	16	33	28	2.3	4.7	4.0
80–84	10.8	14.6	12.7	5.3	6.7	6.0	19	26	24	4.7	7.0	6.4
85–89	13.7	16.8	15.2	5.3	7.0	6.1	33	35	33	7.0	7.0	7.0
90–94	14.6	19.7	17.1	5.2	6.9	6.1	19	40	36	4.7	9.3	8.5
95+	13.4	16.6	15.0	4.5	6.7	5.6	19	30	29	2.3	4.7	4.4
F/χ^2	2.3	3.0	4.9	0.8	0.9	1.0	2.3	3.7	5.1	1.0	1.3	2.3
p	.05	.012	.0002	n.s.	n.s.	n.s.	n.s.	.02	n.s.	n.s.	n.s.	n.s.
All	12.3	15.8	14.1	4.6	6.7	5.7	19	30	27	3.5	5.9	5.3
t-test	$p = .000$			$p = .000$			$\chi^2 = 5.0$ $p = .02$			$\chi^2 = 1.1$ n.s.		

Note. Mean scores on CES-D und HAMD; prevalence rates of depression diagnoses in %.

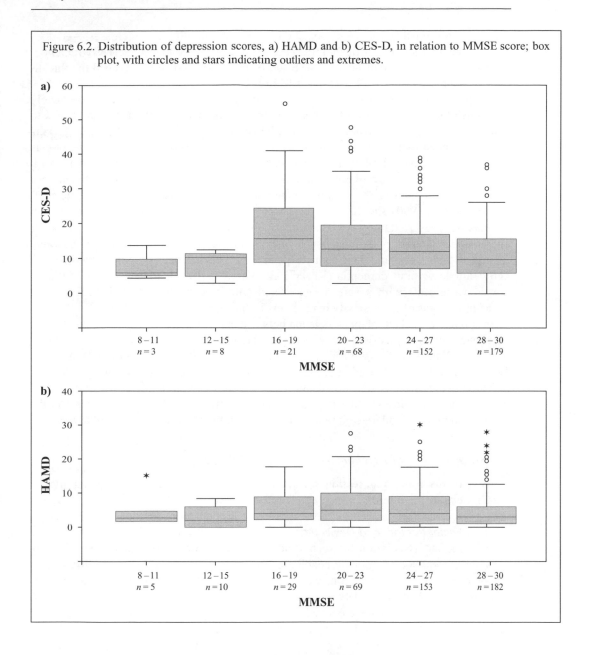

Figure 6.2. Distribution of depression scores, a) HAMD and b) CES-D, in relation to MMSE score; box plot, with circles and stars indicating outliers and extremes.

level of symptoms and syndromes, the relationship appears to be more complex. On the one hand, there is no influence of DSM-III-R specified depression diagnoses on MMSE scores (Reischies & Geiselmann, 1995). On the other hand, an association between mild to moderate cognitive disorders and depressivity can be demonstrated: More persons with increasing cognitive impairment have depressive symptoms. For persons with a mild degree of cognitive impairment, the depressive syndrome becomes significantly stronger than for those without cognitive impairment in both CES-D self-rating (see Fig. 6.2a) and HAMD observer-rating by the psychiatrist (Fig. 6.2b), even after exclusion of symptoms presumably caused by somatic illnesses. Variability also increases. Age does not have an additional significant influence. In contrast, in none of the cases with a high degree of cognitive impairment (MMSE scores under 16) did scores exceed the thresholds for depression (16 in CES-D, 13 or 18 in HAMD).

It remains to be seen whether a severe dementia syndrome can reduce or completely extinguish the manifestation of a depressive syndrome. On the one hand, one needs to take selectivity effects into account (cf. Lindenberger et al., Chapter 2). Some of the persons who ended their participation immediately after the Short Initial Assessment certainly showed signs of both dementia and depression syndromes. Probably, persons with both syndromes are more likely to drop out of field studies, whereas inpatients are not able to end participation, thus leading to the positive correlations reported by some studies (Henderson, 1990). On the other hand, the validity of the assessment of depression in patients with severe dementia is questionable. Presumably, these persons are no longer able to understand properly questions in interviews and questionnaires nor can they give reports on their mood and their bodily experiences. This has been demonstrated in an elderly sample without dementia (Knäuper & Wittchen, 1994). Indeed, for 3 of the 11 BASE participants with severe dementia and with missing values in the CES-D, we found other signs of depressivity in the Short Initial Assessment.

In summary, the lack of an association between categorically diagnosed dementia and depression found in this field study, as opposed to the positive correlation repeatedly reported in clinical studies with inpatients (Henderson, 1990; Lammi et al., 1989; Post, 1962; Reifler, Larson, & Hanley, 1982; Reischies, 1993), could result from a positive association in the early phases of dementia and a negative correlation in cases of severe dementia. The increasing variability of dimensionally measured depressivity scores in the range from mild to moderate cognitive disorders can be interpreted in a similar way.

3.2   Predictors of Psychiatric Morbidity in Old Age

In the following section, we focus on two findings of practical importance which illustrate the interdisciplinary potential of BASE.

3.2.1   Social Factors and Dementia

To examine the association between socioeconomic factors and dementia, specifically between present socioeconomic conditions and specific stresses during the life course and dementia, logistic regressions were calculated with dementia as the dependent variable (Wagner & Kanowski, 1995).[5]

After age and gender were entered into the model as predictors, the following socioeconomic variables were added: level of education and occupational training, social class (cf. Mayer et al., Chapter 8), marital status, and place of residence (institutionalized vs. community-dwelling). Specific stresses during the life course concerning work, family,

[5] In these logistic regressions, the dependent variable consists of a relationship between two likelihoods, the likelihood of a dementia diagnosis versus the likelihood of no diagnosis. This relationship ("odds ratio") can be seen as indicating the "risk" of dementia. The effect coefficients, stating how much the risk of dementia changes if the independent variable increases by one unit, are shown in Table 6.6. If the coefficient equals 1, the variable has no influence on dementia. If it is greater than 1, the likelihood of dementia being present is greater than the likelihood of no dementia.

Table 6.6. *Socioeconomic conditions, selected life course factors, and dementia:*
Logistic regression (N = *516; unweighted data*)

		Odds ratio Exp (b)	
1			
Age	1.12**	1.10**	1.10**
Gender (1 = w, 0 = m)	1.56*	1.17	0.98
2			
Elementary school only		2.72**	2.97**
No occupational training		1.25	1.30
Membership in lower social classes[a]		1.78*	1.90*
Married		0.88	0.87
Institutionalized		5.08**	4.94**
3			
Stressful working conditions[b]			0.90
Experience of divorce			1.20
Number of deaths of children			1.08

* $p < .05$, ** $p < .01$.

[a]The five-step scale of social classes is presented in Chapter 8 (Mayer et al.). Here, the three lower classes were combined to make a single category. The two higher classes are used as the reference category.

[b]Working conditions were measured with von Henninges's scale (1981), which classifies jobs by the extent of stressful demands made on the worker. Four types of demands are distinguished: heavy physical work, work under environmental strain (e.g., wet, cold, hot, or noisy conditions), night or shift work, and restrictive conditions (strongly regulated procedures). We calculated a sum score for all jobs carried out in the course of the occupational career.

and partnership were considered in a third step, including the degree of stressful working conditions, and occurrences of nonnormative familial events such as divorce or a child's death (see Table 6.6).

The analyses support the finding that the risk of dementia increases with age. The risk is 1.12 times higher per year of life beyond 70, and 1.76 (= 1.12^5) times higher in five years. This age association is not affected by socioeconomic factors. Without controlling for other factors, women's risk of dementia is 1.6 times higher than men's. However, this gender effect loses significance when socioeconomic factors are included. Persons with only elementary education have a 2.7 times higher risk of dementia than persons with a higher level of education. Level of education is a stronger predictor than occupational training. Even when education is controlled for, dementia is significantly related to social class membership: Members of the lower classes were more frequently diagnosed with dementia than members of the higher classes. The diagnosis of dementia is independent of participants' marital status at the time of the interview. The institutionalized have a very high risk of dementia as compared to persons living in private households. However, it is most likely not institutionalization that is the cause of dementia; it is the dementia that leads to institutionalization. Finally, the BASE indicators of occupational

Table 6.7. *Comparison of participants with a "pure" depression or dementia diagnosis with the psychiatrically healthy*

	"Pure" depression (n = 61)		"Pure" dementia (n = 59)		No psychiatric diagnosis (n = 269)	
Sociodemographics						
Age	83.2	(7.8)	91.8*	(7.0)	82.7	(8.4)
Gender (% women)	52.5		49.2		44.6	
Institutionalized (in %)	11.5*		50.0*		4.1	
Global health						
Number of chronic somatic illnesses	3.8*	(1.8)	2.9	(1.7)	2.9	(1.9)
Organ functioning[a]						
Kidney	-0.01	(0.94)	-0.37*	(1.04)	0.12	(0.94)
Lung	0.11	(0.96)	-0.57*	(0.84)	0.23	(1.03)
Thyroid	0.22	(0.85)	-0.45*	(0.85)	0.08	(1.01)
Blood count	0.09	(1.11)	-0.33*	(1.23)	0.09	(0.91)
HDL-cholesterol	-0.10	(0.76)	-0.22	(0.76)	0.04	(1.03)
Functional impairment[a]						
Balance/gait	-0.13*	(1.03)	-0.76*	(1.02)	0.37	(0.81)
Hearing	0.16	(1.03)	-0.58*	(0.68)	0.18	(0.99)
Visual acuity	-0.15*	(0.91)	-0.45*	(0.87)	0.20	(1.00)
Medication[b]						
Number of prescibed drugs	5.34*	(2.94)	1.93*	(1.49)	3.58	(2.68)
Risk of adverse drug reactions[a]						
Dementia-related ADR	0.63*	(0.71)	0.30	(0.53)	0.41	(0.54)
Depression-related ADR	0.71*	(0.62)	0.20*	(0.32)	0.46	(0.53)

Note. DSM-III-R specified and nonspecified diagnoses are considered; 127 participants with second psychiatric diagnoses and sleep disorders were excluded, resulting in smaller "pure" groups than those listed in Table 6.3 for depression and dementia. Unweighted data; standard deviations of means in parentheses.
* $p < .05$ as compared with the psychiatrically healthy group.
[a]Aggregations of z-transformed scores.
[b]Medication prescribed for daily use, without self-medication.

and familial strains in the course of life do not have a significant effect on the risk of dementia.

3.2.2   Somatic Risk Factors for Depression and Dementia

Participants with depressive syndromes had a greater number of chronic diseases than the mentally healthy (Table 6.7).[6] Compared with the mentally healthy, participants with dementia generally scored significantly worse in tests of kidney, lung, and thyroid function, in blood count, and in measures of functional impairment.

---

[6] Possible specificity of the associations (e.g., with certain cardiovascular diseases) is analyzed in more detail in Chapter 15 by Borchelt et al.

Drug therapy can also be seen as a risk factor for dementia and depression. For instance, the relatively high number of medicines taken by persons with depressive disorders is associated with an increased risk of adverse psychiatric reactions. Substances such as methyldopa, beta-blockers, steroids, or levodopa can cause depression-like symptoms. Of course, causal attribution is difficult at the individual level. According to international conventions, the occurrence of a symptom that is also known to be an adverse drug reaction is labeled an "adverse event." In BASE, depressive participants have a significantly higher event rate in association with their higher medication use than the comparison group. However, this does not exclude the possibility that at least some of the medicines were prescribed because of depressive complaints, so that the prescription was a consequence and not a cause of depressivity. In any case, somatic comorbidity or medication-related psychiatric impairment must be considered for those with depression or dementia, because this has far-reaching therapeutic consequences.

3.3   Consequences of Psychiatric Illnesses in Old Age

We selected two examples out of a wide range of consequences of psychiatric morbidity: utilization of medication and everyday functioning. Analyses of utilization of medical and nursing care are presented in detail in Chapter 16 by Linden et al.

3.3.1   Utilization of Medication

The BASE data show that psychotropic drugs play an important role in medication prescription. Sixty-seven percent of the population aged 70 and above use some type of psychotropic drugs in the wider sense (i.e., neuroleptics [antipsychotics], antidepressants, tranquilizers, hypnotics, nootropics, and analgesics). One-fourth take strictly defined psychotropic drugs, with benzodiazepine-tranquilizers (13%) making up the largest group (Table 6.8).

Although no significant differences in medication utilization by age and gender were observed, medication and illness state, particularly dementia and depression, are significantly related (Tables 6.9 and 6.10). The number of psychotropic drugs used rises with increasing illness specificity and severity of depression (cf. Table 6.9). This is not primarily due to an increase in antidepressants – it is mainly due to the utilization of benzodiazepines, used as tranquilizers or hypnotics. It must be added that approximately 90% of the participants appeared to use these drugs as permanent medication (for more than six months) and 50% took them daily (Geiselmann, Englert, & Wernicke, 1993).

For dementia, we find the opposite pattern. Participants with a pronounced dementia syndrome received significantly less medications in total than those without (Table 6.10). Interestingly, this also applied to rheologics, which are generally considered appropriate in cases of vascular dementia. Nootropics were also surprisingly rarely prescribed. In contrast, the utilization of neuroleptics increased significantly, apparently playing a role in the treatment of dementia-associated conditions such as organic psychoses, restlessness, or other tranquilizer indications.

The lower overall prescription of medications in cases of dementia could be due to the higher risk of adverse drug reactions in dementia. However, it is also possible that persons with dementia receive less therapeutic attention because they no longer take an active part in their own treatment.

Table 6.8. *Percentage of the population aged 70 and above who take at least one drug from the stated medication group*

Medication[a]	%	M	(SD)[b]	Max.[c]
Antidepressants	3.7	0.03	(0.2)	2
Neuroleptics	4.4	0.05	(0.2)	2
Benzodiazepine-anxiolytics	13.2	0.1	(0.3)	1
Benzodiazepine-hypnotics	4.7	0.05	(0.2)	1
Herbal hypnotics	4.6	0.05	(0.2)	2
Nootropics	4.3	0.05	(0.2)	2
Psychotropics	24.6	0.3	(0.6)	4
Chemically defined psychotropics, hypnotics, and sedatives	29.8	0.3	(0.6)	3
Psychotropics (incl. sedatives, analgesics, etc.)	67.4	1.5	(1.5)	6
All medications	96.4	6.1	(3.8)	24
Prescribed drugs	93.0	4.7	(3.3)	23
Self-medication	57.4	1.2	(1.5)	9

[a]The medications are grouped according to the indication classes in the German *Physician's Desk Reference* ("Rote Liste," 1990).
[b]The mean number of drugs from each group per person (standard deviations in parentheses).
[c]The maximum number of drugs from each group per person.

Treatment quality can only be assessed if all of the information available is taken into account, as is done in consensus conferences between internists and psychiatrists. Almost all (93%) of the so-called chemically defined psychotropics were prescribed and were thus under physicians' responsibility. Nearly 70% of psychotropic prescriptions were appropriate (Table 6.11). Based on the available cross-sectional data, the consensus conference raters judged that 17% of the prescriptions were not necessary, but did not have any objections to them. A clear contraindication was only found in 6% of psychotropic prescriptions. The prescription of psychotropic medication is thus better than often claimed (Beers et al., 1992; Stuck et al., 1994).

The daily dosage was found to be adequate in 64% of prescriptions and too low in 36%. No cases of excessive dosages were observed. This confirms a tendency toward prescribing low dosages to outpatients (Linden, 1987). One can speculate whether physicians are trying to adapt effective dosages to the lower metabolic rate in old age or whether they are conservative when in doubt and prefer to prescribe lower doses.

Finally, considering total medication in specific disease groups, we found undermedication in 4% of cases with dementia, but in 44% of persons with depression. This can be understood in context of the different efficacy of medications for the two illnesses and indicates that treatment possibilities, especially for depression, are not fully exploited in outpatient care.

Table 6.9. *Drug therapy of participants with depressive illnesses*

| Medication[a] | Depressive symptom complex | | | | χ^2 |
	None ($n = 335$)	Symptom level ($n = 48$)	Non-specified depressive illness ($n = 85$)	DSM-III-R specified depressive illness ($n = 48$)	p
Nootropics	3	2	4	4	n.s.
Acetylsalicylic acid	14	15	24	11	.05
Rheologics	22	21	33	35	n.s.
Benzodiazepines	13	15	18	40	.0001
Neuroleptics	3	4	5	2	n.s.
Antidepressants	2	2	4	6	n.s.
Other hypnotics	3	0	5	8	n.s.
Psychotropics in total	16	17	28	40	.0001
All daily medications[b]	5.2 (3.6)	6.1 (4.2)	7.3 (4.0)	8.0 (4.7)	$F = 12.3$ $p = .0001$

Note. Percentage of cases per illness group that were treated with at least one substance from each indication group; unweighted data.

[a]Medication groups according to indication classes of the "Rote Liste" (1990).

[b]Average number of medications taken per day (standard deviations in parentheses).

Table 6.10. *Pharmacotherapy of participants with dementia*

| Medication[a] | Dementia symptom complex | | | χ^2 |
	None ($n = 376$)	Symptom level ($n = 31$)	DMS-III-R specified dementia ($n = 109$)	p
Nootropics	3	3	4	n.s.
Acetylsalicylic acid	16	10	11	n.s.
Rheologics	27	35	13	.05
Benzodiazepines	17	23	12	n.s.
Neuroleptics	2	0	11	.0001
Antidepressants	2	3	4	n.s.
Other hypnotics	4	3	2	n.s.
Psychotropics in total	19	19	26	n.s.
All daily medications[b]	6.3 (3.9)	7.2 (4.6)	4.0 (3.3)	$F = 18.1$ $p = .0001$

Note. Percentage of cases per illness group that were treated with at least one substance from each indication group; unweighted data.

[a]Medication groups according to indication classes of the "Rote Liste" (1990).

[b]Average number of medications taken per day (standard deviations in parentheses).

Table 6.11. *Assessment of participants' psychotropic drug therapy in the consensus conference between psychiatrists and internists*

Domain	%
Prescriber	
Physician	93.0
Patient	5.3
Others	1.7
Indication status	
Contraindicated	6.1
Possibly contraindicated	7.0
Unnecessary	17.4
Possibly appropriate	47.8
Appropriate	21.7
Dosage	
Underdosed	35.7
Correctly dosed	64.3
Overdosed	0.0
Undermedication of dementia	
Yes	3.9
Possibly	16.3
No	79.8
Undermedication of depression	
Yes	44.2
Possibly	23.3
No	32.6

3.3.2   Everyday Functioning

Examining the everyday functioning of older people using the Yesterday Interview, we found several significant differences between the healthy and the mentally ill. Figure 6.3 presents the daily composition of activities during the waking hours of psychiatrically healthy participants, of those diagnosed with dementia, and those with depression. Duration scores were calculated for seven activity categories standardizing for the individual length of day (cf. Table 14.1 in M. M. Baltes et al., Chapter 14). Leisure and social activities took up 48%, while obligatory activities such as grooming, household work, and shopping took up about 38% of the mentally healthy persons' daytime. On average, participants carried out 28 activities of 13 different types. Eighty percent of these took place at home and 60% were carried out alone.

Comparing the daily activity profile of those who were healthy and those with dementia (bottom right circle in Fig. 6.3), one finds the following differences: The latter reported significantly more resting during the day and significantly less time in instrumen-

Figure 6.3. Activity profiles for waking hours by depression or dementia diagnoses. Participants with dementia and depression comorbidity (DSM-III-R specified, not otherwise specified diagnoses or symptom carriers; *n*=49) and persons whose day could not be reconstructed or was implausible (*n*=31) were not included.

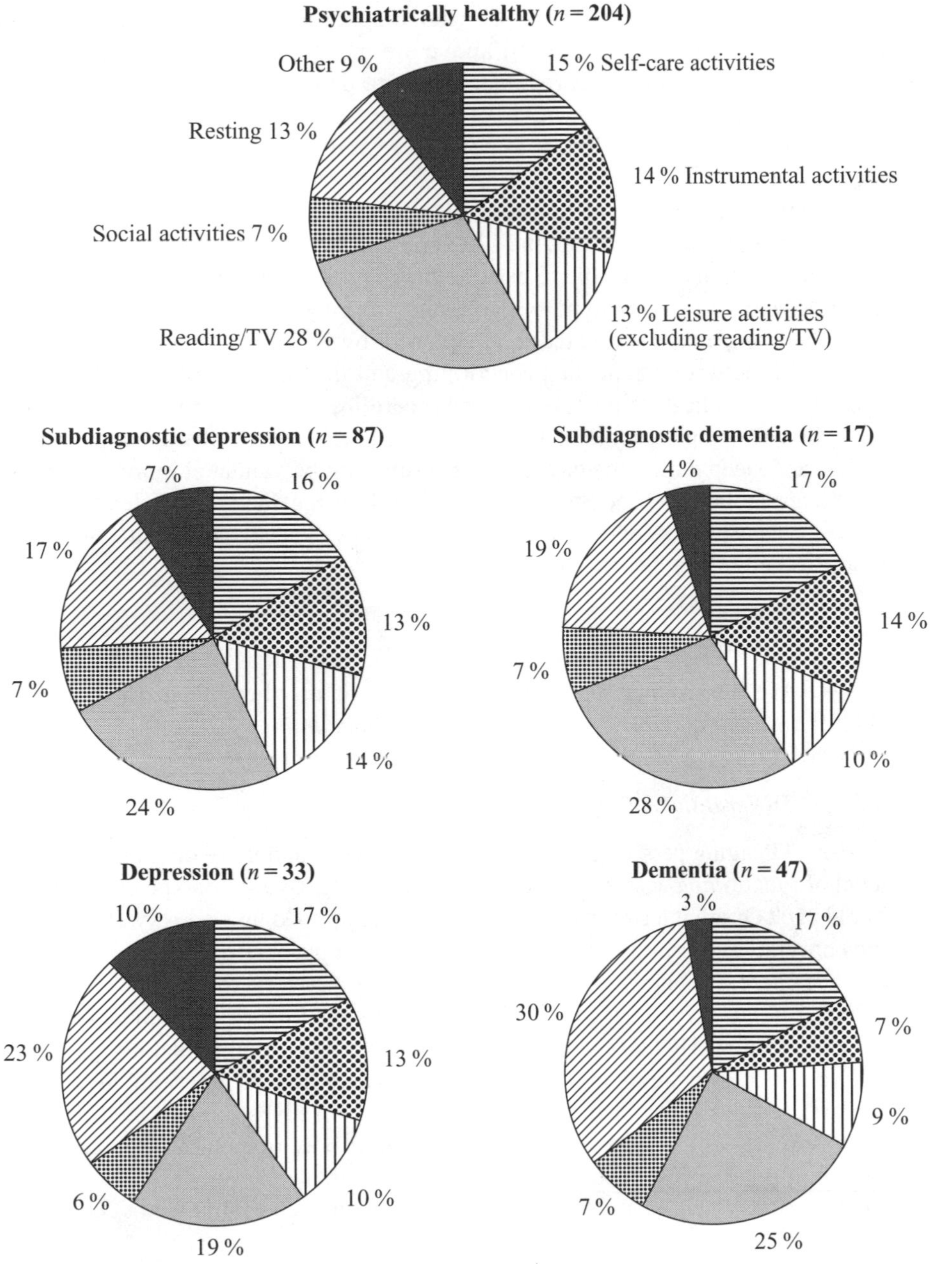

Psychiatrically healthy (*n* = 204)

Other 9 %

15 % Self-care activities

Resting 13 %

14 % Instrumental activities

Social activities 7 %

Reading/TV 28 %

13 % Leisure activities (excluding reading/TV)

Subdiagnostic depression (*n* = 87)

7 %   16 %

17 %

13 %

7 %

14 %

24 %

Subdiagnostic dementia (*n* = 17)

4 %   17 %

19 %

14 %

7 %

10 %

28 %

Depression (*n* = 33)

10 %   17 %

23 %

13 %

6 %

10 %

19 %

Dementia (*n* = 47)

3 %   17 %

30 %

7 %

9 %

7 %

25 %

tal activities.[7] Looking at the variety in everyday activities (i.e., the number of different types of activities), participants with dementia showed less variety (10.3 vs. 13.1) and spent only half as much time outside the house compared with the healthy (12% vs. 21%). However, there was no difference in the time spent alone or with others.

It should be noted that of the 31 persons who did not complete the Yesterday Interview and were therefore excluded, 26 were diagnosed as having dementia. We can thus assume that the findings presented above are more likely to underestimate the differences in activity profiles between persons with dementia and healthy persons. In contrast, the differences in daily activities between persons with depression and those without (bottom left circle in Fig. 6.3) point in a similar direction but are not statistically significant.

In summary, there are relationships between everyday functioning and mental illness, which are significant, however, only in dementia. Although the analyzed data are cross-sectional, it seems reasonable to assume that dementia influences everyday functioning and not vice versa. This hypothesis is supported by the multidisciplinary analyses of everyday competence presented in Chapter 14 by M. M. Baltes et al., which showed a strong link between intellectual functioning and the structure of everyday functioning. The data also indicate that not only is the repertoire of leisure activities reduced, but also the ability to compensate: Lost activities are not replaced by others, but by longer phases of rest and sleep during the day. If these results can be validated in longitudinal studies, the Yesterday Interview could prove very useful for the diagnosis of dementia in its early stages, because the reported changes can also be detected in subdiagnostic dementia cases (see middle circles in Fig. 6.3).

4   Discussion

We discuss our results regarding two of the theoretical orientations guiding BASE: *differential aging* and *continuity versus discontinuity*.

4.1   *Differential Aging*

Do aging persons resemble each other more and more on an increasingly lower level of functioning, as could be assumed from a negative stereotype of dedifferentiation in old age? Or are interindividual differences maintained up into very old age? Our findings provide support for both perspectives. From a psychiatric viewpoint, differences in old age increase mainly because of differences between those who remain mentally healthy up into very old age (a third of old adults) and the rising numbers of mentally ill persons, particularly those with dementia (see Fig. 6.1). Within that group, however, the progressive destructuralizing effect of the illness evens out interindividual differences. Nevertheless, even in old age, mental illnesses themselves can still be differentiated: In contrast to dementia, depression does not become more frequent in old age; persons with dementia receive less medication than those with depression (Tables 6.9 and 6.10); women more often have depressive illnesses than men (Table 6.5). These descriptive

---

[7] Statistical analyses on everyday behavior were carried out by examining contrasts (the group of participants with dementia vs. all other groups) on the basis of univariate variance analyses with separate variance estimates if variances of the contrast groups were inhomogeneous.

characteristics of differential aging point to preconditions and consequences of psychiatric morbidity in old age, which distinguish the continuous processes of "normal" aging and discontinuity because of illness manifestations or "pathological" aging.

4.2   Continuity versus Discontinuity

A central question is whether mental illnesses in old age are only quantitative extensions of "normal" aging associated with an increase in forgetfulness and somatic complaints, or whether dementia and depression are to be distinguished as qualitatively different phenomena. This question is of particular interest when considering mild forms of mental disorders. An answer in favor of discontinuity seems possible when qualitatively new phenomena (such as psychomotoric inhibition or delusions in "endomorphic" depression or aphasic speech disorders in dementia), normally describing severe stages, can be observed in mild manifestations.

In a BASE subsample ($n = 156$), Reischies and Lindenberger (1996) were able to show that age-dependent cognitive decline in the healthy is mainly due to a decrease of psychomotoric speed, while those with dementia are characterized by a different specific pattern of losses in memory and fluency. This indication of discontinuity is supported by the overlapping bimodal distribution of SMMS[8] scores (cf. Fig. 12.6 in Lindenberger & Reischies, Chapter 12). Our finding that the increase of dementia prevalence is possibly halted above the age of 95, at least for men (cf. Fig. 6.1), also argues against the influence of aging alone, but not against the hypothesis of a genetically disposed illness with age-dependent expression (Lishman, 1991; Mohs, Breitner, Silverman, & Davis, 1987). Therefore, it seems likely that between the ages of 65 and 95, the normal age-related decline in intellectual functioning, which may reach the thresholds defining dementia, is complicated or superimposed upon by somatically (e.g., vascularly or genetically) disposed brain diseases leading to dementia.

Because early recognition of beginning dementia is difficult in the individual case, it is desirable to back up a dementia diagnosis with knowledge of risk factors in the patient's previous history and in his or her current situation (Hagnell et al., 1992). The associations between dementia likelihood and multiple disturbances of organ functioning or physical impairments (Table 6.7), as well as level of education (Table 6.6), need to be considered in this context.

The following hypotheses on the effects of risk factors are possible (Helmchen & Reischies, 1998): (1) The risk factor lowers the threshold for diagnostically discernible clinical manifestations (*threshold hypothesis*). (2) Directly or indirectly, the risk factor enhances – or even causes – the illness process (*etiological hypothesis*). (3) The association of the risk factor with the illness is a consequence of the selection effect on the sample examined (*selection hypothesis*). Conversely, negative associations can indicate protective factors (as discussed for the apolipoprotein-E 2 allele; Geßner et al., 1997). The intertwining processes of normal aging and the influence of risk factors have been conceptualized as a diathesis-stress model (Gatz, Kasl-Godley, & Karel, 1996).

Our cross-sectional data do not enable us to decide whether the described somatic risk factors only lower the dementia manifestation threshold, initiate the illness process itself, or only enhance the illness process. The interaction of continuous processes of ag-

---

[8] Short Mini Mental State, short form of the MMSE (Klein et al., 1985).

ing and the discontinuous beginning of pathogenic processes indicates how problematic the continuity/discontinuity paradigm can be for the differentiation between normal aging and illness. For example, previous depressive episodes are associated with a higher dementia risk (Henderson, 1990; Kral, 1982). However, Henderson found an odds ratio of 4.3 if the psychiatrically treated depressive disorder occurred within 10 years before the dementia diagnosis, suggesting that these phases of depression could be interpreted as early symptoms of dementia. Indicators of dementia remaining below the clinical threshold could therefore also predict an increased depression risk. Causes could be an increase of amyloid proteins or their precursors over a 30-year period (Beyreuther, 1992) or a decrease of certain neurotransmitters; for example, a loss of noradrenergic neurons in the nucleus coeruleus in patients with depressive dementia has been described (Chan-Palay & Asan, 1989; Förstl, Levy, Burns, Luthert, & Cairns, 1994). Alexopoulos, Young, Abrams, Myers, and Shamoian (1989) hypothesized that a loss of neurotransmitters causing depression and degenerative dementia is the consequence of the accelerated aging of the brain.

Thus, there are several questions open for further research. First, is dementia in old age related to "premature" aging of the brain? If so, is that premature aging due to normal but accelerated aging processes? This could be interpreted as differential aging. Second, does aging affect neuronal systems differentially and in consequence lead to differential impairments of mental performance? Clinically, this could appear as a discontinuity, presenting a unique symptom pattern of specific age-related illnesses (Lishman, 1991). Analyses of the longitudinal BASE data will allow a closer look at the development of psychiatric morbidity in old age.

References

Alexopoulos, G. S., Young, R. C., Abrams, R. C., Myers, B., & Shamoian, C. A. (1989). Chronicity and relapse in geriatric depression. *Biological Psychiatry, 26*, 551–564.

American Psychiatric Association (APA) (Ed.). (1987). *Diagnostic and statistical manual of mental disorders (DSM-III-R)*. Washington, DC.

Bachman, D. L., Wolf, P. A., Linn, R., Knoefel, J. E., Cobb, J., Belanger, A., D'Agostino, R. B., & White, L. R. (1992). The prevalence of dementia and probable senile dementia of the Alzheimer type in the Framingham study. *Neurology, 42*, 115–119.

Baltes, M. M., Mayr, U., Borchelt, M., Maas, I., & Wilms, H.-U. (1993). Everyday competence in old and very old age: An inter-disciplinary perspective. *Ageing and Society, 13*, 657–680.

Beers, M. H., Ouslander, J. G., Fingold, S. F., Morgenstern, H., Reuben, D. B., Rogers, W., Zeffren, M. J., & Beck, J. C. (1992). Inappropriate medication prescribing in skilled-nursing facilities. *Annals of Internal Medicine, 117*, 684–689.

Berkman, L. F., Berkman, C. S., Kasl, S., Freeman, D. H., Leo, L., Ostfeld, A. M., Cornoni-Huntley, J., & Brody, J. A. (1986). Depressive symptoms in relation to physical health and function in the elderly. *American Journal of Epidemiology, 124*, 372–388.

Beyreuther, K. (1992). Neurobiologie der Alzheimerschen Krankheit. In H. Häfner & M. Hennerici (Eds.), *Psychische Krankheiten und Hirnfunktion im Alter* (pp. 61–78). Stuttgart: Gustav Fischer.

Blazer, D. (1989). Depression in late life. *Current Opinion in Psychiatry, 2*, 515–519.

Blazer, D. (1995). Mood disorders: Epidemiology. In H. I. Kaplan & B. J. Sadock (Eds.), *Comprehensive textbook of psychiatry* (6th ed., pp. 1079–1089). Baltimore: Williams & Wilkins.

Blazer, D., & Williams, C. D. (1980). Epidemiology of dysphoria and depression in an elderly community population. *British Journal of Psychiatry, 137*, 439–444.

Boyle, G. J. (1985). Self-report measures of depression: Some psychometric considerations. *British Journal of Clinical Psychology, 25*, 45–59.

Chan-Palay, V., & Asan, E. (1989). Alterations in catecholamine neurons of the locus coeruleus in senile dementia of the Alzheimer type and in Parkinson's disease with and without dementia and depression. *Journal of Comparative Neurology, 287*, 373–392.

Collegium Internationale Psychiatriae Scalarum (CIPS) (Ed.). (1986). *Internationale Skalen für Psychiatrie*. Weinheim: Beltz.

Cooper, B. (1986). Mental illness, disability and social conditions among old people in Mannheim. In H. Häfner, G. Moschel, & N. Sartorius (Eds.), *Mental health in the elderly* (pp. 35–45). Berlin: Springer-Verlag.

Cooper, B. (1992). Die Epidemiologie psychischer Störungen im Alter. In H. Häfner & M. Hennerici (Eds.), *Psychische Krankheiten und Hirnfunktion im Alter* (pp. 15–29). Stuttgart: Gustav Fischer.

Copeland, J. R., Dewey, M. E., & Griffiths-Jones, H. M. (1986). A computerized psychiatric diagnostic system and case nomenclature for elderly subjects: GMS and AGECAT. *Psychological Medicine, 16*, 89–99.

Copeland, J. R. M., Davidson, I. A., Dewey, M. E., Gilmore, C., Larkin, B. A., McWilliam, C., Saunders, P. A., Scott, A., Sharma, V., & Sullivan, C. (1992). Alzheimer's disease, other dementias, depression and pseudodementia: Prevalence, incidence and three-year outcome in Liverpool. *British Journal of Psychiatry, 161*, 230–239.

Copeland, J. R. M., Dewey, M. E., Wood, N., Searle, R., Davidson, I. A., & McWilliam, C. (1987). Range of mental illness among the elderly in the community. *British Journal of Psychiatry, 150*, 815–823.

Dilling, H., Mombour, W., & Schmidt, M. H. (Eds.). (1991). *Internationale Klassifikation psychischer Störungen: ICD-10, Kapitel V(F). Klinisch-diagnostische Leitlinien. Weltgesundheitsorganisation*. Bern: Huber.

Dilling, H., Weyerer, S., & Castell, R. (Eds.). (1984). *Psychische Erkrankungen in der Bevölkerung*. Stuttgart: Enke.

Emery, V. O., & Oxman, T. E. (1992). Update on the dementia spectrum of depression. *American Journal of Psychiatry, 149*, 305–317.

Folstein, M. F., Folstein, S. E., & McHugh, P. R. (1975). "Mini Mental State": A practical method for grading the cognitive state of patients for the clinician. *Journal of Psychiatric Research, 12*, 189–198.

Förstl, H., Levy, R., Burns, A., Luthert, P., & Cairns, N. (1994). Disproportionate loss of noradrenergic and cholinergic neurons as a cause of depression in Alzheimer's disease: A hypothesis. *Pharmacopsychiatry, 27*, 11–15.

Fratiglioni, L., Grut, M., Forsell, Y., Grafström, M., Holmén, K., Eriksson, K., Viitanen, M., Bäckman, L., Ahlbom, A., & Winblad, B. (1991). Prevalence of Alzheimer's disease and other dementias in an elderly urban population: Relationship with age, sex and education. *Neurology, 41*, 1886–1892.

Fuhrer, R., Antonucci, C., Gagnon, M., Dartigues, J. F., Barberger-Gateau, P., & Alperowitsch, A. (1992). Depressive symptomatology and cognitive functioning: An epidemiological survey in an elderly community sample in France. *Psychological Medicine, 22*, 159–172.

Fuhrer, R., & Rouillon, F. (1989). La version française de l'échelle CES-D (Center for Epidemiologic Studies-Depression Scale): Description et traduction de l'échelle d'autoévaluation. *Psychiatrie et Psychobiologie, 4*, 163–166.

Gatz, M., & Hurwics, M. L. (1990). Are old people more depressed? Cross-sectional data on Center for Epidemiologic Studies-Depression Scale factors. *Psychology and Aging, 5*, 284–290.

Gatz, M., Kasl-Godley, J. E., & Karel, M. J. (1996). Aging and mental disorders. In J. E. Birren & K. W. Schaie (Eds.), *Handbook of the psychology of aging* (4th ed., pp. 365–382). San Diego, CA: Academic Press.

Gebhardt, R., & Kliemitz, H. (1986). Depressive Störungen, Geschlecht und Zivilstand. *Zeitschrift für Klinische Psychologie: Forschung und Praxis, 15*, 3–20.

Geiselmann, B., Englert, S., & Wernicke, T. (1993, October). *Der Gebrauch von Anxiolytika, Sedativa, Hypnotika und Analgetika bei Depressiven und Nicht-Depressiven im höheren Alter*. Paper presented at the "Tagung der Arbeitsgemeinschaft für Neuropsycho-pharmakologie und Pharmakopsychiatrie," Nürnberg.

Gertz, H. J., & Kanowski, S. (1989). Epidemiologie. In M. Bergener (Ed.), *Depressive Syndrome im Alter* (pp. 60–70). Stuttgart: Thieme.

Geßner, R., Reischies, F. M., Kage, A., Geiselmann, B., Borchelt, M., Steinhagen-Thiessen, E., & Köttgen, E. (1997). In an epidemiological sample the apolipoprotein E4 allele is associated to dementia and loss of memory function only in the very old. *Neuroscience Letters, 222*, 29–32.

Goldberg, D., & Sartorius, N. (1990). Introduction. In N. Sartorius, D. Goldberg, G. De Girolamo, J. A. Costa e Silva, Y. Lecrubier, & H. U. Wittchen (Eds.), *Psychological disorders in general medical settings* (pp. 1–5). Göttingen: Hogrefe & Huber.

Grober, E., Buschke, H., Crystal, H., Bank, S., & Dresner, R. (1988). Screening for dementia by memory testing. *Neurology, 38*, 900–903.

Gurland, B. J., Copeland, J., & Kuriansky, J. (1983). *The mind and the mood of aging*. London: Croom Helm.

Häfner, H. (1992). Psychiatrie des höheren Lebensalters. In P. B. Baltes & J. Mittelstraß (Eds.), *Zukunft des Alterns und gesellschaftliche Entwicklung* (pp. 151–179). Berlin: de Gruyter.

Hagnell, O., Franck, A., Grasbeck, A., Öhman, R., Ojesjo, L., Otterbeck, L., & Rorsman, B. (1992). Senile dementia of the Alzheimer type in the Lundby study: 2. An attempt to identify possible risk factors. *European Archives of Psychiatry and Clinical Neurosciences, 241*, 231–235.

Hamilton, M. (1967). Development of a rating scale for primary depressive illness. *British Journal of Consulting and Clinical Psychology, 6*, 278–296.

Hautzinger, M. (1988). Die CES-D Skala: Ein Depressionsmeßinstrument für Untersuchungen in der Allgemeinbevölkerung. *Diagnostica, 34*, 167–173.

Helmchen, H. (1992). Klinik und Therapie depressiver Störungen im höheren Lebensalter. In H. Häfner & M. Hennerici (Eds.), *Psychische Krankheiten und Hirnfunktion im Alter* (pp. 119–138). Stuttgart: Gustav Fischer.

Helmchen, H., & Linden, M. (1993). The differentiation between depression and dementia in the very old. *Ageing and Society, 13*, 589–617.

Helmchen, H., Linden, M., & Wernicke, T. (1996). Psychiatrische Morbidität bei Hochbetagten: Ergebnisse aus der Berliner Altersstudie. *Der Nervenarzt, 67*, 739–750.

Helmchen, H., & Reischies, F. M. (1998). Normales und pathologisches kognitives Altern. *Der Nervenarzt, 69*, 369–378.

Henderson, A. S. (1990). Co-occurrence of affective and cognitive symptoms: The epidemiological evidence. *Dementia, 1*, 119–123.

Henderson, A. S., Jorm, A. F., Mackinnon, A., Christensen, H., Scott, L. R., Korten, A. E., & Doyle, C. (1993). The prevalence of depressive disorders and the distribution of depressive symptoms in later life: A survey using Draft ICD-10 and DSM-III-R. *Psychological Medicine, 23*, 719–729.

Henninges, H. von. (1981). Arbeitsplätze mit belastenden Arbeitsanforderungen. *Mitteilungen aus der Arbeitsmarkt- und Berufsforschung, 4*, 362–383.

Herrath, D. von. (1992). Benzodiazepin-Verordnungen: Vom Verschreibungsmißbrauch zur Abhängigkeit. *Arzneimittelbrief, 26*, 49–52.

Hofman, A., Rocca, W. A., Brayne, C., Breteler, M. M. B., Clarke, M., Cooper, B., Copeland, J. R. M., Dartigues, J. F., da Silva Droux, A., Hagnell, O., Heeren, T. J., Engedal, K., Jonker, C., Lindesay, J., Lobo, A., Mann, A. H., Molsa, P. K., Morgan, K., O'Connor, D. W., Sulkara, R., Kay, D. W. K., & Amaducci, L. (1991). The prevalence of dementia in Europe: A collaborative study of 1980–1990 findings. *International Journal of Epidemiology, 20*, 736–748.

Jorm, A. F., Korten, A. E., & Henderson, A. S. (1987). The prevalence of dementia: A quantitative integration of the literature. *Acta Psychiatrica Scandinavica, 76*, 465–479.

Kay, D. W. K., Beamish, P., & Roth, M. (1964). Old age mental disorders in Newcastle upon Tyne: Part II. A study of possible social and medical causes. *British Journal of Psychiatry, 110*, 668–682.

Kay, D. W. K., Henderson, A. S., Scott, R., Wilson, J., Rickwood, D., & Grayson, D. A. (1985). Dementia and depression among the elderly living in the Hobart community: The effect of the diagnostic criteria on the prevalence rates. *Psychological Medicine, 15*, 771–778.

Klauber, J., & Selke, G. W. (1993). Arzneimittelverordnungen nach Altersgruppen. In U. Schwabe & D. Paffrath (Eds.), *Arzneiverordnungs-Report '93* (pp. 498–507). Stuttgart: Gustav Fischer.

Klein, L. E., Roca, R. P., McArthur, J., Vogelsang, G., Klein, G. B., Kirby, S. M., & Folstein, M. (1985). Diagnosing dementia. Univariate and multivariate analyses of the mental status examination. *Journal of the American Geriatrics Society, 33*, 483–488.

Knäuper, B., & Wittchen, H. U. (1994). Diagnosing major depression in the elderly: Evidence for response bias in standardized diagnostic interviews? *Journal of Psychiatric Research, 28*, 147–164.

Kral, V. (1982). Depressive Pseudodemenz und senile Demenz vom Alzheimer-Typ. *Der Nervenarzt, 53*, 284–286.

Kramer, M., German, P. S., Anthony, J. C., Korff, M. von, & Skinner, E. A. (1985). Patterns of mental disorders among the elderly residents of eastern Baltimore. *Journal of the American Geriatrics Society, 33*, 236–245.

Kukull, W. A., Keopsell, T. D., Inui, T. S., Borson, S., Okimoto, J., Raskind, M. A., & Gale, J. L. (1986). Depression and physical illness among elderly general medical clinical patients. *Journal of Affective Disorders, 10*, 153–162.

Lammi, U. K., Kivela, S. L., Nissinen, A., Punsar, S., Puska, P., & Karvonen, M. (1989). Mental disability among elderly men in Finland: Prevalence, predictors and correlates. *Acta Psychiatrica Scandinavica, 80*, 459–468.

Lauter, H. (1992). Präsenile und senile Demenzen. In H. C. H. Hopf, K. Poeck, & H. Schliak (Eds.), *Neurologie in Praxis und Klinik* (Vol. 2, pp. 73–106). Stuttgart: Thieme.

Linden, M. (1987). *Phase-IV-Forschung*. Berlin: Springer-Verlag.

Linden, M., Borchelt, M., Barnow, S., & Geiselmann, B. (1995). The impact of somatic morbidity on the Hamilton Depression Rating Scale in the very old. *Acta Psychiatrica Scandinavica, 92*, 105–154.

Linden, M., Nather, J., & Wilms, H. U. (1988). Zur Definition, Bedeutung und Messung der Krankheitskonzepte von Patienten: Die Krankheitskonzeptskala (KK-Skala) für schizophrene Patienten. *Fortschritte der Neurologie, Psychiatrie, 55*, 35–43.

Lindesay, J., Briggs, K., & Murphy, E. (1989). The Guy's/Age Concerns Survey. *British Journal of Psychiatry, 155*, 317–329.

Lishmann, W. A. (1991). The evolution of research into the dementias. *Dementia, 2*, 177–185.

McWilliam, C., Copeland, J. R. M., Dewey, M. E., & Wood, N. (1988). The Geriatric Mental State Examination: A case-finding instrument in the community. *British Journal of Psychiatry, 152*, 205–208.

Meller, I., Fichter, M. M., Schröppel, H., & Beck-Eichinger, M. (1993). Mental and somatic health and need of care in octo- and nonagenerians: An epidemiological study. *European Archives of Psychiatry and Clinical Neurosciences, 242*, 286–292.

Mohs, R. C., Breitner, J. C. S., Silverman, J. M., & Davis, K. L. (1987). Alzheimer's disease: Morbid risk among first-degree relatives approximates 50% by 90 years of age. *Archives of General Psychiatry, 44*, 405–408.

Morgan, K., Dallosso, H. M., Arie, T., Byrne, E. J., Jones, R., & Waite, J. (1987). Mental health and psychological well-being among the old and the very old living at home. *British Journal of Psychiatry, 150*, 801–807.

Moritz, D. J., & Petitti, D. B. (1993). Association of education with reported age of onset and severity of Alzheimer's disease at presentation: Implications of the use of clinical samples. *American Journal of Epidemiology, 137*, 456–462.

Mortimer, J. A. (1990). Epidemiology of dementia: Cross-cultural comparisons. *Advances in Neurology, 51*, 27–33.

Moss, M., & Lawton, M. P. (1982). Time budgets of older people: A window on four lifestyles. *Journal of Gerontology, 37*, 576–582.

Murphy, E., Smith, R., Lindesay, J., & Slattery, J. (1988). Increased mortality-rates in late-life depression. *British Journal of Psychiatry, 152*, 347–353.

Naber, D., & Hippius, H. (1989). Psychiatric side-effects of non-pychotropic drugs. In R. Öhman, H. L. Freeman, A. Franck-Holmquist, & S. Nielsen (Eds.), *Interaction between mental and physical illness* (pp. 89–103). Berlin: Springer-Verlag.

Newmann, J. P., Klein, M. H., Jensen, J. E., & Essex, M. J. (1996). Depressive symptom experiences among older women: A comparison of alternative measurement approaches. *Psychology and Aging, 11*, 112–126.

O'Connor, D. W., Pollitt, P. A., & Treasure, F. P. (1991). The influence of education and social class on the diagnosis of dementia in a community population. *Psychological Medicine, 21*, 219–224.

Osterrieth, P. A. (1944). Le test de copie d'une figure complexe. *Archives de Psychologie, 30*, 206–356.

Overall, J. E., & Gorham, D. R. (1962). The Brief Psychiatric Rating Scale. *Psychological Reports, 10*, 799–812.

Parsons, P. L. (1965). Mental health of Swansea's old folk. *British Journal of Preventive and Social Medicine, 19*, 43–47.

Patten, S. B., & Love, E. J. (1993). Can drugs cause depression? A review of the evidence. *Journal of Psychiatry and Neuroscience, 18*, 92–102.

Pilowsky, I., & Spence, N. D. (1983). *Manual of the Illness Behaviour Questionnaire (IBQ)*. Adelaide: University of Adelaide.

Post, F. (1962). *The significance of affective symptoms in old age* (Maudsley Monographs, Vol. 10). London: Oxford University Press.

Radloff, L. S. (1977). The CES-D Scale: A self-report depression scale for research in the general population. *Applied Psychological Measurement, 1*, 385–401.

Radloff, L. S., & Teri, L. (1986). Use of the Center for Epidemiologic Studies-Depression Scale with older adults. *Clinical Gerontologist, 5*, 119–135.

Read, D. E. (1987). Neuropsychological assessment of memory in the elderly. *Canadian Journal of Psychology, 41*, 158–174.

Reifler, B. V., Larson, E., & Hanley, R. (1982). Coexistence of cognitive impairment and depression in geriatric outpatients. *American Journal of Psychiatry, 139*, 623–626.

Reischies, F. M. (1993). *Störungen kognitiver Leistungen depressiver Patienten: Psychopathologie, Verlauf und Analyse von Bedingungsfaktoren*. Unpublished habilitation thesis, Free University of Berlin.

Reischies, F. M., & Geiselmann, B. (1995). Mini Mental State Examination im sehr hohen Alter. In M. Zaudig & W. Hiller (Eds.), *SIDAM: Strukturiertes Interview für die Diagnose einer Demenz vom Alzheimer Typ, der Multiinfarkt- (oder vaskulären) Demenz und Demenzen anderer Ätiologie nach DSM-III-R, DSM-IV und ICD-10; Handbuch* (pp. 107–109). Bern: Huber.

Reischies, F. M., & Lindenberger, U. (1996). Diskontinuität zwischen altersbedingter kognitiver Leistungsbeeinträchtigung und Demenz: Testpsychologisches Profil. In U. H. Peters, M. Schifferdecker, & A. Krahl (Eds.), *150 Jahre Psychiatrie* (Vol. 2, pp. 429–431). Cologne: Martini.

Reischies, F. M., & Spiess, P. von. (1990). Katamnestische Untersuchungen zur depressiven Pseudodemenz. In E. Lungershausen, W. P. Kaschka, & R. Wittkowski (Eds.), *Affektive Psychosen* (pp. 248–253). Stuttgart: Schattauer.

Reitan, R. M. (1958). Validity of the Trail Making Test as an indicator of organic brain damage. *Perceptual and Motor Skills, 8*, 271–276.

Ritchie, K., Kildea, D., & Robine, J. M. (1992). The relationship between age and the prevalence of senile dementia: A meta-analysis of recent data. *International Journal of Epidemiology, 21*, 763–769.

Rodin, G., & Voshart, K. (1986). Depression in the medically ill: An overview. *American Journal of Psychiatry, 143*, 696–705.

Rote Liste. (1990). Aulendorf: Editio Cantor.

Steer, R. A., Beck, A. T., Riskind, J. H., & Brown, G. (1987). Relationship between the Beck Depression Inventory and the Hamilton Psychiatric Rating Scale for Depression in depressed outpatients. *Journal of Psychopathology and Behavioral Assessment, 9*, 327–339.

Stuck, A. E., Beers, M. H., Steiner, A., Aronow, H. U., Rubenstein, L. Z., & Beck, J. C. (1994). Inappropriate medication use in community-residing older persons. *Archives of Internal Medicine, 154*, 2195–2200.

Wagner, M., & Kanowski, S. (1995). Socioeconomic resources, life course, and dementia in old age. In M. Bergener, J. C. Brocklehurst, & S. I. Finkel (Eds.), *Aging, health, and healing* (pp. 475–485). New York: Springer.

Wahl, H.-W. (1990). Auf dem Weg zu einer alltagsbezogenen Gerontopsychologie. Teil 1: Konzeptionelle und methodologische Rahmenbedingungen. *Zeitschrift für Gerontopsychologie und -psychiatrie, 3*, 13–23.

Wallace, J., & O'Hara, M. W. (1992). Increases in depressive symptomatology in the rural
    elderly: Results from a cross-sectional and longitudinal study. *Journal of Abnormal
    Psychology, 101*, 398–404.
Weissman, M. M., Leaf, P. J., Tischler, G. L., Blazer, D. G., Karno, M., Bruce, M. L., & Florio,
    L. P. (1988). Affective disorders in five United States communities. *Psychological
    Medicine, 18*, 141–153.
Weissman, M. M., Myers, J. K., Tischler, G. L., Holzer, C. E., Leaf, P. J., Orvaschel, H., & Brody,
    J. A. (1985). Psychiatric disorders (DSM-III) and cognitive impairment among the
    elderly in a U.S. urban community. *Acta Psychiatrica Scandinavica, 71*, 366–379.
Welz, R., Lindner, M., Klose, M., & Pohlmeier, H. (1989). Psychische Störungen und körperliche
    Erkrankungen im Alter. *Fundamenta Psychiatrica, 3*, 223–228.
Wernicke, T. F., & Reischies, F. M. (1994). Prevalence of dementia in old age: Clinical diagnosis
    in subjects aged 95 years and older. *Neurology, 44*, 250–253.
Weyerer, S., & Dilling, H. (1984). Prävalenz und Behandlung psychischer Erkrankungen in der
    Allgemeinbevölkerung. *Der Nervenarzt, 55*, 30–42.
Wittchen, H. U., Saß, H., Zaudig, M., & Koehler, K. (1989). *Diagnostisches und statistisches
    Manual psychischer Störungen DSM-III-R*. Weinheim: Beltz.
World Health Organization (WHO). (1992). *International classification of mental and
    behavioural disorders (ICD-10)*. Geneva.
Zerssen, D. von. (1976). *Die Beschwerden-Liste*. Weinheim: Beltz.

CHAPTER 7

Trends and Profiles of Psychological Functioning in Very Old Age

Jacqui Smith and Paul B. Baltes

This chapter describes the psychological and psychosocial status of the participants of the Berlin Aging Study (BASE). In the first section, we outline age trends in three domains: intelligence, self and personality, and social relationships. In the domain of intelligence, negative age differences between 70 and 103 years were substantial (representing a 1.8 *SD* difference in performance level and 35% of the interindividual variance) and were closely associated with indicators of biological deterioration. In contrast, age-related differences in personality, self-related beliefs, and social relationships were fewer and considerably smaller (approximately 0.5 *SD*). At a general level, these domains seemed to be less affected by age-related decline than is true for intellectual functioning. Closer examination, however, revealed that age differences on aspects of self, personality, and social relationships were all in a less-than-desirable direction. In advanced old age, individuals may be pushed to the limits of their adaptive psychological capacity.

A further question considered in the chapter concerns the overall systemic nature of psychological functioning in old age. Cluster analysis was used to identify nine subgroups of older individuals with different patterns of functioning across the three psychological domains. Four of these groups reflected various patterns of desirable functioning (47% of the sample), and five, less desirable functioning (53%). The relative risk of membership in the less desirable profile subgroups was 2.5 times larger for the very old (85–103 years) than for people between the ages of 70 and 84 years, and 1.3 times larger for women than for men. On this level of systemic-wholistic analysis, and in comparison with single-variable analyses, the very old appear to be a distinct group psychologically. This finding is consistent with recent predictions about a "fourth age" based on a theoretical analysis of the biological-genetic and sociocultural architecture of life-span development (P. B. Baltes, 1997).

1   Introduction

This chapter reviews the central findings of the BASE Psychology Unit in relation to intellectual functioning, self and personality, and social relationships. When trying to describe psychological functioning in very old age, it is important to keep in mind that age comparisons permit only preliminary (and occasionally false) estimates about age-related change and do not yield any information about individual aging patterns (P. B. Baltes, 1968; Magnusson, Bergman, Rudinger, & Törestad, 1991; Schaie, 1965). In this regard, there is a gap between the data described here and the general theoretical orientation of BASE (cf. P. B. Baltes et al., Chapter 1 in this volume). Thus, although we use the term "psychological aging" in this chapter, we are fully aware of the limits to the interpretation of age comparisons. The data available from the first cross-sectional measurement occasion in BASE do not permit firm conclusions about individual aging or the ontogenesis of age-related variation. Nevertheless, and with this caveat in mind, it is still possible to gain some insight into differential aging by means of cross-sectional data (Birren & Birren, 1990; Thomae, 1979). In particular, we were able to examine (a) interindividual differences, especially age/cohort differences, (b) sources of interindividual and age-related variation, and (c) the systemic interrelationships between the three domains of psychological functioning.

2   Measurement Strategy

To date, there is little consensus about a comprehensive assessment procedure for psychological functioning. Instead, the field is characterized by various theoretical approaches, each with a different focus and empirical method. In BASE we tried to cover the psychological spectrum with constructs and variables from three domains of functioning: (1) intelligence, (2) self and personality, and (3) social relationships. Table 7.1 summarizes the central psychological constructs and measures included in two sections of the BASE Intensive Protocol: in the multidisciplinary Intake Assessment and in three psychology sessions (P. B. Baltes et al., Chapter 1; cf. P. B. Baltes & Smith, 1997; Smith & Baltes, 1993). In approximately six hours of individual psychological assessment in the Intensive Protocol, we employed a multimethod approach, including tape-recorded semistructured interviews, standardized questionnaires with a spoken response format, and computer-presented tests. Testing was carried out in the participants' place of residence (e.g., private home, nursing home, hospital) by trained and supervised research assistants. Below, we describe, in more detail, reasons for the specific approach adopted in each domain and indicate sources for further information.

3   Intelligence

Knowledge about intellectual performance has an important place in gerontology, in part because intellectual functioning has strong implications for independent living and efficiency in everyday life. At one extreme, information about intellectual functioning is fundamental for the clinical diagnosis of dementia (cf. Lindenberger & Reischies, Chapter 12). At another level, findings about typical patterns of intellectual aging and about the potential and limits of performance can also draw attention to the need for societal change. Given appropriate opportunities in the future, perhaps more older adults will be able both to apply and to improve their intellectual capacities so that they can experience and actively create a period of productive and successful aging (P. B. Baltes, 1997; P. B. Baltes & Baltes, 1990).

Central questions in BASE concerned the structure of intellectual functioning in old age, age differences in levels of performance, and correlates of individual and age-related differences. A computerized battery of 14 tests assessing perceptual speed, memory, reasoning, fluency, and knowledge was applied to answer these questions (cf. Lindenberger & Baltes, 1997; Lindenberger, Mayr, & Kliegl, 1993). With the exception of two subtests (Digit Letter and Digit Symbol Substitution), the BASE battery was programmed for presentation in a large-size font on a portable Macintosh SE/30 computer.

This data collection procedure enabled controlled test conditions and benefited from the present-day non-age-related familiarity of concentrating on television screens. Responses were collected using a touch-sensitive screen or, where relevant, tape-recordings of verbal responses. A compatible auditory version of the test battery was developed for blind and severely visually impaired individuals ($n = 57$ in BASE). The computerized data collection procedure was specifically designed to avoid some of the problems typically encountered with timed paper-and-pencil tests. Such measures often prove difficult to use in a standardized way with older adults, because visual and motor impairments make reading and writing difficult.

Some tests in the battery can be matched with medical and psychiatric tests of neurological and cognitive functioning (cf. Lindenberger & Reischies, Chapter 12). Findings from BASE may offer an opportunity to address the question whether dementia is an extreme form of normal cognitive aging or a qualitatively distinguishable process (e.g., Häfner, 1986) and to study the relationship between normal and pathological cognitive aging (e.g., Bäckman, 1991). Each test in the BASE battery was constructed so that a wide range of performance levels could be assessed, from top functioning to dementia. For measures of knowledge and reasoning, items-within-tests increased in difficulty and specific cutoff thresholds were built into the computer program, such that after a succession of three or six consecutive incorrect responses the test was terminated.

3.1   The Structure of Intelligence in Very Old Age

Most theories and research regarding intellectual performance in adulthood suggest that intelligence is a system of more or less interrelated abilities (P. B. Baltes, 1987; Cattell, 1971; Horn & Hofer, 1992; Schaie & Willis, 1993). It is an open question in the literature whether the structure of intellectual abilities remains differentiated in very old age or rather becomes dedifferentiated (integrated) so that fewer and more general factors underlie performance. Dedifferentiation or integration would manifest itself in a decrease of clearly distinguishable ability domains or higher interrelations between different abilities than is typically found in younger cohorts (cf. P. B. Baltes, Cornelius, Spiro, Nesselroade, & Willis, 1980; Hertzog & Schaie, 1986; Reinert, 1970).

As illustrated in Figure 7.1, the BASE data revealed a degree of ability separation but, at the same time, a high level of integration or dedifferentiation (Lindenberger & Baltes, 1997). On the one hand, the multidimensional structure of intelligence found in research with younger adults was also evident in the BASE data. Structural equation modeling distinguished five latent ability factors: (1) perceptual speed, (2) reasoning, (3) memory, (4) fluency, and (5) knowledge. On the other hand, the five ability factors showed higher intercorrelations than have been found in a study with younger adults (P. B. Baltes & Lindenberger, 1997). The median correlation at the level of unit-weighted composites was $r = .70$, and correlations ranged from $r = .63$ to .73. At the latent level, the median correlation was $r = .85$. For estimating the general intellectual capacity of older adults, the strong general factor (g) appears to be a reasonable measure.

Further analyses indicated that the measures of intelligence in BASE also showed ecological validity (Lindenberger & Baltes, 1997). Some studies indicate that psychometric intelligence only moderately predicts everyday competence. In BASE, however, there was a high correlation between intelligence and everyday competence (approximately 40% of the variance in everyday competence could be explained by intelligence; cf. M. M. Baltes et al., Chapter 14; see also Marsiske, Klumb, & Baltes, 1997).

Table 7.1. *Summary of the constructs assessed in BASE from three psychological domains*

Construct	Measure	Source
Intelligence		
Perceptual speed	Digit Letter	Lindenberger, Mayr, & Kliegl, 1993
	Digit Symbol Substitution	Wechsler, 1955
	Identical Pictures	Cf. Ekstrom, French, Harman, & Derman, 1976
Reasoning	Figural Analogies	Cf. Thorndike, Hagen, & Lorge, 1954–68
	Letter Series	Cf. Thurstone, 1962
	Practical Problems	Cf. Educational Testing Service (ETS), 1977
Memory	Activity Recall	Lindenberger et al., 1993
	Memory for Text	Cf. Engel & Satzger, 1990
	Paired Associates	Lindenberger et al., 1993
Knowledge	Practical Knowledge	Cf. HAWIE; Wechsler, 1982
	Spot-a-Word	Cf. Lehrl, 1977
	Vocabulary	HAWIE; Wechsler, 1982
Fluency	Categories (Animals)	Lindenberger et al., 1993
	Word Beginnings (Letter "S")	Lindenberger et al., 1993

Self and personality

Neuroticism	6 items	From NEO (Costa & McCrae, 1985)
Extraversion	6 items	From NEO
Openness to experience	6 items	From NEO
Positive and negative affect	20 items	PANAS (Watson, Clark, & Tellegen, 1988)
Future orientation/optimism	3 items	From LSI-A (Neugarten, Havighurst, & Tobin, 1961)
Social and emotional loneliness	8 items	From UCLA Loneliness Scale (Russell, Cutrona, Rose, & Yurko, 1984)
Subjective well-being	15 items	PGCMS (Lawton, 1975; Liang & Bollen, 1983)
Self-definition: "Who am I?"	10 open-ended statements	Freund & Smith, 1997, in press
Hoped and feared possible selves	4 open-ended statements	From Markus & Nurius, 1986
Highs and lows of life	4 open-ended statements	From Harris, 1975
Subjective age	3 items	From Montepare & Lachman, 1989
Experience of time	4 items	Cf. Staudinger et al., Chapter 11
Personal life investment	10 life domains	Staudinger & Fleeson, 1996
Control beliefs	14 items	Smith, Marsiske, & Maier, 1996
Profile of coping styles	14 items	Cf. Kruse, 1994

Social relationships

Personal social network (size, age/gender composition, relationship type and duration)		After Kahn & Antonucci, 1980 (cf. Antonucci, 1986)
Support (instrumental/emotional; received/given)		
Evaluations of relationships		
Life-span relationships		

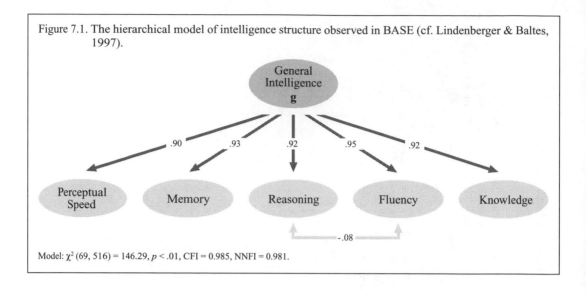

Figure 7.1. The hierarchical model of intelligence structure observed in BASE (cf. Lindenberger & Baltes, 1997).

Model: χ^2 (69, 516) = 146.29, p < .01, CFI = 0.985, NNFI = 0.981.

3.2   Age/Cohort-Related and Individual Differences in Levels of Intellectual Functioning

In younger age groups (up to age 70), performance on two broad categories of abilities, the fluidlike mechanics and crystallized pragmatics of intelligence, exhibits different patterns of maintenance and decline (P. B. Baltes, 1993; Cattell, 1971; Horn & Hofer, 1992; Schaie, 1996). Cross-sectional and longitudinal research has indicated that performance on self-paced knowledge-based tests (such as those on the BASE knowledge and fluency factor) shows a relatively stable development pattern at least into the eighth decade. In contrast, functioning associated with the content-free "mechanics of intelligence" has been found to display instances of decline in middle adulthood (40 to 60 years) and to exhibit robust decline in old age, at least with respect to one or more of its subdimensions (e.g., Hertzog & Schaie, 1988; Kliegl, Smith, & Baltes, 1989; Lindenberger & Baltes, 1994; Salthouse, 1991). The mechanics of intelligence are usually assessed by tests similar to those included in the BASE memory, reasoning, and perceptual speed factors.

Figure 7.2 summarizes results from BASE that speak to questions about differential age change functions in these two global dimensions of intelligence and to more general questions about age-related and individual differences in intellectual performance. The negative age gradients shown for the general factor g (age correlation was r = -.57), for a marker of the mechanics of intelligence (perceptual speed), and for a marker of the pragmatics of intelligence (knowledge), highlight the regularity of age-related performance decline across the ability domains (Lindenberger & Baltes, 1997). In this figure, factor scores are standardized to have a mean of 50 and standard deviation (SD) of 10. As can be seen, there is a very large negative difference (1.8 SD) in performance level between cohorts aged 70 and over 95 years.

Although the findings presented in Figure 7.2 suggest general rather than dimension-specific age trends in the mechanics and the pragmatics of intelligence, theory-consistent

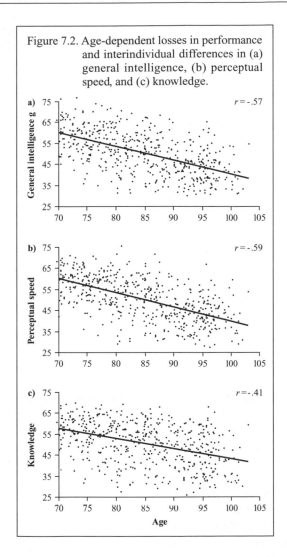

Figure 7.2. Age-dependent losses in performance and interindividual differences in (a) general intelligence, (b) perceptual speed, and (c) knowledge.

differences were also observed (Lindenberger & Baltes, 1997). Negative age correlations for the three mechanic abilities (perceptual speed: $r = -.59$; memory: $r = -.49$; reasoning: $r = -.51$) were significantly higher than those for the two pragmatic abilities (knowledge: $r = -.41$ and fluency: $r = -.46$). We know that, up to the age of 70, the aging trajectory differs for the mechanics and the pragmatics of intelligence. The BASE data suggest that this may hold true for very old age as well, although the differences between the two dimensions of intelligence appear to decrease with increasing age.

What do these age-related differences mean in concrete terms? Consider one of the tasks that loaded in the memory factor: a short-term Paired Associate memory task. In this task participants were presented with a list of eight noun pairs to remember (e.g., tree – lamp). At recall, they received the first noun as a cue and were asked to remember its pair. The final score represented the total number of noun pairs correctly recalled across two trials (i.e., possible range from 0 to 16; BASE M = 4.1). Among the group of BASE participants aged 70 to 79 years, 12% could not retain any pair, whereas 22% recalled 10 or more noun pairs. In contrast, among individuals aged 90 to over 100 years, 43% were at zero and only 2% recalled 10 or more pairs. Consider another example for a test of fluency. Here the participants were asked to name as many different words as possible beginning with the letter "s" within a time limit of 120 seconds (BASE M = 13.6). Only 1% of persons aged 70 to 79 years produced less than 5 words; 17% produced more than 23 words. In contrast, 19% of those aged 90 to over 100 years produced less than 5 words, and only 6% more than 23 words. These examples, together with the data in Figure 7.2, highlight the conclusion that the domain of intellectual functioning is one where processes associated with, or carried by, age are highly visible.

As well as the powerful evidence for ability-general negative trends, the scatterplots in Figure 7.2 also offer another view on the aging mind, namely sizable heterogeneity. In these plots, each dot represents the score of one or more persons. In spite of a general decline in performance, interindividual variability was large throughout the entire age range and across all abilities (see also Lindenberger & Baltes, 1997). The relative high performance of *some* individuals in the oldest cohorts can be seen in Figure 7.2. Some of the very old (including a 103-year-old) were among the highest performers, and some of the 70- to 74-year-olds were among the lowest performers.

3.3   Correlates of Individual and Age-Related Differences in Intellectual Functioning

There are many theories about the sources and driving forces behind individual and age-related differences in intellectual performance in late adulthood. In a comprehensive set of analyses, Lindenberger and Baltes (1997) examined various relationships between intellectual functioning and other measures collected in BASE on sensory and functional capacity and life history. In the present context, three findings are especially important.

First, these analyses revealed that *all* of the age-related variance in intelligence within the BASE sample could be accounted for by differences in vision and hearing acuity or balance (sensory-sensorimotor functioning). These relationships were not significantly reduced when subgroups (such as persons who were blind or deaf, or who had a diagnosis of dementia) are excluded. In a comparative study with younger adults (15 to 54 years; P. B. Baltes & Lindenberger, 1997) the correlation between sensory functioning and intelligence was much lower. Lindenberger and Baltes (1997) believe that this extraordinary nexus between sensory functioning and intelligence demonstrates the importance of brain-related factors in the process of the aging of intelligence.

Second, Lindenberger and Baltes (1997) found that the differential links between genetic-neurobiological and cultural factors and individual differences in the mechanics and pragmatics of intelligence found in younger adults are also manifest in very old age. As can be seen in Figure 7.3, sensory and sensorimotor measures were more related to perceptual speed (a marker of the mechanics of intelligence) than to knowledge (a marker of the pragmatics of intelligence; for all tests of significance $p < .01$). In contrast, education, social prestige, social class, and income were more positively related to knowledge than to speed (for details about these sociobiographical factors, see Mayer et al., Chapter 8).

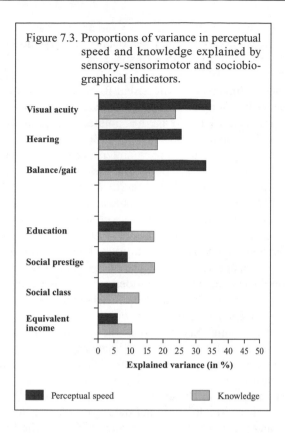

Figure 7.3. Proportions of variance in perceptual speed and knowledge explained by sensory-sensorimotor and sociobiographical indicators.

A third set of analyses examined more closely the relationship between intellectual functioning and life history factors (Lindenberger & Baltes, 1997). Differences in intellectual functioning between socially advantaged and disadvantaged individuals were found to be remarkably consistent throughout the age range 70 to over 100 years. On average, socially advantaged individuals (i.e., those with higher levels of education and professional experience) showed a level of performance of about 1 *SD* higher in all age groups. Nevertheless, the negative age gradient was equivalent for both the socially advantaged and disadvantaged. Thus, with respect to intellectual functioning, old age does not appear to neutralize the diversity in level of intellectual performance that accumulates over the life course as a function of social-structural, biographical, and genetic differences. However, old age does not accentuate these differences or provide protective factors (cf. Rutter, 1987; Staudinger, Marsiske, & Baltes, 1995). In the domain of intelligence, the course of age-related decline seems to be the same for everyone, regardless of previous life conditions.

4   Self and Personality

A broad range of information about personality dispositions, self-related beliefs, and self-regulation processes was collected within BASE (see Table 7.1), with the goal to describe individual differences in adaptation to old and very old age. To date, there have been relatively few empirical studies about self and personality in very old age (see, however, Breytspaak, 1984; Busse & Maddox, 1985; Erikson, Erikson, & Kivnick, 1986; Johnson & Barer, 1997; Lehr & Thomae, 1987). Data on age differences between 70 and over 100 years on the broad range of dimensions collected in BASE thus have the potential to add further to our knowledge in this domain of psychological functioning.

Theoretical work on self and personality in old age has pointed to the importance of understanding the dynamic interplay between aspects of stability and change in functioning and of searching for mechanisms that afford the maintenance of well-being in the face of social loss and health constraints (e.g., Bengtson, Reedy, & Gordon, 1985; Brandtstädter & Greve, 1994; Filipp & Klauer, 1986; Markus & Herzog, 1991; Nesselroade, 1989; Staudinger et al., 1995). Some personality dispositions, especially neuroticism and extraversion, show much structural and mean-level stability (continuity) at least until age 80 (Costa & McCrae, 1980; McCrae & Costa, 1990). Longitudinal analyses of Q-Sort data from the Berkeley Intergenerational Studies, however, revealed consistent group patterns of change (from age 18 to age 60) and large interindividual differences in direction of change on dimensions of self-confidence, cognitive commitment, outgoingness, and dependability (Jones & Meredith, 1996). Personal goals, future and ideal self-concepts (possible selves), control beliefs, and coping styles are expected also to show differential and age-related change and to reflect the dynamic interaction between individuals and their environment. Furthermore, research on general beliefs about change indicates that individuals expect desirable personality characteristics (such as extraversion) to decrease and less desirable ones (such as neuroticism) to increase (Fleeson & Heckhausen, 1997; Heckhausen, Dixon, & Baltes, 1989).

Data collected in BASE, particularly the longitudinal data, will allow us to examine many questions about patterns and predictors of stability and change. In the following sections, we review cross-sectional findings on self-descriptions, age trends in personality characteristics, and age-related differences in reported self-regulatory strategies. Chapter 11 (Staudinger et al.) and Chapter 17 (Smith et al.) discuss further analyses dealing with the concepts of resilience and well-being in very old age. Chapter 9 (M. M. Baltes et al.) presents findings on gender differences in the domain of self and personality (see also Smith & Baltes, in press).

4.1   The Self-Descriptions of Older Adults

Self-descriptions provide some insight into an individual's framing of his or her interactions with the environment and sense of self-worth (e.g., Kihlstrom & Klein, 1994). It is therefore interesting to ask about the range of life domains that older adults include in their self-descriptions and their evaluations of the experience of aging.

4.1.1   Current Self-Definitions
Following the lead of previous studies (e.g., George & Okun, 1985; McCrae & Costa, 1988), BASE used a version of the "Who am I?" task to assess different aspects of self-definitions. What content did we expect? In younger age groups, statements about sociodemographic roles, physical characteristics, and social relationships tend to be predominant in self-descriptions (e.g., Gordon, 1968). In older samples (45 to 70 years), statements about health, life experience, life values, and beliefs increase in frequency (George & Okun, 1985). McCrae and Costa (1988) examined written "Who am I?" re-

sponses in a sample of 32- to 84-year-olds and found positive age correlations for statements about age, health, life situations, life events, interests/hobbies, and personal values. Negative age correlations occurred for statements about family roles, social relationships, and general personality characteristics.

On average, BASE participants used 6.8 different domains to describe themselves (SD = 1.4; for details see Freund & Smith, 1997, in press). The domains most frequently named were individual interests and hobbies at home (62%), everyday activities (48%), family life (47%), community-oriented interests (45%), health (45%), personality characteristics (42%), life review (42%), interpersonal style (41%), and life philosophy (39%). This content reflects an active interest in being engaged with the environment, a concern with the self, and motives to relate to others. Age-related differences in content profile were rather small, but individual differences were substantial. Mention of family, activities outside the home, and interpersonal style decreased with age in the BASE sample, whereas mention of everyday life activities, everyday competence, and sociodemographic characteristics increased.

Only 7% of the sample included a statement about their physical appearance or about death – a finding that sharply contrasts the attributes used by younger adults when asked to describe older persons. Furthermore, contrary to the negative stereotype that older adults "live in the past," the majority of the self-definitions of BASE participants were located in the present, and positive self-evaluations were twice as frequent as negative ones (Freund & Smith, 1997, in press). Approximately 76% of participants spontaneously framed one of their self-descriptive statements (especially those related to personal characteristics, health, everyday competence, and activities) as a comparison (Barnes, 1993). Unlike young adults who compare themselves against peers and significant others (Suls & Wills, 1991), BASE participants typically made comparisons to themselves in the past and gained a sense of continuity from these comparisons (i.e., they concluded that "things have generally stayed the same").

4.1.2 Subjective Aging

Given the overall positive picture of the self-conceptions of BASE participants, it is not surprising to find that they also generally described themselves as feeling 12 years younger than their actual age and as appearing 9.5 years younger. Their preference, however, was to be 25 years younger (see Fig. 7.4). On average, these age discrepancies increased slightly with increasing age ($p < .001$): Individuals in their 90s felt 16 years younger, considered that they looked 14 years younger, and wanted to be in their early 60s. Women considered that they looked 4 years older than men ($p < .001$), and men preferred to be 7 years younger than women ($p < .001$). This pattern of age identities is consistent with the findings of Filipp and Ferring (1989) and the life-span trends reported by Montepare and Lachman (1989), and provides information on the psychological relevance of such comparative evaluations. These investigators found that "feeling young at heart" was not necessarily an expression of fearing or denying one's aging, but rather an expression of a positive self-image.

4.1.3 Future Scenarios (Possible Selves)

The positive self-images of the BASE participants were also reflected in their hoped-for and feared future scenarios (Hauschild, 1996; Smith & Barnes, 1994). The content of one's hopes and fears about the future is seen as being an important source of motivation for action and self-esteem (Markus & Nurius, 1986). Only 6% of the respondents indi-

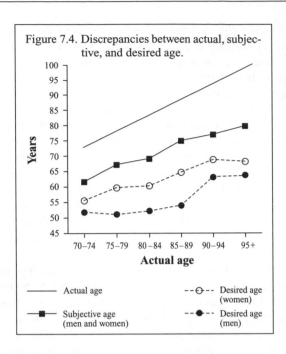

Figure 7.4. Discrepancies between actual, subjective, and desired age.

cated that they had no hopes or fears about the future, whereas 94% generated varied scenarios that covered a range of domains and developmental goals. This is in sharp contrast to the negative stereotype that old age represents a period of disengagement from thinking about the future and a time of "casting off possible selves" (Markus & Herzog, 1991).

The most prominent domains of hopes and fears in future scenarios were personal characteristics (mentioned at least once by 50% of the participants; e.g., "I would like to be someone who can be of help to lots of people," or "I don't ever want to be a malicious, quarrelsome person") and health (e.g., "I don't want ever to have to be nursed"). Activities and interests were not as prominent in future scenarios as in current self-descriptions. Instead, goals of self-acceptance, autonomy, and positive relations with others were the most prominent themes. Contrary to our expectations, the central motive underlying hopes was not to maintain a current life situation, but rather to achieve something new and to reexperience something (e.g., "I would like to go on a long trip again. Two or three months . . . anywhere, I don't care where"; "I would like to be in love with a man again, a really harmonious relationship"). Desires for maintenance were primarily linked to health (e.g., "I hope to stay as healthy and mobile as I am now"). Like the findings for self-definitions, there were few age/cohort differences but substantial individual differences in expressions of future possible selves.

4.2   Age-Related Trends in Desirable and Less Desirable Personality Attributes

Figure 7.5 summarizes age trends in personality characteristics grouped in terms of social and psychological desirability. Desirable characteristics were defined as

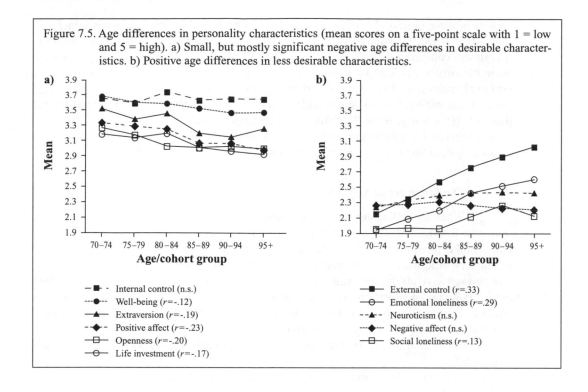

Figure 7.5. Age differences in personality characteristics (mean scores on a five-point scale with 1 = low and 5 = high). a) Small, but mostly significant negative age differences in desirable characteristics. b) Positive age differences in less desirable characteristics.

those which researchers have found to positively influence the process of dealing with life problems; for example, an interest in being with others (extraversion), openness to new ideas and experiences (openness), frequent experience of positive emotions (positive affect), and a feeling of being in control of one's life (internal control). Psychologically less desirable characteristics are those which are known to signal elements of dysfunctionality, such as neuroticism, negative affect, and the belief that one's life is controlled by others (external control).

This categorization of variables as more or less socially desirable reflects a general consensus in the psychological research literature about what "on average" is functional versus dysfunctional, although the categorization is open to debate (e.g., Aldwin, 1991; Pearlin & Mullan, 1992; Snyder & Forsyth, 1991). We acknowledge that the functionality (desirability) of personality characteristics can also be context-specific. For some goals and contexts, characteristics typically thought to be dysfunctional may actually be adaptive. Dysfunctional attributes, such as anger and loneliness, may actually be adaptive in particular contexts if they signalize the necessity for change. Likewise, it might be adaptive (and helpful) for very ill persons to believe that others will care for their well-being (external control). Nevertheless, in the long-term, such less desirable personality characteristics may indeed be dysfunctional, especially if they constitute chronic behavior.

The findings illustrated in Figure 7.5 indicate some negative changes in dimensions that psychologists consider to be central to a sense of psychological well-being. There were age-related decreases in some, but not all, of the desirable characteristics and increases in some undesirable ones. Specifically, as to desirable characteristics, older participants in BASE reported less extraversion, openness, positive affect, and personal life investment compared with participants aged 70 to 84 years. Conversely, in regard to less desirable attributes, older participants felt that their lives were more controlled by others (external control) and reported that they experienced more emotional loneliness. Age correlations were relatively small and, in general, mean differences amounted to less than 0.5 *SD*. Clearly, these "negative" age trends are much smaller in magnitude than those observed for intellectual abilities. As a whole, however, these trends toward increased dysfunction could be interpreted as a type of chronic stress reaction.

4.3   The Structure of Self and Personality in Old Age

What about the interdomain structure of the measures of self and personality assessed in BASE? The outcome was not surprising in its direction, but regarding its extent. Unlike intelligence, where the separate abilities were highly intercorrelated, we found very little structural coherence between the various personality dimensions. Positive and negative affect, for example, were relatively independent dimensions ($r = .04$), extraversion and neuroticism were only minimally correlated ($r = .12$), and so were internal and external control ($r = .07$). An exploratory factor analysis of all the measures of self and personality revealed at least eight factors. This lack of interdomain coherence corresponds to the findings reported in studies with younger samples (e.g., Costa & McCrae, 1980).[1]

There is little evidence that it is possible to construct a homogeneous measure to describe the whole person in the domain of self and personality, equivalent to the general factor expressing individual intellectual performance. As a consequence, generalizations such as "personality declines in old age" should be avoided. On the contrary, within the framework of variables studied in BASE, the dominant outcome was that in very old age self and personality represent a highly differentiated system of characteristics, attitudes, and experiences.

4.4   Self-Regulatory Processes: Control Beliefs as an Example

Much research on self-regulation focuses on issues of "personal control" (M. M. Baltes & Baltes, 1986; Bandura, 1989; Heckhausen & Schulz, 1995; Rodin, Timko, & Harris, 1985; Skinner, 1995). Control beliefs influence how people think, feel, and act. In particular, believing that one's efforts can influence an outcome (i.e., a belief in internal control) increases the likelihood of selecting goals to act upon, investing time and energy in the goals selected, and experiencing subjective well-being in association with the positive outcome of one's efforts (cf. Kunzmann, 1998). This pattern is in contrast to the more negative consequences (in terms of motivation and sense of well-being) thought to be associated with beliefs that other persons (especially powerful others) have control over the events in one's life or that outcomes are rather a matter a chance. For

---

[1] Of course there are moderate correlations between variables measuring similar characteristics. Thus, positive affect and extraversion (with the facet of emotionality) correlate $r = .46$, and negative affect and neuroticism (with the facet of anxiety) correlate $r = .64$ (cf. Watson, Clark, & Tellegen, 1988).

this reason, there has been considerable interest in the literature on aging in determining the extent to which internal control beliefs are maintained and external control beliefs may be avoided (Lachman, 1986).

A scale assessing general beliefs about control over the positive and negative aspects of life was included within BASE (cf. Skinner, 1995; Smith, Marsiske, & Maier, 1996). LISREL analyses confirmed three factors characterizing beliefs about internal control over positive events, internal control over negative events, and external control (powerful others). Consistent with findings from other research groups working specifically with older adults (e.g., Roberts & Nesselroade, 1986), the items in BASE describing a belief in chance did not reliably form a factor. The factors related to internal and external control beliefs did not correlate ($r = .07$), indicating that, in old age as in young adulthood, control beliefs are multidimensional.

The three dimensions of control beliefs showed different age gradients: Whereas beliefs about personal (internal) control over positive and negative events did not differ with age, the belief that others play a significant role in determining the events in one's life (external control) increased significantly with age ($r = .33$). After controlling for age (which explained 10% of the variance) and institutionalization, poor vision, hearing, and mobility were additional significant predictors of external control beliefs (total variance explained was 18%). In the cross-sectional data we could not test specific causal pathways, of course, but these results are consistent with the idea that control beliefs are experience-based (Helgeson, 1992; Rodin et al., 1985). The frailty that comes with advanced age, together with sensory and physical impairment, necessitates increased dependence on others (M. M. Baltes, 1996). This aging process is likely to be reflected in individuals' beliefs that many things in their lives are or will have to be controlled by others.

At the same time, it is important to recall that the age gradient for internal control was almost zero. This suggests that very old people, as far as their own actions are concerned, perhaps maintain an intact self-concept. Furthermore, beliefs about internal and external locus of control were not exclusive. For instance, 27% of the BASE sample tended toward a shared responsibility model, in that they believed that the locus of control lay both with themselves (internal) *and* with others (external).

5   Social Relationships

Previous research has indicated that most older adults are firmly embedded and socially integrated into kin and family contexts (Bengtson & Schütze, 1992; Troll, 1986). This conclusion, however, is primarily linked to the young old. Some of the few studies that have included the very old suggest that, in this age group, social isolation is more likely than is the case for younger cohorts (e.g., Knipscheer, 1986; Lehr & Minnemann, 1987). The availability of kin and social partners also implies a more or less effective exchange system of instrumental and emotional support (Antonucci, 1990; Field & Minkler, 1988) that may be directed by the older persons themselves or their partners, or may reflect reciprocal interests.

From a psychological perspective, the sheer availability of family and kin, as well as the frequency of social contact or instrumental and emotional support, is perhaps less important than the older individual's perception and evaluation of these social contacts (cf. Carstensen, 1993). Individuals may experience social relationships in terms of gains and losses, or as sources of satisfaction (gratification) or strain (stress). Thus, the elderly person's evaluation of his or her social environment and relationships, and the extent to which these evaluations contribute to an individual's sense of well-being, represented important questions to be addressed within BASE.

We were also interested in exploring the concept and implications of loneliness in very old age. The literature generally distinguishes both "living alone" from loneliness as well as social aspects of loneliness from emotional aspects (e.g., Weiss, 1982). It is important to recognize that living alone by itself does not signify loneliness. For psychological loneliness to exist, there has to be a sense of emotional loneliness or a perceived deficit in social sources of emotional attachment, warmth, and comfort. The availability of social interaction partners does not necessarily guarantee absence of psychological loneliness; an individual may have social contacts that provide support and yet experience emotional loneliness. It is often suggested, for instance, that such a pattern may characterize the very old. Family and younger friends may satisfy social requirements, but may not satisfy desires for close contact with peers (Johnson & Troll, 1994; Thomae, 1994).

The data collected in BASE about social relationships (see Table 7.1) represent the study participants' subjective evaluation of their social networks, rather than observed behavior. The "Circle Task" of Kahn and Antonucci (1980; Antonucci, 1986) was used to generate the names of all current and recently lost intimates (first circle), friends (second circle), and acquaintances (third circle) of each individual and the exchanges of support with these people. Much information about the personal networks revealed by this measure is presented in Chapter 10 by Wagner et al. (see also Lang, 1994; Lang & Carstensen, 1994; Schütze & Lang, 1993). We will focus below on the BASE participants' subjective evaluations of their social relationships.

5.1   Composition of Personal Social Networks

The majority of BASE participants were embedded and socially integrated into kin and nonkin contexts. Only 17 BASE participants (3%) nominated no person at all in the Circle Task. Fourteen percent ($n = 71$) named no person in their innermost circle, 17% named no close person for the second circle, and 22% ($n = 115$) named no more distant acquaintances (third circle). Figure 7.6a shows the distribution of persons in the three circles for the 70- to 84-year-old participants and those aged 85 years and older. Approximately 50% of both age groups nominated two to five persons for each circle.

As Figure 7.6b shows, the 70- to 84-year-old participants named significantly more people in their social network ($M = 11.9$) than those 85 years and older ($M = 7.6$, $p < .001$). There was also a significant interaction between age and the number of persons nominated to each of the three circles (cf. Fig. 7.6b, $p < .001$): Specifically, individuals aged 85 to over 100 years named far fewer persons for the outer (second and third) circles of their networks than those aged 70 to 84 years. This result is also reflected in the various age correlations (circle 1: $r = -.14$; circle 2: $r = -.24$; circle 3: $r = -.34$; cf. Lang, 1994; Lang & Carstensen, 1994). In general, participants who nominated more persons for the innermost circle also named more for the second and third circle (correlation between circle 1 and 2: $r = .32$; circle 1 and 3: $r = .23$; circle 2 and 3: $r = .40$). For the very old, only the correlation between circle 1 and 2 was significant ($r = .31$): There was no relationship between circle 1 and 3 ($r = .09$).

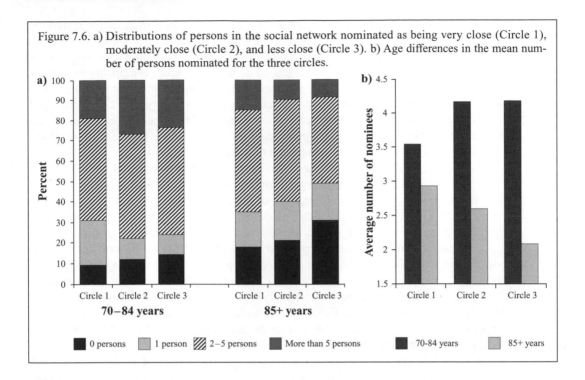

Figure 7.6. a) Distributions of persons in the social network nominated as being very close (Circle 1), moderately close (Circle 2), and less close (Circle 3). b) Age differences in the mean number of persons nominated for the three circles.

Overall, participants aged 85 to 100+ years named fewer social interaction partners, particularly in the periphery of their networks. When all three circles are considered, the age correlation was $r = -.33$. Surprisingly, there was no correlation between age and the reported number of close friends who had recently died ($r = -.03$). These findings about the social microworld of older adults differentiates the stereotype that, with advancing age, people have an increasingly smaller network of relatives, friends, and acquaintances. The data reported by BASE participants suggested a significant tendency in this direction, but the negative age correlation was much smaller than that found for intelligence, for example. Because we do not have data for comparison with younger cohorts, it is difficult to evaluate the absolute size of the social network system in old age.

According to their own reports, very old people appear to be less socially embedded than younger adults (cf. Johnson & Troll, 1994). What is noteworthy, however, is that the negative age gradient is relatively small for the number of intimates (inner circle; cf. Lang & Carstensen, 1994). We had also expected that gender differences would be more apparent than would age differences, particularly with regard to the reported size of social networks. Our analyses, however, did not reveal any significant gender differences (cf. M. M. Baltes et al., Chapter 9).

5.2   Satisfaction with Social Relationships

The majority of BASE participants indicated that they were satisfied with their family life and friendships (on a five-point scale, $M = 3.95$ for family; $M = 3.83$ for friends). There were no age differences. At the same time, 25% indicated that they felt their family had too little time for them, and 21% felt the same way about their friends. Since we do not have data for younger cohorts, it is difficult to interpret these responses in a life-span perspective. By the same token, we do not know how participants would have answered, had we asked them to compare their current situation with that in their past.

More important for general well-being than the desire to simply spend more time with family and friends, however, is the feeling that there is at least one person whom one can trust and rely upon for emotional support in times of need (e.g., Thomae, 1994). Forty-eight percent of the BASE sample indicated that they had no specific person in their network on whom they could rely for emotional support. There were equal numbers of 70- to 84-year-olds and persons aged 85 years and above among the 52% who reported they had such a person to rely on. Further, 19% of the sample indicated that in the last three months they had experienced no affectionate or emotionally close contact with others. Specifically, participants were asked whether, in the last three months, (a) they had spoken to someone about personal worries and concerns (43% had), (b) whether someone had cheered them up at a time when they were feeling sad (31% had experienced this), and (c) whether someone had given them a kiss, or a cuddle, or shown some affection (70% had experienced this, but significantly more younger than older participants, $p <$ .01). As a follow-up, those individuals who indicated that they had not received such emotional support, were asked whether they perceived this as a deficit: This was the case for 13% with regard to an intimate conversation, 18% missed not having been cheered up, and 26% felt a lack of affectionate exchange. Furthermore, 40% of the BASE sample described experiencing some disappointments with individuals (especially children and grandchildren) whom they nevertheless named in their social networks. Disappointments included conflicts regarding money and family possessions, and failure to meet expectations regarding family contact. There were no age differences in these reports.

Although family and friends were named by participants, and relationships were rated overall as being satisfactory, this closer look at specific aspects of social interactions indicates that many individuals in the sample would have liked to see some changes for the better in their relationships with others, especially regarding affectionate exchanges (cf. Carstensen, 1993; Johnson & Troll, 1994). Perhaps reflecting this general feeling, only 19% of the sample mentioned their family as currently being the best thing in their lives (11% considered family to be the most difficult aspect of their lives).

5.3   *Social and Emotional Loneliness*

The literature suggests that feelings of social isolation and emotional distance from other persons represent two different aspects of loneliness (Peplau & Perlman, 1982; Russell, Cutrona, Rose, & Yurko, 1984; Weiss, 1982). LISREL analyses of the BASE data supported two loneliness factors: social loneliness (derived from items asking about perceptions of belonging to a social group and availability of friends) and emotional loneliness (derived from items dealing with feelings of isolation, being alone, and of being secluded from contact with others). These two factors were moderately correlated ($r = .34$). Both factors revealed a positive age gradient: With increasing age, individuals experienced more social loneliness ($r = .13$) and especially more emotional loneliness ($r = .29$). In a sample of young adults, Russell and his colleagues (1984) found that social loneliness was best predicted by a lack of relationships, whereas emotional loneliness was predicted by perceived deficits in intimate attachments to others. Further, each type of loneliness was better predicted by subjective measures of satisfaction than by the reported network size. Stepwise hierarchical regression analyses of the BASE data (separately predicting social and emotional loneliness) supported and extended these earlier findings in younger samples. Together, age and gender explained 10% of the variance in emotional loneliness (i.e., old women and very old persons experienced more emotional loneliness), but did not significantly predict social loneliness. The number of close companions (named in circle 1) contributed to both aspects of loneliness. A measure of satisfaction with family and friends was entered in a final step of the analyses and was found to significantly account for further variance in both factors: 10% of emotional loneliness (total variance accounted 24%) and 7% of social loneliness (total variance accounted 20%). A significant part of both aspects of loneliness was thus found to be related to the participants' subjective evaluation of the extent to which relationships with others satisfied their personal needs (see also Wietzker, 1996).

6   Different Profiles of Psychological Functioning

So far in this chapter, we have presented information about age-related and individual differences *within* the separate psychological domains. In this section, we summarize findings about subgroup differences in profiles of functioning *across* the domains of intelligence, self and personality, and social relationships (Smith & Baltes, 1997). To date, relatively little is known about the nature of the structural and systemic relationships among the domains of psychological functioning (P. B. Baltes & Graf, 1996; P. B. Baltes & Smith, 1997; Birren & Schroots, 1996; Magnusson, 1996). Does functioning in one psychological domain "dominate" (take intelligence as an example), such that decline in this area "triggers" decline in all other areas? Or is there evidence for different profiles of selective maintenance and decline with a fair degree of functional independence (P. B. Baltes & Baltes, 1990)?

In order to examine systemic relationships within the cross-sectional BASE data, we carried out a cluster analysis of 12 constructs selected to broadly represent the central psychological dimensions considered in the research literature on old age: perceptual speed, memory, knowledge, neuroticism, extraversion, life investment, internal and external control, social and emotional loneliness, reported number of close confidants, and perceived support. Several goals underpinned this analysis (Smith & Baltes, 1997). A first goal was to explore the possibility of obtaining a systemic-wholistic view on psychological functioning. We wondered how many subgroups would be revealed in the BASE data by the cluster analysis and how the psychological profiles of these groups would differ in terms of overall level and shape (pattern of high and low scores across the domains). A second goal was to examine whether the subgroups obtained differed in age and gender composition and profile desirability (functional status). Underlying this goal was the desire to gain an impression of the balance of desirable and less desirable psychological profiles in the old and the very old, and for men and women in BASE.

Our use of cluster analysis was not aimed at a taxonomic or content interpretation. We were not interested in identifying subgroups of individuals in the sense of typologies. Rather, we used cluster analysis as an "unbiased" method to identify individuals who were more or less similar to each other and to assign to all individuals based on their cluster membership a ranking in terms of profile desirability.

Table 7.2. *Summary label assigned to each group, membership frequency, percentage of the BASE sample, average age, and gender distribution*

Rank	Subgroup label	n^a	%	Age	% F/M[b]
1	General positive profile: cognitively very fit, extraverted, and not lonely	50	9.8	77.9	48/52
2	General positive profile: high social embeddedness	29	5.7	82.5	45/55
3	Moderately positive profile	119	23.3	81.1	37/63
4	Average profile: cognitively fit, low extraversion, low control, high social loneliness	42	8.2	81.1	55/45
5	Average profile: high neuroticism, high other control, high perceived support	75	14.7	88.0	68/32
6	Average profile: high neuroticism, high loneliness	44	8.6	84.7	50/50
7	Average profile: cognitively impaired, high external (other) control	64	12.5	91.2	53/47
8	Cognitively impaired, low neuroticism, low support, high social loneliness	55	10.7	88.5	36/64
9	General negative profile: severe cognitive impairment, high neuroticism, high loneliness, low extraversion, low internal control	32	6.2	91.2	69/31

[a]Total $N = 510$; see Smith and Baltes (1997).
[b]Percentages of women and men.

Table 7.2 provides an overview of the nine clusters revealed and includes descriptive information about subgroup size, the average age of members, and proportion of men and women (for details, refer to Smith & Baltes, 1997). As can be seen, there was one rather large group containing 119 persons (23% of the sample) and two comparatively small groups ($n = 29$ and 32) each reflecting about 6% of the sample. To estimate average desirability or functional status of each cluster obtained, the unweighted mean was computed of each profile's standardized T-scores on 12 indicators (coded in a direction to reflect their desirability). Higher scores on perceptual speed, memory, knowledge, extraversion, life investment, internal control, perceived support, and close companions were considered as desirable (i.e., more functional). Higher scores on the remaining four variables, neuroticism, external control, social loneliness, and emotional loneliness, were considered less desirable (i.e., less functional). Scores on these latter four variables were recoded so that higher scores on overall desirability (functional status) would indicate positive or desirable functioning (i.e., high scores indicated low neuroticism, low loneliness, etc.). Thus, with this recoding, a desirable status of profile variables was linked to above-average performance and a less desirable status to below-average performance.

The first four groups listed in Table 7.2 (47% of the sample) reflected different patterns of desirable attributes (positive to average functional status). The groups differed in the set of dimensions that defined the peaks of their profile and in the size and location of

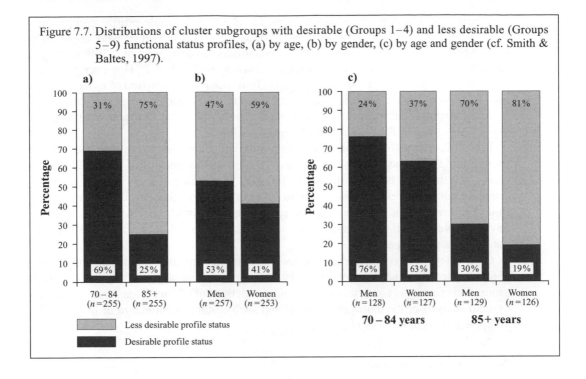

Figure 7.7. Distributions of cluster subgroups with desirable (Groups 1–4) and less desirable (Groups 5–9) functional status profiles, (a) by age, (b) by gender, (c) by age and gender (cf. Smith & Baltes, 1997).

the peaks. One striking feature of the top subgroup ($n = 50$, 10% of the sample) was that, in terms of average level, members were functioning at least 0.5 SD above the sample average on 8 of the 12 dimensions examined. Another feature was that their top performance (> 1 SD) was spread across two domains, intellectual functioning (perceptual speed, memory, and knowledge) and personality (extraversion). The second subgroup ($n = 29$, 6%), also had positive scores across all dimensions on average, but at a lower level than group 1. Group 2 showed only average intellectual functioning but a high involvement in the social side of life. The third and largest subgroup ($n = 119$, 23%) reflected a positive well-balanced spread of average-level functioning across all domains (desirability score = 52.9).

Groups 5 through 9 each exhibited, on average, a less desirable profile (53% of the sample). Groups 5 and 6 reflected two different profiles characterized by relatively high levels of general anxiety (neuroticism > 0.5 SD). The average profiles of cluster groups 7 to 9 were commonly characterized by low to extremely low cognitive function, but had different shapes across the personality and social domains.

As Figure 7.7 illustrates, there were definite differences in the age and gender composition of the clusters characterized as desirable and less desirable. Among the 70- to 84-year-olds in BASE, 69% were included in the high functional status (desirability) groups and 31% in the less desirable profile groups. Among individuals aged 85 years and older, only 25% were in the desirable groups and 75% in the less desirable groups. The relative risk of membership in the less desirable profile subgroup was 2.5 times higher for the very old (85–103 years) than for people between the ages of 70 and 84 years.

Whereas 53% of the men in BASE were members of desirable profile groups, only 41% of the women were. These differences between men and women were apparent in the old (76% men vs. 63% women in desirable groups) and the very old (30% vs. 19%). No subgroup exclusively consisted of men or women (see Table 7.2). However, the sexes were not equally represented in four clusters. Two subgroups consisted of twice as many men as women (groups 3 and 8) and two included twice as many women as men (groups 5 and 9). Overall, the relative risk of being a member of a less desirable profile group was 1.3 times higher for women than for men.

It is, of course, difficult to evaluate the psychological and sociopolitical relevance of these findings because the data are "relative" within the distribution of the BASE participants and there are no absolute norms for what is considered functional or dysfunctional. In our future research, we intend to develop indicators that permit such an evaluation. Furthermore, it is important to recognize the sizable heterogeneity even in advanced old age and not to assume that there is something akin to a prevalent interdomain profile of the aged.

On this level of systemic-wholistic analysis, and in comparison with the single variable analyses described earlier, the very old appear to be a psychologically distinct group. This finding is consistent with recent predictions of a "fourth age" based on a theoretical analysis of the biological-genetic and sociocultural architecture of life-span development (P. B. Baltes, 1997).

7   Overall Conclusion

The intent of this chapter was to provide a general overview of cross-sectional findings in the three domains of psychological functioning investigated in BASE: intellectual functioning, self and personality, and social relationships. At the same time, we tried to address some of the key questions asked in BASE about individual differences (heterogeneity), age-related differences, and possible systemic interrelationships across the domains.

As to individual heterogeneity, the findings provide considerable support for the conclusion that processes of differential aging continue into old age. There are many faces of growing old (P. B. Baltes, 1997). This seems to be as true for 70- to 84-year-olds as it is for the very old. Older adults do not represent a homogeneous group as far as their psychological profiles are concerned. A considerable number of very old individuals continue to exhibit relatively high levels of efficacy in the different domains of psychological functioning. From a systemic point of view, however, the findings indicate that in advanced age, an increasing number of individuals show decline or dysfunction in several domains of psychological functioning, and that these losses also influence facets of subjective well-being (see also P. B. Baltes, 1997; Smith & Baltes, 1997).

These observations on subgroup differences must be complemented by BASE findings regarding domain-specific functioning. Analyses of the three domains of functioning (intelligence, self and personality, and social relationships) did indeed reveal rather different age gradients. In the domain of intellectual functioning, the role of age was paramount. More than one-third of the variance in individual differences was age-related, and the average age gradient was decidedly negative for all the tests of intelligence studied. With regard to intellectual performance, then, old age is a major risk factor.

The age story was somewhat different for the other major psychological constructs considered in BASE. In the domains self and personality as well as social relationships, chronological age accounted for much less variance than in the domain of intelligence. To prevent a possible misunderstanding, let us note that "negative" age trends in such measures as extraversion (less with age), positive affect (less with age), emotional loneliness (more with age), and external social control (more with age) did exist. Their magnitude, however, was typically less than one-half of a standard deviation, and the age correlations accounted for less than 10% of the overall variance. When interpreting these results, it is important to consider two aspects. First, the instruments for the assessment of self and personality as well as social relationships cannot be regarded as "direct" measures of objective reality. Individuals often tend to present themselves in public in a more positive way than they might actually view themselves in private. Second, it is known from research on processes of self-regulation that individuals use a variety of strategies to interpret reality in a self-enhancing way, for example, by changing goals or reorganizing standards of evaluation (cf. Brandtstädter & Greve, 1994; Markus & Herzog, 1991; Staudinger et al., 1995; cf. Staudinger et al., Chapter 11; Smith et al., Chapter 17).

The findings in the domains self and personality and social relationships provide an interesting challenge for psychological research. On the one hand, they contribute to a positive view of the psychological inner world and the capacity reserves of old and very old people. On the other hand, the overall picture of age-related differences, even though each one of them may be relatively small, points to a general trend of less desirable psychological functioning in advanced age. This result indicates that the psychological experience of dealing with aging may be seen as a kind of chronic stress situation (see also Staudinger et al., Chapter 11). The cluster analyses confirmed this view, at least for some subgroups (Smith & Baltes, 1997).

The third major emphasis of our analyses concerned the question whether it is useful to form subgroups of individuals based on their respective similarity across the three domains of psychological functioning (represented by 12 criterion variables) in order to gain a comprehensive picture of the psychological profiles of older persons. The cluster analysis illustrated that, even if individual variable comparisons did not demonstrate major age differences, as, for example, in the domains self and personality and social relationships, combinations of these variables do. Of the nine subgroups extracted, four reflected different patterns of desirable functioning (47% of the sample) and five less desirable functioning (53%). Risk of membership in the less desirable profile subgroups was 2.5 times larger for the very old (85–103 years) than for persons aged 70 to 84 years and 1.3 times larger for women than for men.

We hope that in future analyses, taking into account life history and contextual constellations, we will be able to get more information about the formation of these clusters from a developmental and life-span perspective. As we pursue these questions, we will need to be mindful of two issues. First, it would be desirable to develop criteria by which the resulting clusters could be evaluated in terms of "successful" aging or which would permit the identification of risk versus protective and/or optimizing factors. Second, we need to be careful not to confound cluster analysis (based mainly on similarities) with typological analysis, which often assumes genuine qualitative differences in the basic structure of the psyche. Our data do not indicate any such differences.

In addition to questions of differential aging, we were also interested in the systemic relationships across disciplines, as well as in the predictive value of life history information regarding continuity or discontinuity (cf. P. B. Baltes, 1997; P. B. Baltes & Smith, 1997). The multidisciplinary BASE data permitted the detection of a linkage between biological and psychological functioning. Specifically, P. B. Baltes and Lindenberger (1995, 1997) have pointed to the important role which the sensory and sensorimotor systems seem to play in advanced old age (cf. Marsiske et al., Chapter 13). This is a finding that awaits further study and theoretical discourse, but it suggests the important role that brain physiology and brain integrity play in the process of aging.

As to the potential of using life history information, we concentrated in this chapter on the role of the social life history (education, income, and social prestige) in the process of cognitive aging and compared it with the predictive power of neurobiological factors. First results indicated that individuals with rather different life histories differ only in level in old age, not in their general process of aging. The predictive power of social life history, accounting for some 12% of the variance, was not negligible (Lindenberger & Baltes, 1997) but less than expected, especially in view of the predictive power of neurobiological factors (such as vision and hearing). Sensory and sensorimotor measures accounted for some 50% of the individual variance in intellectual performance and practically for all of the age-related variance. These findings do not exclude a certain continuity based on life history variables, but they do underline discontinuity in old age as a result of neurobiological factors and point to the possible consequences of the relative incompleteness of the architecture of human ontogeny (P. B. Baltes, 1997).

Finally, we would like to mention again the methodological limitations of the present analyses. The data examined represent a cross-sectional and correlative momentary picture. It is an open question whether the aging patterns and the temporal and causal relationships suggested by our findings will be confirmed by longitudinal follow-up studies (cf. P. B. Baltes et al., Chapter 1).

References

Aldwin, C. M. (1991). Does age affect the stress and coping process? Implications of age differences in perceived control. *Journal of Gerontology: Psychological Sciences, 46*, P174–P180.

Antonucci, T. C. (1986). Measuring social support networks: A hierarchical mapping technique. *Generations, 10*, 10–12.

Antonucci, T. C. (1990). Social supports and social relationships. In R. H. Binstock & L. K. George (Eds.), *Handbook of aging and the social sciences* (3rd ed., pp. 205–227). San Diego, CA: Academic Press.

Bäckman, L. (Ed.). (1991). *Memory functioning in dementia*. Amsterdam: North-Holland.

Baltes, M. M. (1996). *The many faces of dependency in old age*. Cambridge: Cambridge University Press.

Baltes, M. M., & Baltes, P. B. (Eds.). (1986). *The psychology of control and aging*. Hillsdale, NJ: Erlbaum.

Baltes, P. B. (1968). Longitudinal and cross-sectional sequences in the study of age and generation effects. *Human Development, 11*, 145–171.

Baltes, P. B. (1987). Theoretical propositions of life-span developmental psychology: On the dynamics between growth and decline. *Developmental Psychology, 23*, 611–626.

Baltes, P. B. (1993). The aging mind: Potential and limits. *The Gerontologist, 33*, 580–594.

Baltes, P. B. (1997). On the incomplete architecture of human ontogeny: Selection, optimization, and compensation as foundation of developmental theory. *American Psychologist, 52*, 366–380.

Baltes, P. B., & Baltes, M. M. (1990). Psychological perspectives on successful aging: The model of selective optimization with compensation. In P. B. Baltes & M. M. Baltes (Eds.), *Successful aging: Perspectives from the behavioral sciences* (pp. 1–34). Cambridge: Cambridge University Press.

Baltes, P. B., Cornelius, S. W., Spiro, A., Nesselroade, J. R., & Willis, S. L. (1980). Integration versus differentiation of fluid/crystallized intelligence in old age. *Developmental Psychology, 16*, 625–635.

Baltes, P. B., & Graf, P. (1996). Psychological aspects of aging: Facts and frontiers. In D. Magnusson (Ed.), *The life-span development of individuals: Behavioral, neuro-biological and psychosocial perspectives* (pp. 427–460). Cambridge: Cambridge University Press.

Baltes, P. B., & Lindenberger, U. (1995). Sensorik und Intelligenz: Intersystemische Wechsel-wirkungen und Veränderungen im hohen Alter. *Akademie-Journal, 1*, 20–28.

Baltes, P. B., & Lindenberger, U. (1997). Emergence of a powerful connection between sensory and cognitive functions across the adult life span: A new window to the study of cognitive aging? *Psychology and Aging, 12*, 12–21.

Baltes, P. B., & Smith, J. (1997). A systemic-wholistic view of psychological functioning in very old age: Introduction to a collection of articles from the Berlin Aging Study. *Psychology and Aging, 12*, 395–409.

Bandura, A. (1989). Human agency in social cognitive theory. *American Psychologist, 44*, 1175–1184.

Barnes, A. (1993). *Spontaneous self-comparisons in old and very old age.* Unpublished master's thesis, Free University of Berlin.

Bengtson, V. L., Reedy, M. N., & Gordon, C. (1985). Aging and self-conceptions: Personality processes and social contexts. In J. E. Birren & K. W. Schaie (Eds.), *Handbook of the psychology of aging* (2nd ed., pp. 544–593). New York: Van Nostrand Reinhold.

Bengtson, V. L., & Schütze, Y. (1992). Altern und Generationenbeziehungen: Aussichten für das kommende Jahrhundert. In P. B. Baltes & J. Mittelstraß (Eds.), *Zukunft des Alterns und gesellschaftliche Entwicklung* (pp. 492–517). Berlin: de Gruyter.

Birren, J. E., & Birren, B. A. (1990). The concepts, models, and history of the psychology of aging. In J. E. Birren & K. W. Schaie (Eds.), *Handbook of the psychology of aging* (3rd ed., pp. 3–20). San Diego, CA: Academic Press.

Birren, J. E., & Schroots, J. J. F. (1996). History, concepts, and theory in the psychology of aging. In J. E. Birren & K. W. Schaie (Eds.), *Handbook of the psychology of aging* (4th ed., pp. 3–23). San Diego, CA: Academic Press.

Brandtstädter, J., & Greve, W. (1994). The aging self: Stabilizing and protective processes. *Developmental Review, 14*, 52–80.

Breytspaak, L. M. (1984). *The development of the self in later life.* Boston: Little, Brown.

Busse, E. W., & Maddox, G. (1985). *The Duke Longitudinal Studies of Normal Aging: 1955–1980.* New York: Springer.

Carstensen, L. L. (1993). Motivation for social contact across the life-span: A theory of socioemotional selectivity. In J. Jacobs (Ed.), *Nebraska Symposium on Motivation* (Vol. 40, pp. 209–254). Lincoln: University of Nebraska Press.

Cattell, R. B. (1971). *Abilities: Their structure, growth, and action.* Boston: Houghton Mifflin.

Costa, P. T., Jr., & McCrae, R. R. (1980). Still stable after all these years: Personality as a key to some issues in adulthood and old age. In P. B. Baltes & O. G. Brim Jr. (Eds.), *Life-span development and behavior* (Vol. 3, pp. 65–102). New York: Academic Press.

Costa, P. T., Jr., & McCrae, R. R. (1985). *NEO: Five-factor personality inventory.* Tallahassee, FL: Psychological Assessment Resources.

Educational Testing Service (ETS). (1977). *Reading: Basic skills assessment program.* Menlo Park, CA: Addison-Wesley.

Ekstrom, R. B., French, J. W., Harman, M. M., & Derman, D. (1976). *Manual for the kit of factor-referenced cognitive tests.* Princeton, NJ: Educational Testing Service.

Engel, R. R., & Satzger, W. (1990). *Kompendium alterssensitiver Leistungstests.* Munich: Psychiatrische Klinik der Universität München.

Erikson, E. H., Erikson, J. M., & Kivnick, H. Q. (1986). *Vital involvement in old age: The experience of old age in our time.* London: Norton.

Field, D., & Minkler, M. (1988). Continuity and change in social support between young-old and old-old or very-old age. *Journal of Gerontology: Psychological Sciences, 43,* P100–P106.

Filipp, S.-H., & Ferring, D. (1989). Zur Alters- und Bereichsspezifität subjektiven Alterserlebens. *Zeitschrift für Entwicklungspsychologie und Pädagogische Psychologie, 21,* 279–293.

Filipp, S.-H., & Klauer, T. (1986). Conceptions of self over the life-span: Reflections on the dialectics of change. In M. M. Baltes & P. B. Baltes (Eds.), *The psychology of control and aging* (pp. 167–205). Hillsdale, NJ: Erlbaum.

Fleeson, W., & Heckhausen, J. (1997). More or less "Me" in past, present, and future: Perceived lifetime personality during adulthood. *Psychology and Aging, 12,* 125–136.

Freund, A. M., & Smith, J. (1997). Die Selbstdefinition im hohen Alter. *Zeitschrift für Sozialpsychologie, 28,* 44–59.

Freund, A. M., & Smith, J. (in press). Content and function of the self-definition in old and very old age. *Journal of Gerontology: Psychological Sciences.*

George, L. K., & Okun, M. A. (1985). Self-concept content. In E. Palmore, E. W. Busse, G. L. Maddox, J. B. Nowlin, & I. C. Siegler (Eds.), *Normal aging III: Reports from the Duke Longitudinal Studies, 1975–1984* (pp. 267–282). Durham, NC: Duke University Press.

Gordon, C. (1968). Self-conceptions: Configurations of content. In C. Gordon & K. J. Gergen (Eds.), *The self in social interaction: Classic and contemporary perspectives* (pp. 115–136). New York: Wiley.

Häfner, H. (1986). *Psychische Gesundheit im Alter.* Stuttgart: Gustav Fischer.

Harris, L. (1975). *The myth and reality of aging in America.* Washington, DC: National Council on Aging.

Hauschild, C. (1996). *Ein Vergleich zukunfts- und gegenwartsbezogener Selbstrepräsentationen im Alter: Zentrale Themen und Implikationen von Distanz.* Unpublished master's thesis, Free University of Berlin.

Heckhausen, J., Dixon, R. A., & Baltes, P. B. (1989). Gains and losses in development throughout adulthood as perceived by different age groups. *Developmental Psychology, 255,* 109–121.

Heckhausen, J., & Schulz, R. (1995). A life-span theory of control. *Psychological Review, 102,* 284–304.

Helgeson, V. S. (1992). Moderators of the relation between perceived control and adjustment to chronic illness. *Journal of Personality and Social Psychology, 63,* 656–666.

Hertzog, C., & Schaie, K. W. (1986). Stability and change in adult intelligence: 1. Analysis of longitudinal covariance structures. *Psychology and Aging, 1*, 159–171.

Hertzog, C., & Schaie, K. W. (1988). Stability and change in adult intelligence: 2. Simultaneous analysis of longitudinal means and covariance structures. *Psychology and Aging, 3*, 122–130.

Horn, J. L., & Hofer, S. M. (1992). Major abilities and development in the adult period. In R. J. Sternberg & C. A. Berg (Eds.), *Intellectual development* (pp. 44–99). Cambridge: Cambridge University Press.

Johnson, C. L., & Barer, B. M. (1997). *Life beyond 85 years: The aura of survivorship*. New York: Springer.

Johnson, C. L., & Troll, L. E. (1994). Constraints and facilitators to friendships in late late life. *The Gerontologist, 34*, 79–87.

Jones, C. J., & Meredith, W. (1996). Patterns of personality change across the life span. *Psychology and Aging, 11*, 57–65.

Kahn, R. L., & Antonucci, T. C. (1980). Convoys over the life course: Attachment, roles, and social support. In P. B. Baltes & O. G. Brim Jr. (Eds.), *Life-span development and behavior* (Vol. 3, pp. 253–283). New York: Academic Press.

Kihlstrom, J. F., & Klein, S. B. (1994). The self as a knowledge system. In R. S. Wyer Jr. & T. K. Skull (Eds.), *Handbook of social cognition* (2nd ed., pp. 153–208). Hillsdale, NJ: Erlbaum.

Kliegl, R., Smith, J., & Baltes, P. B. (1989). Testing-the-limits and the study of adult age differences in cognitive plasticity of a mnemonic skill. *Developmental Psychology, 25*, 247–256.

Knipscheer, K. (1986). Anomie in der Mehrgenerationenfamilie: Kinder und die Versorgung ihrer alten Eltern. *Zeitschrift für Gerontologie, 19*, 40–46.

Kruse, A. (1994). *Kompetenz im Alter: Psychologische Perspektiven der modernen Gerontologie*. Kusterdingen: Spektrum Akademischer Verlag.

Kunzmann, U. (1998). *Being and feeling in control: Two sources of older people's emotional well-being*. Unpublished doctoral thesis, Free University of Berlin.

Lachman, M. E. (1986). Personal control in later life: Stability, change, and cognitive correlates. In M. M. Baltes & P. B. Baltes (Eds.), *The psychology of control and aging* (pp. 207–236). Hillsdale, NJ: Erlbaum.

Lang, F. R. (1994). *Die Gestaltung informeller Hilfebeziehungen im hohen Alter: Die Rolle von Elternschaft und Kinderlosigkeit. Eine empirische Studie zur sozialen Unterstützung und deren Effekt auf die erlebte soziale Einbindung* (Studien und Berichte des Max-Planck-Instituts für Bildungsforschung 59). Berlin: Edition Sigma.

Lang, F. R., & Carstensen, L. L. (1994). Close emotional relationships in late life: Further support for proactive aging in the social domain. *Psychology and Aging, 9*, 315–324.

Lawton, M. P. (1975). The Philadelphia Geriatric Center Morale Scale: A revision. *Journal of Gerontology, 30*, 85–89.

Lehr, U., & Minnemann, E. (1987). Veränderungen von Quantität und Qualität sozialer Kontakte vom siebten bis neunten Lebensjahrzehnt. In U. Lehr & H. Thomae (Eds.), *Formen seelischen Alterns: Ergebnisse der Bonner Gerontologischen Längsschnittstudie (BOLSA)* (pp. 80–91). Stuttgart: Enke.

Lehr, U., & Thomae, H. (Eds.). (1987). *Formen seelischen Alterns: Ergebnisse der Bonner Gerontologischen Längsschnittstudie (BOLSA)*. Stuttgart: Enke.

Lehrl, S. (1977). *Mehrfachwahl-Wortschatz-Test (MWT-B)*. Erlangen: Straube.

Liang, J., & Bollen, K. A. (1983). The structure of the Philadelphia Geriatric Center Morale
    Scale: A reinterpretation. *Journal of Gerontology, 38*, 181–189.

Lindenberger, U., & Baltes, P. B. (1994). Sensory functioning and intelligence in old age: A
    strong connection. *Psychology and Aging, 9*, 339–355.

Lindenberger, U., & Baltes, P. B. (1997). Intellectual functioning in old and very old age:
    Cross-sectional results from the Berlin Aging Study. *Psychology and Aging, 12*,
    410–432.

Lindenberger, U., Mayr, U., & Kliegl, R. (1993). Speed and intelligence in old age. *Psychology
    and Aging, 8*, 207–220.

Magnusson, D. (Ed.). (1996). *The life-span development of individuals: Behavioral,
    neurobiological and psychosocial perspectives*. Cambridge: Cambridge University
    Press.

Magnusson, D., Bergman, L. R., Rudinger, G., & Törestad, B. (Eds.). (1991). *Problems and
    methods in longitudinal research: Stability and change*. Cambridge: Cambridge
    University Press.

Markus, H. R., & Herzog, A. R. (1991). The role of the self-concept in aging. In K. W. Schaie &
    M. P. Lawton (Eds.), *Annual review of gerontology and geriatrics* (Vol. 11, pp.
    110–143). New York: Springer.

Markus, H. R., & Nurius, P. (1986). Possible selves. *American Psychologist, 41*, 954–969.

Marsiske, M., Klumb, P., & Baltes, M. M. (1997). Everyday activity patterns and sensory
    functioning in old age. *Psychology and Aging, 12*, 444–457.

McCrae, R. R., & Costa, P. T., Jr. (1988). Age, personality, and the spontaneous self-concept.
    Journal of Gerontology: Psychological Sciences, 43, P177–P185.

McCrae, R. R., & Costa, P. T., Jr. (1990). *Personality in adulthood*. New York: Guilford.

Montepare, J. M., & Lachman, M. E. (1989). "You're only as old as you feel": Self-perceptions of
    age, fears of aging, and life satisfaction from adolescence to old age. *Psychology and
    Aging, 4*, 73–78.

Nesselroade, J. R. (1989). Adult personality development: Issues in assessing constancy and
    change. In A. I. Rabin, R. A. Zucker, R. A. Emmons, & S. Frank (Eds.), *Studying
    persons and lives* (pp. 41–85). New York: Springer.

Neugarten, B. L., Havighurst, R. J., & Tobin, S. S. (1961). The measurement of life satisfaction.
    Journal of Gerontology, 16, 134–143.

Pearlin, L. I., & Mullan, J. T. (1992). Loss and stress in aging. In M. L. Wykle, E. Kahana, &
    J. Kowal (Eds.), *Stress and health among the elderly* (pp. 117–132). New York:
    Springer.

Peplau, L., & Perlman, D. (Eds.). (1982). *Loneliness: A sourcebook of current theory, research,
    and therapy*. New York: Wiley.

Reinert, G. (1970). Comparative factor analytic studies of intelligence throughout the life span. In
    L. R. Goulet & P. B. Baltes (Eds.), *Life-span developmental psychology: Research and
    theory* (pp. 467–484). New York: Academic Press.

Roberts, M. L., & Nesselroade, J. R. (1986). Intraindividual variability in perceived locus of
    control in adults: P-technique factor analyses of short-term change. *Journal of Research
    in Personality, 20*, 529–545.

Rodin, J., Timko, C., & Harris, S. (1985). The construct of control: Biological and psychosocial
    correlates. In C. Eisdorfer, M. P. Lawton, & G. L. Maddox (Eds.), *Annual review of
    gerontology and geriatrics* (Vol. 5, pp. 3–55). New York: Springer.

Russell, D., Cutrona, C. E., Rose, J., & Yurko, K. (1984). Social and emotional loneliness: An examination of Weiss's typology of loneliness. *Journal of Personality and Social Psychology, 46*, 1313–1321.

Rutter, M. (1987). Psychosocial resilience and protective mechanisms. *American Journal of Orthopsychiatry, 57*, 316–331.

Salthouse, T. A. (1991). *Theoretical perspectives on cognitive aging.* Hillsdale, NJ: Erlbaum.

Schaie, K. W. (1965). A general model for the study of developmental problems. *Psychological Bulletin, 64*, 92–107.

Schaie, K. W. (1996). *Intellectual development in adulthood: The Seattle Longitudinal Study.* Cambridge: Cambridge University Press.

Schaie, K. W., & Willis, S. L. (1993). Age difference patterns of psychometric intelligence in adulthood: Generalizability within and across ability domains. *Psychology and Aging, 8*, 44–55.

Schütze, Y., & Lang, F. R. (1993). Freundschaft, Alter und Geschlecht. *Zeitschrift für Soziologie, 3*, 209–220.

Skinner, E. A. (1995). *Perceived control, motivation, and coping.* Thousand Oaks, CA: Sage.

Smith, J., & Baltes, M. M. (in press). The role of gender in very old age: Profiles of functioning and everyday life patterns. *Psychology and Aging.*

Smith, J., & Baltes, P. B. (1993). Differential psychological ageing: Profiles of the old and very old. *Ageing and Society, 13*, 551–587.

Smith, J., & Baltes, P. B. (1997). Profiles of psychological functioning in the old and oldest old. *Psychology and Aging, 12*, 458–472.

Smith, J., & Barnes, A. (1994). Older adults' concerns about future personal wellbeing. In N. H. Frijda (Ed.), *Multidisciplinary research on emotions* (pp. 355–359). Storrs, CT: ISRE Publications.

Smith, J., Marsiske, M., & Maier, H. (1996). *Differences in control beliefs from age 70 to 105.* Unpublished manuscript, Max Planck Institute for Human Development, Berlin.

Snyder, C. R., & Forsyth, D. R. (Eds.). (1991). *Handbook of social and clinical psychology: The health perspective.* New York: Pergamon Press.

Staudinger, U. M., & Fleeson, W. (1996). Self and personality in very old age: A sample case of resilience? *Development and Psychopathology, 8*, 867–885.

Staudinger, U. M., Marsiske, M., & Baltes, P. B. (1995). Resilience and reserve capacity in later adulthood: Potentials and limits of development across the life span. In D. Cicchetti & D. J. Cohen (Eds.), *Developmental psychopathology: Vol. 2. Risk, disorder, and adaptation* (pp. 801–847). New York: Wiley.

Suls, J., & Wills, T. A. (Eds.). (1991). *Social comparison: Contemporary theory and research.* Hillsdale, NJ: Erlbaum.

Thomae, H. (1979). The concept of development and life-span developmental psychology. In P. B. Baltes & O. G. Brim Jr. (Eds.), *Life-span development and behavior* (Vol. 2, pp. 282–312). New York: Academic Press.

Thomae, H. (1994). Trust, social support, and relying on others: A contribution to the interface between behavioral and social gerontology. *Zeitschrift für Gerontologie, 27*, 103–109.

Thorndike, R. L., Hagen, E., & Lorge, I. (1954–68). *Cognitive Abilities Test.* Boston, MA: Houghton Mifflin.

Thurstone, T. G. (1962). *Primary mental abilities: Grades 9–12. 1962 revision.* Chicago: Science Research Associates.

Troll, L. E. (1986). *Family issues in current gerontology*. New York: Springer.

Watson, D., Clark, L. A., & Tellegen, A. (1988). Development and validation of brief measures of positive and negative affect: The PANAS scales. *Journal of Personality and Social Psychology, 54*, 1063–1070.

Wechsler, D. (1955). *Der Hamburg Wechsler Intelligenztest für Erwachsene (HAWIE)*. Bern: Huber.

Wechsler, D. (1982). *Handanweisung zum Hamburg-Wechsler-Intelligenztest für Erwachsene (HAWIE)*. Bern: Huber.

Weiss, R. S. (1982). Issues in the study of loneliness. In L. Peplau & D. Perlman (Eds.), *Loneliness: A sourcebook of current theory, research, and therapy* (pp. 71–80). New York: Wiley.

Wietzker, A. (1996). *Einsamkeit im Alter: Objektive Lebensbedingungen, Netzwerkgröße und Beziehungsqualität*. Unpublished master's thesis, Free University of Berlin.

CHAPTER 8

Socioeconomic Conditions and Social Inequalities in Old Age

Karl Ulrich Mayer, Ineke Maas, and Michael Wagner

In this chapter we examine the social and economic life circumstances of old and very old people in West Berlin,[1] and the ways different socioeconomic resources influence social participation and aspects of physical and mental health. Information on education, occupational position, household income, housing conditions, forms of household, social activities, and media consumption is analyzed. Three hypotheses about socioeconomic differentiation and its consequences are examined: (a) the hypothesis of age-relatedness, where socioeconomic factors lose importance in comparison to age-related conditions such as health; (b) the hypothesis of socioeconomic continuity, which suggests that socioeconomic differences continue to influence life-styles and activities in old age; and (c) the cumulation hypothesis, where the impact of socioeconomic differentiation increases in old age.

In this study, we mainly find age-associated differences in social activities and social participation, both of which are highly related to health status. In these cases, socioeconomic resources can only partially compensate for health impairments. Until the move into a senior citizens' home, stability in income and housing conditions is found, reflecting the social position attained before retirement. Thus, in terms of the economic situation, age does not discriminate between individuals. Only with regard to utilization of care can we confirm the cumulation hypothesis, where socioeconomic inequality in old age becomes more pronounced: Members (mostly male) of higher social classes are rarely institutionalized and are more likely to be cared for at home. Surprisingly, indicators of somatic and mental health in old age – with the exception of dementia – show only slight differences between social classes.

1   Introduction: From Inequality between Age Groups to Inequality within the Group of Old People

Historically, in all theories of the social structure of society, age has been viewed not only as a fundamental category of horizontal social differentiation, but also as a category of social rank order (Blau, 1974, 1994; Mayer & Wagner, 1993). In the latter view (Riley, Johnson, & Foner, 1972), old and very old people were sometimes ascribed a relatively high social status (Horkheimer, 1975, p. 174). However, more often they lost social respect and prestige (Ehmer, 1990). Right up to the early 20th century,

---

[1] Because this study was planned before the collapse of the Berlin Wall, all BASE participants lived in former West Berlin (cf. P. B. Baltes et al., Chapter 1). As there are likely to be particular socioeconomic differences between persons living in (former) East and West Berlin, we refer to West Berlin and West Berliners throughout this chapter, although this political distinction no longer exists.

people carried on working until it was no longer possible. Those who could not work anymore due to physical and mental deficits were regarded as being old (Borscheid, 1992). Therefore, old age was often associated with economic hardship and a decline in social status for those without property. The parallel link between old age and authority, wisdom, and rank was probably due to the fact that those enjoying high social prestige and wealth were much more likely to survive into very old age (Imhof, 1981, p. 124).

This situation has changed radically since the variation of life expectancies according to socioeconomic status decreased (Kertzer & Laslett, 1995) and a high degree of continuity in life chances was brought about by status-maintaining provisions for old age: "From this conception of retirement as protection from the hazards of old age in an industrial society has grown a positive conception of retirement as a period of potential enjoyment and creative experience which accrues as a social reward for a lifetime of labor" (Donahue, Orbach, & Pollak, 1960, p. 361). With sufficient pensions, old age potentially becomes a phase of autonomy with full social participation (Guillemard & Rein, 1993, p. 471). Furthermore, the societal definition of old age as a phase of poor health is weakening. Old age begins earlier when interpreted as the phase of retirement and "is defined by the majority as the period in which the affected lose their right to work and are consigned to the world of the unproductive" (Guillemard, 1992, p. 631). For most, reaching retirement age is not seen as being linked to impairment of mental and physical functioning. Serious health problems often do not occur until many years after leaving the work force. The large majority of those beginning to need care, becoming physically impaired and dependent on others' help for many years, are well over 80. However, if the phase of old age becomes longer in years, and is characterized by bodily and mental impairment to a lesser degree, one can no longer assume that the socioeconomic situation of old people is uniform.

Apart from the question of inequality *between* age groups – between children, younger adults, and older adults (Preston, 1984) – the question of the degree of social inequality *within* the group of old people, including consequences for the aging process, gains importance. In the following, we provide a summary report on the socioeconomic conditions of persons aged 70 and above living in the area of former West Berlin (see also G. Wagner, Motel, Spieß, & Wagner, 1996). We especially focus on the existence of social and economic disadvantages. On this basis, we can assess whether and to what extent old people need to be regarded as a target group for social policy intervention.

These analyses are complemented in other chapters, particularly in the chapters on cohort differences (Maas et al., Chapter 3 in this volume), on social and familial relationships (M. Wagner et al., Chapter 10), on utilization of care (Linden et al., Chapter 16), and on well-being (Smith et al., Chapter 17).

2   Social Inequalities and Socioeconomic Conditions in Old Age: Three Hypotheses

It is well established that people's occupational qualification and occupational status during their working lives determine their positions in a vertical structure of social inequality. In this way, diverse social conditions may give rise to relatively homogeneous social classes that are augmented by social inclusion and exclusion processes. Social inequalities deriving from the labor market are weakened or strengthened by exchange processes within families and households and by the redistribution of resources via the welfare state. We assume that these early life distinctions remain important in old age, despite, or possibly because of, the fact that differences in income opportunities are standardized and stabilized by the mechanisms regulating provision for old age. Social class membership indicates the economic, social, and cultural resources accessible to individuals and/or households, and – on this basis – their individual welfare.

In the following, we use the construct of social class to measure socioeconomic conditions, but we also add other indicators of social inequality. Looking at potential effects, we concentrate on four aspects: the financial and material situation, social participation, ways of life and social care, and physical and mental health. By *financial and material situation* we mean material resources in a wider sense, particularly objective elements of the standard of living. We conceptualize *social participation* as the use of opportunities in the cultural and political arena. *Ways of life and social care* mainly refer to social relationships that can be used as resources in terms of help and care. We assessed this dimension in three steps. First, we examined whether the older adult lived in a private household or not. Second, we determined the number of people sharing the household and their respective roles. Third, we assessed whether the older adult utilized care from sources outside the immediate household. For *physical and mental health*, we selected indicators judged by psychiatrists and geriatricians as being good and highly aggregated markers of essential health dimensions.

Furthermore, it is important for the understanding of social differentiation to discriminate between those aspects of life circumstances which enable activities and those that constitute activities themselves. Social participation, which always entails social activities, belongs to the latter group. The economic situation and ways of life, conversely, concern economic and social resources available to older people, which, when utilized, can enable certain activities. This distinction between these concepts is important because one might assume, for example, that health impairments have a direct effect on activities, whereas, in reality, they only have indirect effects on activities through changes in activity resources.

As mentioned earlier, we base our analyses on three hypotheses: the hypothesis of age-relatedness, the hypothesis of socioeconomic continuity, and the cumulation hypothesis. These hypotheses specify three possible relations between social class (or other features of social inequality) and conditions, ways of life, and social activities. On the one hand, they can be combined with general concepts of contextual influences on the aging process (e.g., Dannefer, 1992). On the other, there is a strong link to discussions of the social structuring of aging that have particularly emphasized the cumulation hypothesis (Bengtson, Kasschau, & Ragan, 1977).

The first hypothesis of *age-relatedness* claims that age itself is the main cause for socioeconomic conditions in old age. For instance, the common ideas that "old people are poor" or even "old people are poor, because they are old" match this hypothesis. The second hypothesis of *socioeconomic continuity* assumes that the socioeconomic conditions of older adults are primarily determined by the social class they belonged to earlier in life. This hypothesis would apply if we found very few differences among age groups but large differences by socioeconomic situation. The third, *cumulation* hypothesis states that age and socioeconomic situation interact with each other so that persons from the lower classes are even worse off and persons from higher classes are comparatively better off in old age – and thus the impacts of socioeconomic differences are amplified.

The hypothesis of *age-relatedness* is guided by the assumption that the universal process of aging is one of both physical and mental decline, and that this decline primarily and negatively influences the social situation of older people (Mayer & Wagner, 1993, pp. 525–531). This implies that the changes in the socioeconomic situation in old age are dependent on nonsocial factors. Age-related deterioration of the social situation could, however, also set in if pensions decreased or if persons had to cope with income deficits after using up their savings (Kohli, 1990, p. 395). Furthermore, it is possible that more income is needed in old age because of additional costs for health treatment and care, which curb expenditure on other domains such as social and cultural activities.

The hypothesis of *socioeconomic continuity* claims that the social situation in old age depends on social class membership or other features of inequality. Differences in socioeconomic conditions of old people then would not be a consequence of chronological age and associated impairments but, instead, would vary by socioeconomic groups and so be linked to earlier stages of the life course. These links can become manifest in two different ways. First, social class membership affects the material situation, social participation, and relationships early in life, with these characteristics remaining highly stable over the life course. Second, there are direct effects of social class on these characteristics in old age. Both imply that social class membership makes an important contribution toward explaining the social situation in old age. Accordingly, social aging would be a differential process which affects persons depending on their social class.

A hypothesis that has gained importance during the past years runs against the idea of a continuous influence of social class membership on opportunities and individual welfare in old age. It states that traditional class situations have dissolved and been replaced by manifold social milieus and pluralized ways of life and life-styles. If this were the case, it should apply in a special way to older people – particularly in large cities – because they are no longer bound to the obligations of working life. However, continuing and stable effects of social class membership are to be expected even on the basis of social policies alone. Among other things, social policy in Germany aims to enable older adults to maintain an economic position comparable with the one prior to retirement (Zacher, 1992). The effectiveness of this policy can be proved by comparing the stability of average incomes of old and middle-aged adults (Hauser & Wagner, 1992; Motel & Wagner, 1993), and by the decreasing proportions of old people receiving social assistance (Leisering, 1994).

The age-grading in the domain of social and political participation is more difficult to judge than that of economic resources. Social and political participation of old people is hardly institutionalized in society (Riley & Riley, 1992). Culturally, old age is afflicted by negative stereotypes. Although some observers see changes, and claim that older adults are becoming more active (the "new" old) and act increasingly as a political interest group (Klose, 1993), participation and activity norms for elderly people are still moderate. Therefore, social participation in old age presupposes a high degree of individual initiative. In this context, values, life goals, and self-images of older persons play an important role along with economic resources. Cultural resources like these are possibly connected to class or education, and would then also contribute to a continuity of activity patterns specific to social class.

According to the *cumulation* hypothesis, there is an expected interaction between age and socioeconomic differentiation in that the strength of class effects increases in old age. Here, the assumption is that the value of economic and social resources increases when bad health sets in. For example, someone who can no longer walk very far or drive a car only remains mobile if he or she can raise the money for a taxi. Although the need for care is relatively independent of socioeconomic factors such as education, income, or previous job prestige (Mayer & Wagner, 1993), it is possible that the kind of help utilized is specific to social class. Though the social system in Germany guarantees help for all who need care, privately paid nursing and household help may be an alternative. Certain inequities, therefore, may become accentuated when health problems accumulate (cf. Linden et al., Chapter 16).

How previous and continuing class situations influence opportunities and behavior of the old is by no means undisputed. Some authors suppose that class differences decrease during aging. Dowd and Bengtson (1978, p. 428) have called this perspective "advancing age as a leveler." Health deficits and costs for nursing care could reduce the effects of former income differences on current life circumstances. Illness and disability could so restrict mobility and activities that they could no longer be compensated for by individual resources. The leveling of differences would become probable if health, nursing care, and socioeconomic situation were relatively independent of each other.

Another mechanism that could lead to a reduction in class differences and its effects during aging is socially selective mortality (Markides & Machalek, 1984). If members of lower social classes are exposed to stronger risks of mortality, the survivors represent a positive selection from these groups (e.g., in terms of health-enhancing factors). Effects of social class on those social activities that require physical and mental health could thus decrease or even be reversed.

3   Methods

3.1   *Measurement of Social Inequalities*

We use the following indicators for social inequalities: education, social prestige, house ownership, income, and social class. *Education* is measured as the total duration of general education and occupational training in years. *Social prestige* rates the relative social status of the participant's last job using Wegener's (1985) scale. The variable *house ownership* measures whether the participant owns a house or apartment (independently of whether he or she lives in it). Because household *income* has to be made comparable for households of differing size, it is measured as the net household income per head, weighted by the number of people sharing the household (Atkinson, 1983; Motel & Wagner, 1993). To compute this equivalent income, we used the weight of 0.8 for the second and all further household members.

Social class refers to the household and is based on information about the last occupational position held by the participant or his or her spouse before retirement. In BASE, the occupational position was determined for every job held by the participant during his or her working life. A standard measure was used, a slightly different version of which was developed for the German Microcensus Supplementary Survey 1971, and has since become generally established in sociological research (Mayer, 1979). Occupational position differentiates the work force according to criteria of labor law: the self-employed, blue-collar and white-collar workers, civil servants, and helpers in family businesses. Within the group of the self-employed, farmers and academic professionals (physicians, lawyers) are separated from the others. Five subgroups are distinguished within the group of blue-collar workers: The lowest includes unskilled workers, whereas master craftsmen and foremen belong to the highest. Civil servants are ordered by their career track, and white-collar workers by the difficulty of their job and their responsibilities.

The construction of social classes was carried out in two steps. First, occupational positions were grouped in strata on an individual level. Following Mayer (1977) and Handl (1977), five social classes were distinguished: lower, lower middle, middle middle, upper middle, and higher middle class. The distinction of five social classes is mainly pragmatic and due to the size of the sample.

The lower class consists of unskilled and semiskilled workers. The next class includes skilled workers as well as white-collar workers and civil servants with routine tasks. The middle middle class mainly comprises master craftsmen, foremen, civil servants in a middle career track, as well as white-collar workers with more difficult jobs (e.g., book-keepers or technical draftsmen). Civil servants in an upper career track, the dependently employed with limited management responsibilities, as well as the self-employed with up to nine employees are allocated to the upper middle class. The higher middle class consists of the self-employed with larger businesses, academic professionals, civil servants in the higher career track, and the dependently employed with general management responsibilities.

The second step takes into account one assumption of social inequality research, namely that membership of a social class is a feature of households. Thus, children and partners not active in the work force derive their social class from the main wage earner's occupational position (Sørensen, 1994). Therefore, we compared the respective individual social class memberships based on the occupational positions of the interviewees and their partners, and defined the higher of the two as the *class of the household*. For the widowed or divorced, the household situation before the end of the (last) marriage was analyzed. For the unmarried, individual and household classes are identical. On the basis of this construction nearly 50% of women derive their social class from their husbands' occupational positions.

Although the main focus is on social inequality, health and psychological resources are sometimes included in the models as predictors. For their measurement, we refer to Chapter 5 by Steinhagen-Thiessen and Borchelt, and Chapter 7 by Smith and Baltes.

3.2 Measurements of Socioeconomic Conditions

The dependent sociological variables refer to aspects of the socioeconomic situations of older adults. We divide them into the following domains: material situation, social participation, and ways of life and social care. Several indicators are available for each of these domains, but there is no circumscribed set for the definition of socioeconomic conditions to be drawn from previous research. However, the assignment of indicators to domains presented in Table 8.1 is frequently used in quality-of-life research.

As indicators of the *material situation* we use equivalent income as defined above,[2] the number of asset types, monetary assets, living space, house ownership, and satisfaction with living conditions.

---

[2] Thus equivalent income is used as an indicator of social inequality (see Section 3.1) *and* as an indicator of the material situation.

Table 8.1. *Indicators and statistical measures of socioeconomic conditions (unweighted)*

Indicator	Percentage	M	SD	Range
Material situation				
Equivalent income (in DM)[a]	—	2,176	1,099	717–10,000
Number of asset types	—	1.2	0.8	0–5
No monetary assets	18.5	—	—	Yes/no
Social assistance[a,b]	3.6	—	—	Yes/no
Living space	—	1.8	0.9	0.2–7.0
House ownership	13.4	—	—	Yes/no
Satisfaction with living conditions	—	1.0	1.2	0–6
Social participation				
Activity level	—	2.87	2.39	0–11
Media consumption	—	2.14	0.78	0–3
Voting behavior	87.8	—	—	Yes/no
Interest in politics	—	2.93	1.27	1–5
Church visits	—	0.90	1.24	0–5
Ways of life and social care				
Type of household				
Private household, alone	50.3	—	—	Yes/no
Private household, with a partner	28.5	—	—	Yes/no
Private household, with others	7.0	—	—	Yes/no
Institution[c]	14.2	—	—	Yes/no
Sources of help		—	—	
None	54.3	—	—	Yes/no
Informal	9.3	—	—	Yes/no
Professional	17.4	—	—	Yes/no
Informal and professional	4.7	—	—	Yes/no
Institution[c]	14.2	—	—	Yes/no

[a]Excluding the institutionalized.
[b]Data from BASE Intensive Protocol.
[c]Residents of senior citizens' homes, nursing homes, and hospitals for the chronically ill.

    Designating individuals in the lowest quintile of the *equivalent income* distribution as economically disadvantaged yields a threshold income of 1,400 DM. Of course, this value does not represent the relative poverty threshold that exists in the general population. Following international conventions and defining 50% of a population's mean income as the poverty threshold would evince a threshold of 854 DM equivalent income per month (Motel & Wagner, 1993). Instead, the threshold value of 1,400 DM represents an income below which a relative financial disadvantage exists within the West Berlin population. Receiving social assistance is another indicator of economic deprivation, as it shows that those interviewees do not have sufficient financial resources of their own.

Other forms of property are also an important part of financial resources in old age. *Monetary assets* encompass savings (including "piggy bank" and building society savings), life insurances, and stocks. On the one hand, we asked whether participants owned monetary assets at all and, on the other hand, we counted the different *types of assets*. The *standard of living* was evaluated by showing the participants a list of possible faults of their apartments (too expensive, too loud, too cold, etc.). The sum of affirmed defects indicates the degree of dissatisfaction with living conditions. *Living space* counts the number of rooms per household inhabitant.

Social participation includes social activities, media consumption, interest in politics, voting behavior (participation in the last elections), and church visits. To gain a picture of social activities, respondents were shown cards, each illustrating a category of activities (see Table 8.10). Examining the cards in sequence, participants were not only asked whether they had engaged in activities "of this kind" during the previous year, but also to look back at their life and rate their activities before the age of 25 and at 60. The number of different activities in the previous year was defined as their *activity level* (see M. M. Baltes et al., Chapter 14). Participants were also asked about the number of *church visits* during the previous year. The six-point scale ranged from "never" to "several times a week." *Media consumption* was regarded in terms of television, radio, and newspapers. First, participants were asked to answer, on a six- and seven-point scale respectively, how often they watched, or listened to, news programs on television or the radio, and how often they read a newspaper. The answers ranged from "never" to "several times a day." The answers were combined and transformed to a new scale showing how many days a week the participants watched, listened to, or read the news at least once. Media consumption is then measured as an index that refers to the daily use of the three media. A score of "0" indicates no consumption of media at all, and "3" means that the interviewee used all three types at least once daily. The participants' *interest in politics* was measured with a five-point scale ranging from "not at all interested" to "very interested." *Voting behavior* was assessed by asking about participation in the last Berlin election.

Regarding *ways of life and social care*, we distinguish the type of household and the kind of social care received. The *type of household* is indicated by whether participants lived in a private household alone, with a partner, or with others (with or without a partner), or in an institutional setting (senior citizens' home, nursing home, or hospital for the chronically ill). *Social care* regards help received from persons living outside of the private household. This includes informal help from relatives, friends, or acquaintances, as well as professional help from social workers, privately paid household helpers, nurses, and so forth. Institutionalization represents another form of social care (cf. Linden et al., Chapter 16; see also Gilberg, 1997).

4   Results

4.1   *Distributions by Occupational Position, Social Class, and Regional Origin*

Figure 8.1 shows the last occupational positions held by elderly men and women in West Berlin. The distribution is characteristic for a city population of these

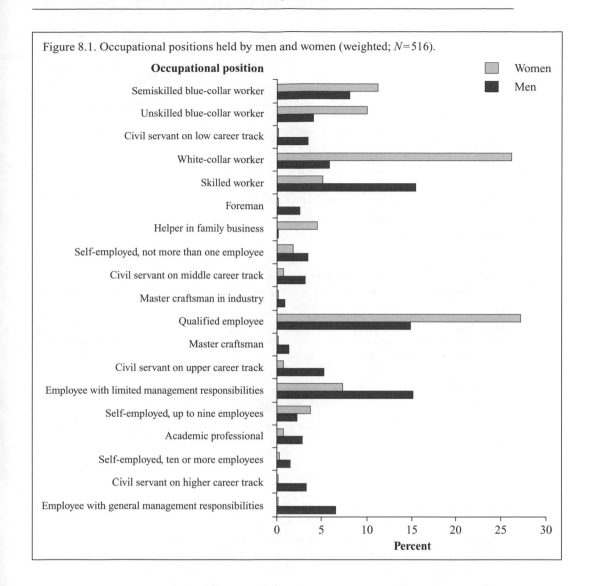

Figure 8.1. Occupational positions held by men and women (weighted; N=516).

birth cohorts. The largest groups are the routine white-collar workers' (20%) and qualified employees' (23%) positions, which were both dominated by women. Taking men and women together, 8% were unskilled, 10% semiskilled blue-collar workers, and 9%, mostly men, were foremen or master craftsmen. Another large group is formed by employees in higher positions (9%). Only a few of the old people in West Berlin held positions as employees in leading positions (2%) or as civil servants (5%). Seven percent can be assigned to the very heterogeneous group of the self-employed and academic professionals.

In Table 8.2, the average social prestige and educational level found for each social class is shown separately for men and women. Social prestige and educational level in-

Table 8.2. *Social classes for men and women by individual social prestige and education (weighted)*

Social class	Men		Women		
	Prestige[a]	Education[b]	Prestige[a]	Education[b]	*n*
Lower class	38.1	8.9	37.0	8.3	44
Lower middle class	46.6	9.9	42.1	9.8	93
Middle middle class	62.3	11.1	51.6	10.4	131
Upper middle class	76.3	12.7	59.1	10.9	170
Higher middle class	118.6	14.3	60.9	11.8	54

[a]Social prestige according to Wegener (1985).
[b]General and occupational education in years.

Table 8.3. *Social class membership of men and women by age (weighted, in %)*

Social class	Men[a]			Women[b]		
	Total	70–84	85+	Total	70–84	85+
Lower class	8.0	8.6	4.7	9.4	8.4	13.2
Lower middle class	22.4	19.7	36.9	18.1	19.6	12.3
Middle middle class	26.4	26.3	26.5	26.8	22.6	42.8
Upper middle class	28.5	29.7	·21.6	36.3	40.2	21.4
Higher middle class	14.8	15.6	10.3	9.4	9.2	10.2

[a]$\chi^2(4) = 3.43$, n.s.
[b]$\chi^2(4) = 19.0$, $p < .001$.

crease by social class for both men and women.[3] This indicates that our measurement of social class does indeed capture a structure of social inequality.

Table 8.3 shows the proportions of old men and women in West Berlin found in the five social classes by age group. As to be expected from the distribution across the occupational positions, the three classes in the middle are most frequent. Among men, 22% are in the lower middle class, which is dominated by unqualified white-collar and trained blue-collar workers, and 26% belong to the middle middle class, which mainly includes qualified employees and civil servants without management responsibilities. For women, we see a somewhat higher proportion in the upper middle class. However, across all categories there is no significant correlation between social class and gender.

---

[3] Separate analyses of data from the Microcensus Supplementary Survey 1971 on West Berlin support this conclusion. In terms of occupational positions at the age of 50, there were only small differences between birth cohorts 1899–1901, 1909–11, and 1920–22. For men, the only obvious differences were an increase in the category of qualified employees, and a decrease of unskilled workers. For women, the employment rate increased in general, as did the proportion of white-collar workers and qualified employees (cf. Maas et al., Chapter 3).

As social class depends on the occupational position held before retirement, it marks the socioeconomic situation at the beginning of the retirement phase. By definition, class mobility is impossible afterward (if one excludes social mobility via marriage, which is rare in old age). Nevertheless, class differences between the old (aged 70–84) and very old (aged 85+) are possible. They could be consequences of cohort differences (see Maas et al., Chapter 3) or of class-specific mortality. Furthermore, differences between age groups could indicate selective migration to Berlin.

As Table 8.3 shows, social class membership is not equally distributed in both age groups. Whereas the proportion of persons belonging to the top and two bottom classes remains constant, there is a shift from the middle to the upper middle class. Thus, members of the younger birth cohorts are less frequent in the middle and more frequent in the upper middle class than are the older cohorts. These age or cohort differences mainly reflect structural changes in the group of women ($\chi^2(4) = 19.0$, $p < .001$). Among men we find no significant correlation between social class and age ($\chi^2(4) = 3.43$, $p = .49$).[4]

The irregular pattern of age differences in class structure does not allow a simple conclusion about socially selective mortality. We analyze this in more depth below. For now, our main finding is that class differences do not contribute much toward explaining age differences in life circumstances since class membership hardly varies by age.

An important piece of background information lies in the fact that today's elderly West Berlin population has been partially influenced by socially selective migration. Remarkably, only a little more than one-third of today's West Berlin population originally comes from West Berlin. Including the East Berliners, half come from Berlin. A fifth immigrated from areas in today's Poland. Many of these were refugees from agricultural regions, which explains the fact that members of the lower class particularly often came from these areas (40%). In contrast, the settlers from former East and West Germany make up a larger proportion of the higher classes. Whereas men and women are equally distributed across the various regional backgrounds, there is a clear age difference in that the 70- to 84-year-olds more often originated from Berlin than those aged 85 and above (57% vs. 40%). The latter were more often born in what is now Poland (19% vs. 29%).

4.2   Material Situation

A measure of relative poverty that is based on 50% of the general population's mean income would result in a poverty rate of 3.3% among older adults in West Berlin. Table 8.4 gives an overview of further aspects of economic deprivation. The results presented here are based on data from the BASE Intensive Protocol ($N = 516$; see also G. Wagner et al., 1996).

Three percent of the community-dwelling older people in West Berlin receive social assistance. Nearly 15% reported that they had no monetary assets, not even a savings account. Six percent live in households with less rooms than inhabitants, or share a room with others in an institution. Comparing age groups, the only obvious differences are in

---

[4] Note that the individual characteristics, social prestige and education, are linked to the household characteristic social class, which, in the case of women, is often derived from the husband's occupational position.

Table 8.4. *Disadvantaged material circumstances by social class and age (weighted, in %)*

	Low income[a]	Social assistance[b]	Without monetary assets	Living in cramped conditions	Low satisfaction with living conditions[b]
Total	20.6	3.3	14.8	5.6	12.7
Age					
70–84	19.7	3.5	13.3	3.8	13.3
85+	25.0	2.3	21.4	12.5	10.1
Social class					
Lower class	33.6	7.6	32.3	13.0	21.0
Lower middle class	32.0	4.9	20.8	5.2	13.3
Middle middle class	18.4	6.1	20.2	6.0	15.3
Upper middle class	14.1	0.2	5.4	3.9	10.8
Higher middle class	11.2	0.7	2.9	0.2	5.7
n	392	468	488	515	471

[a]Lowest quintile of the equivalent income distribution (1,400 DM or less).
[b]Only private households.

Table 8.5. *Per capita household income (equivalent income) in private households by social class and age group (weighted, in DM)*

Social class	Age 70–84		Age 85+	
	M	*(SD)*	*M*	*(SD)*
Lower class	1,670	(545.2)	1,628	(414.6)
Lower middle class	1,660	(476.2)	1,890	(510.4)
Middle middle class	1,962	(887.1)	1,958	(703.0)
Upper middle class	2,260	(768.7)	2,146	(748.0)
Higher middle class	2,983	(1,885.3)	2,083	(1,640.9)

terms of monetary assets and living space. The old (70–84) more often have assets than do the very old (aged 85 and above). The higher proportion of very old persons living in cramped conditions is mainly due to the situation in institutional settings. As to be expected, we find materially disadvantaged circumstances much more often in the lower social classes.

However, we also see that having held higher occupational positions does not always protect old people from having to manage on an income in the lowest quintile. In part, this is due to gaps in the system of provision for old age – for example, when self-employed individuals did not insure themselves adequately. Community-dwelling West Berliners aged 70 and above receive, on average, 2,056 DM per month (net household income weighted by the number of household members; see Table 8.5). Although the in-

Table 8.6. *Determinants of equivalent income in old age: Results of stepwise linear regressions (β-values)*

	All					70–84	85+
1							
Lower class[a]							
Lower middle class	.04	.00	-.01	-.01	-.05	-.05	-.01
Middle middle class	.13	.05	.04	.03	.01	.02	.03
Upper middle class	.29**	.15	.15	.14	.15	.16	.18
Higher middle class	.37**	.22**	.22**	.22**	.21**	.29**	.14
2							
Education		.24**	.26**	.24**	.19**	.17*	.20*
3							
Number of household members			-.12*	-.13**	-.20**	-.27**	-.13
4							
IADL[b]				.02	.07	.05	.06
SMMS[c]				-.01	.02	.08	-.03
Walking mobility[d]				.08	.09	.08	.08
5							
Gender (w = 1, m = 0)					-.21**	-.23**	-.20*
Age					.12		
Adj. *R²*	.11	.15	.16	.16	.21	.23	.14
Δ*R²*		.04**	.01*	.01	.05**		

Note. Excluding the institutionalized.

*p < .05, ** p < .01.

[a]Reference category.

[b]Score on Instrumental Activities of Daily Living Scale (cf. Steinhagen-Thiessen & Borchelt, Chapter 5).

[c]SMMS: Short Mini Mental State Examination score (cf. Helmchen et al., Chapter 6).

[d]Subjective walking distance (Steinhagen-Thiessen & Borchelt, Chapter 5).

come of old adults varies by social class, only the average incomes of the top two classes are significantly different from that of the lower class, which was used as the reference category. Social class alone only explains 11% of income variance. Above, we pointed out one of the reasons for this. The linear regressions shown in Table 8.6 indicate two further reasons. First, differences in qualification within the class structure explain a further 4% of the variance. Second, women are significantly worse off than men. The latter is partly caused by the way the state pension system regulates widows' pensions. However, it is also due to the fact that many women earned less pension entitlements during their working lives (Maas et al., Chapter 3).

The smaller the household is, the larger the equivalent income. This indicates the relatively good financial situation of the widowed, particularly men (Motel & Wagner, 1993). Income is almost independent of age. Only the 70- to 84-year-olds in the higher

Table 8.7. *Types of housing of old people in West Berlin*

	Distribution
Rented accommodations	77%
Private households	69%
Sheltered housing for senior citizens	8%
Privately owned housing	13%
Senior citizens' homes	9%
Other private households	1%

Note.Values are weighted by age and gender; $N = 516$.

Table 8.8. *Living space (rooms) per person by social class and age (weighted)*

	Including the institutionalized		Only private households	
Social class	70–84	85+	70–84	85+
Lower class	1.53	1.55	1.58	1.72
Lower middle class	1.51	1.40	1.57	1.55
Middle middle class	1.71	1.61	1.78	1.83
Upper middle class	2.02	2.10	2.08	2.34
Higher middle class	2.22	2.10	2.22	2.11

middle class appear to be better off than the older group. This is very likely to be a cohort effect.

Chronological age has no influence on income, but neither does functional age as measured by health indicators. The system of provision for old age thus stabilizes both income levels and class-specific income differences during the last phase of life. At the same time, our analyses confirm that social class, qualifications, and gender determine the financial situation of old people.

Nearly four-fifths of the elderly West Berliners live in privately rented accommodations. As is expected for a city, the proportion of persons living in their own property (13%) is very low when compared with the German average (Table 8.7). A proportion of 9% of the elderly West Berliners live in various types of institutional settings (cf. Linden et al., Chapter 16). The institutionalization rate increases with advancing age whereas the distribution of rented or owned accommodations does not change by age group.

On average, elderly West Berliners have 1.8 rooms to live in. However, living space is relatively small in the older age group (85+): 12% live in cramped conditions with more people in the household than rooms. On the other hand, this difference between age groups is not found when the institutionalized are excluded (Table 8.8). In part, this is the result of residents of senior citizens' and nursing homes often having to share rooms with others. There is a weak correlation between social class and living space. Members of the lower classes have an average of 1.5 rooms and those of the higher classes an average of

Table 8.9. *Social participation by social class and age (weighted, in %)*

Age/social class (= 100%)	No activities	Little use of media[a]	No interest in politics	Nonvoters	No church visits
			Low social participation		
All	11.4	3.1	14.9	8.7	48.5
Age					
70–84	8.3	1.9	12.9	7.7	47.1
85+	23.7	7.8	22.5	12.3	54.1
Social class					
Lower class	27.6	0.0	25.7	34.4	61.1
Lower middle class	16.8	1.8	18.5	3.3	40.9
Middle middle class	11.0	5.8	18.8	7.1	49.2
Upper middle class	6.8	2.6	10.0	7.2	48.1
Higher middle class	3.9	0.1	2.3	5.0	50.0
n	511	503	511	507	511

[a]Less than once daily.

more than 2. However, differences in education and income prove to be more important, and those 14% who own their homes have significantly more space per person.

The costs of housing are main determinants of other consumption options. On average, old people in West Berlin spend 633 DM per month (i.e., 25% of their net household income) on private rented accommodations. As to be expected, the relative burden of housing costs in the lowest income group (operationalized as the first quartile) is higher (27%) than in the fourth quartile (19%). Relative housing costs are highest in the second quartile with 29%.

Thirty-eight percent of older adults with living children or grandchildren support them financially. The amount transferred is quite considerable. On average, these donors transfer almost 7,000 DM per year to the younger generation. (Excluding three outliers, the arithmetic mean reaches 4,000 DM. The average sum passed on to grandchildren is much lower, amounting to 2,500 DM.)

4.3   Social Participation

4.3.1   General Findings

Eleven percent of elderly West Berliners do not perform any activities outside their home and can thus be defined as socially isolated (Table 8.9). Three percent make use of the mass media (TV, radio, newspapers) less than once a day, 15% are not interested in politics, 9% claim to be nonvoters, and nearly 50% never go to church. Comparing age groups, a decrease in social participation is noticeable in older age. Two findings related to the clear class effects should be emphasized. First, in comparison to the other classes, members of the lower class (mainly consisting of unskilled and semiskilled workers' households) are conspicuously abstinent in terms of social activities, political interest, and participation, as well as church visits. Twenty-eight percent of the lower class and 4% of the higher middle class are socioculturally inactive. Furthermore, 26% of the lower class state that they are not interested in politics, and 34% report that they did not take part in the last Berlin election.

However, class effects are not equally distributed across all areas of social participation. Whereas the proportions of people without activities and political interest decrease by social class, class differences in media consumption, participation in elections, and church visits are small if the lower class is excluded.

One would expect that reading newspapers, watching television, and listening to the radio could assume greater importance for old people when they become less mobile and more limited in their outside activities. Our empirical results demonstrate that the opposite is true. Even though only very few people do not watch TV at all (5%), and more than one-third (38%) watch programs on TV for more than three hours a day, the following holds true: Those persons who are more active outside their home also use media more often ($r = .35$); with age, their activity level decreases ($r = -.51$), and they read newspapers, watch TV, or listen to the radio less ($r = -.39$). Usage of media, thus, does not compensate for a lower activity level. Accordingly, we find that the institutionalized use the media less often than do community dwellers.[5]

Regression analyses show the conditions for consumption of media in more detail (no table). Class differences do not have a large effect ($\beta = .18$ for the upper middle class, $\beta = .15$ for the higher middle class, $p < .05$, with the lower class as the reference group), whereas institutionalization ($\beta = -.32$, $p < .01$), impairments in physical functioning (score on the Instrumental Activities of Daily Living Scale, IADL; $\beta = .11$, $p < .05$), and nonspecific age effects ($\beta = -.16$, $p < .01$) explain most of the variance.

4.3.2 Continuity of Social Activities in Old Age

We make use of the retrospective data on social activities at younger ages to examine *continuity and discontinuity* across the life course (see also Maas & Staudinger, 1996). Indeed, many studies seem to demonstrate high continuity of the levels of activity and of interindividual differences from youth, into young adulthood, adulthood, and old age (Tokarski & Schmitz-Scherzer, 1984; Ward, 1981–82). Of course, a considerable amount of activities are only learned and taken up during adulthood (Kelly, 1974). As only a few studies have covered the whole life course, it is not yet known how the structure, mean levels, and individual differences of social participation develop over the life course.

Table 8.10 shows a comparison of the activities performed in old age and those already carried out before the age of 25. According to our respondents' reports, there seems to be strong continuity in that most activities that were performed during the last year were also part of the activity pattern in young adulthood (column 2). Volunteer work and political activity are exceptions. However, when starting out from activities carried out in young adulthood (column 3), continuity is much lower. This is mainly due to the fact that social activities in general decrease between young adulthood and old age. Again political activities and volunteer work show rather low continuity. As for po-

---

[5] More detailed analyses show that worsening vision also influences the use of media. Although reading is most impaired by a reduction of visual acuity (see Marsiske et al., Chapter 13), operating television and radio sets also requires good vision.

Table 8.10. *Social activities in old age and in young adulthood (unweighted data)*

Activity	Number of persons carrying out activity in old age	Proportion of those taking part in activity (in %)	
		From the perspective of old age[a]	From the perspective of age 25[b]
Sports	219	79.9	51.6
Dancing	54	83.3	13.8
Day-trips	239	81.6	50.6
Attending cultural events	207	92.8	43.4
Creative activities[c]	65	80.0	20.3
Hobbies	294	59.2	64.7
Traveling	248	66.1	56.0
Volunteer work	45	20.0	14.1
Political activities	31	35.5	18.6

[a]Proportion of those active today who carried out the same activity at the age of 25.
[b]Proportion of those active at the age of 25 who carry out the same activity today.
[c]For example, playing a musical instrument or painting.

litical participation, this might be an artifact, because the members of these generations may very well not want to be reminded of the political activities of their youth. However, this discontinuity could also be real because it is unlikely that those who were politically active during the Nazi period would use this as a resource for later political participation. A closer look at the data on volunteer work shows that the type of volunteer work in young adulthood (e.g., in sport clubs) is different from that in old age (e.g., helping an ill neighbor), attracting other groups of persons (young men in the first case and older women in the latter).

4.3.3 A Model of Continuity and Discontinuity in Social Activities
Taken together, we find indications of both descriptive continuity and discontinuity in social activities. This leads to the question as to whether the explanations for social activities remain constant across the life-span.

It can be assumed that social behavior depends on internal and external resources and restrictions in all phases of life. Thus, descriptive continuity of behavior is presumably related to the continuity of resources. There are indications from several longitudinal studies that internal resources (such as intelligence and personality characteristics) show considerable normative interindividual stability over the life course despite intraindividual changes of various degrees (e.g., Costa & McCrae, 1980; Hertzog & Schaie, 1988). External resources (such as income) might fluctuate more over the life course. Nevertheless, those who come from families with large socioeconomic resources are more likely to establish similar resources for themselves, and to maintain or even increase them over their life course. Another aspect that promotes continuity is the acquisition of social expectations and norms associated with long-term integration in social networks (Kahn & Antonucci, 1980).

Which factors could cause instability and discontinuity? All factors that lead individuals to alter their usual behavior, for even a short period, can lead to discontinuity. As in the case of resources, the disturbing factors might be internal or external, or on the individual (accidents), age-related (marriage), or societal (war) level. In old age, biological and health-related influences are probably the strongest source of discontinuity (e.g., P. B. Baltes & Graf, 1996; Lindenberger & Baltes, 1997; cf. Lindenberger & Reischies, Chapter 12).

To investigate whether the antecedents and correlates of social activities remain the same at different ages of the life-span, we estimated a series of multiple regression models (Fig. 8.2). In the first (Fig. 8.2a), we made sure that the reported descriptive continuity is not an artifact of some participants' impaired mental health (i.e., severity of dementia diagnosis according to DSM-III-R; see Helmchen et al., Chapter 6).

In the second model (Fig. 8.2b), three groups of variables were added to predict reported social activities at three points in the life course: (1) external resources, (2) internal resources, and (3) gender (representing a mixture of internal and external factors). To predict social activities before the age of 25, the participants' educational level and their fathers' social class were entered as external resources. The literature claims that higher class membership of the family of origin and higher educational level are strongly related to higher levels of social participation (Bourdieu, 1984; Lawton, 1985; Scitovsky, 1976). To predict social activities at the age of 60 and at present (i.e., during the year before the interview), we used social class and education as external resources. With regard to the internal resources for all three time points, intelligence and personality measures (extraversion, internal control beliefs, neuroticism) at the time of the interview were entered (cf. Smith & Baltes, Chapter 7). This seems to be justified, as it is known from longitudinal studies that rank orders of persons on these internal resources are very stable across the life-span (e.g., Costa & McCrae, 1980; Schaie, 1983). Gender was entered at all three time points.

In the third model (Fig. 8.2c), we added factors that might be related to discontinuity. The two main processes in adult life, family formation and the occupational career, can both be seen as reasons for interruptions in social participation. It has been shown that mothers with small children (Gordon, Gaitz, & Scott, 1976; Kelly, 1974), unemployed men and women (Kieselbach & Schindler, 1984), and persons who recently moved (Babchuk & Booth, 1969) are less socially active than others. We therefore added the number of geographical moves (between ages 25 and 60), the number of children, and an indicator of unemployment (at least one period lasting a year or more) to predict social activities at age 60. After the age of 60, events such as recent partner loss (not more than two years ago), a move to a senior citizens' home (as external factors), and physical or sensory impairments (visual acuity and subjective walking mobility as internal factors; cf. Steinhagen-Thiessen & Borchelt, Chapter 5) may cause discontinuity between social activities at the age of 60 and the present.

4.3.4   Continuity and Discontinuity of Factors Explaining Social Activities

In model 1 (Fig. 8.2a) we found the expected strong links between the severity of dementia and the number of mentioned social activities for all three assessed time points. These explain a considerable part of the descriptive continuity in social activities. The effect of the early activity level on participation at 60 drops by 14% (from .42 to .36) and the effect of the activity level at 60 on present activities by 17% (from .41 to .34). This is not surprising when one takes into account that recalling activities is a task that requires some degree of mental ability, even if a list of examples is presented. The high correla-

Figure 8.2. Explanatory continuity or discontinuity: Do the same factors influence self-reported social activities throughout life or do they change depending on age?

a) Model 1: Effects of dementia

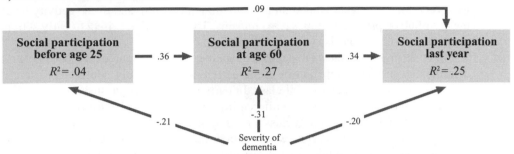

b) Model 2: Effects of internal and external resources

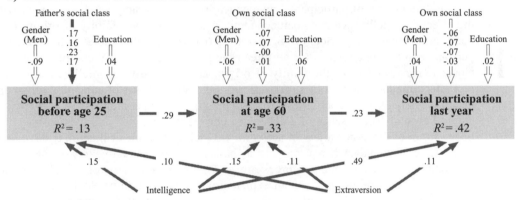

c) Model 3: Effects of age-related changes

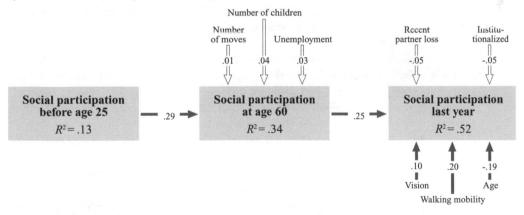

Note. The three models should be regarded cumulatively (i. e., all variables considered in the previous model are also entered in the following, but are not listed again for clarity's sake). If new variables changed effects of previously considered ones, it is discussed in the text. White arrows indicate nonsignificant effects and black ones significant effects.

The lower class is the reference category for social class, and the listed coefficients refer to effects of membership in the lower middle, middle, upper and higher middle class (from top to bottom).

tion between the number of activities in young adulthood and at older ages may therefore reflect a general tendency of older persons with cognitive impairments to mention fewer activities.

However, even after controlling for severity of dementia, a strong effect of the activity level during young adulthood on participation at 60 (.36), and of the activity level at the age of 60 on present activities (.34) remains. The small direct effect of early activities on present participation also remains significant (.09).

Model 2 (Fig. 8.2b) shows that a lack of socioeconomic resources seems to be a main determinant of nonparticipation in social activities during early adulthood. There is a strong effect of the father's social class. In particular, children of unskilled workers report lower activity levels than do children from higher social classes. Surprisingly, it is not the children from the highest class (children of academic professionals or of the self-employed with larger businesses) who mention the most activities, but the children from the class just below (children of civil servants on a higher career track or of the smaller self-employed).

The direct effect of participants' own education is remarkably small compared with the effects of intelligence and socioeconomic resources of their family of origin. Like many other studies (e.g., Schmitz-Scherzer, 1976), we find that more highly educated persons report more activities for all three time points. But when we control for the socioeconomic resources of the family of origin, and especially for intelligence, the direct effect of education becomes insignificant. Of course, effects of education might appear if we only examined activities with high prestige or high complexity (e.g., attending cultural events). The absence of a difference between young men and women may also be the result of the large variety of activities we included. Some of them may have been more attractive to men, whereas others may have been more attractive to women.

Although socioeconomic resources are an important predictor of social activities early in life, they do not provide an explanation for its continuity. Socioeconomic resources measured later in people's career do not have direct effects on their later social activities. As in the case of education, individuals from higher social classes report more activities. However, when controlling for the activity level earlier in life and for internal resources (especially intelligence), the direct effect of socioeconomic resources becomes insignificant.

Taken together, explanatory discontinuity seems to dominate with respect to external resources. The socioeconomic situation plays an important role in determining social activities in young adulthood, but loses its influence later in the life course. Internal resources show a different picture. The more intelligent and the more extraverted individuals report more activities at all three time points, even when external resources are controlled for. In her analysis of social participation, George (1978) found the opposite: Effects of internal resources disappeared when external resources were controlled for. In our model, the effects of external resources were reduced when internal resources were included. Neuroticism and internal control beliefs do not contribute at any time (and therefore are not shown in the figure). The effect of intelligence on reported present participation is very large ($r = .49$). This is probably caused by the correlation between intelligence and age, and thus with health in old age. If we control for these factors (in model 3; see Fig. 8.2c), the effect of intelligence drops to .23.

Thus, one can speak of explanatory continuity regarding internal resources. The same predictors retain their importance throughout the life course. Even the effect sizes remain comparable. Together, intelligence and extraversion explain 22% of the relationship between participation in social activities before the age of 25 and at 60, and 32% of the relationship between participation at 60 and at present.

None of the disrupting factors (migration, number of children, unemployment) affects social participation at the age of 60 if we control for participation during young adulthood. In separate models for men and women we also tested whether the duration of military service during World War II had a negative long-term effect on men's social participation and whether many years of employment increased women's social participation (cf. Lehr, 1983; Lehr & Thomae, 1987), but neither of these two features influence reported activities in old age.

Finally, we examined whether certain characteristics of life after age 60, such as recent partner loss, moving to a senior citizens' home, health, or age itself affect present social activities when participation at the age of 60 is controlled for. In general, no long-term effects of partner loss or institutionalization on activity level are noticeable when controlling for age, walking mobility, and visual acuity. This is consistent with research on self-regulatory processes (e.g., P. B. Baltes & Baltes, 1990; Brandtstädter & Greve, 1994; Staudinger, Marsiske, & Baltes, 1995), which shows that the effects of critical life events are most likely to be identified immediately afterward or when an accumulation of events has exhausted the resilience of the self (Staudinger et al., Chapter 11). All the more unexpected is the highly significant negative effect of recent partner loss for women when we analyze men and women separately. It is unclear why women withdraw from social activities after losing their partner while men do not. However, the period before the spouse's death, during which many women spend a lot of time on nursing care, may be crucial. Alternatively, the effect may be spurious, since the number of recently widowed women in our sample is relatively small ($n = 12$).

Indicators of present health impairment (vision and walking mobility) have clear effects. As to be expected, persons who have difficulty walking longer distances, and those with low visual acuity, report few activities. The remaining strong effect of age itself indicates the existence of further age-related influences that negatively affect social participation.

The general pattern resulting from these regression models is one of moderate descriptive continuity of participation in social activities over the life course. Individual differences come about early in life as a consequence of differential access to socioeconomic resources and differences in internal resources, such as intelligence and personality characteristics. Part of the variance in reported social participation can be explained by the continuity of its association with internal resources across the life course. However, 48% of the variance in participation during the year before the interview cannot be predicted by the examined variables.

The data on social participation show that people withdraw from certain activities during adult life, and begin new ones. These changes do not seem to be connected to characteristics of family life, or occupational and migration history. Declining physical health and increasing frailty seem to be of major importance for discontinuity of reported social participation in old age.

4.4   Ways of Life and Social Care

Table 8.11 shows various household types by social class and age. Nearly 62% of elderly West Berliners live alone in a private household, 25% live with a spouse or partner, and 5% live with others. The remaining 8% live in senior citizens' or nursing homes. Remarkably, the proportion of people living alone does not vary greatly by age

Table 8.11. *Type of household by social class, gender, and age (weighted, in %)*

Age/gender/social class (= 100%)	Alone	Type of household		
		Only with spouse or partner	With other persons[a]	Institution
All	61.4	24.9	5.3	8.4
Age				
70–84	60.6	29.3	4.4	5.8
85+	64.5	7.5	9.1	19.0
Gender				
Men	31.0	61.3	3.5	4.2
Women	72.1	12.0	6.0	9.9
Social class				
Lower class	58.0	16.0	16.0	10.0
Lower middle class	72.1	16.7	2.2	9.0
Middle middle class	63.7	20.1	5.1	11.0
Upper middle class	57.4	32.8	3.9	5.9
Higher middle class	57.7	35.8	6.3	0.2

[a]Including households where persons live with a spouse or partner *and* other persons.

group. However, there is an increase in very old men living alone due to widowhood but a decrease in women, caused by their more frequent institutionalization (see M. M. Baltes et al., Chapter 9; M. Wagner et al., Chapter 10; Linden et al., Chapter 16).

As there is no clear pattern of connections between ways of life and social class, our findings need to be differentiated. First of all, the proportion of old people living alone in a private household is not linearly correlated with social class. But the higher the social class, the more likely it is that older adults share their household with a spouse or partner. Members of the higher classes are not only widowed at a higher age, they are also more likely to find a new partner than are members of the lower classes.

Nonmarital partnerships are relevant here, too: the higher the social class, the greater the likelihood of living together in a nonmarital partnership. Only 2% of the unmarried members of the lower class live with a partner, whereas 13% of the higher middle class do so. One in six members of the lower class shares a household with persons other than a partner. This way of life is hardly observed at all in the other classes. For instance, 12% of the lower class but only 6% of the higher middle class live with a child.

Institutionalization occurs more or less equally among the three lower classes, but hardly at all in the higher middle class. When in need of care, this group relies either on partners or on professional care from outside the household (cf. Gilberg, 1997).

4.5 *Health Impairments*

It is a firm belief of medical sociologists that long-lasting membership in socioeconomic groups and associated differences in life and work conditions are related to

Table 8.12. *Simple partial correlations between socioeconomic features and aspects of physical and mental health (controlled for age and gender)*

	IADL	Walking mobility[a]	Number of illnesses	Visual acuity[b]	Hearing	SMMS
Lower class	-.05	-.07	.02	.00	-.07	-.02
Lower middle class	-.06	-.10**	.06	.01	-.14**	-.09*
Middle middle class	.00	.07*	-.09*	-.02	.00	-.01
Upper middle class	.04	.06	-.02	-.05	.08*	.14**
Higher middle class	.08*	.00	.09*	.07	.12**	.11**
Education in years	.09*	.11**	-.01	.09*	.13**	.17**
Social prestige[c]	.08*	.12**	-.04	.08	.12**	.10**
House ownership[d]	-.03	.03	-.06	.08	.04	.00
Equivalent income[d]	.16**	.15**	-.02	.09	.07	.13**
Presence of household members[d]	.09*	.13**	-.04	.08	-.02	.04

*$p < .05$, ** $p < .01$.
[a]Subjective walking distance (Steinhagen-Thiessen & Borchelt, Chapter 5).
[b]Corrected vision.
[c]Last occupational position before retirement.
[d]Excluding the institutionalized.

differential health and morbidity risks. Evidence for *socially differential morbidity* has been presented by House et al. (1990), Wysong and Abel (1990), Mielck and Helmert (1994), and in the Townsend report (Black, Morris, Smith, & Townsend, 1992). Proof of *socially differential mortality* has been reported by Schepers and Wagner (1989), Vallin, D'Souza, and Palloni (1990), Marmot et al. (1991), and T. Klein (1993). Although these findings seem clear, there has been much controversy about the causes – with the exception of the link between social class and cardiovascular risk factors, such as smoking and obesity (cf. Steinhagen-Thiessen & Borchelt, Chapter 5).

Therefore, we expected to find significant and relatively strong correlations between our indicators of socioeconomic differentiation and functioning, both physical and mental. Table 8.12 presents the partial correlations, after controlling for age and gender, between indicators of inequality (social class, house ownership, and income) and indicators of health (IADL, walking mobility, number of moderate and severe illnesses, visual acuity, hearing, and the risk of dementia as measured by the Short Mini Mental State score [SMMS; L. E. Klein et al., 1985]). This is a rather conservative test, as the possible social background for gender-specific survival likelihoods in the BASE sample is not attributed to socioeconomic features. Here, we only examine whether morbidity and mortality risks are distributed according to socioeconomic characteristics among the surviving age groups of men and women who were interviewed in BASE. However, these coefficients give the maximal influence for each indicator after controlling for age and gender.

The degree of need for assistance with IADL does not differ by social class – with one exception: members of the higher middle class appear to be less impaired. Likewise, higher education, higher individual social prestige, and the presence of others are linked to a slightly higher IADL score. However, in the group of community-dwelling persons, the better off one is economically, the less care seems to be needed.

Physical mobility, as measured by subjective walking distance, also varies by socio-economic group. It is significantly lower in the lower middle class (where many skilled blue-collar workers are household heads), but is higher in the middle middle class, which is dominated by white-collar workers. Again, education, social prestige, living with a partner, and particularly income are associated with better mobility.

In terms of morbidity, members of the middle middle class have significantly more moderate or severe illnesses, whereas members of the higher middle class have less. Members of the lower middle class have poorer hearing than do members of the upper two middle classes. The results on education and social prestige are similar. We find the same pattern for the risk of dementia, including the controversial association with education (see Helmchen et al., Chapter 6; Mayer & Wagner, 1993; M. Wagner & Kanowski, 1995). Finally, there seems to be no correlation between visual acuity corrected by glasses and socioeconomic factors, with education being an exception.

Taking into account the size of the individual correlations and the size of the effect of all mentioned social indicators on health variables (measured by the proportion of explained variance in multiple regression models) demonstrates that these factors have rather low explanatory power. This means that, under the present institutional and social conditions, socioeconomic differences among old people contribute little toward the explanation of differential aging in terms of physical and mental decline (cf. Borchelt et al., Chapter 15). However, one needs to bear in mind that the level of general intellectual functioning and dementia are indeed correlated with socioeconomic factors. In contrast, the rate of decline in intelligence appears to be more or less independent of socioeconomic factors (cf. Helmchen et al., Chapter 6; Lindenberger & Reischies, Chapter 12; see also Lindenberger & Baltes, 1997). For further discussion of socioeconomic factors influencing the utilization of care in old age, refer to Chapter 16 by Linden et al.

5   Discussion

This chapter addressed the question of whether socioeconomic conditions, as measured by social class, education, income, and property, influence life circumstances and social activities of old people. Life circumstances of older adults were examined in terms of material situation, social participation, and ways of life and social care. These domains were selected because physical and mental decline should manifest itself most clearly in the latter two, whereas material resources are likely to be more or less independent of old age due to institutionalized provisions for old age. Regarding the hypothesis of age-relatedness, our results show that, within the BASE age range, age differences determine some aspects of social aging, but not others. Aging is linked to reductions in social participation and autonomy, for example, but not to a worsening of the financial situation. Social participation decreases in all areas – activities outside the home are just as affected as media consumption, interest in politics, and taking part in elections – while the material situation and living standards hardly differ when comparing the old (70–84) and the very old (85+).

Because we have examined age differences using cross-sectional data we cannot be sure that such differences do not reflect cohort differences or selective mortality rather than interindividual aging processes. But as social participation decreases in all aspects we examined – social, cultural, and political – it is very likely that this is due to a general decline in health with age, and not to cohort effects or even selective mortality. The retrospective information on social participation during earlier life phases confirms this interpretation.

The hypothesis of socioeconomic continuity, which assumes a continuous and nearly equal influence of socioeconomic differences, is supported by the stability of the financial situation as mentioned above, but also by the influence of social class and other socioeconomic factors across age groups. Socioeconomic conditions early in life are clearly associated with social participation in early adulthood. Due to the continuity of participation over the life course, these associations can still be found in old age. The relative position in the system of social inequality reached at the end of the working career shapes life circumstances and opportunities in old age. Thus, the material situation in old age is clearly and lastingly linked to social class. Central dimensions of social participation (e.g., social activities, voting behavior, and political interests) are especially low in the class of unskilled and semiskilled blue-collar workers.

These results support the view that social inequalities existing in middle adulthood persist into very old age. However, there were also several indications that in some cases the influence of social class is discontinuous. Thus, the influence of social class on the number of social activities and on media consumption decreases in the group of the very old (85+). Instead, disability and institutionalization become more important determinants in that age group.

The third theoretical expectation, the cumulation hypothesis, claims that age and social inequality effects reinforce each other, so that socioeconomic differences become more pronounced in old age, or certain forms of aging interact with socioeconomic circumstances in a special way. Taken together, our results have mainly confirmed the opposite effect: Socioeconomic influences become weaker with age. This is probably due to the growing importance of functional age for activity. However, some of our findings do support the cumulation hypothesis. The risk of institutionalization is much lower for members of the higher middle class than for the other classes. The opposite is the case for the utilization of professional nursing care (cf. Linden et al., Chapter 16; Gilberg, 1997; Mayer & Wagner, 1996).

The findings on the link between socioeconomic conditions and indicators of physical and mental health are surprising, and therefore need particularly careful interpretation. Illness and frailty in old age are not noticeably associated with socioeconomic disadvantages. We often found only weak individual correlations. Even taken together, the explanatory power of socioeconomic factors is low. Furthermore, we found nonlinear relationships, which rule out simple assumptions about the associations between socioeconomic resources and health.

Three interpretations that are not mutually exclusive can be offered. First, it seems plausible that higher morbidity and mortality risks among socially disadvantaged groups lead to a particularly healthy group of individuals who survive beyond the age of 70, thus decreasing health differences in comparison to more advantaged groups. Second, it is likely that the general health insurance system in Germany enables relatively egalitarian access to medical treatment, so that no additional socioeconomic differentiation effects occur. Indeed, looking at less institutionalized provision of services (such as professional help and care in old age), social differences do after all become obvious (cf. Mayer & Wagner, 1996). Third, physical and mental impairments in old age may be caused by genetically determined organic processes whose course is relatively independent of external circumstances if interventions, such as rehabilitation measures, are not applied to counteract the consequences.

References

Atkinson, A. B. (1983). *The economics of inequality* (2nd ed.). Oxford: Clarendon Press.

Babchuk, N., & Booth, A. (1969). Voluntary association membership: A longitudinal analysis. *American Sociological Review, 34*, 31–45.

Baltes, P. B., & Baltes, M. M. (Eds.). (1990). *Successful aging: Perspectives from the behavioral sciences*. Cambridge: Cambridge University Press.

Baltes, P. B., & Graf, P. (1996). Psychological aspects of aging: Facts and frontiers. In D. Magnusson (Ed.), *The life-span development of individuals: Behavioral, neuro-biological and psychosocial perspectives* (pp. 427–460). Cambridge: Cambridge University Press.

Bengtson, V. L., Kasschau, P. L., & Ragan, P. K. (1977). The impact of social structure on aging individuals. In J. E. Birren & K. W. Schaie (Eds.), *Handbook of the psychology of aging* (pp. 327–353). New York: Van Nostrand Reinhold.

Black, D., Morris, J. N., Smith, C., & Townsend, P. (1992). The Black report. In P. Townsend, N. Davidson, & M. Whitehead (Eds.), *Inequalities in health: The Black report/The health divide* (pp. 31–213). Harmondsworth: Penguin.

Blau, P. M. (1974). Presidential address: Parameters of social structure. *American Sociological Review, 39*, 615–635.

Blau, P. M. (1994). *Structural contexts of opportunities*. Chicago: University of Chicago Press.

Borscheid, P. (1992). Der alte Mensch in der Vergangenheit. In P. B. Baltes & J. Mittelstraß (Eds.), *Zukunft des Alterns und gesellschaftliche Entwicklung* (pp. 35–61). Berlin: de Gruyter.

Bourdieu, P. (1984). *Distinction: A social critique of the judgement of taste*. Cambridge, MA: Harvard University Press.

Brandtstädter, J., & Greve, W. (1994). The aging self: Stabilizing and protective processes. *Developmental Review, 14*, 52–80.

Costa, P. T., Jr., & McCrae, R. R. (1980). Still stable after all these years: Personality as a key to some issues in adulthood and old age. In P. B. Baltes & O. G. Brim Jr. (Eds.), *Life-span development and behavior* (Vol. 3, pp. 65–102). New York: Academic Press.

Dannefer, D. (1992). On the conceptualization of context in developmental discourse: Four meanings of context and their implications. In D. L. Featherman, R. M. Lerner, & M. Perlmutter (Eds.), *Life-span development and behavior* (Vol. 11, pp. 83–110). Hillsdale, NJ: Erlbaum.

Donahue, W., Orbach, H. L., & Pollak, O. (1960). Retirement: The emerging social pattern. In C. Tibbitts (Ed.), *Handbook of social gerontology: Societal aspects of aging* (pp. 330–406). Chicago: University of Chicago Press.

Dowd, J. J., & Bengtson, V. L. (1978). Aging in minority populations: An examination of the double jeopardy hypothesis. *Journal of Gerontology, 33*, 427–436.

Ehmer, J. (1990). *Sozialgeschichte des Alters*. Frankfurt/M.: Suhrkamp.

George, L. K. (1978). The impact of personality and social status factors upon levels of activity and psychological well-being. *Journal of Gerontology, 33*, 840–847.

Gilberg, R. (1997). *Hilfe- und Pflegebedürftigkeit und die Inanspruchnahme von Hilfe- und Pflegeleistungen im höheren Lebensalter*. Unpublished doctoral thesis, Free University of Berlin.

Gordon, C., Gaitz, C. M., & Scott, J. (1976). Leisure and lives: Personal expressivity across the life span. In R. H. Binstock & E. Shanas (Eds.), *Handbook of aging and the social sciences* (pp. 310–341). New York: Van Nostrand Reinhold.

Guillemard, A.-M. (1992). Europäische Perspektiven der Alternspolitik. In P. B. Baltes & J. Mittelstraß (Eds.), *Zukunft des Alterns und gesellschaftliche Entwicklung* (pp. 614–639). Berlin: de Gruyter.

Guillemard, A.-M., & Rein, M. (1993). Comparative patterns of retirement: Recent trends in developed societies. In J. Blake & J. Hagan (Eds.), *Annual review of sociology* (Vol. 19, pp. 469–503). Palo Alto, CA: Annual Reviews.

Handl, J. (1977). Sozioökonomischer Status und der Prozeß der Statuszuweisung: Entwicklung und Anwendung einer Skala. In J. Handl, K. U. Mayer, & W. Müller (Eds.), *Klassenlagen und Sozialstruktur: Empirische Untersuchungen für die Bundesrepublik Deutschland* (pp. 101–153). Frankfurt/M.: Campus.

Hauser, R., & Wagner, G. (1992). Altern und soziale Sicherung. In P. B. Baltes & J. Mittelstraß (Eds.), *Zukunft des Alterns und gesellschaftliche Entwicklung* (pp. 581–613). Berlin: de Gruyter.

Hertzog, C., & Schaie, K. W. (1988). Stability and change in adult intelligence: 2. Simultaneous analysis of longitudinal means and covariance structures. *Psychology and Aging, 3,* 122–130.

Horkheimer, M. (1975). Autorität und Familie. In M. Horkheimer (Ed.), *Traditionelle und kritische Theorie* (pp. 162–230). Frankfurt/M.: S. Fischer.

House, J. S., Kessler, R. C., Herzog, R., Mero, R. P., Kinney, A. M., & Breslow, M. J. (1990). Age, socio-economic status, and health. *Milbank Quarterly, 68,* 383–411.

Imhof, A. E. (1981). *Die gewonnenen Jahre: Von der Zunahme unserer Lebensspanne seit dreihundert Jahren oder von der Notwendigkeit einer neuen Einstellung zu Leben und Sterben.* Munich: Beck.

Kahn, R. L., & Antonucci, T. C. (1980). Convoys over the life course: Attachment, roles, and social support. In P. B. Baltes & O. G. Brim Jr. (Eds.), *Life-span development and behavior* (Vol. 3, pp. 253–283). New York: Academic Press.

Kelly, J. R. (1974). Socialization toward leisure: A developmental approach. *Journal of Leisure Research, 6,* 181–193.

Kertzer, D. I., & Laslett, P. (1995). *Aging in the past: Demography, society, and old age.* Berkeley: University of California Press.

Kieselbach, T., & Schindler, H. (1984). *Psychosoziale Auswirkungen von Arbeitslosigkeit und Hindernisse für eine Aktivierung Arbeitsloser* (Bremer Beiträge zur Psychologie, No. 32). Bremen: University of Bremen.

Klein, L. E., Roca, R. P., McArthur, J., Vogelsang, G., Klein, G. B., Kirby, S. M., & Folstein, M. (1985). Diagnosing dementia: Univariate and multivariate analyses of the mental status examination. *Journal of the American Geriatrics Society, 33,* 483–488.

Klein, T. (1993). Soziale Determinanten der Lebenserwartung. *Kölner Zeitschrift für Soziologie und Sozialpsychologie, 45,* 712–730.

Klose, H.-U. (Ed.). (1993). *Altern der Gesellschaft: Antworten auf den demographischen Wandel.* Cologne: Bund.

Kohli, M. (1990). Das Alter als Herausforderung für die Theorie sozialer Ungleichheit. *Soziale Welt, 7* (Special issue), 387–406.

Lawton, M. P. (1985). The elderly in context: Perspectives from environmental psychology and gerontology. *Environment and Behavior, 17,* 501–519.

Lehr, U. (1983). Altern im sozialkulturellen Kontext: Ein Kommentar. In C. Conrad & H.-J. von Kondratowitz (Eds.), *Gerontologie und Sozialgeschichte: Wege zu einer historischen Betrachtung des Alters* (pp. 121–131). Berlin: Deutsches Zentrum für Altersfragen.

Lehr, U., & Thomae, H. (Eds.). (1987). *Formen seelischen Alterns: Ergebnisse der Bonner Gerontologischen Längsschnittstudie (BOLSA)*. Stuttgart: Enke.

Leisering, L. (1994). Armutspolitik und Lebensverlauf: Zur politisch-administrativen Relevanz der lebenslauftheoretischen Armutsforschung. In W. Hanesch (Ed.), *Sozialpolitische Strategien gegen Armut* (pp. 65–111). Opladen: Westdeutscher Verlag.

Lindenberger, U., & Baltes, P. B. (1997). Intellectual functioning in old and very old age: Cross-sectional results from the Berlin Aging Study. *Psychology and Aging, 12*, 410–432.

Maas, I., & Staudinger, U. M. (1996). Lebensverlauf und Altern: Kontinuität und Diskontinuität der gesellschaftlichen Beteiligung, des Lebensinvestments und ökonomischer Ressourcen. In K. U. Mayer & P. B. Baltes (Eds.), *Die Berliner Altersstudie* (pp. 543–572). Berlin: Akademie Verlag.

Markides, K. S., & Machalek, R. (1984). Selective survival, aging and society. *Archives of Gerontology and Geriatrics, 3*, 207–222.

Marmot, M. G., Smith, G. D., Stansfeld, S., Patel, C., North, F., & Head, J. (1991). Health inequalities among British civil servants: The Whitehall II Study. *The Lancet, 337*, 1387–1393.

Mayer, K. U. (1977). Statushierarchie und Heiratsmarkt: Empirische Analysen zur Struktur des Schichtungssystems in der Bundesrepublik und zur Ableitung einer Skala des sozialen Status. In J. Handl, K. U. Mayer, & W. Müller (Eds.), *Klassenlagen und Sozialstruktur: Empirische Untersuchungen für die Bundesrepublik Deutschland* (pp. 155–232). Frankfurt/M.: Campus.

Mayer, K. U. (1979). Berufliche Tätigkeit, berufliche Stellung und beruflicher Status: Empirische Vergleiche zum Klassifikationsproblem. In F. U. Pappi (Ed.), *Sozialstrukturanalysen mit Umfragedaten: Probleme der standardisierten Erfassung von Hintergrundsmerkmalen in allgemeinen Bevölkerungsumfragen* (pp. 79–123). Königstein/Ts.: Athenäum.

Mayer, K. U., & Wagner, M. (1993). Socio-economic resources and differential ageing. *Ageing and Society, 13*, 517–550.

Mayer, K. U., & Wagner, M. (1996). Lebenslagen und soziale Ungleichheit im hohen Alter. In K. U. Mayer & P. B. Baltes (Eds.), *Die Berliner Altersstudie* (pp. 251–275). Berlin: Akademie Verlag.

Mielck, A., & Helmert, U. (1994). Krankheit und soziale Ungleichheit: Empirische Studien in West-Deutschland. In A. Mielck (Ed.), *Krankheit und soziale Ungleichheit: Sozialepidemiologische Forschungen in Deutschland* (pp. 93–124). Opladen: Leske + Budrich.

Motel, A., & Wagner, M. (1993). Armut im Alter? Ergebnisse der Berliner Altersstudie (BASE) zur Einkommenslage alter und sehr alter Menschen. *Zeitschrift für Soziologie, 22*, 433–448.

Preston, S. H. (1984). Children and the elderly: Divergent paths of America's dependents. *Demography, 21*, 435–457.

Riley, M. W., Johnson, M., & Foner, A. (1972). *Aging and society: A sociology of age stratification* (3rd ed.). New York: Sage.

Riley, M. W., & Riley, J. W., Jr. (1992). Individuelles und gesellschaftliches Potential des Alterns. In P. B. Baltes & J. Mittelstraß (Eds.), *Zukunft des Alterns und gesellschaftliche Entwicklung* (pp. 437–460). Berlin: de Gruyter.

Schaie, K. W. (1983). The Seattle Longitudinal Study: A twenty-one year exploration of psychometric intelligence in adulthood. In K. W. Schaie (Ed.), *Longitudinal studies of adult psychological development* (pp. 64–135). New York: Guilford.

Schepers, J., & Wagner, G. (1989). Soziale Differenzen der Lebenserwartung in der Bundesrepublik Deutschland: Neue empirische Analysen. *Zeitschrift für Sozialreform, 35*, 670–682.

Schmitz-Scherzer, R. (1976). Longitudinal change in leisure behavior of the elderly. In H. Thomae (Ed.), *Patterns of aging: Findings from the Bonn Longitudinal Study of Aging. Contributions to human development* (pp. 127–136). Basel: Karger.

Scitovsky, T. (1976). *The joyless economy: An inquiry into human satisfaction and consumer dissatisfaction.* New York: Oxford University Press.

Sørensen, A. (1994). Women, family and class. In J. Hagan & K. S. Cook (Eds.), *Annual review of sociology* (Vol. 20, pp. 27–47). Palo Alto, CA: Annual Reviews.

Staudinger, U. M., Marsiske, M., & Baltes, P. B. (1995). Resilience and reserve capacity in later adulthood: Potentials and limits of development across the life span. In D. Cicchetti & D. J. Cohen (Eds.), *Developmental psychopathology: Vol. 2. Risk, disorder, and adaptation* (pp. 801–847). New York: Wiley.

Tokarski, W., & Schmitz-Scherzer, R. (1984). Gesundheit und Freizeit im Alter. In A. Kniel (Ed.), *Sozialpädagogik im Wandel: Geschichte, Methoden, Entwicklungstendenzen* (pp. 209–220). Kassel: Gesamthochschulbibliothek.

Vallin, J., D'Souza, S., & Palloni, A. (Eds.). (1990). *Comparative studies of mortality and morbidity: Old and new approaches to measurement and analysis.* London: Oxford University Press.

Wagner, G., Motel, A., Spieß, K., & Wagner, M. (1996). Wirtschaftliche Lage und wirtschaftliches Handeln alter Menschen. In K. U. Mayer & P. B. Baltes (Eds.), *Die Berliner Altersstudie* (pp. 277–299). Berlin: Akademie Verlag.

Wagner, M., & Kanowski, S. (1995). Socioeconomic resources, life course, and dementia in old age. In M. Bergener, J. C. Brocklehurst, & S. I. Finkel (Eds.), *Aging, health, and healing* (pp. 475–485). New York: Springer.

Ward, R. A. (1981–1982). Aging, the use of time, and social change. *International Journal of Aging and Human Development, 14*, 177–187.

Wegener, B. (1985). Gibt es Sozialprestige? *Zeitschrift für Soziologie, 14*, 209–235.

Wysong, J., & Abel, T. (1990). Universal health insurance and high-risk groups in West Germany: Implications for U.S. health policy. *Milbank Quarterly, 68*, 527–560.

Zacher, H. F. (1992). Sozialrecht. In P. B. Baltes & J. Mittelstraß (Eds.), *Zukunft des Alterns und gesellschaftliche Entwicklung* (pp. 305–330). Berlin: de Gruyter.

Interdisciplinary Findings

CHAPTER 9

Men and Women in the Berlin Aging Study

Margret M. Baltes, Alexandra M. Freund, and Ann L. Horgas

The feminization of old age justifies a separate chapter on gender differences despite the fact that they are mentioned in almost every chapter, particularly in the last chapter of this book. The aim of the present chapter is to describe in which biopsychosocial variables – physical, functional, and mental health, personality, and social integration – men and women differ. As a summary statement of the empirical data base in this chapter, we can conclude the following: Gender differences found in the domains examined are small and there are few age differences (from ages 70 to over 100) within the noted gender differences. Of the 27 biopsychosocial variables, when considered separately, 14 show significant gender differences and 4 a significant age-by-gender interaction effect. Most of these differences are in the health domain. When adding the five sociodemographic variables and regarding all variables conjointly, we can correctly classify 78% of the men and 83% of the women. In this context the most significant variables are marital and educational status, physical health, and hearing – that is, not being married and having less education, as well as suffering from a musculoskeletal disease, and having good hearing significantly increase the likelihood of being an old woman. We close the chapter with the question of whether the fact of feminization of old age is rendering a discussion about gender differences in old age obsolete.

1   Introduction

Gender and aging share some intriguing similarities. Both are considered to be "natural phenomena." Yet the fact that these phenomena are universal, and are therefore experienced by most of us, does not necessarily imply that their forms and expressions in most societies represent the "order" of nature. Efforts in gerontology to look beyond the given to what might be possible have created new vistas in aging and for the aged. For example, gerontologists have questioned the automatic association of aging with decline. Similar efforts in gender research have made it clear that "what we have all this time called 'human nature' . . . was in great part only male nature" (Gilman, 1911/1971, cited in Bem, 1993, p. 41).

Gender attributions are pervasive, if not necessarily the same, in all societies, thus leading one author to state that "our society typecasts women and men from birth through death – pink and blue from baby clothes to caskets" (Gailey, 1986, p. 35). The majority of scientists accept the argument that both biological sex and social construc-

This chapter is an evolution from an earlier chapter by M. M. Baltes, Horgas, Klingenspor, Freund, & Carstensen (1996). This version is based on a new set of data analyses.

tions of gender contribute to the differences between men and women. Differences among researchers emerge in the saliency they attach to biological and social forces as well as the theoretical model used to explain the working of such forces (e.g., Bem, 1993). Some feminist researchers adopt a more social learning perspective (e.g., Lott, 1990; Maccoby & Jacklin, 1974), whereas others take up a more cognitive perspective (e.g., Bem, 1993; Gilligan, 1982).

2   Aging and Gender Differences

Gender in old age has received little attention (Barer, 1994). Some pivotal models of late life relied exclusively on studies using male participants (e.g., the Baltimore Longitudinal Study, Shock et al., 1984; Vaillant's [1990] study of Harvard men, as well as Levinson's [1978] study, to name a few). This is particularly surprising in light of the feminization of old age – that is, the widening gap between the number of men and women with increasing age (Neugarten, 1993). Women live longer and, thus, the world of the aged is mostly a women's world. Between the ages of 65 and 70 years, the ratio of men to women is 1 to 1.2; above the age of 85, this ratio reaches 1 to 2.6.

When gender differences were examined in old age, it was primarily in regard to demographic variables such as social class, income or poverty (see also Mayer et al., Chapter 8 in this volume), or health, highlighting the paradox of a long but sickly life of old women (see also Steinhagen-Thiessen & Borchelt, Chapter 5). Thus, much research examined the consequences of "gendered" life courses in old age (Mayer, Allmendinger, & Huinink, 1991), the effects of career exits, loss of partner, or caregiving responsibilities (Niederfranke, 1991). Some research described gender differences in specific domains such as sexuality, female education, or the general life situation of unmarried women.

Because of the unique interdisciplinary nature of the Berlin Aging Study, with equal numbers of women and men distributed across six age/cohort groups from 70 to over 100 years, we believe we can make a real contribution to the description of differences and similarities between old women and men. We selected 32 variables from the following domains: physical, mental, and functional health, personality, and social integration, as well as socioeconomic status. Before presenting our findings, we summarize what is known about gender differences in old age.

2.1   Physical, Functional, and Subjective Health in Old Age

Three areas, longevity, morbidity, and disability, have received the most research attention in the physical health domain (e.g., Ory & Warner, 1990). Longevity refers to the fact that women, on average, live longer than men. Since we cannot contribute to the discussion of the reasons for gender differences in longevity, we want to summarize information on aspects for which we have data in BASE. Gender differences in life expectancy can be partially attributed to differences in the leading causes of death, that is, to physical diseases. Among persons aged 65 and older, cardiac diseases, malignant neoplasms, and cerebrovascular diseases are the first, second, and third leading causes of death for both women and men, with the rank order varying by age group. Despite their prevalence as causes of mortality for both sexes, the actual rate of these diseases is consistently higher for men than for women (Markides, 1990; Verbrugge, 1989). In addition, morbidity and patterns of disease, especially in relation to chronic condi-

tions, show major gender differences (Huyck, 1990). Women and men in advanced age
are diagnosed with similar chronic health problems, but their specific rank order differs.
Among women, arthritis and hypertension are the leading chronic health conditions,
while ischemic heart disease is the most prevalent chronic condition among men (Verbrugge, 1989). These differences in disease conditions are also manifest in drug-taking
behavior, as women are found to use more prescribed and over-the-counter medications
(Dean, 1992).

The implication of chronic disease in late life is often measured in terms of its functional impact (Verbrugge, 1989). The most common assessment of disease-related disability is one's ability to perform Activities of Daily Living (ADL; e.g., dressing and toileting), and Instrumental Activities of Daily Living (IADL; e.g., shopping and using
transportation; see Steinhagen-Thiessen & Borchelt, Chapter 5; M. M. Baltes et al.,
Chapter 14). Consistently, women report higher levels of functional disability than men
(Guralnik et al., 1994; Seeman et al., 1994).

Given the differential subjective evaluation of men and women's functional health
status in late life, it is not surprising that they have different perceptions of their physical
health. In advanced old age, men report better overall physical health than women
(Markides, 1990). Verbrugge (1989) stated that men are more likely to select the extremes of health (i.e., either excellent or poor), whereas women have more moderate responses. In general, subjective health perceptions decline with advanced age, yet gender
differences persist (Levkoff, Cleary, & Wetle, 1987).

In summary, men and women exhibit different physical and functional health conditions and experience health differently in late life. Among those who survive into old
age, the types of prevalent physical conditions are similar across the sexes, but the rank
order of their occurrence for women and men varies. These findings are reflected in the
fact that women suffer more disease-related disability and report more moderate subjective health. In short, men are more likely to suffer from fatal or life-threatening physical
conditions, and women are more likely to have nonfatal but disabling chronic conditions.
In addition, it cannot be overlooked that women have a lower mortality rate for the same
diseases than men (Manton, 1990).

2.2   Mental Health in Old Age

Recent population studies suggest that, with the exception of cognitive disorders, older people experience relatively reduced rates of many psychiatric disorders
(Myers et al., 1984; Robins & Regier, 1991). Empirical investigations have largely failed
to support increasing gender differences with age (Copeland & Abov-Saleh, 1994;
Ebrahim & Kalache, 1996; Gatz, Kasl-Godley, & Karel, 1996; cf. Helmchen et al.,
Chapter 6). In fact, initial onset of psychotic disorders such as schizophrenia in old age is
extremely rare (LaRue, Dessonville, & Jarvik, 1985). Some studies find that psychiatric
disorders lessen in old age (George, 1990; Rodin, McAvay, & Timko, 1988), and some
even suggest that gendered patterns observed in young adulthood reverse such that men
are more likely to be depressed than women (Berkman et al., 1986). Early contentions
that the risk of depression increases linearly with age (e.g., Gurland, 1976) have been
shown to be exaggerated (Futterman, Thompson, Gallagher-Thompson, & Ferris, 1995).
In fact, recent community-based epidemiological investigations of the prevalence of
psychopathology suggest that depression rates are about three times lower among over-

65-year-olds than in middle or early adulthood, with six-month prevalence rates between 1.5% and 2.9% (George, Blazer, Winfield-Laird, Leaf, & Fischback, 1988; Häfner, 1992). Subclinical levels of dysphoria, however, do appear to increase among over-75-year-olds. Indeed, studies suggest that dysphoria (as opposed to clinical depression) shows a small, but reliable, curvilinear pattern with the greatest prevalence among people under 35 and over 75 (Kessler, Foster, Webster, & House, 1992).

Evidence from the Epidemiologic Catchment Area (ECA) studies with regard to prevalence rates in anxiety disorders shows a similar pattern to affective disorders. In comparison to younger and middle-aged adults, the prevalence of anxiety disorders is reduced in the over-65 age group (Myers et al., 1984). Clear gender differences emerged in the ECA studies. With the exception of obsessive-compulsive disorders, women were roughly twice as likely to suffer some type of anxiety disorder as men. The onset of anxiety disorders in old age is rare (Burke, Burke, Regier, & Rae, 1990; Lehtinen et al., 1990).

One clear exception to a general pattern of reduced psychiatric distress with age involves cognitive impairment. Rates of dementia increase with age. Whereas dementia is seen in only 1.5% of 65- to 70-year-olds, rates exceed 10% in the age group of 75- to 85-year-olds, and the prevalence among over-85-year-olds is estimated to be as high as 40% (Cooper & Bickel, 1989; George et al., 1988; cf. Helmchen et al., Chapter 6). In terms of absolute numbers, more women suffer from dementia than men. It is widely assumed, however, that this difference is accounted for by the differences in longevity between women and men as opposed to differences in predisposition for dementia (Gatz, Harris, & Turk-Charles, 1995) and to differences in education (see Helmchen et al., Chapter 6).

In sum, although there is evidence that gender differences in mental illness diminish in old age (George, 1990), methodological problems with much of the available literature threaten the certainty of this claim (see also M. M. Baltes & Horgas, 1997). Relatively small numbers of men survive into old age, rendering the absolute numbers of men in many comparisons extremely low. In other words, age rather than gender is the risk factor (Anthony & Aboraya, 1992; Gatz et al., 1995). Second, cohort differences – which have been well established for affective and somatization disorders – may be influenced by prescribed gender roles of a specific era (Klerman et al., 1985). Rates of depression, for example, are lower among employed women than homemaking women, suggesting that sociocultural changes in the status of women may affect mental health differently in different historic eras. At any rate, cohort effects in prevalence rates render conclusions about gender differences from cross-sectional comparisons precariously tentative.

2.3   Self and Personality

Within the realm of self and personality, questions pertaining to stability versus change have attracted most attention in the adult and aging literature (e.g., Bengtson, Reedy, & Gordon, 1985; Costa & McCrae, 1980; McCrae, 1993). A glance through the books on personality and aging reveals little attention to gender differences. Two classic textbooks, for example, *Personality in adulthood* by McCrae and Costa (1990) and *Adult development* by Whitbourne and Weinstock (1986), do not include sections on gender. The limited amount of research on gender differences in the aging personality may reflect a lack of a comprehensive theory of gender differences in personality development in old age that, in turn, may stem from a general lack of interest in this topic.

Feingold (1994), presenting a meta-analysis of a large number of studies, reported few gender differences in personality characteristics, the two largest ones relating to assertiveness and tender-mindedness. For these two differences, constancy across age, generations, and culture was found. Consistent with this trait-psychology hypothesis of stability of personality and gender differences therein (McCrae & Costa, 1990; Neugarten, 1964), Costa and colleagues (1986) found high stability in a cross-sectional study with a sample aged 32 to 88 years. In contrast to Feingold (1994), however, they report that compared with men, women scored significantly higher on neuroticism and openness to experience across age groups.

With regard to negative and positive affect, young women report more negative affect than men, but the sexes do not differ in the report of positive emotions (e.g., Fujita, Diener, & Sandvik, 1991). With respect to control beliefs, young women are found to be more external than men (e.g., Kunhikrishnan & Manikandan, 1992). Feingold (1994), in his meta-analysis, finds no gender differences in control beliefs across all ages.

Within a life-span developmental perspective (e.g., P. B. Baltes, 1987; Thomae, 1979), change in personality is possible even in old age. In this sense, Jung (1969) suggests that in old age – as the culturally defined sex roles become progressively less prescriptive – gender-related differences in personality are likely to disappear. A similar argument is put forward by Gutmann (1975, 1987): Gender differences should become less pronounced in old age, when the task of raising children and supporting a family is already accomplished. Empirical studies seem to confirm this hypothesis: With increasing age, women endorse more traits that are attributed to the masculinity dimension (e.g., assertive, dominant), whereas men change more in the direction of feminine traits (e.g., emotionally warm, interpersonally concerned; Feldman, Biringen, & Nash, 1981; Lowenthal, Thurnher, & Chiriboga, 1975; Monge, 1975; Ryff & Baltes, 1976; Wink & Helson, 1993; but see Reedy, 1982). Moreover, androgyny in old age seems to be highly adaptive (Fooken, 1987). Due to the cross-sectional nature of BASE, we will not be able to contribute to this discussion.

In sum, according to earlier findings (Maccoby & Jacklin, 1974) and more recent meta-analyses (Feingold, 1994; Hyde, 1991) of gender differences in the domain of personality, few differences have emerged with large effect sizes. Those few domains relate to personality characteristics circumscribed as male agency (i.e., assertiveness) and female community (i.e., nurturance; Bakan, 1966; Feingold, 1994).

2.4   Social Integration

In general, studies looking at gender differences in the social domain have examined behaviors such as aggression, helping, nonverbal communication, and suggestibility (see Eagly, 1987; Hyde, 1991, for review), and deal with younger cohorts. Generally, it seems acceptable to characterize women as more socially related than men. As a group, women are expected to have more communal and fewer agentic qualities than men (M. M. Baltes & Silverberg, 1994). Hagestad (1981) and Marshall and Bengtson (1983) demonstrated the importance of solidarity and the role of women as kinship keepers (see also Kruse, 1983). In this sense, Hagestad (1985) has labeled women ministers of the interior. A number of studies have consistently indicated gender differences in social network size, with married women having larger networks than married men and married men tending to rely on their spouse more exclusively (see Antonucci & Akiyama, 1987).

The importance of social behaviors, such as helping, has found its largest attention in the study of social support. Social support is seen as a potential buffer against the negative effects of stress in times of crises. Both clinically oriented social psychological (Cohen & Wills, 1985; Kessler, Price, & Wortman, 1985) and gerontological literatures (Kahn & Antonucci, 1980) have attested to the importance of social support for well-being throughout the life course and, in particular, in late life (Niederfranke, 1991). Although only positive effects have been considered for a long time, Antonucci and colleagues (e.g., Antonucci & Akiyama, 1987) have reported negative correlations between network size and happiness.

The ambivalent effects of social relations might be related to the fact that women not only receive emotional and social support but are also expected to give it (Rossi & Rossi, 1990). Women are viewed as more qualified in interpersonal relationships and in providing support (Antonucci, 1994; Rossi & Rossi, 1990) and thus women, rather than men, are more likely to be caregivers throughout their lives including old age. Mothers, not fathers, are called by the school if the child is sick (Bem, 1984). Clear gender differences exist in the caregiving role: for wives with regard to their spouses and for women with regard to their social network in general (Kivett & Atkinson, 1984). Most assistance is provided by women, either by wives to their husbands or by daughters to their parents and parents-in-law (Turner, 1994), and this is not always experienced as positive. A great amount of research demonstrates the responsibility and burden experienced by female caregivers (Pillemer & Suttor, 1991; Walsh, Steffen, & Gallagher-Thompson, 1992).

2.5   *Summary*

In general, the research literature regarding gender differences in old age in the domains discussed reveals the following key aspects: (1) Significant gender differences are most likely to be expected in the domain of health, with differences between men and women in the prevalence and type of physical diagnoses, and in the impact of disease on functional capacity and perceived health; (2) sex-based patterns of mental health disorders in late life are less clear; (3) there is support in the literature for some gender differences in personality variables in late life; and (4) women and men appear to differ in relation to social network size and patterns of support, an issue which is confounded with differences in marital status in late life.

Much of this work on gender differences included older people up to the age of 65 or 70. With its age- and sex-stratified sample, the Berlin Aging Study provides a unique opportunity to compare men and women beyond the age of 70. In addition, because of the interdisciplinary nature of BASE, we can investigate gender differences in the major domains of life: health, personality, and social integration. Although we cannot examine variables identical to those reviewed here, we make an attempt to consider some from each domain, including sociodemographic status variables.

3   Methods

On the basis of 32 variables – 12 from the health domain (3 for physical, 4 for functional, 4 for mental, and 1 for subjective health), 10 from the personality domain, 5 from the social network domain, as well as 5 sociodemographic variables – we compare men and women and ask which of the 32 variables discriminate between them. We report

Table 9.1. *Comparison of men and women in BASE with regard to age, as well as marital, residential, and socioeconomic status*

	Women	Men
Mean age (in years)	85.11	84.73
Marital status (in %)		
Married	7	52
Widowed	70	40
Divorced	11	4
Single	12	4
Living arrangement		
Alone	73	43
With other(s)	27	57
Place of residence		
Institutionalized	18	10
Community-dwelling	82	90
Social prestige	70.63	80.94

the odds ratios of a logistic regression analysis that improve the prediction of the constant referring to the 50% chance of falling into the group of men or women. For a first glimpse of possible age differences in gender differences, we present odds ratios separately for persons aged 70 to 84 and those aged 85 and over. In a second step, we examine possible age-by-gender interaction effects more closely by testing each variable for main and interaction effects of gender and age. The means and standard errors in each variable for three age decades are presented graphically in Figures 9.1 through 9.5.

3.1   Characteristics of the Berlin Aging Study Sample

The mean age of the BASE sample was approximately 85 (85.11 for women and 84.73 for men) with a range from 70 to 103 years of age. More women were in the widowed, single, or divorced categories, while more men were in the married group ($\chi^2(3) = 127.96$, $p = .000$). In addition, more women than men lived alone ($\chi^2(1) = 94.01$, $p = .000$) and in institutions ($\chi^2(1) = 6.70$, $p = .01$). With regard to socioeconomic status, we found significant differences in the social prestige scores, in that men had a higher social status than women ($t(504) = 2.93$, $p = .004$). Table 9.1 shows the distribution of women and men with regard to age, and marital, socioeconomic, and residential status. Some of these sociodemographic variables are picked up again in the logistic regression analysis below. As mentioned before, the BASE sample was stratified by age and gender, providing equal numbers of men and women and thereby yielding greater statistical power.

Two caveats must be kept in mind. First, as a result of differential life expectancy, very old men in the BASE sample might represent a more "select" sample than the very old women, thus introducing a positive bias for men. However, this only represents a theoretical concern, because the bias is also reflected in the general population. Second,

Table 9.2. *Overview of variable names, measurement instruments, and responsible research units*

Variable	Instrument	Research unit
Physical health		
Cardiovascular diseases	Physical examination	Geriatrics (cf. Steinhagen-Thiessen
Hyper- and hypotension		& Borchelt, Chapter 5)
Myocardial infarction		
Coronary heart disease		
Arrhythmia		
Congestive heart failure		
Peripheral vascular disease		
Stroke		
Musculoskeletal diseases	Physical examination	Geriatrics (cf. Chapter 5)
Arthritis		
Dorsopathy		
Osteoporosis		
Fractures		
Amputation		
Other somatic diseases	Physical examination	Geriatrics (cf. Chapter 5)
Malignancies		
Thyroid disease		
Diabetes		
Anemia		
Degenerative CNS diseases		
Peripheral neuropathy		
Chronic obstructive lung		
disease		
Liver disease		
Renal failure		
Functional health		
Activities of Daily Living		
(ADL)	ADL Scale	Geriatrics (cf. Chapter 5)
Mobility	Tinetti tests	
Vision	Objective test	
Hearing	Audiometry	
Subjective health	Interview	Geriatrics (cf. Chapter 5)
Mental health		
Depressivity	CES-D	Psychiatry (cf. Helmchen et al.,
Dementia	DSM-III-R	Chapter 6)
Psychopathology	BPRS	
Somatic complaints	Complaint List	
Self and personality		
Neuroticism	NEO	Psychology (cf. Smith & Baltes,
Extraversion		Chapter 7)
Openness		

Table 9.2. *(cont.)*

Variable	Instrument	Research unit

Emotions
   Positive affect
   Negative affect
	PANAS	(Cf. Chapter 7)

Control beliefs
   Internal/positive events
   Internal/negative events
   Powerful others
   Chance
	Questionnaire	(Cf. Chapter 7)

Life satisfaction	Subscale from PGCMS	(Cf. Chapter 7)
Social integration		
Social network size	Network Question-naire	Sociology (cf. Wagner et al., Chapter 10)
Perceived social support		
Received	One item, five-point rating	(Cf. Chapter 10)
Given	One item, five-point rating	
Loneliness	Items from UCLA Loneliness Scale	Psychology (cf. Smith & Baltes, Chapter 7)

gender is significantly associated with marital and residential status. This suggests that gender might be a broad proxy variable that needs more precise specification for the understanding of diverse outcomes (see also Maddox & Clark, 1992).

3.2   *Instruments*

Data on indicators of physical, mental, and functional health, self and personality, social integration, as well as sociodemographic factors, come from a number of different measures used by the BASE research units. Table 9.2 summarizes the instruments by name and research unit and refers to the chapters in which they are described in more detail.

4   Results

4.1   *Systemic Analysis*

In order to estimate the overall predictive power of the 32 variables, from different domains of functioning, in discriminating between older men and women, we conducted a logistic regression analysis including all 32 variables: 27 variables from the domains self and personality, social integration, and physical, mental, functional, and subjective health, and 5 sociodemographic variables (see Table 9.3). The logistic regression analysis revealed a significant improvement in predicting group membership when

Table 9.3. *Odds ratios of logistic regression analysis for 32 variables*

	Odds ratio[a]		
Construct	Entire sample ($n = 465$)[b]	70–84 ($n = 245$)	85+ ($n = 220$)
Self and personality			
Neuroticism	1.39	1.27	1.17
Extraversion	1.22	1.06	0.95
Openness	0.82	0.90	0.81
Control beliefs			
Internal/positive events	0.64[†]	1.08	0.60
Internal/negative events	0.84	0.65	1.03
Powerful others	1.10	0.66	1.53
Chance	1.39	1.56	1.06
Emotions			
Negative affect	1.73	3.29[†]	1.42
Positive affect	1.47	1.26	1.94
Life satisfaction	1.27	1.37	1.21
Social integration			
Emotional loneliness	0.84	1.12	0.69
Social loneliness	0.48	0.35	0.64
Perceived social support			
Received	1.39	1.07	1.68
Given	1.24	2.38[†]	0.83
Social network size	1.02	1.04	1.00
Mental health			
Depressivity	1.00	1.02	1.02
Psychopathology	0.98	0.97	0.98
Dementia	1.26	1.44	1.15
Somatic complaints	1.02	1.04	1.00
Physical health			
Cardiovascular diseases	1.04	1.01	1.01
Musculoskeletal diseases	1.13	1.03	1.29[†]
Other somatic diseases	0.70***	0.81	0.63**
Functional health			
ADL	0.94	1.47	0.92
Hearing	1.98***	2.12***	1.85
Vision	0.84	0.88	0.65
Mobility	0.80	0.85	0.74
Subjective health	0.87	0.94	0.86
Sociodemographics			
Marital status[c]			
Married	0.04***	0.06***	0.07**
Widowed	0.98	1.19	0.52
Single	1.71	1.16	0.81

Table 9.3. *(cont.)*

	Odds ratio[a]		
Construct	Entire sample (*n* = 465)[b]	70–84 (*n* = 245)	85+ (*n* = 220)
Place of residence[d]	0.63	0.19	0.62
Years of education	0.96*	0.96[†]	0.94[†]

[†] $p \leq .05$, * $p < .01$, ** $p < .001$, *** $p < .0001$.
[a]Odds ratios under 1 indicate the likelihood of belonging to the group of men, odds ratios over 1 indicate the likelihood of belonging to the group of women.
[b]Eighty-nine cases were excluded because of missing data on one of the predictor variables: 14 cases in the group of younger men (70–84), 5 cases in the group of older men (85+), 24 cases in the group of younger women (70–84), and 8 cases in the group of older women (85+).
[c]Reference category: divorced.
[d]0 = institutionalized care setting, 1 = private household.

including all 32 variables over a model based on the constant (50%) only ($\chi^2(32) =$ 238.2, $p < .000$) with pseudo-R^2 = 37%, and a correct classification of 79% of the men and 81% of the women. As can be seen in Table 9.3, 2 of the 5 sociodemographic variables, 2 of the 12 health variables, and 1 of the 15 psychosocial variables significantly contributed to the prediction of gender. Odds ratios greater than 1 indicate the likelihood of belonging to the group of women (i.e., better hearing); odds ratios smaller than 1 indicate the likelihood of belonging to the group of men (i.e., being married, having a better education, and suffering from other somatic diseases). When entering the biopsychosocial variables first and sociodemographic variables in a second step, we found a correct classification of 69.68% (69.87% for men and 69.47% for women) on the basis of the biopsychosocial variables alone. If the sociodemographic variables were entered first, we found a correct classification of 74% (57% for men and 91% for women) on the basis of these variables alone.

For a preliminary look at possible age differences in gender differences, logistic regression analyses were run for two age groups (70–84 vs. 85+). Similar results were found. Here too, a significant improvement in the prediction by all 32 variables over the constant could be noted. For the younger age group, the values are pseudo-R^2 = 41%; $\chi^2(32) = 140.5, p < .000$. Correct classification was possible for 78% of the men and 83% of the women. The likelihood of belonging to the group of women was higher when reporting better hearing, more negative affect, and more help given. Being married and having better education significantly predicted belonging to the group of men. For the older age group (pseudo-R^2 = 42.5%; improvement $\chi^2(31) = 129.5, p < .000$, with 81% of the men and 83% of women classified correctly), being married, other somatic diseases, and more years of education significantly predicted being male. For the older women, it was suffering from musculoskeletal diseases and having fewer years of education. Taken together, the strongest predictors were marital status, years of education, auditory functioning, and other somatic diseases, signifying similarity in the predictors across the age range from 70 to over 100 years.

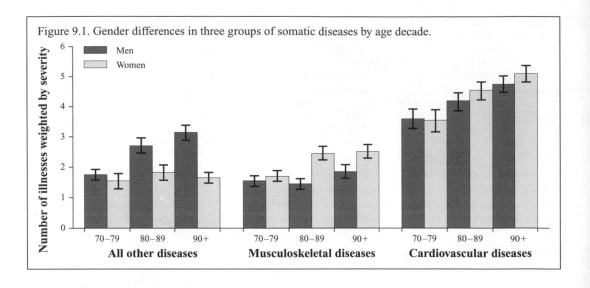

Figure 9.1. Gender differences in three groups of somatic diseases by age decade.

4.2   Bivariate Analyses

In order to more closely identify possible age-by-gender interaction effects we looked at 26 of the 27 health and psychosocial variables separately and tested for statistical significance of gender and age using analyses of variance. (The variable dementia was excluded from these analyses because of its categorical nature.) Figures 9.1 through 9.5 present means and standard errors for all 26 variables, for men and women per age decade.

Figure 9.1 represents the number of moderate and severe illnesses for three groups of diagnoses; musculoskeletal, cardiovascular, and all other somatic diseases. We find a main effect for gender for the musculoskeletal and all other somatic diseases ($F(1, 465) = 15.556$, $p < .000$; respectively $F(1, 465) = 22.893$; $p < .000$) as well as an age-by-gender interaction effect ($F(2, 465) = 3.007$, $p = .003$; respectively $F(2, 465) = 4.914$, $p = .008$). Women were more likely to have a musculoskeletal diagnosis, whereas men showed a greater number of other somatic diseases, and these gender differences increase significantly with age. Gender differences in the cardiovascular diseases were not statistically significant.

Figure 9.2 shows the means for age and sex in the functional and subjective health measures. There were significant gender effects in mobility, vision, hearing, and subjective health. Women showed greater impairment in mobility and vision ($F(1, 465 = 5.873$, $p = .016$, $F(1, 465) = 10.870$, $p = .001$), but less hearing impairment than men ($F(1, 465) = 8.067$, $p = .005$). Women also felt subjectively less healthy ($F(1, 465) = 10.494$, $p = .001$). Only the negative gender difference in mobility increases significantly with age ($F(2, 465) = 4.892$, $p = .008$).

Figure 9.3 represents means and standard errors for men and women on three mental health variables, self-reported depressivity, rated severity of psychopathology, and somatic complaints. Women reported significantly more depressivity ($F(1, 465) = 19.055$, $p = .000$) and somatic complaints ($F(1, 465) = 19.063$, $p = .000$), and had higher ratings

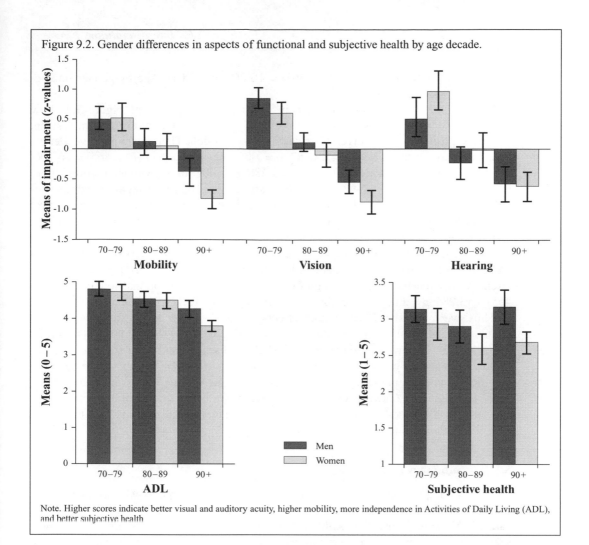

Figure 9.2. Gender differences in aspects of functional and subjective health by age decade.

Note. Higher scores indicate better visual and auditory acuity, higher mobility, more independence in Activities of Daily Living (ADL), and better subjective health

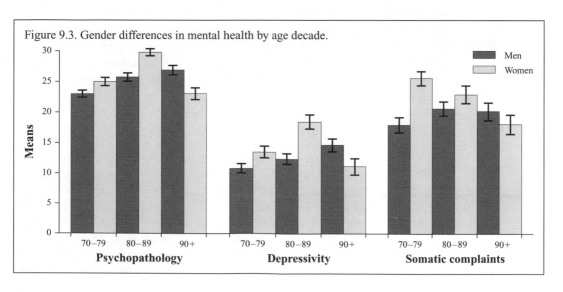

Figure 9.3. Gender differences in mental health by age decade.

in severity of psychopathology ($F(1, 465) = 10.269$, $p = .001$). Age-by-gender interaction effects were not significant.

With regard to the personality domain, the two upper panels of Figure 9.4 show means and standard errors per age decade and gender for neuroticism, extraversion, openness, positive and negative affect, and life satisfaction. There were main gender effects for neuroticism ($F(1, 465) = 28.187$, $p = .000$), negative affect ($F(1, 465) = 16.100$, $p = .000$), and life satisfaction ($F(1, 465) = 9.288$, $p = .002$) in that women reported more neuroticism and negative affect and less life satisfaction. Only with regard to control beliefs (lower panel of Figure 9.4) was there a significant interaction effect for the control dimension "powerful others," in that the older women were more convinced than men and younger women that powerful others control their lives ($F(2, 465) = 3.312$, $p = .037$). In Figure 9.5, gender differences are represented for perceived support received and given, emotional loneliness, social loneliness, and social network size. Gender differences only reached statistical significance in the area of emotional loneliness ($F(1, 465) = 13.085$, $p = .000$). No age-by-gender interaction effects were found.

Thus, we found significant gender effects in 15 of the 26 health and psychosocial variables tested. All effect sizes were small ($\eta = .01-.06$). Only four variables – mobility, control beliefs in powerful others, musculoskeletal diseases, and other somatic illnesses – showed an age-by-gender interaction effect ($\eta = .01-.02$). The fact that there are more significant variables in the separate analyses than in the logistic regression is simply the result of colinearity between variables. Therefore, we argue that there are indeed very few gender differences and that these differences relate almost exclusively to the health and, above all, sociodemographic variables.

5   Summary and Discussion

Taking a systemic view and including biopsychosocial as well as sociodemographic variables, men and women were classified correctly in 78% and 83% of the cases respectively. Consistent with the literature, the obtained results suggest that most sex-related differences are to be found in the domains of physical, mental, and functional health. This underlines the often stated plight that old women live a longer but not necessarily better or healthier life (Barer, 1994). Few gender differences were found in the domains of personality and social integration. Although women reported more negative emotions and scored higher on neuroticism than the men in BASE, the greater similarity than difference in personality and self characteristics is in line with research efforts in younger age groups (Bem, 1993; Hyde, 1991). The same holds true for the social domain. Differences in perceived help received and given did not reach significance. Women, particularly the oldest age group, reported significantly more emotional loneliness, but not more social loneliness. The present findings in the psychosocial and biological domain were small in size, ranging from $\eta = .01$ to .06. This is very much in line with a number of meta-analyses of gender differences published since the early 1980s (for review, see Eagly, 1995; Hyde & Frost, 1993). Most of these meta-analyses repeatedly noted that aggregated gender differences are few and rather small, accounting for no more than 5% of the variance with very few exceptions (Hyde & Plant, 1995). These conclusions are consistent with earlier opinions expressed by Maccoby and others (e.g., Maccoby & Jacklin, 1974). In light of the data from these meta-analyses, one would find it difficult not to agree with Hyde's statement (1991, p. 88): "gender similarities are

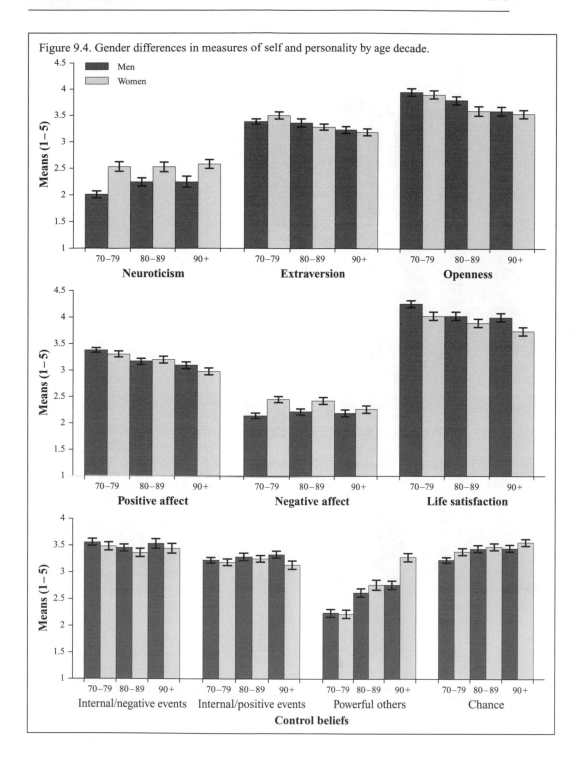

Figure 9.4. Gender differences in measures of self and personality by age decade.

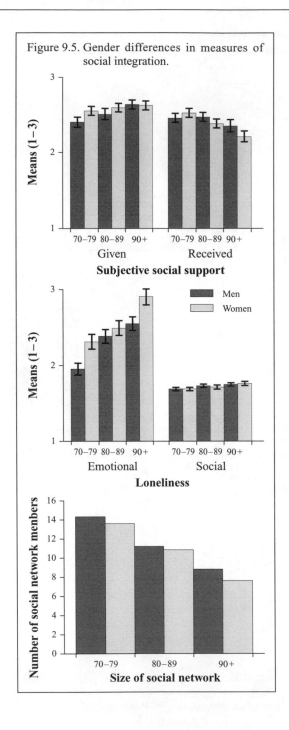

Figure 9.5. Gender differences in measures of social integration.

probably more the rule than gender differences." The argument that interindividual differences in other psychological variables are not larger (see Eagly, 1995) is, first of all, no excuse and, second, not true. For example, there are much larger differences in cognitive functioning between age groups (cf. Lindenberger & Reischies, Chapter 12).

The systemic analysis reveals the driving force of gender differences, namely the sociodemographic factors. The differences in life-styles of men and women, including power and status, are not due to internal barriers, but rather to external ones; the macrostructures in our society affecting education and social status, the societal belief in the incompatibility of achievement and femininity, and the societal practice of job discrimination. Thus, elimination of gender differences will not only require change toward androgyny on the personal level, but much more so on the institutional level. In fact, androgyny is likely to divert attention from the very problem: that is, the analysis of the role of micro- and macrosocial structures in the maintenance of gender differences. Nevertheless, we need to consider the possibility of Gutmann's (1975, 1987) hypothesis on a rapprochement of men and women in late life. Could it be that only those men survive into old age who have become more feminine, and only those women who have become more masculine? Or just the former development, which could explain our finding of few gender differences? As mentioned above, we cannot answer this question due to the cross-sectional nature of our data.

Greater or more differences between men and women might not be detected as long as research relies on an interindividual-differences approach. Some authors, such as Eagly (1987) and Maccoby (1991, 1998), albeit in quite distinct ways, have identified possible reasons for the apparent contradiction between relatively small and equivocal effect sizes reported in the empirical literature and the robust "life" relevance of gender differences.

Eagly (1987) sees the inconsistency as arising from great heterogeneity in samples, settings, and situations represented in empirical research and a general bias toward "agentic" (i.e., male) rather than "communal" (i.e., female) roles in experimental investigation. As a remedy, she proposes more homogeneity in samples, settings, and situations across studies.

In contrast, Maccoby (1991) contends that the *acontextual* measurement inherent in the individual differences approach is to blame. Thus, instead of asking for more homogeneity with regard to context, sample, and situation as Eagly (1987) suggests, Maccoby (1991) asks for systematic inclusions and analyses of diverse contexts. Her argument can be buttressed with a number of empirical findings demonstrating that gender is implicated in a number of behaviors, particularly in the social domain, but its effect is obscured by measuring *across* occasions, situations, and ecologies. Most behaviors, particularly social behaviors, occur in social contexts, and individuals behave differently in different contexts. When context, such as same-sex group versus mixed-sex group, is taken into account, the same behavioral measurements show no gender differences in one context, but dramatic gender differences in others. In Eagly's language, social roles are specified by gender expectations in one context, whereas other expectations might override gender in another. The dramatic effect of context refutes the notion that gender differences are linked to traits or fixed and stable dispositions and suggests instead that they are learned behaviors applied in context-specific ways. Differences between women and men can be reliably found for some behaviors, at some ages, in some situations, at some times, and in some places.

Such a contextual view is the most prominent view of researchers in the field today (Deaux & Major, 1987; Eagly, 1987; Hyde, 1991; Lott & Maluso, 1993). To illustrate, Greeno (1989, cited in Maccoby, 1990) demonstrated that "proximity seeking" behavior, mostly seen as the result of an "affiliative trait" in girls, was only observed when girls were in mixed-sex groups, but not when they were in same-sex groups. Hyde (1991) summarizes work on gender differences in achievement motivation and attributional style that demonstrates the importance of situation. Women only show lower achievement motivation when they are in competitive situations with men, but not when with women (Cronin, 1980). Attributional style varies by whether the task at hand has to do with spatial ability or the establishment of friendship (Frieze, Whitley, Hanusa, & McHugh, 1982). Meyer, Murphy, Cascardi, and Birns (1991) point out that girls display passivity and dependency only when they are in the presence of boys.

Furthermore, gender socialization is very much affected by variations in social class, ethnicity, and family and personal histories. Most behaviors, whether independent or dependent behavior, smiling behavior, aggressive or submissive, nurturing or agentic behavior, are in the behavior repertoire of most people. It is the situational opportunities to exhibit these behaviors that vary drastically between men and women, upper and lower social class, and people of different ethnic and cultural backgrounds.

The contextual perspective presents an interesting trail to follow: If the world becomes increasingly female with age, does it mean that there will be fewer and fewer contexts (e.g., mixed-sex contexts) that appear to elicit gender differences? Is the prevalence of same-sex groups perhaps the reason why we see more self-assertive, agentic behaviors in old women? Longevity might bring women more than just losses. When, and if, contexts (i.e., macro- and microinstitutional environments) change, the future might offer new flexibilities in the distribution of education, work, and leisure over the life course (Riley & Riley, 1994) and, thus, promote gender equality. With important changes in family, economic, and political life, there will be continued reconstruction of social categories, including gender. As a consequence, the greater longevity of women might bring with it greater freedom with regard to independence, mastery, and control of their own destiny.

At the moment and perhaps in the near future, such visions might remain just that. For now, social structures still have a prominent effect on the lives of women. For instance, the cluster analyses presented in Chapter 18 (Mayer et al.) produce "male" and "female" clusters (see also Smith & Baltes, in press). Unfortunately, all "female" clusters are described as containing mostly women who are very old, socioeconomically deprived, physically and mentally impaired, lonely, and unhappy.

References

Anthony, J. C., & Aboraya, A. (1992). The epidemiology of selected mental disorders in later life. In J. E. Birren, R. B. Sloane, & G. D. Cohen (Eds.), *Handbook of mental health and aging* (2nd ed., pp. 26–73). San Diego, CA: Academic Press.

Antonucci, T. C. (1994). A life-span view of women's social relations. In B. F. Turner & L. E. Troll (Eds.), *Women growing older* (pp. 239–269). Thousand Oaks, CA: Sage.

Antonucci, T. C., & Akiyama, H. (1987). An examination of sex differences in social support among older men and women. *Sex Roles, 17,* 737–749.

Bakan, D. (1966). *The duality of human existence*. Chicago: Rand McNally.

Baltes, M. M., & Horgas, A. L. (1997). Long-term care institutions and the maintenance of competence. In K. W. Schaie & S. L. Willis (Eds.), *Societal mechanisms for maintaining competence in old age* (pp. 142–164). New York: Springer.

Baltes, M. M., Horgas, A. L., Klingenspor, B., Freund, A. M., & Carstensen, L. L. (1996). Geschlechtsunterschiede in der Berliner Altersstudie. In K. U. Mayer & P. B. Baltes (Eds.), *Die Berliner Altersstudie* (pp. 573–598). Berlin: Akademie Verlag.

Baltes, M. M., & Silverberg, S. (1994). The dynamics between dependency and autonomy: Illustrations across the life span. In D. L. Featherman, R. M. Lerner, & M. Perlmutter (Eds.), *Life-span development and behavior* (Vol. 12, pp. 41–90). Hillsdale, NJ: Erlbaum.

Baltes, P. B. (1987). Theoretical propositions of life-span developmental psychology: On the dynamics between growth and decline. *Developmental Psychology, 23*, 611–626.

Barer, B. M. (1994). Men and women aging differently. *International Journal of Aging and Human Development, 38*, 29–40.

Bem, S. L. (1984). Androgyny and gender schema theory: A conceptual and empirical integration. *Nebraska Symposium on Motivation, 32*, 179–226.

Bem, S. L. (1993). *The lenses of gender*. New Haven, CT: Yale University Press.

Bengtson, V. L., Reedy, M. N., & Gordon, C. (1985). Aging and self-conceptions: Personality processes and social contexts. In J. E. Birren & K. W. Schaie (Eds.), *Handbook of the psychology of aging* (2nd ed., pp. 544–593). New York: Van Nostrand Reinhold.

Berkman, L. F., Berkman, C. S., Kasl, S., Freeman, D. H., Leo, L., Ostfeld, A. M., Cornoni-Huntley, J., & Brody, J. A. (1986). Depressive symptoms in relation to physical health and function in the elderly. *American Journal of Epidemiology, 124*, 372–388.

Burke, K. C., Burke, J. D., Regier, D. A., & Rae, D. S. (1990). Age at onset of selected mental disorders in five community populations. *Archives of General Psychiatry, 47*, 511–518.

Cohen, S., & Wills, T. A. (1985). Stress, social support, and the buffering hypothesis. *Psychological Bulletin, 98*, 310–357.

Cooper, B., & Bickel, H. (1989). Prävalenz und Inzidenz von Demenzerkrankungen in der Altenbevölkerung: Ergebnisse einer populationsbezogenen Längsschnittstudie in Mannheim. *Der Nervenarzt, 60*, 472–482.

Copeland, J. R. M., & Abov-Saleh, M. T. (Eds.). (1994). *The psychiatry of old age*. London: Wiley.

Costa, P. T., Jr., & McCrae, R. R. (1980). Still stable after all these years: Personality as a key to some issues in adulthood and old age. In P. B. Baltes & O. G. Brim Jr. (Eds.), *Life-span development and behavior* (Vol. 3, pp. 65–102). New York: Academic Press.

Costa, P. T., Jr., McCrae, R. R., Zonderman, A. B., Barbano, H. E., Lebowitz, B., & Larson, D. M. (1986). Cross-sectional studies of personality in a national sample: 2. Stability in neuroticism, extraversion, and openness. *Psychology and Aging, 1*, 144–149.

Cronin, C. L. (1980). Dominance relations and females. In D. R. Omark, F. F. Strazer, & D. G. Freedman (Eds.), *Dominance relations: An ethological view of human conflict and social interaction* (pp. 299–318). New York: Garland Press.

Dean, K. (1992). Health-related behavior: Concepts and methods. In M. G. Ory, R. P. Abeles, & P. D. Lipman (Eds.), *Aging, health, and behavior* (pp. 27–56). Newbury Park, CA: Sage.

Deaux, K., & Major, B. (1987). Putting gender into context: An interactive model of gender-related behavior. *Psychological Review, 94*, 369–389.

Eagly, A. H. (1987). *Sex differences in social behavior: A social-role interpretation*. Hillsdale, NJ: Erlbaum.

Eagly, A. H. (1995). The science and politics of comparing women and men. *American Psychologist, 50*, 145–158.

Ebrahim, S., & Kalache, A. (Eds.). (1996). *Epidemiology in old age*. London: BMJ Publishing Group.

Feingold, A. (1994). Gender differences in personality: A meta-analysis. *Psychological Bulletin, 116*, 429–456.

Feldman, S. S., Biringen, Z. C., & Nash, S. C. (1981). Fluctuations of sex-related self-attributions as a function of stage of the family life cycle. *Developmental Psychology, 17*, 24–35.

Fooken, I. (1987). Älterwerden als Frau. In A. Kruse, U. Lehr, & C. Rott (Eds.), *Gerontologie: Eine interdisziplinäre Wissenschaft* (pp. 238–271). Munich: Bayerischer Monatsspiegel Verlagsgesellschaft.

Frieze, I. H., Whitley, B. E., Jr., Hanusa, B. H., & McHugh, M. C. (1982). Assessing the theoretical models for sex differences in causal attributions for success and failure. *Sex Roles, 8*, 333–343.

Fujita, F., Diener, E., & Sandvik, E. (1991). Gender differences in negative affect and well-being: The case for emotional intensity. *Journal of Personality and Social Psychology, 61*, 427–434.

Futterman, A., Thompson, L., Gallagher-Thompson, D., & Ferris, R. (1995). Depression in later life: Epidemiology, assessment, etiology, and treatment. In E. E. Beckham & W. R. Leber (Eds.), *Handbook of depression* (2nd ed., pp. 494–525). New York: Guilford.

Gailey, C. W. (1986). Evolutionary perspectives on gender hierarchy. In B. B. Hess & M. M. Ferree (Eds.), *Analyzing gender: A handbook of social science research* (pp. 32–67). Newbury Park, CA: Sage.

Gatz, M., Harris, J. R., & Turk-Charles, S. (1995). The meaning of health for older women. In A. L. Stanton & S. J. Gallant (Eds.), *The psychology of womens' health: Progress and challenges in research and application* (pp. 491–529). Washington, DC: American Psychological Association.

Gatz, M., Kasl-Godley, J. E., & Karel, M. J. (1996). Aging and mental disorders. In J. E. Birren & K. W. Schaie (Eds.), *Handbook of the psychology of aging* (4th ed., pp. 365–382). San Diego, CA: Academic Press.

George, L. K. (1990). Gender, age and psychiatric disorders: Why do gender differences in rates of disorders narrow with age? *Generations, 2*, 22–27.

George, L. K., Blazer, D. G., Winfield-Laird, I., Leaf, P. J., & Fischback, R. L. (1988). Psychiatric disorders and mental health service use in later life: Evidence from the Epidemiologic Catchment Area Program. In J. A. Brody & G. L. Maddox (Eds.), *Epidemiology and aging* (pp. 189–219). New York: Springer.

Gilligan, C. (1982). *In a different voice: Psychological theory and women's development.* Cambridge, MA: Harvard University Press.

Gilman, C. P. (1911/1971). *The man-made world; or our androcentric culture.* New York: Johnson Reprint.

Greeno, C. G. (1989). *Gender differences in children's proximity to adults.* Unpublished doctoral thesis, Stanford University, CA.

Guralnik, J. M., Simonsick, E. M., Ferrucci, L., Glynn, R. J., Berkman, L. F., Blazer, D. G., Scherr, P. A., & Wallace, R. B. (1994). A short physical performance battery assessing lower extremity function: Association with self-reported disability and prediction of mortality. *Journal of Gerontology: Medical Sciences, 49*, M85–M94.

Gurland, B. J. (1976). The comparative frequency of depression in various adult age groups. *Journal of Gerontology, 31*, 283–292.

Gutmann, D. L. (1975). Parenthood: Key to the comparative psychology of the life cycle? In N. Datan & L. Ginsberg (Eds.), *Life-span developmental psychology: Normative life crises* (pp. 167–184). New York: Academic Press.

Gutmann, D. L. (1987). *Reclaimed powers.* New York: Basic Books.

Häfner, H. (1992). Psychiatrie des höheren Lebensalters. In P. B. Baltes & J. Mittelstraß (Eds.), *Zukunft des Alterns und gesellschaftliche Entwicklung* (pp. 151–179). Berlin: de Gruyter.

Hagestad, G. O. (1981). Problems and promises in the social psychology of intergenerational relations. In R. W. Fogel, E. Hatfield, S. B. Kiesler, & E. Shanas (Eds.), *Aging* (pp. 11–46). New York: Academic Press.

Hagestad, G. O. (1985). Continuity and connectedness. In V. L. Bengtson & J. F. Robertson (Eds.), *Grandparenthood* (pp. 31–48). Beverly Hills, CA: Sage.

Huyck, M. H. (1990). Gender differences in aging. In J. E. Birren & K. W. Schaie (Eds.), *Handbook of the psychology of aging* (3rd ed., pp. 124–132). San Diego, CA: Academic Press.

Hyde, J. S. (1991). *Half the human experience*. Lexington, MA: D. C. Heath.

Hyde, J. S., & Frost, L. A. (1993). Meta-analysis in the psychology of women. In F. L. Denmark & M. A. Paludi (Eds.), *Psychology of women: A handbook of issues and theories* (pp. 67–103). Westport, CT: Greenwood Press.

Hyde, J. S., & Plant, E. A. (1995). Magnitude of psychological gender differences. *American Psychologist, 50*, 159–161.

Jung, C. G. (1969). *The structure and dynamics of the psyche*. Princeton, NJ: Princeton University Press.

Kahn, R. L., & Antonucci, T. C. (1980). Convoys over the life course: Attachment, roles, and social support. In P. B. Baltes & O. G. Brim Jr. (Eds.), *Life-span development and behavior* (Vol. 3, pp. 253–283). New York: Academic Press.

Kessler, R., Foster, C., Webster, P. S., & House, J. S. (1992). The relationship between age and depressive symptoms in two national surveys. *Psychology and Aging, 7*, 119–126.

Kessler, R. C., Price, R. H., & Wortman, C. B. (1985). Social factors in psychopathology: Stress, social support, and coping processes. *Annual Review of Psychology, 36*, 531–572.

Kivett, V. R., & Atkinson, M. P. (1984). Filial expectations, association and helping as a function of number of children among older rural-transitional parents. *Journal of Gerontology, 39*, 499–503.

Klerman, G. L., Lavori, P. W., Rice, J., Reich, T., Endicott, J., Andreasen, N. C., Keller, M. B., & Hirschfield, R. M. (1985). Birth-cohort trends in rates of major depressive disorder among relatives of patients with affective disorder. *Archives of General Psychiatry, 42*, 689–693.

Kruse, A. (1983). Die Fünf-Generationen-Familie: Interaktion, Kooperation, Konflikt. *Zeitschrift für Gerontologie, 16*, 205–209.

Kunhikrishnan, K., & Manikandan, K. (1992). Sex differences in locus of control: An analysis based on Calicut L.O.C. Scale. *Psychological Studies, 37*, 121–125.

LaRue, A., Dessonville, C., & Jarvik, L. (1985). Aging and mental disorders. In J. E. Birren & K. W. Schaie (Eds.), *Handbook of the psychology of aging* (2nd ed., pp. 664–702). New York: Van Nostrand Reinhold.

Lehtinen, V., Joukamaa, M., Lahtela, K., Raitasalo, R., Jyrkinen, E., Maatela, J., & Aromaa, A. (1990). Prevalence of mental disorders among adults in Finland: Basic results from the Mini Finland Health Survey. *Acta Psychiatrica Scandinavica, 81*, 418–425.

Levinson, D. J. (1978). *The seasons of a man's life*. New York: Ballantine.

Levkoff, S. E., Cleary, P. D., & Wetle, T. (1987). Differences in the appraisal of health between aged and middle-aged adults. *Journal of Gerontology, 42*, 114–120.

Lott, B. (1990). Dual natures or learned behavior: The challenge to feminist psychology. In R. T. Hare-Mustin & J. Marecek (Eds.), *Making a difference: Psychology and the construction of gender* (pp. 65–101). New Haven, CT: Yale University Press.

Lott, B., & Maluso, D. (1993). The social learning of gender. In A. E. Beall & R. J. Sternberg (Eds.), *The psychology of gender* (pp. 99–123). New York: Guilford.

Lowenthal, M. F., Thurnher, M., & Chiriboga, D. (1975). *Four stages of life*. San Francisco, CA: Jossey-Bass.

Maccoby, E. E. (1990). Gender and relationships. *American Psychologist, 45*, 513–520.

Maccoby, E. E. (1991). Gender segregation in the workplace. In M. Frankenhaeuser, U. Lundberg, & M. Chesney (Eds.), *Women, work, and health: Stress and opportunities* (pp. 3–15). New York: Plenum Press.

Maccoby, E. E. (1998). *The two sexes: Growing up apart, coming together*. Cambridge, MA: Harvard University Press.

Maccoby, E. E., & Jacklin, C. N. (1974). *The psychology of sex differences*. Stanford, CA: Stanford University Press.

Maddox, G. L., & Clark, D. O. (1992). Trajectories of functional impairment in later life. *Journal of Health and Social Behavior, 33*, 114–125.

Manton, K. G. (1990). Population models of gender difference in mortality, morbidity, and disability risks. In M. G. Ory & H. R. Warner (Eds.), *Gender, health, and longevity: Multidisciplinary perspectives* (pp. 201–254). New York: Springer.

Markides, K. S. (1990). Risk factors, gender and health. *Generations, 14*, 17–21.

Marshall, V. W., & Bengtson, V. L. (1983). Generations: Conflict and cooperation. In M. Bergener, U. Lehr, E. Lang, & R. Schmitz-Scherzer (Eds.), *Aging in the eighties and beyond* (pp. 298–310). New York: Springer.

Mayer, K. U., Allmendinger, J., & Huinink, J. (Eds.). (1991). *Vom Regen in die Traufe: Frauen zwischen Beruf und Familie*. Frankfurt/M.: Campus.

McCrae, R. R. (1993). Moderated analyses of longitudinal personality stability. *Journal of Personality and Social Psychology, 65*, 577–585.

McCrae, R. R., & Costa, P. T., Jr. (1990). *Personality in adulthood*. New York: Guilford.

Meyer, S. L., Murphy, C. M., Cascardi, M., & Birns, B. (1991). Gender and relationships: Beyond the peer group. *American Psychologist, 46*, 537.

Monge, R. (1975). Structure of the self-concept from adolescence through old age. *Experimental Aging Research, 1*, 281–291.

Myers, J. K., Weissman, M. M., Tischler, G. L., Holyer, C. E., Leaf, P. J., Orvaschel, H., Anthony, J. C., Boyd, J. H., Burke, J. D., Kramer, M., & Stolzman, R. (1984). Six-month prevalence of psychiatric disorders in three communities. *Archives of General Psychiatry, 41*, 959–967.

Neugarten, B. L. (1964). *Personality in middle and late life*. New York: Atherton Press.

Neugarten, B. L. (1993). *New psychological findings of the mysteries of the life-cycle* (Cassette recording No. 8). Alexandria, VA: Audio Transcripts.

Niederfranke, A. (1991). *Ältere Frauen in der Auseinandersetzung mit Berufsaufgabe und Partnerverlust*. Stuttgart: Kohlhammer.

Ory, M. G., & Warner, H. R. (Eds.). (1990). *Gender, health, and longevity: Multidisciplinary perspectives*. New York: Springer.

Pillemer, K., & Suttor, J. J. (1991). "Will I ever escape my child's problems?" Effects of adult children's problems on elderly parents. *Journal of Marriage and the Family, 53*, 585–594.

Reedy, M. N. (1982). Personality and aging. In D. S. Woodruff & J. E. Birren (Eds.), *Aging: Scientific perspective and social issues* (pp. 112–136). Monterey, CA: Brooks/Cole.

Riley, M. W., & Riley, J. W., Jr. (1994). Age integration and the lives of older people. *The Gerontologist, 34*, 110–115.

Robins, N., & Regier, D. A. (Eds.). (1991). *Psychiatric disorders in America: The Epidemiologic Catchment Area Study.* New York: Free Press.

Rodin, J., McAvay, G., & Timko, C. (1988). A longitudinal study of depressed mood and sleep disturbances in elderly adults. *Journal of Gerontology: Psychological Sciences, 43*, P45–P53.

Rossi, A. S., & Rossi, P. H. (1990). *Of human bonding: Parent-child-relationships across the life course.* Hawthorne, NY: de Gruyter.

Ryff, C. D., & Baltes, P. B. (1976). Value transition and adult development in women: The instrumentality-terminality hypothesis. *Developmental Psychology, 12*, 567–568.

Seeman, T. E., Charpentier, P. A., Berkman, L. F., Tinetti, M. E., Guralnik, J. M., Albert, M., Blazer, D., & Rowe, J. W. (1994). Predicting changes in physical performance in a high-functioning elderly cohort: MacArthur Studies of Successful Aging. *Journal of Gerontology: Medical Sciences, 49*, M97–M108.

Shock, N. W., Greulich, R. C., Costa, P. T., Jr., Andres, R., Lakatta, E. G., Arenberg, D., & Tobin, J. D. (1984). *Normal human aging: The Baltimore Longitudinal Study on Aging* (NIH Publication No. 84–2450). Washington, DC: Government Printing Office.

Smith, J., & Baltes, M. M. (in press). The role of gender in very old age: Profiles of functioning and everyday life patterns. *Psychology and Aging.*

Thomae, H. (1979). The concept of development and life-span developmental psychology. In P. B. Baltes & O. G. Brim Jr. (Eds.), *Life-span development and behavior* (Vol. 2, pp. 282–312). New York: Academic Press.

Turner, B. F. (1994). Introduction. In B. F. Turner & L. E. Troll (Eds.), *Women growing older* (pp. 1–34). Thousand Oaks, CA: Sage.

Vaillant, G. E. (1990). Avoiding negative life outcomes: Evidence from a forty-five year study. In P. B. Baltes & M. M. Baltes (Eds.), *Successful aging: Perspectives from the behavioral sciences* (pp. 332–358). Cambridge: Cambridge University Press.

Verbrugge, L. M. (1989). Gender, aging, and health. In K. S. Markides (Ed.), *Aging and health: Perspectives on gender, race, ethnicity, and class* (pp. 23–78). Newbury Park, CA: Sage.

Walsh, W. A., Steffen, A., & Gallagher-Thompson, D. (1992). Depressionsniveau und Belastungsverarbeitung bei Betreuern körperlich und geistig beeinträchtigter älterer Menschen. *Verhaltenstherapie, 2*, 231–236.

Whitbourne, S. K., & Weinstock, C. S. (Eds.). (1986). *Adult development.* New York: Holt, Rinehart, & Winston.

Wink, P., & Helson, R. (1993). Personality change in women and their partners. *Journal of Personality and Social Psychology, 65*, 597–605.

CHAPTER 10

Social Relationships in Old Age

Michael Wagner, Yvonne Schütze, and Frieder R. Lang

The aim of this chapter is to describe the number, nature, and functions of social relationships in old age. The consequences of widowhood, childlessness, and institutionalization on the social relationships and loneliness of elderly people are also examined. The findings are based on the accounts of the Berlin Aging Study (BASE) participants and reveal that it is incorrect to assume that the social integration of older adults is marked by a lack of role in society, or that social relationships remain unchanged in quality and quantity into very old age.

There is a high degree of childlessness among those aged 85 years and older, but this can primarily be interpreted as a cohort effect. Although the loss of relatives from one's own generation is a common occurrence in very old age, the experience of being a great-grandparent also gains in importance. No uniform age differences can be found where nonrelatives are concerned either; whereas the number of friends decreases with age, the proportion of old people who include other nonrelatives in their social network remains relatively constant. The social network of widows and widowers has a structure similar to that of married people. However, the childless have smaller networks than parents, and the institutionalized have smaller networks than those living in private households. Married people feel lonely less frequently, whereas the institutionalized and the childless do so more often. Those aged 85 and older do receive substantially more help than they give, but, remarkably, some very old people still support others.

1   Introduction

Research on social relationships in old age – in comparison with research on the structure and function of social relationships in other phases of life – is a particularly complex matter. The social situation of elderly people has been interpreted as a consequence of structural isolation (Parsons, 1943), disengagement (Cumming & Henry, 1961), desocialization (König, 1965), and the lack of a role in society (Rosow, 1967). According to these theories, retirement, children leaving home, and being widowed represent widespread and, for the most part, irreversible losses of role. What is more, modern societies offer older adults very few opportunities to readopt such central social roles. The average life expectancy has increased over recent years, but this prolonged lifetime is not yet socially structured (Riley & Riley, 1986, 1992).

Some have argued that each individual is surrounded by a "convoy" of interaction partners who accompany him or her throughout life (Antonucci, 1985; Kahn & Antonucci, 1980). A further assumption is that the very old, in particular, shift their attention to those interaction partners to whom they feel closest (Carstensen, 1993; Lang & Carstensen, 1994). It is also maintained that it is especially important for older adults in need of help and care to have a well-functioning social network (M. M. Baltes & Silverberg, 1994).

As far as the loss of role is concerned, Rosenmayr (1983) represents the view that retirement, for example, can also be experienced as a liberation from responsibilities, offering the chance to form new relationships and intensify old ones. Parsons's (1943) thesis of the "structural isolation" of the (nuclear) family gave rise to numerous empirical studies that indicate that contacts between generations continue to flourish despite their living in separate households (Rossi & Rossi, 1990; Shanas, 1979).

The birth of grandchildren can lead to new familial relationships, with grandparents, particularly grandmothers, often involved in a second phase of looking after and bringing up children. Also, widowhood does not preclude older people from forming new partnerships. There does not seem to be any considerable normative pressure that would make it harder for widows and widowers to remarry. However, the loss of a large percentage of widows' or widowers' pensions could pose an obstacle to remarriage. Moreover, children's role regarding a parent's remarriage is not known. As there are far fewer older men than women, unmarried older women do have particular difficulties in finding an unmarried man of the same age (cf. Maas et al., Chapter 3 in this volume).

As for nonfamilial relationships, retirement is often linked to the breaking off of collegial relationships, but this does not necessarily pertain to friendships made at the work place. Even moving to a senior citizens' home provides opportunities to develop new relationships (M. M. Baltes, Wahl, & Reichert, 1991). In view of the undisputed maxim that people are always reliant on others, it is important to ask how social relationships are maintained or perhaps even initiated in old age.

Changes in social relationships in old age have only seldom been examined on a longitudinal basis. The Bonn Longitudinal Study demonstrated that the level of role activity was maintained by two-thirds of participants, but decreased sharply among the remaining third (Lehr & Minnemann, 1987). According to results of the Duke University Longitudinal Studies of Aging, the mean number of contacts remained stable for men and dropped slightly for women (Palmore, 1968). The findings of these two longitudinal studies can be summarized as follows: For a large proportion of old people, the extent of social role activities or contacts remains stable over the aging process. For a smaller proportion it decreases, so that when looking at the entire elderly population, an average drop in the level of social relationships can be seen. Similar results have been observed within the Berkeley Older Generation Study. Field and Minkler (1988) reported that familial relationships remain stable into old age, whereas friendships lose importance, especially for men. Correspondingly, cross-sectional studies showed negative age effects with respect to network size, the number of social roles and social contacts.

Apart from studying the number of social relationships maintained by old people, it is important to examine the functions that these relationships fulfill for the interaction partners involved. Exchange theory assumes that social relationships are constituted and stabilized on the basis of an exchange of material and nonmaterial goods, and a universally valid reciprocity norm, which stipulates that any social exchange must be fair and equally advantageous for each interaction partner (Gouldner, 1960; Walster, Berscheid, & Walster, 1973). The extent to which an unbalanced exchange is accepted depends on the nature of the relationship and resources exchanged, as well as the expectations of the interaction partners. Extremely one-sided relationships are usually seen as unsatisfactory, and are terminated (Roberto, 1989). This does not imply that every action always requires an immediate reaction. Particularly in relationships where the social distance is short, a period of time often elapses before the exchange is completed. In close relationships with family or friends, each interaction partner is more likely to be interested in the well-being of the other person than in the short-term restoration of reciprocity (Clark & Reis, 1988). Exchange theory highlights the fact that older adults themselves have an active part to play in the maintenance of their social relationships, by helping others or engaging in activities with others.

2   Widowhood, Childlessness, Institutionalization, and Their Impact on Social Isolation

The aim of this chapter is to describe the number, nature, and functions of social relationships in old age, and the degree of loneliness among the old and very old. As social exchange relationships were not directly observed within BASE (in contrast to studies on the social behavior of those living in old age homes, for example; see M. M. Baltes, 1996), we are limited to global measures of the functions of social relationships taken from interview data. On the one hand, we differentiate the objectively isolated (i.e., old people who have few or no social relationships) from the subjectively isolated (i.e., those who feel lonely and isolated; cf. Elbing, 1991; Schütze & Lang, 1996). On the other hand, we concentrate on factors that – from both the theoretical and the social policy perspective – are seen to foster social isolation and subjective loneliness; (1) widowhood, (2) childlessness, and (3) institutionalization. What influence do these circumstances exert on the onset of social isolation and loneliness among the old and very old?

Widowhood entails the loss of an often long-standing and emotionally highly loaded relationship. It is immaterial how satisfying or discordant the relationship proved to be (cf. Niederfranke, 1991). The extent to which widowhood affects the structure and functions of the social network has yet to be clarified. It could, for example, imply the loss of a plurality of roles and thus a decrease in the number of friends, or the termination of activities formerly engaged in with the spouse. The counterhypothesis is a compensation or substitution model by which a loss of role in one area of life leads to an increased involvement in another area of life. Widows and widowers are, for example, able to devote more time to friends and acquaintances and intensify their contacts with relatives (Cantor, 1979).

In contrast to widowhood, there has been relatively little research into the effects of *childlessness* on the structure and functioning of social relationships in old age. Most studies report that the childless receive less informal help (Goldberg, Kantrow, Kremen, & Lauter, 1986; Hays, 1984). Some studies also show that the childless are more socially isolated than parents (Bachrach, 1980; Ishii-Kuntz & Seccombe, 1989) and have fewer friends and neighborly contacts (Rempel, 1985). Childless people living alone concentrate more on other relationships such as siblings (Cicirelli, 1982; Taylor, Chatters, & Mays, 1988). Widowed or single childless people express a lower level of subjective well-being and feel lonelier than widowed or single parents, whereas married childless people cannot be differentiated from married parents in this regard (Beckman & Houser, 1982). Thus, we can deduce that childlessness is of serious consequence when it coincides with other factors, such as widowhood. It seems pertinent to take marital status into consideration when investigating the possible effects of childlessness on the structure and functioning of older adults' social networks.

Relationships between parents and children are characterized by normative obligations; they cannot easily be terminated. They are based on both emotional ties – the harmonious nature of which is by no means a certainty – and reciprocal feelings of commitment (Schütze & Wagner, 1991). Children of widowed parents thus feel particularly bound to support their parents; their feelings of responsibility are called on far more than if both parents are still alive. Hence, old parents have a structural advantage over the childless with respect to emotional and practical support. This raises the question as to whether the childless actually do receive less help, or whether alternative ways of securing social support are open to them (Lang, 1994).

Institutionalization is the third condition associated with the idea of social isolation, an image that has been propagated by reports in the mass media. In the social sciences homes are characterized as "total institutions" where inhabitants are "governed" and any scope for individualized interactions is eliminated (Goffman, 1961). However, it is not known whether this appraisal of the social situation in homes corresponds to reality, or whether social networks that help act against social isolation exist even in the conditions of a total institution (cf. M. M. Baltes, 1996).

3   Social Relationships: Terms, Classification, and Assessment Design

Social relationships can be classified using several different methods. One classification commonly used in research refers to *role relationship types*. These can be broadly subdivided into relationships with kin and nonkin. Where kin are concerned, we will deal primarily with spouses and partners, children, and siblings. With respect to nonkin, we will concentrate on friendships and contacts with neighbors.

A further classification criterion differentiates social relationships according to their *function* or *performance*. Here, we distinguish three functional aspects of social relationships. First we examine supportive functions of social relationships; these can be subdivided into instrumental and emotional support (Cobb, 1976; House & Kahn, 1985; Wills, 1985). Second, we look at socializing; despite not strictly counting as help, this is an important function of social relationships (Rook, 1990). Third, we consider affection as a dimension of social interaction which is frequently neglected in social relationship research (cf. Elbing, 1991; Walsh, 1991).

As social relationships can be described in several ways, two different procedures were chosen for the data collection. The Sociology and Social Policy Unit was interested in information about immediate members of the family. All family members were recorded, whether or not the BASE participant had any intensive contact with them. A set of sociodemographic data (e.g., age, sex, marital status, occupation, number of children) was compiled for every sibling, child, and grandchild, irrespective of whether the relative was alive or dead. In cases where the relative was still alive, the frequency of contacts and the features of social support were noted.

The Psychology Unit gathered information on the social network using a modified version of the Network Questionnaire developed by Kahn and Antonucci (1980). BASE participants classified the individuals in their network according to the degree of emotional closeness; thus, the only persons named in this procedure were those to whom the participant felt close. Using a circle diagram, participants positioned persons to whom they felt very close in the first circle, those to whom they felt close in the second circle, and less close but nevertheless important people were placed in the third circle. The following data were compiled for each individual mentioned: nature of the role relationship (e.g., partner, son, neighbor, etc.), duration of the relationship, person's age, frequency of contacts, and changes in the quality of the relationship over the past five years.

Information was also gathered on help given and received. Interviewees stated whom they had helped and/or whom they had received help from in the following areas: (1) help with practical things, (2) help with errands or shopping, (3) nursing care, (4) talking about problems and worries, and (5) encouragement and reassurance. Whereas the first three elements constitute instrumental support, we define the last two as emotional support. Exchange of affection (operationalized as nonsexual physical contact such as hugs and kisses) is treated as an independent dimension of social relationships.

"Socializing" refers to visits received and made, and activities engaged in with others. The frequency with which interviewees met or visited another individual over the past 12 months was ascertained using a seven-point scale ranging from "daily" to "never." This scale was transformed into an index giving the number of days per year (from 0 to 325) on which an interviewee saw a particular person (Frankel & DeWit, 1989). In this chapter we will deal only with the frequency of contacts with children, siblings, and friends. For participants with several children, siblings, or friends, the maximum frequencies are given.

Loneliness was investigated using a slightly modified German version of the eight-item short form of the revised UCLA Loneliness Scale (Russell, Cutrona, Rose, & Yurko, 1984; cf. Smith & Baltes, Chapter 7). The scale reflects two aspects of loneliness: emotional and social. Emotional loneliness refers to statements that describe the feeling of having no close friend and/or being alone in the world, whereas social loneliness deals with the feeling of not being sufficiently embedded in a social network (Elbing, 1991; Weiss, 1973).[1]

The assessment methods of the Psychology and Sociology Units have certain similarities and differences. For example, data about kin with whom there is a close emotional tie or a support relationship are compiled under both procedures. However, the Sociology Unit also gathered information on immediate family members with whom there is no close contact, whereas the Psychology Unit collected data on close emotional relationships to distant kin (nephews, nieces, children-in-law) and nonkin (friends, acquaintances, neighbors).

4   The Structure of Social Networks in Old Age

Who makes up the social network of older adults? In this section we describe the structural features of social networks in older adulthood. We first ask to what extent certain relationships with kin and nonkin are present in old age. As far as familial relationships are concerned, we start with the participants' generation – partners and siblings – and then move directly down the family line to two, three, or four generations, to children, grandchildren, and great-grandchildren. We then turn to the remaining relatives, as well as friends, acquaintances, and neighbors. When looking at parent-child relationships and friendships, we also consider the frequency of contact. Finally, we observe age differ-

---

[1] An exploratory main axis factor analysis with oblique rotation of the factors confirmed the two expected subdimensions and accounted for a total of 43% of the variance of the eight items. The intercorrelation of the rotated factors was .58. In the following we use only the sum totals of the subscales (unit-weighted composite). The internal consistency of the eight z-transformed items is $\alpha = .77$.

Table 10.1. *Percent distribution of role relationships in old age*

	All age groups	70–84	85+
Spouses	23.5 (151)	27.3 (102)	8.8 (49)
Children	72.6 (352)	75.3 (196)	61.9 (156)
Grandchildren	61.2 (306)	62.4 (170)	56.6 (136)
Siblings	44.9 (184)	47.5 (121)	34.6 (63)
Great-grandchildren	18.9 (112)	16.4 (41)	28.9 (71)
Children-in-law	40.5 (184)	41.9 (105)	34.8 (79)
Other kin	66.4 (336)	67.0 (175)	64.1 (161)
Friends	63.5 (281)	68.6 (171)	43.3 (110)
Acquaintances	48.5 (244)	48.2 (123)	50.1 (121)
Neighbors	28.5 (128)	28.2 (68)	29.7 (60)
Other nonkin	14.3 (71)	14.3 (36)	14.3 (35)

Note. Weighted; the number of cases (unweighted) is shown in parentheses.

ences with respect to the size of the complete social network and ask whether these differences can be accounted for by marital status, childlessness, and institutionalization. Table 10.1 shows the distribution of different types of role relationships for two age groups.

4.1   Marriage and Partnership

Let us first deal with the frequency of marriage and partnership (weighted values are used in the following). In former West Berlin, about a quarter of all elderly people are married, and approximately half are widowed. Taking the large age and gender differences into consideration, however, qualifies these values; whereas about three-quarters of all men between 70 and 74 and one-quarter of those aged 95 and above are married, only 20% of 70- to 74-year-old women are married and there are very few very old women (85 and above) whose husbands are still alive. Marital status reveals not only enormous age differences, but also the most distinct gender differences: 63% of men aged 70 and above are married, compared with only 10% of women.

A proportion of the marriages have existed for an extremely long time: One man, for example, has been married for 70 years; another, on the other hand, only for one year. The age at which the current marriage was entered into also spans a broad range; four participants were 21 years old, whereas one man was 84 at his last wedding. Of those who were widowed at the time of the interviews, almost 60% (mainly women) lost their partner before turning 70. As in other phases of life, however, being unmarried does not necessarily mean living without a partner. Fourteen percent of unmarried men and 5% of unmarried women live with their partners. Thus, it is not correct to regard cohabitation as solely a phenomenon of early and middle adulthood.

4.2   Siblings

Just under one-half of all elderly men and women have at least one brother or sister who is still alive (Table 10.1). This mean value is, however, less significant than it may seem, as the proportion of older people who no longer have any siblings increases sub-

Figure 10.1. Current childlessness by age (men: *n*=255; women: *n*=256). Current childlessness means that participants never had children or that that they have survived all of their children. Columns representing men are shown in the front, and women are shown in the back row.

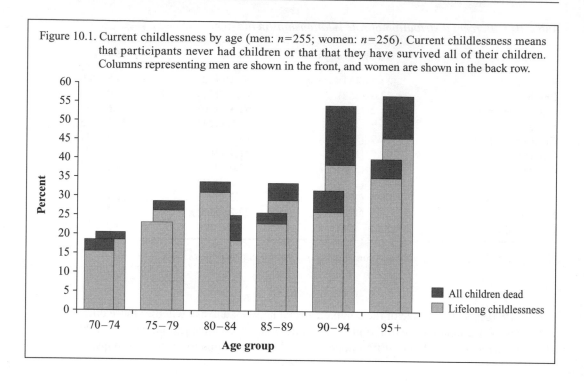

stantially with age. Whereas half of the 70- to 74-year-olds have at least one sibling, only 15% of those aged 95 and older do. The vast majority of older adults had at least one sibling; outliving all of them is clearly an extremely widespread occurrence in very old age.

4.3   Parenthood

The most commonly occurring role relationship in the social networks of men and women aged 70 and over is parenthood. More than 76% of men and 70% of women have at least one child who is still alive. Nearly 86% of married people have children, 76% of widows and widowers, 75% of the divorced, and 15% of singles. Parents see their children on average every four to five days; the frequency increases slightly as the parents grow older.

The level of childlessness among West Berlin's elderly population is very high.[2] Current childlessness can be due to lifelong childlessness or to the fact that all children have already died. As shown in Figure 10.1, a significant proportion of old people have outlived all of their children. It is evident that the probability of outliving a child increases with the age of the parent.

The high level of lifelong childlessness must, however, be interpreted as a cohort effect (Dinkel & Milenovic, 1992; Dorbritz, 1992) that is particularly pronounced in West

---

[2] Comparative studies (the description of which is beyond the scope of this chapter) have shown that the degree of childlessness found in BASE is not only higher than the West German average for these cohorts, but also exceeds that of another large city, Hamburg.

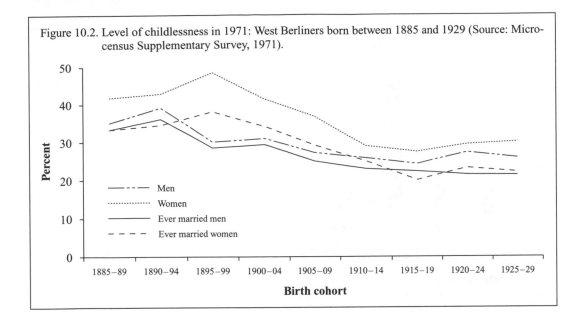

Figure 10.2. Level of childlessness in 1971: West Berliners born between 1885 and 1929 (Source: Microcensus Supplementary Survey, 1971).

Berlin. Figure 10.2 presents data from the Microcensus Supplementary Survey of 1971 (Statistisches Bundesamt [Federal Statistical Office], 1972) showing the proportion of childless West Berliners born between 1885 and 1929. Microcensus interviewees were asked, "Do you have children of your own?" – a question that refers only to blood relatives, but does not differentiate precisely between current and lifelong childlessness.

The levels of childlessness among all old men and women, and in the subgroup of persons who were married at some point in their lives, are also contrasted in Figure 10.2. It is evident that the proportions of childless men and women, and of those who were ever married and remained without children, decrease over the span from the oldest age group (born 1895–99) to the youngest (1915–19). Childlessness is more prevalent among women of every age group, but a particular age/cohort difference can be perceived in those born between 1895 and 1909.

Whereas the only remaining immediate relatives of the lifelong childless are from their *own* generation, parents have frequently become *grandparents and great-grandparents*. As shown in Table 10.1, the proportion of grandparents among the 70- to 84-year-olds is almost as high as that among those aged 85 and over (62% and 57% respectively). The proportion of participants with great-grandchildren increases by age group; 16% of 70- to 84-year-olds have at least one great-grandchild compared with 29% of those aged 85 and over.

4.4   *Size and Generational Structure of Families*

If the size of the family network is defined as the number of immediate family members (i.e., spouse, children, grandchildren, and great-grandchildren), 126 of the BASE participants have no family left. This corresponds to approximately one-quarter

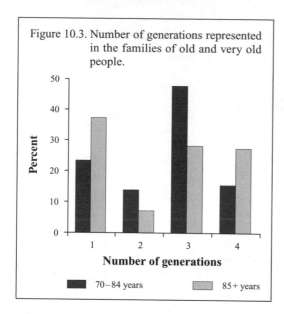

Figure 10.3. Number of generations represented in the families of old and very old people.

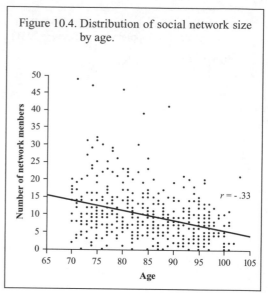

Figure 10.4. Distribution of social network size by age.

of all West Berliners aged 70 and above when projected onto the West Berlin population. In comparison, one interviewee has 33 close relatives. The number of immediate family members decreases only very slightly with age ($r = -.15$), but is always lower for women than for men. In other words, the higher level of childlessness among older participants does not generate a clear reduction in the average size of the family, as it is leveled out by the increasing numbers of grandchildren and great-grandchildren (Johnson & Troll, 1996).

However, the increasing level of childlessness through the age groups leads to a *polarization* with regard to the number of generations in a family. We have already shown that childlessness is predominantly a cohort effect. Here we see that the older age groups include many more persons with no children, but also many more four-generation families than the younger age groups (see Table 10.1 and Fig. 10.3).

4.5   Distant Kin, Friends, and Neighbors

Let us now turn to distant kin and nonkin. Distant kin feature relatively frequently in older people's social networks – they are named by 66%. At least one friend is mentioned by 64% of older adults, 49% have acquaintances, and 29% nominate at least one neighbor (weighted values; cf. Table 10.1).[3] It is striking that only the number of old people who have at least one friend varies clearly over the age groups; 69% of 70- to 84-year-olds have at least one friend, but only 43% of those aged 85 and over (Table 10.1). Those who live in institutional settings are far less likely to have friends than those in private households (34% and 66% respectively). As far as marital status is concerned,

[3] The only differences between men and women are with respect to their attachment to the neighborhood; women are more likely to include neighbors in their network.

singles are most likely to mention a friend (76%), followed by married people (67%), the widowed (61%), and the divorced (61%).

Gauged by the frequency of contact, friends appear to play a very important role in old age. BASE participants meet their friends on average every nine days. Although face-to-face contact with children is more frequent, it is evident that friendships are also cultivated in old age. There are only slight gender and age differences, but obvious differences where marital status is concerned. Widows and widowers see their friends much more regularly than married, divorced, or single people.

However, it is not as easy to determine whether the intensity of relationships with neighbors varies according to age group. There are no distinguishable age differences in the frequency with which neighbors are cited as members of the social network. The average number of neighbors named, however, decreases from 9.4 in the youngest age group (70–74) to 5.5 in the oldest (95+). The amount of help given to, or received from, neighbors also decreases with age (70–74: 24% vs. 95+: 10%).

4.6   Size of the Social Network

In a last step we will examine the size of the egocentered network, that is, the number of persons to whom the interviewee feels emotionally close, and who were named in one of the three circles of the Network Questionnaire. The size of the total network of the BASE participants ranges from 0 to 49 persons; the mean value is 10.9. The average number of persons in each circle did not vary (first circle: 3.5; second circle: 3.8; third circle: 3.7 persons).

Let us now consider the effect of age, marital status, childlessness, and place of residence on the network size. It is evident that the network size diminishes as the participants get older (cf. Fig. 10.4), and that the negative correlation between age and the number of network partners is lowest in the first circle (for details, see Lang & Carstensen, 1994; cf. Smith & Baltes, Chapter 7).

A hierarchical multiple regression shows how the age effect on the network size is mediated by the other independent variables (see Table 10.2). As expected, the influence of chronological age continually decreases as the other variables are included in the model. A significant negative age effect on network size does persist, however. It is notable that the network size of male and female participants is almost identical (cf. Minnemann, 1994). The regression analysis further shows that divorcées have the smallest social networks. Whereas married people name an average of 14.1 network partners, widows and widowers mention 10.6 and divorcées only 7.8 persons. Childless old people have, as expected, relatively small networks (8.1 persons vs. 12.0 persons for parents), as do the institutionalized (only 4.5 network partners compared with 10.3 for those in private households).

5   Functions of Social Relationships in Old Age

What are the functions of the informal social relationships of the old and very old? We will first describe the range of instrumental and emotional social support given and received by older people, the scope of their interaction with visitors and activities with others, and the extent of affectionate exchanges. We will then ask whether these forms of social interaction can lessen feelings of loneliness.

Table 10.2. *Results of a hierarchical multiple regression on the size of the ego-centered network*

Effect	Steps			
	1	2	3	4
1				
Age	-.33**	-.32**	-.24**	-.24**
Gender (w = 1, m = 0)	-.05	.04	.06	.06
2				
Marital status[a]				
Married	—	.13	.12	.12
Divorced	—	-.14**	-.14**	-.14**
Single	—	-.09	-.01	.01
3				
Parental status[b]		—	.17**	.16**
4				
Place of residence[c]	—	—	—	-.18**
ΔR^2	11.0**	4.5**	2.4**	2.9**
R^2	11.0	15.4	17.8	20.8
Adj. R^2	10.6	14.6	16.9	19.7

Note. Network size refers to the number of social relationships given in the circle diagram.

* $p < .01$, ** $p < .001$.

[a]Marital status was dummy coded; the widowed form the reference category.

[b]Parental status: parent (= 1) versus childless (= 0).

[c]Institutionalized (= 1) versus community-dwelling (= 0).

5.1 *Exchange of Support, Socializing, and Affection*

Receiving informal help does not only mean that concrete support is forthcoming, but also symbolizes care and sympathy provided by the social environment. As has been confirmed by numerous empirical findings on the multiplex nature of social relationships (Litwak, 1985; Simons, 1983), they are commonly "multifunctional" in old age.

The great majority of old people have at least one person who helps them (87%) or whom they help (86%). One can assume that the older the person, the more help is needed and received. Here, too, we should bear in mind that the data to which we refer are drawn from participants' self-reports, and thus have already undergone cognitive processing.

These reports indeed indicate that the proportion of persons from whom old people receive emotional or instrumental help (but do not themselves help) increases over the six age groups. Figure 10.5 illustrates that the percentage of relationships in which old people help others decreases sharply when the younger and older age groups are compared. Network members are subdivided into three categories in Figure 10.5: (1) those

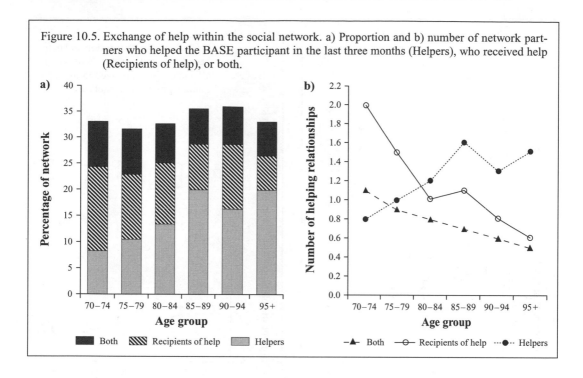

Figure 10.5. Exchange of help within the social network. a) Proportion and b) number of network partners who helped the BASE participant in the last three months (Helpers), who received help (Recipients of help), or both.

who help others, (2) those who are helped, and (3) those who both give and receive help. Figure 10.5a shows the proportion of all network members represented by each of these categories, while Figure 10.5b illustrates the number of relationships in each category. Thus 70- to 74-year-olds characterize 9% of all network members as helpers compared with 20% of those aged 95 and over (this corresponds to an average of 0.8 and 1.5 support relationships respectively). Note, however, that due to sole reliance on self-reports, we do not know how frequently help was actually given and/or received.

Considering support relationships from the perspective of exchange theory, it is evident that in the very old age groups less help is given than received. As Figure 10.5 shows, the proportion and, above all, the number of network members who receive help decreases as the participants grow older. The 70- to 74-year-olds, for example, claimed to help an average of two network members without receiving any help in return. The corresponding value for the oldest age group is only 0.6. If we add the number of network members who only receive help to the number who both give and receive help, we can nonetheless establish that even those aged 95 and over offered emotional or even instrumental help to one person on average over the past three months.

It is also notable that the proportion of informal helpers does not exceed one-quarter of all social relationships in any of the age groups. By far the largest part of the network is made up of people who are not classified as helpers. This means that even in old age social interactions are not centered on social support relationships. After all, the BASE participants named on average 3.7 network partners ($SD = 2.5$) with whom they "socialized." Here we must bear in mind that due to the multifunctional character of informal social interactions in particular, this categorization does not rule out the possibility of the

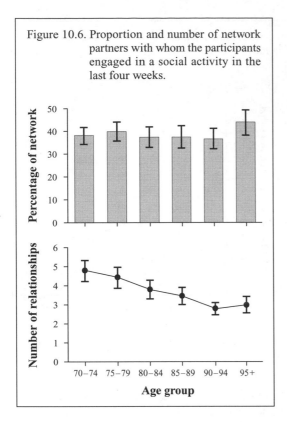

Figure 10.6. Proportion and number of network partners with whom the participants engaged in a social activity in the last four weeks.

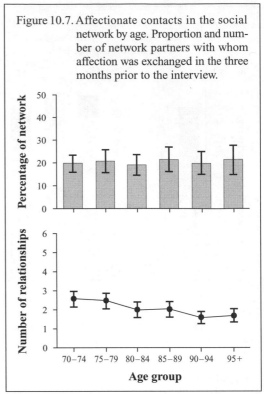

Figure 10.7. Affectionate contacts in the social network by age. Proportion and number of network partners with whom affection was exchanged in the three months prior to the interview.

relationship also including some aspect of help. As we can see from Figure 10.6, the number of people with whom the participants engaged in activities decreases with age, but the proportion of the social network they represent does not. More than a third of BASE participants' social contacts (M = 39%, *SD* = 26.1) consists of interactions with visitors and activities with others.

Older adults name on average two persons (*M* = 2.0, *SD* = 1.8) with whom they exchange affection. Those in the youngest age group (70–74) mention on average one more person than the oldest (95+). The percentage of network members with whom the participants are affectionate remains more or less constant (cf. Fig. 10.7). So, although the actual number of persons with whom the participants are affectionate decreases, members of all six age groups maintained affectionate contact with on average 20% of their network partners (*SD* = 20.5).

5.2 The Functions of Social Relationships with Respect to Marital Status, Childlessness, and Place of Residence

In this section we will first discuss how the functions of social relationships differ when marital status, childlessness, and place of residence are taken into consideration. We will then ask how closely each of these circumstances is connected to a higher

Table 10.3. *The functions of social relationships with respect to marital status, parental status, and place of residence*

	Receiving informal help		Providing help		Socializing		Affection	
Marital status								
Married	1.8	(1.1)	2.2	(1.6)	4.5	(2.7)	2.3	(1.6)
Widowed	2.0	(1.5)	1.6	(1.7)	3.6	(2.4)	1.6	(1.7)
Divorced	1.7	(1.5)	2.1	(2.3)	2.6	(2.2)	1.5	(1.6)
Single	1.5	(1.4)	1.9	(2.0)	2.5	(2.4)	1.3	(1.8)
Effect sizes (η^2)[a]	0.8%		4.5%**		1.6%		0.7%	
Parental status								
Parent	2.0	(1.3)	2.0	(1.9)	4.0	(2.5)	2.3	(1.8)
Childless	1.5	(1.4)	1.5	(1.5)	3.0	(2.4)	1.4	(1.6)
Effect sizes (η^2)[a]	1.9%**		0.3%		0.8%		3.0%**	
Place of residence								
Community-dwelling	2.0	(1.3)	2.0	(1.8)	4.0	(2.5)	2.1	(1.8)
Institutionalized	1.0	(1.1)	0.9	(1.3)	1.8	(1.6)	1.2	(1.6)
Effect sizes (η^2)[a]	5.6%**		1.1%		3.5%**		0.6%	

Note. Values given for all four functions of social relationships are based on statements made about the three months before the interview. Data are given as means, with standard deviations in parentheses.
* $p < .01$, ** $p < .001$ (for univariate F-tests).
[a]Effect sizes were calculated controlling for the factors marital status, parental status, and place of residence, and give the proportion of the total variance accounted for by each factor.

risk of loneliness. Can this risk be accounted for by the fact that certain functions of informal social relationships are not as readily available to the childless, widowed, and institutionalized?

As Table 10.3 shows, older adults with children receive more help and affection than childless older adults. Although parents receive more help, they do not give significantly more help than the childless, and they do not claim to socialize more. Hence, social support and affection are more readily available to old parents, even though the childless help and socialize with others to the same degree. It seems that there is more of a time delay in exchange relationships between parents and children, whereas relationships with others are characterized more by short-term exchanges (Wentowski, 1981). Parents thus make a larger "profit" in the help they receive than the childless.

A different picture emerges where marital status is concerned. Whereas married, widowed, divorced, and single elderly people do not differ significantly in the amount they socialize, receive help, and exchange affection, married people provide more help for others than the widowed and single. Thus, married people help others more, but do not receive more social support or affection than unmarried people. The reason for this may be that married people have comparatively more scope to provide support, in helping the spouse, for example.

Let us now turn to the informal social relationships of those living in institutional settings. The BASE findings concur with the general assumption that the institutionalized receive far less informal help and report less socializing than those living in private households. Here, it is interesting to ask how much emotional support is given by professional caregivers. Our findings show that – from the participants' point of view at least – only a small amount of this form of affection is supplied by professional caregivers. We must bear in mind that the aim of the assessment was to compile a list of those network members to whom the interviewee felt emotionally close, and it is notable that 9% of the institutionalized stated that they receive emotional help from professional caregivers.

We did not deal only with the positive functions of social relationships but also with their deficits; for example, we considered those who needed help but did not receive any. Our results indicate that marital status is strongly linked to the level of social support deficit. Unmarried people miss emotional support and affection more than married people; the desire for more instrumental support is particularly marked among the divorced (13%) and single (20%). The childless do not report any greater deficits in emotional or instrumental help than parents, but their need for more affection was significantly higher (12% for the childless, 6% for parents).

We should also note that the institutionalized do not differ from those living in private households. It seems that the main factor leading to a subjective need for more support is the lack of a partner and/or children rather than the place of residence, as is often assumed. Married people rarely live in institutions (0.4%), whereas 10% of the widowed and divorced, and 21% of singles have given up their own home. More childless old people live in institutions than parents (17% vs. 6%).

6   Loneliness in Old Age

We now ask how the structure of social networks and the functions of social relationships affect the degree of loneliness among elderly people (see also Bundesministerium für Familie und Senioren [Federal Ministry for Family Affairs and Senior Citizens], 1993). Which factors are connected to loneliness in old age? How do the various functions of social relationships contribute to alleviating or intensifying loneliness?

A hierarchical multiple regression analysis was conducted to examine the effects of marital status, parental status (i.e., whether or not the participants have children), and institutionalization on loneliness. Results show that loneliness was greater in older as compared with younger age groups (Table 10.4). Age differences from 70 to 103 years accounted for 7% of the total variance of feelings of loneliness. Men and women did not differ significantly on the 1% level where loneliness is concerned. In a second step, the effects of marital and parental status and institutionalization were investigated. These accounted for a further 8% of the variance. Widows and widowers reported feeling more lonely than married people, but do not differ significantly from the divorced and single. The childless and the institutionalized are more lonely than old people who have children or who live in a private household. A third step examined the functions of social relationships, help given and received, socializing, and affection. These factors accounted for a further 10% of the variance of loneliness; the effect of age lessened progressively.

These findings suggest that the observed age effect is primarily mediated by social relationships. The very old are more lonely than the old if they exchange less affection with others and socialize less. Surprisingly, the exchange of support does not have any

Table 10.4. *Results of hierarchical multiple regression on feelings of loneliness in old age*

Effect	Steps		
	1	2	3
1			
Age	.26**	.16**	.05
Gender (w = 1, m = 0)	.07	-.02	-.04
2			
Marital status [a]			
Married	—	-.16**	-.12
Widowed	—	.08	.03
Single	—	-.07	-.09
Parental status[b]	—	-.17**	-.11*
Place of residence[c]	—	.17**	.10
3			
Help received	—	—	.03
Help given	—	—	-.10
Socializing	—	—	-.19**
Affection	—	—	-.15*
ΔR^2	7.7**	8.3**	9.8**
R^2	7.7	16.0	25.8
Adj. R^2	7.3	14.8	24.1

$* p < .01, ** p < .001.$
[a]Marital status was dummy coded; the widowed form the reference category.
[b]Parental status: parent (= 1) versus childless (= 0).
[c]Institutionalized (= 1) versus community-dwelling (= 0).

direct influence on how lonely older adults feel. The analyses show very distinctly that the number of people with whom one socializes or exchanges affection is the decisive factor where loneliness is concerned. We must bear two aspects in mind when interpreting this result. First, it is theoretically plausible that loneliness, on the one hand, and socializing and affection, on the other hand, have a mutual influence on each other. Second, it is possible that both factors are dependent on personality features (cf. Smith & Baltes, Chapter 7; Staudinger et al., Chapter 11).

7   Discussion

Three aspects of the social relationships of older adults were investigated in this chapter. First, the distribution of role relationships with kin and nonkin was described in detail; second, the extent to which old people give or receive certain forms of social support was examined; and, third, loneliness as a possible result of social isolation was discussed. Particular attention was paid to the effects of widowhood, childlessness, and institutionalization on the social relationships of older adults.

Although the size of the social network decreases with age, and at least one-third of old West Berliners have no immediate relatives (spouse, children, grandchildren, great-grandchildren), a more detailed exploration of each of the role relationships reveals that for a number of reasons it is not productive to make generalizations.

Although parenthood is the role relationship that occurs most often in old age, it is surprising to note that over a quarter of the elderly population of West Berlin is childless. As far as old people of the future are concerned, there will at first be a drop in this high level of childlessness, as the parents of the "baby boomers," born between approximately 1930 and 1940 (the postwar baby boom in Germany reached its peak in 1964), will not reach old age until after the turn of the century (Dinkel & Milenovic, 1992). The higher level of childlessness among those aged 85 and above compared with that of 70- to 84-year-olds is also essentially a cohort effect, even when the fact that the probability of outliving all of one's children increases with age is disregarded. Thus, the widespread prognosis that more and more older adults will be childless in the future, and will therefore be dependent on public institutions, is unfounded – at least for the next few decades. A high level of childlessness has a polarizing influence on the number of relatives in the network. Whereas the number of role relationships increases for those with children due to grandchildren and great-grandchildren, the childless have fewer role relationships.

A further aspect prevents us from making generalizations about social relationships in old age: Some role relationships increase in old age, some remain stable, and some decrease. Here, we must stress that only cross-sectional data were analyzed.

A detailed analysis of familial relationships reveals that the loss of all relatives from one's own generation is a widespread occurrence in very old age. The distribution of grandparenthood barely changes in old age, however, and, as already mentioned, great-grandparenthood becomes more and more common.

Turning to nonfamilial network members, it is evident that the number of old people who report having a friend becomes lower with age. The proportion of older persons who include an acquaintance, neighbor, or nonrelative in their network remains fairly stable, however. This suggests that older adults make distinctions in their concepts of friendship. Whereas acquaintanceships can be struck up easily, they are also more noncommittal; friendships are based on long-lasting relationships and cannot be easily replaced.

Findings on age differences in the frequency of contact with children and friends also contradict the image of a general isolation that increases with age. The frequency of visits between parents and children remains very stable. This is also true for friendships; old people who have friends meet them less than they meet their children, but there are no clear age differences in the frequency of contacts with friends.

It is not correct to assume that old people only receive support from others. The proportion of network members who help older adults does increase with age, but older adults also help others well into very old age. Here, we must remember that data on social relationships were gleaned from self-reports and not from direct observations of behavior.

One question that has not yet been adequately answered is whether the loss of interaction partners in old age is cumulative, or whether it can be compensated by the intensification of other contacts. Divorced people do have relatively small networks, but widows and widowers differ only slightly from married people where their social networks are concerned. It would seem that there are insufficient grounds to suggest that the effect is cumulative.

As far as the institutionalized are concerned, a cumulation of factors contributes to both social isolation and increased loneliness. The institutionalized are often widowed or single, have comparatively few social relationships, are therefore probably more often lonely, and are physically and mentally less fit than those living in private households (cf. Borchelt et al., Chapter 15). We suggest that the social isolation of the institutionalized stems not only from the fact that they have no immediate kin or are worse off where health is concerned; it could be that the institutionalized do not elicit such feelings of responsibility from their environment as do, for example, those living in private households.

In other words, the social relationships of older adults in private households are maintained thanks to everyday gestures, conversations, offers of help, and attention that demand little time or effort. The institutionalized do not have such scope for contact with others; they are cared for merely in the formal sense. They receive only official visits that take up a certain amount of time and demand a different conversational tone than from a visitor who just drops in. Those living alone in private households are integrated in their network partners' everyday lives; this does not apply to the institutionalized and their social relationships.

References

Antonucci, T. C. (1985). Personal characteristics, social support, and social behavior. In R. H. Binstock & E. Shanas (Eds.), *Handbook of aging and the social sciences* (2nd ed., pp. 94–128). New York: Van Nostrand Reinhold.

Bachrach, C. A. (1980). Childlessness and social isolation among the elderly. *Journal of Marriage and the Family, 42,* 627–637.

Baltes, M. M. (1996). *The many faces of dependency in old age.* Cambridge: Cambridge University Press.

Baltes, M. M., & Silverberg, S. (1994). The dynamics between dependency and autonomy: Illustrations across the life span. In D. L. Featherman, R. M. Lerner, & M. Perlmutter (Eds.), *Life-span development and behavior* (Vol. 12, pp. 41–90). Hillsdale, NJ: Erlbaum.

Baltes, M. M., Wahl, H.-W., & Reichert, M. (1991). Successful aging in long-term care institutions? In K. W. Schaie & M. P. Lawton (Eds.), *Annual review of gerontology and geriatrics* (Vol. 11, pp. 311–337). New York: Springer.

Beckman, L. J., & Houser, B. B. (1982). The consequences of childlessness on the social-psychological well-being of older women. *Journal of Gerontology, 37,* 243–250.

Bundesministerium für Familie und Senioren (Ed.). (1993). *Erster Altenbericht: Die Lebenssituation älterer Menschen in Deutschland.* Bonn.

Cantor, M. H. (1979). Neighbors and friends: An overlooked resource in the informal support system. *Research on Aging, 1,* 434–463.

Carstensen, L. L. (1993). Motivation for social contact across the life-span: A theory of socioemotional selectivity. In J. Jacobs (Ed.), *Nebraska Symposium on Motivation* (Vol. 40, pp. 209–254). Lincoln: University of Nebraska Press.

Cicirelli, V. G. (1982). Kin relationships of childless and one-child elderly in relation to social services. *Journal of Gerontological Social Work, 4,* 19–33.

Clark, M. S., & Reis, H. T. (1988). Interpersonal processes in close relationships. In M. R. Rosenzweig & L. W. Porter (Eds.), *Annual review of psychology* (Vol. 39, pp. 609–672). Palo Alto, CA: Annual Reviews.

Cobb, S. (1976). Social support as a moderator of life stress. *Psychosomatic Medicine, 38,* 300–314.

Cumming, E., & Henry, W. (1961). *Growing old: The process of disengagement.* New York: Basic Books.

Dinkel, R. H., & Milenovic, I. (1992). Die Kohortenfertilität von Männern und Frauen. *Kölner Zeitschrift für Soziologie und Sozialpsychologie, 44*, 55–75.

Dorbritz, J. (1992). Nuptualität, Fertilität und familiale Lebensformen in der sozialen Transformation: Übergang zu einer neuen Bevölkerungsweise in Ostdeutschland? *Zeitschrift für Bevölkerungswissenschaft, 18*, 167–196.

Elbing, E. (1991). *Einsamkeit*. Göttingen: Hogrefe.

Field, D., & Minkler, M. (1988). Continuity and change in social support between young-old and old-old or very-old age. *Journal of Gerontology: Psychological Sciences, 43*, P100–P106.

Frankel, B. G., & DeWit, B. G. (1989). Geographic distance and intergenerational contact: An empirical examination of the relationship. *Journal of Aging Studies, 3*, 139–162.

Goffman, E. (1961). *Asylums: Essays on the social situation of mental patients and other inmates*. Garden City, NY: Anchor Books.

Goldberg, G. S., Kantrow, R., Kremen, E., & Lauter, L. (1986). Spouseless, childless elderly women and their social support. *Social Work, 31*, 104–112.

Gouldner, A. W. (1960). The norm of reciprocity: A preliminary statement. *American Sociological Review, 25*, 161–178.

Hays, J. A. (1984). Aging and family resources: Availability and proximity of kin. *The Gerontologist, 24*, 149–153.

House, J. S., & Kahn, R. L. (1985). Measures and concepts of social support. In S. Cohen & S. L. Syme (Eds.), *Social support and health* (pp. 83–105). New York: Academic Press.

Ishii-Kuntz, M., & Seccombe, K. (1989). The impact of children upon social support networks throughout the life course. *Journal of Marriage and the Family, 51*, 777–790.

Johnson, C. L., & Troll, L. E. (1996). Family structure and the timing of transitions from 70 to 103 years of age. *Journal of Marriage and the Family, 58*, 178–187.

Kahn, R. L., & Antonucci, T. C. (1980). Convoys over the life course: Attachment, roles, and social support. In P. B. Baltes & O. G. Brim Jr. (Eds.), *Life-span development and behavior* (Vol. 3, pp. 253–283). New York: Academic Press.

König, R. (Ed.). (1965). *Die strukturelle Bedeutung des Alters in den fortgeschrittenen Industriegesellschaften*. Cologne: Kiepenheuer & Witsch.

Lang, F. R. (1994). *Die Gestaltung informeller Hilfebeziehungen im hohen Alter: Die Rolle von Elternschaft und Kinderlosigkeit. Eine empirische Studie zur sozialen Unterstützung und deren Effekt auf die erlebte soziale Einbindung* (Studien und Berichte des Max-Planck-Instituts für Bildungsforschung 59). Berlin: Edition Sigma.

Lang, F. R., & Carstensen, L. L. (1994). Close emotional relationships in late life: Further support for proactive aging in the social domain. *Psychology and Aging, 9*, 315–324.

Lehr, U., & Minnemann, E. (1987). Veränderungen von Quantität und Qualität sozialer Kontakte vom siebten bis neunten Lebensjahrzehnt. In U. Lehr & H. Thomae (Eds.), *Formen seelischen Alterns: Ergebnisse der Bonner Gerontologischen Längsschnittstudie (BOLSA)* (pp. 80–91). Stuttgart: Enke.

Litwak, E. (1985). *Helping the elderly*. New York: Guilford.

Minnemann, E. (1994). Geschlechtsspezifische Unterschiede der Gestaltung sozialer Beziehungen im Alter: Ergebnisse einer empirischen Untersuchung. *Zeitschrift für Gerontologie, 27*, 33–41.

Niederfranke, A. (1991). *Ältere Frauen in der Auseinandersetzung mit Berufsaufgabe und Partnerverlust*. Stuttgart: Kohlhammer.

Palmore, E. B. (1968). The effects of aging on activities and attitudes. *The Gerontologist, 8*, 259–263.

Parsons, T. (1943). The kinship system of the contemporary United States. *American Anthropologist, 45*, 22–38.

Rempel, J. (1985). Childless elderly: What are they missing? *Journal of Marriage and the Family, 47*, 343–348.

Riley, M. W., & Riley, J. W., Jr. (1986). Longevity and social structure: The potential of the added years. In A. Pifer & L. Bronte (Eds.), *Our aging society: Paradox and promise* (pp. 53–77). New York: Norton.

Riley, M. W., & Riley, J. W., Jr. (1992). Individuelles und gesellschaftliches Potential des Alterns. In P. B. Baltes & J. Mittelstraß (Eds.), *Zukunft des Alterns und gesellschaftliche Entwicklung* (pp. 437–460). Berlin: de Gruyter.

Roberto, K. A. (1989). Exchange and equity in friendships. In R. G. Adams & R. Blieszner (Eds.), *Older adult friendship: Structure and process* (pp. 147–165). London: Sage.

Rook, K. S. (1990). Social relationships as a source of companionship: Implications for older adults' psychological well-being. In B. R. Sarason & G. R. Pierce (Eds.), *Social support: An interactional view* (pp. 219–250). New York: Wiley.

Rosenmayr, L. (1983). *Die späte Freiheit: Das Alter – ein Stück bewußt gelebten Lebens*. Berlin: Severin & Siedler.

Rosow, I. (1967). *Social integration of the aged*. New York: Free Press.

Rossi, A. S., & Rossi, P. H. (1990). *Of human bonding: Parent-child-relationships across the life course*. Hawthorne, NY: de Gruyter.

Russell, D., Cutrona, C. E., Rose, J., & Yurko, K. (1984). Social and emotional loneliness: An examination of Weiss's typology of loneliness. *Journal of Personality and Social Psychology, 46*, 1313–1321.

Schütze, Y., & Lang, F. R. (1996). Integration in family, kinship and friendship networks. In H. Mollenkopf (Ed.), *Elderly people in industrialized societies* (pp. 25–41). Berlin: Edition Sigma.

Schütze, Y., & Wagner, M. (1991). Sozialstrukturelle, normative und emotionale Determinanten der Beziehungen zwischen erwachsenen Kindern und ihren alten Eltern. *Zeitschrift für Sozialisationsforschung und Erziehungssoziologie, 11*, 295–313.

Shanas, E. (1979). The family as a social support system in old age. *The Gerontologist, 19*, 169–174.

Simons, R. L. (1983). Specificity and substitution in the social networks of the elderly. *International Journal of Aging and Human Development, 18*, 121–139.

Statistisches Bundesamt. (1972). *Bevölkerung und Wirtschaft 1872–1972*. Stuttgart: Kohlhammer.

Taylor, R. J., Chatters, L. M., & Mays, V. M. (1988). Parents, children, siblings, in-laws, and non-kin as sources of emergency assistance to black Americans. *Family Relations, 37*, 298–304.

Walsh, A. (1991). *The science of love: Understanding love and its effects on mind and body*. Buffalo, NY: Prometheus Books.

Walster, E., Berscheid, E., & Walster, G. W. (1973). New directions in equity research. *Journal of Personality and Social Psychology, 6*, 435–441.

Weiss, R. (1973). *Loneliness: The experience of emotional and social isolation*. Cambridge, MA: MIT Press.

Wentowski, G. J. (1981). Reciprocity and the coping strategies of older people: Cultural dimensions of network building. *The Gerontologist, 21*, 600–609.

Wills, T. A. (1985). Supportive functions of interpersonal relationships. In S. Cohen & S. L. Syme (Eds.), *Social support and health* (pp. 61–82). New York: Academic Press.

CHAPTER 11

Self, Personality, and Life Regulation: Facets of Psychological Resilience in Old Age

Ursula M. Staudinger, Alexandra M. Freund, Michael Linden, and Ineke Maas

The goal of this chapter is twofold. First, this chapter describes various aspects of self and personality in old age (personality characteristics, self-definitions, experience of time, personal life investment, coping styles, affect) and relates them to individuals' satisfaction with their own aging. Second, based on a model of psychological resilience in old age, we examine whether these aspects of self and personality are protective of aging satisfaction (on a correlational level) in the face of somatic or socioeconomic risks. Taken together, our results indicate that self and personality involve processes and characteristics that help to maintain or minimize the loss of aging satisfaction in the presence of somatic and socioeconomic risk factors. On a correlational level, we observe different adaptive profiles for socioeconomic and somatic risks.

1   Psychological Resilience of Self and Personality in Old Age: A Working Framework

Depressivity and dissatisfaction belong to the negative aging stereotype (cf. Palmore, 1988). In contrast to this negative stereotype, most old and very old people, however, are not depressed and unsatisfied even in the face of somatic and socioeconomic risks. Which features and processes of the aging self are supportive of the maintenance of well-being? In the following, we focus on the correlational analysis of the potentially protective effects of older persons' self-perception, self-evaluation, and general personality characteristics.

Numerous gerontological studies (for review see, e.g., Filipp, 1996; Ruth & Coleman, 1996) have shown that, in contrast to intellectual functioning, self and personality change little with increasing age (cf. Smith & Baltes, Chapter 7; Lindenberger & Reischies, Chapter 12 in this volume). For present purposes, self and personality are broadly defined to include situation-specific as well as dispositional patterns of perception, experience, and behavior that characterize a person in his or her interaction with the environment (e.g., Allport, 1937). Indicators of self-regulatory and personality-related processes such as the feeling of self-worth (e.g., Bengtson, Reedy, & Gordon, 1985), subjective well-being (e.g., Brandtstädter & Wentura, 1994; Costa et al., 1987; Ryff, 1989), low depressivity (e.g., LaRue, 1992), or control beliefs (e.g., Lachman, 1986) exhibit stability rather than negative age differences (Smith & Baltes, Chapter 7; Smith et al., Chapter 17).

In order to gain a better understanding of the weak association between self-related indicators and chronological age in the Berlin Aging Study (BASE) sample, we selected satisfaction with one's own aging (aging satisfaction for short) as an index of the level of adaptivity. This is a subscale (five items; Cronbach's $\alpha = .74$) of the Philadelphia Geriatric Center Morale Scale (PGCMS; Lawton, 1975) for subjective well-being. Age only explains about 6% of the variance in aging satisfaction ($r = -.25$),[1] whereas about 35% of intellectual functioning is explained by age (cf. Lindenberger & Reischies, Chapter 12).

As an expression of self and personality, aging satisfaction seems hardly influenced by age-associated physical and socioeconomic changes (e.g., Filipp, 1996; Staudinger, Marsiske, & Baltes, 1995). In the gerontological and developmental literature on adulthood, this phenomenon is considered a paradox (e.g., P. B. Baltes & Baltes, 1990; Brandtstädter & Greve, 1994) or a protective "illusion" (Taylor & Brown, 1988). These descriptions imply that, in the face of age-related increases of somatic and socioeconomic risks, the aging self has reserve capacities (Staudinger, Marsiske, & Baltes, 1995) that prevent considerable changes in aging satisfaction. Many different solutions have been proposed for this paradox (see, e.g., Brandtstädter & Greve, 1994; Diener, 1994; Staudinger & Fleeson, 1996). For the purposes of this chapter, we have concentrated on the concept of psychological resilience of self and personality (Garmezy, 1991; Rutter, 1987; Staudinger, Marsiske, & Baltes, 1995) to characterize this phenomenon of aging satisfaction maintenance despite increasing risks in old age.

There are at least two reasons for the choice of aging satisfaction as an indicator of psychological resilience. First, satisfaction with aging is at the core of the phenomenon of interest. Assuming that old age is characterized by an increase in risks and a decrease in the reserves to counteract them (e.g., P. B. Baltes, Lindenberger, & Staudinger, 1998), one would expect this to be reflected in satisfaction with aging as the "carrier" of such losses.

The second reason is a methodological one. Indicators of self and personality are usually assessed via self-report. This is true for our measure of resilience as well as for self-regulatory processes and personality characteristics. As our aim is to examine the relationship between observed resilience and self-regulatory as well as personality-related processes, we have to ensure that the argument does not become tautological due to overlap in item content. Not least because of their domain specificity, the items in the aging satisfaction scale (e.g., "With increasing age my life is better than I expected"; "I am just as happy now as I was in younger years"; "The older I become, the less useful I am") appear to be sufficiently independent of the other self-related variables that we examine as potential protective mechanisms.

The concept of psychological resilience was originally developed in the field of developmental psychopathology in childhood and adolescence (Cicchetti, 1989; Garmezy, 1991; Rutter, 1987). The term was coined to describe the fact that certain children do not become socially dysfunctional despite growing up in very bad socioeconomic conditions. Garmezy defined resilience more generally as "the capacity for recovery and maintained adaptive behavior that may follow initial retreat or incapacity upon initiating a stressful event" (Garmezy, 1991, p. 459). For Rutter, resilience is "the positive pole of individual differences in people's response to stress and adversity" (Rutter, 1987, p. 316). In summary, the concept of psychological resilience stands for two types of phenomena: (1) the *maintenance* of normal development despite risks and impairments, and (2) the *recovery* of normal functioning after a traumatic experience. In the literature, resilience describes both the process of dealing with risks and its outcome (Rutter, 1987).

Because of the present study's cross-sectional design we cannot distinguish between these two forms of resilience. As models of psychological resilience usually are process

---

[1] This proportion of variance does not change if persons with a psychiatric diagnosis of severe dementia (DSM-III-R; $n = 39$) or major depression ($n = 28$) are excluded.

Figure 11.1. A working model of correlates, conditions, and consequences of psychological resilience of self and personality in old age.

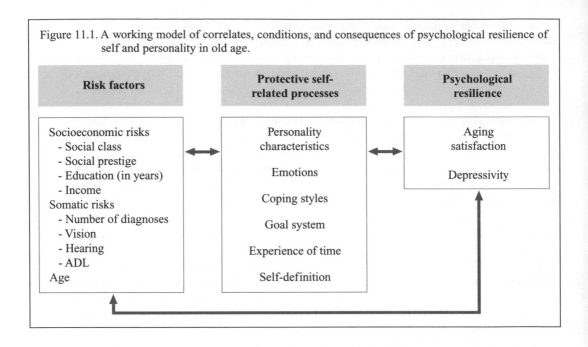

Risk factors	Protective self-related processes	Psychological resilience
Socioeconomic risks - Social class - Social prestige - Education (in years) - Income Somatic risks - Number of diagnoses - Vision - Hearing - ADL Age	Personality characteristics Emotions Coping styles Goal system Experience of time Self-definition	Aging satisfaction Depressivity

models and imply causal effects, we must emphasize that our findings pertain to the process outcome and are based on correlational analyses. We examine the concept of psychological resilience as a cross-sectional correlational relationship between certain risk profiles and aging satisfaction in old and very old age. We can only speculate on the direction of effects and can neither carry out true process analyses nor examine the actual tackling of critical life events. This needs to be remembered when interpreting our findings. However, the longitudinal data on the same population that are currently being collected will make such investigations possible.

As shown in Figure 11.1, models of resilience roughly distinguish between resources and protective factors that support maintenance or recovery of resilience from risk factors that endanger it. Risk and protective factors can be internal (i.e., personal features such as intelligence, genes, health, moods) or external (i.e., characteristics of the social-structural environment such as finances, education, social status; Staudinger, Marsiske, & Baltes, 1995).

This chapter cannot construct a full model of psychological resilience in old age. As indicated by its title, the focus is on the resilience of self and personality as assessed by aging satisfaction. Because of space limitations, we only examine self-regulatory and personality-associated mechanisms, although everyday competence (M. M. Baltes et al., Chapter 14) and intellectual abilities (Lindenberger & Reischies, Chapter 12) certainly also have protective potential.

As risk factors, we selected objective indicators from the socioeconomic and the physical health domain. Whereas somatic risks are clearly age-related, socioeconomic risks are more likely to have influenced a person's life for decades. Both types of risks form individual profiles that challenge older adults' well-being. Social class, social prestige (Wegener, 1988), years of education, occupational training, and income were included as socioeconomic risks (cf. Mayer et al., Chapter 8). Vision and hearing, the number of medical diagnoses (weighted by severity, excluding colds), and the Activities of Daily Living (ADL) score were used as indicators of somatic risks (cf. Steinhagen-Thiessen & Borchelt, Chapter 5).

In order to reduce data and to increase reliability, a factor analysis of all risk factors was carried out. *Risks were recoded such that a higher score always signified a higher risk in the respective domain.* An exploratory factor analysis with oblique rotation resulted in a two-factor solution that explained 50% of the variance. The first factor unites the socioeconomic risks. The somatic risks all loaded on the second factor (factor intercorrelation: $r = .2$). In the following, the factor scores are used as indicators of socioeconomic or somatic risks.[2] Socioeconomic risks are not associated with age ($r = .03$; cf. Mayer et al., Chapter 8) whereas somatic risks are closely age-related ($r = .64$, 41% of the variance).

As to be expected, somatic risks correlate with aging satisfaction more negatively ($r = -.36$, 13% of the variance) than age itself ($r = -.25$; $z = -2.58$, $p = .01$). Socioeconomic risks are not related to aging satisfaction ($r = -.06$, not significant [n.s.]). Considering that the participants could "get used to" their own social situation over a long time and that, in Germany, socioeconomic risks do not seem to be specifically linked to aging (cf. Mayer et al., Chapter 8), this independence is not surprising. Still, it is possible that relationships emerge when self-regulatory mechanisms are included as moderators.

Which resources are available to the aging self to deal with age-related and age-independent risk factors? We consider both self-regulatory, situation-specific, social-cognitive processes, and basic dispositions of perception and behavior (i.e., personality dimensions) that are typically assessed as internal resources of the self. As shown in Figure 11.1, we examine lasting personality characteristics, affect, goal systems and personal life investment, coping styles, experience of time, and self-definition as potentially protective factors of the self. We identify socioeconomic and somatic risk conditions separately and enter risk factors as predictors of aging satisfaction. We present various facets of self and personality, also describing age differences. On a correlational level, we then analyze their protective value in the face of risks.

2   Self-Regulatory Processes, Self-Related Characteristics, and Resilience of the Aging Self

2.1   Personality

First, we examine whether classical psychometric personality dimensions represent protective or risk factors for the aging self and influence resilience. It needs to be taken into account that personality dimensions are conceptualized and operationalized as lasting patterns of experience and behavior that generalize across different life domains. In the gerontological literature, there are indications that personality dimensions are associated with subjective well-being in old age. Costa et al. (1987) found that lower scores on the dimension of neuroticism and higher scores on extraversion are significantly correlated with well-being. We find a comparable pattern of results in the heterogeneous BASE sample (aged 70 to 103 years).

---

[2] Analyses with unweighted composites yielded the same results.

2.1.1   Operationalization and Relationships with Aging Satisfaction
The dimensions of neuroticism, extraversion, and openness to new experiences were assessed with a shortened version of the NEO personality questionnaire (cf. Smith & Baltes, Chapter 7). Their correlations with aging satisfaction are significantly negative (neuroticism: $r = -.45$, $p = .00$), or positive (extraversion: $r = .31$, $p = .00$), and explain 20% and 9%, respectively, of its variance. In contrast, openness to new experiences does not correlate with aging satisfaction ($r = .02$, n.s.).

On a correlational level, the emotionally more unstable or more neurotic report less satisfaction with their aging than emotionally more stable persons. This finding indicates that the patterns of domain-general and long-lasting experience and behavior assessed in personality dimensions can have effects of strain on aging satisfaction (or relief in the case of extraversion). For people higher on neuroticism, it seems likely that the experience of more negative affect (as measured with the Positive and Negative Affect Schedule, PANAS; Watson, Clark, & Tellegen, 1988; cf. Kercher, 1992) could contribute to lower levels of aging satisfaction. The correlations between neuroticism and negative affect ($r = .64$, $p = .00$), and positive affect ($r = -.1$, $p = .05$), support this notion. Indeed, the analysis of the relationship between neuroticism and aging satisfaction after controlling for negative affect shows a reduction of explained variance from 20% to 6%, which, however, does remain significant ($p = .05$).

Accordingly, the relationship between extraversion and aging satisfaction can also be mediated via affect (correlations between extraversion and positive affect: $r = .46$, $p = .01$, and negative affect: $r = -.1$, $p = .05$). In this case, controlling for positive affect reduces the explained variance from 9% to 3%, which again still remains significant ($p = .05$). This supports the hypothesis that, although elderly individuals' dispositional affect does play an important role, the domain-general and lasting patterns of experience and behavior assessed by the constructs of neuroticism and extraversion, have further effects of strain or relief regarding aging satisfaction.

Costa and McCrae (1985) argue that persons high on neuroticism not only experience more negative affect, but are also less able to deal with stressful situations and have less self-control and more unrealistic ideas. Such characteristics may impede the capacity to deal with age-related difficulties, and thus decrease aging satisfaction. In contrast, the persons high on extraversion are distinguished by their increased positive affect, their activity, interest, self-confidence, and outgoingness. Of course, these are characteristics that make it easier to deal with the challenges of old age and increase aging satisfaction. We were more surprised by our finding that the NEO dimension of openness (with variances equaling the other two dimensions) is not related to aging satisfaction. In the literature, at least theoretically, this dimension has often been linked to constructive forms of life management (cf. Whitbourne, 1987). However, one can hypothesize that open individuals are also more curious and probably have higher levels of aspiration, which in turn are more likely to reduce their aging satisfaction. In sum, it seems that on a zero-order level of relationships, extraversion is a protective and neuroticism a risk factor regarding aging satisfaction.

2.1.2   Personality Dimensions and Psychological Resilience
None of the three personality dimensions has a moderating influence on the relationship between age and aging satisfaction ($r = -.25$). This was examined in three separate multiple regression models, first entering the two main effects (i.e., age and each personality

dimension), and then the interactions between age and each dimension as predictors of aging satisfaction. Personality dimensions also had no moderating effect on the relationship between socioeconomic risk factors and aging satisfaction.

However, when considering the relationship between somatic risks and aging satisfaction, neuroticism surprisingly appears to become a "protective" factor. In a three-step multiple regression model, the interaction between neuroticism and somatic risks adds 1% significant predictive variance to the 14% variance explained by neuroticism alone and the 12% explained by somatic risks alone. This may seem a small effect, but if one is interested in basic mechanisms of resilience rather than specific population outcomes, the effect size is less important than significance itself (see Cohen, 1994).

The negative correlation between somatic risks and aging satisfaction of $r = -.36$ for the entire sample is reduced to $r = -.29$ ($n = 258$) for persons with a neuroticism score above the median. For persons with a neuroticism score below the median, the correlation remains practically unchanged ($r = -.35$, $n = 258$). This seemingly counterintuitive moderation effect becomes more comprehensible if one considers the formulation of individual neuroticism items of the NEO questionnaire, such as "When I am under strain I sometimes feel I am breaking down" or "I wish someone would solve my problems." It seems as though it might be quite functional to experience negative feelings like this in cases of strong physical impairments. It is also possible that more neurotic persons are more used to negative emotional states anyway and do not experience the trials of somatic impairments as adversely as persons who are used to positive emotions.

2.2 Affect

Personality development or maturity in adulthood, something akin to psychological resilience, is often discussed in association with the regulation of emotional states. Being able to deal with one's emotions is an aspect of what Erikson (e.g., Erikson, Erikson, & Kivnick, 1986) called "self-integrity." Several studies showed that with increasing age adults become better able to cope with emotional situations (e.g., Blanchard-Fields, 1986; Labouvie-Vief, Hakim-Larson, DeVoe, & Schoeberlein, 1989; Staudinger, 1989).

Despite often being treated as indicators of adaptivity, in the present context, the reported emotional states of individuals are used as a potential resource for resilience based on the above argument. We assume that a person whose positive and negative affects are balanced or whose positive affect outweighs the negative is more likely to be resilient when faced with somatic and socioeconomic risks than an individual whose negative affect predominates (see also Diener & Larsen, 1993). Many studies have shown that a positive affect balance is associated with higher life satisfaction and other indicators of subjective well-being (e.g., Headey & Wearing, 1989; Sandvik, Diener, & Seidlitz, 1993).

2.2.1 Operationalization and Measurement

In the BASE self and personality measurement battery, emotions were assessed with a shortened and translated version of the PANAS (Kercher, 1992; Watson et al., 1988; see Kunzmann, 1994, for discussion of psychometric characteristics and validity). Participants were asked to indicate on a five-point scale (1 = rarely to 5 = very frequently) how often they experienced a certain emotion during the previous year. These frequency rat-

Table 11.1. *Rank order of the experience of positive and negative emotions in old age*

Rank	Positive emotions	*M*	*(SD)*	Rank	Negative emotions	*M*	*(SD)*
1	Interested	3.86	(0.87)	1	Restless	2.83	(1.01)
2	Attentive	3.64	(0.88)	2	Low	2.81	(1.12)
3	Alert	3.51	(0.98)	3	Nervous	2.74	(1.10)
4	Stimulated	3.35	(0.94)	4	Angry	2.56	(1.01)
5	Determined	3.23	(0.97)	5	Moody	2.45	(0.97)
6	Active	3.22	(1.06)	6	Frightened	2.20	(1.06)
7	Enthusiastic	3.20	(1.07)	7	Worried	2.09	(1.01)
8	Expectant	2.94	(0.99)	8	Guilty	1.98	(0.97)
9	Strong	2.56	(1.07)	9	Ashamed	1.95	(0.86)
10	Proud	2.29	(1.13)	10	Hostile	1.55	(0.83)

Note. Taking account of all possible mean comparisons and the Bonferroni correction shows that a difference of more than 0.2 between means is significant on the 1% level.

ings had a position stability above 0.8 over a period of eight weeks (cf. Kunzmann, 1994, p. 95).

The BASE version of the PANAS includes 10 positive and 10 negative emotions. This makes it possible to obtain a score for emotional balance (i.e., the difference between the frequencies of positive and negative affect) as well as scores for negative and positive affect. Consistent with findings in the literature (e.g., Myers & Diener, 1995), the two dimensions were independent of each other in the BASE sample ($r = .05$, n.s.; cf. Smith & Baltes, Chapter 7). Note that aging satisfaction and affect are assessed as separate entities. The former is measured by the agreement with statements on certain expectations and perceptions of age-related states, whereas the latter is rated by the frequency of domain-general and relatively long-lasting emotions. This distinction of the measures is reflected in differing relationships with other indicators of self and personality. For instance, reported emotional balance is significantly correlated with socioeconomic risks ($r = -.19$), but not with aging satisfaction ($r = -.06$). Its association with chronological age is strongly reduced ($r = -.13$) compared with aging satisfaction's ($r = -.26$). In contrast, openness is significantly related to affect ($r = .11$) but not to aging satisfaction ($r = .02$).

2.2.2 *Age Differences in the Experience of Positive and Negative Affect*
Table 11.1 shows the reported frequencies of positive and negative affect in our sample of 70- to 103-year-olds. Please note that the top three positive emotions are indicators of active participation and connectedness with the surroundings (interested, attentive, alert). The top three negative emotions, however, reflect a neurasthenic or depressed mood (restless, low, nervous).

The significant correlations between age and reported frequency of individual emotional states are all negative. It is striking that, as reported in the literature (e.g., Weiner & Graham, 1989), certain negative emotions such as "angry" ($r = -.12, p = .01$), "moody" ($r = -.19, p = .01$), and "nervous" ($r = -.15, p = .00$) are negatively associated with age across an age range of almost 35 years (70–103 years). However, averaged across the 10

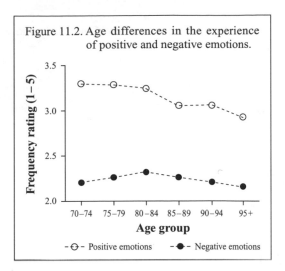

Figure 11.2. Age differences in the experience of positive and negative emotions.

emotions (see Fig. 11.2), negative affect does *not* decrease with age ($r = -.04$, n.s.), whereas positive affect does ($r = -.22$, $p < .01$). On average, the difference between positive and negative emotions (i.e., emotional balance) nevertheless remains positive.

This stability of negative affect and the rank order of emotions can be interpreted as a sign of psychological resilience. In the face of increasing strains and losses in old age, one would expect negative emotions to outweigh the positive. However, the neurasthenic pattern of negative emotions (restless, low, nervous) can be interpreted as consistent with a "stress reaction" (cf. Smith & Baltes, Chapter 7). An increase of agitation, excitability, and fear are discussed as psychological indicators of a stress reaction (e.g., Janke & Kallus, 1995; Lazarus & Launier, 1978). That is, although negative emotions are reported less frequently than positive ones, the pattern of highly frequent negative emotions seems to allow a glimpse behind the self's protection shields and point to the extent of adaptation necessary to deal with old age. Similar findings have been reported from the Georgia Centenarian Study (Martin, Poon, Kim, & Johnson, 1996).

Consideration of age differences in the frequency of positive affect (cf. Fig. 11.2) reveals a slightly negative relationship with age ($r = -.19$, $p < .01$, 4% of variance). This can be interpreted as another sign of the depletion of psychological resources with age. The decrease in reported positive affect becomes more salient around the age of 85 years ($F(1, 514) = 16.64$, $p = .00$, when comparing 70- to 84-year-olds with persons aged 85 and above). The present findings are consistent with other age-comparative studies of emotion. Malatesta and Kalnok (1984), for example, reported that the frequency of negative emotions did not reveal any positive age differences. Levenson, Carstensen, Friesen, and Ekman (1991) were able to show that reactivity in old age is increased due to systemic physiological changes and that this could lead to suppression of emotions to avoid long-lasting agitation. The BASE data show that the reported frequency of emotions, especially the positive ones, decreases significantly from the age of 85 years onward. As people have many emotional experiences over their life courses, it seems likely that the threshold for emotional responses increases with age, thus reducing affect frequency (cf. Schulz, 1985, p. 537). Finally, this decrease could be associated with loss of

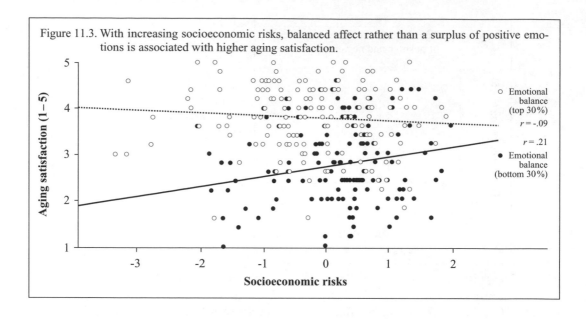

Figure 11.3. With increasing socioeconomic risks, balanced affect rather than a surplus of positive emotions is associated with higher aging satisfaction.

social network partners in old age (cf. Wagner et al., Chapter 10) and reduction of time spent with others (cf. M. M. Baltes et al., Chapter 14), which provides an important context for the experience of emotions (e.g., Carstensen, 1993).

2.2.3 Affect and Psychological Resilience

We now examine the potential moderating effects of emotions and their balance (i.e., difference between positive and negative affect) on the relationship between aging satisfaction, and somatic and socioeconomic risks. First, we consider *age* as a very general risk indicator. In this case, emotional balance explains 28% of the variance in aging satisfaction and 25% after controlling for age. Age and emotional balance thus share 3% of the variance in predicting aging satisfaction. However, the interaction between age and emotional balance does not contribute significantly more to the prediction of age satisfaction. In other words, the predictive relationship between emotional balance and aging satisfaction does not alter depending on age. Nevertheless, a surplus of positive affect explains 25% of the variance in aging satisfaction. Thus, the surplus of positive emotions can be seen as a correlationally protective factor in old age.

If *socioeconomic risks* are considered rather than age, the explained variance in aging satisfaction reaches 29%. The interaction between emotional balance and socioeconomic risks contributes a further significant 1% of variance in aging satisfaction after both main effects are controlled (see Fig. 11.3). As explained above, the importance of this finding lies in the effect's significance and not in its size, because it indicates basic mechanisms of resilience and vulnerability.

This effect means that the weak positive correlation between socioeconomic risks and aging satisfaction found for the entire sample ($r = .07$, n.s.) becomes negative ($r = -.08$, n.s.) for persons with a surplus of positive emotions (top 30% of the distribution). For persons with a lower or no surplus (bottom 30%), the correlation becomes significant and rises from $r = .07$ to $r = .21$ ($p < .01$). This interaction indicates that for elderly persons living under socioeconomically restrictive conditions, balanced emotions (i.e., a small or no surplus of positive emotions) are linked to higher aging satisfaction. To interpret this finding, we should bear in mind that socioeconomic risks have usually taken effect across most of the life-span and the described association could also reflect class-specific emotional patterns. This effect persists after controlling for age and gender. Further analyses have shown again that the difference between persons with high and low socioeconomic risks is a decreased frequency of reported positive emotions, rather than an increase of negative ones. As before, when neuroticism was adaptive under conditions of somatic constraints, positive emotions now seem to have reduced adaptive value under conditions of socioeconomic risk.

2.3   Coping Styles

Another concept with a long research tradition in relation to resilience is that of coping styles (e.g., Filipp & Klauer, 1991). In the late 1970s opinions differed as to whether "regressive" (e.g., giving up responsibility, despair; Pfeiffer, 1977) or "mature" coping strategies (e.g., reinterpretation of the situation, gathering information; Vaillant, 1977) increase with age. Folkman, Lazarus, Pimpley, and Novacek (1987) found that rather than seeking social support or confronting a problem, older adults try to distance themselves and reassess the situation positively. More and more empirical evidence supports the maturation hypothesis (Vaillant, 1977), or at least the assumptions on stability of coping behavior (Aldwin, 1991; Aldwin, Sutton, & Lachman, 1996; Costa & McCrae, 1993; Irion & Blanchard-Fields, 1987; Labouvie-Vief, Hakim-Larson, & Hobart, 1987; McCrae, 1989; Rott & Thomae, 1991). McCrae (1989) was able to show that differences in coping are linked more to age-related differences in situations than to chronological age itself.

2.3.1   Operationalization and Measurement

Given the age distribution of the present sample and limited assessment time, coping styles could not be assessed with the usual questionnaires, which are sometimes long and difficult to understand. Instead, an instrument that included a set of 13 coping styles was developed (Staudinger, Freund, & Smith, 1995), taking into account findings from the Bonn Gerontological Longitudinal Study (Kruse, 1987; Thomae, 1987). In the instructions, participants were asked to rate how well short statements describing coping styles fit their own thinking and behavior in problem situations. The 13 styles were selected to characterize a person's coping pattern, rather than to form a scale.[3] Table 11.2 lists the abbreviations of the 13 coping styles (items) together with means and standard deviations.

We were first interested in the rank order of the 13 styles rated by the participants. Table 11.2 shows that the three "regressive" (cf. Pfeiffer, 1977) styles, "Someone else to take over," "Life loses meaning," and "Giving up," are located at the bottom of the list. This result supports the findings described in the gerontological literature that do *not* as-

---

[3] Applying factor analysis and oblique rotation to the covariance matrix of the 13 styles yields a clear three-factor solution with low intercorrelations ($r = -.12$), which covers 42% of the variance. (This is not surprising as the 13 styles were not constructed to form scales.) The first factor includes styles such as "Giving up" and "Someone else to take over." Styles that are directed toward active coping load onto the second factor. Finally, the third factor includes more passive coping styles.

Table 11.2. *Rank order of coping styles*

Rank	Coping style (abbreviation)	*M*	*(SD)*
1	Comparison with the past	4.19	(0.69)
2	Wish for information	3.98	(0.79)
3	Comparison with others	3.91	(0.88)
4	Keep going	3.90	(0.78)
5	Adaptation to the given	3.63	(0.89)
6	Ups and downs	3.58	(0.86)
7	Faith	3.54	(1.19)
8	Humor	3.27	(1.04)
9	Distraction	3.23	(1.08)
10	Social support	2.82	(1.12)
11	Someone else to take over	2.70	(1.18)
12	Life loses meaning	2.46	(1.08)
13	Giving up	2.46	(1.06)

Note. Taking account of all possible mean comparisons and the Bonferroni correction shows that a difference of more than 0.2 between means is significant on the 1% level.

sume an age-related increase of "regressive" coping styles. This becomes more important considering that the BASE sample represents a very heterogeneous, very old population which is not positively selected for health or social class, as is usually the case. Furthermore, the age range in BASE is much broader than in other gerontological studies, which mostly deal with the "young old."

The top three positions are held by the styles "Comparison with the past," "Wish for information," and "Comparison with others," with "Social support" playing a lesser role (see also Folkman et al., 1987). "Keep going" and "Adaptation to the given" are at fourth and fifth position. This is of interest regarding research on accommodation and assimilation (e.g., Brandtstädter & Greve, 1994) or primary and secondary control (e.g., J. Heckhausen & Schulz, 1995). BASE participants report that they are provided with, and make use of, mechanisms that change the environment *and* allow adaptation (cf. J. Heckhausen & Schulz, 1995).

2.3.2 Age Differences in Coping Styles

The age differences in the reported use of coping styles is presented in Figure 11.4. Roughly, three groups of styles can be distinguished: (1) those that are significantly more frequently used in older age groups such as "Faith" ($r = .24, p < .01$), "Distraction" ($r = .12, p < .01$), and "Adaptation to the given" ($r = .17, p < .01$); (2) those that are used less often in older age groups; and (3) those that do not differ across age groups or are not significantly correlated with age.

The observed age-related increase in adaptive tendencies resembles Brandtstädter's findings on accommodative styles in middle adulthood (up to 60 years; e.g., Brandtstädter & Renner, 1990). The BASE data now show that this trend continues up into very old age. However, it should be noted that we are analyzing participants' reports on the use of coping styles and not their actual behavior.

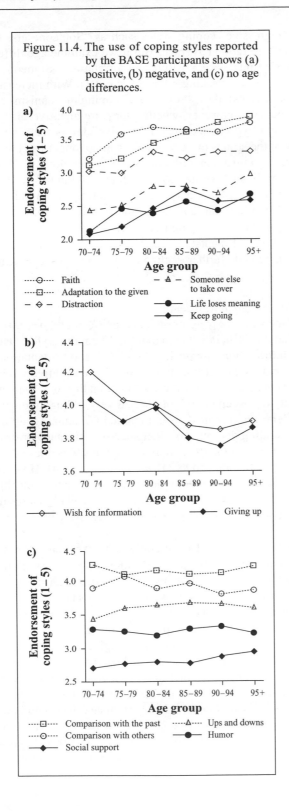

Figure 11.4. The use of coping styles reported by the BASE participants shows (a) positive, (b) negative, and (c) no age differences.

As shown in Table 11.2, "regressive" coping styles such as "Someone else to take over" and "Life loses meaning" are rare on average. But if we examine age differences from 70 to 103 in these styles, we find a weak positive age correlation ("Someone else to take over": $r = .18, p < .01$; "Life loses meaning": $r = .14, p < .01$). With increasing age (and thus with increasing somatic risks), these "regressive" coping mechanisms become more frequent. It remains to be seen, however, whether they are adaptive or dysfunctional in very old age. One could hypothesize that "regressive" styles may indeed become adaptive, because many of the strains of very old age can no longer be changed.

"Comparison with the past," "Comparison with others," "Ups and downs," "Humor," and "Social support" are not significantly related to age while "Giving up" ($r = -.1, p < .05$) and "Wish for information" ($r = -.14, p < .01$) become less frequent in old age. The negative age differences in "Giving up" run parallel to the positive age differences in "Keep going" (see Fig. 11.4). The latter are in contrast to findings from studies carried out with subjects aged up to 60 (e.g., Brandtstädter & Renner, 1990). According to the BASE data set, it seems as if there is no further decline of the assimilative style beyond the age of 70.

2.3.3   *Coping Styles and Psychological Resilience*

Coping styles explain 20% of the variance in aging satisfaction ($R^2 = .20, p = .00$). Using regression analysis, we find that this is mainly due to 6 of the 13 coping styles. "Humor," "Keep going," and "Wish for information" are positively related, and "Adaptation to the given," "Life loses meaning," and "Someone else to take over" are negatively related to aging satisfaction. This very general finding on the dysfunctionality of "Adaptation to the given" and the functionality of "Keep going" in old and very old age indicates that passivity in dealing with problems on average does not maintain or enhance aging satisfaction. Keep in mind that this finding does not consider specific risks and constraints.

If age is regarded as a general risk factor, the pattern of coping styles does not change the relationship between aging satisfaction and age ($r = -.25$ vs. $r = -.24$). However, the correlation between aging satisfaction and somatic risks is altered, when controlling for coping styles, from $r = -.36$ to $r = -.25$ ($z = -2.39, p = .008$). This correlational result indicates that the use of a certain coping pattern is protective in dealing with physical impairments.

Testing the potential protective function of each coping style separately shows that the styles "Wish for information" and "Social support" moderate the association between socioeconomic risks and aging satisfaction significantly in a multiple regression model. Thus, it appears *dysfunctional* for persons with high socioeconomic risks (i.e., low finances and a low level of education and occupational status) to want to know what is going on, whereas it seems protective to seek support from others.

As for somatic risks, it seems *dysfunctional* with regard to aging satisfaction to "Keep going" and to "Wish for information," whereas "Giving up" is protective. Our results on protective coping styles, in particular, show the ones usually identified as regressive in a new light. It does not appear to make sense to generalize certain styles as being regressive. Similar arguments have been raised, for example, by Thomae (1992) and Labouvie-Vief et al. (1987). Rather, life contexts need to be considered when adaptivity of coping is discussed. To avoid misunderstandings, we remind the reader that correlational associations are interpreted as causal here. It will be interesting to test our interpretations predictively with the longitudinal BASE data.

2.4   The Goal System and Personal Life Investment

From an action-theoretical perspective on experience and behavior, the development and pursuit of goals have an important action-regulatory and adaptive role to play (Boesch, 1991). Action theory concentrates on understanding and explaining individual actions. It has been combined, however, with perspectives of life-span developmental psychology (P. B. Baltes, 1987) to refer to larger portions of the life-span or life as a whole. The concept of action regulation has thus been expanded into developmental regulation (e.g., Brandtstädter, 1986; J. Heckhausen, 1998).

In both approaches, the development and pursuit of goals comprise a number of motivational processes. They range from selection processes among various goals, dynamic processes at the nexus between motivation and volition, to the phase of action control in achieving set goals (cf. H. Heckhausen, 1991; Kuhl, 1986).

Our interest is mainly directed toward the last of these, the realization of goals. We concentrate on two aspects. First, we are interested in the energetic aspect of goal pursuit. Because of its crucial importance in old age, we emphasize that personal life investment can be directed toward achieving something new or toward maintenance of the given – as also described in classical motivation theory (e.g., Atkinson, 1964; Lewin, 1926a, 1926b). Second, we are interested in the content of life investment profiles, that is, in examining how goal themes change with age or in different life contexts.

2.4.1   Operationalization and Instruments

We regard the profile and intensity of personal life investment across various life domains as an aspect of life management which may allow the individual to adapt to changing developmental contexts. An instrument was developed for the assessment of life investment into the domains most important to old adults (Staudinger & Fleeson, 1996). On a five-point scale, participants were asked to rate how much they think about, or take action in, a given life topic or life domain (e.g.: "How about your health? To what degree do you think or do something about it?"). Using the instrument, life investment profiles can be assessed, as can an average life investment score, representing a general measure of the intensity of an individual's life investment (for information on the predictive validity of the construct, see Staudinger & Fleeson, 1996).

2.4.2   Life Investment: Associations with Age and Psychological Resilience

First we examine average personal life investment (i.e., investment averaged across all 10 domains), which decreased slightly over the age span covered by the BASE sample ($r = -.17$, $p < .01$, 4% of explained variance). Furthermore, it is weakly associated with aging satisfaction ($r = .1$, $p < .05$).

Using multiple regression models, we analyze interactions with age and somatic risks and their prediction of aging satisfaction. As shown in Figure 11.5a, we find that the relatively high negative correlation between somatic risks and aging satisfaction ($r = -.36$) becomes even more negative ($r = -.42$) for persons with high life investment (i.e., a score above the median) and somewhat less negative for persons with low personal life investment ($r = -.28$). This significant interaction with an effect size of 1% remains after controlling for the frequency of negative emotions, which is done to exclude the possibility that the life investment instrument primarily assesses the degree of rumination. (In Fig.

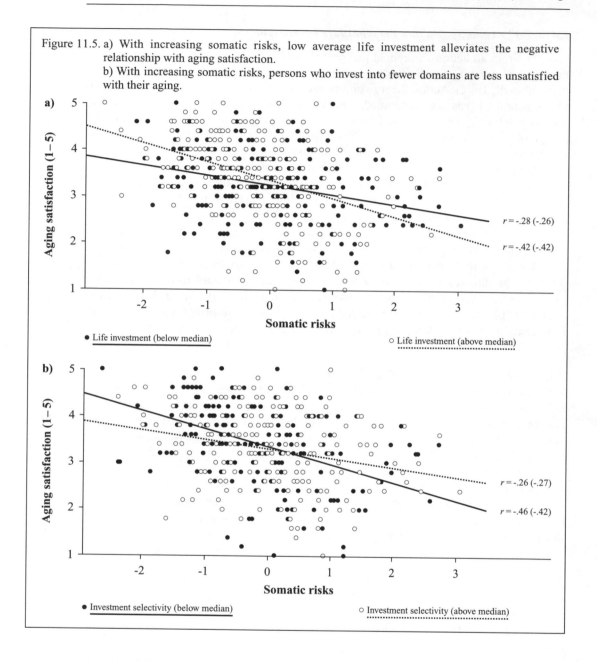

Figure 11.5. a) With increasing somatic risks, low average life investment alleviates the negative relationship with aging satisfaction.
b) With increasing somatic risks, persons who invest into fewer domains are less unsatisfied with their aging.

11.5a, these slightly different correlations are shown in parentheses.) The interaction with age is a little weaker, but has the same direction: With increasing age, low life investment becomes more strongly associated with higher aging satisfaction. A significant interaction is not found for socioeconomic risks.

The finding that life investment can, at least correlationally, buffer the negative effects of somatic risks (even after controlling for rumination and accommodative coping tendencies) is consistent with predictions from the model of successful aging by selective optimization and compensation (Marsiske, Lang, Baltes, & Baltes, 1995). Figure 11.5a shows that for persons with more somatic risks (or older persons), low life investment is associated with higher aging satisfaction. This indicates that increasing selectivity as described by Paul and Margret Baltes (1990) becomes adaptive with increasing age and somatic risks.

However, this interpretation of the protective value of selectivity needs more specific analyses, because a low mean level of life investment can be due to low scores in all domains, or of many very low and some very high scores. Only the latter would be indicative of selectivity. We therefore tried to replicate the interaction effect with a variable called investment selectivity, which is defined as the frequency of very low (score 5) and low (score 4) investment scores. This new variable correlates with average life investment ($r = -.87$) and does indeed yield very similar results (see Figure 11.5b). The assumption that investment selectivity is adaptive under constraining life circumstances seems likely.

The adaptivity of investment selectivity becomes even more obvious if the threshold is not set at the median, but if persons with many somatic risks (top 30%) are compared with those with few somatic risks (bottom 30%). In the high-risk group (top 30%), the correlation between investment selectivity and aging satisfaction is $r = .15$ ($p < .05$) versus $r = -.08$ (n.s.) in the entire sample. However, dysfunctionality of selectivity, or "early" disengagement, becomes manifest in a correlation of $r = -.22$ ($p < .01$) with aging satisfaction in earlier old age, or in cases of low somatic risk (bottom 30%).

2.4.3 Personal Life Investment Patterns across Age and in Association with Psychological Resilience

We now move on to the content of life investment. What occupies persons aged 70 to 103? How do older adults distribute their life investment across different domains? In order to obtain a measure of content preferences that is independent of the average intensity of investment, we controlled the participants' investment scores in each domain for their average life investment.[4]

We can distinguish age-stable investment domains from those increasing or decreasing with age (Table 11.3). For instance, the relative investments into the domains of hobbies and other interests ($r = -.13, p < .00$) and sexuality ($r = .13, p < .00$) decrease by age whereas investment into death and dying ($r = .23, p < .00$) increases. No significant age differences are observed in the domains of health, mental performance, well-being of close relatives, relationships with friends and acquaintances, occupational or comparable activities, and thinking about life.

In particular, stability of the relative investment into health may seem surprising, because it is known from other studies that this domain becomes increasingly important over the life-span. On the one hand, we can assume that, by the age of 70, investment into one's health has reached a level that can hardly become higher (first rank, $M = 3.9$, $SD = .9$). On the other hand, this finding is a reminder of the problem of selective mortality for the interpretation of cross-sectional age differences. It is quite possible that survivors set other priorities than nonsurvivors.

However, the notion of a "ceiling effect" for health investment is supported by a study on middle adulthood that used the same instrument (Staudinger & Fleeson, 1997). Life

---

[4] In each case, an average investment score was calculated out of 9 scores and related to the 10th in order to avoid linear dependencies between quotients.

Table 11.3. *Rank order of the relative investment into 10 goal domains and their correlation with age*

Rank	Goal	M	(SD)	r	(p)
1	Health	1.31	(.38)	.04	(.32)
2	Well-being of close relatives	1.29	(.44)	-.03	(.47)
3	Mental performance	1.19	(.37)	.01	(.79)
4	Relationships with friends and acquaintances	1.11	(.38)	.01	(.83)
5	Thinking about life	1.11	(.37)	.07	(.10)
6	*Hobbies and other interests*	1.02	(.40)	-.12	(.00)
7	Independence	0.96	(.39)	-.01	(.81)
8	*Death and dying*	0.87	(.41)	.22	(.00)
9	Occupational or comparable activities	0.79	(.40)	-.03	(.56)
10	*Sexuality*	0.54	(.29)	-.13	(.00)

Note. Taking account of all possible mean comparisons and the Bonferroni correction shows that a difference of more than 0.09 between means is significant on the 1% level. Italics indicate significant age differences.

investment into health increased continuously over the entire examined age range from 25 to 65 years. Health was ranked ninth for 25- to 35-year-olds ($M = 3.3$, $SD = .9$), fifth for 35- to 55-year-olds ($M = 3.6$, $SD = .9$), and second for the 55- to 65-year-olds ($M = 3.8$, $SD = .9$).

The relative investment pattern averaged across the whole BASE sample can be seen as a reflection of the developmental contexts of old and very old age (e.g., increasing morbidity, time running out, loss of professional and other social roles). Investment is primarily directed toward one's own health and close relatives – following Erikson et al.'s (1986) notion of generativity. The preparation for dying and death increases whereas professional or other social activities decrease in importance. Indeed, if the sample is divided by age, the relative investment patterns differ significantly (after Bonferroni correction) between the 70- to 84-year-olds and the 85- to 103-year-olds ($F(10, 492) = 4.63$, $p = .00$). This difference is primarily due to the 85- to 103-year-olds' lower relative investment into hobbies ($F(1, 501) = 6.06$, $p = .01$) and relatively higher investment into dying and death ($F(1, 501) = 22.86$, $p = .00$).

2.5   *Experience of Time*

Experience of time in old age is usually discussed in terms of time perspective and particularly of so-called future time perspective (i.e., orientation toward the future). From studies on various age groups it is known that a pronounced future perspective, like optimism, has high protective value for subjective well-being and mental health (e.g., Brandtstädter & Wentura, 1994; Reker & Wong, 1988). During recent years, the restriction of investigations of time perspective to the study of its extension and affective tone has been criticized. Time perspective studies have therefore been expanded to include facets such as degree of differentiation, density, and sense of reality in time perspectives (e.g., Lehr, 1967; Rakowski, 1979).

Unfortunately, a differentiated assessment of time perspective was not possible in the BASE battery, but we could include some questions on frequency of thoughts about the present, the future, and the past ("What do you think about most? Past, present, or future? And if you compare the other two, which do you think about more?") as well as the traditional items of future optimism and future time perspective. Furthermore, we asked about subjective proximity to death, and finally, in the tradition of the psychology of perception (e.g., Fraisse, 1963; Levin & Zakay, 1989), posed three questions on the subjective amount and speed of time as explained below.

2.5.1   How Do the Old and Very Old Experience Time?

Before we turn to the potential protective value of the experience of time, we consider the distribution of the reported amount and speed of time across the age groups. According to action-theoretical conceptions, time and its perception play an important role for motivation (e.g., Boesch, 1991; Lewin, 1926a, 1926b). Perception of the passage of time indicates the extent of correspondence between the actual course of actions and individuals' expectations. For instance, time is perceived as shortened when new needs arise and the desire for action grows. Thus, time passes too slowly when one wants to reach a goal soon, and too quickly when one does not want to "arrive."

In the gerontological literature, it is hypothesized that time passes increasingly quickly in old age and is perceived as lessening because of the shortening of the remaining life-span (Bühler, 1933; Wallach & Green, 1961). Combining this hypothesis with the notions of action theory, one could arrive at the formulation that the old are not looking forward to reaching the "goal" of death.

The three items on subjective amount and speed of time were first examined in factor analysis with oblique rotation. Two factors emerge, which explain 65% of the variance and are correlated ($r = .19$). This makes it possible to distinguish two constructs: the *subjective speed* ("How quickly does time pass for you?") and the *subjective amount* of time ("How much time have you got?"). Because of the clear factor solution, these two constructs were each calculated from the averaged three items (unweighted composite; speed: Cronbach's $\alpha = .71$, amount: Cronbach's $\alpha = .7$).

The group mean for speed of time reaches $M = 1.48$ ($SD = .52$) on a scale ranging from 1 ("quickly") to 3 ("slowly"). Time is thus experienced as passing rather quickly. However, on a scale from 1 ("little time") to 3 ("a lot of time"), the average amount of subjective time ($M = 2.28$, $SD = .57$) indicates that participants feel they have enough time. The speed of time is correlated with age ($r = .28$, $p < .01$), that is, older participants experience time as passing more slowly. In comparison, the amount of time is less correlated with age ($r = .11$, $p < .01$). These findings are not altered if persons with dementia or depression diagnoses are excluded. Our results do not support everyday statements of old people, or the gerontological hypothesis that time is experienced as passing increasingly quickly and seems more scarce in old age. Instead, time is experienced as passing more and more slowly across the age range included in the BASE sample.

The *group averages* of items on temporal orientation or time perspective (orientation toward the future, optimism, subjective proximity of death) all lie around 3 on a 5-point scale, with subjective proximity of death ($M = 2.84$, $SD = 1.28$) and orientation toward the future ($M = 2.77$, $SD = 1.3$) remaining slightly below and optimism ($M = 3.51$, $SD = 1.06$) reaching beyond 3. Thus, BASE participants expect their death neither in the very near nor in the distant future, state that they have plans for the next months and the coming year, and are quite optimistic when they think about the future. They also think about the present significantly more than about the past ($t(509) = 4.48$, $p = .00$) or the future ($t(509) = -2.55$, $p = .00$).

Turning to *age differences*, we find that subjective proximity to death increases ($r = .33$, $p < .01$) and orientation toward the future decreases with age ($r = -.39$, $p < .01$). Future optimism also decreases, but only minimally ($r = -.12$, $p < .01$). The time spent on thinking about the present, past, and future hardly changes over the age range from 70 to 103, although there is a tendency toward dwelling more on the past ($r = .21$, $p < .01$).

2.5.2 Does the Experience of Time Contribute toward Psychological Resilience?

In the following, we analyze the potential protective value of the experience of time. First we examine orientation toward the future and optimism. Optimism explains 14% of the variance of aging satisfaction in the BASE sample ("I am optimistic when I think of the future"). Future time perspective ("Do you have plans for the next months and the coming year?") has a smaller, but still significant predictive association with aging satisfaction (10% of the variance). This corresponds to findings reported for general well-being (e.g., Brandtstädter & Wentura, 1994; Spence, 1968).

The BASE sample's broad age range (70–103) makes it possible to test whether the correlationally ascertained protective value of optimism and future perspective reaches into very old age or whether there are changes. The latter seems likely in view of the evidence on changes of time perspective in old age. With age, a far-reaching orientation toward the future is transformed into what Nuttin (1985) called the "open present" (see also Kastenbaum, 1982; Rakowski, 1979): The anticipated units of the future become smaller. However, when we examine this hypothesis in regression models, using optimism and future time perspective as predictors, it is not supported. Both optimism and future time perspective retain their protective function up into very old age.

In the analysis of the association between experience of time and somatic risks, however, the interaction with speed of time reaches significance. For socioeconomic risks, the interaction with orientation toward the future becomes significant in the prediction of aging satisfaction. Figure 11.6 presents these two significant interaction effects. Figure 11.6a shows that the protective function of the perception of time passing quickly declines with increasing somatic risks. In contrast, the perceptions that the speed of time passing is just right or even slow are related to a buffering of the strongly negative correlation between somatic risks and aging satisfaction. Figure 11.6b presents the seemingly counterintuitive finding that a strong orientation toward the future negatively influences aging satisfaction of the socioeconomically disadvantaged.[5]

Taking into consideration that we are discussing correlational evidence, we can nevertheless interpret the evidence within the framework of the model of psychological resilience presented in this chapter. We first concentrate on the protective function of a slower time perception in persons impaired by somatic risks. If we assume that the speed of time passing is related to one's activity level (cf. Boesch, 1991), it seems likely that these individuals have reduced their activities for health reasons, causing time to pass

---

[5] These findings remain unchanged if persons with a psychiatric diagnosis of severe dementia (DSM-III-R; $n = 39$) or major depression ($n = 28$) are excluded.

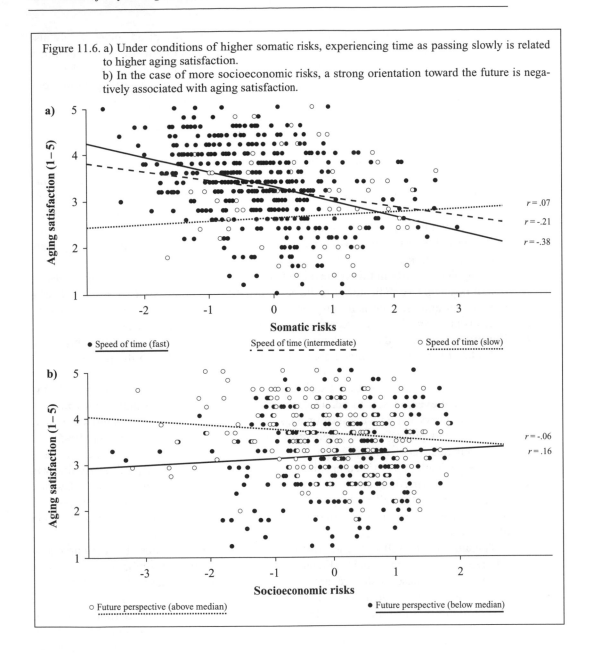

Figure 11.6. a) Under conditions of higher somatic risks, experiencing time as passing slowly is related to higher aging satisfaction.
b) In the case of more socioeconomic risks, a strong orientation toward the future is negatively associated with aging satisfaction.

more slowly. In this case, higher aging satisfaction would be related to the adaptation of activities to physical realities.

In the presence of many socioeconomic risks, aging satisfaction is lower if persons are strongly oriented toward the future. In complete contrast, future time perspective is positively correlated with aging satisfaction for the whole sample ($r = .31, p < .01$). Possibly, plans for the future cannot be realized in cases of high socioeconomic risks and are thus related to low aging satisfaction. The socioeconomically disadvantaged may also have hoped that the restrictions they experienced throughout their life would no longer apply in old age and feel disappointed to find that this is not so. However, this line of argument is purely speculative and can be equally well reversed. Only longitudinal evidence will be able to clarify this.

2.6   *Self-Definition*

Which role does the self-definition play in managing restrictions and losses in old and very old age (Freund, 1995)? First we look at the general function of self-definition. We then present some models dealing more specifically with different features of a self-definition that can contribute to resilience. In contrast to the analyses reported above, we can include a further criterion for psychological resilience, namely depressivity, because the unstructured assessment of the self-definition makes content overlap unlikely (see Section 1).

Using depressivity in this context is interesting because, in contrast to aging satisfaction, it is a negative indicator of resilience. Furthermore, depressivity – or its absence – is a broader and more domain-unspecific indicator of resilience than aging satisfaction, which is more specifically directed toward positive management of age-related changes. However, because of the breadth of the construct and content overlaps with many of the self-related measures examined above, it could not be included in the previously presented analyses.

The self-definition consists of self-related cognitions and concepts that are central to who one believes oneself to be. The self-definition influences an individual's interactions with others and with the surroundings by reducing the manifold of alternative interpretations and purposes in a given situation (Epstein, 1973, 1990; Freund, 1995). As claimed in Section 1, old age is a phase of life during which certain risks to mental health such as the death of a close companion or physical impairments are particularly likely to occur. These restrictions and losses can threaten the stability of self-definition, because various facets of the self no longer correspond to reality (e.g., continuation of sports or out-of-house trips in cases of immobility). How can the self-definition be maintained in old age despite such threats?

A feature of the self-definition that has attracted particular interest is the number of different self-defining domains (Freund, 1995; Linville, 1987; Rosenberg & Gara, 1985; Thoits, 1983). These models regard a large number of circumscribed self-defining domains as a resource to be utilized in case of restrictions and losses. For instance, Linville (1987) found that a complex self-definition (i.e., many distinct self-defining domains) weakens the influence of negative life events on health. Rosenberg and Gara's (1985) model assumes a hierarchical structure of self-defining domains (see also Epstein, 1990). According to this model, superordinate domains facilitate the maintenance of self-definition in the face of losses. Superordinate domains include many different aspects (e.g., "I have varied interests" can comprise interests such as football, music, theater, gardening, and politics). The "richer" a self-defining domain is, the more resistant to restrictions it is supposed to be.

Combining these two approaches, the multifacetedness of the self-definition has been conceptualized as comprising the number of self-defining domains and their richness

(Freund, 1995). In the following, we test the hypothesis that multifacetedness can be regarded as a resource that increases resilience in the face of restrictions.

2.6.1 Measurement Instrument

Self-definition was measured in BASE using the open question "Who am I?" (Bugental & Zehlen, 1950). Participants were instructed to imagine thinking about this question in peace and quiet and to make 10 statements describing themselves. The tape-recorded and transcribed answers were coded for content and variety with a specifically developed category system (for more details, see Freund, 1995). The multifacetedness of the self-definition was operationalized as the number of different self-defining domains weighted by their richness. Thus, a domain (e.g., family) received a higher multifacetedness score if an individual mentioned several aspects (e.g., family members' well-being, outings with them, their financial support).

2.6.2 Self-Definition and Psychological Resilience

In order to examine whether multifacetedness of self-definition can contribute to resilience in old and very old age, we performed separate regression analyses with aging satisfaction and depressivity as criteria. The number of clinical diagnoses was entered as an indicator of physical impairments. The relationship between this indicator and depressivity is significantly positive: The number of diagnoses explained 15% of the variance in depressivity ($p < .000$).

Whereas multifacetedness of self-definition does not significantly buffer the influence of physical impairments on aging satisfaction, it interacts significantly with physical impairments in the prediction of depressivity ($\Delta R^2 = .016$, $\Delta F = 9.57$, $p = .002$). Accordingly, multifacetedness is not positively related to aging satisfaction if physical impairments are present, but is negatively related to depressivity – the larger the number of different domains and the richness of a person's self-definition, the smaller the association between somatic morbidity and depressivity.

3   Conclusions

A model of psychological resilience of self and personality in old age formed the framework of this chapter. We examined which self-related characteristics and mechanisms help individuals to maintain satisfaction with their aging despite facing manifold (somatic and socioeconomic) risks.

Because the available BASE data set is cross-sectional, we were restricted to correlational associations for which causal interpretations are purely hypothetical. The test of causal relationships will only be possible once BASE longitudinal data become available. In the future, it would also be desirable to include other psychological variables such as intellectual functioning and social relationships in the model. Despite these restrictions, we hope that this chapter illustrated the contribution made by self-related processes and characteristics toward resilience in old age. In the following, we summarize and discuss our main findings.

Risk conditions aside, we find the following pattern of relationships between self-related features and aging satisfaction as an indicator of resilience: Persons lower on neuroticism and higher on extraversion are more satisfied with their own aging; persons with a surplus of positive emotions and those who take things humorously do not give up or want to know what is going on, and experience time as passing quickly report that they are more satisfied with their aging.

This pattern is quite radically altered if one takes into account specific development contexts when determining protective mechanisms and characteristics. For instance, endorsement of items indicative of neuroticism becomes adaptive in the face of age-related physical impairments. Conversely, the coping styles, "Keep going" and "Wish for information," as well as the experience of time passing quickly, become dysfunctional. In contrast, personal life investment and multifacetedness of the self-definition are not directly related to aging satisfaction, but lower or more selective investment and a more multifaceted self-definition do become protective given high somatic risks.

The pattern also changes in case of socioeconomic restrictions: Lower rather than higher surpluses of positive emotions become protective whereas the coping style "Wish for information," optimism, and a clear orientation toward the future become dysfunctional.

In summary, our findings show that when investigating the adaptive value of self-related characteristics and processes, one also has to take into account specific (internal or external) developmental contexts or individual constellations. This becomes particularly clear when considering the so-called regressive coping styles.

We also found several more indirect indications of resilience that contradict stereotypes of old age: Positive emotions outweigh the negative up into very old age; "regressive" coping styles are relatively rare; old adults invest more thoughts and actions in health and family than in dying and death or their past; they reach a medium score on optimism and orientation toward the future; the degree of personal life investment does not decrease as much as one would expect from biological models of vitality; and age differences in investment are mainly reflected in changes of content.

Taken together, these results on self and personality present a more positive image of old and very old age than findings on intellectual functioning (cf. Lindenberger & Reischies, Chapter 12). Still, a second look is worthwhile (cf. Smith & Baltes, Chapter 7). The general pattern of experienced emotions can easily be interpreted as the picture of a neurasthenic reaction well known from stress research. And if one considers all of the rather small negative age changes together as a pattern (e.g., decline of extraversion, positive emotions, satisfaction, etc.), one can recognize the substantial adaptation that the aging self has to achieve.

References

Aldwin, C. M. (1991). Does age affect the stress and coping process? Implications of age differences in perceived control. *Journal of Gerontology: Psychological Sciences, 46,* P174–P180.

Aldwin, C. M., Sutton, K. J., & Lachman, M. (1996). The development of coping resources in adulthood. *Journal of Personality, 64,* 837–873.

Allport, G. (1937). *Personality.* New York: Holt.

Atkinson, R. C. (1964). *An introduction to motivation.* Princeton, NJ: Van Nostrand Reinhold.

Baltes, P. B. (1987). Theoretical propositions of life-span developmental psychology: On the dynamics between growth and decline. *Developmental Psychology, 23,* 611–626.

Baltes, P. B., & Baltes, M. M. (1990). Psychological perspectives on successful aging: The model of selective optimization with compensation. In P. B. Baltes & M. M. Baltes (Eds.), *Successful aging: Perspectives from the behavioral sciences* (pp. 1–34). Cambridge: Cambridge University Press.

Baltes, P. B., Lindenberger, U., & Staudinger, U. M. (1998). Life-span theory in developmental psychology. In W. Damon (Ed.) & R. M. Lerner (Vol. Ed.), *Handbook of child psychology: Vol. 1. Theoretical models of human development* (5th ed., pp. 1029–1143). New York: Wiley.

Bengtson, V. L., Reedy, M. N., & Gordon, C. (1985). Aging and self-conceptions: Personality processes and social contexts. In J. E. Birren & K. W. Schaie (Eds.), *Handbook of the psychology of aging* (2nd ed., pp. 544–593). New York: Van Nostrand Reinhold.

Blanchard-Fields, F. (1986). Reasoning on social dilemmas varying in emotional saliency: An adult developmental study. *Psychology and Aging, 1*, 325–333.

Boesch, E. E. (1991). *Symbolic action theory and cultural psychology*. Heidelberg: Springer-Verlag.

Brandtstädter, J. (1986). Personale Entwicklungskontrolle und entwicklungsregulatives Handeln: Überlegungen und Befunde zu einem vernachlässigten Forschungsthema. *Zeitschrift für Entwicklungspsychologie und Pädagogische Psychologie, 18*, 316–334.

Brandtstädter, J., & Greve, W. (1994). The aging self: Stabilizing and protective processes. *Developmental Review, 14*, 52–80.

Brandtstädter, J., & Renner, G. (1990). Tenacious goal pursuit and flexible goal adjustment: Explication and age-related analysis of assimilative and accommodative strategies of coping. *Psychology and Aging, 5*, 58–67.

Brandtstädter, J., & Wentura, D. (1994). Veränderungen der Zeit- und Zukunftsperspektive im Übergang zum höheren Erwachsenenalter: Entwicklungspsychologische und differentielle Aspekte. *Zeitschrift für Entwicklungspsychologie und Pädagogische Psychologie, 26*, 2–21.

Bugental, J. F. T., & Zehlen, S. L. (1950). Investigations into the self-concept: The WAY technique. *Journal of Personality, 18*, 483–498.

Bühler, C. (1933). *Der Lebenslauf als psychologisches Problem*. Göttingen: Hogrefe.

Carstensen, L. L. (1993). Motivation for social contact across the life-span: A theory of socioemotional selectivity. In J. Jacobs (Ed.), *Nebraska Symposium on Motivation* (Vol. 40, pp. 209–254). Lincoln: University of Nebraska Press.

Cicchetti, D. (1989). Developmental psychopathology: Past, present and future. In D. Cicchetti (Ed.), *The emergence of a discipline: Rochester Symposium on Development Psychology* (Vol. 1, pp. 1–12). Hillsdale, NJ: Erlbaum.

Cohen, J. (1994). The earth is round (*p* < .05). *American Psychologist, 49*, 997–1003.

Costa, P. T., Jr., & McCrae, R. R. (1985). *The NEO Personality Inventory: Manual Form S and Form R*. Odessa, FL: Psychological Assessment Resources.

Costa, P. T., Jr., & McCrae, R. R. (1993). Psychological stress and coping in old age. In L. Goldberger & S. Breznitz (Eds.), *Handbook of stress: Theoretical and clinical aspects* (2nd ed., pp. 403–412). New York: Free Press.

Costa, P. T., Jr., Zonderman, A. B., McCrae, R. R., Cornoni-Huntley, J., Locke, B. Z., & Barbano, H. E. (1987). Longitudinal analyses of psychological well-being in a national sample: Stability of mean levels. *Journal of Gerontology, 42*, 50–55.

Diener, E. (1994). Assessing subjective well-being: Progress and opportunities. *Social Indicators Research, 31*, 103–157.

Diener, E., & Larsen, R. J. (1993). The experience of emotional well-being. In M. Lewis & J. M.
    Haviland (Eds.), *Handbook of emotions* (Vol. 28, pp. 405–415). New York: Guilford.

Epstein, S. (1973). The self-concept revisited: Or a theory of a theory. *American Psychologist, 28,*
    404–416.

Epstein, S. (1990). Cognitive-experiential self-theory. In L. A. Pervin (Ed.), *Handbook of
    personality: Theory and research* (pp. 165–192). New York: Guilford.

Erikson, E. H., Erikson, J. M., & Kivnick, H. Q. (1986). *Vital involvement in old age: The
    experience of old age in our time.* London: Norton.

Filipp, S.-H. (1996). Motivation and emotion. In J. E. Birren & K. W. Schaie (Eds.), *Handbook of
    the psychology of aging* (4th ed., pp. 218–235). San Diego, CA: Academic Press.

Filipp, S.-H., & Klauer, T. (1991). Subjective well-being in the face of critical life events: The
    case of successful copers. In F. Strack, M. Argyle, & N. Schwarz (Eds.), *Subjective
    well-being: An interdisciplinary perspective* (pp. 213–234). Oxford: Pergamon Press.

Folkman, S., Lazarus, R. S., Pimpley, S., & Novacek, J. (1987). Age differences in stress and
    coping processes. *Psychology and Aging, 2,* 171–184.

Fraisse, P. (1963). *The psychology of time.* New York: Harper & Row.

Freund, A. M. (1995). *Die Selbstdefinition alter Menschen: Inhalt, Struktur und Funktion*
    (Studien und Berichte des Max-Planck-Instituts für Bildungsforschung 61). Berlin:
    Edition Sigma.

Garmezy, N. (1991). Resilience in children's adaptation to negative life events and stressed
    environments. *Pediatric Annals, 20,* 459–466.

Headey, B., & Wearing, A. (1989). Personality, life events, and subjective well-being: Toward a
    dynamic equilibrium model. *Journal of Personality and Social Psychology, 57,*
    731–739.

Heckhausen, H. (1991). *Motivation and action.* New York: Springer.

Heckhausen, J. (1998). *Developmental regulation in adulthood: Age-normative and socio-
    structural constraints as adaptive challenges.* Cambridge: Cambridge University Press.

Heckhausen, J., & Schulz, R. (1995). A life-span theory of control. *Psychological Review, 102,*
    284–304.

Irion, J. C., & Blanchard-Fields, F. (1987). A cross-sectional comparison of adaptive coping in
    adulthood. *Journal of Gerontology, 42,* 502–504.

Janke, W., & Kallus, K. W. (1995). Reaktivität. In M. Amelang (Ed.), *Enzyklopädie der
    Psychologie: Vol. C-VIII-2. Interindividuelle Unterschiede* (pp. 1–89). Göttingen:
    Hogrefe.

Kastenbaum, R. (1982). Time course and time perspective in later life. In C. Eisdorfer (Ed.),
    Annual review of gerontology and geriatrics (Vol. 3, pp. 80–101). New York: Springer.

Kercher, K. (1992). Assessing subjective well-being in the old-old: The PANAS as a measure of
    orthogonal dimensions of positive and negative affect. *Research on Aging, 14,* 131–168.

Kruse, A. (1987). Coping with chronic disease, dying, and death: A contribution to competence in
    old age. *Comprehensive Gerontology, C1,* 1–11.

Kuhl, J. (1986). Motivation and information processing. In R. M. Sorrentino & E. T. Higgins
    (Eds.), *Handbook of motivation and cognition* (pp. 404–434). New York: Wiley.

Kunzmann, U. (1994). *Emotionales Wohlbefinden im Alter: Struktur, Stabilität und Veränderung.*
    Unpublished master's thesis, Free University of Berlin.

Labouvie-Vief, G., Hakim-Larson, J., DeVoe, M., & Schoeberlein, S. (1989). Emotions and self-
    regulation: A life-span view. *Human Development, 32,* 279–299.

Labouvie-Vief, G., Hakim-Larson, J., & Hobart, C. J. (1987). Age, ego level, and the life-span
    development of coping and defense processes. *Psychology and Aging, 2,* 286–293.

Lachman, M. E. (1986). Personal control in later life: Stability, change, and cognitive correlates. In M. M. Baltes & P. B. Baltes (Eds.), *The psychology of control and aging* (pp. 207–236). Hillsdale, NJ: Erlbaum.

LaRue, A. (1992). *Aging and neuropsychological assessment*. New York: Plenum Press.

Lawton, M. P. (1975). The Philadelphia Geriatric Center Morale Scale: A revision. *Journal of Gerontology, 30*, 85–89.

Lazarus, R. S., & Launier, R. (1978). Stress-related transactions between person and environment. In L. A. Pervin & M. Lewis (Eds.), *Perspectives in interactional psychology* (pp. 287–327). New York: Plenum Press.

Lehr, U. (1967). Attitudes towards the future in old age. *Human Development, 10*, 230–238.

Levenson, R. W., Carstensen, L. L., Friesen, W. V., & Ekman, P. (1991). Emotion, physiology, and expression in old age. *Psychology and Aging, 6*, 28–35.

Levin, I., & Zakay, D. (Eds.). (1989). *Time and human cognition: A life-span perspective* (Advances in psychology, Vol. 59). Amsterdam: North-Holland.

Lewin, K. (1926a). Untersuchungen zur Handlungs- und Affektpsychologie: I. Vorbemerkungen über die psychischen Kräfte und Energien und über die Struktur der Seele. *Psychologische Forschung, 7*, 294–329.

Lewin, K. (1926b). Untersuchungen zur Handlungs- und Affektpsychologie: II. Vorsatz, Wille und Bedürfnis. *Psychologische Forschung, 7*, 330–385.

Linville, P. W. (1987). Self-complexity as a cognitive buffer against stress-related illness and depression. *Journal of Personality and Social Psychology, 52*, 663–676.

Malatesta, C. Z., & Kalnok, M. (1984). Emotional experience in younger and older adults. *Journal of Gerontology: Psychological Sciences, 39*, P301–P308.

Marsiske, M., Lang, F. R., Baltes, P. B., & Baltes, M. M. (1995). Selective optimization with compensation: Life-span perspectives on successful human development. In R. A. Dixon & L. Bäckman (Eds.), *Psychological compensation: Managing losses and promoting gains* (pp. 35–79). Mahwah, NJ: Erlbaum.

Martin, P., Poon, L. W., Kim, E., & Johnson, M. A. (1996). Social and psychological resources in the oldest old. *Experimental Aging Research, 22*, 121–139.

McCrae, R. R. (1989). Age differences and changes in the use of coping mechanisms. *Journal of Gerontology: Psychological Sciences, 44*, P919–P928.

Myers, D. G., & Diener, E. (1995). Who is happy? *Psychological Science, 6*, 10–19.

Nuttin, J. (1985). *Future time perspective and motivation* (Louvain Psychology Series: Studia Psychologica). Leuven, Belgium: Leuven University Press; Hillsdale, NJ: Erlbaum.

Palmore, E. B. (1988). *The facts on aging quiz: A handbook of uses and results*. New York: Springer.

Pfeiffer, E. (1977). Psychopathology and social pathology. In J. E. Birren & K. W. Schaie (Eds.), *Handbook of the psychology of aging* (pp. 650–671). New York: Van Nostrand Reinhold.

Rakowski, W. (1979). Future time perspective in later adulthood: Review and research directions. *Experimental Aging Research, 5*, 43–88.

Reker, G. T., & Wong, P. T. P. (1988). Aging as an individual process: Toward a theory of personal meaning. In J. E. Birren & V. L. Bengtson (Eds.), *Emergent theories of aging* (pp. 214–246). New York: Springer.

Rosenberg, S., & Gara, M. A. (1985). The multiplicity of personal identity. In P. Shaver (Ed.), *Review of personality and social psychology* (Vol. 6, pp. 87–113). Beverly Hills, CA: Sage.

Rott, C., & Thomae, H. (1991). Coping in longitudinal perspective: Findings from the Bonn Longitudinal Study on Aging. *Journal of Cross-Cultural Gerontology, 6*, 23–40.

Ruth, J.-E., & Coleman, P. (1996). Personality and aging: Coping and management of the self in later life. In J. E. Birren & K. W. Schaie (Eds.), *Handbook of the psychology of aging* (4th ed., pp. 308–322). San Diego, CA: Academic Press.

Rutter, M. (1987). Resilience in the face of adversity: Protective factors and resistance to psychiatric disorder. *British Journal of Psychiatry, 147,* 598–611.

Ryff, C. D. (1989). In the eye of the beholder: Views of psychological well-being among middle-aged and older adults. *Psychology and Aging, 4,* 195–210.

Sandvik, K. W., Diener, E., & Seidlitz, L. (1993). Subjective well-being: The convergence and stability of self-report and non-self-report measures. *Journal of Personality, 61,* 317–342.

Schulz, R. (1985). Emotion and affect. In J. E. Birren & K. W. Schaie (Eds.), *Handbook of the psychology of aging* (2nd ed., pp. 531–543). New York: Van Nostrand Reinhold.

Spence, D. L. (1968). The role of futurity in future adaptation. *The Gerontologist, 8,* 180–183.

Staudinger, U. M. (1989). *The study of life review: An approach to the investigation of intellectual development across the life span* (Studien und Berichte des Max-Planck-Instituts für Bildungsforschung 47). Berlin: Edition Sigma.

Staudinger, U. M., & Fleeson, W. (1996). Self and personality in very old age: A sample case of resilience? *Development and Psychopathology, 8,* 867–885.

Staudinger, U. M., & Fleeson, W. (1997). *Life investment in a sample of 20- to 105-year-olds.* Unpublished manuscript, Max Planck Institute for Human Development, Berlin.

Staudinger, U. M., Freund, A. M., & Smith, J. (1995). *Differential coping patterns in old age.* Unpublished manuscript, Max Planck Institute for Human Development, Berlin.

Staudinger, U. M., Marsiske, M., & Baltes, P. B. (1995). Resilience and reserve capacity in later adulthood: Potentials and limits of development across the life span. In D. Cicchetti & D. J. Cohen (Eds.), *Developmental psychopathology: Vol. 2. Risk, disorder, and adaptation* (pp. 801–847). New York: Wiley.

Taylor, S. E., & Brown, J. D. (1988). Illusion and well-being: A social psychological perspective on mental health. *Psychological Bulletin, 103,* 193–210.

Thoits, P. A. (1983). Multiple identities and psychological well-being: A reformulation and test of the social isolation hypothesis. *American Sociological Review, 8,* 174–187.

Thomae, H. (1987). Alltagsbelastungen im Alter und Versuche ihrer Bewältigung. In U. Lehr & H. Thomae (Eds.), *Formen seelischen Alterns: Ergebnisse der Bonner Gerontologischen Längsschnittstudie (BOLSA)* (pp. 92–114). Stuttgart: Enke.

Thomae, H. (1992). Emotion and personality. In J. E. Birren, R. B. Sloane, & G. D. Cohen (Eds.), *Handbook of mental health and aging* (2nd ed., pp. 355–375). San Diego, CA: Academic Press.

Vaillant, G. E. (1977). *Adaptation to life.* Boston: Little, Brown.

Wallach, M. A., & Green, L. R. (1961). On age and the subjective speed of time. *Journal of Gerontology, 16,* 71–74.

Watson, D., Clark, L. A., & Tellegen, A. (1988). Development and validation of brief measures of positive and negative affect: The PANAS scales. *Journal of Personality and Social Psychology, 54,* 1063–1070.

Wegener, B. (1988). *Kritik des Prestiges.* Opladen: Westdeutscher Verlag.

Weiner, B., & Graham, S. (1989). Understanding the motivational role of affect: Life-span research from an attributional perspective. *Cognition and Emotion, 3,* 410–419.

Whitbourne, S. K. (1987). Personality development in adulthood and old age: Relationships among identity style, health, and well-being. In K. W. Schaie & C. Eisdorfer (Eds.), *Annual review of gerontology and geriatrics* (Vol. 7, pp. 189–216). New York: Springer.

CHAPTER 12

Limits and Potentials of Intellectual Functioning in Old Age

Ulman Lindenberger and Friedel M. Reischies

In the first-occasion Intensive Protocol of the Berlin Aging Study ($N = 516$), a psychometric battery of 14 cognitive tests was used to assess individual differences in five intellectual abilities: reasoning, memory, and perceptual speed from the mechanic (broad fluid) domain, and knowledge and fluency from the pragmatic (broad crystallized) domain. In addition, the Enhanced Cued Recall (ECR) test was administered in the context of a separate neuropsychological examination to identify dementia-specific cognitive impairments in cue utilization and learning potential. The overall pattern of results points to sizable and highly intercorrelated age-based losses in various aspects of presumably brain-related functioning, including sensory functions such as vision and hearing. Intellectual abilities had negative linear relations to age, with more pronounced age-based reductions in mechanic than pragmatic abilities. Ability intercorrelations formed a highly positive manifold, and did not follow the mechanic-pragmatic distinction. Gender differences were small in size, and did not interact with age. Indicators of sensory and sensorimotor functioning were strongly related to intellectual functioning, accounting for 59% of the total reliable variance in general intelligence. Even for knowledge, sociobiographical indicators were less closely linked to intellectual functioning than the sensory-sensorimotor variables, and accounted for 24% of the variance in general intelligence. With respect to potentials, results obtained with the ECR test demonstrate that the ability to learn from experience is preserved in normal cognitive aging across the entire age range studied, but severely impaired in individuals with dementia.

1   Introduction

Personal integrity is commonly associated with basic intellectual faculties such as the ability to reflect and remember. Conversely, the decline of these abilities is often linked to illness, need for care, and the disintegration of the self. Hence, the effects of biological aging on intelligence are perceived as particularly threatening. Medical and psychological research on this issue has led to ambiguous results, which strengthen and weaken these concerns. On the one hand, it is worrisome that, with increasing age, a rising proportion of the old and very old is afflicted by Alzheimer's disease and other severe brain disorders (Häfner, 1992; Hofman et al., 1991). On the other hand, the continued existence of learning ability in healthy older adults, the stability and/or increase of predominantly knowledge-based abilities, and the indisputable existence of mentally fit individuals among the very old give rise to optimism (Lindenberger & Baltes, 1994a).

In light of the ambiguity and scarcity of relevant data for the very old segment of the life-span, our primary goal in this contribution is to document and describe intellectual

329

abilities in old and very old age, such as their age gradients, intercorrelations, age-based differences in various aspects of variability, and their embeddedness in sociobiographical as well as aging-related biological systems of influence.[1]

In addition, a related but secondary goal of the present study is to link the major findings emanating from this descriptive enterprise to central themes and concepts of life-span theory (P. B. Baltes, Lindenberger, & Staudinger, 1998) and cognitive aging research (Craik & Salthouse, 1992; Lindenberger & Baltes, 1994a). Typical examples of such themes and concepts include the two-component model of life-span cognition (P. B. Baltes, 1987, 1997; cf. Cattell, 1971; Horn, 1982), the dedifferentiation hypothesis of intellectual aging (P. B. Baltes, Cornelius, Spiro, Nesselroade, & Willis, 1980; Garrett, 1946; Lienert & Crott, 1964; Reinert, 1970), and the distinction between normal cognitive aging and aging with dementia (Buschke, Sliwinski, Kuslansky, & Lipton, 1995, 1997; Nebes, 1992).

We begin this chapter by presenting our general approach and the relevant measures (Section 2). Based on the psychometric battery of intellectual abilities, we then report the age gradients, intellectual-ability intercorrelations, and correlates of intellectual functioning for the total sample (Section 3). Subsequently, we report analyses attempting to separate cognitive aging without dementia from cognitive aging with dementia (Section 4). Finally, we point to the methodological shortcomings of the present data set, summarize the main findings, and discuss the relevance of the observed negative age differences for everyday intellectual functioning in old and very old age (Section 5).

2   Methods

2.1   General Design Features and Sample Description

The data presented in this article refer to all individuals who completed the 14-session Intensive Protocol of the first measurement occasion of BASE ($N = 516$, age range = 70–103 years, mean age = 84.9 years, $SD = 8.7$ years). The sample is stratified by age and gender, resulting in 43 men and 43 women in each of six different age brackets (70–74, 75–79, 80–84, 85–89, 90–94, 95+ years; cf. P. B. Baltes et al., Chapter 1 in this volume; Nuthmann & Wahl, 1996, 1997). Stratification has two interrelated main advantages over the necessarily skewed (e.g., age) and unbalanced (e.g., gender) distributions resulting from representative sampling schemes: (a) It produces equally reliable estimates of population parameters across all levels of the age variable and in both genders; (b) it greatly enhances the likelihood of detecting interactions of age and/or gender with other variables (cf. McClelland & Judd, 1993).

The analysis of sample selectivity has been a central part of the design and analysis of BASE (cf. P. B. Baltes et al., Chapter 1; Lindenberger et al., Chapter 2). With respect to mean-level selectivity, estimates based on repeated applications of the Pearson-Lawley formulae indicate that the Intensive Protocol sample (i.e., the target sample of this chapter, $N = 516$) has a positive selection bias in many domains of functioning such as somatic health, Activities of Daily Living, sensory-sensorimotor and intellectual functioning, social network size, and various personality dimensions such as openness to

---

[1] Some of the findings summarized in this chapter have been published before in English (P. B. Baltes & Lindenberger, 1997; Lindenberger & Baltes, 1997) and German (P. B. Baltes & Lindenberger, 1995; Lindenberger & Baltes, 1995a; Reischies & Lindenberger, 1996).

Table 12.1. *Internal consistencies, interrater or intercoder agreements, and factor loadings of the 14 cognitive tests*

Ability	Name of test[a]	α[b]	r[c]	τ_c[d]	β[e]
Reasoning	Figural Analogies	.90	—	—	.76
	Letter Series	.86	—	—	.79
	Practical Problems	.84	—	—	.82
Memory	Paired Associates	.87	.99	.94	.72
	Activity Recall	.61	.91	.80	.82
	Memory for Text	.57	.96	.86	.66
Perceptual speed	Identical Pictures	.90	—	—	.89
	Digit Letter test	.96	1.00	1.00	.90
	Digit Symbol Substitution	—	1.00	.99	.92
Knowledge	Spot-a-Word	.92	—	—	.66
	Vocabulary	.82	.96	.85	.83
	Practical Knowledge	.82	.95	.84	.87
Fluency	Categories (Animals)	—	.99	.94	.87
	Word Beginnings (Letter "S")	—	.99	.94	.78

[a]Detailed descriptions of the tests are provided in Lindenberger et al. (1993).
[b]Cronbach's alpha. Incorrect responses as well as performance on items that were not attempted were coded as zero.
[c]Intercoder reliability (Pearson's r); not present for tests with computerized response entry.
[d]Intercoder reliability (Kendall's Tau-c); not present for tests with computerized response entry.
[e]Factor loadings (i.e., path coefficients) for a latent factor model with intercorrelated intellectual abilities (for details, see Lindenberger & Baltes, 1997).

experience. The magnitude of these selectivity effects was largest for general intelligence but never exceeded half a standard deviation. Generally, and with the exception of dementia prevalence, where the positive selection bias (e.g., the degree to which dementia prevalence was underestimated) was estimated to be largest in the very old segment of the population (i.e., age 95 and older), observed selectivity did not interact to a sizable degree with age or gender. More importantly, selectivity analyses did not provide any strong evidence in favor of a distortion of variances or covariances as a consequence of sample attrition. This suggests that the structural relations among variables, which figure prominently in this report, were influenced very little by sample selectivity.

2.2   Psychometric Battery of Cognitive Tests

The cognitive test battery comprised 14 tests measuring five intellectual abilities: (a) *perceptual speed* (measured by Digit Letter, Digit Symbol Substitution, and Identical Pictures); (b) *reasoning* (Figural Analogies, Letter Series, and Practical Problems); (c) *memory* (e.g., short-term acquisition and retrieval; Activity Recall, Memory for Text, and Paired Associates); (d) *knowledge* (Practical Knowledge, Spot-a-Word, and Vocabulary); (e) *fluency* (Animals, Letter "S"). A detailed description of the tests has been provided elsewhere (Lindenberger, Mayr, & Kliegl, 1993). The internal consistencies, interrater agreements, and confirmatory factor loadings of the tests for the present sample (i.e., $N = 516$) are reported in Table 12.1. The reliability estimates (i.e., internal consistencies and/or interrater agreements) were satisfactory for all tests in the battery. In accordance with earlier analyses based on a subsample ($n = 156$) of the present data set (Lindenberger & Baltes, 1994b), the correlational structure of the cognitive battery was well described by a hierarchical factor model consisting of five first-order factors representing the five different intellectual abilities and a single second-order factor representing general intelligence (see Fig. 7.1 in Smith & Baltes, Chapter 7; for details, see Lindenberger & Baltes, 1997).

Construction of the battery was informed by the two-component model of intelligence (P. B. Baltes, 1987, 1997), which is closely related to the Cattell-Horn theory of fluid and crystallized intelligence (Gf-Gc theory; Cattell, 1971; Horn, 1982, 1989; for a comparison of the two approaches, see P. B. Baltes et al., 1998). Specifically, perceptual speed, reasoning, and memory represent the "mechanics" of cognition, whereas knowledge and fluency primarily represent the pragmatics of cognition, or individual differences in acquired, culturally relevant bodies of knowledge.

Cognitive testing was assisted by a Macintosh SE/30 equipped with a touch-sensitive screen. With respect to tests related to reasoning and knowledge, items were ordered by ascending order of difficulty, and testing was terminated when subjects made a certain number of *consecutive* failures (three in the case of Figural Analogies, Letter Series, Practical Problems, and Spot-a-Word, six in the case of Vocabulary). With the exception of the Digit Letter and the Digit Symbol Substitution tests, instructions were presented in large fonts on the computer screen. In case of the Digit Letter and the Digit Symbol, instructions were presented in large fonts on a piece of paper.

Testing took place at the residence of the subjects. Tests were administered in the following order: Digit Letter, Spot-a-Word, Memory for Text, Figural Analogies, Letter "S," Vocabulary, Practical Problems, Digit Symbol Substitution, Activity Recall, Identical Pictures, Paired Associates, Animals, Letter Series, and Practical Knowledge. In 81% of the cases, the entire test battery was carried out in a single session. In almost all remaining instances, testing was divided into two sessions. In that case, the first session ended with Activity Recall, the second session began with Identical Pictures, and all tests were administered in the original sequence. Persons who could not work on the computerized version of the battery because of very poor vision or blindness were administered a shortened auditory version of the battery.

Overall, 494 of the total of 7,224 attainable data points (i.e., 516 persons by 14 tests), or 7%, were missing from the psychometric battery data set. Unless stated differently, the data reported in this article refer to the persons-by-variables matrix after replacement of missing data through estimates based on linear regression. Missing data were estimated *within* each of the five intellectual abilities, that is, without the use of information based on tests of the remaining four intellectual abilities (for more information, see Lindenberger & Baltes, 1997).

2.3   *Neuropsychological Assessment*

The psychometric battery of intellectual-ability tests was complemented by a neuropsychological examination (for more information, cf. Reischies & Geiselmann, 1994; Reischies & Lindenberger, 1996). In the following report, we focus on three measures: (a) the Enhanced Cued Recall test (ECR; Grober, Buschke, Crystal, Bank, & Dresner, 1988) to estimate interindividual differences in encoding specificity, which is assumed to be selectively impaired in dementia (Buschke et al., 1995, 1997); (b) the Mini Mental State Examination (MMSE; Folstein, Folstein, & McHugh, 1975); and (c) an index of brain atrophy based on a CT scan of the brain.

In the *Enhanced Cued Recall test,* 16 pictorially represented concrete items are repeatedly shown with and without category cues at both encoding and recall (for a full description of the procedures, see Grober et al., 1988). The present report focuses on cued recall after the first, second, and third learning trial. Both initial level and degree of improvement over consecutive trials are seen as indicators of effective cue utilization, and are assumed to reflect the specificity with which items are encoded during repeated presentation.

The *Mini Mental State Examination* is a standard multi-item checklist, and is often used as a screening device in epidemiological studies of dementia. The German translation followed Zaudig et al. (1991). For the analysis reported in this chapter, we used the short form of the MMSE (SMMS; cf. Klein et al., 1985).

The *brain atrophy index* was determined as part of the medical examination of BASE (Steinhagen-Thiessen & Borchelt, Chapter 5). A CT scan was performed at two different layers of the brain; both internal atrophy (e.g., ventricle size) and external atrophy (e.g., the distance between the brain and the skull) were assessed, and were subsequently rated by an experienced clinician on a four-point scale. The clinician was blind to all other characteristics of the participants including their age. The present score is based on the unit-weighted composite of the indices of inner and outer atrophy, which were moderately intercorrelated, $r = .54$. Primarily for organizational reasons, the CT scan was administered to only 254 of the 516 participants (mean age = 81.5 years, age range = 70–99 years, $SD = 7.7$). Of these 254, 143 were male, and 24 had received a clinical diagnosis of dementia. Additional procedural and descriptive information regarding this measure can be found elsewhere (Reischies, Rossius, & Felsenberg, 1997).

2.4   Other Measures

In addition to the psychometric test battery of intellectual abilities and the neuropsychological measures, a number of other constructs will be considered in this chapter. Most of these constructs refer to sensory-sensorimotor or sociocultural/biographical correlates of intellectual functioning, and allow us to position individual differences in intelligence among old and very old adults in relation to these two systems of influence. Detailed descriptions of these constructs are provided elsewhere (see Lindenberger & Baltes, 1997, as well as the original references provided below). In the following, we restrict ourselves to a brief definition of each variable.

Auditory acuity (i.e., hearing) was assessed in decibels, and refers to reverse-coded hearing thresholds in both ears for pure tones of eight different frequencies (i.e., 0.25, 0.50, 1.00, 2.00, 3.00, 4.00. 6.00, and 8.00 kHz; cf. Lindenberger & Baltes, 1997; Marsiske et al., Chapter 13).

Balance/gait was measured with two clinical assessments of balance and gait, the Romberg trial and the 360° turn (cf. Lindenberger & Baltes, 1997; Marsiske et al., Chapter 13).

Of the 516 participants, 109 (i.e., 21%) received a *clinical diagnosis of dementia* according to DSM-III-R (American Psychiatric Association, 1987) criteria (cf. Helmchen et al., Chapter 6; very mild to mild: $n = 37$; moderate: $n = 33$; severe: $n = 39$).

General somatic morbidity corresponds to the number of distinct clinically relevant diagnoses according to ICD-9 criteria; $M = 8.1$, $SD = 4.0$. A detailed description of somatic morbidity in BASE is provided by Steinhagen-Thiessen and Borchelt (Chapter 5).

Income represents the amount of net income in DM per month per capita on a five-point scale (1 = less than 1,000; 2 = 1,000–1,399; 3 = 1,400–1,799; 4 = 1,800–2,199; 5 = 2,200 and more; $M = 3.44$, $SD = 1.22$). Detailed information regarding the income distribution in this sample can be found elsewhere (cf. Mayer et al., Chapter 8).

Medication refers to the number of prescribed medications; $M = 3.6$, $SD = 2.7$ (for more details, see Steinhagen & Borchelt, Chapter 5; Linden et al., Chapter 16).

Social prestige is based on a standard rating scale of occupational prestige in Germany (cf. Mayer et al., Chapter 8). Ratings refer to the prestige of the participants' last occupation before retirement.

For *social class*, participants were arranged on a continuum of social stratification, ranging from lower class (7% of the sample), lower middle class (20%) to middle middle class (31%), upper middle class (30%), and higher middle class (11%; cf. Mayer et al., Chapter 8).

Visual acuity (i.e., vision) was measured in Snellen decimal units at two different distances using two different standard reading tables (cf. Lindenberger & Baltes, 1997; Marsiske et al., Chapter 13). Measurements were taken without and with the best optical correction (i.e., glasses) available to the subject. Analyses reported in this chapter are based on better values, which in most cases referred to corrected vision.

Years of education represents the number of years spent in formal educational settings. In addition to the number of years spent in elementary school and the different types of high school in Germany (Hauptschule, Realschule, Gymnasium), it also includes formal occupational (e.g., apprenticeships) and academic (e.g., university) training. On average, participants in this sample had 10.8 years of education ($SD = 2.3$).

3   Intellectual Abilities in Old and Very Old Age: Age Gradients, Structure, and Correlates

In this section, we report the age gradients, structure, and correlates in intellectual functioning as assessed by the psychometric battery of intellectual abilities. By default, analyses refer to the entire Intensive Protocol sample ($N = 516$), that is, they include individuals with a clinical diagnosis of dementia. In addition, we also mention results for the sample obtained after excluding individuals with a clinical diagnosis of dementia ($n = 407$, mean age = 83.3 years).

This section's focus on the full sample, rather than the reduced sample, has two reasons. First, it can be argued, from a radically descriptive point of view, that the age-based increase in dementia prevalence forms an integral part of *aging as a population process*. Therefore, if the goal is to describe changes in population parameters, the a priori exclusion of individuals who presumably suffer from some form of dementia leads to a less generalizable picture of age differences in intellectual functioning in old and very old age than results based on age-stratified random samples of the *total* population. The second reason is more methodological in kind. It is commonly assumed that the validity and reliability of a clinical diagnosis of dementia, especially in the very mild to moderate range and among the very old, is not perfect. For this reason, an a priori exclusion of subjects with a dementia diagnosis would have the unwanted consequence that subsequent

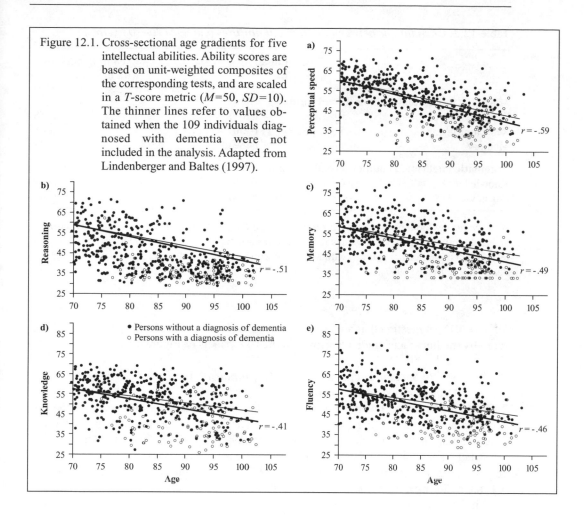

Figure 12.1. Cross-sectional age gradients for five intellectual abilities. Ability scores are based on unit-weighted composites of the corresponding tests, and are scaled in a *T*-score metric (*M*=50, *SD*=10). The thinner lines refer to values obtained when the 109 individuals diagnosed with dementia were not included in the analysis. Adapted from Lindenberger and Baltes (1997).

analyses are conditionalized upon an assessment that may not be more valid and reliable than many of the measures used thereafter.

3.1 Age Gradients of Intellectual Abilities in Old and Very Old Age

3.1.1 Overview

Figure 12.1 shows the age relations of the five intellectual abilities in a *T*-score metric (*M* = 50, *SD* = 10). The linear age relations of the unit-weighted composites ranged from -.41 for knowledge to -.59 for perceptual speed; for latent ability constructs, they ranged from -.49 (knowledge) to -.61 (perceptual speed). The magnitude of age relations was somewhat less pronounced when individuals with a clinical diagnosis of dementia were excluded from the analysis (see Table 12.2, and the thinner regression lines of the panels in Fig. 12.1). Quadratic age trends did not differ significantly from zero (perceptual speed: $r = .03$; reasoning: $r = .09$; memory: $r = .00$; knowledge: $r = .00$; fluency: $r = .00$;

Table 12.2. *Correlations between intellectual abilities and age (70–103 years)*

	Total sample (N = 516)		Excluding persons with dementia	
Mechanic intellectual abilities (broad fluid)				
Perceptual speed	-.59	(-.61)	-.54	(-.58)
Reasoning	-.51	(-.56)	-.44	(-.49)
Memory	-.49	(-.56)	-.39	(-.47)
Pragmatic intellectual abilities (broad crystallized)				
Knowledge	-.41	(-.49)	-.33	(-.41)
Fluency	-.46	(-.53)	-.40	(-.45)

Note. Values without parentheses refer to unit-weighted composites of the indicators, and correspond directly to Figure 12.1. Values in parentheses are based on a latent model positing five intercorrelated intellectual abilities with age as a correlate at the latent level (for details, see Lindenberger & Baltes, 1997).

all ps > .01), suggesting that relations between performance level and age were well captured by the linear age gradients shown in the five panels of Figure 12.1.

3.1.2 Ability-Specific Differences in the Magnitude of Age-Based Decrements: Mechanics versus Pragmatics

Table 12.2 reports the linear age relations of the five intellectual abilities. As expected, negative age relations were more pronounced for the three mechanic than for the two pragmatic abilities (for unit-weighted composites: $z = 4.98$, $p < .01$; for latent ability constructs: $z = 5.34$, $p < .01$).[2] Analyses with the reduced sample (i.e., after exclusion of subjects with dementia) led to analogous results (unit-weighted composites: $z = 4.33$, $p < .01$; latent ability constructs: $z = 4.80$, $p < .01$).

Within the three mechanic abilities, the age relation of perceptual speed ($r = -.59$) was more pronounced than the average age relations of reasoning ($r = -.51$) and memory ($r = -.49$; $z = 3.60$, $p < .01$). In contrast, the age gradients of the two more pragmatic abilities did not differ significantly from each other (knowledge: $r = -.41$; fluency: $r = -.46$; $z = 1.45$, $p > .10$). Analyses excluding individuals with dementia and analyses based on latent ability constructs provided analogous results.

With respect to cross-sectional age gradients, we conclude that the distinction between mechanic (broad fluid) and pragmatic (broad crystallized) intellectual abilities extends into old and very old age. However, compared with earlier periods of the life-span, the distinction in age trajectories appears to be less pronounced. Specifically, earlier differences in directionality (i.e., stability/decrements vs. stability/increments) are con-

---

[2] Differences between (sets of) correlated correlation coefficients were tested for statistical significance using the formulae proposed by Meng, Rosenthal, and Rubin (1992). For instance, differences in the age relations of mechanic and pragmatic abilities were tested with Formula (8) of Meng et al. (1992). This formula allows researchers to specify a contrast to test whether one set of variables (e.g., mechanic abilities) is more highly related to a criterion variable (e.g., age) than another set of variables (e.g., pragmatic abilities).

verted into different degrees of linear decrement. In this context, it is important to note that the three tests of knowledge were administered without any external constraints on testing time, and that instructions, if necessary, were repeated to make sure that participants knew what they were supposed to do. Thus, it is difficult to argue that the negative age gradient for knowledge primarily reflects the operation of age-associated but ability-extraneous performance factors.

3.1.3 Examination of Gender Differences in Level and Age Relations of Intellectual Functioning

Hierarchical regression analyses were computed to examine the possible existence of gender differences in the level and the age relations of intellectual functioning for each of the five intellectual abilities. Due to stratification, age and gender were orthogonal in this sample (average age for men = 84.7 years; average age for women = 85.1 years; correlation between gender and age: $r = .02$, n.s.). Therefore, age, gender, and the age-by-gender interaction orthogonalized with respect to the two main effects were entered simultaneously into the linear regression equation.

In addition to main effects of age, which, reflecting the orthogonality of the predictors, were identical to those reported before, we observed two main effects of gender, one for reasoning and the other for knowledge. In both cases, men had significantly higher scores than women (reasoning: $\beta = -.13$, $t = -3.37$, $p < .002$; knowledge: $\beta = -.15$, $t = -3.68$, $p < .002$; p-values are Bonferroni-adjusted, i.e., .01/5). When expressed in standard deviation units [i.e., $(\text{mean}_{men} - \text{mean}_{women}) / SD_{pooled}$], the effect size of the male advantage was .28 for reasoning and .31 for knowledge. None of the remaining effects were significant. Specifically, there were no indications that age gradients differed significantly as a function of gender.

A possible reason for the observed male advantage refers to the existence of historically stable gender-linked inequalities in societal opportunity structures such as access to formal education. On average, men had received more education than women (men: $M = 11.3$ years, $SD = 2.5$; women: $M = 10.2$ years, $SD = 2.0$; $t = -5.62$, $p < .01$). In accordance with the social-inequality interpretation, gender differences in reasoning and knowledge were no longer significant after statistically controlling for individual differences in education (reasoning: $\beta = -.05$, $t = -1.48$, $p = .14$; knowledge: $\beta = -.06$, $t = -1.66$, $p = .10$). However, we now noticed a significant *female* advantage for memory ($\beta = .12$, $t = 3.13$, $p < .002$). Possibly, this female advantage had been masked by gender-linked individual differences in years of education in the original analysis. Note that the existence of a small but reliable episodic-memory advantage for women is consistent with findings from several other large-scale studies on memory functioning during adulthood and old age (Herlitz, Nilsson, & Bäckman, 1997).

3.2 The Structure of Intellectual Abilities in Old and Very Old Age

We now turn to the structural properties of intellectual functioning in old and very old age. We inspect the intercorrelations of the five intellectual abilities, propose a structural model to capture the structure of old-age intelligence in a more formal manner, and examine possible age differences in ability intercorrelations and interindividual variability.

Table 12.3. *Intercorrelations among intellectual abilities*

	Perceptual speed		Reasoning		Memory		Knowledge		Fluency	
Perceptual speed	—		.72	(.82)	.71	(.85)	.71	(.83)	.73	(.85)
Reasoning	.60	(.73)	—		.64	(.80)	.70	(.86)	.63	(.77)
Memory	.60	(.77)	.52	(.71)	—		.66	(.84)	.70	(.89)
Knowledge	.64	(.77)	.62	(.81)	.58	(.79)	—		.70	(.87)
Fluency	.64	(.79)	.52	(.68)	.61	(.84)	.63	(.83)	—	

Note. $N = 516$. First-order correlations are shown above, age-partialed correlations below the main diagonal. Values without parentheses refer to unit-weighted composites, values in parentheses to intercorrelated latent factors (for details, see Lindenberger & Baltes, 1997).

3.2.1   Intercorrelations of Intellectual Abilities

Table 12.3 reports the intercorrelations among the five intellectual abilities. Correlations were high and uniform throughout all five abilities. For instance, at the level of unit-weighted composites, the median correlation among the five intellectual abilities was $r = .70$, the lowest correlation was $r = .63$, and the highest correlation was $r = .73$. When performing an exploratory factor analysis with principal components extraction over the five unit-weighted ability scores, the first unrotated factor accounted for 75% of the total variance. Finally, at the level of latent constructs (e.g., after correcting for unreliability), the median correlation was $r = .85$, the lowest correlation was $r = .77$, and the highest correlation was $r = .89$.

The magnitude of these intercorrelations is higher than the range commonly observed during earlier phases of the adult life-span (cf. Carroll, 1993). For the purpose of comparison, a recent study from our own laboratory is particularly useful. In that study (P. B. Baltes & Lindenberger, 1997), we administered the identical battery of cognitive tests to a heterogeneous sample of 171 adults aged 25 to 69 years. Using unit-weighted composites, the median intercorrelation among the five intellectual abilities was $r = .38$, the lowest correlation was $r = .22$, and the highest correlation was $r = .42$.

In addition to sheer magnitude, another important feature of the correlational structure was its homogeneity. For instance, correlations *within* mechanic and pragmatic domains were not higher than correlations *between* the two domains (median correlation between perceptual speed, reasoning, and memory: $r = .71$; correlation between knowledge and fluency: $r = .70$; median correlation between the two domains: $r = .70$). Thus, in contrast to age relations, the pattern of intercorrelations did not follow the mechanic-pragmatic distinction.

The finding of uniformly high ability intercorrelations extends the results of earlier studies on age differences in ability intercorrelations (P. B. Baltes et al., 1980; Schaie, Willis, Jay, & Chipuer, 1989), and gives further support to the dedifferentiation or neointegration hypothesis of old-age intelligence (P. B. Baltes et al., 1980, 1998; Deary & Pagliari, 1991; Lienert & Crott, 1964; Reinert, 1970; cf. Garrett, 1946; Spearman, 1927). From a methodological point of view, however, one may object that the magnitude of ability intercorrelations represents little more than the necessary consequence of the magnitude and uniformity of the age relations of the five abilities (Lindenberger & Pötter, 1998; Merz & Kalveram, 1965; Reinert, Baltes, & Schmidt, 1966). To examine this possibility, we also inspected the age-partialed intercorrelations among the five intellectual abilities (see Table 12.3). Ability intercorrelations were lowered by controlling for age, but they still were of greater magnitude and uniformity than comparable correlations during earlier periods of the adult life-span. At the level of unit-weighted composites, the median correlation was $r = .61$, the lowest correlation was $r = .52$, and the highest correlation was $r = .64$. When performing an exploratory factor analysis with principal components extraction over the five age-partialed ability scores, the first unrotated factor still accounted for 68% of the total variance. And finally, when controlling for age at the latent level, we observed a median correlation of $r = .78$.

One may also object that the presence of individuals diagnosed with dementia who scored low across all tests of the battery may have boosted the magnitude of ability intercorrelations. To explore this issue, we examined the magnitude of ability intercorrelations after excluding participants with a clinical diagnosis of dementia ($n = 109$). In the reduced sample ($n = 407$), we observed a median correlation for unit-weighted composites of $r = .61$ before and of $r = .54$ after controlling for individual differences in chronological age (latent level: $r = .79$ vs. $r = .73$).

In sum, the presence of strong and uniform age relations and the inclusion of individuals with a clinical diagnosis of dementia did, in fact, contribute a significant share to the magnitude of ability intercorrelations observed in this sample. However, the magnitude and uniformity of ability intercorrelations remained substantial after controlling for both of these factors, and clearly exceeded the range of ability intercorrelations observed in younger age groups of comparable heterogeneity. Based on this evidence, we conclude that differences in intellectual functioning in old and very old age show a much greater degree of consistency (homogeneity) across abilities and ability domains than differences in intellectual functioning during earlier periods of the adult life-span. In fact, as documented in detail elsewhere (Lindenberger & Baltes, 1997), the observed intellectual-ability intercorrelations can be adequately represented by a hierarchical model of intelligence which posits the existence of a unitary factor of general intelligence, or g, at the second-order level (see Fig. 7.1 in Smith & Baltes, Chapter 7).

3.2.2 Age Differences in Ability Intercorrelations

To examine the possible existence of age-based differences in covariation among the five intellectual abilities *within* the BASE age spectrum, the total sample was split into two subsamples, one labeled as *old* ($n = 258$, mean age = 77.5 years, $SD = 4.3$, age range = 70–84 years) and the other as *very old* ($n = 258$, mean age = 92.4 years, $SD = 4.5$, age range = 85–103 years). First, we compared the magnitude of intellectual-ability intercorrelations in the two groups at the level of unit-weighted composites. The median correlation was .62 in the old and .63 in the very old sample, and there was no evidence for significant differences in the magnitude of ability intercorrelations between the two groups. When individuals with dementia were excluded from the analysis, the median correlation was .55 in the old group ($n = 236$, mean age = 77.2 years, $SD = 4.3$) and .57 in the very old group ($n = 171$, mean age = 91.8 years, $SD = 3.5$). Differences between groups were again not significant. Analyses based on two-group structural models led to comparable results (cf. Lindenberger & Baltes, 1997). Thus, results did not indicate a further increase in ability intercorrelations from old to very old age. Possibly, selective mortality counteracted any subsisting tendency toward continuing dedifferentiation (for more discussion and an analysis of age and ability differences in *intra*individual task variability, cf. Lindenberger & Baltes, 1997).

3.2.3   Age Differences in Interindividual Variability

As reported above, about a third of the interindividual variability in intellectual functioning was related to chronological age. The highest relationship was found for perceptual speed, where age accounted for 38% of the reliable variance. By implication, however, this also means that a substantial portion of interindividual differences was *not* related to chronological age, as demonstrated by the large amount of scatter around the regression lines in Figure 12.1. In fact, a few individuals performed exceptionally well for their age. For instance, with respect to perceptual speed, a 95-year-old performed 1.0 standard deviation units above the mean of the 70-year-olds and 1.5 standard deviation units above the mean of the total sample. Another example is an 89-year-old who, together with a 73-year-old and a 77-year-old, obtained the highest score on the reasoning factor.

To examine whether the amount of interindividual variability increased or decreased with age, we regressed each of the five intellectual abilities and the unit-weighted composite of the five abilities (i.e., general intelligence) on age. To obtain a measure of interindividual variability, we then computed the rank order of the absolute deviations from each of the six regression lines.

Overall, the magnitude of interindividual variability was remarkably stable (see also Table 5 in Lindenberger & Baltes, 1997). Specifically, perceptual speed, fluency, memory, and the general-intelligence composite did not evince any significant changes in interindividual variability with advancing age. Interindividual variability decreased with respect to reasoning ($r = -.30$, $p < .01$), and slightly increased with respect to knowledge ($r = .13$, $p < .01$). Further analyses not reported here showed that the observed pattern of results most likely was not entirely attributable to floor or ceiling effects. For instance, the decrease in interindividual variability for reasoning continued to be significant after excluding individuals diagnosed with dementia ($r = -.25$, $p < .01$) or after excluding all individuals with either missing values or zero scores on any one of the three tests of reasoning ($r = -.19$, $p < .01$). In sum, results indicate that interindividual heterogeneity subsists into very old age, but do not lend support to the stronger claim that individuals become generally more dissimilar as they age (cf. Christensen et al., 1994; Nelson & Dannefer, 1992).

3.3   Correlates of Intellectual Functioning in Old and Very Old Age

We now turn to the correlates of intellectual functioning in old and very old age. Many theoretical conceptions about the structure and life-span ontogenesis of intellectual functioning posit two interrelated but distinct systems of influence: the biological and the cultural. The two systems are seen as antecedents, correlates, and consequents of intellectual functioning. They jointly contribute to the overdetermined or "compound" (Horn, 1989) character of human intelligence (P. B. Baltes, 1987, 1997; cf. P. B. Baltes et al., 1998; Cattell, 1971; Horn, 1982).

In line with these conceptions, we expect that mechanic and pragmatic intellectual abilities are differentially related to biological and sociobiographical correlates. Specifically, we assume that knowledge, as a key marker ability of the pragmatic (broad crystallized) domain, should be closely related to individual differences in past and concurrent sociostructural status and experience. On the other hand, perceptual speed, as a marker ability of the mechanics, should evince a particularly close link to cognition-extraneous indicators of aging-induced biological decrements in brain functioning.

Within the presumably more biologically dominated set of correlates, balance/gait, hearing, and vision were chosen to represent individual differences in the domain of sensory-sensorimotor functioning. As expected, the three sensory-sensorimotor variables and the four sociobiographical variables (i.e., income, social prestige, social class, and years of education) fell into two distinct groups. For instance, an exploratory factor analysis (i.e., principal axis extraction followed by oblique rotation) yielded two, moderately intercorrelated factors ($r = .26$). The divergent nature of the two sets of correlates was further corroborated by the fact that the sensory-sensorimotor variables, but not the sociobiographical variables, were substantially related to chronological age.

3.3.1 The Effect of Life-History Differences on Negative Age Differences in Intellectual Functioning Late in Life: Is Age Kinder to the Initially or Currently Advantaged?

A recurring hypothesis in gerontological research is that individuals with high standing on desirable life-history or sociobiographical dimensions such as social status, social participation, or initial level of cognitive functioning are less likely to experience age-associated decrements in intellectual performance than individuals who score low on any one of these dimensions. According to this line of thought, age is "kinder to the initially more able" (Owens, 1959). Most of the available longitudinal and cross-sectional evidence on this issue does not lend support to this expectation. Instead, with some notable exceptions (e.g., Kohn & Schooler, 1978), the results of numerous investigations seem to suggest that individuals scoring high on desirable dimensions show similar amounts of age changes or age differences as individuals with relatively low scores (for a review, cf. Salthouse, 1991). However, for old and very old age little information about this issue has been available on the same dimensions.

In the BASE sample, all four sociobiographical life-history variables were positively related to general intelligence (see Table 12.4). Among the four, years of education and social prestige were more highly correlated with general intelligence than social class and income ($z = 3.64$, $p < .01$). The multiple correlation of the four correlates with general intelligence was substantial, $R = .48$, $p < .01$. To examine the link of the sociobiographical factors to general intelligence, we computed a unit-weighted composite over the four sociobiographical variables, and compared individuals who scored above the mean ($n = 234$) with those who scored below ($n = 282$). The difference in general intelligence between these two groups amounted to somewhat less than a standard deviation, $E_{SD} = 0.91$, $t = 10.27$, $p < .01$.

As is shown in Figure 12.2, the slope of the cross-sectional age gradients in general intelligence observed in this data set did not vary significantly as a function of social life-history information. The figure displays two freely estimated regression lines, one for individuals above and the other for individuals below the mean on the index of socio-

Table 12.4. *Correlates of general intelligence in old and very old age*

Domain	g	g (age-partialed)	Age
Sociobiographical variables			
Social prestige	.41	.44	*-.08*
Years of education	.39	.38	.14
Social class	.29	.35	*.00*
Income	.28	.31	*-.04*
Multiple correlation (*R*)	.48		
Sensory-sensorimotor variables			
Balance/gait	.59	.36	-.66
Hearing	.51	.28	-.57
Vision	.57	.36	-.59
Multiple correlation (*R*)	.69		
Other medical-biological variables			
Brain atrophy index[a]	-.44	-.20	.51
Number of diagnoses	-.14	*-.08*	.13
Amount of medication	*-.00*	*.04*	*.05*

Note. $N = 516$. Values not significantly different from zero are in italics.
[a] $n = 254$.

biographical differentiation introduced above. The relation of general intelligence to age was identical in the two groups, $r = .58$.[3]

On the one hand, then, past and present sociocultural differences continue to be associated with interindividual differences in intellectual functioning after age 70. On the other hand, there was no evidence in this cross-sectional analysis to suggest that advantages in life history and current sociocultural context protect against age-based reductions in intellectual performance. From a psychometric perspective, our findings suggest that the life periods of old and very old age are not kinder to the initially or presently advantaged. However, a *threshold view* of the matter, which may be more adequate for a variety of practical, ethical, or theoretical reasons, may lead to an opposite interpretation of the same data pattern. According to that interpretation, the sociobiographically more advantaged are much less likely to end up with levels of intelligence that no longer permit an independent life, just because they carry a (presumably constant) advantage into very old age (cf. M. M. Baltes et al., Chapter 14).

[3] To examine the robustness and the generality of this finding, additional analyses were computed using other statistical procedures (e.g., hierarchical regression with a continuous, rather than dichotomous, representation of the independent variable; two-group structural models), different dependent variables (perceptual speed and knowledge, rather than general intelligence), and different independent variables (personality variables such as openness to experience, extraversion, and neuroticism; social participation; age-corrected intelligence). Without exception, interactions with age fell far from statistical significance.

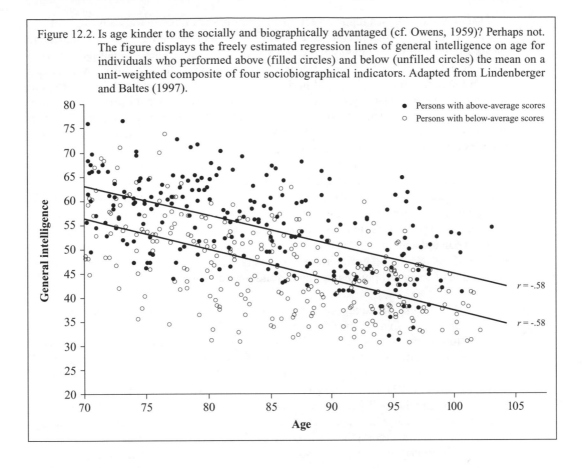

Figure 12.2. Is age kinder to the socially and biographically advantaged (cf. Owens, 1959)? Perhaps not. The figure displays the freely estimated regression lines of general intelligence on age for individuals who performed above (filled circles) and below (unfilled circles) the mean on a unit-weighted composite of four sociobiographical indicators. Adapted from Lindenberger and Baltes (1997).

3.3.2 Biological Factors: The Intersystemic Link to Sensory and Sensorimotor Functions

As can be seen in Table 12.4, the three sensory-sensorimotor variables showed an even more substantial link to general intelligence than the sociobiographical life-history variables, multiple $R = .69$. In contrast, general somatic morbidity was only weakly related to intelligence ($r = -.14, p < .01$), and amount of medication did not show a significant relationship ($r = .00$).

In addition to being strongly related to general intelligence, the sensory-sensorimotor variables and the index of brain atrophy were also strongly related to age. One way to illustrate the predominantly age-based character of the connection between the sensory-sensorimotor variables and general intelligence is to compare the age gradients of general intelligence before and after controlling for individual differences in vision, hearing, and balance/gait. Controlling for individual differences on these three variables reduced the age relation from $r = -.57$ to $r = -.06$ ($p > .05$). In other words, the proportion of the total age-related variance in general intelligence that was shared with vision, hearing, and/or balance/gait did not differ significantly from 100% (e.g., perfect overlap; for methodological caveats in interpreting the results of hierarchical regression, cf. Lindenberger & Pötter, 1998).

In sum, these analyses replicate earlier findings based on the initial subsample of 156 BASE participants (Lindenberger & Baltes, 1994b), demonstrating again that indicators of sensory-sensorimotor functioning emerge as powerful correlates of intelligence in old and very old age. One may wonder whether the magnitude of these relations was primarily due to the fact that a substantial portion of the total sample suffered from very poor hearing or very poor vision (cf. Marsiske et al., Chapter 13). However, additional control analyses found no evidence to suggest that associations between sensory-sensorimotor functioning, general intelligence, and age decreased with increasing sensory-sensorimotor or intellectual performance levels (cf. Lindenberger & Baltes, 1994b).

Elsewhere (P. B. Baltes & Lindenberger, 1997; Lindenberger & Baltes, 1994b), we have argued that the magnitude and the age-relatedness of this intersystemic connection point to the existence of a set of more general, brain-related mechanisms which regulate the aging process in both domains. From this perspective, the sensory-sensorimotor variables are good predictors (in the statistical sense) of age-based differences in general intelligence in old and very old age because they happen to be good indicators of this general set of mechanisms. This interpretation receives additional support by the significant connection of brain atrophy to intelligence and age (cf. Raz et al., 1993).

3.3.3   Ability-Specific Relations to Sociobiographical and Sensory-Sensorimotor Variables: Evidence for Divergent External Validity

We now turn to the issue whether the sociobiographical and sensory-sensorimotor variables assessed in this study were differentially related to mechanic and pragmatic intellectual abilities, as two-component models of intellectual development would predict (P. B. Baltes, 1987, 1997). In a first analysis, we chose knowledge as a marker ability of the cognitive pragmatics and perceptual speed as a marker of the cognitive mechanics to examine whether these two intellectual abilities were differentially related to sensory-sensorimotor and sociobiographical variables. The selection of these two intellectual abilities was guided by theoretical and empirical considerations. Thus, perceptual speed is generally regarded as a highly aging-sensitive ability in the broad fluid domain (Salthouse, 1991), whereas general semantic knowledge is often seen as a reliably measured and socially relevant ontogenetic acquisition.

The emerging correlational pattern was fully consistent with our expectations (see Fig. 7.3 in Smith & Baltes, Chapter 7): Perceptual speed evinced stronger relations to the sensory-sensorimotor variables than knowledge, and knowledge was more strongly related to the sociobiographical variables than perceptual speed. The relevant statistical tests, which compared the correlations of perceptual speed and knowledge with the seven variables, were significant throughout: balance/gait: $z = 5.88$; hearing: $z = 2.75$; vision: $z = 3.69$; income: $z = -2.40$; social prestige: $z = -4.14$; social class: $z = -3.37$; years of education: $z = -3.15$; for all z-values, $p < .01$.

These analyses clearly demonstrate that perceptual speed and knowledge were differentially related to sociobiographical and sensory-sensorimotor correlates of intellectual functioning. Specifically, at least two of the five intellectual abilities assessed in this study displayed meaningful specificity despite the fact that more than 80% of their reliable variance was shared with other intellectual abilities.

Another outcome of this analysis was that both perceptual speed and knowledge appeared to be more strongly related to sensory-sensorimotor functioning than to sociobiographical differences, suggesting a preponderance of sensory-sensorimotor over so-

Table 12.5. *Relations of intellectual abilities to sociobiographical and sensory-sensorimotor correlates: Amounts of shared variance (%) between latent constructs*

	Socio-biographical	Sensory-sensorimotor	z-value
Mechanic intellectual abilities (broad fluid)			
Perceptual speed	19.4	72.4	13.46
Reasoning	22.8	57.9	8.28
Memory	17.7	52.6	8.24
Pragmatic intellectual abilities (broad crystallized)			
Knowledge	37.5	50.4	3.01
Fluency	22.7	59.9	8.83
Average of all five intellectual abilities			
	23.9	59.1	8.34

Note. Results are based on a measurement model with a latent factor of sociobiographical differentiation defined by income, social prestige, social class, and years of education, a latent factor of sensory-sensorimotor functioning defined by balance/gait, hearing, and vision, and five intellectual-ability factors defined by the corresponding tests. The fit of the model was acceptable, $\chi^2(166, 516) = 304.14$, NNFI = .974, CFI = .979, AODSR = .023. The sociobiographical and the sensory-sensorimotor factors had 11.8% of their variance in common. As indicated by the z-values, all five intellectual abilities were more strongly associated with sensory-sensorimotor functioning than with the sociobiographical factor. For further details, see Lindenberger and Baltes (1997).

ciobiographical differences with respect to all five intellectual abilities. To examine this issue more closely, and to control better for differences in reliability between the two sets of correlates, we set up a latent model with a factor of sensory-sensorimotor functioning defined by balance/gait, hearing, and vision, a sociobiographical factor defined by income, social prestige, social class, and years of education, and the five intellectual-ability factors defined by their corresponding tests. The fit of this model was quite acceptable; $\chi^2(166, 516) = 304.14$, NNFI = .974, CFI = .979, AODSR = .023.

Table 12.5 displays the amount of reliable (i.e., latent-factor) variance shared between the five intellectual abilities, on the one hand, and sensory-sensorimotor functioning and a sociobiographical factor, on the other. Three findings are noteworthy. First, all five intellectual abilities were again more strongly related to sensory-sensorimotor functioning than to the sociobiographical factor, suggesting that the previous finding for knowledge and perceptual speed was not only due to differences in reliability between the two sets of correlates. The magnitude of the relationship between perceptual speed and sensory-sensorimotor functioning was especially impressive: The two constructs shared 72% of their variance. Second, we replicated the finding that the link between perceptual speed and sensory-sensorimotor functioning was more pronounced than the link between knowledge and sensory-sensorimotor functioning ($z = 9.64$, $p < .01$). Likewise, the link between knowledge and sociobiographical differences was more pronounced than the link between perceptual speed and the sociobiographical factor ($z = 7.95$, $p < .01$). Finally, the remaining three intellectual abilities showed less distinct correlational profiles, and there was some unexpected crossover between mechanic and pragmatic abilities. Specifically, fluency was more strongly related to sensory-sensorimotor functioning than memory ($z = 3.64$, $p < .01$), but did not differ from reasoning in its relation to the socio-biographical factor status ($z = 0.04$, $p > .10$), which provides further support for the hybrid, rather than predominantly pragmatic, nature of fluency (Salthouse, 1993).

3.3.4   *Correlates of Intellectual Functioning in Old and Very Old Age: A Summary Model*

To summarize relations among age, sensory-sensorimotor functioning, sociobiographical differences, and intelligence in this data set we conclude this section with an overall structural model. As before, sociobiographical differences were indexed by social class, education, social prestige, and income, sensory-sensorimotor functioning by vision, hearing, and balance/gait, and the five intellectual abilities by the corresponding tests. The structural relations among the latent constructs of the model are shown in Figure 12.3.

In this model, chronological age and the sociobiographical factor function as independent variables. It is assumed that age differences in intelligence are connected to sensory-sensorimotor functioning to such a degree that all of the age-related variance in intellectual functioning is shared with the sensory-sensorimotor factor (i.e., it is assumed that the unique effects of age on intellectual functioning after controlling for individual differences in sensory-sensorimotor functioning do not differ significantly from zero). In addition, we expected a specific link between sensory-sensorimotor functioning and perceptual speed, reflecting the close connection between the two domains of functioning. Finally, the sociobiographical factor was related to general intelligence, but also to the sensory-sensorimotor factor. In addition, individual differences captured by the sociobiographical factor were assumed to be specifically linked to knowledge.

The resulting model fits the data quite well, $\chi^2(196, 516) = 372.80$, NNFI = .971, CFI = .975, AODSR = .037, and explained 66% of the total reliable variance in general intelligence. Note that all the links between latent constructs that are missing in this model, such as the link between age and the sociobiographical factor (whose presence would have pointed to the existence of cohort effects), links from age to general intelligence or from age to the five intellectual abilities, and the remaining links from sensory-sensorimotor functioning and the sociobiographical factor to any of the five intellectual abilities, did not differ significantly from zero (i.e., all $ps > .01$).

4   Cognitive Aging with and without Dementia: Direct Comparisons

So far, participants with a clinical diagnosis of dementia were routinely included in the analyses reported in this chapter. This procedure was justified by the argument that aging, as a population process, comprises individuals with and without dementia, and that the reliability and validity of any clinical diagnosis of dementia is not perfect. Nevertheless, it is of interest to examine how individuals diagnosed with dementia differed from other individuals, especially after controlling for age differences between the two groups. In the following, we report three ways to address this issue. First, we examine whether dementia diagnosis and dementia severity were differentially related to the five intellectual abilities assessed by the psychometric test battery. Second, we test the hypothesis that measures of episodic recall performance and learning poten-

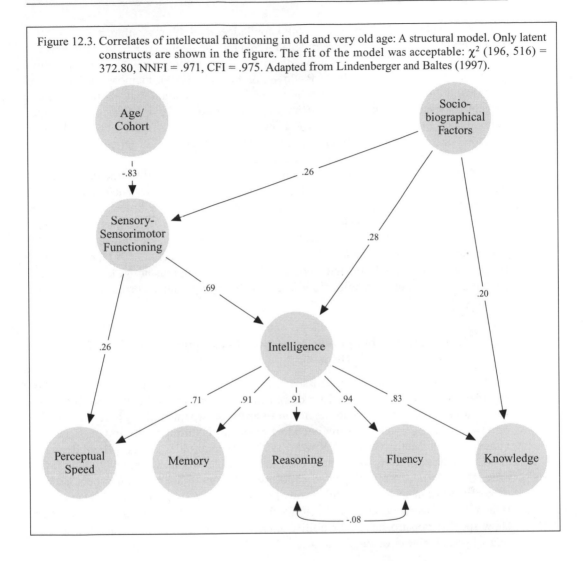

Figure 12.3. Correlates of intellectual functioning in old and very old age: A structural model. Only latent constructs are shown in the figure. The fit of the model was acceptable: χ^2 (196, 516) = 372.80, NNFI = .971, CFI = .975. Adapted from Lindenberger and Baltes (1997).

tial that were designed with the specific goal to be sensitive to individual differences in effective cue utilization, or encoding specificity (Buschke et al., 1995, 1997), such as the ECR test (Grober et al., 1988) used in this study, are especially effective in discriminating between individuals with and without dementia. Third, we report a mixture distribution analysis of the SMMS (Reischies, Schaub, & Schlattmann, 1996) suggesting that the performance distributions of individuals with and without dementia are distinct but appear to converge with advancing age.

4.1 Relationship of Intellectual Abilities to Dementia Diagnosis and Dementia Severity

In the total sample, point-biserial correlations of dementia diagnosis (0 = absent, 1 = present) with intellectual functioning were as follows: memory, r = -.53; perceptual speed, $r = -.52$; fluency, $r = -.50$; knowledge, $r = -.49$; reasoning, $r = -.40$. After controlling for age, relations were reduced in magnitude: memory, $r = -.43$; fluency, $r = -.41$; perceptual speed, $r = -.40$; knowledge, $r = -.40$; reasoning, $r = -.28$. Contrary to expectations (cf. Christensen, Hadzi-Pavlovic, & Jacomb, 1991), memory, in this set of analyses, did not differ significantly in its relation to dementia diagnosis from fluency, perceptual speed, and knowledge (first-order correlations: $z = 1.02$, $p > .10$; age-partialed correlations: $z = 0.93$, $p > .10$). However, reasoning was more weakly related to dementia diagnosis than the other four intellectual abilities (first-order correlations: $z = 4.50$, $p < .01$; age-partialed correlations: $z = 4.69$, $p < .01$).

Within the group of individuals with dementia diagnosis ($n = 109$), the degree of dementia severity (1 = very mild to mild, 2 = moderate, 3 = severe) was negatively related to all five intellectual abilities (raw correlations: memory, $r = -.53$; fluency, $r = -.50$; perceptual speed, $r = -.42$; knowledge, $r = -.29$; reasoning, $r = -.29$; age-partialed correlations: memory, $r = -.52$; fluency, $r = -.49$; perceptual speed, $r = -.40$; knowledge, $r = -.28$; reasoning, $r = -.28$). Consistent with expectations (Christensen et al., 1991), memory and fluency were more highly related to dementia severity than reasoning, knowledge, and perceptual speed (raw correlations: $z = 3.35$, $p < .01$; age-partialed correlations: $z = 3.36$, $p < .01$).

4.2 Cue Utilization in Episodic Memory and Learning: Does It Dissociate Normal Aging from Dementia?

Disproportionately large losses in the ability to learn and remember are often regarded as the central characteristic of dementing disorders. In this context, recent investigations suggest that the ability to profit from environmental support, such as the provision of category cues during encoding retrieval, is differentially impaired in individuals with dementia (Grober & Kawas, 1997). Whereas older adults without dementia appear to make effective use of these cues, and are able to achieve relatively high levels of recall performance after repeated exposure to the to-be-learned items, persons with dementia profit much less from this form of environmental support. According to one interpretation (Buschke et al., 1995, 1997), this suggests that individuals with dementia show specific impairments in the ability to encode to-be-learned materials in a specific (e.g., discriminable or distinct) manner.

4.2.1 Analysis of Recall Level and Learning Gain in the ECR Test

To examine whether initial memory performance and learning gain under supportive conditions differed as a function of dementia status and/or age, we analyzed the trial-by-trial memory performance on the ECR test under conditions of cued encoding and recall. Six groups were distinguished: (a) three age groups of persons without dementia, 70- to 79-year-olds ($n = 162$, mean age = 74.9), 80- to 89-year-olds ($n = 134$, mean age = 84.7), and persons aged 90 and over ($n = 88$, mean age = 94.5); (b) three groups of persons with a diagnosis of very mild to mild ($n = 32$, mean age = 89.6), moderate ($n = 30$, mean age = 89.6), or severe ($n = 31$, mean age = 92.1) dementia. Due to missing data, only 477 individuals were included in this analysis.

A repeated-measures ANOVA with Trial (3) as a within-subjects factor and Group (6) as a between-subjects factor was used to analyze recall performance. A series of five a

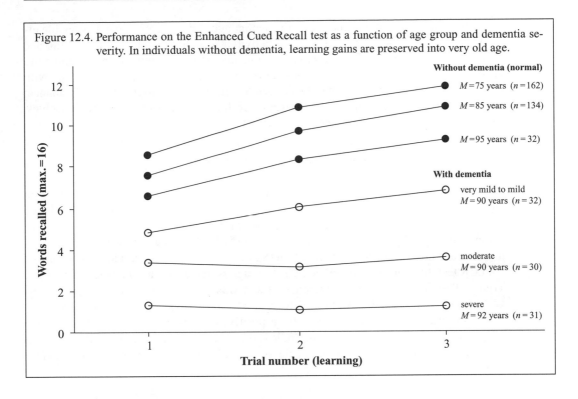

Figure 12.4. Performance on the Enhanced Cued Recall test as a function of age group and dementia severity. In individuals without dementia, learning gains are preserved into very old age.

priori orthogonal contrasts was specified for the Group factor. The first contrast tested individuals without dementia diagnosis versus individuals with a dementia diagnosis. The second and third contrasts tested effects of age *within* individuals without dementia (contrast 2: 70–79 vs. 80+; contrast 3: 80–89 vs. 90+). The fourth and fifth contrasts tested effects of dementia severity (contrast 4: very mild to mild vs. moderate or severe; contrast 5: moderate vs. severe).

The results of the analysis of variance were remarkably clear (see Fig. 12.4). In persons without dementia, recall performance decreased with advancing age, but this decrement did not interact with Trial, indicating that age differences in learning gain were not significant (*Group*: 70–79 vs. 80+: $F(1, 471) = 44.9, p < .01$; 80–89 vs. 90+: $F(1, 471) = 16.0, p < .01$; *Group* $\times$ *Trial*: 70–79 vs. 80+: $F(2, 942) = 0.8, p > .10$; 80–89 vs. 90+: $F(2, 942) = 1.9, p > .10$). In contrast, the comparison of persons with and without a dementia diagnosis revealed both a difference in performance levels as well as a difference in learning gain (*Group* $F(1, 471) = 411.4, p < .01$; *Group* $\times$ *Trial*: $F(2, 942) = 36.4, p < .01$). Within the dementia subsample, persons with very mild to mild dementia differed from those with moderate or severe dementia with respect to both performance level and learning gain (*Group*: $F(1, 471) = 45.2, p < .01$; *Group* $\times$ *Trial*: $F(2, 942) = 6.8, p < .01$). Finally, the comparison between individuals with moderate and severe dementia revealed differences in performance level, *Group*: $F(1, 471) = 11.5, p < .01$, but not in learning gain, *Group* $\times$ *Trial*: $F(2, 942) = 0.11, p > .10$. In fact, a post hoc analysis revealed that the recall performance of those with moderate and severe dementia did not significantly improve across the three trials ($F(2, 118) = 1.23, p > .10$).

In sum, the results of this analysis indicate that age and dementia have dissociable effects on recall level and learning gain. In individuals without dementia, increasing age was associated with lower *levels of recall*, but not with a decrement in the ability to profit from repeated exposure to to-be-learned materials. In contrast, individuals with moderate or severe dementia not only showed lower levels of initial recall performance, but also a drastic reduction in learning gain – in fact, no learning at all (cf. Reischies, Geiselmann, & Lindenberger, 1998).

4.2.2   Predicting Dementia Status: The Specific Contribution of ECR Learning Gain

The discriminating power of learning gain was further confirmed by logistic regression analyses using dementia status (0 = absent, 1 = present) as the dependent variable. Three variables were considered as predictors of dementia status: (a) the intellectual-ability composite of perceptual speed, which can be regarded as a marker variable of normal negative age differences in adult cognition (Salthouse, 1996); (b) recall level at Trial 1 of the ECR test; (c) learning gain in the ECR test, that is, the difference between Trial 3 and Trial 1. Perceptual speed was entered first and was found to predict dementia status, $\chi^2(1, 477) = 135.9$, $p < .01$. Adding ECR recall at Trial 1 significantly reduced the number of misclassified individuals (i.e., false positives and misses) from 72 to 56, $\chi^2(1, 477) = 62.3$, $p < .01$. Finally, entering ECR learning gain in the third step led to a small, but significant further reduction of misclassified individuals from 56 to 52, $\chi^2(1, 477) = 36.6$, $p < .01$.

4.2.3   Matched-Control Analysis

The design of BASE enables us to compare individuals with and without a dementia diagnosis who do *not* differ on the general factor of intelligence and age. Specifically, we matched individuals of similar age and with close-to-identical levels of performance on the general factor of intelligence as defined by the psychometric test battery in a pairwise fashion (i.e., persons with and without dementia). Application of this procedure resulted in 70 pairs. The two groups did not differ in general intelligence ($T_{\text{no dementia}} = 41.9$ vs. $T_{\text{dementia}} = 42.0$, $t = -1.62$) or age ($Age_{\text{no dementia}} = 89.0$ vs. $Age_{\text{dementia}} = 90.7$, $t = -1.52$; t-values refer to dependent t-tests). The scores of the remaining 39 participants with dementia were too low to be matched with a control.

Figure 12.5 shows the recall performance on the ECR test, which was *not* used to assemble the pairs, for the two groups. Despite the equivalence of the two groups in general intelligence and age, significant differences in recall level and learning gain were observed (*Group*: $F(1, 471) = 16.95$, $p < .01$; *Group* $\times$ *Trial*: $F(2, 110) = 4.54$, $p = .013$).

4.2.4   Summary of ECR Analyses

Taken together, the findings obtained with the ECR test support the view that memory-related functioning in older individuals with dementia differs from memory-related functioning in older adults without dementia. Specifically, the findings suggest that the ability to learn from experience (M. M. Baltes, Kühl, & Sowarka, 1992; Willis & Nesselroade, 1990) is disproportionately reduced in persons with dementia, perhaps as a consequence of a disproportionate impairment in mnemonic processes that foster encoding

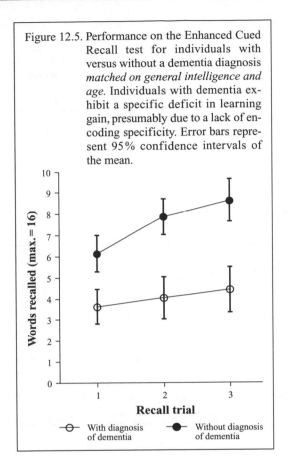

Figure 12.5. Performance on the Enhanced Cued Recall test for individuals with versus without a dementia diagnosis *matched on general intelligence and age.* Individuals with dementia exhibit a specific deficit in learning gain, presumably due to a lack of encoding specificity. Error bars represent 95% confidence intervals of the mean.

specificity. The observation that this impairment increases with disease severity is consistent with previous studies (Bäckman, Josephsson, Herlitz, Stigsdottir, & Viitanen, 1991; Herlitz, Adolfsson, Bäckman, & Nilsson, 1991).

4.3   *Mixture Distribution Analysis*

The observed differences in performance profiles between persons with and without a diagnosis of dementia raise the question of whether measures closely associated with that diagnosis have a bimodal distribution. The SMMS (Klein et al., 1985), which is often used to screen for dementia in random samples of older adults, is well suited to examine this issue. According to the mixture-distribution view, the total distribution of scores on the SMMS is made up of two different distributions, one for the "normal" (i.e., without dementia) portion of the sample, and the other for the portion with dementia. With increasing age, the central tendency of the distribution representing the portion of the population without dementia is expected to be shifted toward the central tendency of the distribution representing the subpopulation with dementia.

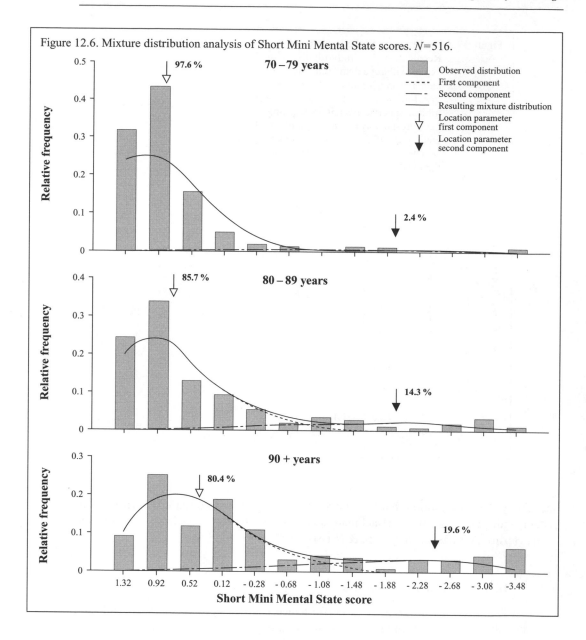

Figure 12.6. Mixture distribution analysis of Short Mini Mental State scores. *N*=516.

Results of a mixture distribution analysis indicate that the frequency distributions of SMMS scores over age are consistent with these predictions (Fig. 12.6; cf. Reischies et al., 1996), and support the claim that normal cognitive aging and aging with dementia are two distinct phenomena (cf. Reischies & Lindenberger, 1995). At the same time, the observed convergence of the two distributions with advancing age indicates that the "signal" of dementia is especially difficult to separate from the "noise" of normal aging in very old age.

5   Discussion

5.1   *Design Limitations of the Present Analyses*

Before concluding, we would like to highlight once more the pitfalls and constraints of cross-sectional studies (P. B. Baltes, Reese, & Nesselroade, 1988; Hertzog, 1996; Lindenberger & Pötter, 1998; cf. P. B. Baltes et al., Chapter 1). With respect to this study, three limitations are especially relevant. First, cross-sectional data sets do not permit direct inferences about intraindividual change and about interindividual differences in intraindividual change. Second, cross-sectional age differences represent complex outcomes of multiple systems of influence and change. In old and very old age, pathological (rather than "normal") aging processes, selective mortality, and generational cohort effects are all likely to be involved. Third, longitudinal (e.g., life-history) interpretations of cross-sectional age differences are necessarily retrospective in character, and need to be corroborated by converging evidence from other sources.

By now, longitudinal follow-up investigations of the sample reported in this study are under way. In addition, we continuously keep track of the mortality history of the BASE participants. It is hoped that the combined analysis of mortality and longitudinal follow-up information will shed further light on the ways in which intraindividual changes, mortality, and generational differences contribute to the age-related cross-sectional differences observed in this study (cf. Keiding, 1991; Nesselroade, 1991).

5.2   *Summary of Findings*

The purpose of this chapter was to delineate the potentials and limits of intellectual functioning in old and very old age. To this end, we reported the age gradients, structure, and correlates of intellectual abilities in old and very old age as observed in the Intensive Protocol of the first wave of the Berlin Aging Study.

Our main findings can be summarized under the dual headings of continuity versus discontinuity and preserved differentiation versus dedifferentiation. According to continuity and preserved-differentiation views, intelligence in old and very old age is assumed to be characterized by predictive, functional, and structural continuity to earlier phases of life. In support of this view, we found: (a) that the different intellectual abilities continue to exist as distinct dimensions of interindividual differences at the first-order level; (b) that there is no general tendency toward a decrease in between-person variability; (c) that life-history differences assessed by sociobiographical variables continue to be associated with intelligence in general, and with knowledge, in particular; and (d) that the ability to learn from experience under highly supportive conditions is well preserved into very old age, as suggested by the findings obtained with the ECR test.

In contrast, the discontinuity and dedifferentiation views posit that old-age intelligence is primarily dominated by aging-induced changes in brain integrity. Albeit such changes are probably present throughout ontogeny, their increasing importance with advancing age is assumed to impose a common and general constraint on many different aspects of intellectual functioning, and to transform old-age intelligence into a distinct developmental phenomenon. In agreement with this view, we found: (a) that the age gradients of predominantly mechanic (broad fluid) and predominantly pragmatic (broad crystallized) intellectual abilities converge to yield a picture of generalized linear decre-

Table 12.6. *BASE participants' performance in Memory for Text (percentage of correct answers)*

"Yesterday Peter, who is seven years old, went to Lake Lead for some fishing. He took his dog Prince along. The lake's banks were flooded due to heavy rain during the previous four days. Peter slipped on the muddy ground and fell into the deep water. He would have drowned if his dog had not jumped in after him and helped him to reach the shore again."

| | Persons without dementia | | | Persons with dementia |
	70–79 (n = 164)	80–89 (n = 138)	90+ (n = 105)	M = 90.8 years (n = 106)
What was the boy's name?	79.3	81.9	70.5	41.3
How old was the boy?	63.4	55.8	52.4	34.9
What was the dog's name?	31.1	26.8	9.5	1.8
What was the lake called?	42.7	26.1	12.4	7.3
Why did the boy fall into the lake?[a]	84.8	81.9	70.5	46.8

Note. One of the six questions ("What is the main episode of the story?") is not presented in the table.
[a]The answer was judged as correct if at least one of the following reasons were mentioned: (a) because he slipped; (b) because it was muddy; (c) because the lake's banks were flooded.

ment (directionality dedifferentiation); (b) that this picture applies to samples both above and below the average on sociobiographical life history variables; (c) that the intercorrelations among intellectual abilities are of greater magnitude and uniformity than commonly observed during earlier phases of life, and are well described by a single factor of general intelligence; and (d) that sensory and sensorimotor variables in combination share about 59% of their total reliable variance with the general factor of intelligence (cf. P. B. Baltes & Lindenberger, 1997; Lindenberger & Baltes, 1997). In addition, the results obtained with the ECR test demonstrate that the ability to learn from experience is severely compromised in individuals with dementia.

To provide an illustration of the average and the range of intellectual functioning in this heterogeneous sample of old and very old individuals, Table 12.6 contains the item-by-item report for one of the three memory tests of the psychometric test battery. In this test, a story about a boy who went fishing, slipped into the water, and was saved by his dog, was presented in large fonts on the computer screen, and read aloud by the research assistant. Immediately thereafter, participants were asked questions about the content of the story. As shown in the table, more than 70% of the individuals without dementia in each of the three age groups (70–79, 80–89, and 90+ years) remembered the name of the boy, and the reason why he had slipped into the water. In contrast, the age of the boy, the name of the dog, and the name of the lake were less likely to be remembered.

5.3   *Outlook: Exploring the Systemic Significance of Intellectual Functioning in Old and Very Old Age*

Taken together, the findings reported in this chapter lend support to the theoretical position that cognitive aging is a relatively unitary and general process, at least within the age period of old and very old age (cf. Li & Lindenberger, in press; Salthouse, 1996). However, in light of the interpretational ambiguity associated with cross-sectional, correlational data (Hertzog, 1996; Lindenberger & Pötter, 1998), additional evidence based on other methods, such as longitudinal, experimental, and simulation designs, is needed to examine further the tenability of this position.

Given their pervasiveness and magnitude, the age-based decrements in intellectual functioning observed in this sample of old and very old individuals are likely to constrain functioning in other domains such as social relations or everyday competence. Other analyses within BASE support this contention (Staudinger et al., Chapter 11; M. M. Baltes et al., Chapter 14; Smith et al., Chapter 17; cf. Reischies & Lindenberger, 1996). According to one interpretation (P. B. Baltes & Lindenberger, 1997; Lindenberger & Baltes, 1994b), the general tendency of intelligence in old age to relate to numerous psychological, social, and behavioral dimensions may reflect the dependency of one's inner, social, and physical life on some minimum amount of intellectual capacity. To complicate matters, this minimum amount is likely to vary as a function of both sampled task difficulty within and across domains and of interindividual differences in intelligence-extraneous resources. Thus, cross-sectional interindividual-difference investigations of the kind presented here need to be complemented not only by real-time longitudinal follow-ups, but also by short-term longitudinal, intraindividual investigations (Molenaar, 1994) to understand better the (presumably nonlinear) links between intellectual and other domains of functioning (P. B. Baltes et al., 1988; Kruse, Lindenberger, & Baltes, 1993; Lindenberger & Baltes, 1995b).

References

American Psychiatric Association (APA) (Ed.). (1987). *Diagnostic and statistical manual of mental disorders (DSM-III-R)*. Washington, DC.

Bäckman, L., Josephsson, S., Herlitz, A., Stigsdottir, A., & Viitanen, M. (1991). The generalizability of training gains in dementia. Effects of an imagery-based mnemonic on face-name retention duration. *Psychology and Aging, 6*, 489–492.

Baltes, M. M., Kühl, K. P., & Sowarka, D. (1992). Testing for limits of cognitive reserve capacity: A promising strategy for early diagnosis of dementia? *Journal of Gerontology: Psychological Sciences, 47*, P165–P167.

Baltes, P. B. (1987). Theoretical propositions of life-span developmental psychology: On the dynamics between growth and decline. *Developmental Psychology, 23*, 611–626.

Baltes, P. B. (1997). On the incomplete architecture of human ontogeny: Selection, optimization, and compensation as foundation of developmental theory. *American Psychologist, 52*, 366–380.

Baltes, P. B., Cornelius, S. W., Spiro, A., Nesselroade, J. R., & Willis, S. L. (1980). Integration versus differentiation of fluid/crystallized intelligence in old age. *Developmental Psychology, 16*, 625–635.

Baltes, P. B., & Lindenberger, U. (1995). Sensorik und Intelligenz: Intersystemische Wechselwirkungen und Veränderungen im hohen Alter. *Akademie-Journal, 1*, 20–28.

Baltes, P. B., & Lindenberger, U. (1997). Emergence of a powerful connection between sensory and cognitive functions across the adult life span: A new window to the study of cognitive aging? *Psychology and Aging, 12*, 12–21.

Baltes, P. B., Lindenberger, U., & Staudinger, U. M. (1998). Life-span theory in developmental psychology. In W. Damon (Ed.) & R. M. Lerner (Vol. Ed.), *Handbook of child psychology: Vol. 1. Theoretical models of human development* (5th ed., pp. 1029–1143). New York: Wiley.

Baltes, P. B., Reese, H. W., & Nesselroade, J. R. (1988). *Life-span developmental psychology: Introduction to research methods.* Hillsdale, NJ: Erlbaum.

Buschke, H., Sliwinski, M. J., Kuslansky, G., & Lipton, R. B. (1995). Aging, encoding specificity, and memory change in the Double Memory Test. *Journal of the International Neuropsychological Society, 1,* 483–493.

Buschke, H., Sliwinski, M. J., Kuslansky, G., & Lipton, R. B. (1997). Diagnosis of early dementia by the Double Memory Test: Encoding specificity improves diagnostic sensitivity and specificity. *Neurology, 48,* 989–997.

Carroll, J. B. (1993). *Human cognitive abilities.* Cambridge: Cambridge University Press.

Cattell, R. B. (1971). *Abilities: Their structure, growth, and action.* Boston: Houghton Mifflin.

Christensen, H., Hadzi-Pavlovic, D., & Jacomb, P. (1991). The psychometric differentiation of dementia from normal aging: A meta-analysis. *Psychological Assessment: A Journal of Consulting and Clinical Psychology, 3,* 147–155.

Christensen, H., Mackinnon, A., Jorm, A. F., Henderson, A. S., Scott, L. R., & Korten, A. E. (1994). Age differences and interindividual variation in cognition in community-dwelling elderly. *Psychology and Aging, 9,* 381–390.

Craik, F. I. M., & Salthouse, T. A. (Eds.). (1992). *The handbook of aging and cognition.* Hillsdale, NJ: Erlbaum.

Deary, I. J., & Pagliari, C. (1991). The strength of g at different levels of ability: Have Detterman and Daniel rediscovered Spearman's "law of diminishing returns"? *Intelligence, 15,* 251–255.

Folstein, M. F., Folstein, S. E., & McHugh, P. R. (1975). "Mini Mental State": A practical method for grading the cognitive state of patients for the clinician. *Journal of Psychiatric Research, 12,* 189–198.

Garrett, H. E. (1946). A developmental theory of intelligence. *American Psychologist, 1,* 372–378.

Grober, E., Buschke, H., Crystal, H., Bank, S., & Dresner, R. (1988). Screening for dementia by memory testing. *Neurology, 38,* 900–903.

Grober, E., & Kawas, C. (1997). Learning and retention in preclinical and early Alzheimer's disease. *Psychology and Aging, 12,* 183–188.

Häfner, H. (1992). Psychiatrie des höheren Lebensalters. In P. B. Baltes & J. Mittelstraß (Eds.), *Zukunft des Alterns und gesellschaftliche Entwicklung* (pp. 151–179). Berlin: de Gruyter.

Herlitz, A., Adolfsson, R., Bäckman, L., & Nilsson, L.-G. (1991). Cue utilization following different forms of encoding in mildly, moderately, and severely demented patients with Alzheimer's disease. *Brain and Cognition, 15,* 119–130.

Herlitz, A., Nilsson, L.-G., & Bäckman, L. (1997). Gender differences in episodic memory. *Memory and Cognition, 25,* 801–811.

Hertzog, C. (1996). Research design in studies of aging and cognition. In J. E. Birren & K. W. Schaie (Eds.), *Handbook of the psychology of aging* (4th ed., pp. 24–37). New York: Academic Press.

Hofman, A., Rocca, W. A., Brayne, C., Breteler, M. M. B., Clarke, M., Cooper, B., Copeland, J. R. M., Dartigues, J. F., da Silva Droux, A., Hagnell, O., Heeren, T. J., Engedal, K., Jonker, C., Lindesay, J., Lobo, A., Mann, A. H., Molsa, P. K., Morgan, K., O'Connor, D. W., Sulkara, R., Kay, D. W. K., & Amaducci, L. (1991). The prevalence of dementia in

Europe: A collaborative study of 1980–1990 findings. *International Journal of Epidemiology, 20,* 736–748.

Horn, J. L. (1982). The theory of fluid and crystallized intelligence in relation to concepts of cognitive psychology and aging in adulthood. In F. I. M. Craik & S. Trehub (Eds.), *Aging and cognitive processes* (pp. 237–278). New York: Plenum Press.

Horn, J. L. (1989). Models of intelligence. In R. L. Linn (Ed.), *Intelligence: Measurement, theory, and public policy* (pp. 29–73). Urbana: University of Illinois Press.

Keiding, N. (1991). Age-specific incidence and prevalence: A statistical perspective. *Journal of the Royal Statistical Society, Series A, 154,* 371–412.

Klein, L. E., Roca, R. P., McArthur, J., Vogelsang, G., Klein, G. B., Kirby, S. M., & Folstein, M. (1985). Diagnosing dementia: Univariate and multivariate analyses of the mental status examination. *Journal of the American Geriatrics Society, 33,* 483–488.

Kohn, M. L., & Schooler, C. (1978). The reciprocal effects of the substantive complexity of work and intellectual flexibility: A longitudinal assessment. *American Journal of Sociology, 84,* 24–52.

Kruse, A., Lindenberger, U., & Baltes, P. B. (1993). Longitudinal research on human aging: The power of combining real-time, microgenetic, and simulation approaches. In D. Magnusson & P. Casaer (Eds.), *Longitudinal research on individual development: Present status and future perspectives* (pp. 153–193). Cambridge: Cambridge University Press.

Li, S.-C., & Lindenberger, U. (in press). Cross-level unification: A computational exploration of the link between deterioration of neurotransmitter systems and dedifferentiation of cognitive abilities in old age. In L.-G. Nilsson & H. Markowitsch (Eds.), *Neuroscience of memory.* Toronto: Hogrefe.

Lienert, G. A., & Crott, H. W. (1964). Studies on the factor structure of intelligence in children, adolescents, and adults. *Vita Humana, 7,* 147–163.

Lindenberger, U., & Baltes, P. B. (1994a). Aging and intelligence. In R. J. Sternberg, S. J. Ceci, J. L. Horn, E. Hunt, J. D. Matarazzo, & S. Scarr (Eds.), *The encyclopedia of human intelligence* (pp. 52–66). New York: Macmillan.

Lindenberger, U., & Baltes, P. B. (1994b). Sensory functioning and intelligence in old age: A strong connection. *Psychology and Aging, 9,* 339–355.

Lindenberger, U., & Baltes, P. B. (1995a). Kognitive Leistungsfähigkeit im Alter: Erste Ergebnisse aus der Berliner Altersstudie. *Zeitschrift für Psychologie, 203,* 283–317.

Lindenberger, U., & Baltes, P. B. (1995b). Testing-the-limits and experimental simulation: Two methods to explicate the role of learning in development. *Human Development, 38,* 349–360.

Lindenberger, U., & Baltes, P. B. (1997). Intellectual functioning in old and very old age: Cross-sectional results from the Berlin Aging Study. *Psychology and Aging, 12,* 410–432.

Lindenberger, U., Mayr, U., & Kliegl, R. (1993). Speed and intelligence in old age. *Psychology and Aging, 8,* 207–220.

Lindenberger, U., & Pötter, U. (1998). The complex nature of unique and shared effects in hierarchical linear regression: Implications for developmental psychology. *Psychological Methods, 3,* 218–230.

McClelland, G. H., & Judd, C. M. (1993). Statistical difficulties of detecting interactions and moderator effects. *Psychological Bulletin, 114,* 376–390.

Meng, X.-L., Rosenthal, R., & Rubin, D. B. (1992). Comparing correlated correlation coefficients. *Psychological Bulletin, 111,* 172–175.

Merz, F., & Kalveram, K. T. (1965). Kritik der Differenzierungshypothese der Intelligenz. *Archiv der gesamten Psychologie, 117*, 287–295.

Molenaar, P. C. M. (1994). Dynamic latent variable models in developmental psychology. In A. von Eye & C. C. Clogg (Eds.), *Latent variables analysis: Applications for developmental research* (pp. 155–180). Thousand Oaks, CA: Sage.

Nebes, R. D. (1992). Cognitive dysfunction in Alzheimer's disease. In F. I. M. Craik & T. A. Salthouse (Eds.), *The handbook of aging and cognition* (pp. 373–446). Hillsdale, NJ: Erlbaum.

Nelson, A. E., & Dannefer, D. (1992). Aged heterogeneity: Fact or fiction? The fate of diversity in gerontological research. *The Gerontologist, 32*, 17–23.

Nesselroade, J. R. (1991). Interindividual differences in intraindividual change. In L. M. Collins & J. L. Horn (Eds.), *Best methods for the analysis of change: Recent advances, unanswered questions, future directions* (pp. 92–105). Washington, DC: American Psychological Association.

Nuthmann, R., & Wahl, H.-W. (1996). Methodische Aspekte der Erhebungen der Berliner Altersstudie. In K. U. Mayer & P. B. Baltes (Eds.), *Die Berliner Altersstudie* (pp. 55–83). Berlin: Akademie Verlag.

Nuthmann, R., & Wahl, H.-W. (1997). *Methodological aspects of the Berlin Aging Study* (Technical report). Berlin: Max Planck Institute for Human Development.

Owens, W. A. (1959). Is age kinder to the initially more able? *Journal of Gerontology, 14*, 334–337.

Raz, N., Torres, I. J., Spencer, W. D., Millman, D., Baertschi, J. C., & Sarpel, G. (1993). Neuroanatomical correlates of age-sensitive and age-invariant cognitive abilities: An in vivo MRI investigation. *Intelligence, 17*, 407–422.

Reinert, G. (1970). Comparative factor analytic studies of intelligence throughout the life span. In L. R. Goulet & P. B. Baltes (Eds.), *Life-span developmental psychology: Research and theory* (pp. 467–484). New York: Academic Press.

Reinert, G., Baltes, P. B., & Schmidt, L. R. (1966). Kritik einer Kritik der Differenzierungs-hypothese der Intelligenz. *Zeitschrift für Experimentelle und Angewandte Psychologie, 13*, 602–610.

Reischies, F. M., & Geiselmann, B. (1994). Neuropsychology of dementia and depression in old age. In A. Beigel, J. J. Lopez Ibor, & J. A. Costa e Silva (Eds.), *Past, present and future of psychiatry. IXth World Congress of Psychiatry* (Vol. 1, pp. 554–558). Singapore: World Scientific.

Reischies, F. M., Geiselmann, B., & Lindenberger, U. (1998). *Recall and learning in very old age and dementia: Qualitative differences*. Submitted manuscript, Department of Psychiatry, Free University of Berlin.

Reischies, F. M., & Lindenberger, U. (1995). Discontinuity of dementia and age-related cognitive decline. In M. Bergener, J. C. Brocklehurst, & S. I. Finkel (Eds.), *Aging, health, and healing* (pp. 204–211). New York: Springer.

Reischies, F. M., & Lindenberger, U. (1996). Grenzen und Potentiale kognitiver Leistungs-fähigkeit im Alter. In K. U. Mayer & P. B. Baltes (Eds.), *Die Berliner Altersstudie* (pp. 351–377). Berlin: Akademie Verlag.

Reischies, F. M., Rossius, W., & Felsenberg, D. (1997). Brain atrophy parameters of very old subjects of a population-based sample with and without dementia: Benign senescent brain atrophy? *Journal of Neuropsychiatry, 9,* 175–176.

Reischies, F. M., Schaub, R. T., & Schlattmann, P. (1996). Normal ageing, impaired cognitive functioning and senile dementia: A mixture distribution analysis. *Psychological Medicine, 26*, 785–790.

Salthouse, T. A. (1991). *Theoretical perspectives on cognitive aging.* Hillsdale, NJ: Erlbaum.

Salthouse, T. A. (1993). Speed and knowledge as determinants of adult age differences in verbal tasks. *Journal of Gerontology: Psychological Sciences, 48*, 29–36.

Salthouse, T. A. (1996). The processing-speed theory of adult age differences in cognition. *Psychological Review, 103*, 403–428.

Schaie, K. W., Willis, S. L., Jay, G., & Chipuer, H. (1989). Structural invariance of cognitive abilities across the adult life span: A cross-sectional study. *Developmental Psychology, 25*, 652–662.

Spearman, C. E. (1927). *The abilities of man.* New York: Macmillan.

Willis, S. L., & Nesselroade, C. S. (1990). Long-term effects of fluid ability training in old-old age. *Developmental Psychology, 26*, 905–910.

Zaudig, M., Mittelhammer, J., Hiller, W., Pauls, A., Thora, C., Morinigo, A., & Mombour, W. (1991). SIDAM: A structured interview for the diagnosis of dementia of the Alzheimer type, multi-infarct dementia and dementias of other aetiology according to ICD-10 and DSM-III-R. *Psychological Medicine, 21*, 225–236.

CHAPTER 13

Sensory Systems in Old Age

Michael Marsiske, Julia Delius, Ineke Maas, Ulman Lindenberger, Hans Scherer, and Clemens Tesch-Römer

In this chapter, three sensory systems (hearing, vision, and balance/gait) are examined. We begin with a descriptive overview of individual differences and age difference patterns in sensory functioning. The pattern of how individual differences in sensory acuity might be related to performance in other psychological and behavioral domains is examined. We reveal a strong, negative pattern of age differences in all three senses studied. These negative age trends have implications for the classification of sensory impairment rates: Although participants in their 70s have levels of sensory acuity that might be classified, on average, as slightly or mildly impaired, by their 90s most participants evince levels that might be classified as moderately to severely impaired, not only in one but in multiple modalities. We also report prevalence rates for the use of commonly occurring compensatory devices and procedures (e.g., hearing aids, glasses, cataract operations). We report the following findings with regard to the relationship of sensory functioning to other domains of psychological and behavioral performance (e.g., intellectual functioning, basic and expanded everyday competence, personality characteristics, well-being, social network size):

(1) Relationships exist between all three sensory domains and the selected outcome domains. The relationships with intellectual functioning and everyday competence are particularly strong.
(2) In all domains studied, the sensory variables can explain or mediate virtually all of the age-related variance in those domains; that is, after statistically controlling for sensory performance, there is essentially no unique effect of chronological age.
(3) For the most part, the effects of sensory variables seem to be additive, rather than interactive, throughout the age range from 70 to over 100 years.

1 Introduction

This chapter reports findings from the Berlin Aging Study (BASE) regarding individual differences in sensory functioning among old and very old persons. The consequences of age-related differences in sensory capabilities for performance in a variety of functional domains are also examined. By considering "functional" consequences of sensory aging, we ask the question of what individuals do, or how they perform, on selected outcome variables in the context of their levels of sensory performance. We focus on three senses: hearing, vision, and balance/gait.

The central importance of effective sensory functioning as a necessary precondition for interaction with the environment is indisputable. Although it may be possible to compensate for some sensory losses, or to function effectively following limited impairments in one or more senses (Whitbourne, 1985), age-associated sensory losses must be thought of as a risk factor restricting effective participation in the everyday world. Since late life is thought of as a time of multiple impairments (see Steinhagen-Thiessen & Borchelt, Chapter 5 in this volume), cumulative risk resulting from losses in more than one sense may have particular importance as a potential source for losses in *other* domains of functioning.

Theoretically, this chapter draws upon the conceptual underpinnings of BASE (discussed in detail in P. B. Baltes et al., Chapter 1; Mayer et al., Chapter 18), particularly the notions of aging as a systemic phenomenon, and differential aging. By viewing *aging as a systemic phenomenon*, we focus on the integration of functioning across systems, and the fact that age-associated changes in some subsystems may have implications for functioning in other systems. One version of this perspective is the "cascade hypothesis" (Birren, 1964), in which the effects of aging losses in some systems seem to have "domino-like" effects for other systems. Sensory performance is a basic domain of functioning. In this domain we can see the most fundamental level of the organism's interaction with its environment. One important question is whether losses in sensory functioning "drive" losses in other, more complex functional domains. It is important to note, however, that the cross-sectional, correlational nature of BASE does not permit us to evaluate the causal status of sensory variables.

Another question embedded in the systemic aging view is whether the "sensory compensation" effect reported earlier in life (e.g., blind persons might hear better or have better tactile sense; Neville, 1990; Rauschecker, 1995) breaks down in later life. Are losses in one sense made up for by stability or gains in other senses? Or are they matched by losses in other senses?

Differential aging, as outlined in detail in Chapter 7 by Smith and Baltes, considers the ways in which the aging process might vary between individuals. A differential perspective might hypothesize, therefore, that the experience of aging may differ for persons with and without severe sensory losses.

To explore late-life sensory functioning and its relations to other domains, this chapter is organized around two major questions. First, we consider, descriptively, the distribution of hearing, vision, and balance/gait functioning in old and very old age, trying to place our findings within the context of other studies, and to illustrate what such losses imply. Second, we also explore the associations of sensory functioning with other domains of performance, and consider what such relationships might mean from systemic and differential perspectives.

2   Descriptive Findings

This section is organized into three parts, each with the aim of describing elements of sensory functioning in BASE participants. First, we consider the distribution of sensory performance in hearing, vision, and balance/gait, focusing on the pattern of age-related individual differences. Second, we explore the implications of these age-related patterns for the classification of sensory impairments (in hearing and vision, where such classification criteria exist). Third, we briefly examine the use of assistive devices and procedures (e.g., hearing aids, glasses, cataract operations) in BASE participants.

Figure 13.1. a) Participants' visual acuity in Snellen decimals by age decade and gender. b) Distribution of binocular distance vision by age.

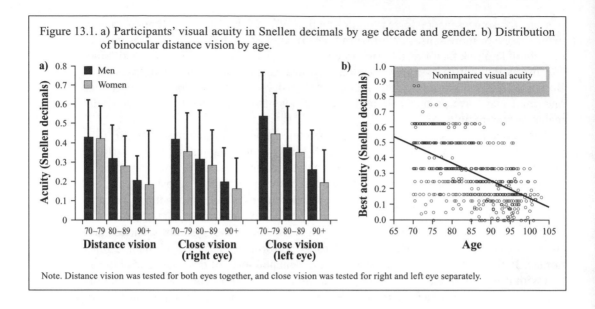

Note. Distance vision was tested for both eyes together, and close vision was tested for right and left eye separately.

2.1   Mean-Level Patterns and Individual Differences

2.1.1   Age Differences in Vision

Within BASE, visual acuity[1] was assessed using standard optometric (clinical) procedures (see also Borchelt & Steinhagen-Thiessen, 1992; Lindenberger & Baltes, 1994; Steinhagen-Thiessen & Borchelt, 1993). It is important to point out that, for the measurement of all senses, process-oriented psychophysical measurements were not available. Close vision was assessed separately for the left and right eyes using a Snellen reading chart presented at an individually determined reading distance (typically about 25 cm); distance vision was assessed binocularly with a Snellen chart 2.5 m away (with greater distances used for persons performing at ceiling under standard assessment). All vision measurements were obtained without and with correction (i.e., participants' glasses, when available). Measurements were taken in Snellen decimal units, where a value of 1.0 is taken to indicate normal (20/20) vision, as normed in younger adults (see below for discussion of thresholds). Over 90% of BASE participants wore glasses, and some analyses in this chapter are based on the *better* performance values (so as to rule out those cases where poor visual correction was clearly a contributor to poor vision).

Figure 13.1a shows the distribution of visual acuity by age and gender within BASE; each additional decade of life was associated with significantly lower visual performance, and women performed significantly more poorly than men. It is important to note that the apparent gender difference may be a spurious consequence of gender-specific selection effects (see Fig. 2.5, Lindenberger et al., Chapter 2), although there is convergent

---

[1] In the following, it is always stated whether visual acuity was measured with or without correction (i.e., participants' glasses). Generally, "vision" encompasses several aspects of visual functioning. In BASE, only acuity was examined. Thus, other functions such as the visual field and color vision are not discussed.

evidence in the geriatric literature that women report a higher rate of visual impairment (e.g., Schmack, 1989).

Figure 13.1b shows the distribution of individual differences in corrected distance vision with age using a scatterplot. The shaded area represents nonimpaired vision as normed in younger adults (Snellen decimal of 0.8 or greater). As the figure shows, not only did very few of the BASE participants meet this criterion for "normal" vision, but there was also a strong trend toward lower performance with advancing age. At the highest ages, most participants were concentrated at the lowest end of the vision distribution; at the youngest ages, most participants were performing closer to (but below) the range of normal vision.

How do the BASE findings regarding visual acuity compare with the results of other studies? A number of cross-sectional and longitudinal investigations of visual aging have documented substantial age-associated losses in vision (for comprehensive reviews, see Fozard, 1990; Kline & Schieber, 1985; Schieber, 1992). Everyday observation suggests that reading glasses become a normative acquisition in midlife; indeed, the epidemiological data suggest that preferred reading distances vary from 10 cm in 20-year-olds to 40 cm in 50-year-olds due to reduced accommodation ability (Bennett & Eklund, 1983a).

Cross-sectional estimates of distance visual acuity show substantial decline after age 50 (Pitts, 1982); visual acuity poorer than 20/50 in the better eye has been reported to occur in about 10% of those aged 60 to 69 years, and in 25–35% of those over age 80 (Anderson & Palmore, 1974; Branch, Horowitz, & Carr, 1989).

In comparison to other studies, the level of visual acuity in BASE participants seems to be substantially lower than that reported in other studies. One reason for this difference may be that other published prevalence estimates of visual impairment actually underestimate true rates of impairment; essentially no studies have studied subjects over 80 years of age as systematically as BASE. Moreover, since most studies of older adults exclude institutionalized individuals, published disability prevalence rates may be further underestimated. At the same time, it must be recalled that BASE participants were tested in their own home and institutional environments. Although this meant that vision was assessed under relatively naturalistic conditions, it was not possible to control the level of target illumination and glare as well as has been done in some other studies. This could have contributed to lower performance levels (Fozard, 1990).

2.1.2   Age Differences in Hearing

In BASE, auditory acuity was assessed with a Bosch ST-20–1 pure-tone audiometer, using headphones. This precluded analysis of corrected versus uncorrected hearing since hearing aids could not be comfortably or securely worn with these headphones. Decibel thresholds were assessed for eight different frequencies, in the following order: 1.0, 2.0, 3.0, 4.0, 6.0, 8.0, 0.5, 0.25 kHz. Testing was started with the ear reported as "better" by participants (the right ear when subjects did not know). Figure 13.2 shows the obtained age-by-gender-by-frequency distribution.

To summarize the results of an analysis of variance on these data, there were significant main effects of age, and frequency, and significant interaction effects included gender by frequency, age by frequency, and age by gender by frequency ($p < .01$). The data suggest that women had lower hearing thresholds (better hearing) than men in frequencies above 0.50 kHz at all ages, and that increasing age was associated with increases in hearing thresholds (i.e., worse hearing). At the lowest frequency (0.25 kHz), men actu-

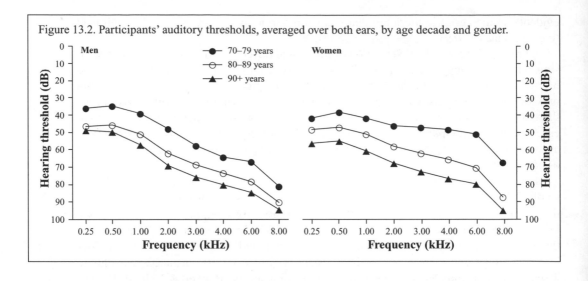

Figure 13.2. Participants' auditory thresholds, averaged over both ears, by age decade and gender.

ally had lower thresholds than women, a result that is consistent with work reported by Corso (1963), Jerger, Chmiel, Stack, and Spretnjak (1993), Pearson et al. (1995), and others. At the same time, there was some narrowing of the gender gap, particularly at higher ages and at higher frequencies. Consequently, the average shapes of the hearing curves, across frequencies, differed by age and gender.

Figure 13.3 displays the variation of uncorrected speech-range auditory acuity (i.e., at 0.5, 1.0, and 2.0 kHz) with age. The shaded area, which runs across the scatterplot, shows normal hearing (normed in younger adults) at speech-range hearing frequencies. Very few participants were performing within this normal range, and most of these persons were at the younger end of the age range. Indeed, with advancing age, there seems to be a shift in both the lowest and highest volumes needed to hear speech-range tones: In the 70s, no one required a tone to be presented at greater than 80 dB; in contrast, in the 80s and 90s, some individuals required tones to be even louder. And while some participants in their 70s could hear tones between 10 and 30 dB, in the 90s virtually no one could hear tones at less than 30 dB.

As with vision, mean levels of auditory acuity are lower in the heterogeneous BASE sample than in many other studies. Two explanations seem likely. First, published prevalence estimates for individuals over 65 may again seriously underestimate the prevalence of hearing loss in the oldest old. Second, the testing of participants in their natural environments means that surrounding noise during the hearing assessment was not as well controlled in BASE as in some other studies, thus raising hearing thresholds to a certain degree.

Despite these caveats, the BASE data reflect patterns that have been widely reported in the research literature. It has been reported that symmetrical (affecting both ears) loss of hearing for high-frequency sounds sets in quite early in life (20+ years), increasing at differing rates (for a review, see Olsho, Harkins, & Lenhardt, 1985; Willott, 1991). This leads to a typical pattern of hearing loss: the higher the frequency, the more severe the hearing loss. Clinically significant hearing loss (defined as 30 dB below the normal 0–15 dB hearing level)[2] is observed in about 30% of men over 65 (e.g., Bess, Lichten-

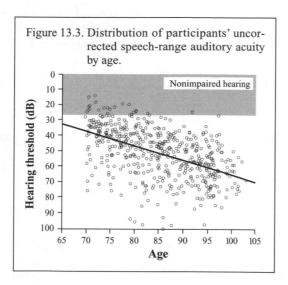

Figure 13.3. Distribution of participants' uncorrected speech-range auditory acuity by age.

stein, Logan, Burger, & Nelson, 1989). Indeed, as Corbin and Eastwood (1986) have noted, hearing loss in the range of 25–35 dB within speech-range frequencies, and 45–50 dB at high frequencies, is considered "normal" for 80-year-olds, although these would constitute clinically significant hearing loss for 40-year-olds. It is also important to note that pure-tone audiometry may underestimate functional hearing impairments in the everyday world. Age-related limitations in speech comprehension, for example, are often more serious than the audiometrically measured pure-tone thresholds in the range of speech frequencies (0.5–2.0 kHz) indicate (for review, see Working Group on Speech Understanding and Aging, 1988). Aging is also associated with an increase in problems like tinnitus and functional deficits, including slowing of signal processing, and limitations in comprehension of distorted speech (e.g., via telephone; Bess et al., 1989).

2.1.3   Age Differences in Balance/Gait

Many reviews of altered sensory functioning in late life do not include balance/gait (but see Corso, 1981), since it is typically not counted as one of the "big five" senses (hearing, vision, taste, touch, and smell).[3] Balance/gait is a "higher order" sense, since the maintenance of orientation in space requires integration of information from many other sensory input channels; coherent ocular, vestibular, proprioceptive, and acoustic information, as well as motor coordination, are necessary for the sensation of stable balance/gait (for review, see Mhoon, 1990). Indeed, many studies have reported that sensory losses, especially in vision, are an important precursor of balance/gait problems (Lord, Clark, & Webster, 1991; Manchester, Woollacott, Zederbauer-Hylton, & Marin, 1989).

---

[2] Different criteria for classification of hearing impairments are used in the literature. According to the World Health Organization (WHO, 1980) a hearing threshold of 0–15 dB is "normal." Impairments of more than 25 dB are termed as mild. The problems associated with setting such criteria are discussed in more depth below.

[3] Although we emphasize sensory functioning throughout this chapter, it is important to underscore that balance/gait also has a motoric component. Where balance/gait is seen to have a unique predictive effect on other variables (below), it may be that this unique variance is primarily motoric.

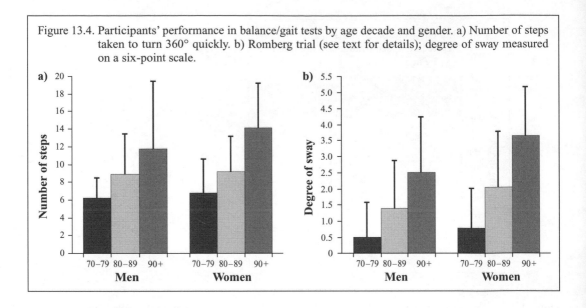

Figure 13.4. Participants' performance in balance/gait tests by age decade and gender. a) Number of steps taken to turn 360° quickly. b) Romberg trial (see text for details); degree of sway measured on a six-point scale.

Much of the research on balance/gait problems has been conducted within the context of research on the prevalence, predictors, and prevention of falls in older adults. Estimates suggest that as many as one-third to one-half of adults over the age of 65 years fall each year (Exton-Smith, 1977; Gryfe, Amies, & Ashley, 1977; Horak, Shupert, & Mirka, 1989; Isaacs, 1985). Survey data also suggest that increasing proportions of adults report subjective difficulties with maintaining equilibrium after age 65 (Gerson, Jarjoura, & McCord, 1989; Ödkvist, Malmberg, & Möller, 1989). According to one review of various investigations, about 60% of women and 30% of men over 65 report attacks of dizziness (Haid, 1993).

Within BASE, a clinical assessment approach derived from Tinetti (1986) was used (for additional details, see M. M. Baltes, Mayr, Borchelt, Maas, & Wilms, 1993; Borchelt & Steinhagen-Thiessen, 1992; Lindenberger & Baltes, 1994; Steinhagen-Thiessen & Borchelt, 1993). In this chapter, we focus on two measures:

(1) For the *Romberg trial*, participants were required to stand with arms extended forward, palms up, eyes closed, and legs together for about one minute. Degree of sway was scored on a six-point scale by physicians in the BASE medical data collection sessions (see Steinhagen-Thiessen & Borchelt, Chapter 5).

(2) For the *360° turn*, participants were asked to turn their body by 360° as quickly and as safely as possible; the number of steps taken was recorded by the medical observers.

Figure 13.4 shows the age and gender distribution of the two balance/gait assessments in BASE. For both measures, as with hearing and vision, there were significant main effects of age and gender ($p < .01$). Increased age was associated with greater difficulty (more sway, more steps), and women performed more poorly than men. Figure 13.5 displays the distribution of postural sway in the Romberg trial. In this task, we see individu-

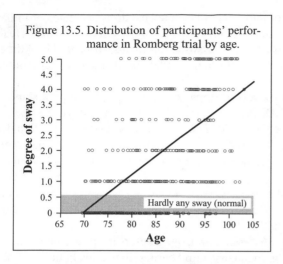

Figure 13.5. Distribution of participants' performance in Romberg trial by age.

als who demonstrated no sway across the full age range studied, although, as the plot densities show, the proportion of individuals who showed the highest levels of sway (4) and who could not perform the task (5) became increasingly larger at higher ages.

2.2   Patterns of Sensory Impairment

What are the implications of these mean and individual difference trends for rates of sensory impairment? Although the estimation of impairment rates is not without problems,[4] we provide estimates for two reasons. First, since much of the research literature on the aging of sensory systems provides estimates of impairment rates, provision of these data here facilitate comparability with other studies. Second, by obtaining information about the proportion of individuals at different levels of functioning within particular age groups, one gains a more concrete understanding of the range of individual performance capabilities among old and very old adults. We present impairment rates for vision and hearing only (i.e., not for balance/gait), since well-agreed-upon impairment criteria for the clinical balance/gait measures discussed in this chapter are not yet available. For further discussion of these measures in connection with disability and impairments of mobility, see Chapter 5 by Steinhagen-Thiessen and Borchelt.

---

[4] It is important to clarify several issues about the impairment classifications in this chapter. First, all systems of impairment classification are essentially arbitrary, and potentially dangerous, because there may be a range of individual competencies at a particular level of auditory or visual acuity, and individuals may have different ways of compensating for impairments. Second, rates of impairment will vary as a function of the classification system used. Third, the impairment classifications discussed below are not specifically normed for older adults. Thus, given normal age-associated losses in hearing and vision, these impairment criteria will lead to the identification of disproportionately more "impaired" older adults than in younger age groups. Fourth, these rates do not speak to remediated versus unremediated impairments, or to the putative origins of such impairments (it is not being suggested, for example, that these impairment rates are indicative of primary or intrinsic aging phenomena, or that they do not include age-related effects on vision and hearing that result from cumulative environment risk and injury, medication, acoustic or optical trauma, etc.).

Although the classification of impairment is somewhat arbitrary (rates of impairment are dependent on the classification system used), we draw upon the World Health Organization (WHO, 1980) "International classification of impairments, disabilities, and handicaps." This system has the benefit of being widely used, and of differentiating several levels of impairment.

For vision, we consider four levels of impairment, focusing here on distance vision averaged across both eyes (WHO, 1980). *No visual impairment* consists of visual acuity at a Snellen decimal of 0.8 or better. *Slight visual impairment* exists for Snellen decimals between 0.8 and 0.3. *Moderate low vision* refers to visual acuity at Snellen decimals between 0.3 and 0.12. *Severe low vision to blindness* includes all individuals with distance visual acuity that is less than 0.12.

For hearing, we also consider four levels of impairment, averaged across both ears. Individuals with *no impairment* are those with hearing in the speech-range frequencies (0.5, 1.0, and 2.0 kHz) between 0 and 25 dB. *Mild impairment* describes speech-range hearing between 26 and 40 dB. *Moderate impairment* refers to speech-range hearing between 41 and 55 dB. All other individuals (with hearing thresholds in the three frequencies that are 56 dB or higher) are classified as having *moderately severe to profound hearing loss*.

In Table 13.1, the resulting impairment rates are shown for three age decades (70–79, 80–89, 90+ years). We report weighted data that correct for the oversampling of men and the very old and, in turn, provide estimated prevalence rates for the West Berlin population of persons aged 70 and above. The weighting procedure, its conceptual basis, and interpretative implications are discussed in detail in Chapter 1 by P. B. Baltes et al.

The impairment patterns reflect the age-patterns in vision already discussed. As Table 13.1 shows for vision, at all ages represented in BASE, very few elderly West Berliners had distance vision that would be classified as "nonimpaired" (as normed in younger adults). However, about 80% of 70- to 79-year-olds showed only slight impairment. In contrast, almost half of 80- to 89-year-olds had moderately low vision. By the age of 90 and above, slightly more than half had moderately low vision, and between one-quarter and one-third had severely impaired vision or blindness.

Table 13.1 also shows impairment rates for hearing in speech-range frequencies. The picture is similar to that obtained with distance vision. At all ages, less than 10% had "normal" hearing (as normed in younger adults). Half of 70- to 79-year-olds were only mildly hearing impaired. Two-thirds of 80- to 89-year-olds were equally divided between moderate and moderately severe hearing impairment. By the age of 90 and above, fully two-thirds of the population had moderately severe hearing impairment or worse.

The picture that emerges then from these data is one of very high prevalence of sensory impairment with advancing age. At the highest ages, nearly everyone in this sample showed some clinically significant loss in hearing or vision.

As suggested above, most prevalence estimates for vision loss and hearing loss in older adults (e.g., Davis, 1983) have been lower, but few studies have included as heterogeneous a subject group as BASE, both in terms of age and residence conditions. Moreover, many studies have not tested older adults in their everyday contexts.

Of course, the examination of impairment separately by modality obscures one of the hallmarks of late life: multimorbidity (e.g., Fries, 1990; cf. Steinhagen-Thiessen & Borchelt, Chapter 5; Borchelt et al, Chapter 15). It has been argued that late life is a time

Table 13.1. *Rates of impairment (in %) in vision and hearing by age*

Distance vision (in Snellen decimals)

| Age group | Impairment[a] | | | |
	None (≥ 0.8)	Slight (0.3–0.8)	Moderate (0.12–0.3)	Severe (< 0.12)
All subjects	0.5	63.2	29.3	7.0
70–79	0.7	79.6	16.3	3.4
80–89	0.0	48.2	44.0	7.8
90+	0.0	19.8	47.3	32.9

Hearing (thresholds in speech-range frequencies)

| Age group | Impairment[a] | | | |
	None (0–25 dB)	Mild (26–40 dB)	Moderate (41–55 dB)	Moderately severe (> 55 dB)
All subjects	5.1	33.5	35.8	25.6
70–79	8.4	42.4	35.7	13.4
80–89	1.5	25.7	37.5	35.2
90+	0.3	6.8	24.2	68.6

[a]Degrees of impairment defined following WHO, 1980.

of particular risk because of the many losses and challenges that must be confronted (e.g., P. B. Baltes & Baltes, 1990). Indeed, in just the two domains of hearing and vision, as the correlations between these domains would suggest (presented below), there is evidence that multiple impairment is common in the age range studied.

One fourth of the population of old people in West Berlin was classified as having at least moderate impairment in both modalities (i.e., moderate uncorrected hearing impairment in speech-range frequencies and moderately low corrected distance vision). When impairment in either sense (hearing, vision, or both) was considered, 68% were adjudged as having an impairment. Breaking these percentages down by age decade, among 70- to 79-year-olds, 10% were classified as having impairment in both senses, and 53% in at least one sense. For the 80- to 89-year-olds, 39% were impaired in both senses, and 85% were impaired in at least one. Finally, for persons aged 90 and above, 73% were classified as impaired in both senses, and 99% were impaired in either hearing or vision. Thus, sensory disability rates, particularly multiple impairments, were very common. Among the oldest individuals, impairment in both hearing and vision seems to become an essentially universal phenomenon.

Statistically, these cross classifications of hearing and vision impairments suggest a high correlation between vision and hearing in this sample. At the same time, there is no hearing-by-vision interaction in these values; the co-occurrence is not more or less frequent than would be expected from their joint probabilities alone. It is striking to note

Table 13.2. *Relationships among age and aggregated hearing, vision, and balance/gait performances*

	Age	Hearing	Vision	Balance/gait
Age	1.00	—	—	—
Hearing	-0.57	1.00	—	—
Vision	-0.56	0.43	1.00	—
Balance/gait	-0.64	0.45	0.49	1.00

what a high proportion of individuals experience multiple impairments at the oldest ages. Table 13.2 illustrates the bivariate Pearson product-moment correlations between hearing, vision, balance/gait, and chronological age in the BASE sample. It shows that the three senses share about 25% of their variance, and each sense is commonly and strongly related to chronological age.

2.3   *Physiological and Pathological Conditions in Hearing and Vision*

Thus far, we have emphasized the patterns of normal sensory aging. One of the strengths of the BASE data set, however, is the availability of a rich amount of clinical data taken from medical examinations of BASE participants. In this section, we briefly consider evidence concerning the occurrence of pathological conditions affecting the visual and auditory system in the BASE sample. It is important to clarify, however, that diagnostic information comes from the participants' medical history, and does not have the same degree of diagnostic validity as the opthalmologic and otologic examinations included in some studies.

With regard to pathological conditions, the BASE data strongly support previous findings that diagnosable visual pathologies become increasingly normative with advancing age. Indeed, when all visual diagnoses were considered (including nonspecific, age-related diagnoses like presbyopia), 452 participants (88%) had a classifiable visual impairment. When only specific conditions (like cataracts, glaucoma, retinal damage) were considered, a relatively high number of subjects (241, 47%) were still adjudged as having a pathological condition. Major visual conditions included glaucoma and cataracts, but simple diagnoses of poor vision were also very common.

BASE physician interviews with study participants about auditory conditions (as with vision) revealed a wide variety, and fairly high prevalence, of self-reported auditory impairments. In contrast to vision, however, substantially fewer participants had a specific auditory diagnosis. Although 477 (92%) had some diagnosed auditory problem, many of these included such general, age-related phenomena as "sensorineural hearing loss." When only specific diagnoses were considered (like otorrhoea, otalgia, tinnitus, eardrum perforations), 71 subjects (14%) had a diagnosed condition of the auditory system. In contrast to vision, relatively few specific conditions seemed to be implicated in age-associated hearing loss.

2.4   *Use of Compensatory Assistive Devices and Procedures for Hearing and Vision*

Having provided basic information regarding the patterns of sensory aging, impairment rates, and pathological conditions in BASE, we turn our focus to an area of interest for many gerontologists: that is, the extent to which these sensory losses can be effectively compensated for (Corso, 1984). In this section,[5] we briefly consider the reported availability of hearing aids and corrective lenses, noting again that these data come from participants' medical history. We also examine the proportion of participants reporting at least one surgery for the removal of cataracts. It is important to note, however, that these data do not speak to the question of whether corrective auditory and visual devices and procedures are appropriately prescribed, or how often they are used. This is an important issue, since there is evidence that many older adults may not have the best correction available. Reinstein et al. (1993), for example, reported that 34% of older adults have an immediately improvable refraction problem in vision which is typically not corrected.

Despite the high prevalence of hearing loss, only 83 participants (16%) reported having at least one hearing aid. With regard to glasses, corrected close vision (i.e., reading glasses) was available for 494 (96%) participants, and distance glasses were available for 388 (75%) participants. Fifty-eight (11%) participants reported having at least one surgery for the removal of a cataract in the last 30 years. Many of these participants reported having multiple surgeries (either for both eyes, or repeated operations on one eye). Most of the reported cataract operations were performed in the four or five years before BASE participation, although a small number of operations (less than 10%) took place at least 10 years before the study. However, none predated 1970.

One interesting finding is that the availability of glasses may not only improve mean-level visual acuity, but it may also increase visual performance variability. Without glasses, most participants were grouped around the lowest level of functioning. With glasses, they were distributed over a wider range of functioning. Figure 13.6 provides a more detailed exploration of the range of visual performance in *close vision* (averaged over left and right eyes). Several points are interesting to note. First, since Snellen decimals lower than 0.3 are typically taken as an indicator of poor vision (WHO, 1980), the substantial majority of study participants had *uncorrected* close vision that was well below levels which would indicate impairment. The right-hand panel in Figure 13.6 also shows the positive effects of visual correction, as well as the limits to visual correctability. Clearly, glasses improve average close visual acuity (although the mean is still below a level classifiable as impaired), but they seem to be differentially efficient in correcting participants' vision, thus leading to greater variability in visual acuity. These results are consistent with the notion that different aging mechanisms (peripheral, central, and pathological processes) affect vision, and that these can be remedied to varying extents by lenses.

[5] Although walking aids are mobility rather than balance aids, we should point out that more than one-quarter of the West Berliners aged 70 and above used such aids. Table 5.7 in Chapter 5 (Steinhagen-Thiessen & Borchelt) shows that more than 20% used a cane, and 2–5% used other aids.

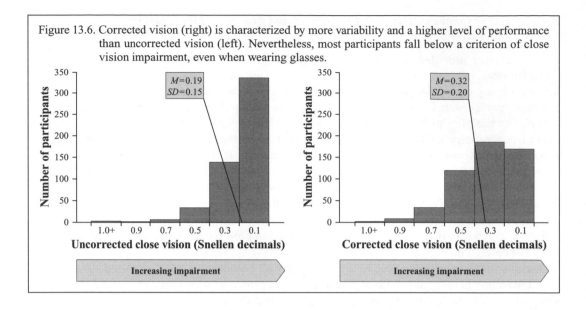

Figure 13.6. Corrected vision (right) is characterized by more variability and a higher level of performance than uncorrected vision (left). Nevertheless, most participants fall below a criterion of close vision impairment, even when wearing glasses.

3   Correlates of Sensory Functioning

Having demonstrated strong, negative trends in hearing, vision, and balance/ gait with advanced age, we turn now to questions of differential aging, and aging as a systemic process. Can sensory variables account for individual differences (both age-related and otherwise) in late life? Is there any evidence that the processes underlying sensory aging are related to a broader process that cuts across multiple domains?

The literature on the relationship between sensory functioning and potential outcome variables is voluminous, and goes beyond the scope of the present chapter. The data suggest that in late life, sensory functioning (hearing, vision, and balance/gait) is a significant predictor of numerous outcome variables including *intellectual functioning* (see Lindenberger & Baltes, 1994, for a review; see also Teasdale et al., 1992), *basic functional competence and leisure participation* (e.g., M. M. Baltes, Wilms, Horgas, & Little, 1998; Branch et al., 1989; Laforge, Spector, & Sternberg, 1992), *social relationships* (e.g., Corso, 1987; Gilhome Herbst, 1983), as well as *aspects of the self* (including well-being; e.g., Bess et al., 1989). These possible outcome variables reflect constructs of substantial interest in the gerontological and adult developmental literature.

To investigate the relationship between hearing, vision, and balance/gait and selected outcome variables within BASE, we created aggregate scores reflecting:

(1) *intellectual functioning*: an aggregate of the five primary intellectual abilities assessed within BASE (see Smith & Baltes, Chapter 7; Lindenberger & Reischies, Chapter 12);

(2) *basic functional competence*: number of self-rated limitations in Activities of Daily Living and Instrumental Activities of Daily Living (ADL/IADL; Lawton & Brody, 1969; Mahoney & Barthel, 1965; see also Steinhagen-Thiessen & Borchelt, Chapter 5; M. M. Baltes et al., Chapter 14);

Table 13.3. *Bivariate correlations between sensory functioning and selected outcome variables*

	Age	Hearing	Vision	Balance/gait
Cognitive-motoric domains				
Intellectual functioning	-.57	.51	.56	.56
	(-.60)	(.56)	(.73)	(.71)
Basic functional competence	-.53	.38	.47	.66
	(-.57)	(.43)	(.60)	(.83)
Expanded competence	-.58	.44	.53	.57
	(-.76)	(.63)	(.86)	(.89)
Self and personality				
Positive openness	-.26	.26	.28	.30
	(-.31)	(.34)	(.43)	(.43)
Anxiety/loneliness	.13	-.14	-.20	-.24
	(.08)	(-.16)	(-.23)	(-.30)
Overall well-being	-.12	.12	.17	.29
	(-.23)	(.22)	(.35)	(.49)
Social relationships				
Social network size	-.34	.25	.29	.33
	(-.34)	(.26)	(.37)	(.39)

Note. Values in parentheses represent correlations between latent constructs disattenuated for measurement error.

(3) *expanded competence*: discretionary activity participation; aggregate of time spent in non-ADL/IADL activities on a typical day, and activity participation in the last year (see M. M. Baltes et al., Chapter 14);

(4) *positive openness*: an aggregate of positive affect, extraversion, and openness to experience (Clark & Watson, 1991; Watson & Clark, 1984; see Smith & Baltes, Chapter 7);

(5) *anxiety/loneliness*: an aggregate of neuroticism, negative affect, and emotional loneliness (cf. Smith & Baltes, Chapter 7);

(6) *overall well-being*: the global score from the Philadelphia Geriatric Center Morale Scale (PGCMS; Lawton, 1975; see Smith et al., Chapter 17); and

(7) *social network size*: (number of very close, close, and less close persons mentioned in the individual's social network (Kahn & Antonucci, 1980; see Smith & Baltes, Chapter 7; Wagner et al., Chapter 10).

Table 13.3 presents the intercorrelations of age, hearing, vision, and balance/gait with each of these outcome variables. The results suggest at least two broad generalizations: First, the relationship between each of the sensory variables and our selected outcome variables tended to be of a similar order of magnitude as the relationship between age and these outcomes. (The exceptions are discussed below.) Second, the outcome domains varied substantially in the magnitude of their relationships with both age and sensory functioning. Variable domains reflecting cognitive-motoric functioning (intellectual

Table 13.4. *Hierarchical communality analyses for the prediction of selected outcome variables: Unique and shared variance percentages*

	Cognitive-motoric domains			Self and personality			Social relation-ships
	1	**2**	**3**	**4**	**5**	**6**	**7**
Total variance explained	47.5	47.3	44.6	12.7	7.4	9.9	14.6
Unique age	1.8	1.3	5.3	0.0	8.5	12.2	6.1
Unique hearing	5.4	0.1	1.3	7.7	1.5	0.3	1.1
Unique vision	10.5	2.8	7.3	10.5	14.7	5.0	6.0
Unique balance/gait	7.2	30.0	9.0	13.9	42.4	67.0	9.7
Shared among sensory functions only	9.4	20.5	6.6	13.1	18.1	13.8	6.0
Shared between sensory functions and age	65.7	45.3	70.5	54.8	14.8	1.7	71.1
Sum	100.0	100.0	100.0	100.0	100.0	100.0	100.0

Note. Column headings: (1) intellectual functioning; (2) basic competence; (3) expanded competence; (4) positive openness; (5) anxiety/loneliness; (6) well-being; (7) social network size.

functioning, basic and expanded functional competence) were relatively strongly related to both age and sensory functioning, whereas the other variable domains showed substantially less relationship to either age or sensory functioning (e.g., positive openness, social network size, well-being).

Table 13.4 shows how well hearing, vision, and balance/gait together accounted for the age-related variance in each of these outcome domains, using the framework of hierarchical regression. The table shows the unique and shared variance components attributable to hearing, vision, balance/gait, and age. A general summary is that sensory functioning not only seemed to account for all or most of the age-related variance in each domain (even where there was only a relatively small proportion of age-related variance), but it typically accounted for a small proportion of unique variance beyond age. While this was generally true, the magnitude of age-related variance (and thus, the magnitude of sensory effects) was substantially larger in the cognitive-motoric behavioral domains of intellectual functioning, basic functional competence, and expanded competence. The largest component of explained variance in most outcomes (intelligence, positive openness, expanded competence, and social network size) could be explained by a complex aggregate of variance *shared* by age and sensory functioning. In the two other domains (anxiety/loneliness, well-being), the largest component of explained variance was attributable to the unique effect of balance/gait, and the second largest component was variance shared by the sensorimotor domains that was independent of age. In these domains, sensorimotor functioning (especially balance/gait) *exceeded* the predictive power of chronological age.

For two variables, expanded competence and well-being, there was a small but significant residual effect of age. The meaning of this residual variance differed substantially for the two domains. For expanded competence, even after controlling for sensorimotor functioning, increased age was associated with lower levels of activity participation.

In contrast, after controlling for sensory functioning, the residual effect of age became *positive* for well-being (it had a weak, negative bivariate correlation with age: $r = -.12$; see Fig. 17.2 in Smith et al., Chapter 17). In other words, sensory functioning (and not age per se) seems to constitute a risk factor for well-being. The positive residual effect of chronological age may reflect the operation of self-regulatory processes, which adjust levels of aspiration and well-being upward to compensate for the negative effects of biological losses (cf. Staudinger et al., Chapter 11; Smith et al., Chapter 17). Of course, this explanation of the positive residual effect of age on well-being is speculative and needs to be confirmed using longitudinal data.

The power of the sensory relationships with the cognitive-motoric domains, and their ability to explain or mediate most age-related variance in many constructs, is striking. Based on the assumption that the predictive power of sensory and sensorimotor functioning is lower in earlier phases of adult life, this could mean that age-correlated biological factors, which are clearly manifested in sensory functioning, become more important in old age (thus indicating "predictive discontinuity"; P. B. Baltes & Lindenberger, 1997; Lindenberger & Baltes, 1997; Lindenberger, Marsiske, & Baltes, 1998). However, in the BASE data there were no indications to show increasing importance of sensory functioning with increasing age. There is one exception in that there *was* a significant, unique age-by-balance/gait interaction, after controlling for sensory predictor main effects, in expanded competence ($F(1, 510) = 8.98$, $p < .001$) – in other words, at higher ages, the effects of balance/gait on leisure participation become increasingly negative (see M. M. Baltes et al., Chapter 14). Results from a study with samples of younger adults indicate that the predictive power of sensory and sensorimotor performance for intellectual functioning clearly increases across the adult age range (P. B. Baltes & Lindenberger, 1997).

Are these sensory predictors simply additive in their effects, or is there "multiple jeopardy" from having impairments in more than one sense? To address this question, we asked whether (in addition to the strong main effects observed in this study) interaction effects among any two, or all three, of the senses might account for additional unique variance in our outcome domains (after controlling for age, balance/gait, hearing, and vision). Only one particular combination of modalities (vision and balance/gait) had a small but significant positive interaction effect that affected social network size ($p < .01$) and expanded competence: Thus, persons with impairments in both senses showed disproportionately lower levels of leisure participation and lower social network sizes.[6]

4   Discussion

In this chapter, we have pursued two goals. First, we provided a descriptive account of sensory functioning in three domains: hearing, vision, and balance/gait. The re-

---

[6] Note that the statistical power for detecting interactions among normally distributed variables is low (McClelland & Judd, 1993).

sults of this descriptive analysis lend strong support to the notion that sensory impairment and loss become increasingly common in the final decades of life, and that there is substantial multimorbidity in sensory functioning. As mentioned in the introduction, these concurrent impairments of different sensory systems may mean that the sensory compensation observed at younger ages (Neville, 1990; Rauschecker, 1995) is no longer possible in old age.

The second goal of the chapter was to investigate possible outcomes of age-associated individual differences in sensory functioning. We selected a broad array of outcome constructs of interest to behavioral and medical scientists. Although the magnitude of relationships between these outcome variables and sensory functioning varied substantially (with cognitive-motoric outcome domains showing the greatest relationships), sensory-sensorimotor functioning accounted for all or most of the age-related variance in each construct. In addition, the unique effects of sensory variables (separately or together) were generally larger than the unique effects of chronological age on each outcome domain.

We began this chapter with a mention of two underlying theoretical underpinnings of BASE: aging as a systemic phenomenon and differential aging. With regard to the differential aging question, we believe that this chapter has persuasively shown that individual differences in a variety of domains of functioning are (sometimes quite strongly) related to individual differences in sensory performance. As we shall discuss in detail below, it is not possible to assign *causal* status to sensory functioning in these data, but it does highlight the practical value of using sensory variables as screening constructs for the identification of individuals "at risk" in a variety of other psychological and behavioral domains. With regard to aging as a systemic phenomenon, we underscore the point that sensory variables account for most of the *age-related* individual differences in the psychological and behavioral domains we examined.

In the cognitive aging literature, many investigators (e.g., Hertzog, 1989; Lindenberger, Mayr, & Kliegl, 1993; Salthouse, 1991) have shown that measures of perceptual speed can mediate, or account for, age-related individual differences in more complex cognitive domains (e.g., reasoning, spatial performance), although much of this research has considered adults younger than BASE participants. From such data, these theorists have argued that one plausible scenario for the aging of the cognitive system is that aging exerts its effects most directly on the speed of intellectual functioning, and that all other cognitive changes may result from this fundamental age effect (e.g., Salthouse, 1994). By extension, the results of this study could similarly be used to support a view of sensory variables as the most direct "recipients" of the effects of aging – reflecting fundamental, underlying aging phenomena in the central nervous system (see Corso, 1981; Era, 1987). As we suggest below, this view of sensory variables does not necessarily mean that sensory aging has as its consequence aging in other domains, but only that sensory aging serves as a useful index of basic aging processes which cut across functional domains (i.e., aging as a systemic phenomenon; P. B. Baltes & Lindenberger, 1997).

Why might sensory functioning (e.g., hearing, vision, and balance/gait) serve as such a powerful predictor? Two broad categories of explanation have been proposed by Lindenberger and Baltes (1998; see also P. B. Baltes & Lindenberger, 1997): *direct effects* (which they discussed mostly in terms of "sensory deprivation" in their work on intelligence), and *common effects* (called the "common cause" hypothesis in their work). The common-effect idea suggests that if "aging" affects outcome X, and "aging" also affects sensory functioning, then the association between sensory functioning and X emerges because of their common causation by "aging." Of course, at its most basic level, the common-effect idea refers to age-associated biological (anatomical or physiological) changes in the brain. There is a rich body of literature about these basic processes (see Corso, 1981, for a detailed discussion), which we cannot discuss in depth. However, it is striking that age-associated changes in sensory performance are frequently linked to neuronal causes (Fozard, 1990). In this context it is important to note that *general* somatic health does not seem to constitute the common underlying feature of relationships between sensory functioning and outcomes. Subjective health was correlated .07, .16, and .26 with hearing, vision, and balance/gait, respectively, and the number of clinically significant diagnoses (Steinhagen-Thiessen & Borchelt, Chapter 5) was correlated -.12, .15, and -.24 with the respective sensory modalities.

A more causal role for sensory functioning is embedded in the direct-effect notion. Of course, it is important to restate that the causal status of sensory functioning cannot be evaluated on the basis of our cross-sectional, correlational data. The direct effect idea assumes that sensory functioning constitutes such a basic ability that effective functioning in a variety of other domains *presupposes* effective sensory capabilities. If one cannot see/hear/remain stable, one cannot do things that require these sensory capabilities (e.g., read, write, interact socially). In this view, sensory functioning is taken to be particularly sensitive to the effects of aging (as we have suggested above), and aging losses in sensory functioning "drag" other functions (which depend on intact senses) with them. This is a version of the "cascade" hypothesis (Birren, 1964), which can be modified to suggest that losses in sensory functioning might *initiate* (i.e., be the most proximal antecedent for) subsequent losses in other domains. Sensory effects can be extremely direct, in the form of *performance effects* (see also Bennett & Eklund, 1983b). Here, the physical inability to perceive implies an inability to perform other tasks.[7]

A second mechanism of sensory effects may be *sensory deprivation*. In this view, loss of sensory inputs leads to active and passive withdrawal from participation in other activities.[8] In addition to the long-standing potential mental health effects of such deprivation (Hebb, 1954), long-term consequences could include reduced intellectual stimulation and practice, as well as social isolation. A third mechanism of sensory effects may be *resource reallocation*, which P. B. Baltes and Lindenberger (1997) have discussed in terms of the attentional costs of sensory loss for intellectual functioning. With regard to intellectual functioning, the argument suggests that losses in sensory functioning mean that more attention must be paid (i.e., more attentional resource must be allocated) to perceiving and interpreting inputs. This increased demand on attentional resources (perhaps combined with other normal age-associated reductions in attentional capacity) may leave less attentional resource for other tasks. In the intellectual and cognitive domain, this attentional

[7] However, in this case, the explanation seems unlikely for two reasons (Lindenberger & Baltes, 1998). First, the correlations between vision and hearing, and the 14 tests of the cognitive test battery were more or less independent of the level of sensory demand during the test. Second, this hypothesis is not able to explain the strong connection between intellectual functioning and balance/gait.

[8] Of course, sensory deprivation effects may not be mutually exclusive of the neurophysiological and anatomical effects we have suggested, and might be a key component of the "common cause" idea. Sensory deprivation could itself contribute to processes of neuronal atrophy (Kaas, 1995).

hypothesis leads to the prediction that persons with sensory impairments will perform less well on cognitive tasks, because they are in a natural situation of divided attention.

In principle, the attentional argument can be extended to other domains of functioning. Social relationships, self-care activities, and even indices of mental health might be expected to suffer if individuals are increasingly attending to, and preoccupied with, their sensory functioning. More precisely stated, in the domain of self and personality, one might expect that impaired sensory functioning could serve as a "personal marker" or cue to the fact that one is growing older. When the awareness of one's experience of aging losses can no longer be denied, negative consequences for well-being might be expected (e.g., Brandtstädter & Greve, 1994; see also Smith et al., Chapter 17). There is further evidence for this "personal marker of aging" idea in the correlational data reported in this chapter. For both anxiety/loneliness and overall well-being, it is the unique effects of sensory functioning and not chronological age that explain the largest proportion of variance (in Chapter 17, Smith et al. offer an interesting perspective on what the underlying processes might be). Smith, Borchelt, and Steinhagen-Thiessen (1992) also present interesting qualitative data to suggest that the self-definitions of persons with severe sensory losses may differ substantially from their age peers. How older adults restructure their sense of self and well-being in the face of sensory impairment is an important question for future research.

Some additional amplification is needed regarding the finding that some variables such as intelligence, basic functional competence, and expanded competence show much stronger relationships to sensory functioning than others. As a general statement, *performance* domains (domains in which individuals actually engage in behaviors) seem to be more affected by sensory aging than *self-evaluation* domains. Colloquially, interaction with the external world may be more compromised by lost sensory capabilities than interaction with the "internal" world. Future research must consider the phenomenology of sensory losses in more detail. Are older persons less "bothered" by hearing and vision losses than theoretically expected because of social cognitive processes like downward social comparisons with age peers (i.e., they compare themselves with those who are worse off)? Are there thresholds beyond which sensory losses are more likely to have negative effects on mental health, self-evaluation, and well-being? Do losses in some modalities lead to more negative consequences than losses in others (cf. Rott & Wahl, 1993; Tesch-Römer & Nowak, 1995)? The relatively weak association between social relationships and sensory functioning also merits further study. Are long-term and close emotional relationships more resistant to sensory losses than more peripheral friendships and acquaintanceships (Antonucci, 1990; Carstensen, 1993)?

The most interesting result of this chapter has been to show strong sensory relationships with a broad array of outcome variables. These findings support a growing body of literature documenting substantial associations between hearing, vision, and/or balance/gait, and cognitive functioning (Anstey, Lord, & Williams, 1997; P. B. Baltes & Lindenberger, 1997; Granick, Kleban, & Weiss, 1976; Lindenberger & Baltes, 1997; Maylor & Wing, 1996; Salthouse, Hancock, Meinz, & Hambrick, 1996; Teasdale, Bard, LaRue, & Fleury, 1993; see also Marsiske, Klumb, & Baltes, 1997, for a detailed consideration of relationships between sensory functioning and activity). Regarding the rich multidisciplinary data set of BASE, we have only "scratched the surface": A large body of constructs remains to be explored in terms of its relationship to sensory functioning, particularly from the underexplored (in this chapter) psychiatric and medical domains.

Although data that precisely address questions of physiological and psychophysical aging, detailed sensory examinations, or occupational history of exposure to particular environmental sensory risks are not available, the detailed life-history and medical data from BASE also hold promise for investigating some potential antecedents for late-life individual differences in sensory performance.

We have tried to provide new evidence, from an older and more heterogeneous sample than has typically been used in sensory research, that (a) sensory systems are subject to a strong age-related decrease of performance, and (b) that sensory performances can be used as powerful indicators of effects of aging in other domains (in the sense of systemic aging phenomena). Indeed, at least for cognitive-motoric domains, the sensory variables in this chapter seem to be among the best predictors of individual, and particularly age-associated, differences in late life.

References

Anderson, B., & Palmore, E. (1974). Longitudinal evaluation of ocular function. In E. Palmore (Ed.), *Normal aging* (pp. 24–32). Durham, NC: Duke University Press.

Anstey, K. J., Lord, S. R., & Williams, P. (1997). Strength in the lower limbs, visual contrast sensitivity, and simple reaction time predict cognition in older women. *Psychology and Aging, 12*, 137–144.

Antonucci, T. C. (1990). Social supports and social relationships. In R. H. Binstock & L. K. George (Eds.), *Handbook of aging and the social sciences* (3rd ed., pp. 205–227). San Diego, CA: Academic Press.

Baltes, M. M., Mayr, U., Borchelt, M., Maas, I., & Wilms, H.-U. (1993). Everyday competence in old and very old age: An inter-disciplinary perspective. *Ageing and Society, 13*, 657–680.

Baltes, M. M., Wilms, H.-U., Horgas, A. L., & Little, T. D. (1998). *Everyday competence in old age: A two-component model.* Submitted manuscript, Department of Gerontopsychiatry, Free University of Berlin.

Baltes, P. B., & Baltes, M. M. (1990). Psychological perspectives on successful aging: The model of selective optimization with compensation. In P. B. Baltes & M. M. Baltes (Eds.), *Successful aging: Perspectives from the behavioral sciences* (pp. 1–34). Cambridge: Cambridge University Press.

Baltes, P. B., & Lindenberger, U. (1997). Emergence of a powerful connection between sensory and cognitive functions across the adult life span: A new window to the study of cognitive aging? *Psychology and Aging, 12*, 12–21.

Bennett, E. S., & Eklund, S. J. (1983a). Vision changes, intelligence, and aging: Part I. *Educational Gerontology, 9*, 255–278.

Bennett, E. S., & Eklund, S. J. (1983b). Vision changes, intelligence, and aging: Part II. *Educational Gerontology, 9*, 435–442.

Bess, F. H., Lichtenstein, M. J., Logan, S. A., Burger, M. C., & Nelson, E. (1989). Hearing impairment as a determinant of function in the elderly. *Journal of the American Geriatrics Society, 37*, 123–128.

Birren, J. E. (Ed.). (1964). *The psychology of aging.* Englewood Cliffs, NJ: Prentice-Hall.

Borchelt, M., & Steinhagen-Thiessen, E. (1992). Physical performance and sensory functions as determinants of independence in activities of daily living in the old and the very old. *Annals of the New York Academy of Sciences, 673*, 350–361.

Branch, L. G., Horowitz, A., & Carr, C. (1989). The implications for everyday life of incident self-reported visual decline among people over age 65 living in the community. *The Gerontologist, 29*, 359–365.

Brandtstädter, J., & Greve, W. (1994). The aging self: Stabilizing and protective processes. *Developmental Review, 14*, 52–80.

Carstensen, L. L. (1993). Motivation for social contact across the life-span: A theory of socioemotional selectivity. In J. Jacobs (Ed.), *Nebraska Symposium on Motivation* (Vol. 40, pp. 209–254). Lincoln: University of Nebraska Press.

Clark, L. A., & Watson, D. (1991). General affective dispositions in physical and psychological health. In C. R. Snyder & D. R. Forsyth (Eds.), *Handbook of social and clinical psychology: The health perspective* (pp. 221–245). New York: Pergamon Press.

Corbin, S. L., & Eastwood, M. R. (1986). Sensory deficits and mental disorders of old age: Causal or coincidental associations? *Psychological Medicine, 16*, 251–256.

Corso, J. F. (1963). Age and sex differences in pure-tone thresholds. *Archives of Otolaryngology, 77*, 385–405.

Corso, J. F. (1981). *Aging sensory systems and perception*. New York: Praeger Publishers.

Corso, J. F. (1984). Technological interventions for changes in hearing and vision incurred through aging. *Audiology, 16*, 146–163.

Corso, J. F. (1987). Sensory-perceptual processes and aging. In K. W. Schaie & C. Eisdorfer (Eds.), *Annual review of gerontology and geriatrics* (Vol. 7, pp. 29–55). Lincoln: University of Nebraska Press.

Davis, A. C. (1983). The epidemiology of hearing disorders. In R. Hinchcliffe (Ed.), *Hearing and balance in the elderly* (pp. 1–43). Edinburgh: Churchill Livingstone.

Era, P. (1987). Sensory, psychomotor, and motor functions in men of different ages. *Scandinavian Journal of Social Medicine, Suppl. 39*, 9–67.

Exton-Smith, A. N. (1977). Clinical manifestations. In A. N. Exton-Smith & G. Evans (Eds.), *Care of elderly: Meeting the challenge of dependency* (pp. 11–16). London: Academic Press.

Fozard, J. L. (1990). Vision and hearing in aging. In J. E. Birren & K. W. Schaie (Eds.), *Handbook of the psychology of aging* (3rd ed., pp. 150–170). San Diego, CA: Academic Press.

Fries, J. F. (1990). Medical perspectives upon successful aging. In P. B. Baltes & M. M. Baltes (Eds.), *Successful aging: Perspectives from the behavioral sciences* (pp. 35–49). Cambridge: Cambridge University Press.

Gerson, L. W., Jarjoura, D., & McCord, G. (1989). Risk of imbalance in elderly people with impaired vision or hearing. *Age and Ageing, 18*, 31–34.

Gilhome Herbst, K. (1983). Psychosocial consequences of disorders of hearing in the elderly. In R. Hinchcliffe (Ed.), *Hearing and balance in the elderly* (pp. 174–200). Edinburgh: Churchill Livingstone.

Granick, S., Kleban, M. H., & Weiss, A. D. (1976). Relationships between hearing loss and cognition in normally hearing aged persons. *Journal of Gerontology, 31*, 434–440.

Gryfe, C. I., Amies, A., & Ashley, M. A. (1977). A longitudinal study of falls in an elderly population: I. Incidence and morbidity. *Age and Ageing, 6*, 201–210.

Haid, C. T. (1993). Schwindel im Alter. In D. Platt (Ed.), *Handbuch der Gerontologie* (Vol. 6, pp. 167–207). Stuttgart: Gustav Fischer.

Hebb, D. O. (1954). Experimental deafness. *Canadian Journal of Psychology, 8*, 152–156.

Hertzog, C. (1989). Influences of cognitive slowing on age differences in intelligence. *Developmental Psychology, 25*, 636–651.

Horak, F. B., Shupert, C. L., & Mirka, A. (1989). Components of postural dyscontrol in the elderly: A review. *Neurobiology of Aging, 10*, 727–738.

Isaacs, B. (1985). Clinical and laboratory studies of falls in older people. *Clinics in Geriatric Medicine, 1*, 513–520.

Jerger, J., Chmiel, R., Stack, B., & Spretnjak, M. (1993). Gender affects audiometric shape in presbyacusis. *Journal of the American Academy of Audiology, 4*, 42–49.

Kaas, J. H. (1995). The reorganization of sensory and motor maps in adult mammals. In M. S. Gazzaniga (Ed.), *The cognitive neurosciences* (pp. 51–71). Cambridge, MA: MIT Press.

Kahn, R. L., & Antonucci, T. C. (1980). Convoys over the life course: Attachment, roles, and social support. In P. B. Baltes & O. G. Brim Jr. (Eds.), *Life-span development and behavior* (Vol. 3, pp. 253–283). New York: Academic Press.

Kline, D. W., & Schieber, F. (1985). Vision and aging. In J. E. Birren & K. W. Schaie (Eds.), *Handbook of the psychology of aging* (2nd ed., pp. 296–331). New York: Van Nostrand Reinhold.

Laforge, R. G., Spector, W. D., & Sternberg, J. (1992). The relationship of vision and hearing impairment to one-year mortality and functional decline. *Journal of Aging and Health, 4*, 126–148.

Lawton, M. P. (1975). The Philadelphia Geriatric Center Morale Scale: A revision. *Journal of Gerontology, 30*, 85–89.

Lawton, M. P., & Brody, E. M. (1969). Assessment of older people: Self-maintaining and instrumental activities of daily living. *The Gerontologist, 9*, 179–186.

Lindenberger, U., & Baltes, P. B. (1994). Sensory functioning and intelligence in old age: A strong connection. *Psychology and Aging, 9*, 339–355.

Lindenberger, U., & Baltes, P. B. (1997). Intellectual functioning in old and very old age: Cross-sectional results from the Berlin Aging Study. *Psychology and Aging, 12*, 410–432.

Lindenberger, U., & Baltes, P. B. (1998). *The dynamics between sensory and cognitive aging: The role of peripheral sensory factors*. Submitted manuscript, Max Planck Institute for Human Development, Berlin.

Lindenberger, U., Marsiske, M., & Baltes, P. B. (1998). *Dual task costs in sensorimotor and intellectual functioning: Increase from early adulthood to old age*. Submitted manuscript, Max Planck Institute for Human Development, Berlin.

Lindenberger, U., Mayr, U., & Kliegl, R. (1993). Speed and intelligence in old age. *Psychology and Aging, 8*, 207–220.

Lord, S. R., Clark, R. D., & Webster, L. W. (1991). Physiological factors associated with falls in an elderly population. *Journal of the American Geriatrics Society, 39*, 1194–1200.

Mahoney, F. I., & Barthel, D. W. (1965). Functional evaluation: The Barthel Index. *Maryland Medical Journal, 14*, 61–65.

Manchester, D., Woollacott, M., Zederbauer-Hylton, N., & Marin, O. (1989). Visual, vestibular and somatosensory contributions to balance control in the older adult. *Journal of Gerontology: Medical Sciences, 44*, M118–M127.

Marsiske, M., Klumb, P., & Baltes, M. M. (1997). Everyday activity patterns and sensory functioning in old age. *Psychology and Aging, 12*, 444–457.

Maylor, E. A., & Wing, A. M. (1996). Age differences in postural stability are increased by additional cognitive demands. *Journal of Gerontology: Psychological Sciences, 51B*, P143–P154.

McClelland, G. H., & Judd, C. M. (1993). Statistical difficulties of detecting interactions and moderator effects. *Psychological Bulletin, 114*, 376–390.

Mhoon, E. (1990). Otology. In C. K. Cassel, D. E. Riesenberg, L. B. Sorensen, & J. R. Walsh (Eds.), *Geriatric medicine* (2nd ed., pp. 405–419). New York: Springer.

Neville, H. J. (1990). Intermodal competition and compensation in development. *Annals of the New York Academy of Sciences, 608*, 71–91.

Ödkvist, L. M., Malmberg, L., & Möller, C. (1989). Age-related vertigo and balance disorders according to a multi-questionnaire. In C. F. Claussen, M. V. Kirtane, & K. Schlitter (Eds.), *Vertigo, nausea, tinnitus and hypoacusia in metabolic disorders* (pp. 423–437). Amsterdam: Elsevier.

Olsho, L. W., Harkins, S. W., & Lenhardt, M. L. (1985). Aging and the auditory system. In J. E. Birren & K. W. Schaie (Eds.), *Handbook of the psychology of aging* (2nd ed., pp. 332–377). New York: Van Nostrand Reinhold.

Pearson, J. D., Morrell, C. H., Gordon-Salant, S., Brant, L. J., Metter, E. J., Klein, L. L., & Fozard, J. L. (1995). Gender differences in a longitudinal study of age-associated hearing loss. *Journal of the Acoustical Society of America, 97*, 1196–1205.

Pitts, D. G. (1982). Visual acuity as a function of age. *Journal of the American Optometric Association, 53*, 117–124.

Rauschecker, J. P. (1995). Compensatory plasticity and sensory substitution in the cerebral cortex. *Trends in Neurosciences, 18*, 36–43.

Reinstein, D. Z., Dorward, N. L., Wormald, R. P. L., Graham, A., O'Connor, I., Charlton, R. M., Yeatman, M., Dodenhoff, R., Touquet, R., & Challoner, T. (1993). "Correctable undetected visual acuity deficit" in patients aged 65 and over attending an accident and emergency department. *British Journal of Ophthalmology, 77*, 293–296.

Rott, C., & Wahl, H.-W. (1993, November). *Relationships between sensory aging, cognitive functioning, coping style, and social activity: Data from the Bonn Longitudinal Study of Aging.* Paper presented at the 46th Annual Scientific Meeting of the Gerontological Society of America, New Orleans, LA.

Salthouse, T. A. (1991). *Theoretical perspectives on cognitive aging.* Hillsdale, NJ: Erlbaum.

Salthouse, T. A. (1994). How many causes are there of aging-related decrements in cognitive functioning? *Developmental Review, 14*, 413–437.

Salthouse, T. A., Hancock, H. E., Meinz, E. J., & Hambrick, D. Z. (1996). Interrelations of age, visual acuity, and cognitive functioning. *Journal of Gerontology: Psychological Sciences, 51B*, P317–P330.

Schieber, F. (1992). Aging and the senses. In J. E. Birren, R. B. Sloane, & G. D. Cohen (Eds.), *Handbook of mental health and aging* (2nd ed., pp. 251–306). San Diego, CA: Academic Press.

Schmack, W. (1989). Geriatrie in der täglichen Praxis des Augenarztes. In D. Platt (Ed.), *Handbuch der Gerontologie* (Vol. 3, pp. 29–40). Stuttgart: Gustav Fischer.

Smith, J., Borchelt, M., & Steinhagen-Thiessen, E. (1992, November). *Links between auditory functioning and profiles of the aged self: Data from the Berlin Aging Study (BASE).* Paper presented at the 45th Annual Scientific Meeting of the Gerontological Society of America, Washington, DC.

Steinhagen-Thiessen, E., & Borchelt, M. (1993). Health differences in advanced old age. *Ageing and Society, 13*, 619–655.

Teasdale, N., Bard, C., Dadouchi, F., Fleury, M., LaRue, J., & Stelmach, G. E. (1992). Posture and elderly persons: Evidence for deficits in the central integrative mechanisms. In G. E. Stelmach & J. Requin (Eds.), *Tutorials in motor behavior* (Vol. 2, pp. 917–931). Amsterdam: Elsevier.

Teasdale, N., Bard, C., LaRue, J., & Fleury, M. (1993). On the cognitive penetrability of posture control. *Experimental Aging Research, 19,* 1–13.

Tesch-Römer, C., & Nowak, M. (1995). Bewältigung von Hör- und Verständnisproblemen bei Schwerhörigkeit. *Zeitschrift für Klinische Psychologie: Forschung und Praxis, 24,* 35–45.

Tinetti, M. E. (1986). A performance-oriented assessment of mobility problems in elderly patients. *Journal of the American Geriatrics Society, 34,* 119–126.

Watson, D., & Clark, L. A. (1984). Negative affectivity: The disposition to experience aversive emotional states. *Psychological Bulletin, 96,* 465–490.

Whitbourne, S. K. (1985). *The aging body.* New York: Springer.

Willott, J. F. (1991). *Aging and the auditory system: Anatomy, physiology, and psychophysics.* London: Whurr Publishers.

Working Group on Speech Understanding and Aging. (1988). Speech understanding and aging. *Journal of the Acoustical Society of America, 83,* 859–895.

World Health Organization (WHO). (1980). *International classification of impairments, disabilities, and handicaps.* Geneva.

Everyday Competence in Old and Very Old Age: Theoretical Considerations and Empirical Findings

Margret M. Baltes, Ineke Maas, Hans-Ulrich Wilms, Markus Borchelt, and Todd D. Little

In this chapter we focus on the construction of a model of everyday competence, differentiating between a basic level of competence (BaCo), defined mainly by self-care related activities, and an expanded level of competence (ExCo), reflecting mostly discretionary or optional activities such as leisure, social, and instrumental activities of daily living. Since BaCo encompasses highly automatized and routinized activities that are necessary for survival, it is thought to be predicted foremost by health-related resources. In contrast, ExCo encompasses activities that are based on individual preferences, skills, motivations, and interests, and therefore should be more dependent on psychosocial resources. To test this model, a multidimensional or multivariable assessment of the two components and their predictors is necessary. The Berlin Aging Study (BASE) provides such a context. The findings support the model: A total of 91% of the reliable variance in ExCo and 86% in BaCo can be explained by the predictors. Furthermore, all age-related variance in everyday competence is accounted for by these health-related and psychosocial predictors. Theoretical and practical implications of the findings are discussed.

1   Introduction

Mastery of one's daily life and effective coping with daily demands are considered prerequisites for independent and autonomous living in old age. In the case of mastery, the person is said to be competent, specifically, to exhibit "everyday competence." We can differentiate at least three lines of research in the domain of everyday competence (see also M. M. Baltes, Wilms, Horgas, & Little, 1998). The first is clinical research focused on the assessment of Activities of Daily Living (ADL), obligatory tasks whose successful completion is critical for the maintenance of independent functioning (Katz, Ford, Moskowitz, Jackson, & Jaffe, 1963). Over the years, this mastery-oriented approach has been differentiated by broadening the scope of activities or skills considered to make up everyday competence. As such, measurements of Instrumental Activities of Daily Living (IADL; Lawton & Brody, 1969) and Advanced Activities of Daily Living (AADL; Reuben, Laliberte, Hiris, & Mor, 1990) were created. Additional methodological efforts by Wolinsky and colleagues (Fitzgerald, Smith, Martin, Freedman, & Wolinsky, 1993; Wolinsky & Johnson, 1991, 1992a, 1992b) have underpinned the meaningfulness of such differentiations. Assessing the need for help with such activities provides a descriptive analysis of the prevalence of dependencies in old age (M. M. Baltes & Wahl, 1987) and, thus, the need for institutionalization, sheltered housing, or home care.

The second line comes from the domain of practical intelligence, specifically from the interest in "context" (Berg, 1990; Sansone & Berg, 1993; Sternberg, 1985), that is, in the relationship between everyday cognitive functioning and performance on intelligence tests. Research on practical intelligence tries to tackle the issue: What kind of intellectual skills are necessary in everyday life? The focus on practical intelligence captures the concern about ecological validity of psychometric intelligence tests for measuring the performance required in everyday life (P. B. Baltes, 1993; Cornelius & Caspi, 1987; Denney, 1989; Marsiske & Willis, 1998; Willis, 1991; Willis & Marsiske, 1991; Willis & Schaie, 1986). This focus is very important in gerontology since it concerns the predictive salience of intelligence tests for independent living versus institutionalization in old age.

The third line is research on time use and/or time budgeting – a favorite topic in demographic sociology – that attempts to get a close description of daily lives, mostly the leisure and work life of adults in terms of time and space constraints (Szalai, 1972; Verbrugge, Gruber-Baldini, & Fozard, 1996; Zuzanek & Smale, 1991). Given these quite distinct lines of research, it is no surprise that everyday competence has been defined and examined from quite different perspectives: that is, a mastery perspective, a context perspective, and a skill perspective (see also Ford, 1985).

In our attempt to construct a model, we combine these different theoretical and methodological perspectives to gain a more comprehensive picture of everyday competence. Given the entity "everyday" – characterized by a temporal, a social, and a geographical or physical dimension (Braudel, 1992; Lehr & Thomae, 1991) – the context perspective seems a necessary prerequisite for the model. The day, the social roles, and the physical environment set the scene for, provide opportunities for, and put restrictions on the occurrence of behaviors. The more often these occurrences are repeated, the more likely it is that they become a behavioral norm on a typical day and represent a characteristic way of behaving. Therefore, to assess everyday competence, we need to assess *all* activities in their social and physical embeddedness as they occur throughout the day. Such a contextual embeddedness of behavior reflects the concept of "Lebensraum" or life space by Lewin (1951) or the concept of environment-person fit (Lawton & Nahemow, 1973). Lewin interprets the life space as a temporal, social, and geographical extension. Lawton argues that everyday competence is not merely the presence of skills, but more so their application when and where needed. He describes a dynamic interaction between competencies and environmental demands in major domains of life (e.g., social, interpersonal, cognitive, and self) and speaks of the "effectance domain." Competence, therefore, can be understood as the orchestration of resources and efforts (Bandura, 1990, 1991) demanded by a certain situation, and resulting in expected outcomes (Sternberg, 1990). Although the aim is autonomy, independence, and life mastery (Willis, 1991), competent organization of daily life can have very different expressions. How autonomy is realized in daily life depends on individual skills, motives, preferences, temperament, and other personality characteristics, as well as on the biographical learning history of the person (Lehr, 1989; Olbrich, 1987). At the same time, when referring to such general goals as independence and autonomy, more or less universal skills (such as dressing, eating, etc.) are required as well (Argyris, 1965).

Thus, in the proposed model of everyday competence we differentiate two components, a basic level of competence (BaCo) and an expanded level of competence (ExCo), which comprise the entire behavioral repertoire necessary for the management of daily life. The theoretical argument for this differentiation is as follows (see also M. M. Baltes, Maas, Wilms, & Borchelt, 1996; M. M. Baltes, Mayr, Borchelt, Maas, & Wilms, 1993; M. M. Baltes & Wilms, 1995a; Horgas, Wilms, & Baltes, in press). Consistent with previous work (Lawton, 1983a, 1983b; Lawton, Moss, Fulcomer, & Kleban, 1982), BaCo reflects basic personal maintenance activities of daily life. In contrast, ExCo relates to discretionary leisure and social activities, as well as instrumental activities of daily living that ensure contact with the outside world and the self. Accordingly, BaCo activities are highly automatized, routinized, and necessary for survival. Thus, they are normative for independent living in adulthood in most societies; that is, all adults should be able to execute these activities. Therefore, we argue that they are relatively free from sociocultural and psychosocial factors, but much more dependent on biological health factors. In contrast, ExCo contains activities that reflect individual preferences, motivations, and specific skills, and should be more heavily influenced by psychosocial factors that vary within and between life biographies. ExCo activities express individuals' engagement with the world around them and with their own development and growth. These activities are necessary for a responsible and satisfactory life in adulthood. Whereas BaCo activities guarantee survival and thereby length or quantity of life, ExCo influences quality of life. Both components together make up everyday competence or the ability to lead an autonomous, responsible, and satisfying life (M. M. Baltes et al., 1998).

Although competence is traditionally defined in psychology as capacity, as opposed to performance, it is operationalized on the behavioral level. As Lawton (1983b) emphasized: "These [capacity-oriented] constructs, however, are usually not directly measurable. Therefore, one way to measure competence is to define behaviors that imply the presence of some element of competence" (p. 350). In this sense, there are efforts in clinical psychology (M. M. Baltes & Kindermann, 1985) and in cognitive intervention research (P. B. Baltes, 1993) to assess competence using testing-the-limits strategies. Such an assessment strategy could not be used in BASE because of its initial cross-sectional design. Nevertheless, we believe that our model of everyday competence with its two components, BaCo and ExCo, allows a rapprochement to "elements of competence."

Because little is known about everyday activities of older adults we will begin with a presentation of descriptive data. In a second step, the relationships between BaCo, ExCo, and age are analyzed. In a third step, the system of predictors is introduced, and the hypothesis concerning the differential prediction of the two components is examined using structural modeling procedures.

2   Methods

2.1   *Sample*

As described in Chapter 1 of this book (P. B. Baltes et al.), the BASE sample is designed to be representative of the western part of the city of Berlin. It oversamples men and the very old. It is a probability sample of community-dwelling and institutionalized individuals between the ages of 70 and over 100 years (14% lived in long-term institutions). The sample was drawn from the city registry (recall that in Germany each citizen must be registered) and consists of 516 participants with equal numbers ($n = 43$

each) of males and females in six age groups (70–74, 75–79, 80–84, 85–89, 90–94, 95+).
Analyses in this chapter are not weighted for age and gender.

2.2   Measurement Instruments

2.2.1   Yesterday Interview
The Yesterday Interview (Moss & Lawton, 1982) attempts a minute-to-minute reconstruction of the sequence and context of activities during the day preceding the day of the
interview. Such a reconstruction allows the assessment of type, frequency, and duration
of activities engaged in by the participant during that day (see Table 14.1), as well as
contextual dimensions of each activity (i.e., location and presence of social partners),
and the level of perceived difficulty of activities (M. M. Baltes et al., 1993, 1998). Interrater reliability assessments for the codings of the activities yielded κ-scores above .80.
The activity score from the Yesterday Interview was defined as the total time (in minutes) spent in six activity categories during the previous day, both at home and away
from home. The six main activity categories were: self-care activities, instrumental activities, leisure activities, social activities, work, and resting (see Table 14.1).

2.2.2   Barthel Index and Lawton and Brody Scale
Subjective ratings by the BASE participants of the degree of help needed with the execution of basic activities such as dressing, toileting, eating, and grooming (see Table 14.2)
were assessed with the Barthel Index (Mahoney & Barthel, 1965) and two items, shopping and transportation, from the IADL Scale by Lawton and Brody (1969). A more detailed description of these scales is given in Chapter 5 (Steinhagen-Thiessen &
Borchelt).

2.2.3   Activity List
The Activity List was part of a sociological interview that contained a detailed life history and a life situation questionnaire, and assessed the level of participation in "out-of-
house" activities (the number of activities people engaged in outside their private domain during the past 12 months; see Mayer et al., Chapter 8, for a description of this
instrument).

3   Descriptive Findings

3.1   Findings from the Yesterday Interview
Table 14.1 contains all activity categories, with the percentages for the six main
activity categories, characteristic of the BASE participants from age 70 to 103. Older
adults spend about equal amounts of time (19% each) with obligatory self-care activities
and resting during their waking hours. This amounts to less than half of their waking day
(38%). An equal amount of time (38%) is spent in leisure activities and another 15% in
instrumental activities. Social activities do not take up much time, only 7% of the day. In
all, however, discretionary activities take up more than half of the waking day, about

Table 14.1. *Percentages of time spent in the main activity categories for all BASE participants, separately for men and women, and for the old (aged 70–84) and very old (aged 85+)*

| Activities | Percentages | | | | |
	Total	Men	Women	70–84	85+
Self-care activities	19.0	19.0	18.9	19.0	18.9
Getting up, personal care, eating, going to bed, shopping, passive transportation, other					
Instrumental activities	15.1	12.4	18.0	16.9	13.2
Light household chores, heavy household chores, handicraft/mending, other housework					
Banking, dealing with authorities, letters and post office, other official business					
Medical treatment, self-treatment					
Leisure activities	38.1	41.1	34.9	42.2	33.6
Active transportation, attending cultural events, continuing education, sports, creative activities, gardening, walking, excursions, reading, writing, playing, watching TV, listening to radio/tapes/records, church activities, political activities, other leisure activities					
Social activities	7.0	7.1	7.0	7.3	6.8
Talking to people, visiting, telephoning, other social activities					
Helping family members, helping other people					
Work	0.7	1.0	0.4	1.3	0.1
Regular paid work, other work					
Resting	18.6	18.1	19.0	12.1	25.5
Sleeping during the day, being inactive					
Missing	1.5	1.3	1.8	1.2	1.9
Waking up, falling asleep, refusal to answer, no reaction					

Note. All activities coded in each category are listed.

60%. Looking more closely at the distribution of activities from morning to evening, self-care activities occur mostly in the morning – as one would expect given our cultural habits – whereas all others (mainly discretionary activities) occur during the afternoon. When considering the social and geographical context of activities, we find that most activities are done alone (64%) and inside the home (80%; see also Horgas et al., in press).

Table 14.1 also shows the average percentages for old (aged 70–84) and very old (85+) participants, and for men and women. Incidentally, the percentages for institutionalized versus community-dwelling persons are not listed because they closely resemble

Table 14.2. *Percentages of limitations ("unable to do" or "need help") in 10 ADLs and 2 IADLs by age, gender, and place of residence*

Activities	Total	70–84	85+	Men	Women	Community-dwelling	Institu-tionalized
Shopping	46.5	22.9	70.2**	39.1	53.9**	40.2	87.1**
Transportation	46.5	20.2	72.9**	39.9	53.1*	40.2	85.7**
Bathing	27.5	8.9	46.1**	20.4	34.5**	21.6	65.7**
Climbing stairs	19.2	5.8	32.6**	12.8	25.6**	13.7	54.3**
Going for walks	20.3	5.8	34.0**	16.3	24.4	17.3	40.0**
Getting dressed	11.0	4.3	17.8**	8.5	13.6	7.2	35.7**
Toileting	6.2	1.6	10.9**	3.5	8.9	2.5	30.0**
Transfer[a]	5.8	1.6	10.1**	3.1	8.5	3.4	21.4**
Grooming	2.5	0.4	4.7	1.6	3.5	2.5	2.9
Eating	1.0	0.4	1.6	0.4	1.6	0.9	1.4
Bladder control	32.4	22.5	42.2**	25.2	39.5**	31.7	37.1
Bowel control	13.8	14.0	13.6	9.3	18.2*	13.0	18.6

* $p < .01$, ** $p < .001$.
[a]Transfer refers to getting into and out of bed.

those for the very old versus old age group. The effects of age and residence are significant for three activities: Resting takes up more time, whereas instrumental and leisure activities take up significantly less time in the very old age group and in the institutionalized group. Men and women differ with respect to two activities; women spend more time in instrumental activities, and men spend more time in leisure activities.

3.2   ADL and IADL Self-Ratings

Looking at the self-ratings of the ability to execute ADLs (Barthel Index) or simple IADLs (Lawton & Brody, 1969), about 32% of the participants report that they do not need help. About half of the participants report that they need some help with shopping and transportation (simple IADLs). Table 14.2 shows some significant differences by gender and residential status. Women report needing more help when engaging in the following six activities: shopping, transportation, bathing, climbing stairs, bladder control, and bowel control. Participants aged 85 and above, as well as those in institutionalized settings, report more difficulty in all activities except eating and grooming.

3.3   Activity List

Table 14.3 lists all "out-of-house" activities mentioned (see also Mayer et al., Chapter 8). Overall, restaurant visits are reported as the most frequent engagement (55%) during the past year, whereas creative and political activities are reported least often. When comparing the two age groups it can be seen that the older participants report significantly lower engagement in all activities. The effects of residential status are similar to those of age, except that there are no differences between community-dwelling

Table 14.3. *Percentages of participants who carried out activities during the past 12 months by age, gender, and residence*

Activities	Total	70–84	85+	Men	Women	Community-dwelling	Institution-alized
Sports	27.5	43.2	11.8**	28.4	26.7	31.1	5.6**
Restaurant visits	55.4	66.1	44.5**	54.3	56.4	60.7	23.3**
Dancing	9.7	17.9	1.6**	14.1	5.4**	11.1	1.4**
Day trips	46.5	59.9	32.9**	46.9	46.1	50.1	24.7**
Attending cultural events	40.5	56.2	24.5**	37.9	43.1	43.6	21.1**
Hobbies	11.1	14.7	3.5*	14.0	8.2	12.7	1.4*
Volunteer work	9.0	14.4	3.5**	10.6	7.4	10.0	2.8
Traveling	48.3	69.0	27.5**	50.0	46.7	55.1	6.9**
Creative activities	3.7	5.8	1.6*	3.5	3.9	4.1	1.4
Playing games	21.8	34.5	9.0**	21.0	22.6	24.9	2.7**
Continuing education	8.6	13.6	3.5**	7.8	9.4	9.5	2.8
Political activities	6.0	8.5	3.5*	9.7	2.3**	7.0	0.0
Total	516	258	258	258	258	442	74

$* p < .01, ** p < .001.$

and institutionalized persons in volunteer work, creative and political activities, and continuing education – all of which are activities that show very low frequencies to begin with. With regard to gender, men report political activities and dancing more frequently than women.

3.4   Summary of Descriptive Findings

The findings regarding the daily activity profile, the out-of-house engagements during the past year, and the subjective ratings of difficulty in ADLs and simple IADLs all show a significant age and residential status effect but only a small gender effect. The very old (aged 85 and above) and the institutionalized both report an overall lower activity level, as well as more difficulties in the execution of activities.

4   Basic and Expanded Levels of Competence

4.1   Relationships between Age, BaCo, and ExCo

4.1.1   Construction of the Dependent Variables, BaCo and ExCo

Both components were each represented by two indicators (see Table 14.4). With regard to the basic level of competence, BaCo, these were based on the self-ratings of the degree of help needed in the execution of 10 basic activities such as dressing, toileting, eating, grooming, and so forth (all from the Barthel Index), and in two instrumental activi-

Table 14.4. *The dependent variables of everyday competence*

Construct	Measure	Author

BaCo
Basic level of competence
	Subjective rating of help needed
	  10 ADLs
	  2 IADLs
		Mahoney & Barthel, 1965
		Lawton & Brody, 1969

ExCo
Expanded level of competence
	Subjective report of engagement
	  in 12 out-of-house categories
	  in Activity List
		Maas & Staudinger, 1996

	Subjective reconstruction of
	  activity sequence in Yesterday
	  Interview
		Moss & Lawton, 1982

ties, shopping and transportation (from the IADL Scale; Lawton & Brody, 1969). To come up with two indicators for BaCo (a prerequisite for the kind of statistical analyses conducted below), the 10 ADL and 2 IADL items were ordered by difficulty and then split into two scales, with the even-numbered items making up the first indicator and the odd-numbered items the second.

The second component of everyday competence, ExCo, was also assessed by means of two indicators. The first indicator of ExCo comes from the Yesterday Interview representing the sum of time spent in all activity categories, except self-care activities and resting. The second indicator stems from the Activity List representing the total number of activities people engaged in outside their home during the past year.

4.1.2   Age/Cohort Differences in BaCo and ExCo

With regard to the interrelationship of age and the two components, two questions were of major interest: (1) What is the relation between age/cohort and the two components of everyday competence? (2) Do the two components represent the same or different portions of age-related variance? Looking at the intercorrelations between the unweighted standardized means of BaCo, ExCo, and age, we find highly significant negative associations, as expected: -.54 between BaCo and age, and -.57 between ExCo and age. Thus, between 70 and 103 years of age there were considerable negative age correlations, but also great heterogeneity or variability unrelated to age, particularly in ExCo, as well as a ceiling effect in BaCo. Quite a few individuals exhibited high levels of basic competence even in very old age.

To answer the question of whether the two components of everyday competence represent the same or different portions of age-related variance, we conducted a hierarchical regression analysis with ExCo as the dependent variable. Entering BaCo in a first step explained 39% of the variance in ExCo ($F(1, 514) = 325.9$, $p < .01$). Age, entered in a second step, explained an additional 6% (change in $F = 52.3$, $p < .01$). The total variance explained in ExCo amounted to 45%. To examine more closely how much of the explained variance is unique or common to BaCo and age, a communality analysis was conducted (Hertzog, 1989). We find that age explains 6% and BaCo explains 11% of specific variance in ExCo; the common variance amounts to 28%. Accordingly, both fac-

Table 14.5. *Latent constructs and indicators*

Construct	Instrument	Author	Research Unit
Distal resources			
Physical health	Number of diagnosed physical illnesses Number of medications		Geriatrics
Socioeconomic status (SES)	Income Magnitude Prestige Scale	G. Wagner, 1991 Wegener, 1988	Sociology
Proximal resources			
Balance/gait	Romberg trial 360° turn	Tinetti, 1986	Geriatrics
Depressivity	HAMD DSM-III-R	Hamilton, 1960, 1967 American Psychiatric Association, 1987	Psychiatry
Fluid intelligence	Reasoning Perceptual speed Memory	Lindenberger, Mayr, & Kliegl, 1993	Psychology
Personality	Extraversion (NEO) Openness (NEO) Life investment	Costa & McCrae, 1985 Staudinger & Fleeson, 1996	Psychology

tors, age and BaCo, are important and independent predictors of ExCo. From this finding, one can deduce that BaCo and ExCo map onto different parts of variance in age, a first indication for the independence of the two components.

4.2   Testing the Two-Component Model

4.2.1   Description of Predictor Variables
According to the theoretical model, predictors consisted of health-related and psychosocial variables (see Table 14.5). Health-related resources were represented by physical health, balance/gait, and depressivity (cf. Steinhagen-Thiessen & Borchelt, Chapter 5; Helmchen et al., Chapter 6). Psychosocial resources were reflected by fluid intelligence, personality, and socioeconomic status (cf. Smith & Baltes, Chapter 7; Mayer et al., Chapter 8). It should be noted that we initially also included control beliefs, as well as contextual resources, such as the place of residence and social network. They will not be shown in the model because they did not explain any additional variance in the two components of everyday competence and actually reduced the fit of the model.

4.2.2   Model Fitting Procedure
To test the two-component model of everyday competence and its differential predictor system, structural equation modeling was conducted using LISREL 8.10 (Jöreskog & Sörbom, 1993). Modeling proceeded in two steps. In a first step, a measurement model

Table 14.6. *Latent correlations among the latent constructs (upper diagonal), and residual correlations among the proximal predictors and between the two outcomes (lower diagonal)*

	1	2	3	4	5	6	7	8	9
1 Age		-.05	.13	-.65	-.64	-.31	.10	-.63	-.72
2 SES	—		.00	.19	.46	.45	.03	.22	.46
3 Physical health	—	—		.30	.15	.03	-.54	.32	.15
4 Balance/gait	—	—	—		.65	.32	-.29	.91	.78
5 Fluid intelligence	—	—	—	.35		.51	-.19	.65	.88
6 Personality	—	—	—	.06	.20		-.13	.32	.62
7 Depressivity	—	—	—	-.19	-.19	-.16		-.35	-.20
8 BaCo	—	—	—	—	—	—	—		.84[a]
9 ExCo	—	—	—	—	—	—	—	.70	

Note. Correlations in italics are not significant at the $p < .05$ level. The residual correlations are from the final model presented in Figure 14.1.
[a]Significantly different from 1.0; $\chi^2(1, 516) = 18.3, p < .001$.

was established, which presented the two components of everyday competence and seven predictors in terms of nine intercorrelated factors. The linear relationships between the seven predictors and the two dependent variables, BaCo and ExCo, are presented in Table 14.6. In a second step, a structural model was tested using the saturated measurement model as a baseline. Theoretically motivated paths between the distal factors and the proximal factors, and between proximal factors and BaCo and ExCo were specified according to our hypotheses (see also M. M. Baltes et al., 1998).[1]

4.3   Findings

4.3.1   The Measurement Model
The latent correlations among the two components, BaCo and ExCo, age, and the six constructs are presented in Table 14.6. When a nine-factor model without constraints on factor intercorrelations is fitted to the variance-covariance matrix, the χ^2 for this saturated model is statistically significant, but the additional fit indices are satisfactory ($\chi^2 = 244.92$, RMSEA = .044, $p = 0.88$, NNFI = 0.96). In this model, an equality constraint was put on the indicators of the dual-indicated constructs, except for the construct physical health. On the basis of a large modification index, the equality constraint was freed on physical health. This implies that this construct is predominantly defined by the number of diagnoses. A high score thus means poor physical health.

---

[1] It is well known that formal fit statistics, such as χ^2, are sample-size dependent (Browne & Cudeck, 1993; Matsueda & Bielby, 1986). Therefore, we will inspect additional fit criteria such as the root mean square error of approximation (RMSEA; Browne & Cudeck, 1993), the Nonnormed Fit Index (NNFI; Bentler & Bonett, 1980), and the Incremental Fit Index (IFI; Bollen, 1989). Generally, the rule applies that χ^2-values should not be more than two to five times larger than the number of degrees of freedom, the RMSEA should be equal or smaller than .08, and NNFI and IFI should be larger than .90.

Table 14.7. *Summary of the model-fitting procedure*

Model	*df*	χ^2	*p*	RMSEA	NNFI	IFI	R^2 BaCo	R^2 ExCo
Saturated model	122	244.92	.00	.044	.96	.97	—	—
Mediated model	135	263.06	.00	.043	.96	.97	.86	.91

4.3.2   The Structural Model

Remember, the hypothesis was that the BaCo component of everyday competence should capture predominantly health-related factors; in contrast, the ExCo component should be determined more by health-nonrelated resources, such as socioeconomic status, intelligence, and personality. Furthermore, all effects of the distal factors should be mediated by the proximal factors, which means that no direct paths from distal factors to BaCo or ExCo were allowed unless required by the data. Accordingly, a model was fit in which balance/gait, depressivity, personality, and fluid intelligence were considered proximal resources; physical health, socioeconomic status, and age were the distal resources. Since differential influences on the two components, BaCo and ExCo, were postulated, direct paths from balance/gait and depressivity to BaCo, and from fluid intelligence and personality to ExCo were expected. Physical health was assumed to exert its effect on BaCo through balance/gait and depressivity. Age and socioeconomic status were assumed to have indirect paths to ExCo through fluid intelligence and personality. Both the distal and the proximal predictors were allowed to intercorrelate among each other. Table 14.6 shows the correlations between the latent constructs as well as the residual correlations. The residual correlations are significant but small. Even the residual correlation of .70 between BaCo and ExCo is based on very small residual variances.

The fit of this constrained, mediational model does not differ significantly from the fit of the saturated model ($\Delta\chi^2(13) = 18.14$, $p = .15$; see Table 14.7). The χ^2 of the structural model amounts to 263.06, which is significant, but other fit indices are satisfactory (RMSEA = .043, NNFI = .96, IFI = .97; Bentler & Bonett, 1980; Bollen, 1989). The model is presented in Figure 14.1; all paths that are not shown are nonsignificant. All remaining paths are significant at the .01 level except the path between personality and ExCo ($p < .05$). Freed paths from distal predictors to BaCo and ExCo were nonsignificant.

Four important results can be deduced from the mediational model. First, the overall explained variance of the reliable variance of BaCo amounts to .86, and to .91 for ExCo. Second, the health-related predictors, physical health, depressivity and balance/gait, exert their influence foremost on BaCo. Third, ExCo is predicted mainly by the psychosocial factors, fluid intelligence and personality. Fourth, the effects of the distal factors on BaCo and ExCo are entirely mediated by the proximal factors. The indirect effect of age on BaCo is -.57, and -.63 on ExCo, the indirect effect of socioeconomic status on BaCo is .17, and .40 on ExCo, and the indirect effect of physical health on BaCo is -.23, and -.08 on ExCo. In the present context perhaps less important, but notable, are the explained variances in the proximal predictors by the distal predictors: $R^2 = .30$ for personality, .61 for fluid intelligence, .53 for balance/gait, and .30 for depressivity.

Figure 14.1. The empirical two-component model of everyday competence.

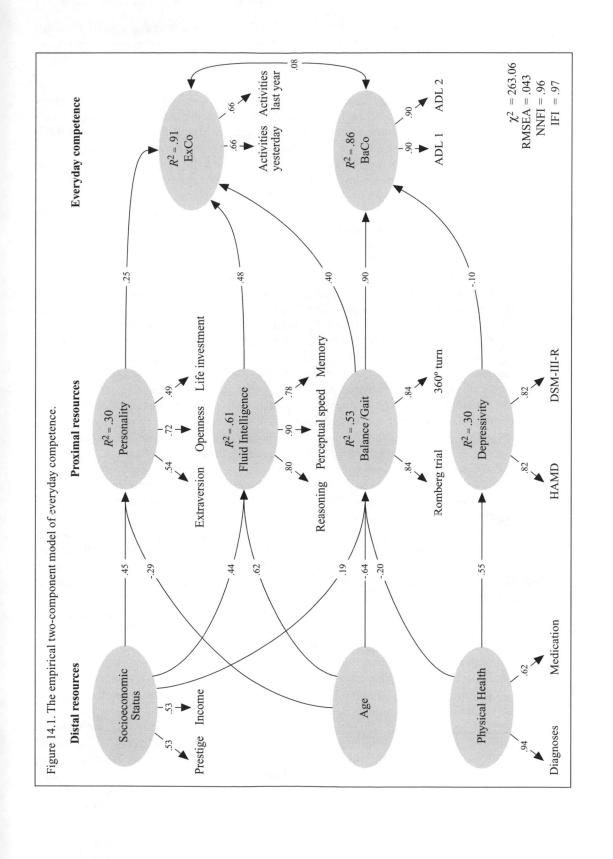

5   Summary and Discussion

This chapter was aimed at providing a description and explanation of elderly persons' everyday competence. How do older adults structure their day and engage in activities crucial for an autonomous, responsible, and satisfying life? What factors influence their everyday competence? The makeup of the average activity profile is somewhat counterintuitive. Leisure activities including reading and watching television (excluding social activities with 7%) take up only 38% of the day, whereas obligatory activities that have to do with personal maintenance still amount to 35%. This is hardly in line with the idea of freedom and autonomy from social roles in old age (i.e., roles that structure young and middle-aged adults' lives).

Surprising, too, is the fact that social activities account for only 7% of a day. Is this a sign of the often cited loneliness among older adults? A look at the ecological parameters would support this interpretation: Older adults spent most of their time at home and alone. We are hesitant, however, to interpret this as an indication of loneliness. Our participants mention an average of 10 people ($SD = 7.1$) in their social network (Lang, 1994; Schulte, 1994; cf. Wagner et al., Chapter 10). Furthermore, the average number of out-of-house activities amounts to 3, and at least half of the participants are independent.

In general, when comparing the profiles of older and younger age groups in the literature, we were surprised to find more similarities than differences. Except for school and work, which take up substantial parts of daily activities in younger age groups (Szalai, 1972; Verbrugge et al., 1996; Zuzanek & Smale, 1991), time spent in social activities and hobbies does not differ much. Old people still keep the same daily organization, with obligatory activities in the morning and nonobligatory activities in the afternoon and evening. Thus, elderly adults do not seem to translate their freedom from social and work roles into a more individualized daily structure.

As expected, there are two basic components of everyday competence, BaCo and ExCo, that show great interindividual variability and are predicted by different resources. BaCo is related mostly to health-related variables, ExCo to psychosocial ones. The paths between ExCo and the proximal predictors differed significantly from each corresponding path between BaCo and the predictors (all $ps < .01$). The significant age effect on everyday competence is entirely mediated by the proximal predictors; thus, the significant age differences in everyday competence seem to be due to either health or psychosocial factors, or some combination of the two.

With the empirical validation of the two-component model, very different research perspectives – the sociological one with its interest in time budgets of work and leisure activities, the clinical one with its interest in ADL/IADL limitations, and the contextual one with its interest in person-environment fit – are brought together for the first time. We believe that the present theoretical frame can enrich the research endeavors in each of the respective fields (see also Ford, 1985). On the methodological level, the use of diverse measurement instruments – subjective ratings of ADL and IADL, subjective reports of out-of-house activities over the past year, and a subjective reconstruction of the previous day (Yesterday Interview) – will yield as "convergent operations" (McCall, 1977) a more comprehensive picture of everyday competence. Such an approach, as elaborated here, can surely be refined and improved upon.

On a theoretical level, there are several points worth mentioning. First, even though balance/gait has a weaker effect on ExCo than BaCo, there is still the effect of a health-related factor on ExCo. We interpret this relationship between balance/gait and ExCo as meaning that a certain neurophysiological performance level is also required for activities that go beyond BaCo. This relationship between balance/gait and ExCo indicates that psychosocial resources such as education, financial security, and openness are necessary but not sufficient to guarantee the realization of ExCo.

A second aspect refers to the highly significant, although mediated, negative age effect on BaCo and ExCo. Despite this strong negative association between age and everyday competence, there is, at the same time, great variability that is in line with the concept of *differential aging*. The reason for this heterogeneity in everyday competence can lie in the factors balance/gait, intelligence, and personality, which moderate the effect of age. This means that age in itself is not responsible for the declines or losses in BaCo and ExCo, rather the health-related and psychosocial factors are. In turn, this would open new avenues for intervention, and the aims of intervention would be different from person to person, or at least from group to group – for instance, persons with dementia versus persons who are mentally healthy (M. M. Baltes & Wilms, 1995b; Wilms & Baltes, 1994).

A third issue relates to the effect of physical health. ExCo and BaCo are affected by health only through balance/gait. One interpretation for the lack of a direct path between health and BaCo is that health deficits are compensated for, as long as they do not affect basic brain processes. It is interesting in this context that there is a strong significant relationship between physical health and depressivity, but a very small and even nonsignificant relationship between depressivity and BaCo, and ExCo. This is very much in contrast to clinical psychiatric experience. Lack of initiative and motivation, key elements of depression, are assumed to affect the activity level of patients. One explanation for this unique finding could be that only three participants in our sample suffered from severe depression. Nevertheless, an interesting issue is to consider depression a consequence rather than an antecedent of changes in BaCo and ExCo. This perspective is very much in accordance with Willis (1991), who proposed that everyday competence is a moderator between well-being and age-related, health-related, and psychosocial losses. Given a situation in which basic activities can no longer be performed, this could very well function as a risk factor for depression.

A fourth aspect, pertaining to the significant relationship between fluid intelligence and balance/gait, requires attention. Does the correlation between fluid intelligence and balance/gait suggest a common neurological base and common neurological processes like speed, identification of schemata, or something similar (Lindenberger & Baltes, 1994; see Lindenberger & Reischies, Chapter 12)? A fifth point worth mentioning is the effect of socioeconomic status on ExCo moderated by personality and intelligence. In other words, financial or economic security alone does not guarantee everyday competence. Instead, personality and intelligence factors facilitate or hamper the effect of socioeconomic status on ExCo.

It seems important to make a point regarding the predictor system of the two-component model here. We emphasized that the structure of a model is dependent upon theoretical assumptions. Undoubtedly, there are others besides the ones we included. For instance, from a biographical perspective it would be personality and intelligence influencing socioeconomic status rather than the reverse. In our model, it is the interplay between age and psychosocial factors that is at the center, and socioeconomic status provides the framework in which this relationship is played out.

In this context it should be reiterated that other context variables, such as residence or residential quality, do not show up as significant factors in the model. The reason might be that these context variables correlate very highly with socioeconomic status in our sample. Single comparisons on the level of activity profiles, for instance, do show effects of residence particularly on ExCo (M. M. Baltes & Horgas, 1997). At the same time, it must be reiterated that we explain 86% of the reliable variance in BaCo and 91% in ExCo. Consequently, efforts should go into understanding the mechanisms by which the factors influence BaCo and ExCo, rather than looking for new predictors.

What are the practical implications that may be deduced from the model and the empirical findings about everyday competence? Although age and socioeconomic status are important influences on everyday competence, they are moderated by factors such as intelligence, personality, and sensorimotor functioning, factors that are open to intervention efforts. Thus, both efforts toward prevention of anticipated losses and rehabilitation after such losses in everyday competence can have different entry points for intervention. In addition, intervention efforts cannot focus on one component of everyday competence alone. The presence of BaCo is not a sufficient, but is a necessary condition for ExCo. Conversely, ExCo is not a prerequisite for BaCo, but is an essential condition for life quality. More detailed knowledge about the interplay between the two components and their age-related changes, as well as between the two and their predictive system, can only be gained from longitudinal data. Such knowledge will point to potentials and limits in compensation, selection, and optimization in everyday competence (Marsiske, Lang, Baltes, & Baltes, 1995).

References

American Psychiatric Association (APA) (Ed.). (1987). *Diagnostic and statistical manual of mental disorders (DSM-III-R)*. Washington, DC.

Argyris, C. (1965). Exploration in interpersonal competence. *Journal of Applied Behavioral Science, 1*, 58–63.

Baltes, M. M., & Horgas, A. L. (1997). Long-term care institutions and the maintenance of competence. In K. W. Schaie & S. L. Willis (Eds.), *Societal mechanisms for maintaining competence in old age* (pp. 142–164). New York: Springer.

Baltes, M. M., & Kindermann, T. (1985). Die Bedeutung der Plastizität für die klinische Beurteilung des Leistungsverhaltens im Alter. In D. Bente, H. Coper, & S. Kanowski (Eds.), *Hirnorganische Psychosyndrome im Alter: Vol. II. Methoden zur Objektivierung pharmakotherapeutischer Wirkungen* (pp. 171–184). Berlin: Springer-Verlag.

Baltes, M. M., Maas, I., Wilms, H.-U., & Borchelt, M. (1996). Alltagskompetenz im Alter: Theoretische Überlegungen und empirische Befunde. In K. U. Mayer & P. B. Baltes (Eds.), *Die Berliner Altersstudie* (pp. 525–542). Berlin: Akademie Verlag.

Baltes, M. M., Mayr, U., Borchelt, M., Maas, I., & Wilms, H.-U. (1993). Everyday competence in old and very old age: An inter-disciplinary perspective. *Ageing and Society, 13*, 657–680.

Baltes, M. M., & Wahl, H.-W. (1987). Dependency in aging. In L. L. Carstensen & B. A. Edelstein (Eds.), *Handbook of clinical gerontology* (pp. 204–221). New York: Pergamon Press.

Baltes, M. M., & Wilms, H.-U. (1995a). Alltagskompetenz im Alter. In R. Oerter & L. Montada (Eds.), *Entwicklungspsychologie* (pp. 1127–1136). Weinheim: Psychologie Verlags Union.

Baltes, M. M., & Wilms, H.-U. (1995b, February). *Alltagskompetenz und Gesundheit.* Paper presented at the "Tagung der Deutschen Gesellschaft für Gerontopsychiatrie," Hamburg.

Baltes, M. M., Wilms, H.-U., Horgas, A. L., & Little, T. D. (1998). *Everyday competence in old age: A two-component model.* Submitted manuscript, Department of Gerontopsychiatry, Free University of Berlin.

Baltes, P. B. (1993). The aging mind: Potential and limits. *The Gerontologist, 33,* 580–594.

Bandura, A. (1989). Human agency in social cognitive theory. *American Psychologist, 44,* 1175–1184.

Bandura, A. (1990). Conclusion: Reflections on non-ability determinants of competence. In R. J. Sternberg & J. Kolligian Jr. (Eds.), *Competence considered* (pp. 315–362). New Haven, CT: Yale University Press.

Bandura, A. (1991). Self-regulation of motivation through anticipatory and self-reactive mechanisms. In R. A. Dienstbier (Ed.), *Nebraska Symposium on Motivation 1990* (Vol. 38, pp. 69–164). Beverly Hills, CA: Sage.

Bentler, P. M., & Bonett, D. G. (1980). Significance tests and goodness of fit in the analysis of covariance structures. *Psychological Bulletin, 88,* 588–606.

Berg, C. A. (1990). What is intellectual efficiency over the life course? Using adults' conceptions to address the question. In J. Rodin, C. Schooler, & K. W. Schaie (Eds.), *Self-directedness: Cause and effects throughout the life course* (pp. 155–182). Hillsdale, NJ: Erlbaum.

Bollen, K. A. (1989). A new incremental fit index for general structural equation models. *Sociological Methods and Research, 17,* 303–316.

Braudel, F. (1992). *The structures of everyday life* (Vol. 1). Berkeley: University of California Press.

Browne, M., & Cudeck, R. (1993). Alternative ways of assessing model fit. In K. A. Bollen & J. S. Long (Eds.), *Testing structural equation models* (pp. 136–162). Newbury Park, CA: Sage.

Cornelius, S. W., & Caspi, A. (1987). Everyday problem solving in adulthood and old age. *Psychology and Aging, 2,* 144–153.

Costa, P. T., Jr., & McCrae, R. R. (1985). *NEO: Five-factor personality inventory.* Talahassee, FL: Psychological Assessment Resources.

Denney, N. W. (1989). Everyday problem solving: Methodological issues, research findings, and a model. In L. W. Poon, D. C. Rubin, B. A. Wilson, & D. Tilson (Eds.), *Everyday cognition in adulthood and late life* (pp. 330–351). Cambridge: Cambridge University Press.

Fitzgerald, J. F., Smith, D. M., Martin, D. K., Freedman, J. A., & Wolinsky, F. D. (1993). Replication of the multidimensionality of activities of daily living. *Journal of Gerontology: Social Sciences, 48,* S28–S31.

Ford, M. E. (1985). The concept of competence: Themes and variations. In J. H. A. Marlowe & R. B. Weinberg (Eds.), *Competence development: Theory and practice in special populations* (pp. 3–49). Springfield, IL: C. C. Thomas.

Hamilton, M. (1960). A rating scale for depression. *Journal of Neurology, Neurosurgery and Psychiatry, 23,* 56–62.

Hamilton, M. (1967). Development of a rating scale for primary depressive illness. *British Journal of Consulting and Clinical Psychology, 6,* 278–296.

Hertzog, C. (1989). Influences of cognitive slowing on age differences in intelligence. *Developmental Psychology, 25,* 636–651.

Horgas, A. L., Wilms, H.-U., & Baltes, M. M. (in press). Daily life in very old age: Everyday activities as an expression of successful living. *The Gerontologist.*

Jöreskog, K. G., & Sörbom, D. (1993). *LISREL 8: User's reference guide.* Chicago, IL: Scientific Software.

Katz, S., Ford, A. B., Moskowitz, R. W., Jackson, B. A., & Jaffe, M. W. (1963). Studies of illness in the aged. The index of ADL: A standardized measure of biological and psychosocial function. *Journal of the American Medical Association, 185,* 914–919.

Lang, F. R. (1994). *Die Gestaltung informeller Hilfebeziehungen im hohen Alter: Die Rolle von Elternschaft und Kinderlosigkeit. Eine empirische Studie zur sozialen Unterstützung und deren Effekt auf die erlebte soziale Einbindung* (Studien und Berichte des Max-Planck-Instituts für Bildungsforschung 59). Berlin: Edition Sigma.

Lawton, M. P. (1983a). Assessment of behaviors required to maintain residence in the community. In T. Crook, S. H. Ferris, & R. Bartus (Eds.), *Assessment in geriatric psycho-pharmacology* (pp. 119–135). New Canaan, CT: Powley.

Lawton, M. P. (1983b). Environment and other determinants of well-being in older people. *The Gerontologist, 23,* 349–357.

Lawton, M. P., & Brody, E. M. (1969). Assessment of older people: Self-maintaining and instrumental activities of daily living. *The Gerontologist, 9,* 179–186.

Lawton, M. P., Moss, M., Fulcomer, M., & Kleban, M. H. (1982). A research and service-oriented multilevel assessment instrument. *Journal of Gerontology, 37,* 91–99.

Lawton, M. P., & Nahemow, L. (1973). Ecology and the aging process. In C. Eisdorfer & M. P. Lawton (Eds.), *Psychology of adult development and aging* (pp. 619–674). Washington, DC: American Psychological Association.

Lehr, U. (1989). Kompetenz im Alter: Beiträge aus gerontologischer Forschung und Praxis. In C. Rott & F. Oswald (Eds.), *Kompetenz im Alter* (pp. 1–14). Vaduz: Liechtenstein.

Lehr, U. M., & Thomae, H. (1991). *Alltagspsychologie.* Darmstadt: Wissenschaftliche Buchgesellschaft.

Lewin, K. (1951). *Field theory in social sciences.* New York: Harper & Row.

Lindenberger, U., & Baltes, P. B. (1994). Sensory functioning and intelligence in old age: A strong connection. *Psychology and Aging, 9,* 339–355.

Lindenberger, U., Mayr, U., & Kliegl, R. (1993). Speed and intelligence in old age. *Psychology and Aging, 8,* 207–220.

Maas, I., & Staudinger, U. M. (1996). Lebensverlauf und Altern: Kontinuität und Diskontinuität der gesellschaftlichen Beteiligung, des Lebensinvestments und ökonomischer Ressourcen. In K. U. Mayer & P. B. Baltes (Eds.), *Die Berliner Altersstudie* (pp. 543–572). Berlin: Akademie Verlag.

Mahoney, F. I., & Barthel, D. W. (1965). Functional evaluation: The Barthel Index. *Maryland Medical Journal, 14,* 61–65.

Marsiske, M., Lang, F. R., Baltes, P. B., & Baltes, M. M. (1995). Selective optimization with compensation: Life-span perspectives on successful human development. In R. A. Dixon & L. Bäckman (Eds.), *Psychological compensation: Managing losses and promoting gains* (pp. 35–79). Mahwah, NJ: Erlbaum.

Marsiske, M., & Willis, S. L. (1998). Practical creativity in older adults' everyday problem solving: Life-span perspectives. In C. E. Adams-Price (Ed.), *Creativity and successful aging: Theoretical and empirical approaches* (pp. 73–113). New York: Springer.

Matsueda, R. L., & Bielby, W. T. (1986). Statistical power in covariance structure models. In N. B. Tuma (Ed.), *Sociological methodology, 1986* (pp. 120–158). San Francisco, CA: Jossey-Bass.

McCall, R. B. (1977). Challenges to a science of developmental psychology. *Child Development, 48*, 333–344.

Moss, M., & Lawton, M. P. (1982). Time budgets of older people: A window on four lifestyles. *Journal of Gerontology, 37*, 576–582.

Olbrich, E. (1987). Kompetenz im Alter. *Zeitschrift für Gerontologie, 20*, 319–330.

Reuben, D. B., Laliberte, L., Hiris, J., & Mor, V. (1990). A hierarchical exercise scale to measure function at the Advanced Activities of Daily Living (AADL) level. *Journal of the American Geriatrics Society, 38*, 855–861.

Sansone, C., & Berg, C. A. (1993). Adapting to the environment across the life span: Different process or different inputs? *International Journal of Behavioral Development, 16*, 215–241.

Schulte, K. (1994). *Der Zusammenhang zwischen dem sozialen Netzwerk, seiner Nutzung im Alltag und Wohlbefinden (Yesterday-Interview)*. Unpublished master's thesis, Free University of Berlin.

Staudinger, U. M., & Fleeson, W. (1996). Self and personality in very old age: A sample case of resilience? *Development and Psychopathology, 8*, 867–885.

Sternberg, R. J. (1985). *Beyond IQ: A triarchic theory of human intelligence*. Cambridge: Cambridge University Press.

Sternberg, R. J. (1990). Prototypes of competence and incompetence. In R. J. Sternberg & J. Kolligian Jr. (Eds.), *Competence reconsidered* (pp. 117–145). New Haven, CT: Yale University Press.

Szalai, A. (Ed.). (1972). *The use of time*. The Hague: Mouton.

Tinetti, M. E. (1986). A performance-oriented assessment of mobility problems in elderly patients. *Journal of the American Geriatrics Society, 34*, 119–126.

Verbrugge, L. M., Gruber-Baldini, A. L., & Fozard, J. L. (1996). Age differences and age changes in activities: Baltimore Longitudinal Study of Aging. *Journal of Gerontology: Social Sciences, 51B*, S30–S41.

Wagner, G. (1991). Die Erhebung von Einkommensdaten im Sozio-oekonomischen Panel (SOEP). In U. Rendtel & G. Wagner (Eds.), *Lebenslagen im Wandel: Zur Einkommens-dynamik in Deutschland seit 1984* (pp. 26–33). Frankfurt/M.: Campus.

Wegener, B. (1988). *Kritik des Prestiges*. Opladen: Westdeutscher Verlag.

Willis, S. L. (1991). Cognition and everyday competence. In K. W. Schaie (Ed.), *Annual review of gerontology and geriatrics* (Vol. 11, pp. 80–109). New York: Springer.

Willis, S. L., & Marsiske, M. (1991). Life-span perspective on practical intelligence. In D. E. Tupper & K. D. Cicerone (Eds.), *The neuropsychology of everyday life: Issues in development and rehabilitation* (pp. 183–198). Boston: Kluwer.

Willis, S. L., & Schaie, K. W. (1986). Practical intelligence in later adulthood. In R. J. Sternberg & R. K. Wagner (Eds.), *Practical intelligence: Nature and origins of competence in the everyday world* (pp. 236–268). Cambridge: Cambridge University Press.

Wilms, H.-U., & Baltes, M. M. (1994, November). *Dementia related influence on everyday competence*. Paper presented at the 47th Annual Scientific Meeting of the Gerontological Society of America, Atlanta, GA.

Wolinsky, F. D., & Johnson, R. J. (1991). The use of health services by older adults. *Journal of Gerontology: Social Sciences, 46*, S345–S357.

Wolinsky, F. D., & Johnson, R. J. (1992a). Perceived health status and mortality among older men and women. *Journal of Gerontology: Social Sciences, 47*, S304–S312.

Wolinsky, F. D., & Johnson, R. J. (1992b). Widowhood, health status, and the use of health services by older adults: A cross-sectional and prospective approach. *Journal of Gerontology: Social Sciences, 47*, S8–S15.

Zuzanek, J., & Smale, B. (1991). *Life cycle variations in across-the-week allocation of time to selected daily activities.* Unpublished manuscript, University of Waterloo, Ontario.

CHAPTER 15

On the Significance of Morbidity and Disability in Old Age

Markus Borchelt, Reiner Gilberg, Ann L. Horgas, and Bernhard Geiselmann

Evidence from gerontological research suggests that physical morbidity and disability in old age are among the most important causes for decline in other functional domains such as social and psychological functioning. However, comprehensive cross-disciplinary analyses on the significance of morbidity and disability in old age and during transition into very old age are scarce.

This chapter examines the strength of associations between (a) somatic and mental health, (b) health and psychosocial status, and (c) objective and subjective health by utilizing multidimensional indicators of physical, mental, psychological, and social functioning from the Berlin Aging Study (BASE) sample ($N = 516$; age range: 70–103 years). The analyses focus on two central questions, namely: (1) To what extent is health an explanatory variable for age differences in other functional domains? (2) Do the associations between health and other domains themselves vary with age?

The results reveal clear age-independent correlations between somatic and psychiatric morbidity as well as between psychosocial factors and health. Moreover, health indicators fully explain the negative effects of age on psychosocial resources and on mental health. However, the significance of objective health for subjective evaluations decreases significantly with age. In this domain, the findings are consistent with recent hypotheses that emphasize manifold intraindividual mechanisms working to maintain positive self-appraisal despite objective decline.

1   Introduction

1.1   Systemic Aspects of Morbidity and Disability in Old Age

Even if old age is not necessarily associated with illness, physical and mental morbidity and disability are prevalent ailments in late life. They are probably the most important causes for decline in various other functional domains (Brody, Brock, & Williams, 1987; Cassileth et al., 1984; Evans & Williams, 1992; Neugarten, 1990; R. C. Taylor & Ford, 1983). Physical illness and disability can play an important role in the development of psychiatric illnesses such as depression or dementia (Katona, 1995; Raskind & Peskind, 1992), both of which can, in turn, lead to the loss of independence (Shanas & Maddox, 1985) or have a strong negative effect on subjective well-being (cf. Smith et al., Chapter 17 in this volume). Vice versa, health is also influenced by psychological and social conditions. Institutionalization, widowhood, loneliness, depression, or dementia can contribute to worsening of physical health, for example, through self-neglect, inadequate diet, and consecutive deterioration of immune functions (Berkman & Breslow, 1983; Maier, Watkins, & Fleshner, 1994; Marmot et al., 1991; J. Rodin, 1986).

Nonetheless, the human capacity to adapt to new conditions (plasticity) does not vanish in old age and needs to be considered in this context (P. B. Baltes & Baltes, 1990). Possibly, the phase of transition into oldest age leaves enough room for subjective adjustments to functional limitations, which Ryff (1991) called "shifting horizons." It seems likely, for instance, that the association between objective and subjective health dynamically changes, that is, becomes weaker, during aging (Brandtstädter & Rothermund, 1994; Heckhausen & Krueger, 1993; Maddox, 1987).

1.2   *Theoretical Orientations, Central Questions, and Sample Definition*

Looking across disciplines at the significance of morbidity and disability in very old age reflects one of the theoretical orientations in BASE that conceptualizes *aging as a systemic phenomenon*. From this contextual and multidisciplinary perspective, morbidity and disability in old age can be regarded as a consequence of complex interactions between biological, psychological, and social factors (Antonucci & Jackson, 1987; Badura & Schott, 1989; Featherman & Lerner, 1985; Häfner, 1992), and also as a predictor, with varying importance of age differences in subjective evaluations and objective states (Maddox, 1987).

In the following, morbidity and disability are defined from a geriatric perspective and analyzed domain-specifically according to correlations with (a) mental health, (b) psychosocial conditions, and (c) subjective perceptions of health. The central question about the significance of morbidity and disability in old age is operationalized by model analyses that focus on the extents to which (1) health indicators are explanatory for age correlations of other domains' indicators, and (2) associations between health and other domains themselves vary with age.

It is important to stress that this approach is explicitly chosen to examine global hypotheses on associations, rather than specific causal links. Hypotheses are based on previous domain-specific empirical findings and assume clear interactions that can be tested against the null hypothesis of a purely age-mediated coincidence. More in-depth analyses will be possible with forthcoming longitudinal data from BASE.

The current analyses were carried out with data from the initial cross-sectional BASE sample. This heterogeneous sample of 516 persons aged 70 to 103 years was randomly drawn from the West Berlin city register and stratified by age and gender (43 women and 43 men in each age group: 70–74, 75–79, 80–84, 85–89, 90–94, 95+; cf. P. B. Baltes et al., Chapter 1).

1.3   *The Geriatric Approach to the Definition and Assessment of Morbidity and Disability*

The geriatric evaluation of morbidity and disability is characterized by a multidimensional viewpoint, which includes a broad range of functional aspects (Rubenstein et al., 1984). It focuses on sensory and sensorimotor impairments (visual acuity, hearing, mobility), the need for help with Activities of Daily Living (ADL), and the complexity of multiple illnesses and medications. In principle, psychiatric morbidity belongs to this context, too. In old age, dementia and depression are the most important psychiatric disorders. Both are associated with considerable psychosocial risks and both can be caused by somatic illnesses (Hall, 1980; Katona, 1995; Raskind & Peskind, 1992; G. Rodin &

Table 15.1. *Geriatric risk groups: Characteristics and definitions*

Characteristic	Definition
Multimorbidity	At least five coexisting, moderate to severe physical illnesses (diagnosed by project physicians)
Multimedication	At least five prescribed drugs (assessed by interviews with participants and their family physicians or by chart review)
Need for help	Inability to perform at least two Activities of Daily Living (ADL/IADL) other than bowel and bladder control (Lawton & Brody, 1969; Mahoney & Barthel, 1965)
Incontinence	Temporary or permanent inability to control bowels and/or bladder (two items of the Barthel Index)
Immobility[a]	Inability to walk or stand upright with eyes closed and/or inability to turn on the spot and/or to bend over (cf. Tinetti, 1986)
Visual impairment	Visual acuity (close and/or distance vision) below 0.2 Snellen decimals
Hearing impairment	Pure-tone hearing thresholds (audiometry) $\geq$ 55 dB (0.25–2.0 kHz) and/or $\geq$ 75 dB (3.0–8.0 kHz)
Dementia	Psychiatric diagnosis of dementia according to DSM-III-R criteria (regardless of severity and without further diagnostic differentiation)
Depression	Depressive disorder according to DSM-III-R criteria including "not otherwise specified depression"

Note. Cf. Steinhagen-Thiessen & Borchelt, Chapter 5; Helmchen et al., Chapter 6.
[a]This characteristic is not to be equated with "immobility" in the clinical sense: It does not indicate subjects who are completely unable to ambulate or bedridden persons; instead, it indicates moderate to severe sensorimotor impairment due to disturbances in balance, gait, and coordination.

Voshart, 1986; Sosna & Wahl, 1983). From this perspective, the entire range of somatic and mental illnesses and disabilities can be subsumed under "geriatric morbidity," although differential aspects and specific associations need to be considered (see Section 2).

The comprehensive, standardized, multidimensional geriatric assessment conducted within BASE provided subjective and objective measures of mobility, sensory functioning, and independence in everyday activities, as well as detailed diagnostic profiles of somatic and mental diseases and related drug use for each participant (cf. Steinhagen-Thiessen & Borchelt, Chapter 5; Helmchen et al., Chapter 6). Based on these measures, nine overlapping risk groups characterized by multimorbidity, multimedication, need for help with ADL, incontinence, immobility, visual impairments, hearing impairments, dementia, and depression were defined according to explicit criteria (Table 15.1).

The individual groups proved to be large enough to examine these aspects (Table 15.2). In size, the groups range from 83 persons with hearing impairments (16%) to 196 multimedicated persons (38%). An overlap of groups, due to the nonexclusive definition of geriatric risks and their positive intercorrelations, needs to be taken into account when interpreting univariate analyses. The largest overlap occurred between groups of persons needing help with ADL and immobile individuals (182 persons altogether, of which 56% were in both groups) whereas all other combinations did not overlap by more than a third.

Table 15.2. *Number of subjects per geriatric risk group and bivariate overlaps between groups: Absolute, relative, and cumulative frequencies*

		1	2	3	4	5	6	7	8	9	Total	Cumulative
1	Multimorbidity	—	34.0	30.7	22.0	34.3	26.5	15.2	27.0	22.3	35.3	35.3
2	Multimedication	96	—	19.9	15.8	22.3	19.2	12.9	28.0	8.2	38.0	54.7
3	Need for help	73	54	—	22.3	56.0	35.0	21.8	25.4	33.0	25.0	62.0
4	Incontinence	49	39	40	—	23.1	15.3	16.1	14.9	18.5	17.4	64.9
5	Immobility	86	64	102	46	—	33.2	24.0	24.7	30.7	30.0	67.6
6	Visual impairment	62	50	63	27	67	—	23.1	16.0	27.4	22.1	69.0
7	Hearing impairment	35	32	38	24	46	37	—	11.9	20.8	16.1	71.3
8	Depression	67	72	53	29	57	34	23	—	14.2	25.8	75.4
9	Dementia	53	23	59	31	62	48	33	30	—	21.1	76.9
Total		182	196	129	90	155	114	83	133	109	—	—
Cumulative		182	282	320	335	349	356	368	389	397	—	—

Note. The absolute number of subjects in two groups (row/column) is given below the diagonal (e.g., 96 subjects belong to the groups with multimorbidity *and* multimedication); the percentage of group overlap is indicated above the diagonal (e.g., 34.0% [$n = 96$] of all subjects with multimorbidity and/or multimedication [$n = 182 + 196 - 96 = 282$] belong to both groups).

Analyzed cumulatively, there was a relatively large group of persons left with none of the geriatric risks ($n = 119$, 23% of the sample; after weighting: 30% of the old West Berliners). This set represents a reference group; it includes men and women of all age groups (age range: 70–96 years, $M = 78.9$, $SD = 6.9$, 44% women).

2   Psychiatric Health in Context of Somatic Morbidity

Various somatic diseases and disabilities can evince typical affective or cognitive symptoms related to the two main psychiatric disorders of old age – dementia and depression (Borson et al., 1986; Ouslander, 1982; Sosna & Wahl, 1983; Wells, Golding, & Burnam, 1988). Due to the age-related increase of somatic and psychiatric morbidity, these associations gain significance with older age. The same applies to mostly reversible pharmacologically induced clinical syndromes with depressive symptoms or delirium. Because of frequent adverse drug reactions, multimedication requires special attention (Borchelt & Geiselmann, 1995; Borchelt & Horgas, 1994; Callahan, 1992; Larson, Kukull, Buchner, & Reifler, 1987; Patten & Love, 1993).

The importance of sensory impairments for affective disorders and intellectual decline is controversial (Eastwood, Corbin, Reed, Nobbs, & Kedward, 1985; Peters, Potter, & Scholer, 1988). Although correlations have often been shown, it remains open whether they are purely age-related coincidences.

From a more global perspective, the significance and direction of associations between somatic and psychiatric morbidity in an old population are still uncertain. Due to the cross-sectional design of the study, the following analyses focus on *correlational patterns* between psychiatric and somatic morbidity in old age, not on causal directions. Factors and processes that possibly contribute to the appearance of significant coincidences will be discussed when interpreting the findings.

2.1   *Variability of Dementia and Depression Prevalence Rates*

The prevalences of depression and dementia in the groups characterized by physical geriatric risks are shown in Figure 15.1. Both disorders were more common in nearly all risk groups than in the entire sample. Depression (sample prevalence 26%) was significantly more frequent among ADL-restricted (41%), multimorbid (37%), immobile (37%), and multimedicated individuals (37%). Dementia (sample prevalence 21%) was more often observed among ADL-restricted (46%), visually impaired (42%), immobile (40%), hearing-impaired (40%), incontinent (34%), and multimorbid individuals (29%), but less frequently in multimedicated persons (11%).

Because of the overlap of geriatric risk groups it must be assumed that the various geriatric features are not independently associated with psychiatric disorders. Testing for all combinations of two features, a maximum rate of depression (56%) was observed among subjects who were ADL-restricted and multimedicated ($n = 54$). Compared with that in the reference group, occurrence was sevenfold (odds ratio = 7.6 [95%-confidence interval: 3.7–15.3]).

The equivalent analysis for dementia showed the highest rate (62%) among subjects who were ADL-restricted and not multimedicated ($n = 75$, odds ratio = 24.5 [10.8–55.6]). Note that this group with low drug utilization had a *higher* number of diagnosed somatic illnesses ($M = 4.6$, $SD = 2.3$) than the remainder ($M = 3.7$, $SD = 2.3$, $F = 9.06$, $p < .01$).

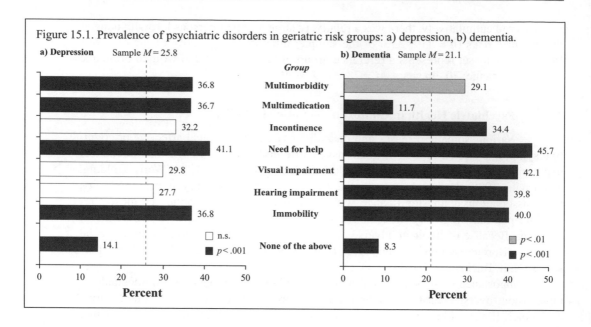

Figure 15.1. Prevalence of psychiatric disorders in geriatric risk groups: a) depression, b) dementia.

Different factors and methodological aspects need to be considered when interpreting these correlative coincidences. On the one hand, multimedication and the need for help can be confounded with general plaintiveness or memory loss because they partially rely on subjective reports. On the other hand, the correlations can reflect potential consequences of psychiatric morbidity – for example, a tendency toward overmedication of depressive patients (Stuck et al., 1994), or underdiagnosis of somatic illnesses and subsequent undermedication of demented patients (Larson, Reifler, Sumi, Canfield, & Chinn, 1985). Furthermore, the need for help is known to be the main psychosocial consequence of dementia as well as a possible consequence of, and cause for, depressive reactions (Helmchen et al., Chapter 5).

Fewer confoundings of this nature are to be expected for somatic multimorbidity, immobility, and visual and hearing impairments. The analysis of interactions of these features revealed additive effects for visual and hearing impairments, and for hearing impairments and immobility that often co-occurred with dementia. Among persons with visual and hearing impairments ($n = 37$), dementia prevalence was 57% (odds ratio = 20.3 [7.9–51.7]), and it was 52% (odds ratio = 16.8 [6.9–41.0]) among persons with hearing impairments and immobility ($n = 46$). In comparison, dementia prevalence among persons aged 85 years and above was just 34% (odds ratio in comparison to the group of 70- to 84-year-olds: 5.5 [3.3–9.1]).

2.2   Explanatory Model: Somatic Morbidity versus Age

The multivariate explanatory model addressed the question of whether the observed coincidence of psychiatric and somatic morbidity can be explained by their individual age correlations alone. In this context, age and gender, which was included due to gender differences found in both health domains (M. M. Baltes et al., Chapter 9), can be

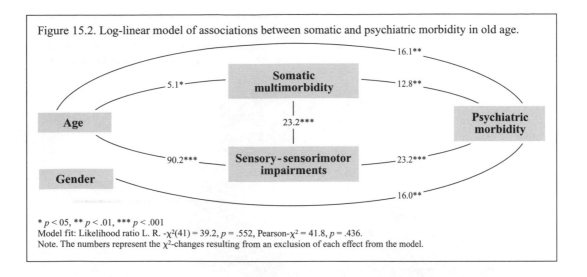

Figure 15.2. Log-linear model of associations between somatic and psychiatric morbidity in old age.

* $p < 05$, ** $p < .01$, *** $p < .001$
Model fit: Likelihood ratio L. R. -$\chi^2(41) = 39.2$, $p = .552$, Pearson-$\chi^2 = 41.8$, $p = .436$.
Note. The numbers represent the χ^2-changes resulting from an exclusion of each effect from the model.

viewed as global indicators that reflect biological, sociodemographic, and psychological aging processes. These were tested against somatic features that are not considered common consequences of psychiatric disorders (i.e., multimorbidity, visual and hearing impairments, immobility).

An initially fully saturated model (hierarchical log-linear analysis) showed that neither higher order interactions nor gender differences in somatic multimorbidity ($\chi^2(1) = 2.6$, $p = .11$) or sensory-sensorimotor impairments ($\chi^2(1) = 0.2$, $p = .63$) need to be taken into account (Fig. 15.2).

As a result, age, gender, sensory-sensorimotor impairments, and somatic multimorbidity were independently associated with psychiatric morbidity. None of these effects could be taken out of the model without significant loss of data fit. From this finding, it can be derived that no alternative model would represent the data as well, but not that all alternative models would fit insufficiently. Therefore, two further models were tested that help to assess the importance of the main effects. The first one, a model without the age effect, proved to be fairly acceptable (likelihood ratio L. R.-$\chi^2(44) = 56.1$, $p = .105$; Pearson-$\chi^2(44) = 59.3$, $p = .062$), whereas the second one, a model without the effect of sensory-sensorimotor impairments, was rejected outright (L. R.-$\chi^2(44) = 63.2$, $p = .030$; Pearson-$\chi^2(44) = 65.4$, $p = .020$).

2.3   Summarizing Discussion

The central finding is that the age correlations with psychiatric and somatic morbidity are not sufficient to explain their significant coincidence in old age. Instead, the results indicate that the age correlation of psychiatric morbidity is canceled when controlling for somatic illnesses as illustrated in Figure 15.3.

Potential causal relationships need to be discussed when interpreting these findings. Our data indicate that somatic multimorbidity and immobility are risk factors for depressive disorders in old age. From other analyses (cf. Steinhagen-Thiessen & Borchelt,

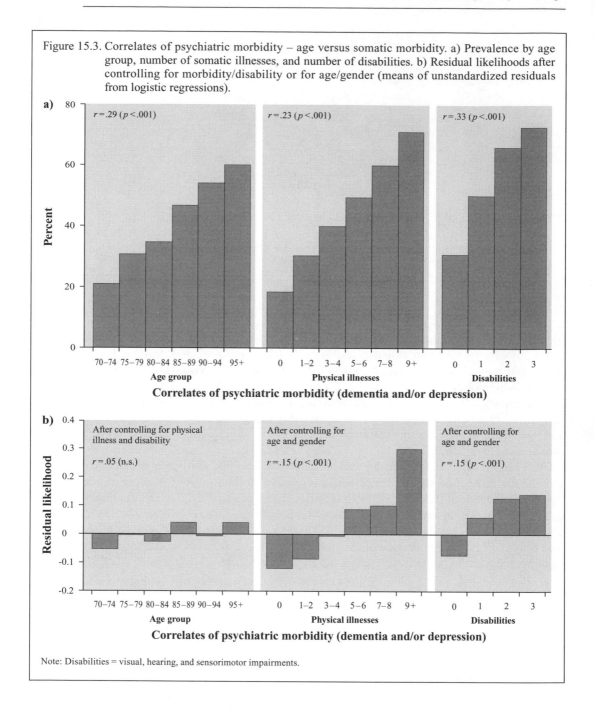

Figure 15.3. Correlates of psychiatric morbidity – age versus somatic morbidity. a) Prevalence by age group, number of somatic illnesses, and number of disabilities. b) Residual likelihoods after controlling for morbidity/disability or for age/gender (means of unstandardized residuals from logistic regressions).

Note: Disabilities = visual, hearing, and sensorimotor impairments.

Chapter 5), we know that loss of mobility is an important somatic risk factor influencing the need for help in old age. Combined with our observation that depression was more frequent in the group of older adults needing help than among the immobile, we can deduce, supported by other studies (Murphy, 1982; Ouslander, 1982), that the need for help due to immobility is an important risk factor in the development of depressive disorders.

Even though sensory-sensorimotor impairments were measured objectively, it is not possible to exclude an overestimation of the associations, as the subjectively assessed need for help could be influenced by aggravation in depressive patients. However, severe depression was not diagnosed in the sample, so an underestimation is equally likely. At any rate, the prevalence of somatic diseases and disability in cases of depression was equivalent to that reported by others (cf. Häfner, 1992).

Regardless of age, dementia was often observed together with somatic multimorbidity, visual and hearing impairments, and immobility. As multimorbidity is mainly due to cardiovascular disorders (Steinhagen-Thiessen & Borchelt, Chapter 5), the first finding can reflect the vascular origin of some dementia syndromes. Furthermore, metabolic-endocrine disorders such as hypothyroidism or diabetes mellitus, which could be diagnosed in BASE with some certainty based on laboratory screening parameters, are known to be the cause of secondary dementia syndromes.

Taken together, the data contradict a purely age-mediated coincidence (Eastwood et al., 1985) and support the assumption that some of the processes leading to sensory, sensorimotor, and intellectual decline have a common neuropathological cause (Fozard, 1990; Johnson, Adams, & Lewis, 1989; Teasdale, Lajoie, Bard, Fleury, & Courtemanche, 1993). Certain impairments of visual acuity, hearing, balance, and coordination can be seen as expressing the same cerebral changes as those leading to dementia. As such, the correlation between dementia and sensory-sensorimotor impairments would reflect a common "normal" and/or "pathological" aging process.

Functional aspects need to be considered, too. Vision, hearing, and mobility are important abilities for the interaction with, and orientation to, the environment (cf. Marsiske et al., Chapter 13). As orientation is an important criterion for the diagnosis of dementia, sensory-sensorimotor impairments are likely to have an effect. However, other factors must also play a role, as blindness or deafness alone are not related to an increased risk of dementia. Vice versa, long-term cognitive deficits (as symptoms of dementia) can lead to deprivation syndromes, which themselves cause losses in other domains (Lindenberger & Baltes, 1994).

Methodological artifacts cannot be excluded, but are likely to be small because of the simple objective tests (audiometry, Snellen charts, balance and gait tests) applied to measure sensory and sensorimotor impairments. In comparison with methods more dependent on participants' cooperation such as spirometry (not recordable in 12% of persons with a diagnosis of dementia vs. 4% of those without), the acuity tests were impossible in only five persons diagnosed with dementia (5% vs. 3% of those without).

Taken together, it was shown that there are strong age-independent relationships between somatic and psychiatric morbidity in late life. Accordingly, persons with dementia and depression were included as further geriatric risk groups to be examined for differences in psychosocial characteristics and subjective health perceptions.

3   Psychosocial Status in Context of Geriatric Morbidity

Life situations of older adults are often existentially influenced by psychosocial events such as the loss of a partner or the clearance of their household. Somatic and psychiatric morbidity can be both cause and consequence of psychosocial changes, and the examination of these relationships has a long social-medical tradition (Elliot & Eisdorfer, 1982). As a kind of "counterweight," research on protective factors or resources has

Table 15.3. *Definitions of psychosocial risks and resources in old age*

Category	Source/Definition[a]
Risks	
Recent household move[b]	Information about duration of living at present place of residence (two years or less: $n = 54$)
Institutionalization[b]	Observed place of residence (senior citizens' home, nursing home, or hospital for the chronically ill: $n = 74$)
Poverty[b]	Information on household income, assets, and social assistance (lowest category of income, i.e., below 1,400 DM, and no assets; or dependent on social welfare: $n = 78$)
Social isolation[b]	Information on living situation and social network (living alone, no children in Berlin, and no close companions: $n = 61$)
Recent losses	Information on recently deceased close companions (at least two in the past two years: $n = 259$)
Resources	
Partnership[b]	Information on living situation (living with partner: $n = 162$)
Life and aging satisfaction[b]	Satisfaction with life and aging (both rated as "good" or "very good": $n = 119$)
Wealth[b]	Information about financial resources (highest category of household income, i.e., above 2,200 DM plus assets and/or estate: $n = 109$)
Large circle of friends[b]	At least two close companions mentioned ($n = 127$; median: 4 close companions)
Education	Information about schooling and occupational training (both completed: $n = 118$)
Children living in Berlin	Information on children living in Berlin (at least one: $n = 276$)

[a]See also Mayer et al., Chapter 8.
[b]Factors potentially influenced by illness/disability.

developed in sociology (Cassel, 1975), psychiatry (Alloway & Bebbington, 1987; Rutter, 1987), and psychology (Staudinger, Marsiske, & Baltes, 1995).

Many studies consider critical life events such as the move to a senior citizens' home (Bickel & Jäger, 1986) or widowhood (Magaziner, Cadigan, Hebel, & Parry, 1988) as general psychosocial risks. Psychosocial resources such as education (House et al., 1990; Siegrist, 1989; Williams, 1990), income (Fox & Carr-Hill, 1989; George, 1989; Haan & Kaplan, 1986; Kitagawa & Hauser, 1973), social relationships (Cohen & Syme, 1985; Kaplan & Haan, 1989; Sabin, 1993), or psychological concepts of adaptivity (resilience) are usually seen as protective factors (Staudinger et al., Chapter 11).

On the basis of these studies we followed the work of R. C. Taylor (1992) and first identified the most important psychosocial risks (poverty, social isolation, loss of close companions, recent household move, institutionalization) and resources (high education, wealth, partnership, large circle of friends, children living in Berlin, above-average life and aging satisfaction). These factors were further differentiated as those influenced by current health and those either beyond individual control (e.g., death of close companions) or established earlier in life (e.g., education; see Table 15.3 for definitions). Since personality characteristics such as coping styles (Lachman, 1986) cannot be easily defined as risk factors or resources, they are not included (but see Staudinger et al., Chapter 11).

First, we examine whether certain psychosocial risks and resources are distributed differentially among geriatric groups. This could give a first indication of the significance of morbidity and disability for psychosocial situations.

3.1   *Variability of the Prevalence of Psychosocial Characteristics*

The group-specific prevalences of *psychosocial risks* are shown in Figure 15.4. A household move within the previous two years had been experienced by 28% of those with dementia, 25% of those in need of help, 22% of those with visual impairments, 19% of those with immobility, but only by 3% of those in the reference group (Fig. 15.4a). Unsurprisingly, 41 (76%) of the 54 persons who had moved had transferred to a senior citizens' home, nursing home, or hospital for the chronically ill. Nevertheless, due to the cross-sectional nature of the data, it is not possible to determine whether these moves were consequences, antecedents, or only indirect correlates of the health situation.

The proportion of institutionalized persons in each geriatric risk group reflects these relationships (Fig. 15.4b) and adds further aspects. Among the incontinent there were more persons in homes (21% vs. sample prevalence of 14%). Previous research indicates that institutionalization is frequently the cause for incontinence (Cassileth et al., 1984), and this association is still supported by the implicit "dependence training" applied in many homes. The significantly low prevalence of institutionalized persons among the multimedicated should also be noted. This reflects the interaction between dementia and medication discussed above.

Poverty (Fig. 15.4c) was significantly more frequent among persons in need of help (26%), the immobile (25%), and the hearing-impaired (25%). However, these findings are difficult to interpret without taking into account age and gender differences. Fitting a hierarchical log-linear model to the data on poverty revealed that the individual relationships could all be explained by the effect of need for help that remained after controlling for age and gender differences. The relative risk of poverty was 2.6 times higher for persons in need of help than for the independent (95%-confidence interval: 1.5–4.3). This result is very plausible considering that individual financial resources have to be used to pay for nursing care services (cf. Linden et al., Chapter 16). Social isolation (Fig. 15.4d) was only marginally more frequent in geriatric risk groups than in the entire sample or the reference group.

The situation is reversed regarding *psychosocial resources* (Fig. 15.5). In comparison to the reference group, geriatric risk groups were mainly characterized by a lower prevalence of partnership, and lower life and aging satisfaction. Whereas there were some differences between rates of living with a partner (Fig. 15.5a), good or very good life and aging satisfaction hardly occurred in any geriatric risk group (Fig. 15.5b).

Wealth was also rarer among the geriatric risk groups (Fig. 15.5c). Even if this was due to health differences caused by social class membership (Kitagawa & Hauser, 1973), the reverse also applies – just as for the relationship between poverty and the need for help. The higher frequency of wealth among the multimedicated cannot be adequately explained without taking into account other factors (age, gender, depression). Turning to large circles of friends (Fig. 15.5d), the geriatric risk groups did not differ significantly from the sample (25%).

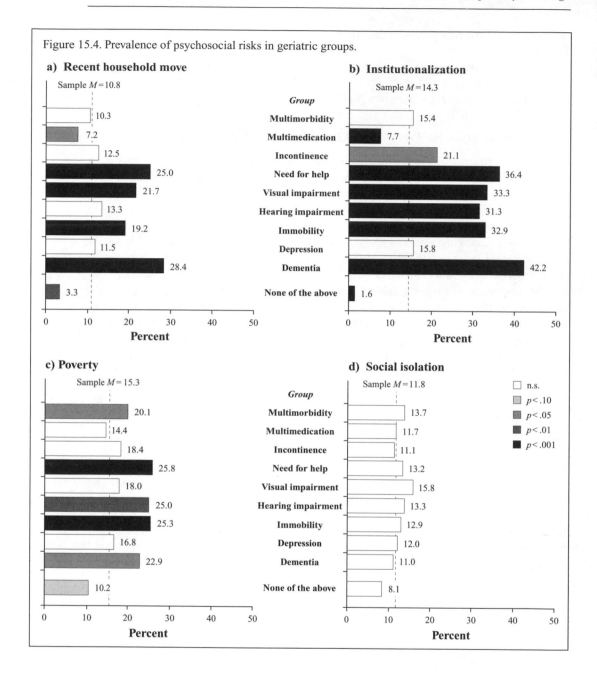

Figure 15.4. Prevalence of psychosocial risks in geriatric groups.

These descriptive analyses already give an indication of how differently individuals age (P. B. Baltes et al., Chapter 1; Maddox, 1987; Steinhagen-Thiessen & Borchelt, 1993). However, age and gender can also be assumed to play an important role. We therefore used a theory-based model to test the extent to which morbidity and disability may influence psychosocial situations independent of age and gender.

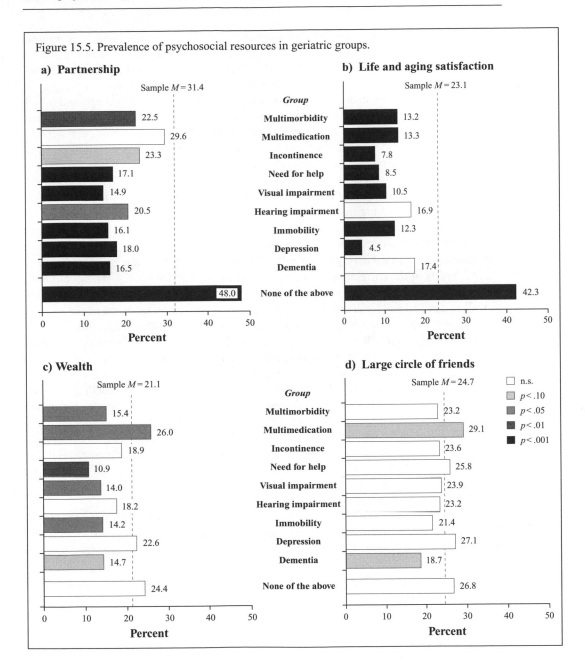

Figure 15.5. Prevalence of psychosocial resources in geriatric groups.

3.2   *Explanatory Model: Morbidity versus Age*

There are various models of interactions between individual psychosocial factors and their causal relations to health (Waltz, 1981). On the one hand, it is assumed that negative consequences of psychosocial or behavioral stressors are either (1) continuously modulated by individual resources (*triggering model*) or (2) completely resisted up to a certain threshold (*shield model*; Caplan, 1974). On the other hand, it is thought that (3) lack of resources can be seen as an additional risk factor (*additive model*; Wheaton, 1980) or (4) certain resources only become effective in the presence of specific risks as a kind of "social immune system" (*buffering model*; Cassel, 1975; Cobb, 1976). It is undecided whether these models remain relevant in very old age and which factors are still important. To what degree can morbidity and disability explain the loss of psychosocial resources and the increase of risks in very old age?

Following the models on additive and interactive effects between psychosocial and health factors, the number of psychosocial resources and risks were each constructed and interpreted as global indicators of cumulated psychosocial factors (additive model).[1] Assuming that resources continuously modulate the interactions between health and psychosocial risks (triggering model), the difference between resources and risks was also calculated and regarded as a hypothetical indicator of "psychosocial reserves." Not least because of the low intercorrelation between resources and risks ($r = -.32$), this measure was characterized by relatively broad and stable variability across age groups.

The results of the correlational analyses are presented in Table 15.4. The continuous variables used to define the geriatric groups and the constructed psychosocial indicators, as well as age and gender, were entered. The resulting partial correlations are crucial for our question on age-independent correlations between social and health factors.

We found that, regardless of age and gender, the number of psychosocial resources decreased most strongly with worsening close-vision impairment, speech-range hearing impairment, and dementia, whereas the number of psychosocial risks increased with dementia severity, the need for help with ADL, and close-vision impairment. The number of prescribed drugs, incontinence, and depression were not correlated to any psychosocial indicator.

The inclusion of the number of "psychosocial reserves" did indeed improve the representation of these associations as indicated by the increase in the multiple correlation between psychosocial resources and health factors from $R = .48$ to $R = .52$ ($\Delta R^2 = +.03$, $p < .001$). Accordingly, all correlations with psychosocial resources described above remained, but medication, incontinence, and depression were still uncorrelated.

The significant partial correlations prove an age- and gender-independent association between cumulated psychosocial factors and health characteristics. We also found that the clear (raw) correlations between the three global psychosocial indicators and age disappeared when health indicators were partialed out, but the significant gender differences did not (bottom of Table 15.4). Taken together, this means that age differences in psychosocial situations can be explained by health differences. However, gender differences in psychosocial reserves remain, regardless of morbidity and disability.

3.3 Summarizing Discussion

Our findings support the hypothesis that the correlational associations between health and psychosocial factors cannot be explained by pure age-mediated coincidence. Instead, morbidity and disability can explain age differences in psychosocial status. We

---

[1] Despite some overlaps, the correlations between factors were remarkably low ($-.20 \leq r \leq +.20$). Exceptions were household moves and institutionalization ($r = +.50$), wealth and poverty ($r = -.39$), as well as children living in Berlin and social isolation ($r = -.40$).

Table 15.4. Correlations between psychosocial factors and indicators of geriatric morbidity

	Psychosocial factors					
	Number of resources		Number of risks		Difference (reserves)	
	Raw correlation[a]	Partial correlation[b]	Raw correlation[a]	Partial correlation[b]	Raw correlation[a]	Partial correlation[b]
Health variables						
Number of diagnoses	-.20***	-.10*	.12**	—	-.21***	-.10*
Number of prescribed drugs	-.01	—	-.05	—	-.02	—
Incontinence	-.13**	-.08†	.04	—	-.11**	—
Need for help with ADL	-.26***	-.09*	.25***	.17***	-.31***	-.15***
Immobility	-.27***	-.10*	.24***	.12***	-.31***	-.13**
Hearing impairment (0.25–2.0 kHz)	-.27***	-.14**	.21***	.12*	-.30***	-.16***
Visual impairment (close vision)	-.31***	-.18***	.24***	.16**	-.34***	-.20***
Depression	-.11*	—	.05	—	-.10*	—
Dementia	-.25***	-.14**	.27***	.20***	-.31***	-.21***
Age and gender						
Age	-.30***	—	.22***	—	-.33***	—
Gender	-.29***	-.25***	.13**	.08†	-.28***	-.23***
R	.48***		.37***		.52***	

† $p < .10$, * $p < .05$, ** $p < .01$, *** $p < .001$.

[a] Pearson's r.

[b] Partial correlations are provided only if $p < .10$; age and gender are partialed out for health variables, whereas all health indicators are partialed out for age and gender.

restrict ourselves to the discussion of the two most obvious competing interpretations (psychosocial factors affecting health and vice versa). Again it should be noted that our analyses do not allow statements on causal directions. We can only examine whether correlational patterns confirm hypotheses on causes.

Our first conclusion refers to the important influence that psychosocial risks and resources may have on health in late life. Partnership, life and aging satisfaction, and wealth can be regarded as protective factors, whereas recent household moves, institutionalization, and poverty are seen as risk factors. Taken together, this perspective coincides with interpretations of other empirical results on such factors' significance for health, including the lack of a correlation between social isolation and morbidity (R. C. Taylor, 1992).

It is striking that this perspective predominates (Sabin, 1993; Wheaton, 1980). Only sporadically has a second viewpoint (health impairments affecting psychosocial situations) complemented the first – for example, when considering the psychosocial consequences of incontinence or the health determinants of institutionalization or reduced life satisfaction (R. C. Taylor & Ford, 1983). Based on our findings, partnership, income, and wealth should be added as psychosocial resources, which are mainly threatened by sensory-sensorimotor impairments, the need for help, somatic multimorbidity, and dementia. Strengthening this perspective seems necessary in order to give more plausible answers to several questions.

Assuming that partnership is a factor protecting against visual or sensory-sensorimotor impairments necessitates the assumption of additional mediating factors of social (support) or psychological nature (well-being). The reverse claim that somatic or mental illness and disability reduce elderly individuals' chances of maintaining or beginning partnerships would explain the association directly. This underlines the psychosocial significance of morbidity and disability in old age, as partnership is an important resource that can buffer or even prevent psychosocial consequences of morbidity and disability (e.g., institutionalization).

This type of interaction between psychosocial and health factors can also be discussed regarding the significant correlation between the need for help and income. Health risks are known to be distributed differentially among the population according to social class. Chronic material hardship mainly affects old women and is regarded as a stressful life condition, which can lead to an increased risk of mental and physical impairments. The need for care can then increase social inequality by draining any remaining financial resources. However, we only found a rather small but significant gender effect (for more detailed discussion of gender differences, see M. M. Baltes et al., Chapter 9).

4   Subjective Health Perception in Context of Geriatric Morbidity

The question of personal (subjective) health perception is an important component of gerontological research, allowing the examination of the individual importance of morbidity and disability. Although it has often been reported that subjective evaluations correlate highly with objective professional assessments, neither complete agreement nor systematic incongruence between subjective and objective health in old age has been found (Kaplan & Camacho, 1983; Maddox & Douglass, 1973; Svanborg, 1988). Still, despite a clear negative age correlation of objective health in late life, subjective evaluations appear to be relatively age-invariant (Brandtstädter & Greve, 1994; Heckhausen & Schulz, 1995), leading to the assumption that the association between subjective and objective health must change in old age.

However, most studies have not examined subjective health as a dependent variable, but as a predictor for other medical and psychological aspects (e.g., functional capacity, intellectual functioning, or general well-being; Hultsch, Hammer, & Small, 1993; Mossey & Shapiro, 1982; Rakowski & Cryan, 1990; Staats et al., 1993). Idler, Kasl, and Lemke (1990) were able to show higher mortality in persons with lower subjective health ratings, independent of objective health.

Which aspects of somatic or mental health influence subjective health perceptions in late life most and whether these perceptions remain constant into very old age are open questions. On the one hand, there are several indications that illnesses leading to functional limitations have stronger effects on subjective evaluation than other chronic illnesses (Jylhä, Alanen, Leskinen, & Heikkinen, 1986; Levkoff, Cleary, & Wetle, 1987; Svanborg, 1988). On the other hand, subjective ratings could also be strongly influenced by the number of prescribed drugs, age, gender, education, and psychiatric disorders such as dementia and depression (Verbrugge, 1989).

The influence of old age, particularly very old age, remains unclear: Some studies documented a negative age correlation, that is, subjectively declining health with age (Jylhä et al., 1986; Levkoff et al., 1987), whereas others observed positive correlations (Linn & Linn, 1980; Maddox & Douglass, 1973).

4.1   *Variability of Subjective Health Perceptions*

The responses of BASE participants to the global question "How do you rate your present physical health?" were not correlated with age ($r = -.01$). This stability is in clear contrast to the negative age correlations of objective somatic ($r = -.28$) and functional ($r = -.57$) health. Equally obvious is the contrast with the *positive* age correlation of subjective evaluation "compared to people of your age" ($r = +.19, p < .001$). Still, both subjective indicators' correlations with objective measures were negative (the number of somatic diseases correlated $r = -.33$ with global subjective health, and $r = -.22$ with subjective health as compared with age peers).

From these findings, some of which are known as the "age-invariance paradox" of global subjective ratings (P. B. Baltes & Baltes, 1990; Brandtstädter & Greve, 1994; cf. Staudinger et al., Chapter 11; Smith et al., Chapter 17), we hypothesize that individual perceptions of objective health status do not remain stable during late life. As indicated by psychological research (P. B. Baltes, 1993; Brandtstädter & Greve, 1994; Heckhausen & Krueger, 1993), it is more probable that *adaptation* to changes in physical health and functioning occurs with increasing age (e.g., by cognitive reorganization of rating criteria or by new internal comparison processes; cf. Staudinger et al., 1995).

Possibly, "good health" in old age no longer means absence of illness or disability, but absence of tormenting complaints or just that one's own health is perceived as better than that of age peers (Heckhausen & Krueger, 1993). A further option is that the subjective significance of a chronic illness or long-term treatment is large to begin with, but decreases over time (*diminution*). Alternatively, relatively subordinate medical problems can gain importance over the years (*amplification*).

Although the existence of dynamic processes such as adaptation, diminution, or amplification can only be examined longitudinally, it is possible to model "age-dynamic"

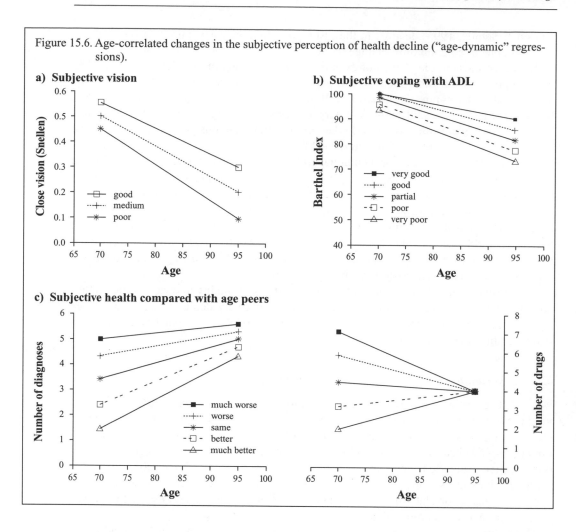

Figure 15.6. Age-correlated changes in the subjective perception of health decline ("age-dynamic" regressions).

correlations between objective and subjective health with cross-sectional data by using interaction terms (i.e., by multiplication of age with subjective or objective indicators). Different age trends for health indicators can then be estimated and tested statistically in regression analyses.

4.2   Simple Explanatory Model: Age-Dynamic Correlations

Apart from the subjective health measures mentioned above, we were able to use the subjective assessment of ability to perform ADL as well as subjective vision and hearing. All three assumed age-dynamic processes could be exemplified by simple regressions (Fig. 15.6). The individual rating of vision was a good example of subjective adaptation to functional limitations (Fig. 15.6a). With age, the subjective thresholds shifted in parallel. Thus, one cannot conclude that objective visual acuity is equal when 70- and 90-year-olds report the same degree of visual impairment.

We did not find a convincing example for age-correlated amplification of certain health aspects. The association between subjective ADL and the need for help with ADL was just significant (Fig. 15.6b), but the age-dependent spread of the regression lines (β = .31, $p < .10$)[2] may well only reflect increasing variance of Barthel Index scores with age.

In contrast, the age-dynamic models of associations between global measures of objective and subjective somatic health (Fig. 15.6c) were highly significant. Both the importance of the number of diagnoses (β = -.51, $p < .001$) and the number of drugs (β = -.72, $p < .001$) clearly decreased with age. Whereas 70-year-olds' subjective ratings differed congruently with their somatic morbidity and medication, this was no longer the case for 95-year-olds, although the objective and subjective variable variances remained stable over age.

This already indicates that, with increasing age, objective health can explain less and less of the variance of subjective health, thus losing subjective importance age-dynamically. The following multivariate analyses of this phenomenon are based on the theoretical model that cognitive mechanisms used to transform objective status (mainly processes of comparison) become stronger with increasing age (P. B. Baltes & Baltes, 1990; Brandtstädter & Greve, 1994; Heckhausen & Schulz, 1995; Ryff, 1991).

4.3 Complex Explanatory Model: Age Dynamics of Intraindividual Processes of Comparison

In order to model age-dependent dynamic processes in subjective health perception, multiple regression analyses were carried out for three indicators of subjective somatic health (global rating, comparison with age peers, changes over the last year). The continuous variables used for the definition of geriatric risk groups were entered as indicators of objective health and complemented by psychosocial factors (recent household move, institutionalization, poverty, social isolation, partnership, life and aging satisfaction, education, and wealth). The latter were included assuming that factors might be identified whose importance increases with age in contrast to objective health. The results of these analyses are summarized in Table 15.5.[3]

The interpretation of β_{In} is dependent on β and the direction of their signs. If both coefficients are significant, but one is positive and the other negative (e.g., number of diagnoses, number of drugs, and incontinence), the initial effect decreases with age. If both have the same sign, the effect is enhanced with age (e.g., need for help with ADL). If

---

[2] Here, and in the following, β refers to the regression coefficients for the interaction of the predictor with chronological age.

[3] Methodologically, objective health indicators, psychosocial factors, age, and gender were entered first. We then examined whether entering the age interaction of each indicator separately significantly contributed explained variance (based on t-tests of the β_{In} scores for age-dynamic variables). The significances of the individual interaction terms were not tested within the models due to the difficulty of controlling their intercorrelations (18 variables multiplied by age). The total contribution to explained variance (as a percentage of entire variance) by age-dynamic modeling of the variable groups (objective health vs. psychosocial factors) was ascertained by a global statistical test (F-value of the R^2-change). In Table 15.5, the columns titled β present the standardized regression coefficients for models with all indicators, but without interaction terms. The columns titled β_{In} show coefficients for the interaction with age if the interaction term was included. Accordingly, ΔR^2 refers to the change of R^2 after entering all interaction terms at once.

Table 15.5. *Age-dynamic regression analyses of objective health indicators and psychosocial factors on different subjective health indicators*

| | Subjective health indicators[a] | | | | | |
| | Global | | Comparison | | Change | |
	β[b]	β_{ln}[c]	β[b]	β_{ln}[c]	β[b]	β_{ln}[c]
Objective health indicators						
Number of diagnoses	-.14**	.17***	-.09†	.15***	-.14**	.17***
Number of prescribed drugs	-.14**	.08†	-.15**	.19***	-.10†	—
Incontinence	-.07	—	-.09†	.16***	-.05	—
Need for help with ADL	-.13*	-.10*	-.13*	—	-.15*	—
Hearing impairment (0.25–2.0 kHz)	.00	-.11*	.09†	—	-.09	—
Visual impairment (close vision)	.01	-.11*	.03	—	-.02	—
Depression	-.07	—	.03	—	-.09†	—
Dementia	.04	—	-.07	—	.16**	—
Psychosocial factors						
Partnership	-.02	—	-.04	—	.07	—
Life and aging satisfaction	.36***	—	.20***	-.11*	.09	-.10*
High education	.06	—	.04	—	.03	—
Wealth	.08†	—	.03	—	.00	—
Household move	-.06	—	.04	—	-.04	—
Institutionalization	.10	—	.04	—	.09	.09†
Poverty	-.03	.09*	.03	—	.05	—
Social isolation	.05	—	.00	—	.16***	—
Age and gender						
Age	.12*	—	.44***	—	-.15*	—
Gender	-.01	—	-.01	—	-.01	—
ΔR^2	.35***	.06**	.26***	.09***	.18***	.06†

† $p < .10$, * $p < .05$, ** $p < .01$, *** $p < .001$.
[a]Global: "How do you rate your present physical health?"; comparison: "How do you rate your physical health compared with people of your age?"; change: "Has your health changed over the last 12 months?"
[b]Standardized regression coefficient β.
[c]β_{ln} for the interaction term with age if it is entered in the analysis at the next step (only stated if $p < .10$).

only the interaction term is significant, an effect sets in at a later age (e.g., close-vision or hearing impairments).

The clearest effects in these models (number of diagnoses and number of drugs) indicated that the correlation between objective and subjective health did indeed weaken with age. However, effects of psychosocial factors did not increase. In fact, subjective evaluation was directly influenced very little by psychosocial factors, apart from a strong association with life and aging satisfaction. We have no good explanation for the unexpected finding that the socially isolated experienced a positive health change during the preceding year.

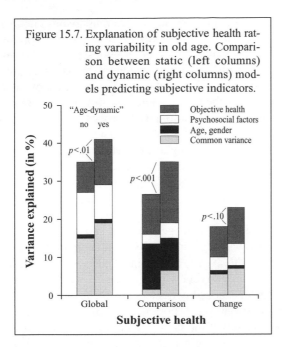

Figure 15.7. Explanation of subjective health rating variability in old age. Comparison between static (left columns) and dynamic (right columns) models predicting subjective indicators.

The percentages of explained variance in subjective measures shown in Figure 15.7 illustrate differences in specific relationships with objective health and psychosocial factors as well as the gain achieved by age-dynamic modeling, which is mainly due to the objective health indicators. The strong, singular age effect on the subjective comparison with persons of the same age is striking. The other two indicators (i.e., global rating and intraindividual temporal comparison) proved to be relatively age-invariant.

4.4   Summarizing Discussion

Apart from the finding that the correlations between objective and subjective health change with age, it should be noted that age itself explains differing portions of variance in subjective measures of health (Fig. 15.7). Taken together, the observed correlation patterns show that the association between objective and subjective health is weakened with increasing age and that the psychological processes of comparison develop in opposite directions: Intraindividual temporal comparison worsens with age (i.e., subjective decline of health over time), whereas interindividual comparison improves (i.e., subjective improvement of health compared with age peers).

Why is the comparison with age peers more strongly age-dependent than global rating or assessment of changes during the previous year? Psychological research on late life has been able to show that many indicators of self-perception such as well-being, control beliefs, self-efficacy, and life satisfaction are very stable in old age (M. M. Baltes & Baltes, 1986; Filipp & Klauer, 1986; Lachman, 1986; cf. Staudinger et al., Chapter 11; Smith et al., Chapter 17). In this context, interindividual social comparison, downward comparison in particular, has received most attention among the psychological processes providing stability (Heckhausen & Krueger, 1993; Staudinger et al., 1995; S. E. Taylor & Lobel,

1989; Wood, 1989). According to this notion, interindividual comparisons mainly refer to persons who are worse off than oneself, resulting in more positive self-perceptions.

Regarding the evaluation of health changes over the previous year, our results confirm a phenomenon that Ryff (1991) calls "shifting horizons," that is, older adults rate the past more positively than younger adults. The combination of positive evaluations of past health and subdued expectations for the future could possibly limit the range of potentially perceivable changes of one's own situation. This process of protective adjustment could enable the maintenance of a constant level of global evaluation.

What is the explanation for the relatively strong age effect on the rating of one's own health in comparison with persons of the same age? Possibly, this expresses the discrepancy between implicit and explicit comparisons. When older adults are asked to rate their own health in comparison with age peers, this could be taken as an explicit demand to extend their reference group upward and to compare themselves with healthier individuals. This could result in more "realistic" and age-sensitive self-perceptions.

However, our findings show that, with age, interindividual comparisons become increasingly favorable to one's own health. Nevertheless, intraindividual changes of one's own health are perceived increasingly negatively with age. Hence, the age-invariant subjective global rating of somatic health is possibly made up of these two contrasting age-related components: With increasing age, the experienced decline of health over time worsens, but the comparison with persons of the same age improves. Based on the results of our age-dynamic regressions, it can be assumed that these internal processes of comparison become increasingly detached from objective reality in old age.

From a different perspective, we can deduce objective health status more precisely from self-ratings of 70-year-olds than from those of 90-year-olds. Except for the slightly increasing importance of sensory impairments and the need for help with ADL, no factors were identified as particularly helpful in explaining subjective health ratings of the very old. In other words, the subjectivity of ratings increases with age and the influence of objective health and psychosocial factors decreases. Specifically, incontinence and the number of diagnoses and of drugs appear to influence the responses of persons aged 90 and above much less than those of 70- to 75-year-olds.

However, potential methodological problems need to be remembered. For instance, due to selective survival, elderly samples possibly contain more persons with certain personality characteristics such as resistance to objective conditions. Although subjective health appears to be associated with mortality independent of objective health (Idler et al., 1990; Mossey & Shapiro, 1982), it seems unlikely that all of our findings are consequences of selective mortality, as we could not document an age-dependent decrease of subjective health variability. This would be the case if persons with certain subjective health ratings had a higher survival likelihood than others. Thus, we can assume that the described age dynamics of subjective health are based on intraindividual psychological processes of life and aging management rather than interindividual differences in mortality.

References

Alloway, R., & Bebbington, P. (1987). The buffer theory of social support: A review of the literature. *Psychological Medicine, 17,* 91–108.

Antonucci, T. C., & Jackson, J. S. (1987). Social support, interpersonal efficacy, and health: A life course perspective. In L. L. Carstensen & B. A. Edelstein (Eds.), *Handbook of clinical gerontology* (pp. 291–311). New York: Pergamon Press.

Badura, B., & Schott, T. (1989). Zur Bedeutung psychosozialer Faktoren bei der Bewältigung einer chronischen Krankheit. In M. M. Baltes, M. Kohli, & K. Sames (Eds.), *Erfolgreiches Altern: Bedingungen und Variationen* (pp. 149–154). Bern: Huber.

Baltes, M. M., & Baltes, P. B. (Eds.). (1986). *The psychology of control and aging*. Hillsdale, NJ: Erlbaum.

Baltes, P. B. (1993). The aging mind: Potential and limits. *The Gerontologist, 33*, 580–594.

Baltes, P. B., & Baltes, M. M. (1990). Psychological perspectives on successful aging: The model of selective optimization with compensation. In P. B. Baltes & M. M. Baltes (Eds.), *Successful aging: Perspectives from the behavioral sciences* (pp. 1–34). Cambridge: Cambridge University Press.

Berkman, L. F., & Breslow, L. (1983). *Health and ways of living*. New York: Oxford University Press.

Bickel, H., & Jäger, J. (1986). Die Inanspruchnahme von Heimen im Alter. *Zeitschrift für Gerontologie, 19*, 30–39.

Borchelt, M., & Geiselmann, B. (1995). Are there specific physical health characteristics in depression versus dementia in old age? In M. Bergener, J. C. Brocklehurst, & S. I. Finkel (Eds.), *Aging, health, and healing* (pp. 427–440). New York: Springer.

Borchelt, M., & Horgas, A. L. (1994). Screening an elderly population for verifiable adverse drug reactions: Methodological approach and initial data analysis of the Berlin Aging Study (BASE). *Annals of the New York Academy of Sciences, 717*, 270–281.

Borson, S., Barnes, R. A., Kukull, W. A., Okimoto, J. T., Veith, R. C., Inui, T. S., Carter, W., & Raskind, M. A. (1986). Symptomatic depression in elderly medical outpatients: I. Prevalence, demography, and health service utilization. *Journal of the American Geriatrics Society, 34*, 341–347.

Brandtstädter, J., & Greve, W. (1994). The aging self: Stabilizing and protective processes. *Developmental Review, 14*, 52–80.

Brandtstädter, J., & Rothermund, K. (1994). Self-percepts of control in middle and later adulthood: Buffering losses by rescaling goals. *Psychology and Aging, 9*, 265–273.

Brody, J. A., Brock, D. B., & Williams, T. F. (1987). Trends in the health of the elderly population. *Annual Review of Public Health, 8*, 211–234.

Callahan, C. M. (1992). Psychiatric symptoms in elderly patients due to medications. In J. W. Rowe & J. C. Ahronheim (Eds.), *Annual review of gerontology and geriatrics* (Vol. 12, pp. 41–75). New York: Springer.

Caplan, G. (1974). *Support systems and community mental health*. New York: Behavioral Publications.

Cassel, J. C. (1975). Psychiatric epidemiology. In G. Caplan (Ed.), *American handbook of psychiatry* (pp. 401–410). New York: Basic Books.

Cassileth, B. R., Lusk, E. J., Strouse, T. B., Miller, D. S., Brown, L. L., Cross, P. A., & Tenaglia, A. N. (1984). Psychosocial status in chronic illness: A comparative analysis of six diagnostic groups. *New England Journal of Medicine, 311*, 506–511.

Cobb, S. (1976). Social support as a moderator of life stress. *Psychosomatic Medicine, 38*, 300–314.

Cohen, S., & Syme, S. L. (Eds.). (1985). *Social support and health*. New York: Academic Press.

Eastwood, M. R., Corbin, S. L., Reed, M., Nobbs, H., & Kedward, H. B. (1985). Acquired hearing loss and psychiatric illness: An estimate of prevalence and co-morbidity in a geriatric setting. *British Journal of Psychiatry, 147*, 552–556.

Elliot, G. C., & Eisdorfer, C. (1982). *Stress and human health*. New York: Springer.

Evans, J. G., & Williams, T. F. (Eds.). (1992). *Oxford textbook of geriatric medicine*. Oxford: Oxford University Press.

Featherman, D. L., & Lerner, R. M. (1985). Ontogenesis and sociogenesis: Problematics for theory and research about development and socialisation across the lifespan. *American Sociological Review, 50,* 659–676.

Filipp, S.-H., & Klauer, T. (1986). Conceptions of self over the life-span: Reflections on the dialectics of change. In M. M. Baltes & P. B. Baltes (Eds.), *The psychology of control and aging* (pp. 167–205). Hillsdale, NJ: Erlbaum.

Fox, J., & Carr-Hill, R. (1989). Health inequalities in European countries: Introduction. In J. Fox (Ed.), *Health inequalities in European countries* (pp. 1–18). Aldershot: Gower.

Fozard, J. L. (1990). Vision and hearing in aging. In J. E. Birren & K. W. Schaie (Eds.), *Handbook of the psychology of aging* (3rd ed., pp. 150–170). San Diego, CA: Academic Press.

George, L. K. (1989). Social and economic factors. In E. W. Busse & D. G. Blazer (Eds.), *Geriatric psychiatry* (pp. 203–234). Washington, DC: American Psychiatric Press.

Haan, M. N., & Kaplan, G. A. (1986). The contribution of socioeconomic position to minority health. In *Report of the Secretary's Task Force on Black and Minority Health* (Vol. 2, pp. 69–103). Washington, DC: U.S. Department of Health and Human Services.

Häfner, H. (1992). Psychiatrie des höheren Lebensalters. In P. B. Baltes & J. Mittelstraß (Eds.), *Zukunft des Alterns und gesellschaftliche Entwicklung* (pp. 151–179). Berlin: de Gruyter.

Hall, R. C. W. (Ed.). (1980). *Psychiatric presentations of medical illnesses.* Lancaster: MTP Press.

Heckhausen, J., & Krueger, J. (1993). Developmental expectations for the self and most other people: Age-grading in three functions of social comparison. *Developmental Psychology, 25,* 539–548.

Heckhausen, J., & Schulz, R. (1995). A life-span theory of control. *Psychological Review, 102,* 284–304.

House, J. S., Kessler, R. C., Herzog, R., Mero, R. P., Kinney, A. M., & Breslow, M. J. (1990). Age, socio-economic status, and health. *Milbank Quarterly, 68,* 383–411.

Hultsch, D. F., Hammer, M., & Small, B. J. (1993). Age differences in cognitive performance in later life: Relationships to self-reported health and activity style. *Journal of Gerontology, 48,* 1–11.

Idler, E. L., Kasl, S. V., & Lemke, J. H. (1990). Self-evaluated health and mortality among the elderly in New Haven, Connecticut, and Iowa and Washington counties, Iowa, 1982–1986. *American Journal of Epidemiology, 131,* 91–103.

Johnson, C. A., Adams, A. J., & Lewis, R. A. (1989). Evidence for a neural basis of age-related visual field loss in normal observers. *Investigative Ophthalmology and Visual Sciences, 30,* 2056–2064.

Jylhä, E., Alanen, E., Leskinen, A. L., & Heikkinen, E. (1986). Self-rated health and associated factors among men of different ages. *Journal of Gerontology, 41,* 710–717.

Kaplan, G. A., & Camacho, T. (1983). Perceived health and mortality: A nine-year follow-up of the Human Population Laboratory cohort. *American Journal of Epidemiology, 117,* 292–304.

Kaplan, G. A., & Haan, M. N. (1989). Is there a role for prevention among the elderly? Epidemiological evidence from the Alameda County Study. In M. G. Ory & K. Bond (Eds.), *Aging and health care: Social science and policy perspectives* (pp. 27–51). London: Routledge.

Katona, C. L. E. (1995). *Depression in old age.* Chichester: Wiley.

Kitagawa, E. M., & Hauser, P. M. (1973). *Differential mortality in the United States: A study in socioeconomic epidemiology*. Cambridge, MA: Harvard University Press.

Lachman, M. E. (1986). Personal control in later life: Stability, change, and cognitive correlates. In M. M. Baltes & P. B. Baltes (Eds.), *The psychology of control and aging* (pp. 207–236). Hillsdale, NJ: Erlbaum.

Larson, E. B., Kukull, W. A., Buchner, D., & Reifler, B. V. (1987). Adverse drug reactions associated with global cognitive impairment in elderly persons. *Annals of Internal Medicine, 107*, 169–173.

Larson, E. B., Reifler, B. V., Sumi, S. M., Canfield, C. G., & Chinn, N. M. (1985). Diagnostic evaluation of 200 elderly outpatients with suspected dementia. *Journal of Gerontology, 40*, 536–543.

Lawton, M. P., & Brody, E. M. (1969). Assessment of older people: Self-maintaining and instrumental activities of daily living. *The Gerontologist, 9*, 179–186.

Levkoff, S. E., Cleary, P. D., & Wetle, T. (1987). Differences in the appraisal of health between aged and middle-aged adults. *Journal of Gerontology, 42*, 114–120.

Lindenberger, U., & Baltes, P. B. (1994). Sensory functioning and intelligence in old age: A strong connection. *Psychology and Aging, 9*, 339–355.

Linn, B. S., & Linn, M. W. (1980). Objective and self-assessed health in the old and very old. *Social Science and Medicine, 14a*, 311–315.

Maddox, G. L. (1987). Aging differently. *The Gerontologist, 27*, 557–564.

Maddox, G. L., & Douglass, E. B. (1973). Self-assessment of health. *Journal of Health and Social Behavior, 14*, 87–93.

Magaziner, J., Cadigan, D. A., Hebel, J. R., & Parry, R. E. (1988). Health and living arrangements among older women: Does living alone increase the risk of illness? *Journal of Gerontology: Medical Sciences, 43*, M127–M133.

Mahoney, F. I., & Barthel, D. W. (1965). Functional evaluation: The Barthel Index. *Maryland Medical Journal, 14*, 61–65.

Maier, S. F., Watkins, L. R., & Fleshner, M. (1994). Psychoneuroimmunology: The interface between behavior, brain, and immunity. *American Psychologist, 49*, 1004–1016.

Marmot, M. G., Smith, G. D., Stansfeld, S., Patel, C., North, F., & Head, J. (1991). Health inequalities among British civil servants: The Whitehall II Study. *The Lancet, 337*, 1387–1393.

Mossey, J. M., & Shapiro, E. (1982). Self-rated health: A predictor of mortality among the elderly. *American Journal of Public Health, 72*, 800–808.

Murphy, E. (1982). Social origins of depression in old age. *British Journal of Psychiatry, 141*, 135–142.

Neugarten, B. L. (1990). Social and psychological characteristics of older persons. In C. K. Cassel, D. E. Riesenberg, L. B. Sorensen, & J. R. Walsh (Eds.), *Geriatric medicine* (2nd ed., pp. 28–37). New York: Springer.

Ouslander, J. G. (1982). Physical illness and depression in the elderly. *Journal of the American Geriatrics Society, 30*, 593–599.

Patten, S. B., & Love, E. J. (1993). Can drugs cause depression? A review of the evidence. *Journal of Psychiatry and Neuroscience, 18*, 92–102.

Peters, C. A., Potter, J. F., & Scholer, S. G. (1988). Hearing impairment as a predictor of cognitive decline in dementia. *Journal of the American Geriatrics Society, 36*, 981–986.

Rakowski, W., & Cryan, C. D. (1990). Associations among health perceptions and health status within three age groups. *Journal of Aging and Health, 2*, 58–80.

Raskind, M. A., & Peskind, E. R. (1992). Alzheimer's disease and other dementing disorders. In J. E. Birren, R. B. Sloane, & G. D. Cohen (Eds.), *Handbook of mental health and aging* (2nd ed., pp. 477–513). San Diego, CA: Academic Press.

Rodin, G., & Voshart, K. (1986). Depression in the medically ill: An overview. *American Journal of Psychiatry, 143*, 696–705.

Rodin, J. (1986). Aging and health: Effects of the sense of control. *Science, 233*, 1271–1276.

Rubenstein, L. Z., Josephson, K. R., Wieland, G. D., English, P. A., Sayre, J. A., & Kane, R. L. (1984). Effectiveness of a geriatric evaluation unit. *New England Journal of Medicine, 311*, 1664–1670.

Rutter, M. (1987). Resilience in the face of adversity: Protective factors and resistance to psychiatric disorder. *British Journal of Psychiatry, 147*, 598–611.

Ryff, C. D. (1991). Possible selves in adulthood and old age: A tale of shifting horizons. *Psychology and Aging, 6*, 286–295.

Sabin, E. P. (1993). Social relationships and mortality among the elderly. *Journal of Applied Gerontology, 12*, 44–60.

Shanas, E., & Maddox, G. L. (1985). Health, health resources, and the utilization of care. In R. H. Binstock & E. Shanas (Eds.), *Handbook of aging and the social sciences* (2nd ed., pp. 696–726). New York: Van Nostrand Reinhold.

Siegrist, J. (1989). Steps towards explaining social differentials in morbidity: The case of West Germany. In J. Fox (Ed.), *Health inequalities in European countries* (pp. 353–371). Aldershot: Gower.

Sosna, U., & Wahl, H.-W. (1983). Soziale Belastung, psychische Erkrankung und körperliche Beeinträchtigung im Alter: Ergebnisse einer Felduntersuchung. *Zeitschrift für Gerontologie, 16*, 107–114.

Staats, S., Heaphey, K., Miller, D., Partlo, C., Romine, N., & Stubbs, K. (1993). Subjective age and health perceptions of older persons: Maintaining the youthful bias in sickness and in health. *International Journal of Aging and Human Development, 37*, 191–203.

Staudinger, U. M., Marsiske, M., & Baltes, P. B. (1995). Resilience and reserve capacity in later adulthood: Potentials and limits of development across the life span. In D. Cicchetti & D. J. Cohen (Eds.), *Developmental psychopathology: Vol. 2. Risk, disorder, and adaptation* (pp. 801–847). New York: Wiley.

Steinhagen-Thiessen, E., & Borchelt, M. (1993). Health differences in advanced old age. *Ageing and Society, 13*, 619–655.

Stuck, A. E., Beers, M. H., Steiner, A., Aronow, H. U., Rubenstein, L. Z., & Beck, J. C. (1994). Inappropriate medication use in community-residing older persons. *Archives of Internal Medicine, 154*, 2195–2200.

Svanborg, A. (1988). Aspects of aging and health in the age interval 70–85. In J. J. F. Schroots, J. E. Birren, & A. Svanborg (Eds.), *Health and aging: Perspectives and prospects* (pp. 133–141). New York: Springer.

Taylor, R. C. (1992). Social differences in an elderly population. In J. G. Evans & T. F. Williams (Eds.), *Oxford textbook of geriatric medicine* (pp. 24–32). Oxford: Oxford University Press.

Taylor, R. C., & Ford, E. G. (1983). The elderly at risk: A critical examination of commonly identified risk groups. *Journal of the Royal College of General Practitioners, 33*, 699–705.

Taylor, S. E., & Lobel, M. (1989). Social comparison activity under threat: Downward evaluation and upward contacts. *Psychological Bulletin, 96*, 569–575.

Teasdale, N., Lajoie, Y., Bard, C., Fleury, M., & Courtemanche, R. (1993). Cognitive processes involved for maintaining postural stability while standing and walking. In G. E. Stelmach & V. Hömberg (Eds.), *Sensorimotor impairment in the elderly* (pp. 157–168). Dordrecht: Elsevier.

Tinetti, M. E. (1986). A performance-oriented assessment of mobility problems in elderly patients. *Journal of the American Geriatrics Society, 34*, 119–126.

Verbrugge, L. M. (1989). Gender, aging, and health. In K. S. Markides (Ed.), *Aging and health: Perspectives on gender, race, ethnicity, and class* (pp. 23–78). Newbury Park, CA: Sage.

Waltz, E. M. (1981). Soziale Faktoren bei der Entstehung und Bewältigung von Krankheit: Ein Überblick über die empirische Literatur. In B. Badura (Ed.), *Soziale Unterstützung und chronische Krankheit* (pp. 40–119). Frankfurt/M.: Suhrkamp.

Wells, K. B., Golding, J. M., & Burnam, M. A. (1988). Psychiatric disorders in a sample of the general population with and without chronic medical conditions. *American Journal of Psychiatry, 145*, 976–981.

Wheaton, B. (1980). The sociogenesis of psychological disorder. *Journal of Health and Social Behavior, 21*, 100–124.

Williams, D. R. (1990). Socioeconomic differentials in health: A review and redirection. *Social Psychology Quarterly, 53*, 81–99.

Wood, J. V. (1989). Theory and research concerning social comparisons of personal attributes. *Psychological Bulletin, 106*, 231–248.

CHAPTER 16

The Utilization of Medical and Nursing Care in Old Age

Michael Linden, Ann L. Horgas, Reiner Gilberg, and Elisabeth Steinhagen-Thiessen

The increasing number of older people in Western societies has made dealing with their needs for help and care a pressing matter. In the interdisciplinary context of the Berlin Aging Study (BASE), involving geriatricians, psychiatrists, psychologists, and sociologists, it was possible to examine how older adults utilize health care and which predicting factors are important.

Major areas of health care utilization are: (1) physician contacts, (2) medication use, (3) different levels of caregiving, including informal, formal, and institutional care, and (4) inpatient treatment for acute illness episodes in hospitals. Results from the BASE assessments show that 85% of persons aged 70 and above had regular physician contact and that 96% used at least one medication. Thirty-one percent received some kind of informal or formal caregiving assistance. Multiple regression analyses revealed differential predictive relationships for each of the three dependent health care utilization variables. Higher use of medications was most strongly predicted by increased numbers of somatic diagnoses, better intellectual functioning, and particular health attitudes. Physician contact was weakly predicted by somatic health variables, hypochondriasis, and living alone. In contrast, living alone was the strongest predictor of the utilization of caregiving services, whereas children living in Berlin served as a protective factor against the need for more formal care. Thus, utilization of health care is a multidimensional phenomenon that continues to depend on the interaction between physical and mental health, attitudinal, and social factors in old age.

1   Introduction

The "aging society" is a well-known phrase used to describe current demographic trends (Dinkel, 1992; Myers, 1985). The age structure of modern Western societies has changed, with more and more people reaching advanced old age, so that the "age pyramid" has been replaced by an "age cylinder." Longevity, however, is regularly associated with an increase in morbidity and chronic disease in late life, and often fewer financial and social resources to manage them. Thus, the age cylinder has led to a paradox wherein society as a whole is healthier, but more people have chronic disease conditions (Krämer, 1992; Verbrugge, 1989).

These demographic and health changes create a social problem, since they are associated with increased health care costs and need for services in late life (Crimmins, Saito, & Ingegneri, 1989). For instance, in comparison to an average 28-year-old man, an average 73-year-old man uses 4 times the amount of outpatient services, 10 times the amount of hospital treatment, and 12 times the amount of prescription medication (Krämer, 1992).

In addition, older adults often need assistance in maintaining daily functioning and require help through family and/or professional caregivers or special residential settings such as senior housing or long-term care institutions. Available surveys say that among community-dwelling older adults, approximately 5–8% of those over the age of 65 in the United States and Germany have limitations in performing Activities of Daily Living (ADL; Guralnik & Simonsick, 1993; Wahl, 1993). There is a steep increase with age, as only 2% of those aged 65 to 69, but 26% of those 85 years and older require regular care (Schneekloth & Potthoff, 1993). The estimated need for assistance with Instrumental Activities of Daily Living (IADL) is on average even higher, extending to 20% of old people (Bäcker, Dieck, Naegele, & Tews, 1989). In Germany, for instance, about 55% of persons over the age of 85 showed either ADL or IADL limitations (Schneekloth & Potthoff, 1993; see also Steinhagen-Thiessen & Borchelt, Chapter 5 in this volume). These findings are the same in the United States (Brock, Guralnik, & Brody, 1990) and Sweden (Zarit, Johansson, & Berg, 1993). Caregiving services to compensate for these physical limitations are, of course, associated with considerable costs to individuals, families, and societies.

Understanding or even predicting the utilization of medical and caregiving services is highly important for the planning and improvement of services, but is a difficult task that requires consideration of a number of factors (Hansell, Sherman, & Mechanic, 1991; Lundeen, George, & Toomey, 1991; Spore, Horgas, Smyer, & Marks, 1992). First, it is important to distinguish between different forms of medical and nursing services used most often by older adults, including physician visits, medication use, hospital admissions, informal caregiving by family and neighbors, formal professional assistance by home health services, and formal long-term care in senior housing and nursing homes. Second, there is a variety of possible predictors such as health variables, attitudinal, personality, social-structural, and life-situational variables that are all thought to have an important impact on the availability, use, and outcome of health-related services.

There have been several theoretical models to describe determinants of health care utilization (Schwarzer, 1990). A first distinction has to be made between person-centered and provider-centered factors (Linden & Priebe, 1990). Provider-centered factors include availability, type, spectrum, familiarity, and affordability of services while person-centered factors include attitudes or type and severity of disorders. Furthermore, there have been several attempts to integrate the many factors into explanatory models, most of which give special emphasis to patient-centered variables. Most important are health locus of control models (B. S. Wallston, Wallston, Kaplan, & Maides, 1976), the health belief model (Rosenstock, Strecker, & Becker, 1988), and the social-psychological model suggested by Andersen and Newman (1973).

In particular, the social-psychological model (Andersen & Newman, 1973) integrates multiple domains of predictors by differentiating between predisposing, enabling, and need factors as determinants of the use of health services such as hospital and dental care, professional home health and personal care, and nursing home placement (Bass, Looman, & Ehrlich, 1992; Branch & Jette, 1982; Coulton & Frost, 1982; Evashwick, Rowe, Diehr, & Branch, 1984; Jette, Branch, Sleeper, Feldman, & Sullivan, 1992; Strain, 1991; Wan, 1982, 1989; Wan & Arling, 1983; Wan & Odell, 1981; Wolinsky et al., 1983; Wolinsky & Johnson, 1991). "Need variables" include subjective and objective evaluations of health conditions or functional limitations. "Enabling variables" are those that support or impede the attainment of health services when they are needed, such as income, health insurance, or service availability. "Predisposing factors" pertain to individual characteristics, such as age, gender, socioeconomic status, education, marital status, and family size and structure, as well as health attitudes, beliefs, and motivational variables. Limitations of this model include a lack of clear differentiation between enabling and predisposing factors, an emphasis on predicting formal health care services to the neglect of informal care and social support, and a conception of service use as a dichotomous event that ignores different levels of care utilization (Pescosolido, 1991, 1992).

Drawing on the background of these theoretical considerations, the purpose of this chapter is to test domain-specific constructs under a patient-centered perspective, in an integrated manner. That is, we consider the role of somatic health, mental health, health attitudes, and social-structural variables on health care utilization. In addition, we have incorporated a more comprehensive view of health care utilization by examining the use of three types of health services: physician contact, medication use, and level of help utilized. Further, we conceptualize the use of help more broadly by examining not only the presence or absence of institutionalization, but also the level of formal and/or informal help received by older adults.

Important questions to be answered are: (1) What is the extent of health care service utilization (e.g., physician contact, medication use, and informal or formal caregiving) among very old adults in a representative, urban sample? (2) What is the relationship between somatic health, mental health, health attitudes, and social-structural variables and health service use, and which of these patient variables are most predictive of different types of service utilization?

The impact of personal variables on health care utilization can be particularly well studied under the conditions of the German health care system. All old people are fully insured, so that they can ask for any type of respective help without any immediate costs. In some ways, this is also true for care in institutions, although in this case persons with higher income must contribute to the costs. Furthermore, there is no gate-keeping structure in the German health care system, so that every patient can choose to see any physician at any time. Such a client-centered system of care makes individual characteristics of patients the most important variable to influence the utilization of care.

2   Methods

2.1   Sample

As described by P. B. Baltes et al. (Chapter 1), the BASE sample of 516 persons aged 70 to 103 was randomly drawn from the city register of the western districts of Berlin and stratified by age and gender. Participants were seen wherever they were living, be it in their private homes or in institutions. In order for the sample to be representative of the Berlin population, the descriptive data provided below were weighted by age and gender. Accordingly, the mean age was 79.8 years, and 56% of older West Berliners were widowed. The majority (83%) lived in private households, 8% lived in sheltered housing for old people, 6% in senior citizens' homes, and 3% in nursing homes.

2.2   Procedures

The BASE Intensive Protocol consisted of 14 sessions (cf. P. B. Baltes et al., Chapter 1). Interviews and assessments were carried out in participants' homes and in a

Table 16.1. *Variables and their measures*

Variables	Measures
Utilization of care	
Number of physician visits	Semistructured interview by psychiatrists
Number of medications	Medication interviews, consensus conference
Need for help or care	Activities of Daily Living (ADL) in Barthel Index (Mahoney & Barthel, 1965), Internal Medicine Interview
Level of care	Semistructured interview, Sociology Unit
Physical health	
Number of diagnoses	Physical examinations, consensus conference
Mobility	Subjective maximum walking distance
Mortality risk	Mortality Index based on Body Mass Index (Andres, 1985)
Mental health	
Depression	Center for Epidemiologic Studies-Depression Scale (CES-D; Radloff, 1977); Hamilton Depression Scale (HAMD; Hamilton, 1986)
Dementia	Mini Mental State Examination (MMSE; Folstein, Folstein, & McHugh, 1975)
Psychiatric morbidity	Brief Psychiatric Rating Scale (BPRS; Overall & Gorham, 1962); Geriatric Mental State Examination, community version A (GMS-A; McWilliam, Copeland, Dewey, & Wood, 1988)
Health attitudes	
Hypochondriasis	Health concerns: Whiteley Index (Pilowsky & Spence, 1983)
Number of nonspecific complaints	Complaint List (von Zerssen, 1976)
Illness beliefs	Illness Concepts Scale (Linden, Nather, & Wilms, 1988)
Social situation	
Level of education	Sociology Interview
Social prestige	Magnitude Prestige Scale (Wegener, 1985)
Living alone	Sociology Interview
Number of children in Berlin	Sociology Interview

geriatric clinic by research assistants, internists, and psychiatrists. A summary of the constructs and measures used in the present analyses are presented in Table 16.1.

2.3   Measures

2.3.1   Health Care Utilization Variables

To determine *physician contact*, participants were asked to report the number of visits they had to any physician within the previous year and the specialty of these physicians. This information was cross-validated in a telephone interview with the participants' family physicians.

For *medication use*, the use of all types of medications, both prescribed and nonprescribed, at the time of the interview was assessed by the examining internist and psychiatrist independently. The participants' family physicians were also asked about their prescriptions. During the at-home interviews, participants were asked to present to the examining physician all the medications that they currently used. The drug name, dosage, duration, and frequency of use, and whether it was physician- or self-prescribed were recorded. In a consensus conference of psychiatrists and internists, a final summary of the present medication regimen was made on the basis of all available information.

A categorical variable on *level of help utilization*, reflecting type and level of caregiving help used, was created according to Gray (1988). Four mutually exclusive levels of caregiving were identified: none, informal help via family and friends, professional help via nursing services, and institutionalization. Every person was characterized by the highest level of care he or she received.

Based on a taxonomy used in the German nursing care insurance rules ("Pflege-Versicherungsgesetz," 1994), we additionally created an index of the *need for care* which takes account of the ability to perform basic ADL (Katz, Ford, Moskowitz, Jackson, & Jaffe, 1963) and walking mobility. Level A refers to persons who need no help with ADL and can walk at least 100 meters (approximately 110 yards). Persons on level B are *in need of help* and require assistance with at least one ADL, but can walk at least 100 meters, or need no help with ADL, but can only walk up to 100 meters. Level C includes persons needing help with at least one ADL several times a week and walking less than 100 meters. Level D refers to persons needing daily assistance with at least one ADL, who can not walk more than several steps or are bedridden. Finally, level E describes persons needing constant help with all ADL. Levels C, D, and E roughly correspond to levels I, II, and III as defined by the German nursing care insurance. In the following, the persons on these three levels are considered as *in need of nursing care*.

2.3.2   Independent Variables

To determine *physical health*, all BASE participants underwent comprehensive physical examinations by internists, together with radiographic, ultrasound, and laboratory testing (Steinhagen-Thiessen & Borchelt, Chapter 5). A complete psychiatric evaluation was made by psychiatrists (Helmchen et al., Chapter 6). Furthermore a phone interview was conducted with the participants' family physician. Based on this information, diagnoses were classified for each subject according to the International Classification of Diseases (ICD-9; World Health Organization, 1978) and cross-validated in consensus conferences between the internists and psychiatrists. The total number of diagnoses was used as one indicator of physical health. Only diagnoses that were verified by the investigators and were judged to be at least moderately severe were considered. In addition, the Mortality Index (Andres, 1985) was used as another index of physical health status. This measure is a standardized Body Mass Index known to be related to mortality risk, signaling under- or overweight. As an indicator of functional health, mobility was assessed on a self-reported, seven-point maximum walking distance scale. Scores on this scale ranged from (1) "cannot walk at all" to (7) "able to walk more than five kilometers [approximately 3.1 miles] without difficulty."

For *mental health*, psychiatrists made psychiatric diagnoses based on the Geriatric Mental State Examination, community version A (GMS-A; McWilliam, Copeland, Dewey, & Wood, 1988; cf. Helmchen et al., Chapter 6). Severity of depression was assessed via the Center for Epidemiologic Studies-Depression Scale (CES-D; Hautzinger, 1988; Radloff, 1977) and the Hamilton Depression Scale (HAMD; Hamilton, 1986). Dementia was assessed using the Mini Mental State Examination (MMSE; Folstein, Folstein, & McHugh, 1975). Global psychiatric illness was evaluated using the Brief Psychiatric Rating Scale (BPRS; Overall & Gorham, 1962).

Several measures were utilized to assess *health attitudes.* The Whiteley Index (Pilowsky & Spence, 1983) was applied to measure participants' concern with their health. The Illness Concepts Scale (Linden, Nather, & Wilms, 1988) was used to assess participants' perceptions of, and attitudes toward, illness and treatment. Based on the theoretical models of Becker et al. (1982) and B. S. Wallston et al. (1976; cf. K. A. Wallston et al., 1983), this measure consists of six subscales: susceptibility, trust in physicians, belief in chance, trust in medications, expectation of side effects, and self-confidence. Finally, the level of subjective health complaints was assessed using the Complaint List, a questionnaire that asked about the presence and severity of 24 unspecific somatic symptoms (von Zerssen, 1976).

To determine *social situation*, age, gender, educational level, occupational training, social prestige, place of residence, household composition, and income were assessed during the Sociology Interview (cf. Mayer et al., Chapter 8). Educational level was based on the highest level of formal schooling completed. Social prestige was based on the Magnitude Prestige Scale (Wegener, 1985) and was calculated using the highest social prestige attained by the participants or their spouses (depending on whose prestige was higher). In addition, home ownership was assessed as another indicator of financial status and resources. The place of residence, including type of institutional setting for those not living in a private household, was also assessed. Participants residing in senior citizens' or nursing homes and hospitals for the chronically ill were considered to be institutionalized. Finally, the size and composition of each subject's household was assessed, and two variables were created to indicate whether participants lived alone or with others and the number of children living in Berlin.

3   Results

3.1   Utilization of Care

3.1.1   Physician Contact

Eighty-five percent of the community-dwelling elders in West Berlin were regularly seeing a family physician, and 6% received care through an institutional or residentially affiliated physician. Only 7% had no contact with any physician. Forty-two percent of the family physicians were general practitioners and 56% were internists. Family physicians said that they had seen their older patients on average 6.3 times within the three months prior to the interview. Only 11% of the old persons had not made any visits during this time interval. On average, they had been seeing their family physician for more than seven years. Only 17% reported receiving one or more house visits from their physician. Use of emergency medical treatment within the three months preceding the interview was relatively infrequent (4%).

In addition to contact with family physicians, 60% of old people also went to see another specialist; 21% reported visiting two and 3% reported visiting three or more additional doctors. Thirty-seven percent reported seeing ophthalmologists; 13%, orthope-

Table 16.2. *The distribution of the need for help and care (in %)*

Need for care	Men	Women	Total
A None	76.9	81.1	78.0
B In need of help	14.7	13.6	14.4
C Nursing level I: several times a week	2.1	2.7	2.3
D Nursing level II: daily	4.1	1.1	3.3
E Nursing level III: permanently	2.2	1.5	2.0

Note. See text for definitions of levels A–E. Percentages are weighted by age and gender.

dists; 8%, otolaryngologists; 7%, urologists; 6%, gynecologists; and 4%, dermatologists. Less than 4% reported seeing a psychiatrist. Furthermore, nearly 10% reported seeing a massage or physical therapist.

3.1.2   Medication Use

Almost all (96%) reported using at least one medication, including both prescription and nonprescription drugs. On average, older adults reported using 6 drugs per day (ranging from 0 to 23). Ninety-three percent were taking at least 1 prescribed drug, and 57% reported using at least 1 nonprescription or over-the-counter medication. These numbers of drugs have to be seen in context of an average of 7.4 medical diagnoses per person. More detailed information on medication and its quality is presented by Steinhagen-Thiessen and Borchelt (Chapter 5) and Helmchen et al. (Chapter 6).

3.1.3   The Need for Help with Activities of Daily Living

The ADL Index (Katz et al., 1963; Katz & Akpom, 1976; cf. Steinhagen-Thiessen & Borchelt, Chapter 5; M. M. Baltes et al., Chapter 14) assesses participants' ability to perform basic everyday activities. In West Berlin, almost 1% of older adults needed help with eating, 3% with toileting, 3% with getting out of bed, 6% with dressing, and 16% with bathing or taking a shower. When each participant's mobility was additionally taken into account as described above, 8% of older adults were found to need some form of nursing care (levels C–E), and a further 14% required help to some lesser extent (level B; see Table 16.2). Equally important is the fact that 78% of old people were independent and did not need help with basic ADL from others.

3.1.4   Utilization of Nursing Care

We found that 70% of the old people in Berlin did not mention external help with household work or nursing care. Examining those 22% of the older population who were in need of some form of help or care, it became clear that assistance from outside the family is of major importance (see Table 16.3). More than 26% of these persons were cared for in homes, about 20% received formal (professional) help in private households, and 26% were helped by relatives in their household (mainly by wives) or by relatives living elsewhere. Neighbors and other acquaintances only helped in 7% of these cases. Nearly 26% lived alone and did not receive any help in spite of respective needs as defined by ADL assessments.

Table 16.3. *Provision of help and care to those who need it (weighted by age and gender, in %)*

Sources of help	Total		Children in Berlin		No children in Berlin	
	All	Only private households	All	Only private households	All	Only private households
Help from children[a]	5.4	7.5	7.5	8.7	—	—
Help from other relatives[a]	1.3	1.7	2.9	3.4	0.9	1.6
Help from outside the family[a]	7.4	10.0	6.9	8.0	9.6	16.1
Only formal help[a]	18.8	25.5	16.9	19.6	21.0	35.2
Formal and familial help[a]	0.7	1.0	1.0	1.1	0.4	0.7
Formal and extrafamilial help[a]	1.6	2.2	—	—	3.6	6.0
No external help, living with family members	12.7	17.2	22.0	25.6	1.9	3.1
No external help, living alone	25.8	34.9	28.8	33.6	22.2	37.3
Institutionalized	26.2	—	14.2	—	40.3	—
Total	100.0	100.0	100.0	100.0	100.0	100.0
Living with family members	21.5	25.1	30.9	33.2	6.7	11.6
External help from family or living with family	26.3	32.1	37.6	41.0	7.7	13.5

Note. Help and care entails help with shopping or household work, or nursing care received during the past four weeks.

[a]Help from outside the household.

Only 5% of the old individuals in need of care were helped by children living outside the household. This proportion remained small (8%) when only those living in private households were examined. In these cases, informal help from relatives (27%) was just as important as professional services. Almost 35% of those in need of care in private households stated that they neither received help nor care.

These findings emphasize the importance of professional care in and outside institutions, and also the significance of living partners. When one compares older individuals with and without children in town, the significance of the latter also emerges. The proportion of those living alone who did not receive help with shopping, housework, or nursing care is more or less equal, whether they had children living in Berlin or not. But there is a difference in the likelihood of living in a home – 14% for those with children in Berlin versus 40% for those without. Furthermore, older adults with children in Berlin more frequently shared a household with relatives (26% vs. 3%). Of course, children living close by are important when help and nursing care become necessary, but this does not necessarily mean that old people without children nearby have less access to help. Professional services and – to a lesser degree – extrafamilial helpers replace children. Types of care are thus substitutive or compensatory, and not cumulative (cf. Gilberg, 1997).

3.2   Predictors of the Utilization of Health Care Services

3.2.1   Social-Structural Characteristics

We examined the bivariate correlation matrix for *age*. No significant relationships emerged between age and either the number of medications used or the number of physician contacts (see Table 16.4). This finding is consistent with global pharmacoepidemiological data indicating that the increase in medication use occurs between the ages of 40 and 70 (Klauber & Selke, 1993), rather than in very late life.

There is, however, a significant age effect on the level of caregiving services used. Figure 16.1 shows the proportion of persons who use no help, informal help, professional help, and institutional help across the five-year age intervals between 70 and 103. Eighty-seven percent of the participants aged 70 to 74 used no help, but only 20% of those aged 90 and older were similarly independent. The need for professional help and institutionalization increased with age so that by 95 years of age, 37% of the sample resided in a caregiving institution. Most persons aged 80 to 94 lived in sheltered housing for old people and senior citizens' homes, whereas most aged 95 and older resided in nursing homes.

Gender does not make a significant difference with respect to physician contact (women: $M = 3.0$, $SD = 4.4$; men: $M = 2.6$, $SD = 3.3$) or number of medications used (women: $M = 6.0$, $SD = 3.9$; men: $M = 5.7$, $SD = 4.0$). In addition, men and women were equally likely to be fully independent, or to use informal or formal care (no help: women, 52%, men, 56%; informal help: women, 8%, men, 11%; formal help: women, 22%, men, 23%). The only significant difference was found in relation to institutional caregiving in that 10% of men and 18% of women resided in senior citizens' or nursing homes ($\chi^2(1) = 6.7$, $p = .01$).

Social situation assessment showed that indicators of social status (e.g., education, occupation, home ownership) and social network (e.g., living alone and the number of children living in town) had only very little or no relationship to medication use or physi-

Table 16.4. *Bivariate correlations between physical health, mental health, attitudinal, and social-structural variables and the utilization of help*

Predictor variable	Number of drugs[a]	Number of physician contacts[a]	Level of help utilized[b]
Physical health			
Number of diagnoses	.58**	.21**	.22**
Mortality risk	-.01	.16**	.33**
Subjective walking distance	-.08	-.13**	.47**
Mental health			
BPRS	.12**	.04	.42**
MMSE	.19**	.01	.56**
CES-D	.24**	.12**	.25**
HAMD	.31**	.16**	.16*
Health attitudes			
Complaint List	.47**	.17**	.15*
Whiteley Index	.45**	.21**	.15**
Illness Concepts Scale	.30**	.07	.13*
Social situation			
Education	.03	-.07	.16**
Occupational training	.04	-.01	.12
Social prestige	.08	-.04	.25**
Home ownership	-.04	-.02	.10
Living alone[c]	-.07	.11**	.27**
Number of children in Berlin	-.00	.01	.21**
Age	.00	.06	.99***
Gender	.04	-.05	.11

* $p < .05$, ** $p < .01$, *** $p < .001$.
[a]Product-moment correlation.
[b]η or contingency coefficient, referring to no help, informal, formal, and institutional care.
[c]Institutionalized participants were coded according to prior residential status.

cian visits among older adults. Only living alone was significantly associated with having more physician contacts ($r = .11$, $p < .01$). In contrast, these variables were significantly related to the use of caregiving services. Living alone ($\eta = .27$, $p < .01$), having children in Berlin ($\eta = .21$, $p < .01$), higher levels of education ($\eta = .16$, $p < .01$), and higher social prestige ($\eta = .25$, $p < .01$) were positively correlated with using more formal help.

3.2.2   Physical Health

There is a significant positive correlation (see Table 16.4) between the number of diagnoses and use of medications ($r = .58$, $p < .01$), more frequent physician contacts ($r = .21, p < .01$), and use of more formal support ($\eta = .22, p < .01$). In addition, a higher level

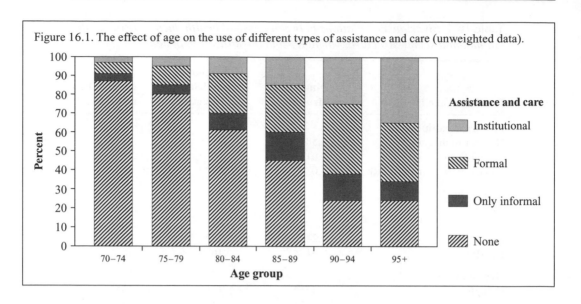

Figure 16.1. The effect of age on the use of different types of assistance and care (unweighted data).

of mortality risk was significantly correlated with more physician contacts ($r = .16$, $p <$ .01) and use of formal professional services ($\eta = .33$, $p < .01$), but not with more drug use. Similarly, mobility limitations were significantly related to fewer physician visits ($r = -.13$, $p < .01$) and more formal caregiving ($\eta = .47$, $p < .01$).

3.2.3   Mental Health

It is interesting to see that dementia, as measured by the MMSE, was not significantly related to the number of physician contacts (Table 16.4). There was a significant association with less overall medication use ($r = .19$, $p < .01$). Also, dementia was strongly associated with the need for formal care such as institutionalization ($\eta = .56$, $p < .01$). Depression in late life was significantly related to each of the three dependent variables. Scores on the Hamilton Depression Scale (HAMD) or the self-rating CES-Depression Scale were significantly related to more drug use (HAMD: $r = .31$; CES-D: $r = .24$, $p < .01$), more physician contacts (HAMD: $r = .16$, $p < .01$; CES-D: $r = .12$, $p < .01$), and use of formal care (HAMD: $\eta = .16$, $p < .05$; CES-D: $\eta = .25$, $p < .01$). A similar pattern of relationships holds for psychopathology in general as measured by the Brief Psychiatric Rating Scale. Higher levels were positively associated with more medication use ($r = .12$, $p < .01$) and utilization of formal caregiving ($\eta = .42$, $p < .01$), but not with increased physician contact.

3.2.4   Health Attitudes and Beliefs

As seen in Table 16.4, the number of unspecified health complaints was significantly correlated with the number of medications used ($r = .47$, $p < .01$), number of physician contacts ($r = .17$, $p < .01$), and use of formal care ($r = .15$, $p < .05$). The same is true for hypochondriasis in relation to each of the three health utilization variables (see Table 16.4). Illness concepts, or one's attitudes and beliefs about health and illness, were significantly related to both medication use ($r = .30$, $p < .01$) and level of care ($\eta = .13$, $p <$ .05), but not to the number of physician visits. In particular, the subscales of trust in medications ($r = .27$, $p < .01$) and belief in susceptibility to illness ($r = .25$, $p < 01$) were significantly associated with more medication use; the subscales of expectation of side effects ($r = -.18$, $p < .01$) and self-confidence ($r = -.10$, $p < .01$) were significantly related to less medication use. Though the number of general health complaints, hypochondriasis, and some illness concept subscales were significantly related to the level of caregiving help, the magnitude of these correlations was generally lower than those noted for medication use.

3.3   An Integrated Model of Health Care Utilization

As shown in the previous bivariate analyses, the utilization of therapeutic help is related to a variety of variables. In order to evaluate their relative impact while controlling for all others, a series of regression models was calculated to predict physician contact, medication use, and use of care through somatic health, mental health, health attitudes, and social-structural variables.

3.3.1   Predicting Medication Use

The number of medical diagnoses was the strongest predictor for medication use (β = .43, $p < .01$; see Table 16.5). Dementia was the only powerful psychiatric variable, as reduced intellectual abilities were related to less drug use. All three of the attitudinal variables significantly predicted medication use. Higher levels of hypochondriasis, more health complaints, and higher levels of positive beliefs about medication and treatment were associated with more drug use. Relatively few of the social-structural variables were significantly predictive in this model, though older participants and those with higher social prestige scores used more drugs, and persons who lived alone used fewer drugs. Overall, this model accounted for 46% of the total variance in medication use.

3.3.2   Predicting Contacts with Physicians

Prediction of the number of physician contacts from the same health, attitudinal, and social-structural variables turned out to show far fewer significant relationships and to account for very little of the total variance ($R^2 = .08$; see Table 16.5). Only mortality risk and number of diagnoses showed weak, positive associations with physician contact, and hypochondriasis was the only attitudinal variable with a significant relationship to visits to a doctor (β = .15, $p < .01$). With regard to social-structural predictors, only living alone was significantly predictive of physician visits (β = .10, $p < .01$). Thus, it appears that physician contacts are by and large independent of acute variations in health status and are not influenced very much by social-structural factors either.

3.3.3   Predicting Caregiving Help

As already noted in the bivariate analyses, the factors associated with utilization of caregiving help are different from those related to utilization of medical help. Using a series of logistic regression analyses, three dummy variables were created with the "no help" category as the reference group coded as 0 (see Table 16.6). The odds ratios in Table 16.6 reveal that different levels of help are differentially predicted by the independent variables. Use of informal help by family and neighbors increases with advanced age, living alone, and having children in the area, and is negatively related to dementia. The use of professional help at home is significantly associated with immobility, older age, living

Table 16.5. *Multiple regresssion analyses predicting the use of medical care from physical health, mental health, attitudinal, and social-structural variables (standardized regression coefficients)*

Predictor variable	Number of drugs	Number of physician contacts
Physical health		
Number of diagnoses	.43**	.12*
Mortality risk	-.09	.17**
Subjective walking distance	.03	-.07
Mental health		
BPRS	.03	-.09
MMSE	.12*	-.05
CES-D	-.05	.02
Health attitudes		
Complaint List	.20**	-.01
Whiteley Index	.11*	.15*
Illness Concepts Scale	.19**	.04
Social situation		
Education	-.01	-.04
Occupational training	.02	.02
Social prestige	.08*	-.03
Home ownership	-.04	-.02
Living alone	-.09*	.10*
Number of children in Berlin	-.03	.03
Age	.13**	-.05
Gender	-.07	.01
Adj. R^2	.46	.08

$*p < .05, ** p < .01.$

alone, higher levels of education and social prestige, and less hypochondriasis. Finally, institutional care is predicted largely by mental health variables (e.g., dementia and depression), though immobility, living alone, owning a home, and advanced old age also make a significant contribution. Taken together, it appears that increased levels of utilization of nursing care are primarily associated with somatic impairment at lower levels of care, and with mental and physical comorbidity at higher levels of formal caregiving.

4   Discussion

This chapter describes the utilization of health care among older adults and their correlation with selected patient-centered factors. Health care utilization, in this regard, refers to service use per se, and does not address the important issue of health care costs.

Table 16.6. *Logistic regression analyses predicting use of caregiving services from physical health, mental health, attitudinal, and social-structural variables (odds ratios)*

Predictor variable	Informal vs. no help	Formal vs. no help	Institution vs. no help
Physical health			
Number of diagnoses	1.06	1.03	1.06
Mortality risk	1.04	0.70	0.73
Subjective walking distance	1.04	0.55**	0.43**
Mental health			
BPRS	0.98	1.02	1.04
MMSE	0.88*	0.91	0.77**
CES-D	1.02	1.01	1.14*
Health attitudes			
Complaint List	1.01	1.04	0.99
Whiteley Index	0.98	0.83**	0.68**
Illness Concepts Scale	1.02	1.01	0.98
Social situation			
Education	1.18	1.87*	1.14
Occupational training	0.92	2.09	1.34
Social prestige	1.00	1.02**	0.98
Home ownership	0.32	1.03	0.10*
Living alone[a]	4.55**	4.96**	3.37*
Number of children in Berlin	1.41*	1.00	0.55
Age	1.11**	1.12**	1.10*
Gender	2.09	1.78	2.91

$*p < .05$, $**p < .01$.
[a]Institutionalized participants were coded according to prior residential status.

The data presented here refer to adults aged 70 years and older residing in the former West Berlin. The medical and caregiving system in this metropolitan area is cost-free to the individual, offers an abundance of physicians of all specialties, and includes the highest per capita rate of caregiving institutions in Germany. As such, the generalizability of the results to other regions, countries, and cultures is an open question. The issue of representativeness is particularly relevant for some social-structural variables, since Berlin has a higher than average proportion of widows, higher rates of female employment, and fewer homeowners than other areas of Germany. The multivariate analyses should be less affected by these issues of representativeness, however, since these individual factors are statistically controlled. Despite these caveats, the nature of the health care system in Berlin makes it especially interesting to study the impact of personal variables on care utilization, as there are relatively optimal provider conditions.

Further strengths of the Berlin Aging Study lie in its multidisciplinary design, in which internists, psychiatrists, sociologists, and psychologists thoroughly investigated each of the constructs studied using state-of-the-art assessments. Thus, individual variables were measured as precisely as possible. Medication use patterns in this sample provide an example of this interdisciplinary and comprehensive assessment procedure. This process included: (a) a psychiatric interview of subjective health complaints and related medication use, (b) an inspection of medications used during the at-home psychiatric visit, (c) a medication assessment during the examination by internists, (d) cross-validation interviews with participants' personal physicians, and (e) consolidation of medication data during consensus conferences between psychiatrists and internists. This unique feature of the Berlin Aging Study represents a major advantage in terms of the reliability and validity of the data presented.

Another strength of BASE lies in the age distribution of the study sample. Since men and the very old were oversampled, equal proportions of men and women were included in the study. In addition, old persons in each five-year age interval were equally represented. These design features increase the certainty with which conclusions regarding age and gender differences in health care utilization can be made. Alternatively, the sample can be weighted to represent the population characteristics of West Berlin.

In this regard, 78% of older Berlin adults can be called independent in Activities of Daily Living, 14% required some help, and about 8% needed intensified care (see Table 16.2). These figures are somewhat lower than those generally reported in other studies (Brock et al., 1990; Zarit et al., 1993).

Not surprisingly, the increased rate of somatic and mental health disorders among older adults shows significant associations with the increased use of physician services and the need for caregiving assistance (Sager et al., 1996; Welch, Verrilli, Katz, & Latimer, 1996). General practitioners and internists as family physicians are the most important source of medical care and therefore primarily responsible for health care of older adults. Nevertheless, 60% of old persons also visit specialists, most often ophthalmologists or orthopedists. Despite the high incidence of mental health morbidity in late life and its associated implications for cost and caregiving, psychiatrists play a relatively minor role. This supports the finding by German, Shapiro, and Skinner (1985) that family physicians remain the primary consultants for mental health disorders.

In conjunction with the high rates of morbidity, older adults take a high number of prescribed and nonprescribed medications (Bressler, 1987). This polypharmacy, together with age-related changes in the pharmacokinetics and pharmacodynamics of drugs, places old people at greater risk for adverse drug reactions (Vestal, 1990). An interesting observation is that the number of medications taken does not significantly increase after the age of 70, which is comparable to results from other studies that used different methodologies. This indicates a quantitative boundary beyond which the therapeutic benefit of additional drugs must be carefully weighed in relation to potential negative consequences. With widespread multimorbidity in old age, it is a special challenge for physicians to determine criteria on the illnesses that need to be treated and those where compromises should be made (Linden, Geiselmann, & Borchelt, 1992).

There are interesting combinations of somatic and mental disorders in the prediction of the use of caregiving services. In particular, mobility limitations were associated with the need for professional at-home care, whereas dementia, in combination with mobility limitations and living alone, was predictive of the need for institutional caregiving. This relationship between health impairment and service utilization can be seen into very advanced old age.

The utilization of medical and caregiving help, however, is not exclusively explained by health factors. As seen in younger age groups (Wilms & Linden, 1992) and as predicted from the theoretical model of Andersen and Newman (1973) and others, a significant relationship exists between subjective health experiences, health attitudes, and the use of health services (McCormick et al., 1996). This is particularly true for the use of drugs. Patients in general are not just passive recipients of treatment, they also actively influence the type and amount of care they receive. It is important to note that this is not different in advanced age. Individual differences in illness experience and symptom presentation continue to play an important role in selection or rejection of help or treatment. In this context, it is also noteworthy that 26% of old persons living alone who are in need of assistance with ADL do not receive help.

The use of nursing care, especially professional and institutional services, is particularly dependent on social factors as well as illness factors. Persons who live alone without children nearby and those who have minimal social networks show a high probability of using professional help. As such, life circumstances play an important role in determining the utilization of care (George & Maddox, 1989).

As advanced old age is closely associated with illness and frailty, it can also be characterized by increasing needs for care. Therefore older adults are especially dependent on a good health care system (Engelhardt et al., 1996). It is important to stress that health care is not a uniform phenomenon and that different types of care are used and needed by different persons for different reasons. The system of care must adapt to the changing needs of old individuals in a very flexible way. It should not take responsibilities away from persons who still can look after themselves in many areas just because they need help in selected domains. However, help should not only be available, but also be brought to the persons requiring it when the need arises. Our data show that a considerable proportion of older adults report that they need some kind of assistance, but are nevertheless left alone. The need for help can also imply the inability to ask for it.

In the same context, our results show that, despite the high interrelationships between age, illness, and health care, a differential perspective must be maintained. To a certain degree it is a very personal decision when, how, and whom to ask for help and how to cope with health problems and reduced abilities. In this respect, our results clearly illustrate the differential experience of aging in relation to health status and the use of medical and caregiving services. Individuality and self-determination are highly apparent in late life. Finally, these results reiterate the fact that health care utilization is not only a medical, but also a psychological and social phenomenon.

References

Andersen, R., & Newman, J. F. (1973). Societal and individual health determinants of medical care utilization in the United States. *Milbank Quarterly, 51*, 92–124.

Andres, R. (1985). Mortality and obesity: The rationale for age specific height-weight tables. In R. Andres, E. L. Bierman, & W. R. Hazzard (Eds.), Principles of geriatric medicine (pp. 311–318). New York: McGraw-Hill.

Bäcker, G., Dieck, M., Naegele, G., & Tews, H. P. (1989). *Ältere Menschen in Nordrhein-Westfalen: Wissenschaftliches Gutachten zur Lage der älteren Menschen und zur Altenpolitik in Nordrhein-Westfalen zur Vorbereitung des zweiten Landesaltenplans.*

Düsseldorf: Ministerium für Arbeit, Gesundheit und Soziales des Landes Nordrhein-Westfalen.

Bass, D. M., Looman, W. J., & Ehrlich, P. (1992). Predicting the volume of health and social services: Integrating cognitive impairment into the modified Andersen framework. *The Gerontologist, 32*, 33–43.

Becker, M. H., Maiman, L. A., Kirscht, J. P., Häfner, D. P., Drachman, R. H., & Taylor, D. W. (1982). Wahrnehmungen des Patienten und Compliance: Neuere Untersuchungen zum "Health Belief Model." In R. B. Haynes, D. W. Taylor, & D. L. Sackett (Eds.), *Compliance Handbuch* (pp. 94–131). Munich: Oldenbourg.

Branch, L. G., & Jette, A. M. (1982). Elders' use of informal long-term care assistance. *The Gerontologist, 23*, 51–56.

Bressler, R. (1987). Drug use in the geriatric patient. In L. L. Carstensen & B. A. Edelstein (Eds.), *Handbook of clinical gerontology* (pp. 152–174). New York: Pergamon Press.

Brock, D. B., Guralnik, J. M., & Brody, J. A. (1990). Demography and epidemiology of aging in the United States. In E. L. Schneider & J. W. Rowe (Eds.), *Handbook of the biology of aging* (3rd ed., pp. 3–23). San Diego, CA: Academic Press.

Coulton, C., & Frost, A. (1982). Use of social and health services by the elderly. *Journal of Health and Social Behavior, 23*, 330–339.

Crimmins, E. M., Saito, Y., & Ingegneri, D. (1989). Changes in life expectancy and disability-free life expectancy in the United States. *Population and Development Review, 15*, 235–267.

Dinkel, R. H. (1992). Demographische Alterung: Ein Überblick unter besonderer Berücksichtigung der Mortalitätsentwicklungen. In P. B. Baltes & J. Mittelstraß (Eds.), *Zukunft des Alterns und gesellschaftliche Entwicklung* (pp. 62–93). Berlin: de Gruyter.

Engelhardt, J. B., Toseland, R. W., O'Donnell, J. C., Richie, J. T., Jue, D., & Banks, S. (1996). The effectiveness and efficiency of outpatient geriatric evaluation and management. *Journal of the American Geriatrics Society, 44*, 847–856.

Evashwick, C., Rowe, G., Diehr, P., & Branch, L. (1984). Factors explaining the use of health care services by the elderly. *Health Services Research, 19*, 357–382.

Folstein, M. F., Folstein, S. E., & McHugh, P. R. (1975). "Mini Mental State": A practical method for grading the cognitive state of patients for the clinician. *Journal of Psychiatric Research, 12*, 189–198.

George, L. K., & Maddox, G. L. (1989). Social and behavioral aspects of institutional care. In M. G. Ory & K. Bond (Eds.), *Aging and health care: Social science and policy perspectives* (pp. 116–141). London: Routledge.

German, P. S., Shapiro, S., & Skinner, E. A. (1985). Mental health of the elderly: Use of health and mental health services. *Journal of the American Geriatrics Society, 33*, 246–252.

Gilberg, R. (1997). *Hilfe- und Pflegebedürftigkeit und die Inanspruchnahme von Hilfe- und Pflegeleistungen im höheren Lebensalter.* Unpublished doctoral thesis, Free University of Berlin.

Gray, M. (1988). Living environments for the elderly: 1. Living at home. In N. Wells & C. Freer (Eds.), *The aging population: Burden or challenge?* (pp. 203–216). London: Macmillan.

Guralnik, J. M., & Simonsick, E. M. (1993). Physical disability in older Americans. *Journal of Gerontology, 48* (Special issue), 3–10.

Hamilton, M. (1986). HAMD (Hamilton Depression Scale). In Collegium Internationale Psychiatriae Scalarum (CIPS) (Ed.), *Internationale Skalen für Psychiatrie*. Weinheim: Beltz.

Hansell, S., Sherman, G., & Mechanic, D. (1991). Body awareness and medical care utilization among older adults in an HMO. *Journal of Gerontology, 46*, 151–159.

Hautzinger, M. (1988). Die CES-D Skala: Ein Depressionsmeßinstrument für Untersuchungen in der Allgemeinbevölkerung. *Diagnostica, 34*, 167–173.

Jette, A. M., Branch, L. G., Sleeper, L. A., Feldman, H., & Sullivan, L. M. (1992). High risk profiles for nursing home admission. *The Gerontologist, 32*, 634–640.

Katz, S., & Akpom, C. A. (1976). A measure of primary sociobiological functions. *International Journal of Health Services, 6*, 493–508.

Katz, S., Ford, A. B., Moskowitz, R. W., Jackson, B. A., & Jaffe, M. W. (1963). Studies of illness in the aged. The index of ADL: A standardized measure of biological and psychosocial function. *Journal of the American Medical Association, 185*, 914–919.

Klauber, J., & Selke, G. W. (1993). Arzneimittelverordnungen nach Altersgruppen. In U. Schwabe & D. Paffrath (Eds.), *Arzneiverordnungs-Report '93* (pp. 498–507). Stuttgart: Gustav Fischer.

Krämer, W. (1992). Altern und Gesundheitswesen: Probleme und Lösungen aus der Sicht der Gesundheitsökonomie. In P. B. Baltes & J. Mittelstraß (Eds.), *Zukunft des Alterns und gesellschaftliche Entwicklung* (pp. 563–580). Berlin: de Gruyter.

Linden, M., Geiselmann, B., & Borchelt, M. (1992). Multimorbidität, Multimedikation und Medikamentenoptimierung bei alten Patienten. In E. Lungershausen (Ed.), *Demenz: Herausforderung für Forschung, Medizin und Gesellschaft* (pp. 231–240). Berlin: Springer-Verlag.

Linden, M., Nather, J., & Wilms, H. U. (1988). Zur Definition, Bedeutung und Messung der Krankheitskonzepte von Patienten: Die Krankheitskonzeptskala (KK-Skala) für schizophrene Patienten. *Fortschritte der Neurologie, Psychiatrie, 55*, 35–43.

Linden, M., & Priebe, S. (1990). Arzt-Patient-Beziehung. In R. Schwarzer (Ed.), *Gesundheitspsychologie* (pp. 415–425). Göttingen: Hogrefe.

Lundeen, T. F., George, J. M., & Toomey, T. C. (1991). Health care system utilization for chronic facial pain. *Journal of Craniomandibular Disorders, 5*, 280–285.

Mahoney, F. I., & Barthel, D. W. (1965). Functional evaluation: The Barthel Index. *Maryland Medical Journal, 14*, 61–65.

McCormick, W. C., Uomoto, J., Young, H., Graves, A. B., Vitaliano, P., Mortimer, J. A., Edland, S. D., & Larson, E. B. (1996). Attitudes toward use of nursing homes and home care in older Japanese-Americans. *Journal of the American Geriatrics Society, 44*, 769–777.

McWilliam, C., Copeland, J. R. M., Dewey, M. E., & Wood, N. (1988). The Geriatric Mental State Examination: A case-finding instrument in the community. *British Journal of Psychiatry, 152*, 205–208.

Myers, G. C. (1985). Aging and worldwide population change. In R. H. Binstock & E. Shanas (Eds.), *Handbook of aging and the social sciences* (2nd ed., pp. 173–198). New York: Van Nostrand Reinhold.

Overall, J. E., & Gorham, D. R. (1962). The Brief Psychiatric Rating Scale. *Psychological Reports, 10*, 799–812.

Pescosolido, B. A. (1991). Illness careers and network ties: A conceptual model of utilization and compliance. In G. Albrecht & J. Levy (Eds.), *Advances in medical sociology* (pp. 161–184). Greenwich, CT: JAI Press.

Pescosolido, B. A. (1992). Beyond rational choice: The social dynamics of how people seek help. *American Journal of Sociology, 97*, 1096–1138.

Pflege-Versicherungsgesetz. (1994). Gesetz zur sozialen Absicherung des Risikos der Pflegebedürftigkeit. *Bundesgesetzblatt, 30* (May 28th, 1994), 1014.

Pilowsky, I., & Spence, N. D. (1983). *Manual of the Illness Behaviour Questionnaire (IBQ)*. Adelaide: University of Adelaide.

Radloff, L. S. (1977). The CES-D Scale: A self-report depression scale for research in the general population. *Applied Psychological Measurement, 1*, 385–401.

Rosenstock, I. M., Strecker, V. J., & Becker, M. H. (1988). Social learning theory and the health belief model. *Health Education Quarterly, 15*, 175–183.

Sager, M. A., Rudberg, M. A., Jalaluddin, M., Franke, T., Inouye, S. K., Landefeld, C. S., Siebens, H., & Winograd, C. H. (1996). Hospital Admission Risk Profile (HARP): Identifying older patients at risk for functional decline following acute medical illness and hospitalization. *Journal of the American Geriatrics Society, 44*, 251–257.

Schneekloth, U., & Potthoff, P. (1993). *Hilfs- und Pflegebedürftige in privaten Haushalten* (Report on the project "Potentials and limits of independent living" funded by the German Federal Ministry for Family Affairs and Senior Citizens). Stuttgart: Kohlhammer.

Schwarzer, R. (Ed.). (1990). *Gesundheitspsychologie*. Göttingen: Hogrefe.

Spore, D. L., Horgas, A. L., Smyer, M. A., & Marks, L. N. (1992). The relationship of antipsychotic drug use, behavior, and diagnoses among nursing home residents. *Journal of Aging and Health, 4*, 514–535.

Strain, L. A. (1991). Use of health services in later life: The influence of health beliefs. *Journal of Gerontology: Social Sciences, 46*, S143–S150.

Verbrugge, L. M. (1989). Gender, aging, and health. In K. S. Markides (Ed.), *Aging and health: Perspectives on gender, race, ethnicity, and class* (pp. 23–78). Newbury Park, CA: Sage.

Vestal, R. E. (1990). Clinical pharmacology. In W. R. Hazzard, R. Andres, E. L. Bierman, & J. P. Blass (Eds.), *Principles of geriatric medicine* (2nd ed., pp. 201–211). New York: McGraw-Hill.

Wahl, H.-W. (1993). Kompetenzeinbußen im Alter: Eine Auswertung der Literatur zu "Activities of Daily Living" und Pflegebedürftigkeit. *Zeitschrift für Gerontologie, 26*, 366–377.

Wallston, B. S., Wallston, K. A., Kaplan, G. D., & Maides, S. A. (1976). Development and validation of the Health Locus of Control Scale. *Journal of Consulting and Clinical Psychology, 44*, 580–585.

Wallston, K. A., Smith, R. A., King, J. E., Forsberg, P. R., Wallston, B. S., & Nagy, V. T. (1983). Expectancies about control over health: Relationship to desire for control of health care. *Personality and Social Psychology Bulletin, 9*, 377–385.

Wan, T. T. (1982). Use of health services by the elderly in low-income communities. *Milbank Quarterly, 60*, 82–107.

Wan, T. T. (1989). The behavioral model of health care utilization by older people. In M. G. Ory & K. Bond (Eds.), *Ageing and health care: Social science and policy perspectives* (pp. 52–77). London: Routledge.

Wan, T. T., & Arling, G. (1983). Differential use of health services among disabled elders. *Research on Aging, 5*, 411–431.

Wan, T. T., & Odell, B. (1981). Factors affecting the use of social and health services for the elderly. *Ageing and Society, 1*, 95–115.

Wegener, B. (1985). Gibt es Sozialprestige? *Zeitschrift für Soziologie, 14*, 209–235.

Welch, W. P., Verrilli, D., Katz, S. J., & Latimer, E. (1996). A detailed comparison of physician services for the elderly in the United States and Canada. *Journal of the American Medical Association, 275*, 1410–1416.

Wilms, H. U., & Linden, M. (1992). Die Patientenperspektive in der Langzeitbehandlung. In H. Helmchen & M. Linden (Eds.), *Die jahrelange Behandlung mit Psychopharmaka* (pp. 205–214). Berlin: de Gruyter.

Wolinsky, F. D., Coe, R., Miller, D., Prendergast, J., Creel, M., & Chavez, N. (1983). Health services utilization among the noninstitutionalized elderly. *Journal of Health and Social Behavior, 24*, 325–337.

Wolinsky, F. D., & Johnson, R. J. (1991). The use of health services by older adults. *Journal of Gerontology: Social Sciences, 46*, S345–S357.

World Health Organization (WHO). (1978). *Manual of the international statistical classification of diseases, injuries, and causes of death. Based on the recommendations of the Ninth Revision Conference, 1975, and adopted by the 29th World Health Assembly.* Geneva.

Zarit, S. H., Johansson, B., & Berg, S. (1993). Functional impairment and co-disability in the oldest-old: A multidimensional approach. *Journal of Aging and Health, 5*, 291–305.

Zerssen, D. von (1976). *Klinische Selbstbeurteilung-Skala (KSb-S) aus dem Münchener Psychiatrischen Informations-System.* Weinheim: Beltz.

CHAPTER 17

Sources of Well-Being in Very Old Age

Jacqui Smith, William Fleeson, Bernhard Geiselmann, Richard A. Settersten Jr., and Ute Kunzmann

In this chapter, we examine ideas about the sources and processes of well-being in the context of a model derived from the work of Campbell, Converse, and Rodgers (1976). The model allows an integration of medical, sociological, and psychological perspectives. We describe the levels of well-being reported by the participants in the first cross-sectional measurement phase of the Berlin Aging Study (BASE), and examine the extent to which objective and subjective indicators of specific life domains predict overall individual well-being. Results from this investigation were multifaceted. The majority of participants reported satisfaction with their present life conditions. However, older women, individuals aged 85 and over, and persons living in institutions reported less frequent experience of positive emotions, an important component of well-being. Path analysis indicated that subjective domain evaluations (especially subjective health) were stronger predictors of subjective well-being than were the objective measures of domain status. This finding is consistent with the theoretical framework of Campbell et al. (1976). It suggests that the self-regulation processes that contribute to adaptation to changing life conditions (e.g., changes in aspiration levels and comparison targets) operate effectively in old age. We argue, however, that the cumulative challenges and losses of very old age could tap the limits of these adaptive processes. For this reason, it is essential to implement measures supportive of well-being in late adulthood. There is much room, for example, for improving living conditions through technological development, political measures, and social change.

1   Introduction

No study of very old age would be complete without some general measures of the quality of life experience. To this end, assessments of well-being and quality of life are widely employed in the gerontological literature as indicators of the effectiveness of social policies and welfare programs, the success of medical and psychiatric treatments, as global indicators of psychological adjustment, and successful aging (P. B. Baltes & Baltes, 1990, 1992; Lawton, 1983, 1991; Patrick & Erickson, 1993; Rowe & Kahn, 1987; Ryff, 1989; Thomae, 1987). Despite this widespread use, the concepts "well-being" and "quality of life" remain ill-defined, and their appropriate measurement is hotly contested. It is not uncommon to find these concepts used interchangeably in the literature. This, in part, contributes to the definitional debate since the two concepts have different connotations across disciplines.

In this chapter, we use the term "well-being" because it has few roots in any particular discipline (cf. Schuessler & Fisher, 1985). We take a multidisciplinary perspective on questions about well-being in very old age by examining the predictive interplay of sub-group differences, objective life conditions, and subjective evaluations of domain status.

Although there is consensus across the disciplines of medicine, sociology, psychiatry, and psychology that well-being is a multidimensional phenomenon, there is less agreement about the mechanisms underlying a sense of well-being and the way to measure the concept. Between disciplines there is disagreement as to whether the focus should be on self-reports or external (objective) criteria of well-being. Within disciplines there is disagreement as to whether self-reported well-being is best assessed with (1) single- or multi-item measures, (2) scales tailored for healthy populations or frail older persons, or (3) measures that address either the affective or cognitive components of subjective well-being, or some combination of these components (cf. Andrews & McKennell, 1980; Birren, Lubben, Rowe, & Deutchman, 1991; Campbell et al., 1976; Diener, 1994). Measures biased toward the affective components of well-being ask about the experience of enjoyment and happiness, the preponderance of happiness and pleasant feelings over unpleasant feelings, or the absence of emotional upset. More cognitively oriented measures focus on judgments of life quality, meaningfulness, and satisfaction. Whereas some disciplines focus on the *presence* of the positive cognitive and affective dimensions of subjective well-being, others focus on assessing the *absence* of negative factors. Various researchers have also introduced other dimensions (e.g., adjustment, mastery, morale, or mental health; Lawton, 1975; Ryff & Essex, 1991). In the following sections, we briefly elaborate upon these different measurement approaches, outline an integrative heuristic model based on the work of Campbell et al. (1976), and (in the context of this model) review proposals about specific predictors of subjective well-being in very old age. After this, we describe the levels of well-being reported by participants in the first cross-sectional measurement sample of the Berlin Aging Study (BASE, $N = 516$).

1.1   General Approaches to Studying Well-Being

What constitutes well-being in very old age? Researchers have taken two main routes toward answering this question. These routes roughly correspond to common-sense (naive) theories that attribute the source of well-being either to individuals' material resources or to their subjective experience and evaluation of their life circumstances.

As might be expected, approaches that focus on defining well-being in terms of *material resources and life conditions* are primarily represented in the fields of sociology, economics, internal medicine, and mental health (Land, 1983; Lawton, 1991; Schuessler & Fisher, 1985). Here researchers are interested in determining a so-called *objective* set of social-normative criteria that specify the prerequisite physical, material, and personal life conditions that could potentially contribute to successful aging and a "good life" in old age. One would examine whether older persons have (1) acceptable housing (e.g., comfortable, fitted with appliances that support independent living in late life), (2) access to a wide range of health care and community services, (3) opportunities for family-related and general social activities, (4) sufficient financial resources, and (5) nonhandicapping physical and mental health. Following this approach, an individual would theoretically be considered as having well-being (or the potential for well-being) if a set of specific resources and/or functioning criteria is met.

The second approach to studying well-being, which emphasizes the importance of *the individual's subjective experience of life*, is taken primarily by psychologists (e.g.,

Campbell et al., 1976; Diener, 1984, 1994; Herzog, Rodgers, & Woodworth, 1982; Ryff & Essex, 1991; Thomae, 1987), but also has advocates in sociology and medicine (e.g., Bullinger & Pöppel, 1988; Glatzer, 1992; Glatzer & Zapf, 1984; Lehman, 1983). This approach defines well-being in terms of individuals' cognitive evaluations of their lives and their emotional experience (positive or negative) associated with their life circumstances. Thus, the criteria for well-being within this approach are set by the individuals themselves.

Defining well-being in terms of the individual's subjective experience of life avoids the difficult task of establishing consensus about criteria of quality that satisfy both individuals and social institutions. The standards and/or needs of one target individual or group may not always match the standards and the criteria of an observer (e.g., professional caregiver, government department, institution). Furthermore, objectively equivalent life conditions may be interpreted differently by people with different life histories, and so have differential influences on perceived and reported personal well-being (Schwarz & Strack, 1991; Tsevat et al., 1994; Veenhoven, 1991). This is not to say that the approach that focuses on individual subjective definitions of well-being views objective conditions as being unimportant. On the contrary, objective life conditions are what individuals subjectively evaluate, so there ought to be some correspondence between objective status and subjective judgment. Indeed, the prime research questions within this approach involve detecting the processes that underlie subjective evaluation. For example, researchers ask what evaluative standards individuals use, whether these standards might change depending on age and objective life circumstances, and whether status in some specific life domains especially contributes to individuals' overall evaluations of well-being.

This chapter in part integrates these two traditions. On the one hand, we use as outcome measures older adults' subjective evaluations of their overall personal well-being and satisfaction with life. On the other hand, we ask whether objective life conditions (especially poor physical and mental health, financial difficulty, and reduced social activities) influence these evaluations, both directly and indirectly. This integrative strategy, derived from the theory and research of Campbell et al. (1976), is illustrated in Figure 17.1. This theory was selected because it offered the best solution to our dual goals of describing the cross-sectional survey data available from BASE and presenting a multidisciplinary overview of well-being in this heterogeneous sample.[1] Furthermore, it allowed an examination of whether the model implied in Figure 17.1 about the sources and processes underlying reported well-being applied to data from the very old.

1.2   Outline of the Integrative Campbell et al. Model

The heuristic model in Figure 17.1 (modified after Campbell et al., 1976, p. 16) posits that overall subjective well-being is a function of the *direct* and *indirect* effects of social-structural and demographic variables (e.g., age, gender, marital status), objective life conditions (e.g., housing, income, social network and activities, physical and mental health), and subjective experiences of these domain-specific life conditions (see also Brief, Butcher, George, & Link, 1993; Filipp & Schmidt, 1994; George, Okun, & Lan-

---

[1] This chapter reports analyses on unweighted data, and so results refer to the BASE participants rather than to the elderly population of the western districts of Berlin.

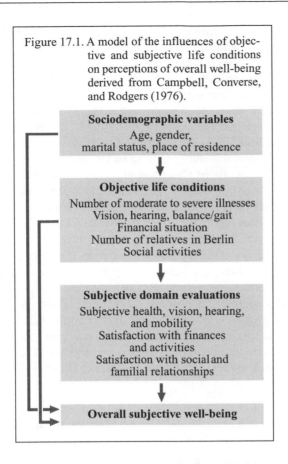

Figure 17.1. A model of the influences of objective and subjective life conditions on perceptions of overall well-being derived from Campbell, Converse, and Rodgers (1976).

Sociodemographic variables
Age, gender,
marital status, place of residence

Objective life conditions
Number of moderate to severe illnesses
Vision, hearing, balance/gait
Financial situation
Number of relatives in Berlin
Social activities

Subjective domain evaluations
Subjective health, vision, hearing, and mobility
Satisfaction with finances and activities
Satisfaction with social and familial relationships

Overall subjective well-being

derman, 1985; Herzog et al., 1982; Lehman, 1983). The directions of the arrows in the model represent the idea that objective life conditions may have a direct effect on subjective well-being, as well as an indirect effect through individuals' subjective domain evaluations.

Campbell et al. (1976) have argued (on the basis of data from adults aged 20 to 80 years) that typically the effects of specific objective life conditions on subjective well-being are filtered through subjective evaluations of these conditions. That is, enduring objective life conditions as such have only a minimal direct effect on reports of well-being. They can, however, have substantial indirect effects because they influence the way individuals evaluate these conditions. There may or may not be a close relationship between objective status in a domain and subjective satisfaction with that domain. A concrete example from recent discussions in medicine can be used to illustrate these ideas. Two patients with osteoarthritis may have the same limitations as assessed by an objective health status scale, but they might assign very different levels of importance to their incapacity as a function of their life background and personal preferences (Tsevat et al., 1994). There are large individual differences in the amount of time, discomfort, money, and risk that patients are prepared to invest in undertaking treatment, as well as how individuals rate the limitations caused by one illness compared with another health state.

Judgments of domain satisfaction, according to Campbell et al. (1976), reflect the complex operation of different value and motivational systems. Within social groups, there are common values about status and achievement in various life domains and age-related expectations about the relative importance of life domains for individual identity and well-being (see also Hagestad & Neugarten, 1985; Rosow, 1985). Individuals are motivated to comply and conform to these social values and expectations by setting personal life goals and standards that reflect social norms. Individuals' feelings of subjective well-being are believed to reflect some mental calculation of the "gap" or ratio of discrepancies between the social ideals that they aspire to and what they perceive themselves as having (Andrews & Withey, 1976; Campbell et al., 1976; Michalos, 1985). Judgments of satisfaction are presumed to decline the greater the gap between socially desired standards and actual circumstances. Based on this argument alone, we would expect the proportion of populations that report positive life satisfaction to reflect only the upper percentiles of the social distribution of social goods and resources (Rawls, 1971).

Campbell and others, however, described various mechanisms that help to explain why more individuals than might be expected, based on objective criteria, typically report positive well-being. These mechanisms, which involve a complex interplay of attribution, personal preference, and comparison processes, intervene in the processes of making a judgment about one's own level of satisfaction. For example, it is suggested that older adults and individuals in less advantaged social groups may maintain high levels of subjective well-being by careful selection of comparison targets and lowering of aspiration levels (e.g., P. B. Baltes & Baltes, 1990; Brandtstädter & Greve, 1994; Suls & Wills, 1991).

1.3 Questions from the Campbell et al. Model Addressed within the Berlin Aging Study

Data collected within BASE (cf. P. B. Baltes et al., Chapter 1 in this volume) provided a unique opportunity to examine three central questions about subjective well-being in old age in the context of the various parts of the heuristic model in Figure 17.1.

1.3.1 *How Satisfied with Their Lives Are the BASE Participants?*

Survey studies including individuals aged 20 to 70 years typically find that the majority of respondents report positive life satisfaction, even despite sometimes substantial differences in objective life conditions (e.g., Andrews & Withey, 1976; Campbell et al., 1976; Diener, 1984; Glatzer & Zapf, 1984; Myers & Diener, 1995). There are, however, conflicting proposals regarding expected levels of reported well-being in the period of very old age.

One set of proposals argues for lower levels (cf. Atchley, 1991). It is suggested that the declines associated with very old age overwhelm individuals to such a degree that they moderate their expression of well-being. In addition, researchers point to the possible implications of the general negative stereotype of very old age, which conjures an image of loss (particularly in physical and mental health), of increased illness and pain, of death, and of decreased life enjoyment (Heckhausen, Dixon, & Baltes, 1989). The more positive stereotypes of earlier phases of the life course are associated with pervasive social and age-appropriate norms that it is better to report that "life is fine" than to complain (Miller & Prentice, 1996; Taylor, 1989). The mechanisms of compliance to these norms (e.g., comparison processes) are said to explain the relatively small effects of age and objective life conditions on reported levels of well-being typically found in surveys of 20- to 70-year-olds (Emmons & Diener, 1985; Herzog et al., 1982). The existence of the negative stereotype about old age suggests that it may be more socially acceptable for the very old to report reduced well-being (Carstensen & Cone, 1983). For individuals over 85 years, the social pressures to comply to the "life is fine" norm may be less pervasive.

Another set of proposals about expected levels of reported well-being in the period of very old age argues that, just as in earlier parts of the life course, large numbers of individuals should report high well-being (e.g., P. B. Baltes, 1991; Brandtstädter & Greve, 1994; Brim, 1992; George et al., 1985; Herzog et al., 1982; Lawton, 1991). These researchers suggest that individual changes in evaluative standards used to judge satisfaction and the operation of self-protective mechanisms contribute to the maintenance of reported positive well-being even in very old age. Lawton (1985), for example, demonstrated how some impaired, homebound individuals successfully optimized, managed, and gained pleasure from their lives by arranging "control centers" around their beds or living-room chairs. The "control centers" usually consisted of a telephone (for social contact), television or radio (for information and social participation), together with personal mementos (which provide cues for reliving good times in the past). Each of these objects were used proactively to obtain and maintain different positive life experiences.

1.3.2 Are Some Subgroups of BASE Participants More at Risk Than Others for Lower Perceived Well-Being?

Here we examine group differences associated with age, social-structural variables (i.e., gender, marital status, institutionalization), and with suspected dementia. The BASE sample design was rather unique in that it included a sufficient number of individuals in their 70s, 80s, and 90s to allow an investigation of possible age-related differences in well-being *during* the period of old age. Most earlier studies, which report few age differences in subjective well-being, have compared differences between young and older adults, with the younger group aged 20 to 40 years and the older age group usually comprising individuals in their 60s and 70s (e.g., Diener, 1984; Glatzer, 1992; Herzog et al., 1982; Larson, 1978). Increased risk of frailty, loss, and poor health during the period of very old age (from 85 to 100+ years) may, however, place limits on life satisfaction (Birren et al., 1991). Furthermore, these risks may be inequitably distributed across subgroups of the aged population (e.g., those still married vs. widowed; community-dwelling vs. institutionalized).

1.3.3 What Combination of Variables Best Predicts Overall Subjective Well-Being in the BASE Sample?

Data collected within the various sessions of the multidisciplinary BASE Intensive Protocol (see P. B. Baltes et al., Chapter 1) allowed the investigation of both objective *and* subjective domain-specific predictors of subjective well-being. Objective and subjective measures were available for domains found to be important for well-being in younger age groups (i.e., financial situation, family life, social participation) as well as for those thought to be critical for well-being in very old age (i.e., physical health and functional capacity; George et al., 1985). We were interested not only in the relative contribution of each of these domains to predicting well-being, but also in the relative contributions of the objective and subjective predictors from these domains.

As described above, studies with younger samples typically find that subjective evaluations rather than objective assessments of important life domains are the best direct predictors of overall reported well-being (supporting the Campbell et al. model). It is still an open question whether this result also holds true for the period of very old age. BASE provided a unique chance to examine this question. First, as a function of the multidisciplinary character of BASE, we were able to capitalize on the availability of independently obtained measures of domain functioning. A second unique feature involved the availability of comprehensive, clinically based assessments of health. In general, previous studies of well-being in old age that have examined a predictive model similar to Figure 17.1 have had access to few (if any) objective measures of physical health and functional capacity (e.g., George et al., 1985). The BASE data included clinically based assessments of physical health (multimorbidity) together with measures of vision, hearing, and balance/gait (mobility). Furthermore, we were able to examine the effects of diagnosed poor mental health (especially dementia) on reported well-being.

BASE was limited in that it was not suited to a microanalytic study of the standards and strategies underlying individual judgments or the specific effects of temporal and situational life changes (cf. Filipp & Ferring, 1989; Schwarz & Strack, 1991). However, BASE did provide the rare advantage of a heterogeneous sample of the very old (a feature often overlooked in microanalytic studies). Further, it provided objective measures of those life conditions considered to be important bases for well-being by the sociological, medical, and psychiatric disciplines.

2   Subjective Well-Being: Findings from BASE

BASE included several single-item measures of past, present, and expected future *life satisfaction*, a standard measure of *positive and negative affect* (Positive and Negative Affect Schedule, PANAS; Watson, Clark, & Tellegen, 1988), and a 15-item measure of *overall subjective well-being* specifically designed for use with older adults (Philadelphia Geriatric Center Morale Scale, PGCMS; Lawton, 1975; Liang & Bollen, 1983; McCulloch, 1991). The items regarding past and present life satisfaction together with the PGCMS were included in the BASE Intake Assessment. The other items were presented in an interview about aspects of self and personality in the BASE Intensive Protocol. Items in all measures were read aloud by an interviewer and simultaneously presented visually in large font. The subject's response to each item on a five-point scale was recorded by the interviewer.

Results are described in three sections, corresponding to the central questions outlined earlier (for further details, refer to Smith, Fleeson, Geiselmann, Settersten, & Kunzmann, 1996). To begin, we describe average levels of reported well-being across the entire BASE sample. Then we examine age-related and subgroup differences in subjective well-being. After reporting these data, we turn to the third question about predictors of subjective well-being. Here we report the results of a series of hierarchical multiple regressions examining the predictive model outlined in Figure 17.1. The goal of these analyses was to determine the cumulative direct and indirect contributions of sociodemographic characteristics, objective life conditions, and subjective domain evaluations to predicting overall subjective well-being. The PGCMS was used as the outcome measure.

2.1   *Average Levels of Subjective Well-Being Reported by the BASE Participants*

Overall 63% of BASE participants reported that they were satisfied or very satisfied with their life at present ($M = 3.7$ [max. = 5], $SD = .97$), 83% reported that they were satisfied or very satisfied when they looked back over their life ($M = 4.1$ [max. = 5], $SD = .84$), and 63% expected to be satisfied in the future ($M = 3.5$ [max. = 5], $SD = 1.1$). These levels are similar to those reported from earlier West German social welfare surveys (Glatzer, 1992; Glatzer & Zapf, 1984). Responses for the three time frames of life satisfaction, moreover, were moderately related to each other (correlations ranged from .14 to .38), indicating that although average satisfaction ratings were similar, older adults distinguished between these three perspectives on life satisfaction (cf. Brandtstädter & Wentura, 1994; Shmotkin, 1991).

In general, the BASE participants also reported experiencing positive affect more often ($M = 3.2$, $SD = .59$) than negative affect ($M = 2.3$, $SD = .61$; $F(1, 508) = 621.05$, $p < .001$; see also Kunzmann, 1998). The correlation between positive affect and negative affect was essentially zero (.04), as is typically found in younger samples, supporting the notion that the experience of these two affect dimensions is independent and that they contribute differentially to overall well-being. Positive affect was positively correlated with life satisfaction ($r = .30$, .30, and .17 for the present, future, and past respectively), and negative affect was negatively correlated with satisfaction ratings ($r = -.35$, -.26, and -.10 respectively).

Overall well-being (mean score on the 15-item PGCMS) was positive ($M = 3.56$, $SD = .62$; interitem consistency, Cronbach's $\alpha = .85$). This overall score correlated $r = .20$ with positive affect, $r = -.60$ with negative affect, $r = .36$ with past life satisfaction, and $r = .34$ with expected future satisfaction (satisfaction with present life is included as a dimension of the PGCMS). In the literature, the PGCMS has always been reported in terms of an overall score (see Liang & Bollen, 1983; McCulloch, 1991). In the BASE sample, however, LISREL modeling suggested that three first-order factors could be extracted (nonagitation, satisfaction with aging, and life satisfaction), although these factors were correlated (nonagitation with aging satisfaction, $r = .51$; nonagitation with life satisfaction, $r = .71$; aging satisfaction with life satisfaction, $r = .76$). In this chapter, we nevertheless retained the traditional procedure of using the overall score.

Although ratings on all measures were generally positively skewed, there were still considerable individual differences. Figure 17.2 illustrates this finding for the PGCMS. Each point in this figure represents one or more persons. This figure also shows the location in the total distribution of those individuals in the BASE sample who were diagnosed as having some level of dementia (cf. Helmchen et al., Chapter 6). As can be seen, individuals in this subgroup also exhibited substantial individual differences in general well-being.

2.2   *Age/Cohort and Subgroup Differences in Overall Subjective Well-Being*

Within the cross-sectional BASE sample, there was some indication that overall subjective well-being (PGCMS), expected future life satisfaction, and especially the experience of positive emotions including happiness may decrease from age 70 to over 100. Each of these measures showed significant but relatively small negative age corre-

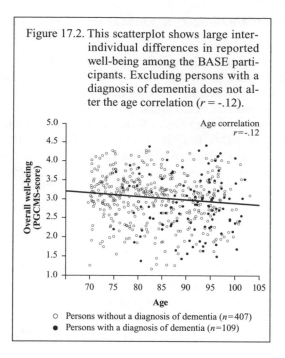

Figure 17.2. This scatterplot shows large inter-individual differences in reported well-being among the BASE participants. Excluding persons with a diagnosis of dementia does not alter the age correlation ($r = -.12$).

lations: for overall well-being, $r = -.12$ ($p < .01$); expected future life satisfaction, $r = -.12$ ($p < .01$); and positive affect, $r = -.22$ ($p < .01$; cf. Smith & Baltes, Chapter 7). Of the PGCMS subscales, satisfaction with one's own aging showed the highest negative correlation with age, $r = -.25$. Age was *not* correlated with the reported experience of negative affect ($r = -.04$), past life satisfaction ($r = .05$), or with present life satisfaction ($r = -.06$). These findings extend the age-related trends reported in studies that have compared age groups from 20 to 75 years (e.g., Brandtstädter & Wentura, 1994; Campbell et al., 1976; Herzog et al., 1982; McNeil, Stones, & Kozma, 1986; Shmotkin, 1990). Subsequent analyses of longitudinal follow-ups of the BASE sample have indicated that these small age-related correlations do represent age-related change (Maier, Kunzmann, & Smith, 1997).

The zero-order correlations reported above of course capture only linear relationships between age and well-being. We also examined the possibility of nonlinear relationships with age/cohort groups and compared the levels for other subgroups within the cross-sectional BASE sample. Results are illustrated in Figure 17.3.

As the graphic presentation of mean levels suggests, subgroup differences within BASE were relatively small. The data in Figure 17.3 have been standardized to an overall mean of 50 and a standard deviation of ±10. In fact, most of the significant results described below represent differences of less than half a standard deviation. Our regression analyses (reported in the next section) indicated that taken together, age, gender, marital status, and institutionalization accounted for 6% of the variance in subjective well-being (a level that is similar to studies with younger samples; e.g., Diener, 1994).

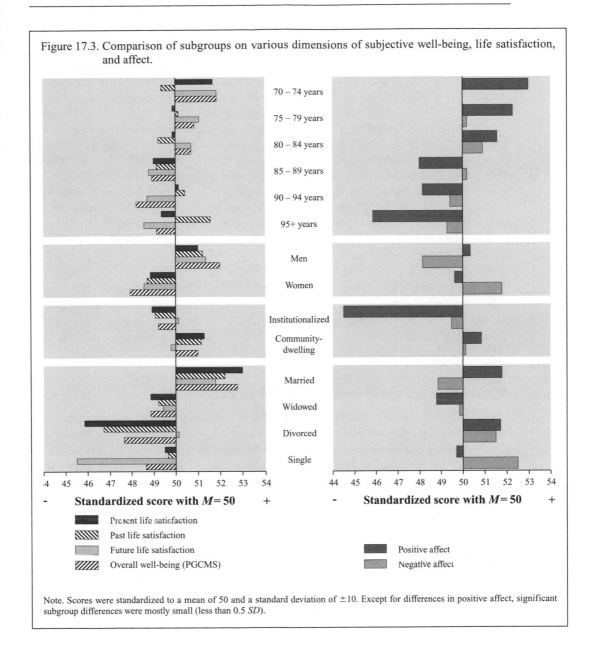

Figure 17.3. Comparison of subgroups on various dimensions of subjective well-being, life satisfaction, and affect.

Note. Scores were standardized to a mean of 50 and a standard deviation of ±10. Except for differences in positive affect, significant subgroup differences were mostly small (less than 0.5 *SD*).

Within the BASE sample (*N* = 516), significant subgroup differences in life satisfaction and overall well-being (all at *p* < .01) were found for gender, marital status, and institutionalization, but did not reach significance for comparisons of the six age/cohort groups. The largest differences in present life satisfaction, past life satisfaction, and overall well-being were found for comparisons of married versus divorced persons. For expected future satisfaction, the largest differences were between married and single persons. This pattern of results is similar to that found in most large population surveys:

Married persons generally report higher subjective well-being than all categories of un-married persons (Andrews & Withey, 1976; Campbell et al., 1976). In the BASE sample, many more men than women were currently married (or living with a partner), so that the significant but small gender difference also reflects these differences in life circum-stances (see M. M. Baltes et al., Chapter 9; Smith & Baltes, in press).

As Figure 17.3 also shows, there were subgroup differences in the reported experi-ence of positive and negative affect. Here age/cohort group, marital status, and institu-tionalization produced significant differences (all at $p < .001$) in the reported experience of positive affect (happiness and enjoyment). In fact, for positive affect (besides institu-tionalization, see below), age proved to have the most decisive negative effect: 70- to 84-year-olds differed from adults aged 85 and above by half a standard deviation. With re-gard to negative affect, only gender ($p < .001$) made a difference. Women in all age groups have been found to report feeling more negative affect and emotional upset than men (Campbell et al., 1976; Spreitzer & Snyder, 1974), a finding that was replicated within the BASE sample.

As several authors (e.g., Birren et al., 1991; Lawton, 1991; Okun, Stock, Haring, & Witter, 1984) have also pointed out, the institutionalized are an identifiable subgroup of older adults who appear to be at risk for lowered well-being, and this was also found in the institutionalized subgroup of BASE. Participants living in institutions reported less frequent experience of positive affect compared with participants living in private house-holds (the difference was 0.5 *SD*).

2.3   *Prediction of Overall Subjective Well-Being*

The descriptive analyses reported above indicated that the sociodemographic variables (age, gender, marital status, and place of residence) provide only limited ex-planatory power for subjective well-being in old age (except, perhaps, for the results on positive affect). Being older in the period of late adulthood apparently represents only a small risk for lower overall well-being but a somewhat higher risk for less frequent expe-riences of positive affect.

We expected that, compared with age, objective life conditions and subjective domain-specific evaluations would be stronger predictors of individual differences in subjective well-being. As reviewed earlier in this chapter, previous studies with younger age groups have suggested that personal evaluations of health, financial conditions, in-terpersonal and family relationships, and participation in social activities are powerful determinants of subjective well-being (Campbell et al., 1976; Herzog et al., 1982). To date, the few studies that have examined objective status in these life domains report stronger links between domain satisfactions and overall subjective well-being than be-tween objective status and subjective well-being (Krause, 1991; Larson, 1978; Lehman, 1983; Okun et al., 1984).

2.3.1   *Results for the Predictive Model Presented in Figure 17.1*
In the following, we consider the various parts of a predictive path analysis in detail (cf. the model presented in Fig. 17.1). We systematically compared the relative direct and in-direct effects of objective and subjective variables within and across domains in predict-ing overall subjective well-being (the total PGCMS score). The arrows in Figure 17.1 suggest causal directions resulting from theory-based statistical analyses. Within the

constraints of the present cross-sectional data from BASE, we are of course restricted in interpretation with regard to cause and outcome as well as temporal relationships. We take the lead from other principal researchers in the field, however (Campbell et al., 1976; George et al., 1985), and consider the regression results as providing tentative evidence for the theoretical causal model.

Six pairs of objective and subjective measures from domains assessed in BASE were used in the hierarchical regression analyses (see also Fig. 17.4). Three of the six pairs represented different aspects of health associated with psychological stress in old age (namely, multimorbidity, physical impairment, and sensory functioning) and the other three represented other important life conditions (financial situation, social participation, family network). Descriptive information about these 12 constructs can be found in other chapters of this book.

The objective measure of multimorbidity (number of diagnosed moderate to severe physical illnesses, $M = 3.69$) was based on thorough medical examinations by professional physicians (see Steinhagen-Thiessen & Borchelt, Chapter 5). This was paired with a standard single-item self-evaluation of health status (five-point scale, $M = 2.91$). Physical mobility impairment (balance and gait) was assessed objectively with tasks adapted from Tinetti (1986) and paired with a subjective evaluation of the distance that could be walked without pain (six-point scale of subjective mobility; see also Steinhagen-Thiessen & Borchelt, Chapter 5). Audiometric and standard visual tests were used to measure sensory acuity (for details, see Marsiske et al., Chapter 13). In this domain, participants were also asked to rate subjectively their difficulties in hearing and vision.

Details about the indicators of the financial situation, social participation, and the family network are given in Chapter 8 by Mayer et al. Equivalent income was used as an objective measure of financial situation and was paired with a self-report of satisfaction with current finances (four-point scale, $M = 3.21$). A detailed interview regarding social participation in the previous year provided a fairly objective measure of the frequency of social activities outside the home which could be paired with reported satisfaction with these social activities. The number of kin living in Berlin was derived from family documents and from information obtained in the family history inventory (see also Wagner et al., Chapter 10). In addition, as part of the interview on the personal support network, participants were asked how satisfied they were with contacts with their family and friends.

The results of the path analysis are summarized graphically in Figure 17.4. The central finding was that *subjective domain evaluations were stronger predictors of subjective well-being than were the objective measures of domain status.*[2] In Figure 17.4, five of the six arrows pointing directly to subjective well-being come from subjective domain evaluations (namely, subjective health, vision, finances, activities, and satisfaction with social relationships). There are no direct arrows (i.e., significant direct predictions) from the objective measures of status and functioning in these domains to subjective well-being, and only one direct arrow is carried through from the sociodemographic level (gender).[3]

---

[2] Note that this finding is not the result of overlapping (circularity). None of the items used for assessing predictors and outcome variables is identical.

[3] Adding interaction terms, we ran additional analyses to find out whether age moderates the relationships between general well-being, and objective and subjective predictors. None of these interactions was significant.

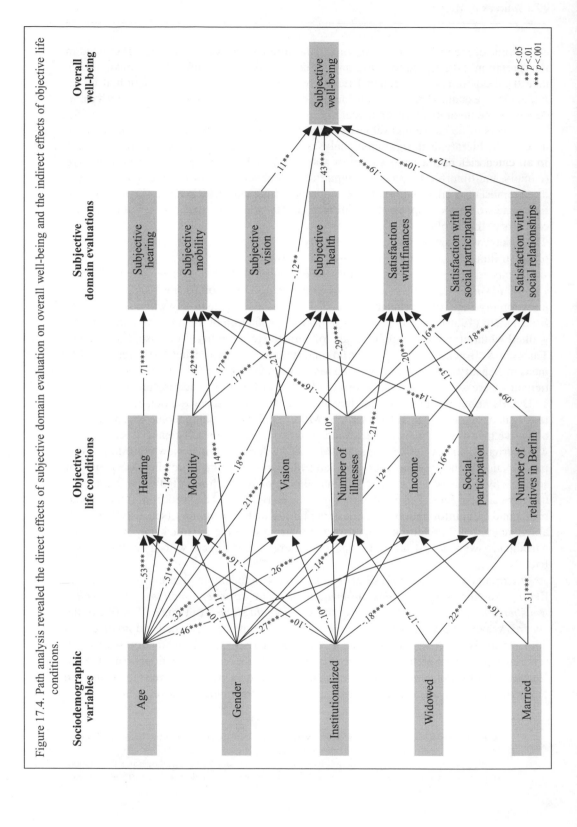

Figure 17.4. Path analysis revealed the direct effects of subjective domain evaluation on overall well-being and the indirect effects of objective life conditions.

For clarity of presentation in Figure 17.4, we have only included arrows (and standardized β-levels) between variables where predictive relationships proved to be significant. However, all possible direct and indirect cross-relationships were tested in the hierarchical regressions. That is, we examined a fully saturated model in which all categories of variables (sociodemographic and objective status, and subjective domain evaluations) had an equal chance to predict subjective well-being. It is important to note when considering this figure that the path β-values represent correlations after all other variables in all categories prior to the dependent variable have been controlled. For example, the β-value -.29 from the number of illnesses to subjective health is the result after controlling for all other objective domain measures and for all of the sociodemographic variables. Likewise, the β-value of .43 from subjective health to subjective well-being is the result after controlling for all subjective, objective, and sociodemographic variables. Thus, these values may differ from the zero-order and partial correlations reported elsewhere in this chapter and in other chapters of this book.

The total model explained 42% of the variance in overall subjective well-being. As a further look at the associations between subjective well-being and the sociodemographic, objective, and subjective variables, we ran separate regression analyses in which we entered only the variables of one category (i.e., only the sociodemographic status, the objective status, or the subjective domain evaluations). These analyses confirmed our hypotheses. For example, the sociodemographic variables (age together with gender, marital status, and institutionalization) accounted for 6% of the variance in overall subjective well-being, the indicators of objective life circumstances together accounted for 10%, whereas the domain-specific subjective evaluations together accounted for 38% in overall subjective well-being. Thus, subjective well-being is primarily related to the subjective evaluation of different life domains.

2.3.2 The Direct and Indirect Influence of Life Circumstances on Subjective Well-Being

What then is the overall predictive route toward subjective well-being? As it would take too long to describe and interpret all of the paths in Figure 17.4 (the within-domain relationships have in any case been outlined and discussed in many of the other chapters of this book), we focus on the overall picture. In doing so, we will highlight findings that speak to the relative predictive power of objective domain status versus subjective domain evaluations. We also note, once again, that any implications regarding the causal direction of relationships have to be treated with caution, given that cross-sectional data were analyzed.

The model begins with individual differences in fundamental life circumstances defined by the sociodemographic variables: age, gender (males = 1; females = 2), place of residence (institutionalized = 1; community-dwelling = 0), marital status (married = 1; not married = 0), and widowhood (yes = 1; no = 0). In general, age, gender, and institutionalization (after controlling for the other sociodemographic variables) show varying relationships to most of the objective life conditions sampled. These sociodemographic variables also directly predict subjective domain evaluations (even after controlling for objective domain status).

Of the five sociodemographic variables, only gender remained at the end of the path model as a unique direct predictor of subjective well-being. The negative β-value (-.12) indicates that males in the BASE sample generally reported higher subjective well-being than females, a finding consistent with most population surveys (e.g., Andrews & Withey, 1976; Campbell et al., 1976; Glatzer, 1992; Glatzer & Zapf, 1984). These reports of higher satisfaction and well-being are usually coupled with findings that elderly males form the more financially and socially advantaged groups in samples of older adults.

The middle section of the model (Fig. 17.4) reveals an intricate pattern of relationships between objective indicators of domain functioning and subjective evaluations of these domains. With the exceptions of social participation and family life, the within-domain relationships between objective status and subjective evaluation were significant (for hearing, $\beta = .71$; mobility, $\beta = .42$; vision, $\beta = .21$; number of illnesses, $\beta = .29$; and finances, $\beta = .20$).

In the domains of health, sensory functioning, and mobility, BASE participants were not asked directly about their domain-specific satisfaction, but were asked instead to evaluate their capacities. Although not ideal (e.g., it is possible for instance that "satisfaction" judgments do not match "goodness" or "capacity" judgments), these "subjective" measures were nevertheless included in the regression analyses out of pragmatic necessity. There is also considerable support for this procedure in the gerontological literature (see George, 1981; Okun et al., 1984).

The finding that objective and subjective measures of social participation and family life did not correspond is not particularly surprising, especially given the type of objective variables included in the present analyses. Although one might have a large network of kin in close residence, this does not guarantee the frequent or even enjoyable contact that might afford subjective well-being (Antonucci, 1990; Rook, 1984). It is also possible to imagine that for some individuals, one significant other could provide more satisfying experiences than several social partners (Carstensen, 1993). Similarly, a large number of different activities may not be the best route to satisfaction. More likely, individual standards of evaluation relate to particular types of activity rather than to their sheer number.

Objective status in some domains also had pervasive effects on satisfaction with other domains. As might be expected, this was especially true for physical health (as measured by the number of moderate to severe illnesses), followed by mobility. For example, physical health (after controlling for all other objective and sociodemographic variables) predicted the subjective evaluation of physical impairment (-.15), satisfaction with social participation (-.16), and satisfaction with social relationships (-.18). Furthermore, objective status in family life (number of relatives) and social participation (number of social activities) also showed cross-domain relationships: Both were significant predictors of satisfaction with finances.

It is interesting to note that, in this analysis of BASE data, income was only related to its own subjective measure ($\beta = .20$). This finding is consistent with reports from other representative samples of older adults (Krause, 1991; Krause & Baker, 1992; Larson, 1978). These studies have also found that, although the relationship between actual income and overall subjective well-being is significant, income itself accounts for only a small proportion (between 1% and 5%) of the variance in well-being. Compared with younger adults, adults over 70 years are less likely to report that they worry about their present and future material resources (Herzog et al., 1982). Satisfaction with the current financial situation is, nevertheless, a powerful predictor of life satisfaction and happiness (Herzog et al., 1982; Krause, 1991; Lawton, 1983). This was also the case in BASE ($\beta = .19$).

2.3.3 Direct Predictors of Well-Being in the BASE Model

After controlling for all these cross-domain relationships, the following *direct* paths to subjective well-being remained significant (the right-hand section of Fig. 17.4): subjective health (.43), subjective evaluation of vision (.11), satisfaction with current finances (.19), satisfaction with social relationships (.13), satisfaction with social participation (.10), and gender (-.12). Clearly, after controlling for all categories of variables, there were more direct paths remaining from subjective evaluations to subjective well-being than from objective indicators or sociodemographic variables, supporting previous findings from younger samples.

Subjective health proved to be the strongest predictor, followed by satisfaction with current finances. Furthermore, we found that in addition to evaluations of the prime areas of life (health, wealth, and love), two other aspects of life were significant, namely, subjective evaluation of visual acuity and satisfaction with social participation. We did not find support for theoretical expectations that judgments of life satisfaction and well-being increase with advancing age if the disadvantages of poor health and other losses are controlled for (George et al., 1985; Herzog et al., 1982). However, being female represented a risk factor for lower subjective well-being, even after controlling for all other variables in this model (cf. M. M. Baltes et al., Chapter 9; Smith & Baltes, in press).

Since the strongest predictors were subjective evaluations, we wondered to what extent diagnosed dementia and/or depression might have influenced our findings. To investigate this, we ran the same regression analyses, excluding all participants with diagnosed dementia or major depression. These analyses produced similar predictive patterns to those reported in Figure 17.4.

3   Objective Life Conditions and Subjective Well-Being: A Paradox?

Did the objective life conditions of the older adults in the BASE sample in any way represent a "risk" for subjective well-being? In order to interpret the results of the predictive analyses with regard to the paradox mentioned earlier (i.e., the frequently found discrepancy between life conditions and reported positive well-being), we decided to take a closer look at the actual status of BASE participants on these domains. Specifically, we asked whether objective life conditions exhibited negative age-related trends. Significant negative age group differences (indicative of decline) in objective life conditions (e.g., more illnesses, less income, fewer kin in close residence) could be considered as risks for lowered subjective well-being.

Figure 17.5 illustrates age/cohort group mean-level trends for objective status in those domains considered in the predictive model and, as a comparison, those for subjective well-being (PGCMS). For ease of comparison, all scores in Figure 17.5 were standardized to a sample mean of 50 and standard deviation of ±10. Results for different domains are offset in separate rows to highlight different trends.

As already reported, age-related variation in subjective well-being was minimal but significant in the BASE sample. What becomes apparent from Figure 17.5 is that there were also *minimal* variations in the so-called prime domains of life (Larson, 1978; Law-

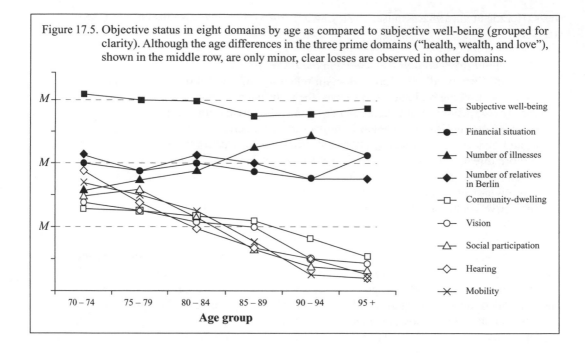

Figure 17.5. Objective status in eight domains by age as compared to subjective well-being (grouped for clarity). Although the age differences in the three prime domains ("health, wealth, and love"), shown in the middle row, are only minor, clear losses are observed in other domains.

ton, 1983): health (here number of moderate to severe illnesses, BASE sample average $M = 3.6$), wealth (equivalent monthly income, $M = 2,017$ DM),[4] and love (number of relatives residing in Berlin, $M = 4$). This pattern contrasts sharply to the negative trends evident on other measures: especially, sensory functioning (vision and hearing), physical mobility, social participation, and likelihood of institutionalization (on average, more than one standard deviation).

What does this mean in terms of the paradox described earlier (i.e., regarding the frequently found discrepancy between life conditions and reported positive well-being)? The answer is twofold. It is generally expected that old age brings negative changes in life conditions – and, indeed, that objective life conditions further deteriorate over the years from 70 to over 100. As Figure 17.5 illustrates, however, the age groups in the BASE sample differed little in some indicators of the central life domains and substantially in others. Of course, this pattern of results could be misleading. For example, the measures plotted here might not be the best indicators of actual status and/or functioning in each of these domains (compare these trends with those for other domain variables reported by Steinhagen-Thiessen & Borchelt, Chapter 5; Helmchen et al., Chapter 6; Mayer et al., Chapter 8; Wagner et al., Chapter 10; Borchelt et al., Chapter 15). It could also be that substantial changes, especially in the domains of health, wealth, and love, occur before the age of 70. Nevertheless, it is particularly interesting to find that the objective indicators of prime domains proposed to predict well-being show so little varia-

---

[4] This equivalent income was computed by excluding one participant who was still working and had reported a rather high monthly income.

tion across the BASE age groups, and that these age-related trends correspond with those obtained in subjective well-being.

Thus, the first answer is that part of the paradox does not even exist: The prime objective life conditions were rather similar for the old and the very old in BASE. The second part of the answer is what we have stressed throughout: Namely, objective life conditions primarily have indirect effects on subjective well-being. Thus, even when objective conditions do deteriorate, the effects on subjective well-being appear to be cushioned by the individual's interpretation of change.

4   Final Comments

In this chapter, we have attempted to integrate two traditions in well-being research. Rather than setting our own criteria for what constitutes "a good life," we accepted as outcome measures the BASE participants' own reports of their personal well-being and life satisfaction. Our central analyses focused, however, on asking whether objective life conditions (e.g., many illnesses, low income) or individuals' evaluations of domain functioning would be the best predictors of subjective well-being. Specifically, we wondered whether age-related decline in health would be so overwhelming in its impact (especially in the later decades of old age), that participants would lower their expressions of well-being.

The obtained pattern of findings is multifaceted. On the one hand, the results indicate a high level of stability in old age and point to the power of processes associated with self-regulation and social expectation. Overall, 63% of BASE participants reported that they were satisfied or very satisfied with their present life and that they were optimistic about the future. On the other hand, the results indicate that some aspects of well-being do show negative age trends in later life (70 to 100+ years; see also Maier et al., 1997). For example, participants aged 85 and above reported less frequent experience of positive affect and less satisfaction with aging than those aged 70 to 84.

Predictive analyses indicated that BASE participants' general sense of well-being represented a compound of their satisfactions with the specific facets of health, visual acuity, finances, family and friends, and social participation. The effects of specific objective life conditions on overall subjective well-being were filtered through these subjective domain-specific evaluations. Furthermore, age, gender, and sociodemographic variables (i.e., marital status, institutionalization) together accounted for only a small amount (6%) of the variation in overall subjective well-being. In the overall predictive model, these variables (apart from gender) also only showed indirect paths to subjective well-being.

A closer look at the objective life conditions of the BASE participants revealed that some showed little variation across the age groups from 70 to over 100 years. This was particularly so for those life domains that have been principally related to well-being in previous research, namely, health, wealth, and love (i.e., social life). Perhaps the prevailing expectation that very old age is a life phase beset by more losses than gains and a shrinking life perspective is mistaken. Many losses (especially in vision, hearing, mobility, and in intellectual functioning) occur gradually (cf. other chapters in this book), and their onset may be in late middle age. It is possible that the processes of progressive adjustment to these life changes are already well in place by the age of 70. These changes of the aging body and mind are perhaps also seen as being inevitable and beyond control. Perceived losses in the domains of family, social life, and finances, and increased number and severity of chronic illnesses are perhaps more critical because they are considered to be subject to personal control and intervention.

Overall, the BASE data on subjective well-being suggest a rather positive picture of old age. The majority of the BASE participants reported being satisfied with the lives they had led, somewhat contented with the present, and relatively free from anxiety about the future. But it is important, once again, to emphasize that these subjective reports of life satisfaction represent the end product of complex psychological processes geared at presenting a positive "face" to the world. Even in the face of severe life constraints, positive well-being is maintained by means of gradual adaptation, change of comparison standards, and lowering of aspirations.

There may well be limits to this capacity for psychological adaptation or resilience (cf. Staudinger et al., Chapter 11), as indicated by a closer look at individual aspects of subjective well-being in specific subgroups (cf. Fig. 17.3; see also Smith & Baltes, Chapter 7). Furthermore, a more detailed look at specific components of well-being (e.g., the experience of positive affect or satisfaction with aging) may provide a different perspective on the challenges to life satisfaction that accumulate with increasing age.

The picture of well-being gained from self-reports says little about the potential that exists to increase the levels of well-being attained in old age. There is much room for improving the life conditions of older adults (cf. Mayer et al., Chapter 18). In spite of the recognition of self-regulatory adaptation processes, future technological and political developments should provide for improvements in the life conditions of older adults. It is this group of the very old that will form an increasingly large part of the total population in the future, entailing many new challenges for our society. Only by taking into account this development and by implementing special policies for the improvement of life circumstances will it be possible to promote a positive "culture of aging" (P. B. Baltes & Baltes, 1992).

References

Andrews, F. M., & McKennell, A. C. (1980). Measures of self-reported well-being: Their affective, cognitive, and other components. *Social Indicators Research, 8,* 127–155.

Andrews, F. M., & Withey, S. B. (1976). *Social indicators of well-being: America's perception of life quality.* New York: Plenum Press.

Antonucci, T. C. (1990). Social supports and social relationships. In R. H. Binstock & L. K. George (Eds.), *Handbook of aging and the social sciences* (3rd ed., pp. 205–227). San Diego, CA: Academic Press.

Atchley, R. C. (1991). The influence of aging or frailty on perceptions and expressions of the self: Theoretical and methodological issues. In J. E. Birren, J. E. Lubben, J. C. Rowe, & D. E. Deutchman (Eds.), *The concept and measurement of quality of life in the frail elderly* (pp. 207–225). San Diego, CA: Academic Press.

Baltes, P. B. (1991). The many faces of human ageing: Toward a psychological culture of old age. *Psychological Medicine, 21,* 837–854.

Baltes, P. B., & Baltes, M. M. (1990). Psychological perspectives on successful aging: The model of selective optimization with compensation. In P. B. Baltes & M. M. Baltes (Eds.), *Successful aging: Perspectives from the behavioral sciences* (pp. 1–34). Cambridge: Cambridge University Press.

Baltes, P. B., & Baltes, M. M. (1992). Gerontologie: Begriff, Herausforderung und Brennpunkte. In P. B. Baltes & J. Mittelstraß (Eds.), *Zukunft des Alterns und gesellschaftliche Entwicklung* (pp. 1–34). Berlin: de Gruyter.

Birren, J. E., Lubben, J. E., Rowe, J. C., & Deutchman, D. E. (Eds.). (1991). *The concept and measurement of quality of life in the frail elderly.* San Diego, CA: Academic Press.

Brandtstädter, J., & Greve, W. (1994). The aging self: Stabilizing and protective processes. *Developmental Review, 14,* 52–80.

Brandtstädter, J., & Wentura, D. (1994). Veränderungen der Zeit- und Zukunftsperspektive im Übergang zum höheren Erwachsenenalter: Entwicklungspsychologische und differentielle Aspekte. *Zeitschrift für Entwicklungspsychologie und Pädagogische Psychologie, 26,* 2–21.

Brief, A. P., Butcher, A. H., George, J. M., & Link, K. E. (1993). Integrating bottom-up and top-down theories of subjective well-being: The case of health. *Journal of Personality and Social Psychology, 64,* 646–653.

Brim, O. J., Jr. (1992). *Ambition: Losing and winning in everyday life.* New York: Basic Books.

Bullinger, M., & Pöppel, E. (1988). Lebensqualität in der Medizin: Schlagwort oder Forschungsansatz. *Deutsches Ärzteblatt, 85,* 504–505.

Campbell, A., Converse, P. E., & Rodgers, W. L. (1976). *The quality of American life: Perceptions, evaluations, and satisfactions.* New York: Russell Sage Foundation.

Carstensen, L. L. (1993). Motivation for social contact across the life-span: A theory of socioemotional selectivity. In J. Jacobs (Ed.), *Nebraska Symposium on Motivation* (Vol. 40, pp. 209–254). Lincoln: University of Nebraska Press.

Carstensen, L. L., & Cone, J. D. (1983). Social desirability and the measurement of psychological well-being in elderly persons. *Journal of Gerontology, 38,* 713–715.

Diener, E. (1984). Subjective well-being. *Psychological Bulletin, 95,* 542–575.

Diener, E. (1994). Assessing subjective well-being: Progress and opportunities. *Social Indicators Research, 31,* 103–157.

Emmons, R. A., & Diener, E. (1985). Factors predicting satisfaction judgments: A comparative examination. *Social Indicators Research, 16,* 157–167.

Filipp, S.-H., & Ferring, D. (1989). Zur Alters- und Bereichsspezifität subjektiven Alterserlebens. *Zeitschrift für Entwicklungspsychologie und Pädagogische Psychologie, 21,* 279–293.

Filipp, S.-H., & Schmidt, K. (1994). Die Rolle sozioökologischer Variablen in einem Bedingungsmodell der Lebenszufriedenheit alter Menschen: Eine Übersicht. *Zeitschrift für Entwicklungspsychologie und Pädagogische Psychologie, 26,* 218–240.

George, L. K. (1981). Subjective well-being: Conceptual and methodological issues. In C. Eisdorfer (Ed.), *Annual review of gerontology and geriatrics* (Vol. 2, pp. 345–382). New York: Springer.

George, L. K., Okun, M. A., & Landerman, R. (1985). Age as a moderator of the determinants of life satisfaction. *Research on Aging, 7,* 209–233.

Glatzer, W. (1992). Die Lebensqualität älterer Menschen in Deutschland. *Zeitschrift für Gerontologie, 25,* 137–144.

Glatzer, W., & Zapf, W. (1984). *Lebensqualität in der Bundesrepublik: Objektive Lebens-bedingungen und subjektives Wohlbefinden.* Frankfurt/M.: Campus.

Hagestad, G. O., & Neugarten, B. L. (1985). Age and the life course. In R. H. Binstock & E. Shanas (Eds.), *Handbook of aging and the social sciences* (2nd ed., pp. 35–61). New York: Van Nostrand Reinhold.

Heckhausen, J., Dixon, R. A., & Baltes, P. B. (1989). Gains and losses in development throughout adulthood as perceived by different age groups. *Developmental Psychology, 255*, 109–121.

Herzog, A. R., Rodgers, W. L., & Woodworth, J. (1982). *Subjective well-being among different age groups* (Research Report Series). Ann Arbor: University of Michigan, Institute for Social Research, Survey Research Center.

Krause, N. (1991). Stress and isolation from close ties in later life. *Journal of Gerontology: Social Sciences, 46*, S183–S194.

Krause, N., & Baker, E. (1992). Financial strain, economic values, and somatic symptoms in later life. *Psychology and Aging, 7*, 4–14.

Kunzmann, U. (1998). *Being and feeling in control: Two sources of older people's emotional well-being.* Unpublished doctoral thesis, Free University of Berlin.

Land, K. C. (1983). Social indicators. In R. H. Turner & J. F. Short Jr. (Eds.), *Annual review of sociology* (Vol. 9, pp. 1–26). Palo Alto, CA: Annual Reviews Inc.

Larson, R. (1978). Thirty years of research on the subjective well-being of older Americans. *Journal of Gerontology, 33*, 109–125.

Lawton, M. P. (1975). The Philadelphia Geriatric Center Morale Scale: A revision. *Journal of Gerontology, 30*, 85–89.

Lawton, M. P. (1983). Environment and other determinants of well-being in older people. *The Gerontologist, 23*, 349–357.

Lawton, M. P. (1985). The elderly in context: Perspectives from environmental psychology and gerontology. *Environment and Behavior, 17*, 501–519.

Lawton, M. P. (1991). A multidimensional view of quality of life in frail elders. In J. E. Birren, J. E. Lubben, J. C. Rowe, & D. E. Deutchman (Eds.), *The concept and measurement of quality of life in the frail elderly* (pp. 3–27). San Diego, CA: Academic Press.

Lehman, A. F. (1983). The well-being of chronic mental patients: Assessing their quality of life. *Archives of General Psychiatry, 40*, 369–373.

Liang, J., & Bollen, K. A. (1983). The structure of the Philadelphia Geriatric Center Morale Scale: A reinterpretation. *Journal of Gerontology, 38*, 181–189.

Maier, H., Kunzmann, U., & Smith, J. (1997, November). *Subjective well-being in old age: Longitudinal evidence for both stability and change.* Poster presented at the 50th Annual Scientific Meeting of the Gerontological Society of America, Cincinnati, OH.

McCulloch, B. J. (1991). A longitudinal investigation of the factor structure of subjective well-being: The case of the Philadelphia Geriatric Center Morale Scale. *Journal of Gerontology: Psychological Sciences, 46*, P251–P258.

McNeil, J. K., Stones, M. J., & Kozma, A. (1986). Subjective well-being in later life: Issues concerning measurement and prediction. *Social Indicators Research, 18*, 35–70.

Michalos, A. C. (1985). Multiple discrepancies theory. *Social Indicators Research, 16*, 347–413.

Miller, D. T., & Prentice, D. A. (1996). The construction of social norms and standards. In E. T. Higgins & A. W. Kruglanski (Eds.), *Social psychology: Handbook of basic principles* (pp. 799–829). New York: Guilford Press.

Myers, D. G., & Diener, E. (1995). Who is happy? *Psychological Science, 6*, 10–19.

Okun, M. A., Stock, W. A., Haring, M. J., & Witter, R. A. (1984). Health and subjective well-being: A meta-analysis. *International Journal of Aging and Human Development, 19*, 111–132.

Patrick, D. L., & Erickson, P. (1993). *Health status and health policy: Quality of life in health care evaluation and resource allocation.* New York: Oxford University Press.

Rawls, J. (1971). *A theory of social justice.* Cambridge: Cambridge University Press.

Rook, K. S. (1984). The negative side of social interaction: Impact on psychological well-being. *Journal of Personality and Social Psychology, 46*, 1097–1108.

Rosow, I. (1985). Status and role change through the life cycle. In R. H. Binstock & E. Shanas (Eds.), *Handbook of aging and the social sciences* (2nd ed., pp. 62–93). New York: Van Nostrand Reinhold.

Rowe, J. W., & Kahn, R. L. (1987). Human aging: Usual and successful. *Science, 237*, 143–149.

Ryff, C. D. (1989). Happiness is everything, or is it? Explorations on the meaning of psychological well-being. *Journal of Personality and Social Psychology, 57*, 1069–1081.

Ryff, C. D., & Essex, M. J. (1991). Psychological well-being in adulthood and old age: Descriptive markers and explanatory processes. In K. W. Schaie & M. P. Lawton (Eds.), *Annual review of gerontology and geriatrics* (Vol. 11, pp. 144–171). New York: Springer.

Schuessler, K. F., & Fisher, G. A. (1985). Quality of life research and sociology. In R. H. Turner & J. F. Short Jr. (Eds.), *Annual review of sociology* (Vol. 11, pp. 129–149). Palo Alto, CA: Annual Reviews.

Schwarz, N., & Strack, F. (1991). Evaluating one's life: A judgment model of subjective well-being. In F. Strack, M. Argyle, & N. Schwarz (Eds.), *Subjective well-being: An interdisciplinary perspective* (pp. 27–47). Oxford: Pergamon Press.

Shmotkin, D. (1990). Subjective well-being as a function of age and gender: A multivariate look for differentiated trends. *Social Indicators Research, 23*, 201–230.

Shmotkin, D. (1991). The role of time orientation in life satisfaction across the life span. *Journal of Gerontology: Psychological Sciences, 46*, P243–P250.

Smith, J., & Baltes, M. M. (in press). The role of gender in very old age: Profiles of functioning and everyday life patterns. *Psychology and Aging.*

Smith, J., Fleeson, W., Geiselmann, B., Settersten, R., & Kunzmann, U. (1996). Wohlbefinden im hohen Alter: Vorhersagen aufgrund objektiver Lebensbedingungen und subjektiver Bewertung. In K. U. Mayer & P. B. Baltes (Eds.), *Die Berliner Altersstudie* (pp. 497–523). Berlin: Akademie Verlag.

Spreitzer, E., & Snyder, E. (1974). Correlates of life satisfaction among the aged. *Journal of Gerontology, 29*, 454–458.

Suls, J., & Wills, T. A. (Eds.). (1991). *Social comparison: Contemporary theory and research.* Hillsdale, NJ: Erlbaum.

Taylor, S. E. (1989). *Positive illusions.* New York: Basic Books.

Thomae, H. (1987). Alternsformen: Wege zu ihrer methodischen und begrifflichen Erfassung. In U. Lehr & H. Thomae (Eds.), *Formen seelischen Alterns: Ergebnisse der Bonner Gerontologischen Längsschnittstudie (BOLSA)* (pp. 173–195). Stuttgart: Enke.

Tinetti, M. E. (1986). A performance-oriented assessment of mobility problems in elderly patients. *Journal of the American Geriatrics Society, 34*, 119–126.

Tsevat, J., Weeks, J. C., Guadagnoli, E., Tosteson, A. N. A., Mangione, C. M., Pliskin, J. S., Weinstein, M. C., & Cleary, P. D. (1994). Using health-related quality-of-life information: Clinical encounters, clinical trials, and health policy. *Journal of General Internal Medicine, 9*, 576–582.

Veenhoven, R. (1991). Is happiness relative? *Social Indicators Research, 24*, 1–34.

Watson, D., Clark, L. A., & Tellegen, A. (1988). Development and validation of brief measures of positive and negative affect: The PANAS scales. *Journal of Personality and Social Psychology, 54*, 1063–1070.

Overview and Outlook

What Do We Know about Old Age and Aging? Conclusions from the Berlin Aging Study

Karl Ulrich Mayer, Paul B. Baltes, Margret M. Baltes, Markus Borchelt,
Julia Delius, Hanfried Helmchen, Michael Linden, Jacqui Smith,
Ursula M. Staudinger, Elisabeth Steinhagen-Thiessen, and Michael Wagner

1   Introduction

Our central goal in this concluding chapter is to make the presentation of BASE findings accessible to readers from different backgrounds and to elucidate some implications for social policy and application. To this end, a certain degree of overlap in the material presented is unavoidable.

To begin, we address readers with a general interest in aging research. Our aim is to show discrepancies between social expectations of old age and the evidence obtained in the Berlin Aging Study. We employ a format developed by Palmore (1988) in the Facts on Aging Quiz that confronts readers with a list of assertions about old age and aging. Using new questions and BASE findings, we then reveal the "correct" response (see Section 2).

In Section 3, we address specialists in the field of gerontology and summarize important results from each of the four BASE research units. In Section 4, we take a systemic perspective, combine these discipline-specific findings, and examine whether certain groups of older people or patterns of aging can be distinguished. In a sense, the observations offered in Section 4 are the closest we come to a wholistic view of aging, one of the stated primary objectives of BASE.

Finally, in the light of BASE findings, we consider whether current images of old age are too positive or too negative. We also discuss the implications of BASE results in terms of the theoretical conceptions of differential aging, continuity versus discontinuity, and systemic aspects of aging. Does very old age represent a continuation of previous life phases, or are there discontinuities that indicate that this final period of life is different and needs to be seen as akin to a "fourth" age of life?

2   Images of Old Age and Aging

The consequences of our beliefs and knowledge about old age and aging are manifold. Stereotypical perceptions of old age influence the way individuals regulate their own aging and our day-to-day interactions with older people. In this sense, stereotypical conceptions, beliefs, and attributions are also reflected in older adults' own attitudes about themselves, in the attitudes of the numerous persons working with and for old people, and social policies.

For some time now, gerontologists have condemned the one-sidedness of negative aging stereotypes and have promoted findings on "active," "productive," and "successful" aging. For instance, the introduction of a distinction between the "young old" and the "old old" (Karl & Tokarski, 1989; Neugarten, 1974) made it possible to uphold both a positive and a negative image of aging.

475

More recently, however, doubts have arisen suggesting that the repudiation of negative images may have gone too far – that our search for a positive image of old age may reflect our tendency to deny the existence of frailty, suffering, and death, our hopes for a long and healthy life. Just as evidence for the existence of relatively healthy and active elders may open up opportunities for individual autonomy, so the rejection of negative images focusing on decline and impairment may hinder opportunities for taking necessary compensatory action. There are probably few research areas in which scientists' and society's beliefs about what is desirable and essential influence the selection of research questions and interpretation of findings as strongly as in gerontology (P. B. Baltes & Staudinger, 1993).

In this final chapter, therefore, we follow up on Palmore's (1977, 1981) Facts on Aging Quiz approach. We pose a list of questions about old age, summarize information accumulated within the Berlin Aging Study (BASE), and contrast it with extant stereotypic beliefs. This approach will also permit readers to examine their own beliefs about old age with the presumed reality as it has so far revealed itself in BASE. Specifically, we present a list of statements about old age and aging that can be rated as "true" or "false" (Table 18.1). The following selection criteria were used: (a) The statements should refer to important aspects of old age and aging, (b) statements should be either counterintuitive or controversial in gerontology or public opinion, and (c) it should be possible to test each statement with BASE data.

2.1   Internal Medicine and Geriatrics

A1   The majority of old people are prescribed too many medications

BASE Result: False

The BASE data do not support the view that, on average, older persons take too many drugs. However, it is true that most older adults regularly receive prescription drugs. According to the BASE data (weighted to represent the population of elderly West Berliners), 92% of persons aged 70 and above take at least one drug, and 24% take five or more drugs simultaneously (Steinhagen-Thiessen & Borchelt, Chapter 5, Table 5.5). Based on individual case conferences involving various medical staff working in BASE, it was possible to assess whether these figures indicate that old people take *too many* medications.

Fourteen percent of BASE participants were judged as taking medication that was either not indicated by the individual case diagnosis or even contraindicated. Furthermore, irrespective of individual diagnoses, 19% of BASE participants took a medication that experts judged to be inappropriate for treating old people (Beers et al., 1991; Stuck et al., 1994). Thus, a total of 28% of the sample took a prescribed drug that was either not indicated, contraindicated, or inappropriate for their age group. However, despite the generally high rate of medication, instances of undermedication (i.e., untreated moderate to severe somatic diseases) were identified in 24% of the BASE sample. The main problem of drug-related medical treatment in old age, then, appears to lie in its quality rather than its quantity (Borchelt, 1995).

A2   Most old people have at least one illness

BASE Result: True

It is not easy to confirm this statement as it is highly dependent on the definition of illness (see also Statement A3). From a medical perspective, nearly all persons aged 70 and

Table 18.1. *Statements about old age and aging*

	True	False
A1 The majority of old people are prescribed too many medications.	❏	❏
A2 Most old people have at least one illness.	❏	❏
A3 Most old people report that their health is poor.	❏	❏
A4 Old women live longer and therefore have fewer illnesses than men.	❏	❏
A5 The majority of very old women need assistance in bathing or showering.	❏	❏
A6 Most biochemical reference values do not change in old age.	❏	❏
B1 Depressive disorders become more frequent in old age.	❏	❏
B2 Most persons aged 70 and above have serious impairments in intellectual functioning.	❏	❏
B3 About half of those aged 90 years and over exhibit severe mental decline (dementia).	❏	❏
B4 Most old people receive too many psychotropic drugs.	❏	❏
B5 Everyday life for older adults consists mainly of passive activity and rest.	❏	❏
C1 Old people are preoccupied with death and dying.	❏	❏
C2 Memory gets worse with age.	❏	❏
C3 Most old people are no longer able to learn new things.	❏	❏
C4 A good education and a challenging job are protective against age-related intellectual decline.	❏	❏
C5 Most old people believe that they can no longer control what happens in their life.	❏	❏
C6 Only very few older persons still have life goals.	❏	❏
C7 Older adults live mainly in the past.	❏	❏
C8 Most old people have a confidant with whom they can talk about difficult problems.	❏	❏
D1 In West Berlin, many older adults are poor.	❏	❏
D2 The number of social relationships decreases with old age.	❏	❏
D3 Most persons aged 95 and above are institutionalized.	❏	❏
D4 Children are the main caregivers of old persons who live in private households.	❏	❏
D5 People who were more socially active in their youth also participate more in social life when they are old.	❏	❏
D6 In old age, the rich are healthier than the poor.	❏	❏
D7 Women who were housewives for most of their lives are worse off in old age than women who were in paid employment.	❏	❏

Note. Follows Palmore, 1988.

above in BASE were diagnosed as having at least one illness according to the terms of the International Classification of Diseases (ICD-9; World Health Organization [WHO], 1978). Even after restricting the range of illnesses and their level of severity, 96% of the BASE sample were evaluated as having at least one moderate to severe internal, neurological, or orthopedic disease (Steinhagen-Thiessen & Borchelt, Chapter 5, Section 3.3).

Based on these data, then, it is correct to conclude that most old people have an illness. However, it is not true that most older adults are ill with an acute or medium-term threat to life. Life-threatening illnesses such as coronary heart disease or congestive heart failure were observed in less than half of the BASE sample (33%).

A3   *Most old people report that their health is poor*

BASE Result: False

On a subjective level, 29% of BASE participants aged 70 and above rated their somatic health as good or very good, 38% as satisfactory, and only 33% as fair (19%) or poor (14%). When asked to compare their health with that of their age peers, 62% perceived their own health to be better or much better, 18% to be the same, and only 10% worse or much worse.

Ratings of subjective health were not correlated with age ($r = -.01$), a finding that contrasts with indicators of objective physical health ($r = -.28$). Furthermore, with rising age, there was an increase in the tendency to perceive one's own health as better than that of one's age peers ($r = .19$; cf. Borchelt et al., Chapter 15, Section 4.1).

A4   *Old women live longer and therefore have fewer illnesses than men*

BASE Result: False

Although women have a longer life expectancy, as a group their profile of illnesses is not really very different from that of men of the same age (M. M. Baltes et al., Chapter 9, Section 4.2). In some aspects men are, in fact, healthier than women.

For example, old women are more often affected by multiple chronic illnesses than are old men (41% of women vs. 30% of men aged 70 and above had five or more somatic illnesses). Moreover, old women's functional health is worse than old men's: women have more disabilities (cf. Statement A5; Steinhagen-Thiessen & Borchelt, Chapter 5, Section 6.2). This more dysfunctional health status of women is also evident in cluster analyses where many variables are considered simultaneously (see below; cf. Smith & Baltes, 1997).

A5   *The majority of very old women need assistance in bathing or showering*

BASE Result: True

As many as 60% of women aged 85 and above, but only 32% of men reported that they needed assistance in bathing or showering (Steinhagen-Thiessen & Borchelt, Chapter 5, Table 5.7). In total, 16% of the BASE sample said that they required such assistance.

Note that this perceived need for assistance may not equate fully with professional judgments of actual "need for care" as defined by nursing care and health insurance agencies (cf. Linden et al., Chapter 16, Section 3.1.3). However, when restricting the expectation to very old women (aged 85 and above) and the specific behavior considered (bathing, taking a shower), the statement squares with the evidence collected in BASE.

A6   *Most biochemical reference values do not change in old age*

BASE Result: True

There were few significant age-related deviations from the reference values for younger adults on the broad range of biochemical analyses of blood parameters carried out in BASE (Kage, Nitschke, Fimmel, & Köttgen, 1996; Steinhagen-Thiessen & Borchelt, Chapter 5, Section 3.1). Notable exceptions included reference values for kidney function (creatinine and urea), blood formation, and calcium metabolism.

The evidence available in BASE, however, does not imply what one might call "untreated aging." Thus, it should be noted that the parameters measured may already have been regulated or influenced by medication.

2.2   Psychiatry

B1   Depressive disorders become more frequent in old age

BASE Result: False

The prevalence of clinically diagnosed depression did not differ significantly across the BASE age groups from 70 to over 100. However, self-reports of depressive symptoms using the Center of Epidemiologic Studies-Depression Scale (CES-D) showed positive age differences. The apparent discrepancy between diagnoses and self-reports is probably due to the fact that the CES-D also registers physical complaints and feelings of strain which occur with increasing multimorbidity (cf. Helmchen et al., Chapter 6, Section 3.1).

In sum, then, there is no evidence in BASE that clinical depression increases with age. This includes people of advanced old age such as 80- and 90-year-olds.

B2   Most persons aged 70 and above have serious impairments in intellectual functioning

BASE Result: False

This question focuses on "serious" impairments. BASE data indicate that approximately 17% of persons aged 70 and above exhibit some form of pathological cognitive impairment, with 14% affected by dementia (only two-thirds of these cases are characterized as moderate to severe and require nursing care; Helmchen et al., Chapter 6, Table 6.3).

In sum: Although there is a general decline of intellectual functioning with old age (Smith & Baltes, Chapter 7, Section 3.2; Lindenberger & Reischies, Chapter 12, Section 3.1), it is not large enough to evince pathological scores in most elderly persons. In fact, as shown by research on learning, most old persons continue to have the potential to benefit from new learning experiences.

B3   About half of those aged 90 years and over exhibit severe mental decline (dementia)

BASE Result: True

This statement highlights the negative side of cognitive decline among the oldest old. The prevalence of dementia increases steeply with age. In BASE, no cases of dementia were diagnosed in the group of 70- to 74-year-olds, but 43% of those aged 90 and over were found to be affected by some level of dementia (Helmchen et al., Chapter 6, Fig. 6.1). Considering sample selection effects (e.g., due to participants' inability to give consent or incapacity to be examined because of physical frailty), the prevalence rate for dementia in persons aged 95 and over was estimated to be around 60% (Lindenberger et al., Chapter 2, Fig. 2.6).

In advanced old age, then, more and more persons suffer from dementia involving serious losses in intellectual functioning. This is an instance where it is very important to distinguish between the evidence for the young old and the old old.

B4   Most old people receive too many psychotropic drugs

BASE Result: False

It is often said that older adults take too many psychotropic drugs. What is the evidence? In BASE, two-thirds of older adults were judged to be taking psychotropic drugs in a wider sense (including herbal tranquillizers, sedatives, and analgesics), and a quarter to be taking psychotherapeutic drugs as formally defined in the German *Physician's Desk Reference* ("Rote Liste," 1990).

Whether this signifies overmedication can only be decided by evaluating individual cases as was done in BASE. According to this assessment, 70% of prescribed psychotropics were medically necessary, and in a further 17% of cases there were no objections to the prescription. Possible or definite contraindications were observed in 13% of the sample. Underdosage was detected in more than a third of psychotropic drug prescriptions, whereas overdosage was not found at all. Undermedication (i.e., nonprescription of indicated medication) was determined in 4% of persons with dementia and in a remarkable 44% of persons with depression.

In summary, the BASE evidence does not suggest a general overmedication involving psychotropic drugs. However, as was true for other medications, the evaluation of psychotropic drug prescriptions requires careful inspection, particularly in view of increased multimorbidity in old age. Most psychotropics are appropriately prescribed, but a more than negligible share of prescriptions is possibly or definitely contraindicated (Helmchen et al., Chapter 6, Section 3.3.1).

B5   Everyday life for older adults consists mainly of passive activity and rest

BASE Result: False

Reconstructing the typical day of BASE participants shows that, on average, only 19% of waking hours were spent resting. However, there was an age-related increase in the percentage of the day spent resting: from 12% in the 70- to 84-year-old group to 26% in the group aged 85 and above (M. M. Baltes et al., Chapter 14, Table 14.1). There is also a significant difference in resting time between psychiatrically healthy old people in BASE and those with dementia (Helmchen et al., Chapter 6, Section 3.3.2).

This evidence from BASE does not suggest that the daily lives of older adults consist mainly of inactivity and rest. However, it is true that the activities decrease in scope and take more time (see also M. M. Baltes & Lang, 1997).

2.3   Psychology

C1   Old people are preoccupied with death and dying

BASE Result: False

People often believe that thinking about death and dying is common in old age. In BASE, participants were asked about their investment (thought, effort) in ten domains of life including death and dying. Of ten life domains, 70% of BASE participants reported that the well-being of family and relatives occupied their thoughts and actions to a large degree and 60% said that they were most concerned with their intellectual functioning.

Only 30% claimed to think a lot about death and dying (Staudinger et al., Chapter 11, Section 2.4.3). This percentage barely differed between the younger (70–84: 27%) and the older age group (85+: 32%). Only 7% of BASE participants mentioned the topic of death and dying in spontaneous self-descriptions (Smith & Baltes, Chapter 7, Section 4.1.1; cf. Freund & Smith, 1997, in press). In the psychiatric interviews, 8% of participants expressed death wishes and 1% were suicidal. These rates are comparable with younger age groups (Barnow & Linden, 1997).

C2   Memory gets worse with age

BASE Result: True

Sizable negative correlations were found between age and performance on the memory tasks of the BASE cognitive test battery ($r = -.49$; Lindenberger & Reischies, Chapter 12, Fig. 12.1; cf. Lindenberger & Baltes, 1997). This negative association remained when persons with diagnosed dementia were excluded. Two examples of memory tasks illustrate this finding. From a list of eight pairs of words, 35% of those aged 90 and above versus 9% of the 70- to 79-year-olds could not remember any of the eight pairs (this involves only those persons without dementia who could carry out the visual version of the test; Smith & Baltes, Chapter 7, Section 3.2).

In a Memory for Text task, participants generally remembered important features, rather than details of the story told to them. Age differences in memory were larger for questions on details than for questions on the story's central features (Lindenberger & Reischies, Chapter 12, Table 12.6). Interestingly, participants with dementia also remembered the story's central features (46%) better than its details (2%).

C3   Most old people are no longer able to learn new things

BASE Result: False

Older people (at least those without dementia) are capable of learning new things even into very old age despite memory decline. The learning ability of BASE participants was measured with the Enhanced Cued Recall test in which a list of 16 words was memorized in three trials. On average, participants learned 7.8 words in the first trial and 10.9 in the third. Nearly two-thirds of participants were able to improve their performance by two or more words across the three trials.

However, hardly any learning improvement occurred among the BASE participants diagnosed as having moderate or severe dementia (Lindenberger & Reischies, Chapter 12, Fig. 12.4). Indeed, learning difficulties are thought to be an important early indicator of dementia (cf. M. M. Baltes, Kühl, & Sowarka, 1992).

C4   A good education and a challenging job are protective against age-related intellectual decline

BASE Result: False

Many believe that education and a challenging work environment slow down the aging process. BASE data are less supportive of this view, although we need to note that the evidence is cross-sectional. Persons with an above-average education, socially prestigious and cognitively demanding professions, and higher incomes do, on average, show a higher level of intellectual functioning in old age. However, the rate or amount of intellectual decline (from the age of 70 onward) for individuals with these above-average sociostructural-biographical resources is virtually equal to that of individuals with below-average resources ($r = -.58$ vs. $r = -.59$; Lindenberger & Reischies, Chapter 12, Fig. 12.2; cf. Lindenberger & Baltes, 1997).

Thus, the magnitude of cross-sectional aging loss in intellectual functioning from age 70 onward is identical for people in above-average and below-average life circumstances. Note, however, that even though the magnitude of age-related loss is similar, persons with higher resources accumulated in their life histories maintain higher levels of intellectual functioning throughout old age due to their initial advantage. This may also enhance their ability to confront everyday problems associated with increasing physical impairment.

C5   *Most old people believe that they can no longer control what happens*
        in their life

BASE Result: False

One of the major psychological questions is to what degree people have a sense of control over their lives. The majority (70%) of BASE participants stated that they felt in control of their lives. Twenty-seven percent believed that what happened in their lives was to some extent a function of their own actions, but also to a large degree dependent on the actions of others.

On the self-report level, then, most older persons indicated that they felt in control of their lives. As more detailed questions were asked (Smith & Baltes, Chapter 7, Section 4.4), the picture became more differentiated, but there is still no evidence that the majority would report no control or very little control across various domains of life.

C6   *Only very few older persons still have life goals*

BASE Result: False

The social expectation is that old age is characterized by little future-oriented purpose in life. In contrast, almost all (94%) of the BASE participants described scenarios for the future that covered a broad range of life domains and goals (Smith & Baltes, Chapter 7, Section 4.1.3).

The correlation of $r = -.17$ between personal life investment in ten domains of life and age indicated that persons between 70 and 100+ did not differ greatly in their reports about having life goals (Staudinger et al., Chapter 11, Section 2.4.2). Thus, older persons in the age range studied in BASE continue to report much investment in thoughts and action for the achievement or maintenance of life goals.

C7   *Older adults live mainly in the past*

BASE Result: False

Contrary to the expectation of a radically altered time perspective in old age, 40% of BASE participants reported thinking mostly about the present, 30% about the past, and 25% said that their thoughts were mostly future-oriented (Staudinger et al., Chapter 11, Section 2.5). Their self-descriptions mainly referred to the present (Smith & Baltes, Chapter 7, Section 4.1.1; cf. Freund & Smith, 1997, in press).

Thus, older persons, on average, continue to participate in all aspects of life: prospective, concurrent, and retrospective. This is true even though they also report that the lifetime available for future-oriented behavior is shrinking and that this is a topic of concern.

C8   *Most old people have a confidant with whom they can talk about difficult problems*

BASE Result: False

Nearly half (45%) of the BASE participants said that they had nobody with whom they could talk about personal problems (Smith & Baltes, Chapter 7, Section 5.2). It seems that older adults may have too few close companions. Among other reasons, this may be due to the fact that old friends have died. Strictly speaking, we do not know whether this finding is specific to old age. It would be necessary to compare these findings for old people with those for younger age groups.

2.4   Sociology and Social Policies

D1   *In West Berlin, many older adults are poor*

BASE Result: False

It is difficult to make noncontroversial statements about absolute poverty rates. However, following scientifically accepted conventions on relative poverty, we found a poverty rate of 3% for the West Berliners aged 70 and above. This is below the rate for the entire German population. Although poverty is higher among very old women (85+: 8%) and the divorced (10%), late life in West Berlin is not, on the whole, associated with large financial disadvantages (Motel & Wagner, 1993; G. Wagner, Motel, Spieß, & Wagner, 1996; cf. Mayer et al., Chapter 8, Section 4.2).

From other German studies, it is well known that younger unmarried women with children are more affected by poverty than old people (Hauser, 1996; Hauser & Wagner, 1996). However, financial needs can rise disproportionately in very old age – for example, when household help is needed because of frailty and disability.

D2   *The number of social relationships decreases with old age*

BASE Result: True

On average, BASE participants named ten persons in their social network. However, network size differed between age groups ($r = -.33$; M. Wagner et al., Chapter 10, Fig. 10.4). Whereas 70- to 74-year-olds nominated 13 persons for their social network, participants aged 95 and above only named 7. Age differences in network size could, of course, represent generational or cohort differences. For instance, many of the West Berlin women over 90 years never had children (cf. M. Wagner et al., Chapter 10, Fig. 10.1). Childlessness by itself (after age, gender, marital status, and place of residence were taken into account) was minimally related to feelings of loneliness ($r = .17$; M. Wagner et al., Chapter 10, Table 10.4).

In general, then, the statement that the number of social relationships decreases with age is true. There is another finding, however, which suggests that the closest circle of relationships reported by old people is less affected by this decline (Lang & Carstensen, 1994; but this is in contrast to the finding reported in Statement C8, which relies on another method of measurement).

D3   *Most persons aged 95 and above are institutionalized*

BASE Result: False

Approximately 9% of all West Berliners aged 70 and above live in a senior citizens' or nursing home. For those aged 95 and above, however, the rate is 37% (Linden et al., Chapter 16, Sections 2.1 and 3.2.1). A previous survey of homes estimated the institutionalization rate to be 5% for over 70-year-olds in the former West German states (Krug & Reh, 1992). In addition to the 14% institutionalized BASE participants, 1.5% were hospitalized. It is likely that the proportion of hospital patients was higher among dropouts from the BASE sample (because they could not be reached or were unable to give consent). This assumption is based on the fact that about a fifth of participants stated that they had been in the hospital at least once during the previous year. However, at any given point in time, the majority of even very old persons does not live in senior citizens' or nursing homes.

Note, however, that this one-time cross-sectional view of the population of older persons does not address the individual probability of ever living in an institutional setting. Using BASE data, it has been estimated that at age 85 the probability of ever being institutionalized is 20% for women and 5% for men, rising to 60% for women and 45% for men at age 95 (Gilberg, 1997).

D4   *Children are the main caregivers of old persons who live in*
          private households

BASE Result: False

According to BASE findings, children were not the prime caregivers for elderly parents. Only 54% of the BASE sample who were in need of assistance and care had children in Berlin. Of these, only 8% received regular household assistance or nursing care from their children.

Prime sources of regular assistance and care at home were spouses (mostly female) and professional community or nursing services (Linden et al., Chapter 16, Section 3.1.4). As these findings rely on participants' self-reports, however, the often considerable efforts to organize care undertaken by children or daughters-in-law may be underestimated. Indeed, parents who were in need of care did report that their children provided other forms of support: 65% indicated that their children helped with practical matters and 40% said their children gave much emotional support (Gilberg, 1997). The low rate of children's regular everyday commitment to the provision of care does not appear to be due to their own old age. The average age of the children of BASE participants requiring assistance or care was 56; only 35% were over 60.

D5   *People who were more socially active in their youth also participate more in*
          social life when they are old

BASE Result: True

This statement concerns another facet of a life-span continuity view. Indeed, there was a positive association between former and current levels of social activities reported by BASE participants. Those who stated they had been socially active in earlier life remained so in late life. The evidence available in BASE comes from retrospective accounts. For instance, the correlation between reported activity level as a young adult and at age 60 was $r = .42$. A similar correlation was found between the activity level after the age of 70 and the retrospectively rated level for age 60 ($r = .41$; Mayer et al., Chapter 8, Section 4.3.2; cf. Maas & Staudinger, 1996).

D6   In old age, the rich are healthier than the poor

BASE Result: False

That poverty is a major condition for poor health in old age is a widespread belief. In BASE, perhaps surprisingly, there were few differences in physical or mental health associated with social class or financial situation (Mayer et al., Chapter 8, Section 4.5; Borchelt et al., Chapter 15, Section 3.3). Perhaps members of lower social classes who survive into very old age are healthier because of selective mortality. A notable exception to this general finding is the higher proportion of individuals with lower education levels among persons with diagnosed dementia (Helmchen et al., Chapter 6, Section 3.2.1).

The statement, then, that the rich are healthier in old age, is false if assessed by BASE findings. This finding calls for cross-national analysis. One compatible hypothesis might be that German health insurance provides relatively equal access to medical services and therefore diminishes socioeconomic differences.

D7   Women who were housewives for most of their lives are worse off in old age
*   than women who were in paid employment*

BASE Result: False

This statement is of much interest to current debates on gender discrimination. In BASE, and contrary to our own expectations, the duration of employment of the married and widowed BASE women was not related to household financial status in old age (cf. Maas & Staudinger, 1996; G. Wagner et al., 1996). The situation of married and widowed women was similar to that of single women who had usually been in paid employment for longer and more continuous periods. This can be explained by the fact that married and widowed women owe most of their financial resources in old age to their husbands. Furthermore, even if these women were in paid employment for a long time, they were often not able to accumulate sufficient pension entitlements in the German system (Allmendinger, 1994).

In sum: In the BASE cohorts of older women, there is little evidence for a strong benefit of paid employment for the financial status in old age. Aside from the other reasons given, this finding may also be a reflection of the German social welfare state.

3   Main Discipline-Specific Findings

This section focuses on the most central findings of the four BASE research units – Internal Medicine and Geriatrics, Psychiatry, Psychology, Sociology and Social Policy – and thus represents a summary of the major results reported in the preceding chapters.

3.1   *Internal Medicine and Geriatrics*

From the medical geriatric examinations in BASE, it was possible to gain a comprehensive picture of the *spectrum of physical health* represented in a heterogeneous sample of older adults. Our central interests lay in the prevalence of physical illnesses and multimorbidity, pharmacotherapy and multimedication, sensory-sensorimotor impairments and functional disabilities, and the specific links between morbidity, medication, and functional limitations in old age (cf. Steinhagen-Thiessen & Borchelt, Chapter 5).

The major findings can be summarized as follows (results weighted to represent the population of old West Berliners): 96% of persons aged 70 and above have at least one, and 30% at least five medical, neurological, or orthopedic illnesses. Cardiovascular diseases are the most prevalent, greatly decreasing life expectancy: 36% of old people exhibit moderate to severe cardiovascular diseases such as coronary heart disease (CHD), peripheral vascular disease (PVD), and cerebral atherosclerosis (CAS) and 24% have moderate to severe congestive heart failure. A fifth of the persons with one of these illnesses died within 28 months of the examination, compared with 6% of the rest of the sample. Mortality within 28 months was also higher among the multimorbid with five or more illnesses (26%) than among those with less than five diagnoses (9%).

Taken together, these findings indicate that nearly all persons aged 70 and above are medically "ill" in some way, and a third are afflicted with life-threatening illnesses. Furthermore, although many objective diseases require treatment (e.g., hypertension, fat metabolism disorders), they often produce only few or even no subjective complaints. "Morbidity" in this sense is thus not the same as "feeling ill."

Nonetheless, old age is often equated with illness. One reason, of course, is that physical "morbidity" in the objective medical sense is indeed very frequent in old age. However, the prevalence of medically defined diseases can at best be equated with the rate of treatment requirements, not with the rates of subjective feelings of illness or objective life-threatening diseases. BASE findings show that, even among the very old (85+), 44% are free of clinically manifest vascular diseases and have an accordingly low mortality rate (cf. Steinhagen-Thiessen & Borchelt, Chapter 5, Section 4.3). Furthermore, diseases of the musculoskeletal system such as osteoarthritis and osteoporosis cause more subjective complaints than cardiovascular disorders. Forty-nine percent of old people reported moderate to severe complaints (mostly chronic pain) due to osteoarthritis, osteoporosis, or dorsopathy, with osteoarthritic pain at the top of the list (32%). These findings support the assumption that objective and subjective meanings of illness differ quite a bit in very old age and underscore proposals that "morbidity" in old age needs to be considered in a very differentiated way.

Regarding gender differences in physical health, we found that old women have a higher risk of musculoskeletal disorders. This was especially evident in indicators of mobility (e.g., Romberg trial and 360° turn) and functional capacity (ADL/IADL; see Steinhagen-Thiessen & Borchelt, Chapter 5, Section 6.2; M. M. Baltes et al., Chapter 9, Section 4.2).

Findings on the *quantity and quality of pharmacotherapy* corresponded to those on observed morbidity in old age. Nearly all persons aged 70 and above were treated with prescribed drugs (92%), with almost a quarter (24%) receiving five or more drugs at once. Based on detailed case- and diagnosis-related consensus conferences between BASE geriatricians and BASE psychiatrists, it was shown that the high prevalence in medication treatment involved over- and inappropriate medication (in 28% of cases), but also undermedication (in 24% of cases). Inappropriate medication (i.e., nonindicated or contraindicated treatment) was mainly observed for psychotropic drugs (3% of the sample), gastrointestinal medications (2%), and diuretics (2%). Undermedication (i.e., no adequate medication prescribed for individuals with moderate to severe somatic ill-nesses) was mainly found in cases of hypertension, fat metabolism disorders, congestive heart failure, and diabetes.

These findings suggest that the widespread negative image of multimedication as overmedication is a false assumption. If present treatment regimens were modified ac-cording to the criteria of individually necessary and optimal medication as adopted by the BASE consensus conferences, the overall prevalence rate of pharmacotherapy in old age would barely change.

This purely quantitative perspective, however, should not obscure qualitative charac-teristics of pharmacotherapy in old age. In BASE, it was also possible to compare data on the quality of individual medication with general criteria for geriatrically inadequate pharmacotherapy (medication that is inappropriate in old age on principle). Here we followed Beers et al. (1991) and Stuck et al. (1994), who recommend the avoidance of certain substances that are considered very problematic in old age (e.g., diazepam, reser-pine). We estimated that 19% of the elderly population were taking such age-inappropriate medication. A cumulative consideration of the various aspects of pharmacotherapeutic quality indicated that the total prevalence of under-, over-, or inappropriate medication for older persons in West Berlin was about 44% and that 1% of older persons may be si-multaneously under-, over-, *and* inappropriately medicated.

In summary, the BASE findings show that the qualitative optimization of geriatric pharmacotherapy remains a challenge. The avoidance of under-, over-, and inappropriate medication is important, although the actual quantity of medication prescribed would probably not change very much. However, we should add that in our view, other types of treatment, such as dietary and physical therapy, physio- and occupational therapy, and other rehabilitative procedures (prescription of physical aids, refurbishment of apart-ments, etc.), should be utilized much more often. Although detailed analyses of BASE data on these aspects are not available yet, it is obvious from first inspections of the data that these intervention types only played a minimal role in the outpatient care and treat-ment of BASE participants.

Another important perspective for the assessment of morbidity in old age is the fre-quency and manifestation of *functional impairment*. In comparison with somatic mor-bidity, the BASE data revealed a much lower rate of basic ADL disability, that is, of dys-function in everyday bodily and behavioral capacities. For example, 16% of persons aged 70 and above needed assistance when taking a bath or shower and 6% required help when getting dressed. A third of all old persons reported needing assistance with Instru-mental Activities of Daily Living (IADL) such as shopping or transportation; this pro-portion reached 70% for those aged 85 and above.

The age-related increase in need for assistance with everyday activities is mainly as-sociated with functional impairment in the sensory (hearing and vision), sensorimotor (balance/gait), motor (mobility and strength), and intellectual domains. For example, go-ing by a WHO impairment classification (WHO, 1980), the vision of one-third of elderly West Berliners was moderately to severely impaired.[1] This group includes less than 20% of septuagenarians, but approximately 80% of nonagenarians. The (uncorrected) hearing

---

[1] In this case, visual acuity was assessed without correcting glasses. But even with glasses, the visual acuity mean of BASE participants remains below the WHO threshold of moderate impairment (cf. Marsiske et al., Chapter 13, Fig. 13.1).

of six out of ten old persons was moderately to severely impaired (according to the WHO classification). Nearly half of the septuagenarians were affected, and more than 90% of the nonagenarians. A quarter of old people were moderately to severely impaired in both sensory modalities (vision and hearing), with an increase from 10% of the septuagenarians to 70% of the nonagenarians (see Marsiske et al., Chapter 13, Section 2.2).

Each of the functional domains mentioned above is, in turn, affected by somatic morbidity. However, it is important to note that neither the changes in functional capacity in these domains nor changes in the need for assistance with ADL/IADL can be explained by somatic morbidity alone. Our analyses suggest that unavoidable biological aging processes play a role in the development of physical disabilities independently of morbidity. Only half of the negative age effect in ADL/IADL can be explained by factors such as somatic and psychiatric illness, the psychosocial situation, or medication. Apart from age, numerous other factors (several of which are modifiable; see also Fries, 1990) seem to facilitate or hinder changes in functional capacity (mainly risk factors for atherosclerosis, quality of medication, psychiatric comorbidity, and psychosocial factors).

Turning to aspects of diagnosis and therapy, we emphasize four findings. First, the analyses show that the risk of *atherosclerosis* (judged by risk factor profiles) is much higher among the atherosclerosis-free or healthy 70- to 84-year-olds (mainly due to fat metabolism disorders) than among those aged 85 and above (Steinhagen-Thiessen & Borchelt, Chapter 5, Section 4.3). This implies that atherosclerosis-free older adults should be considered for treatment of relevant risk factors such as hypertension and hypercholesterolemia.

Second, the detailed medication analyses in BASE indicated that individual profiles of symptoms and diagnoses, particularly pathological laboratory findings, can very often be related to drugs inducing adverse reactions (ADR; Borchelt, 1995). In the context of this cross-sectional study (in which ADR cannot be proved), these can be considered ADR-like symptoms (Borchelt & Horgas, 1994; Steinhagen-Thiessen & Borchelt, Chapter 5, Section 5.4). BASE observations suggest that a coincidence of medication and adverse symptoms can be expected in 87% of older adults. Based on our cross-sectional assessment of these constellations and taking account of participants' retrospective reports of their medical history, in approximately 58% of cases at least one symptom or pathological finding could not be explained by an existing illness and could therefore possibly constitute an ADR. Aldosterone antagonists (74% with suspected ADR), diuretics (70%), and antihypertensives (62%) head the list of drugs associated with possible ADR (see Steinhagen-Thiessen & Borchelt, Chapter 5, Table 5.6) This argument for serious consideration of drug-induced adverse reactions, however, needs modulation. For most other medications, ADR were found in less than one in three cases. Although ADR cannot be completely avoided as concomitants of pharmacotherapy, increased ADR-prevalence in old age may well gain importance as having negative effects on general functioning. Indeed, we found a negative correlation between the number of objective ADR-like findings (pathological laboratory tests, ECG or spirometry) and global functional capacity in terms of sensory-sensorimotor functioning and ADL-independence ($r = -.25$).

Third, laboratory blood tests indicated that, on the whole, there are no major differences between *reference values for older adults* and younger adults (Kage et al., 1996; cf. Steinhagen-Thiessen & Borchelt, Chapter 5, Table 5.2). Like other studies, we observed a morbidity-unrelated, age-correlated decrement in indicators of renal functioning such as creatinine ($\beta = .26$) and urea ($\beta = .24$), blood formation such as hemoglobin ($\beta = -.35$), and calcium metabolism (calcium: $\beta = -.24$). Note, however, that this absence of age differences in most medical reference values is accompanied by an age-correlated increase in medication, much of which is oriented toward the regulation of these reference values.

Fourth, the dental examinations in BASE suggested that the *quantity and quality of German dental treatment* for older adults does not reach modern standards (Nitschke & Hopfenmüller, 1996; cf. Steinhagen-Thiessen & Borchelt, Chapter 5, Section 3.5). Three-quarters of BASE participants were in need of periodontal treatment, 73% needed denture repair, and 23% required surgical treatment. In contrast, the participants' subjective evaluations of their dental health were very positive. Thus, it seems very important to ensure that the elderly population, particularly the large group of edentulous older persons (52% of the sample), has regular dental checkups. Badly fitting dentures, for example, can lead to speech problems or chewing difficulties, both of which can contribute to disengagement from social contacts and activities.

3.2   Psychiatry

Psychiatric research topics in BASE concerned the types and distribution of mental disorders in old age, as well as risk factors for, and consequences of, psychiatric morbidity. We first present prevalence rates and then proceed to describe a more differentiated picture of the age relatedness of psychiatric illnesses in late life (cf. Helmchen et al., Chapter 6).

BASE findings on the distribution of mental disorders show that the proportion of persons aged 70 and above with a diagnosed mental disorder (24%)[2] is not higher than in younger years. On the one hand, this means that old age is not inevitably associated with mental disorders – the majority of old people are healthy from a psychiatric point of view. On the other hand, this prevalence of 24% is high enough to constitute a sizable problem (Helmchen et al., Chapter 6, Table 6.5). Mental disorders not only imply dementia, but also other mental illnesses such as depression. When we also take into account those mental "subthreshold" disturbances that are judged as requiring treatment and thus as having illness value (Table 6.5: 17%) while not fulfilling the criteria (e.g., number, duration, intensity of psychopathological symptoms) for a psychiatric disorder according to the current diagnostic system, DSM-III-R (American Psychiatric Association, 1987), the prevalence rate increases to 40%. The rates range from 30% among 70- to 74-year-olds to nearly 70% among persons aged 95 and above due to increasing dementia (Helmchen et al., Chapter 6, Fig. 6.3). Most of these subthreshold or "subdiagnostic" psychiatric disturbances are affective disorders.

Subthreshold psychiatric morbidity represents a research focus in BASE. Subthreshold morbidity not only affects a sizable proportion of the elderly population (17%), but also has many consequences, particularly regarding the utilization of care and medication (Helmchen et al., Chapter 6, Table 6.6). It is unclear whether psychological problems below the threshold of specified DSM-III-R diagnoses are equally frequent at younger ages (because such epidemiological surveys have not yet been carried out in

---

[2] All frequencies are given as prevalences (at a set date), that is, as rates weighted to represent the population of old West Berliners.

Germany). Comparable research, however, suggests that this is the case (Linden et al., 1996).

The most frequent mental disorders in old age are dementias and depressions. BASE data indicate that 14% of older adults have some form of *dementia*. The prevalence of moderate and severe dementias is estimated to be 8%, which is equivalent to findings from other studies (Helmchen et al., Chapter 6, Section 3.1). The age-correlated increase in dementia is discussed below.

The second most frequent group of disorders is *depression* with a prevalence of 9%, of which 25% are mild, 68% moderate, and 7% severe. Treatment needs for mild depressions should not be underestimated, however, because these are linked to risks such as suicidal feelings or above-average use of medication (Helmchen et al., Chapter 6, Table 6.9). This becomes particularly important when we consider that depression rises to the top of the list of mental disorders in old age (27%) when mild (55%) to moderate (45%) "subdiagnostic morbidity" is taken into account (cf. Gatz, Kasl-Godley, & Karel, 1996). Nevertheless, we must emphasize that major depression in old age is not more frequent than in younger years.

The next largest group of mental disorders are the much rarer (4%) primary anxiety disorders. To arrive at this diagnosis, those anxiety syndromes (18%) that are part of other disorders such as depression were excluded. Drug addiction plays no role in the examined age groups, dependence on medication has a low prevalence (0.7%), and alcohol dependence and abuse are also clearly less frequent than in younger age groups (1.1%; Helmchen et al., Chapter 6, Table 6.5).

Of the mental disorders, dementia is the one that exhibits a strong *age-dependency*. Prevalence of dementia in BASE increases dramatically from about 0% among 70- to 74-year-olds to over 40% among 90- to 94-year-olds. This age-dependence holds for mild, moderate, and severe levels of dementia (Helmchen et al., Chapter 6, Fig. 6.3). The exponential increase beyond the age of 95 predicted by previous studies was not observed in the BASE sample itself. Based on data not corrected for sample selection effects, dementia prevalence among BASE participants aged 95 and above remained below 40% and was thus similar to that of the 90- to 94-year-olds. This finding particularly applied to moderate to severe dementia and to men. It is possible, however, that a further increase of dementia in very old age was not detected because older persons with dementia were likely to drop out early in the BASE assessment protocol. Indeed, selectivity analyses revealed an estimated dementia prevalence of about 60% for persons aged 95 and above (Lindenberger et al., Chapter 2, Fig. 2.6).

In contrast to dementia, there was no clear increase in depression across the examined age groups. This cross-sectional finding should be interpreted with care. We cannot exclude the possibility that depression in very old age is underdiagnosed, be it due to somatic comorbidity or a decline in the ability to express emotions. The latter, however, is a highly controversial assumption in psychological gerontology. Neither can we exclude a negative association between depressivity and severe dementia (Helmchen et al., Chapter 6, Fig. 6.2).

What about *predictors of psychiatric morbidity*? When considering somatic and social risk factors for psychiatric morbidity in old age, clear associations between psychiatric and somatic morbidity can be shown. Depressive older adults are more likely to suffer from chronic somatic illnesses and sensory-sensorimotor impairments than their psychiatrically healthy peers (see also Borchelt et al., Chapter 15, Section 2.3). In contrast, malfunctioning of certain organs (such as the thyroid) was more frequently observed among BASE participants with dementia (Helmchen et al., Chapter 6, Table 6.7). It remains to be shown whether somatic illnesses lead to mental disorders, just as mental disorders can cause somatic morbidity (e.g., through impaired mobility, dietary, or medication behavior).

There were also associations between sociodemographic factors and mental disorders. Of particular theoretical and practical interest was the replicated finding that level of education and dementia are negatively correlated (education with dementia as indicated by the Mini Mental State Examination [MMSE]: $r = -.30$; with clinically diagnosed dementia: $r = -.14$). This association is important since it could account for the higher prevalence of dementia in women (Helmchen et al., Chapter 6, Table 6.6). The finding is in itself clear: Persons with a higher level of education are less often diagnosed with dementia. Its explanation, however, remains open (see also Fratiglioni et al.,1991).

Does education protect against dementia? Do better-educated persons have life-styles that lower the risk of dementia (in aspects of diet or work, for example)? Can persons with higher educational levels mobilize resources to delay the beginnings of dementia? Can they compensate or cover up cognitive decline for a longer period, thus postponing the crossing of the diagnosis-related threshold, even though the level of illness is as high as in persons with lower intellectual functioning? In the latter case, the gradient of cognitive decline over time should be an important diagnostic criterion. However, only longitudinal follow-ups, as are currently being carried out in BASE, can clarify whether the negative association between education and dementia is resolved when dementia is diagnosed by gradients of decline. All of the proposals mentioned open new vistas for further research and have practical consequences.

Possible consequences of psychiatric morbidity have been explored, as far as this is possible with correlational one-time data, in respect to social adaptation and utilization of medical care. Assessments of everyday activities in BASE confirmed that dementia is associated with different activity profiles: Periods of resting during the day increase at the expense of activities (Helmchen et al., Chapter 6, Fig. 6.6). Dementia is also a main factor in determining the need for care and institutionalization (Linden et al., Chapter 16, Section 3.2.3). Depressive disorders are associated with an increased utilization of psychotropics and general medication.

Within the BASE medical consensus conference, epidemiological medication data could be evaluated in terms of medication adequacy under the condition of age typical multimorbidity. According to these analyses and contrary to popular belief, the primary problem of *psychotropic drug therapy* in old age is undermedication rather than overmedication (Helmchen et al., Chapter 6, Table 6.13). Only 10% of older adults with depressive disorders receive specifically antidepressive medication. Note, however, that where overall pharmacotherapy is concerned (see previous section of this chapter), there was equal evidence for under- and overmedication.

3.3   *Psychology*

The Psychology Unit concentrated on three domains: (1) intellectual functioning, (2) self and personality, and (3) social relationships. From the broad range of findings presented in Chapters 7 (Smith & Baltes), 11 (Staudinger et al.), 12 (Lindenberger & Reischies), 13 (Marsiske et al.), and 17 (Smith et al.), we primarily emphasize results on age differences and point to findings that contradict general assumptions about psychological aging.

When considering the three psychological domains, a most striking finding is that it is not possible to speak of a unitary or uniform process of psychological aging. To a large extent, intelligence, self and personality, and social relationships age independently of each other. This is a central finding because it shows that there is no general marker of psychological aging. Therefore, it is necessary to present our main results separately for each domain. It is possible, however, that the degree of uniformity increases in advanced old age (P. B. Baltes & Smith, 1997; Smith & Baltes, 1997).

With regard to *intellectual functioning* in BASE (Smith & Baltes, Chapter 7, Section 3; cf. P. B. Baltes & Lindenberger, 1997; Lindenberger & Baltes, 1997), there was, as expected, a substantial negative age correlation in the general factor of intelligence ($r = -.57$). This negative age gradient remained after excluding persons with diagnosed dementia. Surprisingly, in terms of directionality, the same negative age gradient was also observed irrespective of socioeconomic differences. In other words, while socially advantaged individuals had a higher performance level on average (approximately 0.9 SD above the disadvantaged), their negative age gradients were practically identical (Lindenberger & Reischies, Chapter 12, Fig. 12.2).

The age-related "loss" (note again that these are cross-sectional data) in intellectual functioning from 70 to 103 years of age amounts to 1.5 SD in performance level and is equivalent to 35% of the entire variance. For the crystallized pragmatic abilities that are more strongly determined by cultural factors, the negative age gradient was less pronounced (fluency: $r = -.47$; knowledge: $r = -.41$) than for the fluid mechanic abilities (perceptual speed: $r = -.59$; reasoning: $r = -.51$; memory: $r = -.49$). As predicted by a life-span theory of intelligence, experiential life history factors continue to regulate crystallized pragmatic functioning in old age, though at a lower level than neurobiological factors.

Overall, an age-related decline was observed across all facets of intelligence (and on all 14 tests). The findings suggest a dedifferentiation (homogenization) in the *structure* of intellectual functioning in old age as compared with that in early and middle adulthood (P. B. Baltes & Lindenberger, 1997; Lindenberger & Baltes, 1997). Furthermore, the remarkably high correlation between intellectual and sensory-sensorimotor functioning (hearing, vision, balance/gait) suggests that age-related intellectual decline is strongly associated with neurobiological processes of brain aging (Lindenberger & Reischies, Chapter 12, Fig. 12.3; Marsiske et al., Chapter 13, Section 4; cf. P. B. Baltes & Lindenberger, 1997; Lindenberger & Baltes, 1994).

Second, however, considerable interindividual differences in performance across age coexist with this picture of robust decline across all intellectual abilities. For example, 4% of nonagenarians achieved scores near the mean for septuagenarians and about 5% of septuagenarians lay below the mean for nonagenarians. Furthermore, the majority of older persons were still able to learn new things, even though the extent of their learning capacity decreased with age. However, this considerable plasticity of intellectual functioning was not observed among those with moderate or severe dementia (Lindenberger & Reischies, Chapter 12, Fig. 12.4; cf. M. M. Baltes et al., 1992).

Considering *self and personality*, few large age differences were observed on the level of single variables, very much in contrast to intelligence. Where present, the relatively weak negative age differences in self and personality signify losses in characteristics generally considered to be desirable (e.g., decreased life satisfaction) or increases in characteristics that clinical research regards as dysfunctional (e.g., more loneliness). The age differences found were all in the less desirable direction. Compared with the 70- to 84-year-olds, the very old reported less frequent experiences of positive emotions ($r = -.22$), less satisfaction with their own aging ($r = -.25$), more emotional loneliness ($r = .28$), and were more likely to believe that others controlled the events in their lives ($r = .32$). The extent of these negative age effects all remained below 0.5 SD, accounting for a maximum of 10% of the variance.

In our opinion, these relatively small age losses in measures of self and personality provide evidence for the continued operation of adaptive processes, and indicate the psychological resilience or plasticity of self and personality in old age (Staudinger, Marsiske, & Baltes, 1995). However, there are also indications that these processes of self-regulation may be pushed to their limits in the face of increasing life constraints and accumulating losses. The overall negative trend, together with profile patterns of self-related dimensions revealed in systemic analyses (Smith & Baltes, 1997), is suggestive of a chronic stress reaction (see also Smith & Baltes, Chapter 7, Section 4.2; Staudinger et al., Chapter 11, Section 2.2.2). In other words, if many self and personality variables are considered at once, the oldest of the old display a profile that is similar to the one often reported in research on stress (e.g., fewer positive emotions, more external control beliefs, etc.).

The negative global trend across many self and personality variables suggests, then, that old and, more so, very old age represent a demanding stress-like situation that requires considerable adaptation. Not surprisingly, and in contrast to young and middle adulthood when developmental tasks associated with career, family, and friends are central, the BASE participants reported that most of their thoughts and actions were invested in their health and intellectual functioning (Staudinger & Fleeson, 1996). On an overall subjective level, this investment seems to be successful, because the majority also claimed to be generally satisfied with their lives at present (Smith et al., Chapter 17, Section 2.1). Perhaps adaptation to old age can be conceived as a threshold model where the steady increase of demands and loss in compensatory opportunities ultimately lead to the collapse of this "life management system."

With regard to *social relationships,* as expected, BASE participants nominated fewer persons to whom they felt close at the time of the interviews than typically reported by middle-aged adults. They appear to be less socially embedded than younger adults as far as the total number of their social network partners is concerned (cf. Section 3.4 below). This is also reflected in the findings from the Yesterday Interview (cf. M. M. Baltes et al., Chapter 14, Section 3.1) showing that BASE participants spent most of their waking time alone. Of course, time spent alone cannot be equated with experience of loneliness. Although an increase in reported emotional loneliness was observed with age ($r = .28$), its extent did not mirror the decrease of social network size and the increase of time spent alone. This is also reflected in the stability of the number of persons to whom the old feel very close (Smith & Baltes, Chapter 7, Fig. 7.6; M. Wagner et al., Chapter 10, Section 4.6) and in findings from the Yesterday Interview (cf. M. M. Baltes et al., Chapter 14, Section 5).

What are the patterns of psychological functioning across all three domains? Cluster analysis of 12 measures of intellectual, self- and personality-related, and social functioning revealed nine subgroups of BASE participants (ranging in size from 6% to 23% of the sample) with different profiles of psychological functioning (Smith & Baltes, Chapter 7, Section 6; cf. Smith & Baltes, 1997). This emphasizes the heterogeneity of older adults. Using the distributional patterns observed in BASE as well as inferences from clinical psychology, four of the nine extracted groups reflected patterns of desirable functioning (47% of the sample) and five reflected less desirable profiles (53%). For instance, one of the groups with a desirable profile was characterized by relatively high intellectual functioning, another by high social embeddedness, and a third by positive to average functioning across all three psychological domains. Different, less desirable profiles were also revealed – for example, one group with severe cognitive impairment and high neuroticism, another one also cognitively impaired but socially isolated with low neuroticism. Note that these groups are not types in any sense of exclusiveness. However, these findings point to marked differences in profiles of psychological functioning, thus supporting the notion of differential aging.

What about the role of age and gender in defining membership in these groups (see also Smith & Baltes, 1997)? The age and gender effects obtained represent a major new finding in psychological aging research. The risk of membership in the less desirable profile groups was 2.5 times larger for the very old than for persons aged 70 to 84, and 1.25 times larger for women than for men. Thus, if we take a more systemic or wholistic perspective, negative aspects of psychological aging become more obvious. Therefore, one should not underestimate the psychological vulnerability and risk status – especially for the very old – caused by the age-related increase in challenges and constraints. In another context (see below; cf. P. B. Baltes, 1997) such data and related results, such as findings on the age-related increase in dementia, were used to explore the notion of a "fourth" age.

3.4   *Sociology and Social Policy*

The Sociology and Social Policy Unit aimed to answer questions on old people's *social and economic situation* (cf. Mayer et al., Chapter 8; M. Wagner et al., Chapter 10; see also Maas et al., Chapter 3; Linden et al., Chapter 16). For instance, are older adults poor and economically disadvantaged? Do they voluntarily retreat from society or are they forced into retreat? How do socioeconomic conditions influence mental and physical aging processes? Are there social differences in access to care in old age?

What are the expectations of scientists and the general public regarding these questions? It is often assumed that older adults are dependent on others, are economically constrained, that they have few friends and social contacts, and are lonely and withdrawn. Likewise, it is a common belief that the less well off are not only less healthy and have a shorter life expectancy, but that they receive less help. The well-off are thought to retain the "younger" life-style for longer.

In the following section, we emphasize findings that characterize the population of older West Berliners from which the BASE sample was drawn. Therefore, the data reported are weighted data aimed at representing the West Berlin elderly population as it existed at the time of data collection (for comparable U.S. data, see Myers, 1997).

What about *income* status? When the income of older West Berliners is compared with that of people currently on the labor market, they do not appear to be less well provided for (Mayer et al., Chapter 8; cf. Motel & Wagner, 1993; G. Wagner et al., 1996). During the period of assessment (1990–93), elderly West Berliners living in private households had an average monthly per capita income (equivalent income)[3] of between 1,900 and 2,000 DM; this is roughly similar to the average per capita income of the West German population (cf. Hauser & Wagner, 1992). However, depending on the criterion applied, we can still isolate a group of 3% who were poor and 25% who were economically disadvantaged. Specifically, about 3% had a per capita income below the poverty threshold of about 850 DM per month (cf. Motel & Wagner, 1993).

More than 15% had no assets at all, and 25% did not have a savings account. The number of economically disadvantaged individuals was particularly high among very old and divorced women. The financial situation of the institutionalized was equally critical. Their pensions were entirely used up on accommodation costs, and they were therefore dependent on social assistance. In contrast, we also found a group representing about 4% of the older population who can be regarded as wealthy.[4] Note again, however, that both of these economically extreme groups are rather small in size.

To summarize, our findings confirm that the present German old-age pension system to a large extent fulfills its aim of providing sufficient financial security and resources in old age – as measured against the general population's income and against individual income prior to retirement. At the same time, this means that the disparities resulting from previous employment continue to have effects in old age.

Our analyses suggest three main deficits of the system. These are in the provision for (1) women who do not receive a widow's pension and were not able to gain sufficient pension entitlements despite having worked for long periods, (2) divorced women, and (3) persons in need of nursing care. As long as basic conditions do not worsen, improvement is to be expected in all three areas due to better insurance provisions being made for future generations of pensioners. However, we need to be alert to the need for further analysis and reform. Although our results confirm, for instance, that old people no longer make up the main group afflicted by poverty in German society, one cannot claim that the old are an economically privileged group, since this analysis is based on the population of one large city. Furthermore, when social policy analysts and policy makers compare the financial situations of older and younger persons, they need to take into account that many older adults require greater financial resources to cover additional costs due to frailty and the need for care.

Elderly persons in West Berlin cannot be characterized as a risk group in terms of their *housing conditions* either. On average, in 1992 their monthly rent was 630 DM. On average, this means less than 30% of their net household income. It is estimated that the households of 10% of older men and 4% of older women are below standard (i.e., no bath/shower or central heating). On average, elderly community-dwelling West Berliners occupy one-bedroom apartments; 13% own their homes. These findings reflect general city housing conditions and the particular situation in Berlin (G. Wagner et al., 1996). Thus, old West Berliners are just as well provided for with housing as other age groups in the city. On the surface, then, there is no particular need for action regarding the inappropriate distribution of living space. However, one should not conclude that the

---

[3] Equivalent income represents a finer "per capita calculation," because it takes into account that the same income can be utilized more efficiently by larger than smaller households (cf. Mayer et al., Chapter 8, Section 3.1).

[4] They have at least twice the average equivalent income of the entire German population at their disposal.

available apartments are adequately equipped when the need for care arises: There is certainly a shortage of apartments architecturally and technologically equipped to fulfill the needs of very old and disabled persons (see also Kruse, 1992).

In terms of the *household composition*, about 60% of old West Berliners live alone in a private household (72% of these are women). A quarter live with a spouse or partner, 5% with other persons (e.g., children), and 9% live in senior citizens' or nursing homes.[5] Many old women live alone, partly as a consequence of their higher life expectancy, but also due to lower rates of marriage and remarriage (after widowhood or divorce) for women in the examined cohorts (Maas et al., Chapter 3, Section 5.1). Women are overrepresented in the subgroup of institutionalized older adults, but men without spouses or partners are also particularly likely to live in homes. Eighty percent of persons aged 85 and above still live in private households and 20% are institutionalized. The better-off more often share a private household with a partner and hardly ever live in institutions, whereas members of lower classes more often live with their children.

What about age differences in *family relationships* and *social participation*? Nearly two-fifths of very old (85+) West Berliners have no children: first, as a consequence of a historically linked cohort effect particularly specific to Berliners; second, because very old parents may have outlived their children (M. Wagner et al., Chapter 10, Section 4.3; see also Maas et al., Chapter 3, Section 5.2). Among the very old, we therefore find two contrasting groups, very much in line with the notion of differential aging: a quarter with no close relatives at all and nearly two-fifths who belong to four-generation families with children, grandchildren, and great-grandchildren.

As expected, the total size of the social network decreases with increasing age ($r = -.33$). However, there are hardly any age differences in the frequency of visits to children and friends (among older Berliners who have children and/or friends). The proportion of acquaintances, neighbors, and other nonrelatives among social network partners does not differ significantly between the old (70–84) and the very old (85+).

Surprisingly, very old persons, particularly women, continue to report that they not only receive support, but also provide support for others. About 40% of old people with children said that they give their children money (on average, 4,000 DM a year, excluding extreme values; G. Wagner et al., 1996). This is not only an indication of the modesty of this generation, but also symbolizes older parents' continued interest in relationships with their children and grandchildren and processes of generational transfer.

The number of companions nominated for the social network did not differ between married, widowed, and single BASE participants. Only divorced persons mentioned fewer social network partners. Certainly, children are of great significance for social contacts: Old persons with children have larger networks and feel less lonely than the childless (M. Wagner et al., Chapter 10, Section 6). Married people feel less lonely than those who were never married. From BASE data, it appears that widowed and single older persons do not have a larger social network than their married peers, and that older persons with partners do not isolate themselves. However, most married older adults are men, and the majority of widowed, divorced, or single old people are women. In the literature, it is often suggested that women are responsible for the organization and maintenance of social networks in old age. From our data, it is impossible to determine whether

---

[5] This quota of 9% relies on weighted data from the Intensive Protocol. If the less biased Intake Assessment data are used for weighting, the home quota is 6% (Gilberg, 1997).

women have greater social skills or resources in arranging social interactions for themselves and/or their partners. The networks of married men may very well be maintained primarily by their wives.

What about the *out-of-house activity profile* and *social participation* of elderly West Berliners? In general, they are still very active outside their homes: On average, they named nearly 4 (of 12 given) types of activities, mostly visits to restaurants, trips and excursions, sports, and cultural activities such as visits to the cinema, theater, or concerts. Nearly 40% were members of a club (33% active members), 11% did volunteer work, and 13% took part in educational activities (14% of 70- to 84-year-olds, 6% of those aged 85 and above). Lecture attendance (8%) was the most frequent educational activity mentioned. Activities outside the home were less frequent in the older age groups due to health impairments (Mayer et al., Chapter 8, Table 8.9; M. M. Baltes et al., Chapter 14, Section 5).

Despite large interindividual differences in social participation, there were no great differences between social classes and/or between men and women. However, the low degree of sociocultural integration of persons who had formerly lived in unskilled or semiskilled worker households is striking. This is not only obvious in their activity profiles, but also in their lack of political interest and low participation in elections (34% of those from unskilled and semiskilled worker households were nonvoters compared with an average of 9% of nonvoters in the elderly population at large; Mayer et al., Chapter 8, Table 8.9). We also found a high degree of continuity of social participation in relation to previous life history. Those who described themselves as more active in their youth were very likely to be more active in late life as well (Mayer et al., Chapter 8, Section 4.3).

A politically explosive topic in Germany, as well as in many other countries, concerns adequate *support and nursing care* for the old. About 70% of old West Berliners living in private households reported that they did not receive regular assistance from professional services. In all, 92% of community dwellers were completely independent or only in need of slight assistance, and 8% were in need of care (following criteria of the German nursing care insurance law). Sixty percent of those in need of care live in private households and are cared for by relatives or professional services, and the remaining 40% live in long-term care institutions.

All of these indicators of need for care vary strongly with age. A fifth of the very old (85+) are in need of care, and nearly a third in need of assistance (Linden et al., Chapter 16, Section 3). Children who live in Berlin assist their elderly parents when they become dependent. For example, 65% of those who had children and were in need of assistance and care reported that they received some household assistance from their children. Nevertheless, children hardly ever replaced professional services.

We did not find a simple linear relationship between social class and the utilization of care. Likewise, and this may be surprising to many readers, there was no straightforward social class dependence in the use of informal and professional assistance (Mayer et al., Chapter 8, Section 4.4). However, the members of the higher middle class distinguish themselves from the other groups in that they hardly receive any informal assistance, but much more assistance from professional services (33%), and are only very rarely institutionalized (cf. Gilberg, 1997).

Are *socioeconomically disadvantaged old people* more ill, disabled, and in need of care? Some aspects of functional and mental health (e.g., reported maximal walking distance, hearing, dementia, and the need for assistance with ADL) are correlated with indicators of socioeconomic conditions. However, the correlations are small and their explanatory power is low. The findings can be interpreted such that socioeconomically advantaged old people are somewhat better able to compensate for impairments, for example, by organizing assistance. In addition, education, income, and the presence of a partner seem to function as effective protective factors against the development of morbidity and the need for care. Low education and social class, for example, are important factors in predicting women's risk of dementia, and the probability of being institutionalized is related to the absence of a partner, low income, and social class.

On the whole, however, we were surprised about the relatively low correlations between health impairments of persons aged 70 and above and socioeconomic factors. On the one hand, this could be a function of selective survival: Perhaps severely socioeconomically disadvantaged persons do not survive to the age of 70, or only the healthiest members of the lower social classes live to an old age. On the other hand, these findings could be explained by the German health insurance system, which allows fairly egalitarian access to medical treatment, and by other aspects of the German social welfare state.

In addition, we have several findings showing that, for the very old (85+), the effects of socioeconomic inequality on out-of-house activities or media consumption, for example, are weaker than for the old (70–84). There are hardly any indications that the impact of social differences increases with age. For West Berlin, then, it appears that the process of aging and associated increases in states of morbidity reduce social inequality rather than magnifying it, as is occasionally argued in the gerontological literature (Mayer et al., Chapter 8, Section 5).

4   Profiles and Patterns of Old Age and Aging

In the preceding sections, we presented central BASE findings from the perspective of the individual scientific disciplines involved. Apart from the depth of discipline-specific assessment, however, the scope of this study offered special opportunities to carry out interdisciplinary analyses dealing with systemic relationships between different domains and dimensions of old age. To this end, we made efforts to conduct research which makes explicit that aging is a physical, mental, social, and institutional process.

Throughout this book and in other publications we have documented many systemic interrelations, for example, between sensory and intellectual functioning (Smith & Baltes, Chapter 7; Marsiske et al., Chapter 13; cf. P. B. Baltes & Lindenberger, 1997; Lindenberger & Baltes, 1994), between social prestige, intelligence, and social participation (Mayer et al., Chapter 8; Lindenberger & Baltes, 1997), between physical and sensory impairments and depressivity (Borchelt et al., Chapter 15), between intelligence, health, sensory functions, personality, and everyday competence (M. M. Baltes et al., Chapter 14; Marsiske, Klumb, & Baltes, 1997), and between the different life courses of men and women and their multidomain profiles of functioning in old age (M. M. Baltes et al., Chapter 9; Smith & Baltes, 1997).

In this section, we attempt to move beyond the scope of these analyses and identify systemic patterns of old age across a wider range of functions and domains. For this purpose, we report the results of a multidisciplinary cluster analysis[6] which was aimed at

---

[6] For information on methods and limitations of cluster analysis, see Smith and Baltes (1997).

one overall consideration of central data collected in each of the four research units. Using cluster analysis, we considered conjointly the role of a total of 23 constructs (cf. P. B. Baltes, 1997, Smith & Baltes, in press). We were interested in the following questions:

(1) How many subgroups of BASE participants can be distinguished based on their profiles across the 23 constructs?

(2) How can these groups be characterized (e.g., with regard to positive or negative views of old age, functioning, and forms of successful aging)?

(3) Are the groups differentiated by age and/or gender? Are more men than women in the desirable groups or more of the younger old than very old?

4.1   *Constructs Considered in Cluster Analysis*

Table 18.2 includes a list of the constructs considered. Of the 23 constructs, 6 were selected from internal medicine and geriatrics (cf. Steinhagen-Thiessen & Borchelt, Chapter 5): the number of diagnoses of moderate to severe cardiovascular, musculoskeletal, and other illnesses, as well as measures of functional capacity (ADL/IADL), sensory acuity (an unweighted construct of hearing and vision, cf. Marsiske et al., Chapter 13), and subjective health. From the psychiatry protocol, two constructs were included: measures of depressivity (Hamilton Depression Scale, HAMD) and dementia (Mini Mental State Examination, MMSE; cf. Helmchen et al., Chapter 6). Seven constructs came from the sociological protocol: social prestige of the household head (Mayer et al., Chapter 8), number of years in education (school and occupational training), number of close kin (cf. M. Wagner et al., Chapter 10), number of activities outside the home as a measure of social participation (Mayer at al., Chapter 8), and different facets of the social network (the number of very close companions, subjective instrumental and emotional support received, and emotional loneliness; M. Wagner et al, Chapter 10). Psychological domains were represented by eight constructs: a general measure of intelligence and various facets of personality characteristics and self-regulatory processes (extraversion, positive affect, neuroticism, internal and external control beliefs, as well as personal life investment; cf. Smith & Baltes, Chapter 7; Staudinger et al., Chapter 11). A measure of subjective well-being was also included in the analysis (PGCMS; Smith et al., Chapter 17).

Using cluster analysis (cf. Milligan & Cooper, 1987), 11 groups were identified within the BASE sample of old West Berliners.[7] Table 18.2 presents an overview of the groups and their standardized scores for all 23 selected variables. The groups were rank ordered (from 1 to 11) to reflect the average score of the positive and negative characteristics of their profile. Table 18.3 provides an overview of the groups' size (number of members and proportion of the sample) and the descriptive labels that were decided among representatives of all four research units. From a methodological point of view, note that such clusters or subgroups are not types or unrelated to each other. On the contrary, cluster analysis organizes the entire sample in such a manner that people within clusters are more similar to each other (in level and profile of functioning) than they are to other individuals in the overall sample (see Smith & Baltes, 1997, for further discussion).

---

[7] One additional group of three persons was obtained in a first analysis step, but its members were subsequently excluded because they were characterized by extremely large multigenerational families (with 7–11 children and 27–46 relatives altogether). Five further persons were excluded from all analyses because of missing data.

Table 18.2. *Profiles of the 11 subgroups across 23 constructs (standardized T-scores; M = 50, SD = 10)*

						Subgroups					
Construct	1 (n = 28)	2 (n = 18)	3 (n = 44)	4 (n = 56)	5 (n = 47)	6 (n = 69)	7 (n = 55)	8 (n = 67)	9 (n = 44)	10 (n = 45)	11 (n = 35)
Average score	57	56	55	53	52	52	48	48	47	45	43
Internal Medicine/Geriatrics											
Number of diagnoses[a]											
Cardiovascular diseases	59	52	56	50	42	57	48	47	48	48	47
Musculoskeletal diseases	53	52	50	55	47	55	48	48	49	48	44
Other diseases	58	50	51	53	48	53	49	44	48	50	50
Need for help with ADL/IADL[a]	57	53	56	55	53	56	43	49	51	39	35
Subjective health[a]	60	53	52	50	56	53	50	42	47	42	38
Sensory functioning (hearing, vision)[a]	62	52	56	54	47	53	43	51	49	42	42
Psychiatry											
Depressivity (HAMD)[b]	58	52	53	52	55	55	53	37	51	53	34
MMSE[b]	56	55	56	53	51	55	48	52	52	27	46

Psychology

Intelligence	*64*	*56*	*62*	*55*	*48*	*54*	*43*	*49*	*48*	*36*	*40*
Extraversion	*60*	*56*	*50*	*52*	*54*	*51*	*54*	*48*	*41*	*46*	*41*
Positive affect	*60*	*57*	*54*	*53*	*52*	*54*	*53*	*51*	*39*	*40*	*40*
Subjective well-being (PGCMS)	*59*	*54*	*55*	*51*	*58*	*54*	*50*	*38*	*51*	*51*	*35*
Life investment	*55*	*59*	*52*	*55*	*49*	*50*	*50*	*55*	*39*	*42*	*49*
Neuroticism[c]	*57*	*53*	*56*	*51*	*59*	*53*	*49*	*40*	*51*	*51*	*35*
Internal control	*54*	*54*	*45*	*51*	*52*	*52*	*57*	*49*	*41*	*49*	*47*
External control[c]	*57*	*55*	*55*	*47*	*57*	*54*	*40*	*49*	*57*	*43*	*43*

Sociology/Social Policy

Social prestige	*51*	*56*	*68*	*50*	*52*	*47*	*46*	*50*	*45*	*43*	*46*
Education in years	*57*	*52*	*65*	*50*	*52*	*47*	*45*	*50*	*45*	*45*	*47*
Number of very close companions	*49*	*84*	*52*	*53*	*51*	*47*	*50*	*49*	*44*	*45*	*46*
Received social support	*49*	*51*	*51*	*57*	*52*	*42*	*54*	*55*	*41*	*46*	*53*
Emotional loneliness[c]	*63*	*58*	*55*	*55*	*56*	*50*	*47*	*42*	*48*	*49*	*38*
Number of relatives	*45*	*58*	*53*	*53*	*54*	*47*	*48*	*48*	*47*	*48*	*47*
Activity level	*60*	*57*	*59*	*58*	*48*	*53*	*43*	*50*	*44*	*41*	*42*

Note. All constructs were standardized so that higher scores signify higher levels of functioning. All scores above 55 or below 45 are printed *in italics*.

[a]Higher scores: better somatic health.

[b]Higher scores: better mental health.

[c]Higher scores: more positive psychological functioning (e.g., low neuroticism, low loneliness).

Table 18.3. *Overview of the 11 subgroups with the numbers of their members and their relation to the BASE sample*

Groups	Characteristics	n	%
1	Physically and mentally fit, vitally involved	28	5.5
2	Socially embedded, committed, and happy	18	3.5
3	Cognitively fit, active, high social status	44	8.7
4	Average functioning, active, and supported	56	11.0
5	Cardiovascular disease, but satisfied with life	47	9.3
6	Relatively healthy and independent	69	13.5
7	Impaired and dependent, but in control	55	10.8
8	Sick, depressive, anxious, and lonely	67	13.2
9	Withdrawn, passive, bored with life	44	8.7
10	Extreme cognitive and sensory deficits (demented)	45	8.9
11	Very frail, depressive, and lonely	35	6.9

Because the scores were computed in the direction of putative desirability of functional status, the groups with above-average mean scores (groups 1–6) can be interpreted as representing the more positive and desirable patterns of old age, whereas those with below-average scores (7–11) represent more negative and undesirable patterns. This method based on distribution characteristics was selected because, for most of the 23 constructs, a threshold or criterion value that allows a distinction between functionality and dysfunctionality is not available. Only the directions of functionality (desirability) versus dysfunctionality (undesirability) can be specified (see also Smith & Baltes, 1997). Therefore, for ease of comparison across constructs, the *T*-scores for all variables were recoded so that higher values signify better functioning.[8]

4.2 Description of Groups

Table 18.3 offers a first account of the key characteristics of the subgroups identified. The labels assigned to the groups should be interpreted with caution, however. They are only abbreviations of the departures from the average in the profiles shown in Table 18.2. Our use of these descriptive labels emphasizes that we do not claim to have identified a typology of aging. The reader should remember that the labels overgeneralize the characteristics common to the group members and do not signal the variability within each group or the intergroup similarities (e.g., Woodbury & Manton, 1982).

We begin with the more desirable and better functioning profiles. The first three groups (*n* = 90, 17.7% of the BASE sample; cf. Fig. 18.1b for weighted percentages) include persons who were relatively healthy for their age, were socially active, and had good intellectual functioning compared with the BASE sample as a whole. The groups differ primarily in psychological and social aspects and to a lesser extent in terms of their

[8] With *M* = 50 and *SD* = 10 for physical health, the score of 60 means a step of one standard deviation above the mean in a positive direction, signifying relatively good health. For a score of 40, the reverse applies: It lies one standard deviation below the mean, signifying worse health.

illness profiles or subjective health. Members of groups 1 ($n = 28$) and 2 ($n = 18$) were more outgoing with higher degrees of extraversion and life investment than the members of group 3. Whereas persons in groups 1 and 2 believed in personal (internal) control over their lives, members of group 3 believed that what occurred in their lives was controlled both by themselves (internal control) and by significant others (external control).

Group 3 ($n = 44$) stood out in terms of social status: Individuals in this group were advantaged regarding social prestige and education (on average 14 years). Group 2 ($n = 18$) included persons with strikingly large family and social networks: Members had an average of 8 direct kin and nominated 27 persons for the inner circle of their social networks.

Members of groups 4, 5, and 6 ($n = 172$, 33.3%) were characterized by average levels of psychological and intellectual functioning, but different socioeconomic contexts and health. Members of group 4 ($n = 56$) reported receiving much instrumental and emotional support, whereas members of group 6 ($n = 69$) who had fewer kin ($M = 2$) reported receiving very little of such support. In comparison, the profile of persons in group 5 ($n = 47$) seems strongly characterized by the presence of cardiovascular illnesses (with an average of three out of six possible diagnoses). Although those in group 5 were in objectively poor health, they were nevertheless satisfied with life in general.

The remaining five groups (7–11) reflect the least positive pictures of old age ($n = 246$, 48.4%). The profiles of groups 7, 10, and 11 identify persons with different levels of intellectual, somatic, and sensory impairments – often multiple impairments (85% of the 67 institutionalized persons in BASE were in these groups). Groups 8 and 9 reflect two different profiles of depressivity: those who are physically ill and depressive, and those who appear withdrawn, lonely, and bored with life. Group 10 mainly included persons diagnosed with moderate to severe dementia ($n = 45$, 8.5%; cf. Helmchen et al., Chapter 6).[9]

4.3   Age and Gender as Risk Factors for Group Membership

For the BASE sample, Figure 18.1a presents the relative proportions of the old (aged 70 to 84) and very old (aged 85 and above), and of men and women in the groups. To obtain information on the likely distribution in the entire West Berlin population of older persons, Figure 18.1b compares the distribution of the 11 subgroups in the BASE sample with the estimated distribution in the elderly population of West Berlin based on weighting. As expected due to the oversampling of men and the very old in the BASE sample, the groups including more women or 70- to 84-year-olds (groups 1, 2, 3, 6, and 8) are larger after weighting, whereas groups 7, 10, and 11 are smaller.

As to age and gender membership, results of both analyses suggest the same outcome. Membership in different groups is clearly age-related. More of the 70- to 84-year-olds were found in groups with desirable characteristics (1, 2, 3, 4, and 6; $RR = 2.5$), and more of the older individuals (85–100+) were in groups with less desirable features ($RR = 2.3$). As to gender, women were overrepresented in the dysfunctional groups, 10 and 11 ($RR = 2.5$), and men were overrepresented in the high-functioning groups, 3 and 5 ($RR = 1.3$). *Thus, being older and being a woman are significant risk factors for belonging to a dysfunctional group.*

---

[9] In fact, later analyses showed that all persons with a diagnosis of severe dementia are indeed gathered in this group.

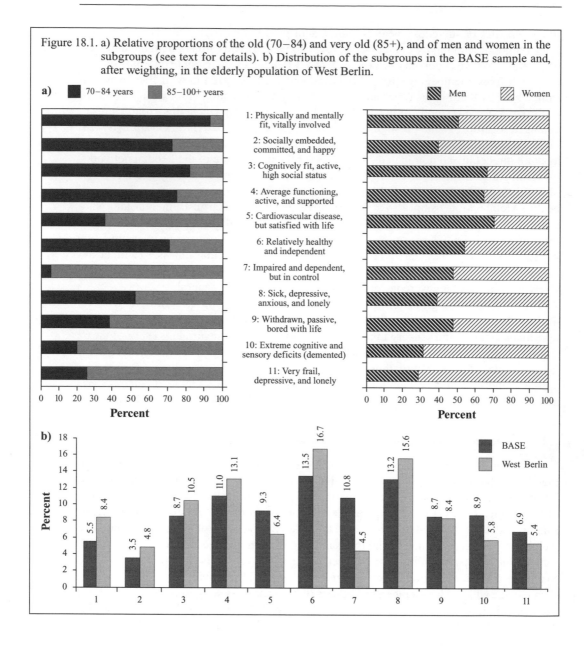

Figure 18.1. a) Relative proportions of the old (70–84) and very old (85+), and of men and women in the subgroups (see text for details). b) Distribution of the subgroups in the BASE sample and, after weighting, in the elderly population of West Berlin.

Another visual representation of this finding is offered in Figure 18.2a. It summarizes the relative proportions of persons in each age group whose social and psychological situation, mental and physical health can be characterized as good (groups 1–3), average (groups 4–6), poor (groups 7–9), and very poor (10, 11). This figure makes very clear the different life conditions of individuals in their 70s, 80s, and 90s and the increasing likelihood of negative and less desirable profiles in very old age. The slight increase of per-

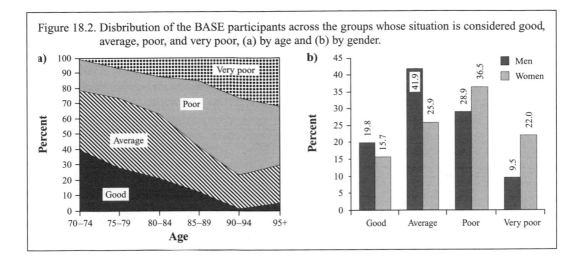

Figure 18.2. Disbribution of the BASE participants across the groups whose situation is considered good, average, poor, and very poor, (a) by age and (b) by gender.

sons aged 95 and above in "good" and "average" groups may indicate the selective survival of persons with high levels of functioning.

Figure 18.2b also shows that men are more likely to be found in the more positive and women in the more negative groups. This clearly illustrates gender's role as a risk factor (see also Smith & Baltes, in press). Although women live longer on average, they are more likely than men to be afflicted by frailty and have a 2.5 times higher risk of belonging to the most dysfunctional groups (10 and 11; see Fig. 18.1a). The reasons for this gender risk factor are many. Our related analyses suggest that life history differences in social conditions are among the relevant factors.

Some questions resulting from this analysis can only be answered with data from the ongoing longitudinal data collection of BASE. On a very general level, the open questions refer to how, why, and when persons move into dysfunctional groups and which somatic, psychological, and social conditions are protective for maintaining a good or average profile. For instance, one could assume that the psychologically robust but physically impaired groups and the socially embedded and supported have a better chance of maintenance of adequate status than the subjectively and objectively lonely and withdrawn. However, the answers to questions like these await the availability of longitudinal information.

5   Summary and Conclusions

We are aware of the danger that lies in reducing the differentiated and complex findings obtained in the Berlin Aging Study to just a few conclusions and perspectives. Nevertheless, not least because of important implications for social policy as well as providing a first basis for cross-national comparisons, we will try to highlight some aspects of our results. As a reference framework, we once again take up the study's theoretical orientations, which were introduced in Chapter 1 (P. B. Baltes et al.): reserve capacity in old age, differential aging, continuity versus discontinuity (with a focus on very old age), and aging as a transdisciplinary systemic phenomenon. Subsequently, we attempt some general observations on future theory and research in gerontology as well as on matters of social policy.

5.1   *Resources, Reserves, and Their Limits: Positive and Negative Aspects of Old Age and Aging*

We begin with the more positive aspects of the BASE results on aging and old age.[10] BASE has produced a great deal of empirical support for the notion that, on average, old age is *not* foremost a negative and problem-ridden phase of life. Findings contradicting negative images can be observed in the subjective well-being of older adults. Most old people were satisfied with their lives. Two-thirds felt healthy, nearly two-thirds perceived themselves as healthier than their peers, and nearly a fifth felt just as healthy. Such positive comparisons even increase in very old age: The older they were, the more healthy people felt compared with others of the same age. More than two-thirds believed that they had control over their lives and thereby felt self-reliant and independent. More than nine out of ten of the BASE participants still had goals, and only a third were strongly oriented toward the past. Less than a tenth of elderly West Berliners spent a lot of time thinking about death and dying.

Along the same lines, many of the BASE findings also confirm positive aspects of the status of older persons in more objective indicators. Most older adults not only felt self-reliant, they also lived independently. More than nine out of ten lived in private households. Despite a high rate of childlessness because of the special situation of Berlin and historical generational experiences, less than 10% of Berlin's older population lived in institutional settings. Three-quarters of community-dwelling old persons received no help from outside the household. Nine out of ten were not in need of nursing care. Even among the very old aged 85 and above, only a fifth needed nursing care and a third required help with everyday activities. Note, however, that these findings on independent living in old age are more positive for men than women.

Another positive result of BASE shows that less than a quarter of those aged 70 and above had specified psychiatric disorders, and only a tenth had mental illnesses involving the need for care. These prevalence rates are similar to younger age groups. Moreover, depressive disorders did not increase with age. Furthermore, old age and frailty should not be equated. Nearly half of the sample were free of serious complaints related to musculoskeletal diseases, and almost half of those aged 85 and above were free of cardiovascular illnesses. A further remarkable BASE finding is that hardly any differences in morbidity and treatment requirements were due to social class and other features of socioeconomic inequality. In part, this could be due to selective morbidity before the age of 70, but it is probably also due to certain aspects of the German welfare state, such as an efficient health insurance system and medical treatment that does not discriminate according to financial or insurance status.

The image of old age as a phase of social isolation, withdrawal, and inactivity in everyday life can also be rejected. BASE findings show many older adults to be active, both at home and outside the household. Although the very old reported fewer social re-

---

[10] With the exception of statements referring to age groups, all reported numbers are weighted to represent the population of elderly West Berliners.

lationships and felt emotionally lonelier, they nominated the same number of very close companions as the younger group of old persons. There were hardly any age differences in the frequency of contacts with children and friends either. Furthermore, old persons were neither particularly poor nor did they live in bad housing. An important finding is that most of the old people in BASE received help and nursing care when they needed and requested it. Furthermore, older adults not only received support, they also stated that they very often helped others. Thus, they made an important contribution to their families and society.

However, these positive perceptions of old age and of themselves offered by the BASE participants can and should not be interpreted as a reflection of their objective situation. Subjective evaluations are typically better than objective conditions. To a significant degree, the mainly positive assessments are the result of effective self-regulation processes employed by the old to adapt to, and deal with, unfavorable conditions; in addition, they are likely to be the consequence of generation-specific norms of modesty and unselfishness.

At the same time, however, BASE findings also offer a window to the more negative aspects of aging and old age. For instance, our results also confirm the inevitability of physical and mental decline, the increase of chronic illnesses with age, and the manifold consequences of sensory, mental, and somatic limitations for an active and independent way of life. Feeling healthy is not the same as objectively being healthy. Nearly all of the BASE participants had at least one moderate to severe illness, and about a third had a life-threatening disease. Nearly half suffered from chronic, painful musculoskeletal illness. Dementia prevalence increased rapidly in very old age, affecting between 40% and 60% of the oldest age group (95+). Both harmful overmedication and considerable undermedication were observed. A particularly grave deficit was revealed in dental treatment: Three-quarters of old people required treatment. There was also a clear decline in sensory functioning (hearing and vision) due to physiological and pathological processes in old age.

On average, there was a gradual decline in intellectual functioning. Of course, longitudinal information is necessary to see whether this negative age gradient applies to all individuals. Not only memory, but all other intellectual abilities continuously worsened from age group to age group. This applied to indicators of the pragmatics of intelligence (vocabulary and practical knowledge), but particularly to the mechanics (e.g., reasoning and perceptual speed). Not surprisingly, therefore, the learning of new things also decreased with increasing age, although, on average, BASE participants demonstrated continued ability to learn. Because of the strong connection of this aging of intelligence with measures of vision, hearing, and motor balance, it is likely that the average intellectual losses observed are the consequences of brain aging rather than lack of practice (Lindenberger & Baltes, 1997).

Negative aspects of aging also appeared in the area of self and personality when a magnifying lens was applied. Thus, despite relatively high life satisfaction, negative personality traits such as less openness, less positive affect, and feelings of external control increasingly emerged in the older age groups. One possible interpretation is that the considerable psychological adaptation capacities of old people reach their limits in very old age. As mentioned above, the very old felt lonelier. Social activities decreased with age, mainly because of health impairments. Nearly half of the old people had no confidant.

However, we do not know how this compares with younger adults. Residents of senior citizens' and nursing homes had particularly little contact to the outside world.

Nearly half of those older BASE participants we judged to be in need of assistance or care stated that they received no support. This could mean that provision of care for the old and very old is less than optimal and intervention is necessary for at least some of those observed to be living independently. Despite much reserve capacity, then, limits and constraints in functional status cannot be overlooked, especially in the very old aged 85 and above. Our attempt to characterize conditions of old age across many dimensions and domains not only revealed that a third of old people were physically, sensorily, and mentally impaired, severely ill and disabled, but also that this situation was associated with a very negative mental and psychological status in at least a quarter of the participants. In this context, we should emphasize that more than half of the very old (aged 85+) and two-thirds of those aged 90 and over belonged to the groups whose overall profile of functioning was characterized as less desirable. The negative aspects of late life thus accumulate with increasing age from 70 to 100.

5.2   *Differential Aging into Very Old Age*

A second focus of BASE asks whether the variability of aging between persons and between domains continues into very old age. The answer seems unambiguous, but does need qualification. The range of interindividual variation (differences between persons) is equally large throughout old age, from 70 to over 100. Age groups differ in their means, but not in their distributions. This impression of continued heterogeneity prevails through all chapters of this book and includes geriatric and psychiatric findings. This finding of continued heterogeneity is a very significant result because it underlines the importance of asserting a differentiated picture of old and advanced old age.

At the same time, there are some important exceptions. For instance, certain medically relevant indicators are no longer observed in very old age in the BASE sample. Very low prevalences of the apolipoprotein genotypes Apo-E 2/2 and 4/4 (genetic markers of a very high atherosclerosis risk) were observed (cf. Steinhagen-Thiessen & Borchelt, Chapter 5, Section 4.1). Such deviations from heterogeneity and the distributional composition of indicators observed for younger age groups can be significant because the lack of certain features may indicate age-related morbidity and selective mortality processes.

However, the picture of heterogeneity (variability) is less age-resistant *within* individuals across domains. In terms of intraindividual variability, we find that the various levels of functioning become more similar across domains. For instance, on the pathological level, multimorbidity increases. The strong merging of different intellectual abilities in old age provides another pronounced example (cf. Lindenberger & Baltes, 1997). The emergence of a very close relationship between sensory functioning and intelligence in old age is also striking. This is an important finding, although the explanation of the dedifferentiation of intelligence structure and its linkage to sensory functioning is not yet clear.

In other words, considerable and undiminished interindividual variability remains in old age, but each person experiences age-related changes that tend to be oriented in the same direction and therefore reduce within-person variability. In the age range studied, then, the individual's system of functioning changes toward more uniformity with age, that is, as a whole in the same direction. The main exceptions are personality characteristics and self-regulatory mechanisms which appear to be particularly resilient to the unifying tendency of the aging process. Nevertheless, the warning given at the beginning of this book still applies. We must await analyses of the BASE longitudinal data in order to answer the questions surrounding differential aging with the necessary methodological precision. At present, strictly speaking, we can only address age/cohort averages, not individual trajectories.

5.3   Focusing on Very Old Age: A New Perspective?

A third focus of BASE lies on very old age, the age spectrum from age 85 onward. This focus on advanced old age was chosen because most gerontological research deals with the so-called young old in their 60s and 70s and because most open theoretical and social questions about old age concern the growing number of the oldest old. Is advanced old age, for instance, simply a continuation of what happens in young old age? Is it possible to generalize the relatively positive results on the vitality and reserve capacities of the younger old to those surviving into very old age? Or is there discontinuity?

We cannot yet offer a final answer to these questions since this requires longitudinal data. However, based on our cross-sectional findings, it seems that those surviving into very old age represent new constellations. Whether they reflect the impact of selective survival or aspects of discontinuity remains open to date.

By and large, our findings on the young old confirm the view developed in the past decade that assigns to older adults surprisingly high levels of physical, psychological, and social functioning (P. B. Baltes & Mittelstraß, 1992; Bortz, 1991; Fries, 1990; Karl & Tokarski, 1989; Lehr, 1991; Riley & Riley, 1992; Schaie, 1996; Willis, 1996). Indeed, our results support the conclusion: "The young old are on the move." The young old have a considerable degree of optimism and vitality, and "young old age" is stretching out to higher ages. There is much hope for the future of old age in this age range. Our observations and measurements provide an empirical foundation for this optimistic perspective.

However, BASE findings also revealed a different picture beyond the eighth decade of life. Very old age represents a considerable challenge to psychological resilience and coping capacities. The rather isolated and specific loss of intellectual functioning observed in younger old age extends to a general decline of performance across all abilities in very old age. And this decline appears to include those whose life courses were characterized by above-average personal and socioeconomic resources.

This image of a qualitative change from young old to old old age is particularly supported by psychiatric findings. In contrast to other mental disorders, the prevalence of dementia clearly changes in very old age. Beyond the age of 80, its prevalence increases rapidly, reaching 40% to 60% among nonagenarians and centenarians. This means that many very old persons exhibit a new "quality" – sometimes so much so that they are no longer recognizable as the individuals they once were.

The geriatric findings on the need for care and multimorbidity also support the view that very old age constitutes a new stage. Social conditions are also qualitatively different in very old age: Emotional loneliness increases, social participation outside the household decreases, and, foremost, institutionalization increases. On a systemic level, increasing numbers of the very old, particularly women, belong to groups whose functioning and life circumstances are associated with unsatisfactory constellations and real risks (cf. Figs. 18.1 and 18.2).

In our opinion, this general finding challenges gerontological theory and leads to the formation of new hypotheses. For these and other reasons (e.g., P. B. Baltes, 1997), some of us argue that it is useful to consider advanced old age as a kind of "fourth age" (see also below). For example, very old age may be increasingly determined by factors (e.g., biological-genetic factors) that are independent of previous conditions and that can be less well controlled by sociocultural resources than in younger adulthood (but see also McGue, Vaupel, Holm, & Harvald, 1993; Yashin & Iashine, 1994, on the issue of genetic vs. nongenetic determinants of aging).

5.4   Aging as a Systemic Phenomenon

With its fourth focus, researchers in BASE attempted to capture what gerontologists have always considered the main characteristic of old age: As age simultaneously constitutes a biological, psychological, social, and institutional phenomenon, gerontological studies should be designed to include a wide range of disciplinary and interdisciplinary research (e.g., Birren & Schaie, 1996; Maddox, 1995; Mittelstraß et al., 1992; Rowe & Kahn, 1987). Although our efforts in this direction are far from complete (e.g., the deep-frozen blood samples have not been thoroughly investigated for genetic markers), several bodies of results indicate how worthwhile this effort is.

One example is the multidisciplinary cluster analysis presented before in this chapter and its power in demonstrating essential differences between the old and very old and between men and women on an aggregated level of profile analysis. This multidisciplinary macroscope allows a view of the characteristic effects of old age and gender beyond individual variability and single-variable age trajectories. We therefore expect the profile results shown in Figure 18.1 and 18.2 to be regarded as new and significant. These profiles of subgroups allow the subsequent decomposition of age and gender in terms of social and biological factors as well as their interactions. They may also permit us to track individual changes into and out of groups differing in functional status; for instance, based on therapeutic interventions or other changes in life circumstances.

The consensus conferences carried out by geriatricians and psychiatrists provide another example of the fruitfulness of an interdisciplinary approach. For instance, the consensus conference made it possible to determine the limits of validity of certain medical categorizations and to assess the quality of medication – with a result surprising to those without medical training: Old people are not generally overmedicated. Depending on the domain examined, we found that the degree of undermedication is more or less equal to that of inappropriate drug treatment and overmedication.

Finally, the advantages of an interdisciplinary approach are endorsed by our discovery of a remarkably strong association between sensory functioning and intelligence. Although there are very many studies of intelligence in old age, this finding is new – mainly because such close cooperation between physicians and psychologists has been rare. Now that this link is established, completely new questions about the decline of intelligence in old age arise, questions that appear to demand close cooperation between biological and behavioral scientists. In fact, based on first publications of these findings in journals (e.g., Lindenberger & Baltes, 1994), this line of new research is already underway.

5.5   *Prospects for the Future*

As mentioned in Chapter 1, a book providing an extensive overview of the status and perspectives of gerontology (P. B. Baltes & Mittelstraß, 1992) was the first major product of the Berlin-Brandenburg Academy of Sciences study group "Aging and Societal Development." This volume laid the foundation for the present study. It also dealt with questions of furthering gerontological research in general (Mittelstraß et al., 1992) and of gerontological and social political practice in particular (Mayer et al., 1992). We now respond to some of the issues raised in this earlier work, issues that, of course, are also at the center of other major publications on the state of the art in gerontology and age-related social policy (Binstock & George, 1996; Birren & Schaie, 1996; Maddox, 1995; Schneider & Rowe, 1996; Suzman, Willis, & Manton, 1992).

The aim of our study was to gather new information on old age and to contribute to gerontological theory. The funding agencies also stimulated us in the direction of issues of application and policy. Few of the BASE scientists are experts in practical or social application – and hardly any of the results point to such unambiguous and compelling practical consequences that they elicited a clear consensus among the BASE scientists. However, individuals from the BASE group have published articles that deal explicitly with questions of application and aging policies (e.g., M. M. Baltes & Montada, 1996; P. B. Baltes, 1996; Helmchen, Linden, & Wernicke, 1996; Linden, Horgas, Gilberg, & Steinhagen-Thiessen, 1997; Mayer, 1994; Staudinger, 1996; G. Wagner, 1995), and with implementation in a model of geriatric rehabilitation (Borchelt & Steinhagen-Thiessen, 1995; Steinhagen-Thiessen, Gerok, & Borchelt, 1994).

In this concluding section, we make an effort to explore some issues of application and policy. In this vein, we aim to initiate scientific and societal discussion rather than providing recipes to solve concrete problems.

5.5.1   *On the State of Gerontological Research*

BASE has not only shown that an interdisciplinary approach to aging from 70 to over 100 years is feasible and useful. Medical researchers, clinicians, and social and behavioral scientists were able to discuss their different and occasionally controversial understandings of reality and theory development, allowing joint measurements and cooperative analyses. However, it is clear that even the broad spectrum of disciplines in BASE, ranging from biochemistry and diagnostic radiology to psychological and social-structural analysis and biographical case interpretation, is by no means sufficient. Specifically, the present analyses fall short on two counts. In our view, the inclusion of molecular genetic analyses (of the collected blood samples) has high priority for future work. Furthermore, we think that assessments more strongly linked to intervention models are urgently needed – not only within the narrow bounds of technological aids, but also in a more theory-driven context such as the study of residential transfer to institutional settings and the onset of critical events such as the loss of close companions or partners.

These observations on as yet unexplored territory of interdisciplinary collaborative work, however, permit us to make a plea for the sustenance of large-scale interdisciplinary research. In our case, we have received much support from sponsors in extending the Berlin Aging Study to a longitudinal follow-up. However, as we know from others, this is not always the case. To ensure that interdisciplinarity is not only present in groups, but also becomes rooted in individual minds, we encourage funding institutions to commit themselves to the view that long-term interdisciplinary cooperation is a foundation for major advances in the social sciences and not only in the natural sciences. Future priorities in gerontology should be to safeguard interdisciplinary research affiliations over a long period in addition to supporting research on aging in individual disciplines.

A further topic concerning the state of gerontological research in Germany and elsewhere comes to the fore when considering our results. The reported findings stem from the initial, cross-sectional BASE data on the old in their special historical context. Our results emphasize the necessity of longitudinal studies and cohort comparisons (see also Maddox, 1995). BASE has revealed many links whose causal mechanisms can only be sufficiently understood and tested with longitudinal data on large samples followed from early old age to death. Thus, we encourage strong support for longitudinal work (see also Magnusson, 1996; Magnusson & Casaer, 1993; Moen, Elder, & Lüscher, 1995).

However, single-cohort longitudinal research is not enough. It underplays the important role of cultural-historical change. For instance, the new integration of sociological life course research (Elder, 1997; Mayer, 1992; Schaie, 1996; Settersten & Mayer, 1997) or psychological life-span work (P. B. Baltes, Lindenberger, & Staudinger, 1998) into gerontology has made it clear that studies of "old" persons are always examinations of members of historically specific generations, regarding, for instance, the motive systems of particular generations, the proportion of childless people, or the pattern of occupational careers. Some of the factors influencing BASE participants' old age and aging were determined even before World War I (e.g., early childhood nutrition or female education). The world economic crisis between the wars, World War II, and the period immediately afterward have shaped the lives of BASE cohorts in specific ways. Longitudinal studies of different cohorts, so-called cohort-sequential longitudinal studies (P. B. Baltes, Reese, & Nesselroade, 1988; Schaie, 1996), would allow the identification of universal characteristics of aging, of historical particularities, and of changing trends. In this sense, BASE can be considered only as a "base-line" study to which further cohort studies should be added.

This observation puts constraints on the policy implications that can be derived from BASE. Simple extrapolations into the future can easily be misleading because natural and social environments as well as the resources and orientations of future older generations are changing rapidly (P. B. Baltes, 1996; Bengtson & Schütze, 1992). One very probable outcome of these changes is a further increase in the survival likelihood in very old age (Jeune & Vaupel, 1995; Kannisto, 1994; Lutz, 1994; Suzman et al., 1992). In particular, recent biomedical and rehabilitation developments give rise to hopes for a longer life-span and better quality of life. Therefore, when evaluating the BASE findings, one should remember that they may already have been made obsolete by societal changes – and these are not necessarily positive.

5.5.2   Social Policy Guidelines

Despite these constraints, we suggest a series of concepts to serve as guidelines in coming discussions on the future of aging. First, we deem it necessary to emphasize the heterogeneity in aging among groups, individuals, domains, and age processes. Differential aging is not a BASE discovery, of course; it goes back to previous gerontological research (P. B. Baltes & Baltes, 1992; Birren, 1959; Lehr & Thomae, 1987; Maddox, 1987; Nelson & Dannefer, 1992). However, BASE has been able to measure this variability in a larger number of dimensions and features, and, foremost, it has extended its range to advanced old age (i.e., for 80- to 100-year-olds). Our findings do suggest that the many faces of age continue into very old age and thus call for political and human acceptance of the very old in their individuality and exceptionality.

A second guideline for the public discourse about aging policy refers to the modifiability of aging. A good part of what we have learned about old people may neither be inevitable nor necessary. Many impairments of old age could be revoked, reduced, rehabilitated, or suspended – there are many untapped reserves and potentials that stake out a large area of individual and societal modifiability. Thus, the search for new forms of institutional, social, and cultural support in old age comes into focus.

Improvements in the provision for old age and in the nursing care insurance system, the development of consumer-oriented nursing care and counseling as well as new technologies (e.g., in health care, communication, and transport) seem necessary. A particularly pressing issue is society's task to provide late life with a sense of purpose (M. M. Baltes & Montada, 1996; Rentsch, 1992; Rosenmayr, 1990; Staudinger & Dittmann-Kohli, 1992). Opportunities to lead a subjectively "productive" and independent life in old age are lacking. Old people should have the chance to live a life that is not characterized only by passive consumption and being the object of social policies. However, general precepts of productivity in old age need to be detached from ideas of economic usefulness. Because of the high proportion of women among old people and considering that feminine attributes and achievements are generally less highly esteemed, much reorientation and rethinking is called for (M. M. Baltes, 1996b; Friedan, 1996).

Another aspect in this context is developing new avenues in health policies that strive to support the relative independence and autonomy of old people (M. M. Baltes, 1996a). More often than not, the "burden" of age-related health costs is discussed, rather than the savings possible through purposeful prevention and rehabilitation (see also Fries, 1990). The BASE findings on latent reserve capacities in old age illustrate that there is more scope for successful intervention than one would expect. In particular, somatic and psychiatric-psychological methods of diagnosis and therapy should be further developed and offered to old persons. Equally, intervention in the domains of intellectual and sensory functioning appears promising (Willis, 1996).

5.5.3   A Fourth Age?

There is a third guideline involving a differentiation between the young old and the old old. The policy observations offered so far are characterized by basic optimism. However, the Berlin Aging Study reveals a much less positive and optimistic view of very old age. In very old age, the *finitude and vulnerability of life* and the strains and suffering associated with the approach of death become predominant. In our summary assessment (see also P. B. Baltes, 1996, 1997) we conclude that the ages from 70 to the early 80s are characterized by many continuities from previous periods of life. In this phase of life, which is often called "young old age" or "the third age," the majority of old people still have the reserves to live their lives autonomously, especially if they have a partner or other close companions and sufficient economic resources and social support. In this phase of young old age, there is a great deal of room for improvement: More persons can reach this age and live independently.

It has become clear to us, however, that the optimistic basic position that promulgated positive images of old age in the 1980s is less adequate for the ages of 85 and above (see also Cole, 1991; Suzman et al., 1992). At present and in the foreseeable future, the groups of the very old (which currently consist mainly of women) are increasingly affected by biological-organic impairments. In another context, one of us (P. B. Baltes, 1996) has spoken of the image of "hope with a mourning band" and argued that a belle époque of very old age does not await us in the immediate future. In gerontological theory development and aging policy, therefore, it may be useful to differentiate within the range from 70 to over 100 years. One option is to consider a "fourth age" following the third age as proposed by historian Peter Laslett (1991). This differentiated view of the age spectrum may be a logical consequence of ever more persons surviving into older ages, not unlike the increased differentiation of age in earlier periods of life.

In our view, then, *the greatest zone of insecurity regarding the future of old age surrounds the aging of the very old.* It cannot be excluded that a further extension of life – which is fairly likely – will simultaneously mean prolongation of the phase of severe somatic and mental impairments (but see Committee on National Statistics, 1994). At the same time, we are aware of the fact that such a concerned view of the aging of the very old may be a transitional phenomenon. In the past, the optimization of aging has moved up in the life-span, for instance, from 60 to 70 years of age. Could this trend not simply continue? Yes, but as P. B. Baltes (1997) has argued, for example, there may be powerful factors (evolutionary and ontogenetic) that make the optimization of aging more and more difficult as advanced old age is reached.

In BASE, we do not have the data to draw a definite conclusion about the special significance of a kind of "fourth age." However, we are persuaded that it is of utmost importance to collect more data on the quality of life and functional status in advanced old age and to orient gerontological research and medical, psychiatric, psychological, and sociopolitical practice toward this period of life. It is necessary to find new ways of life in and with very old age, a period that is at present strongly determined by mental and sensory deficits, frailty, and the need for care. The developmental progress of a society will not only be assessed by the provision of opportunities for the young old, the third age, but also by its achievements in developing and supporting humane ways of life in its final period. In advanced old age, beyond the age of 85, personal, familial, and social problems are most acute, and these very old persons and their caregivers belong to the neglected part of our society.

References

Allmendinger, J. (1994). *Lebensverlauf und Sozialpolitik: Die Ungleichheit von Frau und Mann und ihr öffentlicher Ertrag.* Frankfurt/M.: Campus.

American Psychiatric Association (APA) (Ed.). (1987). *Diagnostic and statistical manual of mental disorders (DSM-III-R).* Washington, DC.

Baltes, M. M. (1996a). *The many faces of dependency in old age.* Cambridge: Cambridge University Press.

Baltes, M. M. (1996b). Produktives Leben im Alter: Die vielen Gesichter des Alters – Resümee und Perspektiven für die Zukunft. In M. M. Baltes & L. Montada (Eds.), *Produktives Leben im Alter* (pp. 393–408). Frankfurt/M.: Campus.

Baltes, M. M., Kühl, K.-P., & Sowarka, D. (1992). Testing for limits of cognitive reserve capacity: A promising strategy for early diagnosis of dementia? *Journal of Gerontology: Psychological Sciences, 47,* P165–P167.

Baltes, M. M., & Lang, F. R. (1997). Everyday functioning and successful aging: The impact of resources. *Psychology and Aging, 12*, 433–443.

Baltes, M. M., & Montada, L. (Eds.). (1996). *Produktives Leben im Alter*. Frankfurt/M.: Campus.

Baltes, P. B. (1996). Über die Zukunft des Alterns: Hoffnung mit Trauerflor. In M. M. Baltes & L. Montada (Eds.), *Produktives Leben im Alter* (pp. 29–68). Frankfurt/M.: Campus.

Baltes, P. B. (1997). On the incomplete architecture of human ontogeny: Selection, optimization, and compensation as foundation of developmental theory. *American Psychologist, 52*, 366–380.

Baltes, P. B., & Baltes, M. M. (1992). Gerontologie: Begriff, Herausforderung und Brennpunkte. In P. B. Baltes & J. Mittelstraß (Eds.), *Zukunft des Alterns und gesellschaftliche Entwicklung* (pp. 1–34). Berlin: de Gruyter.

Baltes, P. B., & Lindenberger, U. (1997). Emergence of a powerful connection between sensory and cognitive functions across the adult life span: A new window to the study of cognitive aging? *Psychology and Aging, 12*, 12–21.

Baltes, P. B., Lindenberger, U., & Staudinger, U. M. (1998). Life-span theory in developmental psychology. In W. Damon (Ed.) & R. M. Lerner (Vol. Ed.), *Handbook of child psychology: Vol. 1. Theoretical models of human development* (5th ed., pp. 1029–1143). New York: Wiley.

Baltes, P. B., & Mittelstraß, J. (Eds.). (1992). *Zukunft des Alterns und gesellschaftliche Entwicklung*. Berlin: de Gruyter.

Baltes, P. B., Reese, H. W., & Nesselroade, J. R. (1988). *Life-span developmental psychology: Introduction to research methods*. Hillsdale, NJ: Erlbaum.

Baltes, P. B., & Smith, J. (1997). A systemic-wholistic view of psychological functioning in very old age: Introduction to a collection of articles from the Berlin Aging Study. *Psychology and Aging, 12*, 395–409.

Baltes, P. B., & Staudinger, U. M. (1993). Über die Gegenwart und Zukunft des Alterns: Ergebnisse und Implikationen psychologischer Forschung. *Berichte und Mitteilungen der Max-Planck-Gesellschaft, 4*, 154–185.

Barnow, S., & Linden, M. (1997). Suicidality and tiredness of life among very old persons: Results from the Berlin Aging Study (BASE). *Archives of Suicide Research, 3*, 171–182.

Beers, M. H., Ouslander, J. G., Rollingher, I., Reuben, D. B., Brooks, J., & Beck, J. C. (1991). Explicit criteria for determining inappropriate medication use in nursing home residents. *Archives of Internal Medicine, 151*, 1825–1832.

Bengtson, V. L., & Schütze, Y. (1992). Altern und Generationenbeziehungen: Aussichten für das kommende Jahrhundert. In P. B. Baltes & J. Mittelstraß (Eds.), *Zukunft des Alterns und gesellschaftliche Entwicklung* (pp. 492–517). Berlin: de Gruyter.

Binstock, R. H., & George, L. K. (Eds.). (1996). *Handbook of aging and the social sciences* (4th ed.). San Diego, CA: Academic Press.

Birren, J. E. (1959). Principles of research on aging. In J. E. Birren (Ed.), *Handbook of aging and the individual: Psychological and biological aspects* (pp. 3–42). Chicago: University of Chicago Press.

Birren, J. E., & Schaie, K. W. (Eds.). (1996). *Handbook of the psychology of aging* (4th ed.). San Diego, CA: Academic Press.

Borchelt, M. (1995). Potentielle Neben- und Wechselwirkungen der Multimedikation im Alter. *Zeitschrift für Gerontologie und Geriatrie, 28*, 420–428.

Borchelt, M., & Horgas, A. L. (1994). Screening an elderly population for verifiable adverse drug reactions: Methodological approach and initial data analysis of the Berlin Aging Study (BASE). *Annals of the New York Academy of Sciences, 717*, 270–281.

Borchelt, M., & Steinhagen-Thiessen, E. (1995). Medikamentöse Therapie. In I. Füsgen (Ed.), *Der ältere Patient: Problemorientierte Diagnostik und Therapie* (2nd ed., pp. 538–572). Munich: Urban & Schwarzenberg.

Bortz, W. M. (1991). *Living short and dying long*. New York: Bantam.

Cole, T. R. (1991). *The journey of life: A cultural history of aging in America*. Cambridge: Cambridge University Press.

Committee on National Statistics (Ed.). (1994). *Trends in disability at older ages: Summary of a workshop*. Washington, DC: National Academy Press.

Elder, G. H., Jr. (1997). The life course and human development. In W. Damon (Ed.) & R. M. Lerner (Vol. Ed.), *Handbook of child psychology: Vol. 1. Theoretical models of human development* (5th ed., pp. 939–991). New York: Wiley.

Fratiglioni, L., Grut, M., Forsell, Y., Grafström, M., Holmén, K., Eriksson, K., Viitanen, M., Bäckman, L., Ahlbom, A., & Winblad, B. (1991). Prevalence of Alzheimer's disease and other dementias in an elderly urban population: Relationship with age, sex and education. *Neurology, 41*, 1886–1892.

Freund, A. M., & Smith, J. (1997). Die Selbstdefinition im hohen Alter. *Zeitschrift für Sozialpsychologie, 28*, 44–59.

Freund, A. M., & Smith, J. (in press). Content and function of the self-definition in old and very old age. *Journal of Gerontology: Psychological Sciences*.

Friedan, B. (1996). Retirement as a new beginning. In M. M. Baltes & L. Montada (Eds.), *Produktives Leben im Alter* (pp. 14–28). Frankfurt/M.: Campus.

Fries, J. F. (1990). Medical perspectives upon successful aging. In P. B. Baltes & M. M. Baltes (Eds.), *Successful aging: Perspectives from the behavioral sciences* (pp. 35–49). Cambridge: Cambridge University Press.

Gatz, M., Kasl-Godley, J. E., & Karel, M. J. (1996). Aging and mental disorders. In J. E. Birren & K. W. Schaie (Eds.), *Handbook of the psychology of aging* (4th ed., pp. 365–382). San Diego, CA: Academic Press.

Gilberg, R. (1997). *Hilfe- und Pflegebedürftigkeit und die Inanspruchnahme von Hilfe- und Pflegeleistungen im höheren Lebensalter*. Unpublished doctoral thesis, Free University of Berlin.

Hauser, R. (1996). Die Entwicklung der Einkommensverteilung in den neuen Bundesländern seit der Wende. In M. Diewald & K. U. Mayer (Eds.), *Zwischenbilanz der Wiedervereinigung: Strukturwandel und Mobilität im Transformationsprozeß* (pp. 165–188). Opladen: Leske + Budrich.

Hauser, R., & Wagner, G. (1992). Altern und soziale Sicherung. In P. B. Baltes & J. Mittelstraß (Eds.), *Zukunft des Alterns und gesellschaftliche Entwicklung* (pp. 581–613). Berlin: de Gruyter.

Hauser, R., & Wagner, G. (1996). Die Einkommensverteilung in Ostdeutschland: Darstellung, Vergleich und Determinanten für die Jahre 1990–1994. In R. Hauser (Ed.), *Soziale Probleme der deutschen Einheit* (pp. 165–188). Berlin: Duncker & Humblot.

Helmchen, H., Linden, M., & Wernicke, T. (1996). Psychiatrische Morbidität bei Hochbetagten: Ergebnisse aus der Berliner Altersstudie. *Der Nervenarzt, 67*, 739–750.

Jeune, B., & Vaupel, J. W. (Eds.). (1995). *Exceptional longevity: From prehistory to the present*. Odense, Denmark: Odense University Press.

Kage, A., Nitschke, I., Fimmel, S., & Köttgen, E. (1996). Referenzwerte im Alter: Beeinflussung durch Alter, Medikation und Morbidität. In K. U. Mayer & P. B. Baltes (Eds.), *Die Berliner Altersstudie* (pp. 405–427). Berlin: Akademie Verlag.

Kannisto, V. (Ed.). (1994). *Development of oldest-old mortality, 1950–1990: Evidence from 28 developed countries*. Odense, Denmark: Odense University Press.

Karl, F., & Tokarski, W. (1989). *Die neuen Alten*. Kassel: Gesamthochschulbibliothek.

Krug, W., & Reh, G. (1992). *Pflegebedürftige in Heimen: Statistische Erhebung und Ergebnisse* (Schriftenreihe des Bundesministeriums für Familie und Senioren, Vol. 4). Stuttgart: Bundesministerium für Familie und Senioren.

Kruse, A. (1992). Alter im Lebenslauf. In P. B. Baltes & J. Mittelstraß (Eds.), *Zukunft des Alterns und gesellschaftliche Entwicklung* (pp. 331–355). Berlin: de Gruyter.

Lang, F. R., & Carstensen, L. L. (1994). Close emotional relationships in late life: Further support for proactive aging in the social domain. *Psychology and Aging, 9*, 315–324.

Laslett, P. (1991). *A fresh map of life: The emergence of the Third Age*. London: Weidenfeld.

Lehr, U. (1991). *Psychologie des Alterns* (7th ed.). Heidelberg: Quelle & Meyer.

Lehr, U., & Thomae, H. (Eds.). (1987). *Formen seelischen Alterns: Ergebnisse der Bonner Gerontologischen Längsschnittstudie (BOLSA)*. Stuttgart: Enke.

Linden, M., Horgas, A. L., Gilberg, R., & Steinhagen-Thiessen, E. (1997). Predicting health care utilization in the very old: The role of physical health, mental health, attitudinal and social factors. *Journal of Aging and Health, 9*, 3–27.

Linden, M., Meier, W., Achberger, M., Herr, R., Helmchen, H., & Benkert, O. (1996). Psychische Erkrankungen und ihre Behandlung in Allgemeinarztpraxen in Deutschland: Ergebnisse aus einer Studie der Weltgesundheitsorganisation (WHO). *Der Nervenarzt, 67*, 205–215.

Lindenberger, U., & Baltes, P. B. (1994). Sensory functioning and intelligence in old age: A strong connection. *Psychology and Aging, 9*, 339–355.

Lindenberger, U., & Baltes, P. B. (1997). Intellectual functioning in old and very old age: Cross-sectional results from the Berlin Aging Study. *Psychology and Aging, 12*, 410–432.

Lutz, W. (Ed.). (1994). *The future population of the world*. London: Earthscan.

Maas, I., & Staudinger, U. M. (1996). Lebensverlauf und Altern: Kontinuität und Diskontinuität der gesellschaftlichen Beteiligung, des Lebensinvestments und ökonomischer Ressourcen. In K. U. Mayer & P. B. Baltes (Eds.), *Die Berliner Altersstudie* (pp. 543–572). Berlin: Akademie Verlag.

Maddox, G. L. (1987). Aging differently. *The Gerontologist, 27*, 557–564.

Maddox, G. L. (Ed.). (1995). *The encyclopedia of aging* (2nd ed.). New York: Springer.

Magnusson, D. (Ed.). (1996). *The life-span development of individuals: Behavioral, neuro-biological and psychosocial perspectives*. Cambridge: Cambridge University Press.

Magnusson, D., & Casaer, P. (Eds.). (1993). *Longitudinal research on individual development: Present status and future perspectives*. Cambridge: Cambridge University Press.

Marsiske, M., Klumb, P., & Baltes, M. M. (1997). Everyday activity patterns and sensory functioning in old age. *Psychology and Aging, 12*, 444–457.

Mayer, K. U. (1992). Bildung und Arbeit in einer alternden Bevölkerung. In P. B. Baltes & J. Mittelstraß (Eds.), *Zukunft des Alterns und gesellschaftliche Entwicklung* (pp. 518–543). Berlin: de Gruyter.

Mayer, K. U. (1994). Wider die einfachen Rezepte. *Argumente (SPD-Bundestagsfraktion [Ed.], Schlagseite–Bevölkerungsentwicklung und politisches Handeln)*, 54.

Mayer, K. U., Baltes, P. B., Gerok, W., Häfner, H., Helmchen, H., Kruse, A., Mittelstraß, J., Staudinger, U. M., Steinhagen-Thiessen, E., & Wagner, G. (1992). Gesellschaft, Politik und Altern. In P. B. Baltes & J. Mittelstraß (Eds.), *Zukunft des Alterns und gesellschaftliche Entwicklung* (pp. 721–757). Berlin: de Gruyter.

McGue, M., Vaupel, J. W., Holm, N. V., & Harvald, B. (1993). Longevity is moderately inheritable in a sample of Danish twins born 1870–1880. *Journal of Gerontology: Biological Sciences, 48,* B237–B244.

Milligan, G. W., & Cooper, M. C. (1987). Methodology review: Clustering methods. *Applied Psychological Measurement, 11,* 329–354.

Mittelstraß, J., Baltes, P. B., Gerok, W., Häfner, H., Helmchen, H., Kruse, A., Mayer, K. U., Staudinger, U. M., Steinhagen-Thiessen, E., & Wagner, G. (1992). Wissenschaft und Altern. In P. B. Baltes & J. Mittelstraß (Eds.), *Zukunft des Alterns und gesellschaftliche Entwicklung* (pp. 695–720). Berlin: de Gruyter.

Moen, P., Elder, G. H., Jr., & Lüscher, K. (Eds.). (1995). *Examining lives in context: Perspectives on the ecology of human development.* Washington, DC: American Psychological Association.

Motel, A., & Wagner, M. (1993). Armut im Alter? Ergebnisse der Berliner Altersstudie (BASE) zur Einkommenslage alter und sehr alter Menschen. *Zeitschrift für Soziologie, 22,* 433–448.

Myers, G. C. (Ed.). (1997). Asset and Health Dynamics among the oldest old (AHEAD): Initial results from the longitudinal study. *Journal of Gerontology: Psychological and Social Sciences, 52B* (special issue).

Nelson, A. E., & Dannefer, D. (1992). Aged heterogeneity: Fact or fiction? The fate of diversity in gerontological research. *The Gerontologist, 32,* 17–23.

Neugarten, B. L. (1974). Age groups in American society and the rise of the young-old. *Annals of the American Academy of Political and Social Sciences, 9,* 187–198.

Nitschke, I., & Hopfenmüller, W. (1996). Die zahnmedizinische Versorgung älterer Menschen. In K. U. Mayer & P. B. Baltes (Eds.), *Die Berliner Altersstudie* (pp. 429–448). Berlin: Akademie Verlag.

Palmore, E. (1977). Facts on aging: A short quiz. *The Gerontologist, 17,* 315–320.

Palmore, E. (1981). The facts of aging quiz: Part 2. *The Gerontologist, 21,* 431–437.

Palmore, E. B. (1988). *The facts on aging quiz: A handbook of uses and results.* New York: Springer.

Rentsch, T. (1992). Philosophische Anthropologie und Ethik der späten Lebenszeit. In P. B. Baltes & J. Mittelstraß (Eds.), *Zukunft des Alterns und gesellschaftliche Entwicklung* (pp. 283–304). Berlin: de Gruyter.

Riley, M. W., & Riley, J. W., Jr. (1992). Individuelles und gesellschaftliches Potential des Alterns. In P. B. Baltes & J. Mittelstraß (Eds.), *Zukunft des Alterns und gesellschaftliche Entwicklung* (pp. 437–460). Berlin: de Gruyter.

Rosenmayr, L. (1990). *Die Kräfte des Alters.* Wien: Edition Atelier.

Rote Liste. (1990). Aulendorf: Editio Cantor.

Rowe, J. W., & Kahn, R. L. (1987). Human aging: Usual and successful. *Science, 237,* 143–149.

Schaie, K. W. (1996). *Intellectual development in adulthood: The Seattle Longitudinal Study.* Cambridge: Cambridge University Press.

Schneider, E. L., & Rowe, J. W. (Eds.). (1996). *Handbook of the biology of aging* (4th ed.). San Diego, CA: Academic Press.

Settersten, R. A., Jr., & Mayer, K. U. (1997). The measurement of age, age structuring, and the life course. In J. Hagan & K. S. Cook (Eds.), *Annual review of sociology* (Vol. 23, pp. 233–261). Palo Alto, CA: Annual Reviews.

Smith, J., & Baltes, M. M. (in press). The role of gender in very old age: Profiles of functioning and everyday life patterns. *Psychology and Aging.*

Smith, J., & Baltes, P. B. (1997). Profiles of psychological functioning in the old and oldest old. *Psychology and Aging, 12*, 458–472.

Staudinger, U. M. (1996). Psychologische Produktivität und Selbstentfaltung im Alter. In M. M. Baltes & L. Montada (Eds.), *Produktives Leben im Alter* (pp. 344–373). Frankfurt/M.: Campus.

Staudinger, U. M., & Dittmann-Kohli, F. (1992). Lebenserfahrung und Lebenssinn. In P. B. Baltes & J. Mittelstraß (Eds.), *Zukunft des Alterns und gesellschaftliche Entwicklung* (pp. 408–436). Berlin: de Gruyter.

Staudinger, U. M., & Fleeson, W. (1996). Self and personality in very old age: A sample case of resilience? *Development and Psychopathology, 8*, 867–885.

Staudinger, U. M., Marsiske, M., & Baltes, P. B. (1995). Resilience and reserve capacity in later adulthood: Potentials and limits of development across the life span. In D. Cicchetti & D. J. Cohen (Eds.), *Developmental psychopathology: Vol. 2. Risk, disorder, and adaptation* (pp. 801–847). New York: Wiley.

Steinhagen-Thiessen, E., Gerok, W., & Borchelt, M. (1994). Innere Medizin und Geriatrie. In P. B. Baltes, J. Mittelstraß, & U. M. Staudinger (Eds.), *Alter und Altern: Ein interdisziplinärer Studientext zur Gerontologie* (pp. 124–150). Berlin: de Gruyter.

Stuck, A. E., Beers, M. H., Steiner, A., Aronow, H. U., Rubenstein, L. Z., & Beck, J. C. (1994). Inappropriate medication use in community-residing older persons. *Archives of Internal Medicine, 154*, 2195–2200.

Suzman, R. M., Willis, D. P., & Manton, K. G. (Eds.). (1992). *The oldest old*. New York: Oxford University Press.

Wagner, G. (1995). *Kriterien einer rationalen Organisationsreform der gesetzlichen Rentenversicherung*. Discussion paper, Ruhr University Bochum, Social Science Faculty.

Wagner, G., Motel, A., Spieß, K., & Wagner, M. (1996). Wirtschaftliche Lage und wirtschaftliches Handeln alter Menschen. In K. U. Mayer & P. B. Baltes (Eds.), *Die Berliner Altersstudie* (pp. 277–299). Berlin: Akademie Verlag.

Willis, S. L. (1996). Everyday cognitive competence in elderly persons: Conceptual issues and empirical findings. *The Gerontologist, 36*, 595–601.

Woodbury, M. A., & Manton, K. G. (1982). A new procedure for analysis of medical classification. *Methods of Information in Medicine, 21*, 210–220.

World Health Organization (WHO). (1978). *Manual of the international statistical classification of diseases, injuries, and causes of death. Based on the recommendations of the Ninth Revision Conference, 1975, and adopted by the 29th World Health Assembly*. Geneva.

World Health Organization (WHO). (1980). *International classification of impairments, disabilities, and handicaps*. Geneva.

Yashin, A. I., & Iashine, I. A. (1994). *Environment determines 50% of variability in individual frailty: Results from a study of Danish twins born 1870–1900* (Population Studies of Aging 10). Odense, Denmark: Center for Health and Social Policy, Odense University.

Notes on Contributors

Margret M. Baltes, Ph.D., Professor of Psychological Gerontology and head of the Psychological Gerontology research unit in the Department of Gerontopsychiatry at the Free University of Berlin. Research interests: everyday competence and dependency in old age; cognitive plasticity and Alzheimer's disease; successful aging.

Paul B. Baltes, Prof. Dr. phil., director of the Center for Lifespan Psychology at the Max Planck Institute for Human Development in Berlin, Professor of Psychology at the Free University of Berlin. He is the chairman of the Berlin-Brandenburg Academy of Sciences study group "Aging and Societal Development" and codirector of the Berlin Aging Study and its Psychology Unit. Research interests: life-span psychology; psychology of intelligence and personality; gerontology; theories of successful development and successful aging.

Markus Borchelt, Dr. med., deputy head of the Geriatrics research group at the Evangelisches Geriatriezentrum Berlin, Medical Faculty of the Humboldt University, and deputy director of the BASE Internal Medicine and Geriatrics Unit. Research interests: geriatric drug therapy and drug epidemiology; functional capacity in old age; geriatric assessment; nutrition in old age.

Cornelia Borchers, M.A., occupational therapist and social scientist, now working for the German Stroke Foundation, Gütersloh. Until 1993 she was a member of the BASE Project Coordination Center.

Julia Delius, Dr. med., coordinating editor and translator for the Berlin Aging Study. Interests: neurobiological development of the visual system; sensory systems in old age; interdisciplinary research approaches.

William Fleeson, Ph.D., Assistant Professor of Psychology at Wake Forest University, Winston-Salem, NC. Postdoctoral fellow at the Center for Lifespan Psychology, Max Planck Institute for Human Development in Berlin until 1996. Research interests: personality and personality change; well-being; self-concepts; motivation.

Alexandra M. Freund, Dr. phil., research scientist at the Center for Lifespan Psychology, Max Planck Institute for Human Development in Berlin. Research interests: processes of developmental regulation; selection and pursuit of goals across the lifespan; motivational, emotional, and social-cognitive antecedents and consequences of selection, optimization, and compensation; development of content, structure, and function of self-related cognitions and emotions over the life-span.

521

Bernhard Geiselmann, Dr. med., neurologist and psychiatrist, senior registrar at the Department of Geriatric Psychiatry of the Max Bürger Center, Berlin. Psychiatric examination of BASE participants at the first occasion of measurement. Research interests: correlates of subthreshold syndromes; psychiatric case definitions.

Reiner Gilberg, Dr. phil., research worker for Infas Social Research in Bonn. Doctoral student at the Center for Sociology and the Study of the Life Course, Max Planck Institute for Human Development in Berlin until 1997. Research interests: utilization of assistance and care in old age; medical sociology; social policies; empirical social research methods.

Hanfried Helmchen, Prof. Dr. med., director of the Department of Psychiatry at the Free University of Berlin and director of the BASE Psychiatry Unit. Research interests in BASE: ethical issues; epidemiology of psychiatric disorders; subdiagnostic morbidity.

Ann L. Horgas, Ph.D., Assistant Professor of Gerontology and Nursing at Wayne State University, Detroit, MI. Postdoctoral fellow at the Psychological Gerontology research unit, Free University of Berlin until 1995, sponsored by a U.S. National Research Award (Grant no. 1 F32 H000 77). Research interests: health and functioning in older adults; pain; mental health.

Siegfried Kanowski, Prof. Dr. med., deputy director of the Department of Psychiatry at the Free University of Berlin, director of the Department of Gerontopsychiatry. Research interests: conditions of psychiatric morbidity in old age; psychotropic drug therapy; ethical issues; diagnosis and therapy of dementias.

Ute Kunzmann, Dr. phil., postdoctoral fellow at the University of California, Berkeley. Former doctoral student at the Center for Lifespan Psychology, Max Planck Institute for Human Development in Berlin. Research interests: personality across the life-span; emotional regulation and coping in old age.

Frieder R. Lang, Dr. phil., research scientist at the Psychological Gerontology research unit, Department of Gerontopsychiatry at the Free University of Berlin. Research interests: development of social behavior, social motivation, and social relationships across the life-span; criteria and mechanisms of successful development; everyday competence in adulthood.

Michael Linden, Prof. Dr. med. Dipl.-Psych., head of the Outpatient Therapy research group at the Department of Psychiatry, Free University of Berlin, deputy director of the BASE Psychiatry Unit. Research interests: provision of assistance and care; therapy evaluation; compliance; anxiety disorders; depression.

Ulman Lindenberger, Dr. phil., research scientist at the Center for Lifespan Psychology, Max Planck Institute for Human Development in Berlin. Research interests: measurement, development, composition, and structure of intellectual abilities across the life-span; working memory and cognitive control; methodological issues in developmental psychology.

Todd D. Little, Ph.D., Assistant Professor of Psychology at Yale University, CT. Research scientist at the Center for Lifespan Psychology, Max Planck Institute for Human Development in Berlin until July 1998. Research interests: modeling individual differences and developmental processes; contextual influences on motivation and action-control regulation.

Ineke Maas, Dr. (Sociology), senior scientist at the Center for Sociology and the Study of the Life Course, Max Planck Institute for Human Development in Berlin. Research interests: social participation in old age; aging and the life course; social mobility and inequality.

Michael Marsiske, Ph.D., Assistant Professor of Gerontology and Psychology at Wayne State University, Detroit, MI. Postdoctoral fellow at the Center for Lifespan Psychology, Max Planck Institute for Human Development in Berlin until July 1995. Research interests: life-span developmental psychology; development and plasticity of intelligence across the life-span; intellectual aspects of everyday competence; relationships between sensory-sensorimotor functioning and cognition in adulthood.

Karl Ulrich Mayer, Prof. Dr. rer. soc., director of the Center for Sociology and the Study of the Life Course at the Max Planck Institute for Human Development in Berlin. He is codirector of the Berlin Aging Study and its Sociology and Social Policy Unit and deputy chairman of the Berlin-Brandenburg Academy of Sciences study group "Aging and Societal Development." Research interests: analysis of social structure; social inequality and mobility; labor market processes; sociology of the life course; empirical social research methods.

Reinhard Nuthmann, Dr. rer. pol., senior manager and head of research administration at the Max Planck Institute for Demographic Research in Rostock. He was head of the BASE Project Coordination Center at the Max Planck Institute for Human Development in Berlin from 1990 until 1996. Research interests: aging and societal development; education and employment.

Ulrich Pötter, Dr. rer. pol., research scientist at the Institute for Social Science Methodology and Statistics, Ruhr University in Bochum. He worked at the Center for Sociology and the Study of the Life Course at the Max Planck Institute for Human Development in Berlin until 1996. Research interests: statistics with incomplete data; semiparametric models.

Friedel M. Reischies, Priv. Doz. Dr. med., neurologist and psychiatrist, senior registrar at the Department of Psychiatry, Free University of Berlin, and head of the Neuropsychology and Brain Imaging research group. Research interests: neuropsychological assessments; diagnosis of dementia and depression.

Hans Scherer, Prof. Dr. med., director of the Ear, Nose, and Throat Clinic at the Benjamin Franklin Clinic, Free University of Berlin. Research interests: research of balance; equilibrium in conditions of weightlessness; laser surgery.

Yvonne Schütze, Dr. phil., Professor of Sociology and Education at the Humboldt University Berlin. Research interests: development of the family across the life course; socialization; social relationships; migration.

Richard A. Settersten Jr., Ph.D., Assistant Professor at the Department of Sociology, Case Western Reserve University, Cleveland. Postdoctoral fellow at the Center for Sociology and the Study of the Life Course, Max Planck Institute for Human Development in Berlin until 1993. Research interests: formal and informal organization of the life course; structuring of old age; individual and cultural interpretation of old age and the life course.

Jacqui Smith, Ph.D., senior scientist at the Center for Lifespan Psychology, Max Planck Institute for Human Development in Berlin, codirector of the BASE Psychology Unit. Research interests: longevity from a psychological perspective; self-concepts and self-regulatory processes in old age; life planning and life-span development of everyday knowledge.

Ursula M. Staudinger, Priv. Doz. Dr. phil., senior scientist at the Center for Lifespan Psychology, Max Planck Institute for Human Development in Berlin. Research interests: life-span development of intellectual abilities and personality; interactive minds; life as unit of psychological research; societal and individual potentials of aging.

Elisabeth Steinhagen-Thiessen, Prof. Dr. med., director of the Evangelisches Geriatriezentrum Berlin and Professor of Internal Medicine at the Charité, Campus Virchow Clinic, Humboldt University Berlin. She is the director of the BASE Internal Medicine and Geriatrics Unit. Research interests: geriatrics; gerontology; age-dependent changes of the musculoskeletal system; atherosclerosis; lipid metabolism; geriatric treatment concepts; rehabilitation of hemiplegic patients.

Clemens Tesch-Römer, Priv. Doz. Dr. phil., head of the German Center of Gerontology, Berlin. Research interests: coping with stress in old age; psychosocial consequences of presbycusis; rehabilitation in old age; biographical life-span analysis.

Michael Wagner, Prof. Dr. phil., Professor of Sociology at the University of Cologne. Senior scientist at the Center for Sociology and the Study of the Life Course, Max Planck Institute for Human Development in Berlin until 1997. Codirector of the BASE Sociology and Social Policy Unit. Research interests: life course research; marriage and the family; geographic mobility. In BASE: social inequality in old age; later phases of the family course.

Thomas Wernicke, Dr. med., neurologist and psychiatrist, senior registrar at the Department of Neurology, Free University of Berlin. Psychiatric examination of BASE participants at the first occasion of measurement. Research interests: epidemiology of psychiatric morbidity; treatment of depression and dementia; pharmacoepidemiology; severity of psychiatric disorders.

Hans-Ulrich Wilms, Dr. phil., research scientist at the Department of Psychiatry at the University of Leipzig. Research scientist at the Psychological Gerontology research unit, Department of Gerontopsychiatry, Free University of Berlin until 1997. Research interests: everyday competence in old age; illness concepts; computer-aided diagnostic methods.

Abbreviations

ADL: Activities of Daily Living
ADR: Adverse drug reactions
ANOVA: Analysis of variance
AODSR: Average off-diagonal standardized residual
Apo-E 2/2: apolipoprotein E, genotype 2/2
BaCO: basic competence
BASE: Berlin Aging Study
BMFuS: Bundesministerium für Familie und Senioren [Federal Ministry for Family Affairs and Senior Citizens]
BPRS: Brief Psychiatric Rating Scale
CAS: cerebral atherosclerosis
CES-D: Center for Epidemiologic Studies-Depression Scale
CFI: Comparative Fit Index
CHD: coronary heart disease
CIPS: Collegium Internationale Psychiatriae Scalarum
CT: computer tomography
DM: deutschemark
DSM-III-R: *Diagnostic and Statistical Manual of Mental Disorders* (3rd revision)
EAS: European Atherosclerosis Society
ECA: Epidemiologic Catchment Area
ECR: Enhanced Cued Recall
ECG: electrocardiography
EGZB: Evangelisches Geriatriezentrum Berlin
ExCo: expanded competence
FU: Free University (of Berlin)
GAF Scale: Global Assessment of Functioning Scale
GMS-A/HAS: Geriatric Mental State Examination, Version A/History and Aetiology Schedule
HAMD: Hamilton Depression Scale
HAWIE: Hamburg Wechsler Intelligenztest für Erwachsene [Hamburg Wechsler intelligence test for adults]
HDL: high-density lipoprotein
HU: Humboldt University (Berlin)
IADL: Instrumental Activities of Daily Living
ICD-9: *International Classification of Diseases* (9th revision)
ICD-10: *International Classification of Diseases* (10th revision)
ICIDH: *International Classification of Impairments, Disabilities, and Handicaps*
IFCC: International Federation of Clinical Chemistry

527

IFI: Incremental Fit Index
LDL: low-density lipoprotein
LISREL: linear structural relationships
L. R.: likelihood ratio
LSI-A: Life Satisfaction Index A
M: mean
MMSE: Mini Mental State Examination
MPI: Max Planck Institute (for Human Development)
MZ71: 1%-Mikrozensus-Zusatzerhebung 1971 [1% Microcensus Supplementary Survey 1971]
NEO: neuroticism, extraversion, openness
NNFI: Nonnormed Fit Index
n.s.: not significant
NSAID: nonsteroidal anti-inflammatory drugs
PANAS: Positive and Negative Affect Schedule
PDR: *Physician's Desk Reference*
PGCMS: Philadelphia Geriatric Center Morale Scale
PVD: peripheral vascular disease
qCT: quantitative computer tomography
RMSEA: root mean square error of approximation
RR: relative risk
SD: standard deviation
SMMS: Short Mini Mental State Examination
WHO: World Health Organization

Author Index

529

Subject Index

accommodation and assimilation, 312
activities
    leisure/social, 76, 186–187, 228–231, 241–247,
        250–251, 387–390, 460, 497
    out of house, 241, 243, 250, 387–390, 396, 497
    political, 242, *see also* interests, political
    profile, 30, 186–188
Activities of Daily Living (ADL) (*see also* functional
        capacity; need for help), 170, 261, 372–373,
        384, 387–391, 404, 434, 436
    and functional capacity, 149–151, 153
    and psychiatric morbidity, 170, 176, 186–188
    and sample selectivity, 74–75
Activities of Daily Living Index, 149, *434*
Activity List, *234*, 387, 389–390
adaptation processes, *see* self-regulatory processes
adaptive fit perspective, 385
ADL, *see* Activities of Daily Living
adverse drug reactions (ADR), *144*, 147–149, 154,
        183, 407, 488
affect, 209–210, 219, 307–311, 456–460
affection, 214, 285, 286, 292–296
age
    chronological, 23, 219, 230
    as design variable in BASE, 19–20, 34–35
    and sample selectivity, 61, 64
    social status, 228
    very old, 17, 508–510, 514
age differences, 20, 353, 503–505
    in dementia and depression, 168–169, 172–180
    in dental status, 137
    in functional capacity, 155–160
    in intelligence, 202–205
    in medication, 144–149
    in need for help, 438, 440
    in objective and subjective health, 159, 418–424
    in participation in BASE, 62
    in psychological profiles, 217–219
    in psychosocial resources and risks, 415–416
    in selectivity, 66, 76–77
    in self and personality, 205–211, 315, 320
    in sensory functioning, 362–367
    in social relationships, 211–215, 286–291
age groups in BASE, *34–35*
aging
    differential, 22–23, 159, 188–189, 198, 361, 376,
        397, 414, 508–509
    normal vs. pathological, 23, 189, 199, 330, 352–353
    psychological, 197–226
    subjective, *see* subjective aging
    successful, *see* successful aging
    as a systemic phenomenon, 22, 24–25, 159,
        215–218, 361, 376, 378–379, 404, 510,
        see also interdisciplinarity
aging satisfaction, 42, 302–328, 413, 421–422, 457
analgesics, 183
anamnesis, *85–86*

androgyny, 263, 275
antidepressants, 183–185
anxiety, 48, 217, 262, 373, 490
apolipoproteins, 140, 189
apoplexy, *see* cerebral atherosclerosis; stroke
assets, 232, 234, 237–238, 495
assistance (*see also* help; support), 249, 434,
        436–438, 440, 444–445, 484
atherosclerosis, 140–144
    risk factor model, 140–144
attention, 377–378

BaCo, *see* basic competence
balance/gait (*see also* sensorimotor functioning),
        150, 154–155, 182, 204, 333, 365, *366*–367,
        372–375, 392, 394, 397
Baltimore Longitudinal Study of Aging, 260
Barthel Index, 149, 154–155, 397
BASE, *see* Berlin Aging Study
basic competence (BaCo), 372, 378, 385–386,
        390–391, 392–398
benzodiazepines, 183–185
Berkeley Older Generation Study, 283
Berlin (West), special conditions, 42–43
Berlin Academy of Sciences and Technology, 2
Berlin Aging Study (BASE), 3–4, 16–19
    aims, 16–19
    organizational aspects, 3–4
    overview and foci, 3–4, 16–33
Berlin Wall, 84, 114
Berlin-Brandenburg Academy of Sciences, 2–3
biochemical reference values, 133–134, 488–489
biological decline (*see also* central nervous changes),
        204–205, 309, 329, 343–344, 492
blood
    formation indicators, 134
    samples, 132
Body Mass Index, 70, 78, 434
Bonn Gerontological Longitudinal Study, 29, 283, 311
brain, aging, *see* central nervous changes
Brief Psychiatric Rating Scale (BPRS), 435, 440

cardiovascular diseases (*see also* atherosclerosis),
        140–144, 159
care (*see also* assistance; help; services), 430–449,
        484, 497
    costs, 230, 430, 442
    formal, 430–432, 436–438, 445
    informal, 430–432, 436
    institutional, 430–432, 445
    insurance, *see* nursing care insurance
    levels, *434*
    for partner, 436
caregiver, 264
cataract, 370
Center for Epidemiologic Studies-Depression Scale
    (CES-D), 173–180, 435, 440

Note. Measurement and/or assessment methods are explained on the pages shown in italics.